EIGHTH EDITION

# *Interpretations of* AMERICAN HISTORY

## Patterns and Perspectives

| VOLUME ONE | *Through Reconstruction*

*Edited by*

**FRANCIS G. COUVARES**
**Amherst College**

**MARTHA SAXTON**
**Amherst College**

**GERALD N. GROB**
**Rutgers University**

**GEORGE ATHAN BILLIAS**
**Clark University**

D0145220

**BEDFORD/ST. MARTIN'S**

Boston • New York

**To Gerald F. Linderman and Alexander Saxton, teachers and historians**

**For Bedford/St. Martin's**

*Publisher for History*: Mary V. Dougherty
*Executive Editor*: William J. Lombardo
*Director of Development for History*: Jane Knetzger
*Senior Editor*: Sara Wise
*Developmental Editor*: Jim Strandberg
*Editorial Assistant*: Lynn Sternberger
*Production Supervisor*: Sarah Ulicny
*Executive Marketing Manager*: Jenna Bookin Barry
*Text Design*: Brian Salisbury
*Project Management*: Books By Design, Inc.
*Index*: Books By Design, Inc.
*Cover Design*: Sara Gates
*Composition*: Achorn International
*Printing and Binding*: RR Donnelley & Sons Company

*President*: Joan E. Feinberg
*Editorial Director*: Denise B. Wydra
*Director of Marketing*: Karen R. Soeltz
*Director of Editing, Design, and Production*: Marcia Cohen
*Assistant Director of Editing, Design, and Production*: Elise S. Kaiser
*Manager, Publishing Services*: Emily Berleth

Library of Congress Control Number: 2008923367

Manufactured in the United States of America.

3   2   1   0   9   8
f   e   d   c   b   a

*For information, write:* Bedford/St. Martin's, 75 Arlington Street, Boston, MA 02116   (617-399-4000)

ISBN-10: 0-312-48049-0
ISBN-13: 978-0-312-48049-3

# *Preface*

We are very pleased to offer readers a thoroughly revised edition of *Interpretations of American History,* now published by Bedford/St. Martin's. First conceived by George Billias and Gerald Grob more than three decades ago, this collection has provided students of American history with a unique introduction to the major debates in American history, from the nature of the earliest settlements to contemporary conflicts. We intend this new edition of *Interpretations of American History* to provide students with selections of the best recent and classic works in American history, as well as updated historiographical essays that help them understand what is at stake when thoughtful historians disagree.

*Interpretations of American History* has long been a popular choice for both undergraduate and graduate historiography and methods courses, and a valued resource for historians. Based on positive feedback from reviewers, we have retained the general structure and format of the book. The book is again published as a two-volume paperback, with the chapter on Reconstruction appearing in both volumes. Each volume includes eleven chapters, and every chapter opens with a historiographical essay that tracks the major debates about the events or era covered in that chapter. Each chapter's historiographical essay is followed by two readings by outstanding scholars who offer differing viewpoints on — or approaches to — the general topic of that chapter. In many cases, we have chosen selections that overlap or complement each other to show students how historians build on the work of others to advance the field. By moving beyond a simple "either-or" format, we invite a deeper understanding of how historians work, why discourses take the shape they do, and how and why this changes over time.

## New to This Edition

While the overall structure of the book remains the same, the eighth edition has been seriously revised and freshened. Each of the opening historiographical essays has been rewritten to reflect the most recent scholarship, with dozens of new books and articles discussed in the essays and hundreds of new historical works added to the extensive footnote citations. Volume One includes the newest scholarship on the struggles between Native Americans and colonists over the settlement of North America, the slave trade, the

Revolution, and the Constitution, as well as the Civil War and Reconstruction. Volume Two has been updated to reflect the latest interpretations of Progressivism and immigration and includes significantly revised coverage of the debates over the causes and consequences of the Cold War, the inclusivity of Second Wave feminism, and the evolution of the New Right. Beyond this crucial updating of our opening essays, fully half of the readings are new to this edition — Volume One includes twelve new readings, while eight new readings appear in Volume Two.

In the last decade, an explosion of historical writing has interpreted events in an international perspective. A rich and continuing harvest of comparative history has broadened the array of themes within which students must now consider our past. This dramatic development often challenges long held notions of American exceptionalism and, even more important, offers broader perspectives with which to judge the distinctive and common elements of historical experience across national and regional borders. Nearly every chapter of the eighth edition includes reference to this extensive new comparative, transnational scholarship. This new scholarship is reflected mostly in the historiographical essays but is not ignored in the new readings. For example, in Chapter 3 of Volume One, a new reading by Claudio Saunt analyzes the Choctaw-Cherokee conflict in the Old Southwest as a proxy war in the global struggle between the French and the British. In Volume Two, the new essay on the Cold War shows that even a field long committed to international perspectives has been transformed by new transnational approaches. The essay reviews older debates about the origins of the Cold War, most of which weighed the relative responsibility of the Soviet Union and the United States for the origins and evolution of conflict. Going beyond these debates, some contemporary historians increasingly take a "pericentric" approach that emphasizes the efficacy of nations that became independent after World War II, each with an agenda of its own, each tugging at the two superpowers. A new reading for the chapter by Odd Arne Westad shows that this new paradigm helps account for the duration and intensity of superpower conflict, even after many of the premises of a Euro-centered rivalry had outlived their purpose.

These volumes also emphasize even more than previous editions the centrality of race in American history. Work on the slave trade and the Black Atlantic provided early models for transnational history, while studies of race influenced later work on gender, ethnicity, and immigration — all fields that transcend nationality. In this edition, race figures importantly, not only with regard to obvious subjects such as the slave trade, slave culture, Reconstruction, and civil rights, but also in essays on Jacksonian politics, labor-capital conflict, immigration, Progressivism, Second Wave feminism, and the origins of the New Right.

In addition to the new scholarship that enlivens this edition, we also include classic arguments that have generated enduring debates within the discipline. For example, the first essay on the slave trade reaches back to Eric Williams, whose seminal 1944 book, *Capitalism and Slavery*, argued that slave traders acted out of a desire for profit, not racism, and that those profits propelled the Industrial Revolution in England and other capitalist countries. Economic historian David Eltis counters that Europeans targeted Africans for enslavement only because they considered them sufficiently "other" to be excluded from European notions of individual rights. The fast growing and conceptually adventurous historiography of the slave trade exemplifies both the centrality of slavery and race in U.S. history and the transnational turn in almost all fields of history today.

In Volume One, we have brought back a chapter on Jacksonian democracy to reflect recent scholarship that has reinvigorated study of that period. This revision's treatment of the Jacksonian era focuses on the Democratic Party's policies toward blacks and Native Americans. Sean Wilentz emphasizes the profound democratizing of politics that brought working men and farmers into the Jacksonian Democratic coalition. He defends the Democratic Party against proslavery charges, arguing that the diverse, sometimes antislavery northern Jacksonians of earlier years should not be confused with the more thoroughly proslavery party of the 1850s. In contrast, Lacy Ford insists that Jacksonian Democrats in the South widely and continuously supported slavery, reinforcing Alexander Saxton's demonstration that white workingmen's constructions of blackness and whiteness were fundamental to their ideas of democracy in the antebellum years and beyond.

While race is a central concern of these volumes, the chapter on the rise and possible fall of the New Right in Volume Two shows just how difficult it is to interpret late-twentieth-century politics through that lens. A new selection by Matthew Lassiter argues forcefully that the so-called Southern Strategy does not account for Republican victories in the last decades of the century. Rather, a Suburban Strategy linked middle-class Americans of all regions not only in resisting the politics of racial equality, but also in joining anti-crime, anti-tax, anti-abortion, and anti-busing movements. While many historians have explained the new conservatism as the southernization of the nation's politics, this new reading suggests that class concerns intermixed with racial ones in ways that transcended region.

We hope that this new edition of *Interpretations of American History* leads students to find in history what we and many others have discovered: an opportunity to explore the record of human thought and action with a commitment to accuracy, thoroughness, and imaginative sympathy.

## Acknowledgments

For their important help in evaluating the seventh edition and helping us to identify which readings to keep or replace, we wish to thank the following reviewers: Steven J. Bucklin, University of South Dakota; William W. Cutler III, Temple University; Andrew Darien, Salem State College; Charles W. Eagles, University of Mississippi; Michael Frisch, University at Buffalo, The State University of New York; Larry G. Gerber, Auburn University; Kurt E. Leichtle, University of Wisconsin–River Falls; Lisa Levenstein, University of

North Carolina–Greensboro; Greg O'Brien, University of Southern Mississippi; Bradford Sample, Indiana Wesleyan University; and Matthew Avery Sutton, Washington State University.

We also wish to thank many people for their invaluable assistance on this project, including Mary Dougherty, Jane Knetzger, Sara Wise, Emily Berleth, Nancy Benjamin, Mary Sanger, Sybil Sosin, Jim Strandberg, Christopher Tullis, Rhea Cabin, Enrico Ferorelli, Betty Couvares, Eric Foner, Bruce Laurie, David Blight, Celso Castro-Alves, Joyce Avrech Berkman, and Gregory Call.

# Contents

# Introduction to U.S. Historiography

These volumes reflect our understanding that history is an act of interpretation. They also reflect the dramatic changes in the practice of history over the last four decades. Fifty years ago, historians primarily interpreted politics, diplomacy, and war. Since then, the civil rights, antiwar, and women's movements have dramatically opened up what historians and readers think of as history, while bringing into the profession women, African Americans, Hispanics, and Native Americans. Contemporary American historians write about nearly everything that has affected nearly everybody — from war to childbirth, agriculture to housework, illness to leisure, and banking systems to sewer systems. The expansive new history and the influx of new and diverse historians have linked the past more strongly to the present. Over a hundred years ago, the Italian philosopher Benedetto Croce observed, "Every true history is contemporary history."[1] He was trying to cast doubt on arguments of late-nineteenth-century historians (called "historicists" or "positivists") that history was a science and could recover objective truths if properly practiced. Croce insisted that the past "in itself" is unknowable and that history represents our collective effort to make sense of the world. Inviting into the practice of history groups previously excluded from the profession has demonstrated the validity of Croce's view in new ways. Views of the past vary not only with generations but also because of divergent experiences stemming from the historian's gender, ethnicity, class, and race. This does not mean that we cannot find out anything solid about the past. But it does mean that no account of the past is free of the perspectives, prejudices, and priorities of its author and that the more varied the range of historians, the more likely their collective output will achieve a balanced totality.

When we read history, we are reading a particular historian's encounter with the world. The historian is devoted to the "facts," spends years of his or her life combing through the archives, and believes that the story she or he comes away with represents reality. But in writing, the historian renders this material into a story. The design of a narrative reflects its author's

---

[1]Benedetto Croce, *History: Its Theory and Practice* (New York, 1921), develops ideas he first articulated in 1893; for a sampling of the work of Croce and other philosophers of history in the first half of the twentieth century, see Hans Meyerhoff, ed., *The Philosophy of History in Our Time* (New York, 1959); and Patrick Gardiner, ed., *Theories of History* (Glencoe, Ill., 1959). See also Fritz Stern, ed., *Varieties of History: From Voltaire to the Present* (Cleveland and New York, 1956). An excellent guide through these philosophical thickets, designed especially for students, is Michael Stanford, *A Companion to the Study of History* (Oxford, 1994).

circumstances, values, ideology, nationality, school of thought, or theoretical and methodological preference. One historian is, we say, a Jeffersonian liberal, another a neo-Marxist, another a progressive or a conservative, still another a feminist or postmodernist. We note that Perry Miller's account of the Puritans reflects his alienation from twentieth-century American liberalism, John Hope Franklin's or Eric Foner's account of Reconstruction is shaped by his engagement with the civil rights movement, Oscar Handlin's or George Sanchez's history of immigration reflects his own ethnic experience, or Kathryn Sklar's ideas about Progressivism are informed by her feminism. In doing so, we acknowledge that personal perspective influences the angle of vision and the character of illumination that the historian brings to the historical landscape.

If history is partly craft and partly personal perspective, however, it is also partly science. An error as common as thinking history is "just the facts" is thinking it is "just your story." Whereas the nineteenth-century positivists thought that scientific method could guarantee objective truth in history just as it does in physics, some present-day postmodern theorists maintain that history is inescapably opinion. Postmodern criticism has encouraged historians to be more attentive to the possible layers of meaning in their documents, to their unacknowledged theoretical commitments, and to their use of language in writing history. But those postmodernists who assert that historians cannot arrive at truth, or that history is no different than fiction, err like the positivists but in the opposite direction. However parallel some of the techniques of ideologue, novelist, and historian, the historian is constrained by the record in a way the other two are not. One literary critic has written that, like other writers of nonfiction, the historian's "allegiance is to fact."[2] Historians willingly acknowledge that no account is absolutely true and is certainly never final, but they also insist that some histories are better than others. Something other than the historian's political, moral, or esthetic preferences comes into play in judging one history better than another, something, for want of a better term, objective.

While committed to a particular interpretation, the historian remains faithful to the evidence and determined to test the accuracy and the adequacy of every historical account. History succeeds when it tells us how things were, yet at the same time reminds us that the only access we have to the past is through the imagination of a finite and very contemporary human being. A historian reveals the contours of a landscape from a distinct perspective, but he or she does not invent the landscape.[3] The British

[2]Sue Halpern, "The Awful Truth," *New York Review of Books* (September 25, 1997): 13.

[3]The most recent denial of history's truth claims is Peter Novick, *That Noble Dream: The "Objectivity Question" and the American Historical Profession* (Cambridge, 1988). Dorothy Ross, "Grand Narrative in American Historical Writing: From Romance to Uncertainty," *American Historical Review* 100 (June 1995): 651–77, offers brilliant critiques of historians' narrative strategies and somewhat elusive postmodernist suggestions about alternatives. Arguments for a middle ground between objectivism and Novick's relativism can be found in James T. Kloppenberg, "Objectivity and Historicism: A Century of American Historical Writing," *American*

historian Mary Fulbrook has recently affirmed convincingly that there are reasonable "criteria for preferring one historical approach or interpretation to another; and that these criteria need not be, as the postmodernists would have it, purely based on moral, political, or aesthetic considerations."[4] Fulbrook insists that, when theoretically alert, historians can deploy "empirical evidence and inter-subjective professional dialogue" to produce "progress" in historical knowledge.[5]

In practical terms, historians make progress and get closer to the truth by arguing with one another. And so history relies on historiography, the study of history and its changing interpretations.[6] Every historian begins work by immersing himself or herself in the subject and remains in dialogue with others interested in similar matters. Most books by serious historians include historiographical essays that locate the work within the context of related works. Historiography reminds us that history is not a closed book, not a collection of inarguable facts. There is always something to argue about in history, something that makes us think about the conduct of our contemporary lives. Thus, in a world of liberation movements and resurgent nationalism, it matters how we tell the story of the American Revolution or of the growth of America's overseas empire. In a society riven by conflicts over racism, sexual exploitation, and growing disparities between rich and poor, it matters how we narrate the history of labor, or the New Deal, or the rights movements of the 1960s and 1970s. Knowing that African American state governments during Reconstruction effectively delivered services while suffering only modest corruption makes it impossible to cast African American disfranchisement as a by-product of cleaning up government. It may also affect our judgments about contemporary liberals' confidence in elections as the road to equality and of conservatives' recent efforts to prevent "voter fraud." Similarly, knowing that some turn-of-the-century migrants to the United States returned to their homelands in great numbers might require us to adjust ideas about assimilation. It may also change the way we think about the dual loyalties of contemporary migrants.

---

*Historical Review* 94 (October 1989): 1011–30; Thomas L. Haskell, "Objectivity Is Not Neutrality: Rhetoric vs. Practice in Peter Novick's *That Noble Dream*," *History and Theory* 29 (1990): 129–57; David Hollinger, *In the American Province: Studies in the History and Historiography of Science* (Bloomington, Ind., 1985); and "*AHR* Forum: Peter Novick's *That Noble Dream*: The Objectivity Question and the Future of the Historical Profession," *American Historical Review* 96 (June 1991): 675–708, with contributions from Hollinger and others and with a reply from Novick. See also Joyce Appleby, Lynn Hunt, and Margaret Jacoby, *Telling the Truth about History* (New York, 1994); Alan B. Spitzer, *Historical Truth and Lies about the Past: Reflections on Dewey, Dreyfus, de Man, and Reagan* (Chapel Hill, N.C., 1996); and Richard J. Evans, *In Defense of History* (New York, 1999). A more conservative and alarmist defense of objectivity is Keith Windschuttle, *The Killing of History: How Literary Critics and Social Theorists Are Murdering Our Past* (New York, 1997).

[4]Mary Fulbrook, *Historical Theory* (London, 2002), ix–x.
[5]Ibid., 188, 30.
[6]J. H. Hexter defines historiography as "the craft of writing history" or the "rhetoric of history," in "The Rhetoric of History," originally published in the *International Encyclopedia of the Social Sciences*, vol. 6 (New York, 1968), 368–94, and republished in revised form in his *Doing History* (Bloomington, Ind., 1971), 15–76.

Historical scholarship is thus in continual flux. But for careful students of historiography, disagreement is more interesting than agreement could ever be, for it holds the key to a better understanding not just of the past but of the present and possibly the future as well.

What follows is a sketch of the evolution of American history as a discipline over the course of the last two centuries.[7] As with all attempts to fit diverse strands of thought and experience into a single story, ambiguities haunt this narration or are suppressed in the interest of a continuous story line. As much as possible, the following overview tries to balance human complexity with narrative simplicity.

Broadly speaking, the writing of American history has passed through four stages: the providential, the rationalist, the nationalist, and the professional. The ministers and magistrates of the seventeenth and eighteenth centuries, and most of the women who wrote history through the Civil War, wrote a form of providential history. The Puritan practitioners who originated this form wished to justify the ways of God to man, and vice versa. Their history was a holy chronicle, revealing his Providence toward his Chosen People and their efforts to build a New Canaan in the wilderness. The preeminent work in this tradition was William Bradford's *Of Plimoth Plantation*. Written during the 1630s and 1640s when Bradford was governor of the colony, the book recounts the fate of a tiny band of Puritans who fled England for Holland and then for the New World. They rested in the certainty that God's hand led them forward, that their disasters were his rebukes, their successes his merciful rewards. Governor John Winthrop of Massachusetts wrote such a history, as did Cotton Mather in the next century. Mary Rowlandson's eyewitness account of her own captivity employed the same providential themes. Well into the nineteenth century, male and female historians, including Mercy Otis Warren, Elizabeth Peabody, and Hannah Adams, viewed the story of America as an extension of the history of the Protestant Reformation. The Revolution became for them a triumph of reformed Christianity over paganism and Catholicism. And the United States as a whole took the place of New England as the model of Christian virtue for the corrupt Old World to emulate.[8]

In the late eighteenth century, as the European Enlightenment came to America, history took on a secular and naturalistic cast. A new class of intellectuals, influenced by Newton, Locke, and the French philosophes, had come to see history, like the physical universe, as subject to natural law. These rationalist historians flourished alongside and sometimes superseded the clerics who had once dominated the educated class in the colonies. The new story they told was of progress, reason — and, indeed, "the progress of reason" — in human affairs. Although a few Protestant ministers responded to the new

---

[7]On the development of the historical profession in America, see John Higham, *History: Professional Scholarship in America* (New York, 1973). See also works cited in footnote 3.

[8]Nina Baym, *American Women Writers and the Work of History* (New Brunswick, N.J., 1995), particularly "History from a Divine Point of View," 46–66.

intellectual currents,[9] most historians in the late eighteenth century were lawyer-politicians, planter-aristocrats, merchants, professionals, and, in the case of Judith Sargent Murray, the daughter and wife of a minister. Among the most prominent were Thomas Hutchinson, leading merchant and royal governor of Massachusetts; William Smith, physician, landowner, and prominent politician of New York; and Robert Beverley and William Byrd of Virginia, both planter-aristocrats and officeholders. These men possessed classical educations, fine private libraries, and the leisure time to use both. Their writing was more refined and allusive than the studiously plain prose of their Puritan predecessors. They wrote history for their own satisfaction, but also to explain to the enlightened world the success of men like themselves — free, bold, intelligent, and ambitious men who built fortunes and governed provinces that embodied a perfect balance between liberty and order.

Thomas Jefferson's *Notes on the State of Virginia* (written in the midst of revolutionary turmoil and finally published in 1785) is a highly evolved product of this rationalist tradition. America is for Jefferson, as it was for the Puritans, a model for the world, but natural law takes the place of divine providence in directing its affairs. Self-interest, not piety, motivates men; reason, not faith, allows them to discover and pursue their destiny. The fruits of liberty include not only astonishing material prosperity and advances in knowledge but moral progress as well. The new nation is destined to open the way toward a new era in human history not only because its natural resources are vast but also because free people are virtuous and possessed of the moral energy to change the world. Some evangelical Protestants called Jefferson a "confirmed infidel" and a "howling atheist" for his emphasis on human as opposed to divine agency. But Jefferson's most potent enemies were political: in the 1790s, he led the Republican opposition to the Federalist Party of Washington, Hamilton, and Adams. During the brutal presidential election campaigns of 1800 and 1804, both of which Jefferson won, Federalist writers combed the *Notes* to find ammunition against Jefferson the infidel, the apologist for slavery, the lover of French revolutionary excess. Their charges reveal, among other things, that history had already become politicized. History was a story about how wealth, power, rights, and wrongs came to be in this world — how causes produced effects, and how human actions could change those effects. But the story for the rationalists was no more open-ended than it was for the providentialists: it still pointed toward improvement. Through most of the nineteenth century and into the early twentieth, American history remained the story of the progress of the "Empire of Liberty."

As the nineteenth century wore on, historians began to temper their Enlightenment assurance about human beings' capacity for rational improvement. They increasingly believed that races possessed different inherent capacities and viewed the rise of America as the triumph of Anglo-Saxon

---

[9]See Edmund S. Morgan, *The Gentle Puritan: A Life of Ezra Stiles, 1727–1795* (New Haven, Conn., 1962).

people over inferior races. Similar strains of thinking in Europe helped to justify colonization. George Bancroft, the most distinguished American historian of the mid-nineteenth century, organized the history of America around three themes: progress, liberty, and Anglo-Saxon destiny. Bancroft deviated from his own rationalist background after studying in Germany, where he absorbed the romantic emphasis on the inborn virtues of the "folk." The idea that Teutonic peoples (who included Anglo-Saxons) were racially destined to spread freedom across the globe was central to this romantic nationalism. In twelve volumes published between 1834 and 1882, Bancroft chronicled the spread of Anglo-Saxon ideas of political freedom, their perfection in American democratic institutions, and their realization in Jacksonian democracy.[10]

Even women historians such as Hannah Adams, Susanna Rowson, Elizabeth Peabody, and Emma Willard, whose evangelical commitments made them political enemies of the Jacksonian Democratic Party, manifested romantic nationalist thinking not unlike Bancroft's. In her *Pioneer Women of the West* (1852), Elizabeth Ellet focused on conflict between white settlers and indigenous people. As Nina Baym put it in 1995, Ellet "is as close to a genocidal writer as one is likely to find."[11] Some women, however, did break the barriers of gender and nationalist history. Helen Hunt Jackson explored white-Indian relations in both fiction and history. Her *Century of Dishonor* (1881) — which she sent to every member of Congress — documented the American nation's shameful dealings with Indians. Intent on reaching a wider popular audience, she then published a novel, *Ramona*, that dramatized white appropriation of Indian lands and other cruelties. At the same time, white and Indian anthropologists began studying native cultures, some because they thought Indians were disappearing, others because they wished to counteract racist myths by displaying the vigor and richness of Indian cultures.[12] Unfortunately, neither criticism nor ethnographic knowledge seriously affected the trajectory of mainstream history. Not until the arrival of the inclusionary politics of the late twentieth century would the work of anthropologists and ethnographers find its way into the pages of historical scholarship.

By the 1870s, Bancroft's self-congratulatory epic history had become conventional wisdom. But changes were afoot in the discipline. The first change was in leadership: amateur writers increasingly gave way to professional historians. As college education became more common among middle-class Americans and as industrialization reinforced the value of technical and scientific knowledge, historians increasingly concerned themselves with specialized training, research methodology, and educational credentials. History became a profession like any other. This meant, among other things,

---

[10]On Bancroft and other romantic historians, see David Levin, *History as Romantic Art* (New York, 1963).

[11]Baym, *American Women Writers*, 219, 238; other enemies of Jackson, such as historians Francis Parkman and W. H. Prescott, wrote a similar kind of romantic-racial epic: see Levin, *History as Romantic Art.*

[12]See Chapter 11.

that it would be practiced by the only people who had access to advanced education — white men. Many of them were trained in Germany, but in 1876 Johns Hopkins University became the first exclusively graduate research institution in the United States. Soon thereafter, graduate study spread to the midwestern land-grant universities and the Ivy League. The newly minted historians usually planned careers in the same university system that had trained them. They prided themselves on rigorous research and a capacity to distinguish scientifically verified truth from romantic notion. Reflecting on these developments in 1894, Henry Adams imagined this new professional historian "dreaming of the immortality that would be achieved by the man who should successfully apply Darwin's method to the facts of human history."[13]

Along with Frederick Jackson Turner, Adams exemplified the first generation of professional historians, which held sway from about 1870 to 1910. A scion of the great family that had produced presidents and statesmen, Adams might appear at first to be a throwback to the era of patrician amateurs. Politics was the career he had hoped for, while history seemed an avocation. But as his political hopes dimmed, his professional ambitions ignited. In 1870, he was invited to Harvard to teach the first seminar ever devoted to historical research at that institution. Adams taught the meticulous methods of German scholarship and insisted that history's goal was to develop knowledge every bit as sound as that in physics. His exhaustively researched nine-volume history of the Jefferson and Madison administrations represented the fruit of his commitment to the scientific method and remains a classic. Although he left Harvard after a few years, his career exemplified the new professionalism that would permanently transform the discipline.

Turner could not have been more different from Adams in background and personal circumstances. Born of modest means in a rural town in Wisconsin, he attended the University of Wisconsin, received a Ph.D. in history at Johns Hopkins, and went on to teach at Wisconsin and Harvard. While different from Adams in so many ways, Turner shared the belief that history should be a science. He fulfilled Adams's prophecy in using Darwin's evolutionary theory to explain the genesis of the American character. Just as one species surpassed another, he argued in his famous "The Significance of the Frontier in American History," so one frontier environment succeeded another in the course of American expansion. As successive frontiers grew more remote from European antecedents, they increasingly nurtured the distinctive American virtues of self-reliance, egalitarianism, tolerance, practicality, and realism.[14] Although he embodied the new scientific history, Turner's sweeping generalizations and his assumptions about the "progress of the

---

[13]Henry Adams, "The Tendency of History," *Annual Report of the American Historical Association for the Year 1894* (Washington, D.C., 1895), 19.

[14]Turner's essay, originally delivered as his presidential address to the American Historical Association in 1893, can be found in *The Frontier in American History* (New York, 1920). For more on Turner, see John Higham, *Writing American History: Essays on Modern Scholarship* (Bloomington, Ind., 1970), 118–29; see also the discussion in Chapter 7.

race" linked him to his nationalist predecessors. He conflated America with capitalism, democracy, and the heroic deeds of the pioneers.

Between 1910 and 1945, a second generation of professional scholars — the Progressive historians — rose to prominence. They were identified with the Progressive movement in politics, which worked to combat corporate and political corruption and the suffering of working families in early-twentieth-century America.[15] They observed that modernity — industrialization, urbanization, and class conflict — had fundamentally transformed the society. If democracy was to survive, people needed a materially based history of changing institutions and economic interests, not fables about the progress of liberty and justice. Progressives saw history as politics, not science or art. To be sure, science was needed to produce usable facts and art to persuade people to act on them, but Progressive historians wanted their history to provoke political action above all. Neither genteel amateurs nor morally neutral scientists, Progressives were muscular intellectuals — or, as they would have gladly called themselves, reformers.

In 1913, the most famous Progressive historian, Charles A. Beard, published *An Economic Interpretation of the Constitution,* one of the most influential books ever written in American history. It argued that the Constitution was the product not of wise men intent on balancing liberty and order, but of a clique of wealthy merchants and landowners who wanted a central government strong enough to defend their privileges against the unruly masses. A series of books culminating in *The Rise of American Civilization* (1927), which Beard wrote with his wife, Mary Ritter Beard, elaborated the thesis that American history was a succession of conflicts between economic interest groups. Although critics found flaws with his economic determinism and faith in Progressive reform, Beard managed to inspire a generation to look to history for answers to the questions that pressed most insistently on the democratic citizenry.

With a literary flair that exceeded that of either Turner or Beard, Vernon L. Parrington brought the Progressive interpretation to intellectual history in *Main Currents in American Thought.* His story was arrestingly simple: all of American history was shaped by the contest between Jeffersonian and Hamiltonian ways of thinking. Jefferson, champion of the people, represented decentralized agrarian democracy; Hamilton, tribune of the privileged, stood for centralized commercial aristocracy. From the moment the Revolution ended, these two ideas fought for control of American minds. In whatever guise — Federalist versus Republican, Whig versus Jacksonian, Conservative versus Progressive — all these conflicts reflected a continuous economic dynamic that animated American history. The function of history was to uncover the economic basis of political ideas and thereby to educate the citizenry. Parrington wanted his fellow citizens to take on the task of fighting reaction and pushing reform.

---

[15]See Volume Two, Chapter 6.

Progressive history challenged the profession in another way: it insisted that historical knowledge is relative. In an essay published in 1935 entitled "That Noble Dream," Charles Beard observed that one bar to objectivity is that the historian's documentation is always partial. More important, like Croce he insisted that the historian is never neutral and therefore must write an interpretation, not a scientific re-creation, of the past. The dream of objectivity must be discarded by the serious and honest historian. Acknowledging one's politics and prejudices does not weaken the value of the historian's work, Beard insisted, but rather strengthens it. An interpretation — which he defined as an "overarching hypothesis or conception employed to give coherence and structure to past events" — should be measured not by whether it is correct or incorrect but by whether it is useful to people who are trying to improve their world.[16] Carl L. Becker, a Progressive historian of early America, made the promotion of relativism one of the central purposes of his career. In his 1931 presidential address to the American Historical Association, "Everyman His Own Historian," and in other essays, Becker repeated that, however indispensable the scientific pursuit of facts, history meant nothing unless it was yoked to the political necessities of real people. History's obligation is not to the dead but to the living; its account of the past is "perhaps neither true nor false, but only the most convenient form of error."[17]

Female and African American scholars challenged the profession in still other ways, though historians were not yet ready to respond. Mary Ritter Beard, for example — who published many works with her husband and many books about women on her own, culminating in *Woman as a Force in History* in 1946 — achieved little or no recognition from the profession. She entered Columbia graduate school with her husband in 1902, but dropped out two years later and subsequently nurtured a hostility for academics and for college education for women. She chose to wear her amateur status like a crown in the face of a profession that refused to welcome her.[18] Other women in the Progressive Era who chose to write women's history similarly saw their work ignored by their male colleagues.[19]

African American historians fared little better. At the American Historical Association meeting in 1909, W. E. B. Du Bois, having earned a Ph.D. from Harvard, offered a startling reinterpretation of Reconstruction that focused on the lives of poor blacks and whites. In the face of a daunting tradition condemning Reconstruction, he argued that it had briefly

---

[16]Charles A. Beard, "That Noble Dream," *American Historical Review* 41 (October 1935): 74–87.

[17]This and related essays may be found in *Everyman His Own Historian* (New York, 1935). See also Phil L. Snyder, ed., *Detachment and the Writing of History: Essays and Letters of Carl L. Becker* (Ithaca, N.Y., 1958). For more on historical relativism, see Higham, *History;* a neo-relativist argument can be found in Novick, *That Noble Dream*, and other works cited in note 3, above. Still very useful as a philosophical guide is Jack W. Mieland, *Scepticism and Historical Knowledge* (New York, 1965).

[18]Ann J. Lane, *Mary Ritter Beard, A Sourcebook* (New York, 1977), 33, 53–54.

[19]Helen Sumner's *Women and Industry in the U.S.* and Edith Abbott's *Women in Industry*, both published in 1910, were barely noticed by the male profession.

provided the South with democratic government, public schools, and other needed social programs. Like other Progressives, Du Bois found economic causes underlying political events; unlike them, however, he included black people as legitimate historical subjects. This simple act of inclusion irrevocably altered his assessment of Reconstruction. Published in 1935, his book attracted many favorable reviews, but most historians ignored it. Du Bois's views did not enter the mainstream of the profession until John Hope Franklin's and Kenneth Stampp's revisionist interpretations appeared in the 1960s.[20]

The Progressives' economic determinism and their relativism both had an enormous impact on the history profession, but neither Beard nor Becker held the center stage exclusively or for long. Critics of both progressive and relativist assertions began to multiply. In part, the critics were responding to the rise of totalitarianism, which made faith in progress seem naive and relativism seem cowardly. The fact that Charles Beard quite conspicuously continued to oppose American involvement in World War II, at a time when most left-wing intellectuals were rapidly shifting from pacifism to intervention, seemed to many intellectuals to emphasize the narrow-mindedness of the Progressive point of view. In the face of Hitler and Stalin, and especially after the horrors of Auschwitz, Dresden, and Hiroshima, American historians asked themselves if Progressive history had ill-prepared them and their fellow citizens for the harrowing obligations of the twentieth century. But it was not just the weight of tragic events that shifted the historiographical terrain.

In the 1930s and into the 1950s, younger historians increasingly found the Progressive historians' psychology shallow, their social analysis predictable, and their moral judgments superficial. Like the philosophers and theologians who were criticizing liberalism for its facile optimism and obtuseness in the face of human tragedy, these critics charged that Progressive historians underestimated humankind's propensity for evil, overestimated its capacity for good, and turned history into a simple morality play. More important, they found the Progressive insistence on explaining most events as the product of conflict between rich and poor, East and West, reactionaries and reformers, and the like to be more hindrance than help in making sense of specific historical problems. More and more historians were insisting that, for better *and* worse, consensus rather than conflict marked American political history, that the absence of European-style class conflict had indelibly shaped American institutions and ideas. In Europe, the crises of depression and war led many historians in radical directions; here, under the influence of the Cold War, it led toward what came to be called "consensus history."

The caricature of consensus historians is that they asserted the unity and homogeneity of America's past, the stability of basic institutions, and the existence of a homogeneous national character. When they did acknowl-

---

[20]W. E. B. Du Bois, *Black Reconstruction in America, 1860–1880* (New York, 1992), vii–viii, xvi. For more on the historiography of Reconstruction, see Chapter 11.

edge that conflict occurred between sections, classes, and groups, the consensus historians insisted that contestants fought within a common liberal framework and never really disagreed over fundamentals. Moreover, this caricature continues, consensus historians doubted the value of social change and, having observed a world brutalized by fascism and communism, feared mass movements of any kind. In this reading, consensus historians trimmed the sails of history to the conservative and anti-Communist winds of the McCarthy era. In fact, so-called consensus historians were remarkably diverse, and many were liberals. Some were indeed "Cold War liberals" who believed that a defense of American values and institutions was more important than social criticism at a moment when totalitarianism threatened to take over the world. However, there was no simple correlation between Cold War attitudes and consensus historiography. Arthur M. Schlesinger Jr., who never departed from the Progressive camp, was the leading Cold War liberal in the history profession. On the other hand, the distinguished Columbia University historian Richard Hofstadter, who was called a consensus historian and was a sharp critic of Progressive historiography, was equally if not more critical of the consensus he found in American history.

Some consensus history did prove useful to cold warriors. In his influential *The Liberal Tradition in America*, Louis Hartz argued that because America lacked a feudal tradition, it escaped the struggles between reactionaries, liberals, and socialists that characterized the history of most European countries. The United States instead had a three-century-long tradition of liberal consensus, wherein all Americans subscribed to the Lockean tenets of individualism, private property, natural rights, and popular sovereignty. The differences among Americans, Hartz maintained, were over means rather than ends. And thus America had very little class conflict and little ground for the breeding of class-based ideologies. Socialism could mean little in America because nearly everyone had access to a middle-class way of life. Conservatism, too, could mean little because the only thing to conserve — the only continuous tradition — was liberalism.[21]

Another postwar consensus historian, Daniel Boorstin, wrote a three-volume epic story of settlement, westward migration, and community building. Although he echoed the Progressive Turner in many ways, Boorstin described characters who were largely uninterested in politics and ideology. Most of them were pragmatic, energetic, healthy-minded "Versatiles," ready to conquer a continent, invent the balloon-frame house, experiment with popular democracy, and in the process develop the freest and most prosperous society on earth. Boorstin's approach was social-historical. Like the more radical social historians who would soon transform the discipline,

---

[21]Louis Hartz, *The Liberal Tradition in America: An Interpretation of American Political Thought since the Revolution* (New York, 1955). A brilliant critique (and also appreciation) of Hartz can be found in James T. Kloppenberg, "From Hartz to Tocqueville: Shifting the Focus from Liberalism to Democracy in America," in Meg Jacobs, William J. Novak, and Julian E. Zelizer, eds., *The Democratic Experiment: New Directions in American Political History* (Princeton, N.J., 2003), 350–80.

Boorstin insisted that American society and culture were decisively shaped by millions of ordinary people, not by elites. But for Boorstin, those anonymous masses were middle class at heart and yearned for nothing so much as a house with a picket fence and a little room to breathe. Distinct from most of the other consensus historians, Boorstin preached a political message that might be called conservative populism.

If Hartz's insistence on ideological homogeneity and Boorstin's populist social history seemed to affirm a Cold War consensus, the political tonality of Richard Hofstadter's work proved harder to gauge. Beginning in 1948 with the publication of *The American Political Tradition and the Men Who Made It*, Hofstadter argued that the liberal tradition had failed to escape the acquisitive and individualistic assumptions that had shaped it. Supposed reformers such as the Populists and Progressives looked back with nostalgia to an era of self-made men, rather than facing up to the fundamental problems of an industrialized and corporate America. Even Franklin Delano Roosevelt, who did not share the nostalgia common to the Progressive tradition, was primarily a pragmatist whose strength lay in the force of his personality rather than in any consistent ideology or philosophy. In *The Age of Reform: From Bryan to F.D.R.*, Hofstadter exposed what he saw as the curious blend of racism, nativism, and provincialism that shaped the Populists and would later manifest itself in paranoid scares such as McCarthyism in the 1950s. All such movements meant "to restore the conditions prevailing before the development of industrialism and the commercialization of agriculture."[22] Hofstadter maintained that American political conflict reflected not the clash of economic interests but the search by different ethnic and religious groups for a secure status in society. By the latter third of the nineteenth century, the middle-class offspring of Anglo-Saxon Protestant families found themselves displaced from traditional positions of leadership by a nouveau-riche plutocracy, on the one hand, and urban immigrant political machines, on the other. Responding to this displacement, the elite launched a moral crusade to resuscitate older Protestant and individualistic values — the Progressive movement. In this campaign "to maintain a homogeneous Yankee civilization," Hofstadter wrote, "I have found much that was retrograde and delusive, a little that was vicious, and a good deal that was comic."[23]

Hofstadter emerged from within the Progressive historiographical tradition, briefly flirted with Marxism in the 1930s, and thereafter, though his sympathies remained on the left, considered himself effectively nonpolitical.[24] In a sense, his entire career can be seen as a lover's quarrel with liberalism, in the course of which he recognized its promise but relentlessly

---

[22]Richard Hofstadter, *The Age of Reform: From Bryan to F.D.R.* (New York, 1955), 62.
[23]Ibid., 11.
[24]For a brief assessment of the historian, see Eric Foner, "The Education of Richard Hofstadter," in *Who Owns History? Rethinking the Past in a Changing World* (New York, 2002), 25–46; other assessments are cited in his footnotes. For a fuller picture, see Richard S. Brown's fine biography, *Richard Hofstadter* (Chicago, 2006).

exposed its inadequacies, delusions, and failures. Despite his own leftist tendencies, Hofstadter resisted completely the temptation to find heroic victories for the people in what he saw as a depressing chronicle of consensus based on common cupidity. America was more illiberal than the Progressive historians would prefer; they wrote history that fostered the illusion of liberal reform, but he would not.

Hofstadter's powerful critique of American liberalism was shaped not only by his evolving political views, but also by his reading of twentieth-century social science research. Based on that reading, he began to address in new ways a familiar set of questions about American society. Who were American reformers, and what did they want? Hofstadter used the findings of social scientists to explain the significance of status in shaping social behavior. If abolitionists, Populists, and Progressives had not in fact democratized America, just what had they accomplished? Hofstadter looked to the sociology of bureaucracy and complex organizations, as well as research into the modernization of societies in the European and non-European world, to illuminate an era in which Americans were moving from small towns to big cities, from simple and homogeneous to complex and pluralistic social structures. To explain the reformers' passions, he employed social-psychological concepts such as projection, displacement, scapegoating, and the authoritarian personality.

If Hofstadter derived critical insights from social science, another consensus historian, Edmund S. Morgan, looked elsewhere. A student of Perry Miller, the distinguished Harvard historian of early American religion and culture, Morgan echoed his mentor's distrust of Progressive history and of liberalism generally. Liberalism, Miller had believed, possessed few intellectual resources with which to criticize the modern pursuit of individualism, self-expression, and material success. In the premodern and therefore pre-liberal Puritan world, Morgan (like Miller) found depths of wisdom that seemed lacking in the twentieth century. Wary of those who applied present-day assumptions to the task of understanding the past, Morgan refused to see Puritans as sexually repressed and obsessed with sin. And he refused to see colonial dissidents as anticipators or forerunners of latter-day democratic liberalism. Thus, in his earliest works, he portrayed Anne Hutchinson and Roger Williams not as progressive critics of Puritan oligarchy, but as self-righteous zealots, nihilists even. In contrast, Governor John Winthrop was not a repressive Puritan oligarch but a man striving to live responsibly in a deeply imperfect world that required order more than individual freedom for visionaries.[25]

If Progressives and Marxists insisted that economic interests and material forces shaped history, Morgan would follow his mentor Perry Miller in insisting that ideas mattered. Winthrop and his adversaries were obsessed with ideas, led by them, willing to suffer and even die for them. In 1967, in a striking demonstration of this belief, Morgan admitted that he had been wrong

---

[25]See especially Edmund S. Morgan, *The Puritan Dilemma: The Story of John Winthrop* (Boston, 1958).

about Roger Williams. In *Roger Williams: The Church and the State*, Morgan now acknowledged that Williams's ideas were momentous. Williams had understood that conscientious protest was an act "not so much of defiance as of discovery." What Williams discovered — what John Winthrop could not — was that separation of church and state was absolutely necessary, first, to preserve religion from being corrupted by the state and, second, to protect the state from becoming the engine of religious intolerance. Thus, the historian who began his career by rebuking modern liberals for misrepresenting the strange world of seventeenth-century Puritanism found himself in the 1960s affirming the connection between Puritanism and the tradition of civil-libertarian protest that became a hallmark of the later democratic republic.[26] Perhaps the America he and his students encountered in the 1960s forced this most scrupulous of historians to reflect on what Croce called the contemporaneous character of history.

Morgan's work spanned a great variety of subjects from Puritan thought, to the Revolution, to slavery. Although he never abandoned his faith in the power of ideas, by the late 1960s his research into the origins of slavery had plunged him deeply into social history, that is, into the realm of group experience and collective fate that seemed very far away from the world of intellectuals and political leaders that had once so occupied him. Executing a dazzling intellectual pirouette, Morgan came to insist that there was nothing incompatible between asserting that consensus dominated mainstream American political and intellectual history and insisting that the most egregious form of oppression — slavery — lay at the heart of the American social experience. Indeed, he claimed, it was precisely because white America relied on slavery to keep the lowest of the low under control, thereby minimizing class conflict among the free, that liberal democracy was able to flower in the late eighteenth and nineteenth centuries.

Morgan's *American Slavery, American Freedom* is the book named "most admired" more frequently than any other in a 1994 poll of American historians.[27] Morgan's complex argument cannot be summarized here, but its power can be attributed to its capacity to span the historiography wars that marked the history profession in the 1960s and for several decades thereafter. What historian John Higham called the "Cult of American Consensus" had made American history tame and predictable.[28] Within that consensus perspective, eighteenth-century America appeared to be the spawning ground for middle-class democracy; the Revolution was a largely intellectual movement; radicals, abolitionists, Reconstructionists, and socialists were maladjusted sufferers of status anxiety; and the Cold War was a noble (if reluctant) effort to save the world from totalitarianism. In the face of this antiseptic treatment of the past, dissenters predictably arose. A new

---

[26]Edmund S. Morgan, *Roger Williams: The Church and the State* (New York, 1967).

[27]Edmund S. Morgan, *American Slavery, American Freedom: The Ordeal of Colonial Virginia* (New York, 1975); the historians' poll and commentary on it can be found in *Journal of American History* 81 (December 1994).

[28]John Higham, "The Cult of 'American Consensus': Homogenizing Our History," *Commentary* 27 (February 1959): 93–100.

generation of neo-Progressives began to insist that conflict, not consensus, marked the American past.

The assault on consensus history reflected the erosion of political consensus in 1960s America. Already in the late 1950s, the emergence of the civil rights movement signaled the reemergence of the African American struggle against inequality and racism in American society. For a time, the movement could be subsumed under the rubric of liberal reform, welcomed as a perfection of liberal democracy rather than a fundamental challenge to it. But by the mid-1960s, the racial animosity and poverty that had once been invisible to whites, and for a time appeared readily curable, came to seem more endemic and intractable. Radical inequality would require radical measures — at least, some insisted, measures more radical than integration or voting rights. When New Left critics of American society looked for radical antecedents in prominent historical accounts, they found chronicles of consensus — but not for long. Increasingly, younger historians found in older Progressive historical works and in neo-Marxist scholarship from Europe the inspiration to rewrite American history as a chronicle of struggle — for working-class power, for racial equality, for women's rights, for ethnic identity, and for all forms of social justice. The Vietnam War added immense energy to this endeavor. As college campuses became centers of protest against the war, historians absorbed the growing suspicion that the U.S. foreign policy establishment served interests quite distinct from the national interest. They condemned all forms of concentrated power — corporations, political parties, government bureaucracies, professional organizations, and the like — that seemed to profit from inequality and promote injustice in the United States and around the world.

Methodological innovation involving the increased interaction of history with social science, comparative history, and quantitative methods only reinforced tendencies toward radical critique. While Hofstadter, Hartz, and other historians had already begun to pay attention to social science research and comparative approaches, the move to quantification was new. With the exception of economic historians, most historians had no acquaintance with the use of scientifically measurable historical data. One of the attractions of quantitative techniques was quite old-fashioned: like the positivists of the late-nineteenth and early-twentieth centuries, modern-day quantifiers sought the authority of science. They also wanted to strengthen their claim to the growing pools of research money available in the postwar United States from both government and private funders of social science research. At the same time, the urge to quantify drew energy from a democratic urge to capture the reality of ordinary lives through social history. Peasants, workers, slaves, migrants — whole categories of human beings — were invisible because they had been "inarticulate," that is, illiterate and ignored by those who left written documents. Quantitative history suggested a way to make them speak: through records that traced collective behavior and from which ideas, values, intentions, and beliefs might be inferred. Thus John Demos surprisingly could bring in view the interior lives of the earliest settlers of Plymouth colony through the analysis of wills, deeds, contracts, and probate records.[29] On a broader canvas, Paul Kleppner's quantitative analysis of voting records revealed the ethnic motives of voters in the nineteenth-century Midwest; and as a result of computer analysis of manuscript censuses and other data, Stephen Thernstrom discovered the astounding geographical (and limited social) mobility of working-class New Englanders in the industrial era.[30]

Quantitative historians drew inspiration not only from the social and behavioral sciences but also from the work of historians associated with the French journal *Annales*. Led by Lucien Febvre and Marc Bloch, who had begun using quantitative techniques in the 1930s and 1940s, these French historians strove for "total history" — a history that recorded the myriad experiences of masses of people, not just the dramatic events that featured prominent actors. In the hands of a leading figure in the *Annales* school, Fernand Braudel, history became a slow, majestic procession of material change — change in population, agricultural production, prices, trade, and so on — that created, unbeknownst to any individual, the true conditions of life in medieval and early modern Europe. This version of social history was "history with the politics left out," indeed, history with all the usual markers of individual consciousness left out.[31]

Others trying to write a new social history took a very different tack. For them, social history meant history from the bottom up. Though sometimes inspired by the quantifiers' capacity to occupy a distant perch and from there comprehend a vast historical terrain, these new social historians more closely observed institutional change and group action. They refused to believe that the masses were inaccessible to creative historical research. In fact, social historians began to find copious evidence of conscious thought and action among the lower orders. Slave narratives, diaries of farm wives and artisan workers, letters and articles in obscure newspapers, broadsides and pamphlets, court and police records, institutional memoranda and reports — these and many other sources began to give up their secrets. The new social historians were neo-progressives, in a way, but far more radical than Beard and Becker. Piecemeal political reform would not easily remake a society hideously distorted by racism and sexism, dominated by immense corporations, regulated by "therapeutic" bureaucracies, and dedicated to the systematic exploitation of the third world. Not Progressive reformers, but militant, even revolutionary activists — like the artisan revolutionaries in the 1770s, the abolitionists and radical Reconstructionists in the nineteenth

---

[29]John Demos, *A Little Commonwealth: Family Life in Plymouth Colony* (New York, 1970). See also Kenneth A. Lockridge, *A New England Town: The First Hundred Years* (New York, 1970); a later community study focusing on the Chesapeake is Darrett B. and Anita H. Rutman, *A Place in Time: Middlesex County, Virginia, 1650–1750* (New York, 1984).

[30]Paul Kleppner, *The Third Electoral System: 1853–1892: Parties, Voters, and Political Cultures* (Chapel Hill, N.C., 1979); Stephen Thernstrom, *Poverty and Progress: Social Mobility in a Nineteenth-Century City* (Cambridge, Mass., 1964), and *The Other Bostonians: Poverty and Progress in an American Metropolis* (Cambridge, Mass., 1973).

[31]Of Braudel's many works, perhaps the most accessible is *Capitalism and Material Life, 1400–1800* (New York, 1967).

century, and the most combative unionists in the 1930s — became models for latter-day radicals in the 1960s and 1970s.[32]

As Chapter 3 in Volume Two makes clear, among the first subjects to respond to this approach was labor history or, as it came increasingly to be called, working-class history. Inspired especially by the English neo-Marxist E. P. Thompson, new labor historians rewrote the history of unions and unionization but, more importantly, of working-class families and communities, working-class politics and culture. The people whom they studied, far from seeming to be either aspirants to middle-class status or alien radicals, came to seem at once both more militantly class-conscious and more deeply rooted in American society and culture. Other fields, such as immigration history, African American history, and women's history, similarly experienced a dramatic renaissance. Both white and black scholars helped turn the history of slavery into one of the most exciting and fruitful fields of history. Recovering the seminal scholarship of African American historians such as W. E. B. Du Bois and Eric Williams, and plunging into previously ignored archival sources, the historians of the 1960s found not passivity but agency among slaves, not imitation of white culture but cultural resistance and the endurance of African traditions and practices. They insisted that the Civil War had been fought to abolish slavery, that African Americans played a crucial part in its conduct and success, and that only force and betrayal — not the alleged cultural deprivation or political immaturity of blacks — had led to the failure of Reconstruction.[33]

Women's historians began to effect a similarly profound change in the standard narrative of American history. If women had been excluded from the conventionally male realms of power and privilege, they had no less been excluded from the pages of American history. Inspired by the women's liberation movement and the simultaneous arrival of history from the bottom up in the 1960s and 1970s, male and especially female historians began to hear the voices of women and transfer them to the pages of

---

[32]See, for example, Alfred F. Young, ed., *The American Revolution: Explorations in the History of American Radicalism* (DeKalb, Ill., 1976); John Hope Franklin, *Reconstruction: After the Civil War* (Chicago, 1961); Kenneth M. Stampp, *The Era of Reconstruction, 1865–1877* (New York, 1965); and Daniel J. Leab, ed., *The Labor History Reader* (Urbana, Ill., 1980), which includes classic essays published over a twenty-year period. A sweeping narrative (and celebration) of the rise of radical history can be found in Jonathan M. Wiener, "Radical Historians and the Crisis in American History, 1959–1980," *Journal of American History* 76 (September 1989): 399–434, part of a roundtable that includes criticism and commentary from a variety of historians and a response from Wiener.

[33]On slavery, see John W. Blassingame, *The Slave Community: Plantation Life in the Ante-Bellum South* (New York, 1972); George P. Rawick, *From Sundown to Sunup: The Making of the Black Community* (Westport, Conn., 1972); and Leslie Howard Owens, *This Species of Property: Slave Life and Culture in the Old South* (New York, 1976). On African Americans in the Civil War, the classic study is Benjamin Quarles, *The Negro in the Civil War* (Boston, 1953), which James M. McPherson built upon in *The Negro's Civil War: How American Negroes Felt and Acted during the War for the Union* (New York, 1965). On Reconstruction, the epic work is C. Vann Woodward, *Origins of the New South* (Baton Rouge, La., 1951); see also works by Franklin and Stampp cited in footnote 32 and others cited in Chapters 4 and 9.

history.[34] In the suffrage movement and the labor movement; in the records of settlement houses and women's academies and colleges; in the records of births and marriages, of prostitution arrests and temperance campaigns; in the copious records of literary and moral reform publications, in which women argued both for equality and for recognition of their distinctive feminine gifts; and in many other sources, historians of women rewrote the story of America from its very beginnings up to the recent past. They did not merely give women a place in the existing narratives; rather, they reconceived whole fields of history. Thus, for example, the culture of slavery appears to be a realm not simply of *either* accommodation *or* resistance, but — when women are brought centrally into its historical reconstruction — a realm of endurance and cultural creativity.[35] Likewise, the history of progressive reform becomes the story of women, denied direct access to political office, asserting their rights to set the public agenda and to demand maternalist state action in the interest of reforming the social household.[36]

In these and many other ways, historians of women and of African Americans joined a broader wave of socially critical scholarship that had moved very far away from even the history of the most progressive men of earlier generations. Today it seems that every man and woman has become his and her own historian in a way even Carl Becker would have found surprising (and cheering). Considerable success in democratizing the academy in the wake of civil rights and women's rights movements has unseated dominant perspectives and opened the way for more diverse and more politically critical schools of interpretation in history and other disciplines. So unsettling have these developments been that by the 1980s many historians complained that both interpretive coherence and objectivity had vanished from the profession. They feared that fragmentation threatened to consign scholars to increasingly microscopic and specialized enclaves, making it impossible to communicate with one another, let alone with a broader public. To others, this lack of coherence seemed a healthy state of ferment and pluralistic openness: "Maybe drift and uncertainty," one such historian remarked, ". . . are preconditions for creativity."[37] It is probably true that coherence and fragmentation, harmony and polytonality, the pursuit of

---

[34]A few early works include Gerda Lerner, *The Woman in American History* (Menlo Park, Calif., 1971); William H. Chafe, *The American Woman: Her Changing Social, Economic and Political Roles, 1920–1970* (New York, 1972); and Nancy F. Cott, *The Bonds of Womanhood: "Woman's Sphere" in New England, 1780–1835* (New Haven, Conn., 1977). See also classic essays in Linda K. Kerber and Jane DeHart Matthews, eds., *Women's America: Refocusing the Past* (New York, 1982), and other works cited in Volume Two, Chapter 10.

[35]See Chapter 9.

[36]See Volume Two, Chapter 6, and also Chapter 8 in this volume.

[37]On the perils of fragmentation, see Thomas Bender, "Wholes and Parts: The Need for Synthesis in American History," *Journal of American History* 73 (June 1986): 120–36; see the ensuing debate on Bender's essay in "A Round Table: Synthesis in American History," *Journal of American History* 74 (June 1987): 107–30. See also John Higham, "The Future of American History," *Journal of American History* 80 (March 1994): 1289–1309. The quotation is from Jackson Lears, "Mastery and Drift," *Journal of American History* 84 (December 1997): 979–88.

the microscopic and the synthetic are parallel rather than alternative practices within the history profession. In the end, moreover, diversity of perspectives does not rule out a broadly synthetic multicultural history. The ambition to make sense of a complex past — to narrate a big story — should not be confused with an urge to drown difference in a wave of false or oppressive homogeneity.

The charge that history had descended into political partisanship gained more energy from forces outside the academy than from within. To be sure, historians as different as the Marxists Elizabeth Fox-Genovese and Eugene D. Genovese, the liberals Arthur Schlesinger Jr. and Diane Ravitch, and the conservative Gertrude Himmelfarb, to name a few, pilloried the profession for allowing social history to descend into what they considered tendentious, multiculturalist special pleading. Several of them helped organize a new professional organization, the Historical Society, which published a new journal designed to avoid the pitfalls of the "balkanized" history and restore dispassion and breadth of view to the profession.[38] Its founding manifesto announced the aim of "reorienting the historical profession toward an accessible, integrated history free from fragmentation and over-specialization." For the most part, however, despite manifestos, the new journal features articles that are mostly indistinguishable from those published in mainstream journals.[39] Moreover, the vigor of debate in professional journals and meetings belies the charge that conformity on ideological or methodological matters has stifled free inquiry.

In the realm of public history, however, the highly politicized claims about leftist bias in history have sparked real rancor. The controversy over the National History Standards in the mid-1990s generated much heat and throws a little light on the "history wars."[40] In 1994, spurred by Lynne Cheney, who headed the National Endowment for the Humanities under the first President Bush, and directed by the eminent historian of early America, Gary Nash, the project — after years of discussion, preparation,

---

[38]The *Journal of the Historical Society* began publication in 2000. On the Historical Society, see Elizabeth Fox-Genovese and Elisabeth Lasch-Quinn, eds., *Reconstructing History: The Emergence of a New Historical Society* (New York, 1999); it should be noted that the Historical Society's founders included liberals such as Sean Wilentz, who shared very few of his cofounders' views other than an allegiance to publicly accessible narrative history.

[39]See Elizabeth Fox-Genovese and Eugene D. Genovese, "The Political Crisis of Social History: A Marxist Perspective," in Peter N. Stearns, ed., *Expanding the Past* (New York, 1988): 16–32; Arthur Schlesinger Jr., *The Disuniting of America* (New York, 1992); Diane Ravitch's views have appeared mostly in occasional essays and articles, several of which are cited, along with a host of other works representing many views, in a special issue of the *Journal of Social History* 29 (1995) entitled "Social History and the American Political Climate — Problems and Strategies"; Gertrude Himmelfarb, *The New History and the Old: Critical Essays and Reappraisals* (Cambridge, Mass., 1987). See also "AHR Forum: The Old History and the New," *American Historical Review* 94 (June 1989), with contributions from Himmelfarb along with other historians of various persuasions.

[40]See Gary B. Nash, Charlotte Crabtree, and Ross E. Dunn, *History on Trial: Culture Wars and the Teaching of the Past* (New York, 1997), and Diane Ravitch, "The Controversy over the National History Standards," in Fox-Genovese and Lasch-Quinn, *Reconstructing History*, 242–52.

and consultation — published preliminary guidelines for the teaching of history in public schools. Critics exploded with outrage. Diane Ravitch and Arthur Schlesinger Jr. leveled measured critiques of the pedagogical strategies recommended by the drafters, but less temperate right-wing pundits blasted the standards as anti-American. Cheney herself, now "in opposition" to the Clinton administration, turned on the project she had helped spawn, and in early 1995 the U.S. Senate voted ninety-nine to one to condemn the standards. Although revised standards eventually won broad support, other battles in the history wars erupted around the same time and in similar ways. Most notoriously, several exhibitions at the Smithsonian Institution museums in Washington, D.C., evoked cries of anti-Americanism from conservative critics. In response to such criticism, the National History Museum removed "excessive" references to genocide from its exhibition "The American West," and the Air and Space Museum abandoned its Enola Gay exhibition when it could not find a way to both celebrate the patriotic struggle against Japan and take note of the horrors of nuclear destruction.[41]

The most important challenge to American historians in the twenty-first century comes not from those demanding more patriotic narratives but from those advocating the "internationalization" of American history. Sometimes advocating "global" or "transnational" or "postnational" history, these critics insist that Americans' "exceptionalism" distorts both the national record and the reality of historical change. In the modern and postmodern world, almost none of the important forces shaping events are nation-based, they argue. Wars and revolutions, racial hierarchies and forms of economic dominance and subordination, markets, migrations, and media, among other phenomena, all emerge and develop in response to forces well beyond state boundaries. Most historians seem to welcome the new effort, although disagreements arise as soon as they try to clarify what it means.

In a collection of essays entitled *Rethinking American History in a Global Age*, Thomas Bender celebrates the urge to "deprovincialize" and "defamiliarize" American history.[42] Another contributor to that volume, the eminent diplomatic historian Akira Iriye, proposes that international history means comparative history, an immersion into more than one national archive, usually requiring skill in more than one language. But he also insists that comparison must incorporate peoples, cultures, and non-state movements, not just states. The character and outlines of such an approach remain elusive, but Iriye believes that a more international approach will one day generate a truly global or transnational history of human affairs.[43] For other diplomatic historians, internationalizing means turning the tables on U.S.-centered,

---

[41]See Edward T. Linenthal and Tom Engelhardt, eds., *History Wars: The Enola Gay and Other Battles for the American Past* (New York, 1996). See also Mike Wallace, *Mickey Mouse History and Other Essays on American Memory* (Philadelphia, 1996).

[42]Thomas Bender, "Introduction: Historians, Nations, and the Plenitude of Narratives," in Bender, ed., *Rethinking American History in a Global Age* (Berkeley, Calif., 2002).

[43]Akira Iriye, "Internationalizing International History," in Bender, *Rethinking*, 47–62.

hegemonic renderings of history. While Louis A. Perez Jr. finds many of the goals of transnational history admirable, he spots a worm in the global apple. "A new historiography that celebrates the promise of borderlessness seems entirely congruent with the larger assumptions through which to validate the assumptions of globalization. Is the new international history the handmaiden to globalization?" He insists that the nation that sponsors and reaps the most immense rewards from globalization — the United States — must remain clearly in the historian's focus. Similarly, Marilyn Young warns historians to distinguish between "de-centering" U.S. history and creating "a world free of [America's] overwhelming military power"; she continues, "it is crucial to remember the difference" and to make sure that "the effort to de-center American history" does not "run the danger of obscuring what it means to illuminate."[44]

A different view of transnational history emerges from the work of historians of migration, gender, and race. For them, "diasporic" approaches offer the opportunity to comprehend the meaning of lives in motion, not primarily defined by nations but by the spaces created by capitalist markets, international political movements, and mass communication. Such approaches sometimes begin with the subnational — family economies, local religious cultures, regional environments — but proceed to link them to phenomena of the largest scale — capitalism, imperialism, patriarchy, and the like. When grounded in exhaustive archival and oral research, as in the work of Dirk Hoerder and Donna Gabaccia, such studies succeed in reframing what once seemed a simple story of immigrants reaching and assimilating into the Promised Land into a far more complex tale of migration, reverse migration, and the simultaneous construction of national, racial, and ethnic identities among both settlers and sojourners within many different national contexts.[45]

Felipe Fernandez-Armesto takes another approach to the challenge of transnational history, writing a history of the continent that highlights the starkly different fates of North America and America south of the Rio Grande. He treats the rise and fall of indigenous societies and colonization comparatively and then asks, Why did these two regions, similar for so long, diverge so dramatically in the nineteenth century? The south had conspicuously provided much of the wealth for the development of Western capitalism, but in the nineteenth century, Canada and the United States began exploiting their resources with unparalleled success while maintaining political stability. The reverse was true for the south. In light of this comparison,

---

[44]Louis A. Perez Jr., "We Are the World: Internationalizing the National, Nationalizing the International," *Journal of American History* 89 (September 2002): 564; Marilyn B. Young, "The Age of Global Power," in Bender, *Rethinking*, 291.

[45]See Dirk Hoerder, "From Euro- and Afro-Atlantic to Pacific Migration System: A Comparative Migration Approach to North American History," in Bender, *Rethinking*, 195–235; Donna R. Gabaccia, "When the Migrants Are Men: Italy's Women and Transnationalism as a Working-Class Way of Life," in Gabaccia and Vicki L. Ruiz, eds., *American Dreaming, Global Realities: Rethinking U.S. Immigration History* (Urbana, Ill., 2006), and other works cited therein and in Volume Two, Chapter 5.

Fernandez-Armesto identifies crucial conditions and resources that facilitated the remarkable economic growth and political stability of the north. He sees a constellation of these opportunities presently taking shape in the south and wonders if that region will be able to take advantage of them.[46]

In *The Theft of History*, Jack Goody radically reappraises most histories of the Western world since the sixteenth century, in which Europe and the United States were the measure of all other civilizations. This "provincial" perspective obviated careful studies of societies marked by significantly different forms of land tenure, market activity, and communal traditions. If provincialism deprived historians of models of social and cultural difference, it also blinded them to similarities. Thus, Goody asserts, abundant evidence shows that romantic love, freedom, and humanism, usually characterized as essentially European values, appeared elsewhere.[47] Thomas Bender's *A Nation among Nations* offers a different worldwide perspective on U.S. history. He sees in the age of discovery the beginning of global history, which, he emphasizes, began with the importation and exploitation of millions of Africans. He treats the American Revolution as one event in the long war between England and France that began in 1689 and continued until 1815. He connects the Civil War with the Europeans' revolutions of 1848, the failure of Reconstruction with European failures to realize the ideals of its revolutions. Similarly, for Bender the Spanish-American War makes sense only in the larger context of European imperialism, progressive reform only as one of many global responses to industrial capitalism. Although Bender uses comparative history explicitly to explain American developments, *A Nation among Nations* never becomes a triumphant tale of economic progress or political virtue.[48]

Despite the benefits of transnational history, some historians have raised cautionary flags. They worry that transnational insights claimed by American historians suggest an ironic reverse imperialism. Just as the United States appropriates resources, labor, and cultural space around the world, these critics imply, American historians appropriate the right to tell everybody's story.[49] In a very different way, some scholars qualify their endorsement of transnational approaches with reminders about the enduring significance of the nation as an idea and a reality in human history.[50] Ian Tyrell applauds the exploitation of "new, non-national records" to "suggest models of transnational processes," but insists that historians have long transcended narrow nationalism. He notes that nation-focused and transnational approaches will together be required to account adequately for the overwhelming power of the United States within the world. Recalling the comparative and global tendencies of historians often thought to be avatars of "American exception-

---

[46]Felipe Fernandez-Armesto, *The Americas, A Hemispheric History* (New York, 2003).

[47]Jack Goody, *The Theft of History* (New York, 2006), 1–8, 240, 246, 286.

[48]Thomas Bender, *A Nation among Nations: America's Place in World History* (New York, 2006), 3–9, 290–301.

[49]Doubts of this sort surface in essays by Ron Robin and a few others in Bender's *Rethinking*.

[50]See John Higham, "The Future of American History," *Journal of American History* 80 (March 1994): 1289–1307.

alism," from Frederick Jackson Turner to Louis Hartz, Tyrell, like Bender, advocates the enrichment and complication of American history, not its dissolution into the sea of transnationalism.[51]

However one reads the opportunities and challenges of the transnational turn in historiography, that turn cannot be ignored. This edition of *Interpretations of American History* pays greater attention to the global dimensions of the transatlantic economy, slave trade, and abolitionist movements. It addresses transnational approaches to the study of migration, to state-making and Progressive reform, to the role of multiple states and non-state actors, not just great powers, in shaping international relations during and after the Cold War, and to many other subjects. Yet it also heeds the words of several of the participants in the *Journal of American History*'s recent "Interchange," cited above, who affirm history's intense empirical focus and openness to different approaches and who warn that some kinds of "interdisciplinarity . . . narrow rather than widen inquiries." History's "eclecticism" has, as David Hollinger notes, always made it "easier for us to absorb and use a variety of theories and methods . . . without being captured by any." History's "methodological integrity," he goes on, remains a solid bottom on which to navigate the shifting seas of transnational and other approaches to the study of human affairs. As Joyce Appleby and others have noted, moreover, if people desire "to chart their lives by what they believe to be true," then they will turn to history, which "offers a variety of tools for effecting liberation from intrusive authority, outworn creeds, and counsels of despair."[52] In responding to that demand, historians will continue to write narratives both broad and narrow and to argue about them strenuously in the decades to come.

A final note about the way these chapters present competing interpretations of historical phenomena. While interpretive argument undoubtedly remains among the most common and necessary practices in the discipline, it is equally true that the either-or format can distort the true nature of historians' arguments. Indeed, burlesquing this format is a happy pastime common in graduate student lounges all over the country (Fat-Free Mozzarella: Noble Experiment or Tragic Error?). We have, in fact, tried wherever possible to offer differences in interpretation that are not polar or mutually exclusive, but rather partially overlapping and complementary. Sharp differences there are, and sometimes hot debate produces light. But

---

[51] Ian Tyrell, "Making Nations/Making States: American Historians in the Context of Empire," *Journal of American History* 80 (March 1994): 1015–44; see also Richard White, "The Nationalization of Nature," *Journal of American History* 80 (March 1994): 976–86. On a more theoretical level, see Craig Calhoun, *Nations Matter: Culture, History, and the Cosmopolitan Dream* (London, 2007). On both traditional comparative approaches and the recent "transnational turn" (as well as cultural studies, subaltern studies, and approaches that focus on religion, gender, and race), see the enlightening "Interchange: The Practice of History," *Journal of American History* 90 (September 2003): 576–611. See also Michael Adas, "From Settler Colony to Global Hegemon: Integrating the Exceptionalist Narrative of the American Experience into World History," *American Historical Review* 106 (December 2001): 1692–1720.

[52] Appleby et al., *Telling the Truth about History*, 301, 308.

historians usually do not differ by excluding each other's evidence or utterly demolishing each other's arguments. More often, they try to incorporate as much of the former and recast as much of the latter as possible in order to better explain a historical phenomenon. Thus, for example, whereas Progressive historians might have once portrayed the New Deal as a radical advance in liberal reform, and New Left historians as a triumph of corporate hegemony, the liberal William Leuchtenberg and the radical Alan Dawley in their essays in Volume Two acknowledge a good deal of common ground, even while clearly disagreeing over important points. Whether the New Deal was "radical within limits" or "conservative with radical implications" remains truly a matter of opinion, but the common ground shared by these two historians makes clear the cumulative and "objective" quality of scholarship on the subject. In coming to a judgment on this and other questions posed in the following chapters, we hope that students will find in the debates, and the historiographical essays that precede them, a pathway to understanding the world in which they live and an encouragement to change that world for the better.

# The Puritans: Orthodoxy or Diversity?

**P**uritanism occupies a crucial position in the mainstream of American thought. The name Puritanism identifies the religious philosophy and intellectual outlook that characterized New England's first settlers. But, for some, it has also come to stand for an important thread in the development of American civilization. Indeed, one historian of colonial America has gone so far as to remark, "Without some understanding of Puritanism . . . there is no understanding of America."[1]

Just what Puritanism means, however, is a matter of dispute. To one group of historians, the Puritans were reactionary bigots — people opposed to freedom of thought, religious liberty, and the idea of democratic government. For these historians, Massachusetts represents a perfect case study of the kind of undemocratic colony the Puritans founded. Massachusetts was a theocracy — a state in which the civil government was under the control of the ministers or churches. Resisting change and repressing all dissenting views, Puritan oligarchs banished independent thinkers like Anne Hutchinson and Roger Williams whose radical religious ideas represented a threat to the stability of the colony. They rejected the new ideas of Newtonian science and remained indifferent to cultural matters; they imposed a "glacial period" on the intellectual life of the colony from the 1630s to the outbreak of the American Revolution.

A second group of historians, however, took a much more sympathetic view of the Puritans and the society they created. To them, the Puritans were the torchbearers of religious liberty and political freedom — brave pioneers of American democracy. The strict discipline and control exercised by the Puritan oligarchy in Massachusetts was necessitated by the demands of a frontier environment. Within these parameters, the Puritan clergy did everything possible to stimulate intellectual activity, founding the first college and public school system in the American colonies.

This favorable image of the Puritans survived well into the nineteenth century because the writing of American history and literature was dominated by the descendants of Puritans. The so-called filiopietist school of historians, reflecting both ancestor worship and provincial pride, identified the Puritans as the source of all virtues attributed to the American people — thrift, hard work, and moral earnestness. The accepted view among these

---

[1]Perry Miller, *American Puritans: Their Prose and Poetry* (New York, 1956), ix.

historians was that America's contemporary political and religious liberty sprang from the seventeenth-century Puritan tradition.

John Gorham Palfrey took this approach in his five-volume *History of New England* (1858–1890). A descendant of early seventeenth-century New England stock, Harvard graduate, and Unitarian clergyman from Boston, Palfrey deeply admired his ancestors, and his work was one long paean to them. "In the colonial history of New England," he wrote, "we follow the strenuous action of intelligent and honest men in building up a free, strong, enlightened, and happy state."[2]

In the 1920s, there was a marked change in attitude toward New England Puritanism as historians and commentators began to reexamine different aspects of American culture. Disillusioned with the ambiguous results of World War I and worried by the Russian Revolution, they turned to history with the hope of discovering what was unique and indigenous in the American tradition and in search of a heritage that seemed a logical predecessor to the current national character.

The rise of intellectual history in the post–World War I period was as important a force as cultural nationalism in directing attention of scholars to the study of Puritanism. Throughout the nineteenth and early twentieth centuries, historians who wrote about Puritanism dealt almost exclusively with its political and institutional aspects, not ideas and culture. In the 1920s, however, American historians threw off the old distrust of the study of ideas that had characterized much of nineteenth-century scholarship. Historians now forged ahead on the assumption that the study of Puritan thought was significant.

Pro-Puritan and anti-Puritan tendencies continued to shape historians' views into the late twentieth century. The Progressive historians, who tended to read the social conflicts of their own day back into the nation's past, mistrusted the Puritans. They rewrote American history in terms of economic conflict — as a continuous struggle between the forces of liberalism and conservatism, aristocracy and democracy, and the rich and the poor. The progressives saw the Puritans as reactionaries.

Three Progressive scholars in particular — James Truslow Adams, Vernon L. Parrington, and Thomas J. Wertenbaker — pictured Puritans as authoritarian, bigoted, and hypocritical and derided the idea that the Puritans had founded American democracy. James Truslow Adams inaugurated this cult of anti-Puritanism with *The Founding of New England* in 1921. Adams thought Puritans repressed private choice and were intolerant in public life of any deviation from the ruling orthodoxy.[3] No detail of the Puritans' personal conduct was too small to escape a ruling by the oligarchy: "The cut of clothes, the names he bore, the most ordinary social usages, could all be regulated in accordance with the will of God," concluded Adams.[4] In Adams's opinion,

---

[2] John Gorham Palfrey, *History of New England*, 5 vols. (Boston, 1875), vol. 4, x.
[3] James T. Adams, *The Founding of New England* (Boston, 1921), 143.
[4] Ibid., 79.

the Puritan leaders' desire for control was economically, not religiously, motivated. Once in America, "they looked with fear, as well as jealousy, upon any possibility of allowing control of policy, of law and order, and of legislation concerning persons and property, to pass to others."[5]

In *The Colonial Mind*, the first volume of his literary history *Main Currents in American Thought*, published in 1927, Vernon Parrington helped redirect Puritan studies toward intellectual history. To Parrington, orthodox Puritanism was a reactionary theology. A succession of liberal heroes, like Roger Williams and Anne Hutchinson, who rose up to oppose such reactionary views represented the liberal tradition that was America's destiny.[6]

The anti-Puritan writers of the 1920s were followed in the 1930s by a number of historians at Harvard University favorably disposed to Puritanism. Samuel Eliot Morison, Clifford K. Shipton, and Perry Miller proceeded to rehabilitate the battered reputation of the early Puritan leaders. Rather than pit Puritanism against twentieth-century liberalism, the Harvard historians studied them in the context of their own age and background.

In 1930, Samuel Eliot Morison published his elegantly written *Builders of the Bay Colony*, transforming the rigid Puritans of Adams, Parrington, and Wertenbaker into living human beings. As he recalled two decades later, his was a lonely voice at the time "crying in the wilderness against the common notion of the grim Puritan . . . steeple-hatted [and] long-faced living in a log cabin and planning a witch-hunt . . . as a holiday diversion."[7] Morison humanized many of the major Puritan figures by showing that they were not averse to the simple pleasures of life — sex, strong drink, and colorful clothes — but that their zeal to lead godly lives provided them with even greater satisfaction. In his second work, *The Puritan Pronaos*, published in 1936, three hundred years after the Puritans had founded Harvard, Morison emphasized the rich intellectual lives of the Puritans.[8]

Clifford K. Shipton, the second of the Harvard historians, militantly defended the Puritan contribution to American democratic thought. Shipton argued that Puritans were open-minded and receptive to new ideas. "Far from being narrow bigots, the ministers were the leaders in every field of intellectual advance in New England."[9]

The work of Perry Miller, the third of the Harvard historians, constituted a landmark in American intellectual history. In the 1930s, Miller published two works — *Orthodoxy in Massachusetts* and *The New England Mind: The Seventeenth Century* — that dissected the Puritans' principal ideas. Miller argued that reason had played a major role in Puritan theology; Puritans looked upon man as an essentially rational and responsible being despite

---

[5]Ibid., 143.

[6]Vernon L. Parrington, *Main Currents in American Thought*, 3 vols. (New York, 1927–1930), vol. 1, iv.

[7]Samuel Eliot Morison, "Faith of a Historian," *American Historical Review* 56 (January 1951): 272.

[8]Samuel Eliot Morison, *The Puritan Pronaos: Studies in the Intellectual Life of New England in the Seventeenth Century* (New York, 1936), 264. This work was reissued under the title *The Intellectual Life of Colonial New England* (New York, 1956).

[9]Clifford K. Shipton, "A Plea for Puritanism," *American Historical Review* (April 1935): 467.

their belief that he was tainted by original sin. By holding such views, the Puritans were taking part in the great intellectual revolution that was being fought all over Europe — the revolt against scholasticism.[10] In *Orthodoxy in Massachusetts*, published in 1933, Miller showed the seriousness with which people in the early 1600s took their religious ideas and their willingness to create a church and a life that conformed to those ideas. Most of the problems the Puritans encountered in putting their ideas of church government into practice in Massachusetts arose more from their experiences in New England than in opposition from old England. Much of what Miller had to say in this work was not new, but he demonstrated as never before that the history of the Bay Colony during its first two decades could be "strung on the thread of an idea."[11]

Six years later, Miller produced *The New England Mind: The Seventeenth Century*, a more detailed analysis of the ideas of New England Puritanism and their relationship to one another. He described the interlocking system of covenants — the covenant of grace, the social covenant, and the church covenant — that formed the core of Puritan theology. He demonstrated more conclusively than earlier scholars had that the doctrine of the covenant was the keystone to Puritanism, and he argued that this covenant theology made room for man's activity in the process of his own salvation; thus Puritanism, rather than being fatalistic in outlook, was a stimulus to action. Running throughout this work was the major theme of the New World's transformation of Puritan thought as experience and time made an impact upon the ideas the settlers had originally brought over.[12]

In the second volume of *The New England Mind*, published in 1953 and subtitled *From Colony to Province*, Miller explored change as the second and third generations of Puritans became more provincial and began grappling with the day-to-day problems in the New World. Material success, which sprang from the Puritan idea of a calling — faithfully doing God's appointed work here on earth — undermined spiritual life; Christian brotherhood and Puritan consensus gave way to personal squabbles; theological conflicts were replaced by political struggles; and secular values triumphed over religious aims. Miller's description of the decline of Puritan zeal from the arrival of the first settlers in the 1620s to the 1720s thereby became a tale of irony as well as change.

Miller's works lifted the study of New England Puritanism out of the narrow framework of national history and placed it within the much broader context of European intellectual history. He was able to uncover hitherto unsuspected connections between New England Puritanism and Renaissance humanism, the Reformation, and scholasticism. In his hands, the study of Puritanism became more than a history of the ideas of the New England founders; it became instead a study of an important epoch in the intellectual history of the

---

[10]Perry Miller, *The New England Mind: The Seventeenth Century* (New York, 1939), viii.
[11]Perry Miller, *Orthodoxy in Massachusetts 1630–1650* (Cambridge, Mass., 1933), xii.
[12]Ibid., passim.

Western world. The first selection presents Miller's point of view and is drawn from a book of readings he wrote with Thomas H. Johnson.

In the decades since the 1960s, the direction of the study of American Puritanism entered an entirely new phase marked by four main lines of approach. The first was characterized by the direct revisionist critiques of Miller's monumental work, often by intellectual historians. The second involved studies by scholars of literature who, in the 1970s, brought literary analysis to bear on Puritan texts and sometimes expanded upon or attacked Miller's hypothesis. Then came the contributions of the new social historians, who began in the 1960s to study Puritanism within the microcosm of New England communities as well as reveal the experience of women, Native Americans, and African Americans within the Puritan world. This mounting scholarship was as diversified as it was massive: it was estimated that more than one thousand books, articles, and dissertations were written on the Puritans between 1960 and 1987.[13] Finally, beginning in the 1990s, Puritan studies entered what David D. Hall has called a postrevisionist phase, in which historians are working to integrate the insights of the revisionists into a satisfying whole — both vindicating and reshaping earlier interpretations. In recent years, postrevisionists have paid particular attention to the connections — social, economic, political, and, of course, religious — among Massachusetts Puritans and those in England and Holland. Perhaps in response to the post-9/11 world, some historians have focused on conflict and conflict containment among Puritans as a group and between Puritans and those they considered "other."

The first historians after Miller worked, by necessity, in his shadow. Some revered him not only as the most important Puritan scholar but also as the greatest American historian of the twentieth century. They considered his reconstruction of the Puritan intellectual world to be the towering achievement of American scholarship in their time. According to other scholars, however, especially the new social historians of the 1960s, Miller's perspective was flawed. He wrongly focused on elites and gave little attention to the thinking, beliefs, and behavior of ordinary people. Therefore, his view of Puritanism, they argued, was unrepresentative. Second, Miller concentrated on the evolution and interplay of abstract ideas and disregarded the social and economic forces from which such ideas sprang. Third, he assumed a unity in Puritan experience that was belied by a multiplicity of believers and sects. Fourth, he erroneously held that the New England Puritans had formulated their covenant theology to free themselves from the terrible uncertainty of a strict, predestinarian Calvinism — that is, a religious view in which God had, at the beginning of time, already determined who would be saved and who would be damned. And finally, he incorrectly pictured Puritanism as being in a process of gradual spiritual decline; Miller postulated a "declension," or falling away from early piety and communitarian ideals, of the New England mind and a trend toward secularism and materialism during the seventeenth century.

---

[13]David D. Hall, "On Common Ground: The Coherence of American Puritan Studies," *William and Mary Quarterly*, 3rd Ser., 44 (1987): 193.

Intellectual historians in the 1950s and 1960s argued that Miller had overintellectualized the Puritan experience at the expense of their emotional engagement. Others showed that there was no declension in church membership among women, only among men. And Michael Walzer, a political scientist, made the case for Puritans as radicals attempting to change not only society and politics but also religion.[14]

The intellectual historian David D. Hall, one of Miller's sharpest critics in the 1970s, examined the relationship between Puritan ideas and the New England social and economic environment. His study of the Puritan ministry in *The Faithful Shepherd* showed that the migration from England posed new problems for ministers, forcing many to rethink the teachings they had inherited. Most significantly, New Englanders were of more than one mind, much as their ministers may have wished "to regulate their attitudes and practices of their congregations. Yet much slipped away or was ignored."[15] Still, Hall concluded, the ideas and values derived from the mother country were undoubtedly influential in shaping the New England ministers.[16]

Many other intellectual historians challenged Miller's interpretation on different grounds in the 1970s. Robert Middlekauff, for example, in a thoughtful multiple biography of members of the Mather family, disagreed with Miller's depiction of a declension in the Puritan sense of mission. Examining three generations of Mather ministers — Richard, Increase, and Cotton — Middlekauff found a different pattern, one that showed a spiritual strengthening and growing piety over time.[17]

Historians critical of Miller, like Philip Gura, objected that Miller, in his *New England Mind* in particular, had treated Puritan literature as though it were the product of a single homogeneous group. Gura, like others before him, noted the well-known presence of prominent dissenters from the tradition. People like Roger Williams and Anne Hutchinson and groups like Quakers, certain Baptist sects, and some millenarians constituted a long line of radicals who were just as Puritan as John Winthrop's mainstream orthodox establishment.[18]

---

[14]Alan Simpson, *Puritanism in Old and New England* (Chicago, 1955); Norman Pettit, *The Heart Prepared* (New Haven, Conn., 1966); Robert G. Pope, *The Half-Way Covenant* (Princeton, N.J., 1969); and Michael Walzer, *The Revolution of the Saints* (Cambridge, Mass., 1965).

[15]David D. Hall, *The Faithful Shepherd* (Chapel Hill, N.C., 1972). In "Understanding the Puritans," in Herbert J. Bass, ed., *The State of American History* (Chicago, 1970), 330–49, Hall summarized some of the critical reaction to Miller's account of the relationship between Puritanism and Calvinism. James Hoopes, a supporter of Miller, organized a conference on his work in 1982 at Babson College, taking up the issue of declension and popular religious beliefs in New England. Hoopes argued for the internal coherence of Miller's work. James Hoopes, "Art as History: Perry Miller's New England Mind," *American Quarterly* 34 (1984): 3–25. Scholars including David D. Hall, Joyce Appleby, P. M. G. Harris, and Margaret Sobczak attacked declension. Joyce Appleby, "History as Art: Another View," 1; David D. Hall, "A Readers' Guide to the New England Mind: The Seventeenth Century," 31–36; P. M. G. Harris, "Of Two Minds, Falsely Sundered: Faith and Reason, Duality and Complexity, Art and Science in Perry Miller and in Puritan New England," 36–42; and Margaret Sobczak, "Hoopes' Symposium on Perry Miller," 43–48. In 1982, Francis T. Butts defended Miller, claiming the revisionists were attacking a caricature rather than Miller's real assumptions. See "The Myth of Perry Miller," *American Historical Review* 87 (1982): 665–91.

[16]David D. Hall, ed., *Puritans in the New World: A Critical Anthology* (Princeton, N.J., 2004), xiv.

[17]Robert Middlekauff, *The Mathers* (New York, 1972).

[18]Philip Gura, *A Glimpse of Sion's Glory* (Middletown, Conn., 1984).

Other intellectual historians attacked the Miller thesis from different angles. Theodore D. Bozeman in *To Live Ancient Lives* provided an important corrective to Miller's "errand" hypothesis. Miller had argued in his influential essay "Errand into the Wilderness" that the Puritans intended the Massachusetts Bay Colony to be a shining example to save England from its excesses by providing a perfect model society. Bozeman insisted, however, that a careful reading of the primary sources, taking seriously the Puritans' own words, failed to justify such a conclusion.[19]

In a work subsequent to *The Faithful Shepherd,* David D. Hall focused upon the lay or popular beliefs of New Englanders to challenge Miller's depiction of one New England mind. In *Worlds of Wonder, Days of Judgment* (excerpted below), Hall demonstrated the importance of folk beliefs, the appeal of "magic," the popular "wonder" books of the era, rates of literacy, and common rituals of the conversion process to show how broad their role was in shaping religious beliefs in America. By revealing the impact of popular beliefs and practices on New England culture, Hall showed that organized religion was only one way in which the Puritans viewed their place in the cosmos.[20]

By introducing popular culture into the religious perspective, Hall completely changed the parameters of the debate about Puritanism and scored a permanent blow for the Miller critics. Whether scholars defended, extended, or criticized Miller's work, they had to take into account the new broadened picture of New England culture. So, Harry S. Stout read several thousand sermons in manuscript and showed that Miller's picture of the pervasiveness of Puritanism in New England society and culture held up. Norman Fiering suggested that the inner life of New Englanders developed over a long time and that new theories of the mind led to a more subjective life that subsequently gave rise to more complicated theories. Charles L. Cohen analyzed the conversion experience along the lines of emerging ideas about the construction of the self. His work, like that of Stout, Fiering, Bozeman, and others, showed that the intellectual history approach, which had generally fallen into disrepute, proved to be one of the most fruitful perspectives employed in deepening our understanding of Puritanism throughout the 1980s.[21]

In Bozeman's 2004 study, *The Precisionist Strain: Disciplinary Religion and Antinomian Backlash in Puritanism to 1638,* he looks at what he defines as

---

[19]Theodore D. Bozeman, *To Live Ancient Lives* (Chapel Hill, N.C., 1988).

[20]David D. Hall, *Worlds of Wonder, Days of Judgment: Popular Religious Belief in Early New England* (New York, 1989).

[21]Harry S. Stout, *The New England Soul* (New York, 1986); Norman Fiering, *Moral Philosophy at Seventeenth-Century Harvard* (Chapel Hill, N.C., 1981); James Hoopes, *Consciousness in New England* (Baltimore, 1989); Charles L. Cohen, *God's Caress* (New York, 1986); David D. Hall, "Religion and Society: Problems and Reconsiderations," in Jack P. Greene and J. R. Pole, eds., *Colonial British America* (Baltimore, 1984), 325. Michael McGiffert, a historian of religion, showed how preachers in Elizabethan England groped their way to new concepts of the covenant of grace and the covenant of works in the late seventeenth century. See Michael McGiffert, "Grace and Works: The Rise and Division of Covenant Theology in Elizabethan Puritanism," *Harvard Theological Review* 7S (1982): 463–502, and "Tyndale's Conception of Covenant," *Journal of Ecclesiastical History* 32 (1981): 167–84. See also the important work of another historian of religion, Charles Hambrick-Stowe, *The Practice of Piety* (Chapel Hill, N.C., 1980).

Puritans' fundamental tension between the "precisionist" or regulatory aspect of Puritanism and those who found such ascetic discipline too difficult. This division, he argues, underlay the Hutchinson controversy, pitting those who believed in the efficacy of faith alone for salvation against those who also believed in faith but saw an ascetic life or "exact walking" as a necessary counterpart to salvation. In tracing this fault line back through previous decades in England and Holland, he links Massachusetts' earliest years with its transatlantic past and with the Civil War to come in England, and he stresses the importance of practice and emphasis in distinguishing the major currents within any religion.[22]

The second line of approach in post-Miller Puritan studies used the methods of literary criticism to analyze religious and social phenomena. These scholars, who were not focused specifically on doing battle with Miller, brought about a dramatic change in the understanding of the Puritan imagination and the relationship between literature and ideas by employing new theories such as deconstruction, psychoanalysis, semiotics, and gender analysis. They suggested that the ideas developed in New England had given rise to a powerful myth — the myth of New England as the place God had chosen to create his millennial kingdom on earth as the New Jerusalem. The Puritan vision originated the notion of New England as a separate and exceptional place. This regional self-identity, in turn, morphed into the national myth of American exceptionalism — the idea that America was unique and fundamentally different from Europe and the rest of the world. Perry Miller himself, of course, had been an exemplar of American exceptionalism, and many literary scholars drew their inspiration from him. Criticism in this vein also shone light for the first time on negative aspects of American exceptionalism, particularly its racism and violence.

Sacvan Bercovitch, perhaps better than any other literary scholar, expanded upon Miller's notion of a Puritan mission and the concept of American identity. In his *Puritan Origins of the American Self*, Bercovitch explored the essence of Puritan rhetoric through literary analysis of the language, symbolism, and myth. To Bercovitch, early New England rhetoric provided the religious framework for the production of values, later to become secular, with which America would become identified: human perfectibility, individualism, technological progress, and democracy. In Bercovitch's view, American writers like Ralph Waldo Emerson came directly from the Puritan rhetorical tradition.[23]

In a later study, *The American Jeremiad*, Bercovitch revised Miller's somewhat pessimistic view of this kind of political sermon, which stressed the failings of the people of New England as a way to explain their political and social difficulties. Where Miller's interpretation of the jeremiad led to declension, Bercovitch concluded that the Puritan cry of declension was part of a strategy designed to revitalize the idea of an "errand into the wilder-

---

[22]Theodore Bozeman, *The Precisionist Strain: Disciplinary Religion and Antinomian Backlash in Puritanism to 1638* (Chapel Hill, N.C., 2004).

[23]Sacvan Bercovitch, *Puritan Origins of the American Self* (New Haven, Conn., 1975).

ness." Where Miller saw decline in the seventeenth century, Bercovitch argued that Puritanism succeeded in giving rise to a myth of an eternal American mission that has characterized middle-class culture.[24]

Some literary scholars uncovered and pursued the dark side of Bercovitch's narrative, finding violent intolerance toward the "other" implicated in the same myth. Richard Slotkin's *Regeneration through Violence* explores these themes, particularly as Puritan and later national ideology sanctioned Indian killing. Following on Slotkin, Ann Kibbey, a feminist literary scholar, found a link to violence, particularly toward Indians, in the way Puritans constructed supernatural power. In 1998, Jill Lepore, in a sweeping literary analysis of the New England histories of King Philip's War in 1676–1677, connected these writings to the development of American identity. She argued that "wounds and words — the injuries and their interpretation — cannot be separated, that acts of war generate acts of narration." Analyzing these accounts, she showed the ways the Puritan prose depicted in gory detail the ritual Native American torture of individual captives, horrific, but few in number compared to the total war the Puritans waged, slaughtering whole Indian villages, sparing neither women, nor old people, nor children. Puritans interpreted these acts of unprecedented violence in the experience of Native Americans into enactments of God's wisdom and purposes, linking Puritan piety with deadly force against native people.[25]

Other literary scholars, like intellectual historians, did not agree with Miller. Andrew Delbanco, for example, denied that there was any grand "errand" or journey toward the millennium in the minds of the Puritans when they came to America. The Puritans, according to him, were fleeing the chaos they found in England and in themselves.[26]

The third major development in Puritan studies was the appearance of the new social historians beginning in the early 1960s. They rejected Miller's approach that claimed the early history of New England could be strung "on the thread of an idea." Writing New England's local history from the bottom up, these scholars studied secular records — wills, deeds, tax lists, town records, and registers of births, marriages, and deaths — to reconstruct the development of Puritan communities and to understand the dynamics of the communitarian values that shaped them. They were concerned with precise conclusions and insights from such other disciplines as social psychology, historical demography, and cultural anthropology.

A whole host of community studies of New England written between 1960 and the end of the 1980s analyzed the impact of Puritanism on the everyday life of the early settlers. Historians explored a number of themes that Miller

---

[24]Sacvan Bercovitch, *The American Jeremiad* (Madison, Wis., 1978). For a searching review essay from which much of this discussion is drawn, see Gordon S. Wood, "Struggle over the Puritans," *New York Review of Books*, November 8, 1989.

[25]Richard Slotkin, *Regeneration through Violence: The Mythology of the American Frontier, 1600–1860* (Middletown, Conn., 1973); Ann Kibbey, *The Interpretation of Material Shapes in Puritanism: A Study of Rhetoric, Prejudice, and Violence* (New York, 1986); Jill Lepore, *The Name of War: King Philip's War and the Origins of American Identity* (New York, 1998).

[26]Andrew Delbanco, *Puritan Ordeal* (Cambridge, Mass., 1989).

had either failed to look at, such as family dynamics, inheritance patterns, and witchcraft, or that he had written about without providing a socioeconomic base, for example, the idea of a declension, or a falling away from communitarian ideals. While all this history revised the belief that intellectual history alone was a sufficient way to understand the Puritans, some of the revisionists challenged Miller's idea with their research, while others ended up confirming or elaborating on observations he had made.

Kenneth Lockridge traced the evolution of local institutions in Dedham, Massachusetts, over a one hundred year period. He concluded that the town during its first fifty years was a "Christian Utopian Closed Corporate community." But in the second fifty years, conflicts eroded the prevailing consensus, shattered the Puritan vision of a perfect society, and gave rise to a modern provincial town. Lockridge's story refined the declension theme by providing it with an economic and political base.[27]

In another view of the religious and social stresses caused by increasing economic success, Paul Boyer and Stephen Nissenbaum studied witchcraft in *Salem Possessed.* Severe tensions developed in Salem because merchant capitalism was emerging from a commercial base while the explosive population growth meant the decreasing availability of land. These material developments rewarded some people and challenged traditional farmers, dividing the town and provoking the outbreak of witchcraft hysteria, which, according to Boyer and Nissenbaum, was caused more by these stresses than by the Puritan dogmatism and bigotry emphasized in the older and more traditional interpretations.[28]

Virginia DeJohn Anderson focused on a community within a community, some seven hundred people of the Great Migration generation. Applying new social historical methods to a theme Perry Miller had explored, Anderson was searching for the origins of Puritan exceptionalism. She looked to the experience of crossing the ocean, town planting, and community building to explain the distinctive legacy of the Puritans. Meanwhile, other revisionists like David Cressy were challenging precisely this notion and arguing, as the Progressives had, that there was nothing particularly religious about the motivation of the emigrants and that there was nothing particularly Puritan about most of the residents of New England.[29]

---

[27]Kenneth Lockridge, *A New England Town* (New York, 1970). See also Sumner Chilton Powell, *Puritan Village: The Formation of a New England Town* (Middletown, Conn., 1963), and David Grayson Allen, *In English Ways: The Movement of Societies and the Transferral of English Local Law and Custom* (Chapel Hill, N.C., 1981). The literature on Puritan community studies is voluminous, and the studies cited are merely representative of certain theses or generalizations. Among the first of the community studies to challenge Miller's findings directly was Darrett Rutman, *Winthrop's Boston* (Chapel Hill, N.C., 1965); see also his *American Puritanism: Faith and Practice* (Philadelphia, 1970). For the relationship between law and society, see David T. Konig, *Law and Society in Puritan Massachusetts: Essex County, 1629–1692* (Chapel Hill, N.C., 1982).

[28]Paul Boyer and Stephen Nissenbaum, *Salem Possessed: The Social Origins of Witchcraft* (Cambridge, 1979).

[29]Virginia DeJohn Anderson, *New England's Generation: The Great Migration and the Formation of Society and Culture in the Seventeenth Century* (Cambridge and New York, 1991); David Cressy, *Coming Over: Migration and Communication between England and New England in the Seventeenth Century* (New York, 1987).

In recent years, historians of the Puritans, as in so many other fields, have enlarged the communities they study and have made transnational connections when possible. Using the Atlantic World as an organizing principle, Alison Games in *Migration and the Origins of the English Atlantic World* studied the entire Great Migration of 1635 to Massachusetts, Providence Island in the Caribbean, and Virginia to demonstrate that the broad culture from which it was drawn was not "singular, uniform or harmonious." She also showed how the "tensions and ambiguity latent in Puritanism" in England when practitioners had only one enemy were free to proliferate in the New World and resulted in a "decade of dispute and transformation in ecclesiastical polity, Puritanism, and relations between ministers and laity." The Atlantic focus blunts claims for exceptionalism and points to conflict and diversity among migrants, while providing a richer social and political context for the beginnings of New England.[30]

Studies of the colonial family by the new social historians also provided important insights into the Puritan value system and behavior. John Demos in his study of the Plymouth colony in the seventeenth century, *A Little Commonwealth*, pioneered an exploration of Puritan child-rearing practices and resorted to the techniques of demography, psychoanalysis, social psychology, and archaeology to arrive at his conclusions. Philip Greven in *Four Generations* argued, as did Demos, that the family was the key institution in socializing the individual within the Puritan community. Greven studied changes within the family, household, and community structure in Andover, Massachusetts, over four generations, and concluded that landholding practices, geographic mobility, birth and death rates, marriage customs, inheritance law, and intergenerational relationships all helped shape the outlines of this Puritan town in ways that were no longer English.[31]

But there was increasing disenchantment with the large number of community studies that had appeared by the end of the 1980s. Although the studies were interesting individually, skeptics felt they offered collectively little in the way of new generalizations about Puritanism or Puritan society as a whole. No community could be taken as being typical of a region or colony or as representative of the American colonies as a whole. As Darrett Rutman pointed out, moreover, American colonial historians assumed that Puritanism led to communal cohesiveness, while English historians saw Puritans as a divisive force in the villages of the mother country. Thus, the definition of the term *Puritan* itself came under question. To use community studies to discover more about Puritanism, Rutman concluded, new social historians would have to explore outward linkages — economic, governmental,

---

[30]Alison Games, *Migration and the Origins of the English Atlantic World* (Cambridge, Mass., 1999), 9, 133.

[31]John Demos, *A Little Commonwealth: Family Life in Plymouth Colony* (New York, 1970), and Philip Greven, *Four Generations: Population, Land, and Family in Colonial Andover, Massachusetts* (Ithaca, N.Y., 1970). The work on this subject by the new social historians was preceded by Edmund S. Morgan's *Puritan Family* (Boston, 1944). Judith Graham's newer study, *Puritan Family Life: The Diary of Samuel Sewall* (Boston, 2000), attempts to portray the family as less dour and more loving than other accounts have suggested.

political, religious, and intellectual — between individual communities and surrounding places.[32]

Michael Winship's new view of the Anne Hutchinson trial in Boston as a political crisis, more than a theological or social one, rises to Rutman's challenges. Winship narrated the unfolding events in their transatlantic political context, revealing a highly unstable Puritanism that was constantly shaping and reshaping itself through "dynamic coalitions." He agreed with Rutman that the label Puritan suggested a homogeneity that did not exist and referred to them instead as "hot Protestants," among other names. He recast the effort of the prosecutors to focus on Hutchinson as a political tactic designed to avoid focusing on more important radicals like John Cotton and particularly on Henry Vane, who would become a regicide. Winship's Puritans are a "ramshackle entity," and the free grace controversy of Anne Hutchinson was "transatlantic in its scope. In England it played a not inconsiderable role in the 1640s and 1650s, magnifying Puritanism's systematic capacity for disorder." By placing this controversy in a transatlantic context, Winship illuminates not only the shifting alliances that propelled it, but also similar and more violent upheavals to come across the ocean. Published in 2002, this book offers insight into the significance of a religious-political struggle that transcended geographical confines. It is one of a number of new studies on what individual disputes can teach us about long-term conflicts among believers and the permeable borders between the religious and the political.[33]

Historians of women who had been influenced by the new social history looked at Puritan life from the standpoint of gender to understand more about power relations among Puritans and women's roles in preserving communitarian values and to challenge Miller's idea of a single, declining New England spirituality. Laurel Thatcher Ulrich's *Good Wives* (1980) focused on women's experience in the family, in household economy, and among neighbors. She retrieved women's experiences by looking at them through several well-defined biblical roles. By studying northern New England, she showed that strict Puritan theology was diluted in daily life by English village culture. Robert Saint George, in an article on slander in Puritan communities, observed how women took a significant role policing the moral bounds of the community. Mary Maples Dunn, however, looked at Puritan sources for women's religious and moral activism and compared these unfavorably with the experience of Quaker women.[34]

---

[32]Darrett Rutman, "Assessing the Little Communities of Early America," *William and Mary Quarterly*, 3rd Ser. (1986): 163–78.

[33]Michael Winship, *Making Heretics: Militant Protestantism and Free Grace in Massachusetts, 1636–1641* (Princeton, N.J., 2002).

[34]Laurel Thatcher Ulrich, *Good Wives: Image and Reality in the Lives of Women in Northern New England, 1650–1750* (New York, 1980); Robert Saint George, "'Heated Speech' and Literacy in Seventeenth-Century New England," in *Seventeenth-Century New England* (Boston, 1985); Mary Maples Dunn, "Saints and Sinners: Congregational and Quaker Women in the Early Colonial Period," *American Quarterly* 30 (1978): 582–601; see also E. Jennifer Monaghan, "Literacy Instruction and Gender in Colonial New England," *American Quarterly* 40 (March 1988): 18–41 for a discussion of how and why so many Puritan women learned to read.

Looking at the law from the perspective of gender provided insight into Puritan methods of enforcing their moral — particularly, their sexual — code. Nancy Hull, studying the Puritan legal system and its effect on women, found them particularly susceptible to being punished for sexual transgressions and found that disproportionate punishment increased dramatically when the women were black. Later, Cornelia Dayton Hughes, studying women and the law in the highly orthodox New Haven colony, found that women under the Puritans fared better in the legal process of the seventeenth century than they did in the more secular atmosphere of the eighteenth century.[35]

In 1987, Carol Karlsen was the first, astonishingly, to analyze witchcraft from the standpoint of gender. In *The Devil in the Shape of a Woman*, she employed tools from psychology and cultural anthropology, as had John Demos in his earlier study, *Entertaining Satan*. Her work revealed how Puritan ideology, despite its emphasis on the equality of male and female souls in the eyes of God, saw specific spiritual vulnerabilities in women that led to a greater likelihood that they would be perceived as practicing witchcraft. Her study also found a significant correlation between displays of women's independence — especially ownership of property — with witchcraft accusations. Elizabeth Reis, in *Damned Women*, has explored the ideological origins of Puritan views of women's characteristic weaknesses, which opened them to charges of witchcraft.[36]

Other new social historians employed interdisciplinary approaches to demonstrate Puritan strategies of dealing with dissent. Kai T. Erikson, for example, used sociological and psychological theories to study the groups Puritans defined as deviants. He then showed what constituted the boundaries of acceptable behavior within Puritan society. Michael Zuckerman, using cultural anthropology, concluded that a kind of communal consensus created peace, order, and harmony within a number of eighteenth-century towns based in part on a carryover of Puritan cultural ideals. These communities remained "peaceable kingdoms" until the eve of the Revolution, according to Zuckerman, despite underlying social tensions.[37]

All these different lines of approach to Puritanism resulted in shattering or questioning Miller's synthesis, but they gave rise to problems of their own. Social historians, particularly those involved in community studies to explore Puritanism, appeared to have foundered on the problem of how representative these communities were. Intellectual historians dismantled Miller's notion

---

[35]Nancy E. Hull, *Female Felons: Women and Serious Crime in Colonial Massachusetts* (Urbana, Ill., 1987); Cornelia Hughes Dayton, *Women before the Bar: Gender, Law, and Society in Connecticut, 1639–1789* (Chapel Hill, N.C., 1995).

[36]Carol Karlsen, *The Devil in the Shape of a Woman: Witchcraft in Colonial New England* (New York, 1987); John Demos, *Entertaining Satan: Witchcraft and the Culture of Early New England* (New York, 1982); Elizabeth Reis, *Damned Women: Sinners and Witches in Puritan New England* (Ithaca, N.Y., 1997).

[37]Kai T. Erikson, *Wayward Puritans: A Study in the Sociology of Deviance* (New York, 1966), and Michael Zuckerman, *Peaceable Kingdoms: New England Towns in the Eighteenth Century* (New York, 1970).

of the covenant as a compromise provoked by the unbearably high anxiety engendered by predestination, but no one could come up with a convincing theory that seemed to define Puritans as a group and about what held New England together. Literary historians, with their new perspectives, provided new overviews of New England and its mythology, but their analytic methods, such as deconstruction, and the absence of economic and social evidence did not persuade most traditional historians.

In 1998, Darren Staloff argued that the revisionist or anti-Miller synthesis was an essentially conservative and incorrect view of the Puritans.[38] Revisionists like David Hall, for example, have rejected the notion of a broad consensus on Puritanism, as it left out the bottom half of the population entirely and homogenized many differences of belief among the others. Scholars continue to argue that Miller and subsequent defenders have overemphasized ideas and underemphasized the social and economic differences among dissenters. Staloff's new synthesis took into consideration the social, political, and institutional influences on Puritanism but simultaneously stressed the immense importance of the Puritan clergy. Staloff argued that this group's struggle for power and status mobilized the middling and lower orders into the Puritan cause. "The flowering of Puritan divinity was then, in part at least, the religious mobilization of the 'popular' elements of the political nation by a semiunderground ministry."[39] Staloff attempted to fold in the arguments of the (now older) new social historians like Michael Walzer as to the democratic urgency of Puritanism by finding political radicalism in the Puritan emphasis on the authority of the Bible over church hierarchy. Puritan ministers interpreted the Bible, to be sure, and therein lay the source of their own power. But ultimately, in its emphasis on literacy and the individual's ability to read and understand scripture for himself, the Puritan message could undermine all temporal authority. This radical realization of Puritanism could only have happened in the New World with the dramatic increase in the power of the educated gentry, professionals, and clergy who crossed the Atlantic. "New England is thus key to unfolding the radical nature of Puritan dissent. . . . A postrevisionist interpretation puts New England back at the center" of the Calvinist world.[40]

Staloff's account gave precedence to a relatively small group of individuals whose concern about their own status overlapped fortuitously with the democratic desires of middling and lower sorts. Since then, Louise Breen has argued to the contrary that the "social context drove the theological debate. . . . [F]ew Puritans lived without the temptation to free themselves from the confining intellectual and social bonds" of Winthrop's city on a hill. In her view, the radicalism of the poor was economic, ideological, and

---

[38]Darren Staloff, *The Making of an American Thinking Class: Intellectuals and Intelligentsia in Puritan Massachusetts* (Oxford, 1998). Staloff's invaluable appendix B (192–205) is the basis for these remarks on postrevisionism and Perry Miller.

[39]Ibid., 202.

[40]Ibid., 204.

divisive. And Thomas N. Ingersoll, in his marvelously titled 1999 article, "'Riches and Honor Were Rejected by Them as Loathsome Vomit': The Fear of Levelling in New England," presented the Puritan clergy lumping both radical religious sectarians and the undeferential poor together with horror. He showed these two often overlapping groups managing to inch the Puritan elite, kicking and screaming, toward greater democracy.[41]

Lisa M. Gordis undermines Staloff's argument from quite a different perspective in her careful study of how freely Puritans read and interpreted scripture. She describes a spectrum ranging from approaching the text as an account of God's will to an interpretive approach that could include "prophesying . . . a divinely enabled activity." In Gordis's view, the clergy contested the right of the unsaved to interpret scripture. Over time, ministers tended to restrict this activity to themselves, but, as Gordis writes, interpretation remained a source of "conflict and struggle [yet] they resisted the impulse to trade the open text for a closed book."[42]

Joseph Conforti's *Saints and Strangers: New England in British North America* is a compact social, economic, and political synthesis of New England history. Conforti puts the region in the context of the lively Atlantic trade, other colonies of transplanted Europeans, and the large number of Native Americans and small but increasing number of Africans and others who helped build the new colony. English New Englanders regarded the latter as strangers, yet they managed to establish cultural pockets for themselves within the larger English world. Conforti's title points to the book's focus on New England's continuing relationship with Great Britain. He sees its most dominant influence as its English heritage rather than Puritanism, although he does not neglect the latter.[43] Conforti resists making claims for New England's outsized influence on the United States or Puritanism's continuing hold on the psyches of Americans.

Reaching across the Atlantic and south into the lands being conquered by Spain, Jorge Cañizares-Esguerra has compared the English conquest of what became New England with the Iberian conquests to the south. In *Puritan Conquistadors: Iberianizing the Atlantic, 1550–1700,* he argues that, contrary to repeated English portrayals of differences with Spain, the two countries employed remarkably similar discourses in their colonizing projects. Although England claimed moral superiority in its treatment of native peoples and created the Black Legend to describe Spanish atrocities toward Indians, both nations depicted the struggle to overcome Native Americans as one between holy Christianity and Satan. Both identified Indians as demons in the New

---

[41]Louise Breen, "Religious Radicalism in the Puritan Officer Corps: Heterodoxy, the Artillery Company, and Cultural Integration in Seventeenth-Century Boston," *New England Quarterly* (1995): 3–43. Thomas N. Ingersoll, "'Riches and Honor Were Rejected by Them as Loathsome Vomit': The Fear of Levelling in New England," in Carla Gardina Pestana and Sharon Salinger, eds., *Inequality in Early America* (Hanover, N.H., 1999), 48.

[42]Lisa M. Gordis, *Opening Scripture: Bible Reading and Interpreting Authority in Puritan New England* (Chicago, 2002), 2, 216.

[43]Joseph Conforti, *Saints and Strangers: New England in British North America* (Baltimore, 2006).

World, and both also feared the works of the devil hiding insidiously among their own. Cañizares-Esguerra argues that we have hitherto focused on the differences between the conquests of Reformation England and Catholic Spain because we have been thinking about them as nations, but in taking a transnational approach, the similarities between the colonization ideology and tactics of the two powers become much more apparent. In what promises to be a rich field for exploration, we can expect to learn much more about the Puritans from a transnational approach that extends beyond England.[44]

Without knowing yet how influential Conforti's synthesis will be or where Cañizares-Esguerra's bold lead will take us, familiar questions persist about Puritanism and its relation to New England and America. Were Puritans bigots obsessed with ridding themselves of the other, or consensus-minded community builders? Were the Puritans pious idealists concerned mainly with maintaining their special Protestant way of life? Or were they practical-minded pioneers, simply seeking to make their way and establish viable settlements in the New World? Were they a radical movement that needed the institutional vacuum of the New World to realize its potential for religious and intellectual innovation? Was Puritanism as a cultural movement restricted to its own time in terms of its influence? Did it give rise to a New England myth and later a national myth of manifest destiny, or was it merely one of several cultural strands that fed into the United States? Was Puritan devotion repressive or essentially progressive in its effect on daily life? Can liberalism emerge from a theocratic state? New questions include whether Puritanism was sufficiently coherent to deserve one name. Was Puritanism's secret of success that it learned to thrive on dissent, not orthodoxy? These are some of the questions that occur in trying to determine the precise role of the Puritans and their proper place in American history.

---

[44]Jorge Cañizares-Esguerra, *Puritan Conquistadors: Iberianizing the Atlantic, 1550–1700* (Stanford, Calif., 2006).

PERRY MILLER AND THOMAS H. JOHNSON

*from* The Puritans   [1938]

**PERRY MILLER** (1905–1963) was professor of American literature at Harvard University until his death. He was the author of numerous articles and books, including *The New England Mind,* 2 vols. (1939–1953), *Jonathan Edwards* (1949), *Errand into the Wilderness* (1956), and *The Life of the Mind in America: From the Revolution to the Civil War* (1965).

**THOMAS H. JOHNSON** (1902–1986) taught for many years at the Lawrenceville School in New Jersey as well as at a number of universities. He was the author of *Emily Dickinson: An Interpretive Biography* (1955) and *The Oxford Companion to American History* (1966).

Puritanism may perhaps be described as that point of view, that philosophy of life, that code of values, which was carried to New England by the first settlers in the early seventeenth century. Beginning thus, it has become one of the continuous factors in American life and American thought. Any inventory of the elements that have gone into the making of the "American mind" would have to commence with Puritanism. It is, indeed, only one among many: if we should attempt to enumerate these traditions, we should certainly have to mention such philosophies, such "isms," as the rational liberalism of Jeffersonian democracy, the Hamiltonian conception of conservatism and government, the Southern theory of racial aristocracy, the Transcendentalism of nineteenth-century New England, and what is generally spoken of as frontier individualism. Among these factors Puritanism has been perhaps the most conspicuous, the most sustained, and the most fecund. Its role in American thought has been almost the dominant one, for the descendants of Puritans have carried at least some habits of the Puritan mind into a variety of pursuits, have spread across the country, and in many fields of activity have played a leading part. The force of Puritanism, furthermore, has been accentuated because it was the first of these traditions to be fully articulated, and because it has inspired certain traits which have persisted long after the vanishing of the original creed. Without some understanding of Puritanism, it may safely be said, there is no understanding of America.

Yet important as Puritanism has undoubtedly been in shaping the nation, it is more easily described than defined. It figures frequently in controversy of the last decade, very seldom twice with exactly the same connotation. Particularly of recent years has it become a hazardous feat to run down its meaning. In the mood of revolt against the ideals of previous generations which has swept over our period, Puritanism has

Perry Miller and Thomas H. Johnson, eds., *The Puritans* (New York: American Book Company, 1938), 1–19. Reprinted with omissions by permission of the American Book Company.

become a shining target for many sorts of marksmen. Confusion becomes worse confounded if we attempt to correlate modern usages with anything that can be proved pertinent to the original Puritans themselves. To seek no further, it was the habit of proponents for the repeal of the Eighteenth Amendment during the 1920s to dub Prohibitionists "Puritans," and cartoonists made the nation familiar with an image of the Puritan: a gaunt, lank-haired killjoy, wearing a black steeple hat and compounding for sins he was inclined to by damning those to which he had no mind. Yet any acquaintance with the Puritans of the seventeenth century will reveal at once, not only that they did not wear such hats but also that they attired themselves in all the hues of the rainbow, and furthermore that in their daily life they imbibed what seem to us prodigious quantities of alcoholic beverages, with never the slightest inkling that they were doing anything sinful. True, they opposed drinking to excess, and ministers preached lengthy sermons condemning intoxication, but at such pious ceremonies as the ordination of new ministers the bill for rum, wine, and beer consumed by the congregation was often staggering. Increase Mather himself — who in popular imagination is apt to figure along with his son Cotton as the archembodiment of the Puritan — said in one of his sermons:

> Drink is in it self a good creature of God, and to be received with thankfulness, but the abuse of drink is from Satan; the wine is from God, but the Drunkard is from the Devil.

Or again, the Puritan has acquired the reputation of having been blind to all aesthetic enjoyment and starved of beauty; yet the architecture of the Puritan age grows in the esteem of critics and the household objects of Puritan manufacture, pewter and furniture, achieve prohibitive prices by their appeal to discriminating collectors. Examples of such discrepancies between the modern usage of the word and the historical fact could be multiplied indefinitely. It is not the purpose of this volume to engage in controversy, nor does it intend particularly to defend the Puritan against the bewildering variety of critics who on every side today find him an object of scorn or pity. In his life he neither asked nor gave mercy to his foes; he demanded only that conflicts be joined on real and explicit issues. By examining his own words it may become possible to establish, for better or for worse, the meaning of Puritanism as the Puritan himself believed and practiced it.

Just as soon as we endeavor to free ourselves from prevailing conceptions or misconceptions, and to ascertain the historical facts about seventeenth-century New Englanders, we become aware that we face still another difficulty: not only must we extricate ourselves from interpretations that have been read into Puritanism by the twentieth century, but still more from those that have been attached to it by the eighteenth and nineteenth. The Puritan philosophy, brought to New England highly elaborated and codified, remained a fairly rigid orthodoxy during the seventeenth century. In the next age, however, it proved to be anything but static; by the middle of the eighteenth century there had proceeded from it two distinct schools of thought, almost unalterably opposed to each other. Certain elements were carried into the creeds and practices of the evangelical religious revivals, but others were perpetuated by the rationalists and the forerunners of Unitarianism. Consequently our conception of Puritanism is all too apt to be colored by subsequent happenings; we read ideas into the seventeenth century which belong to the eighteenth, and the real nature of Puritanism can hardly be discovered at all, because Puritanism itself became two distinct and contending things to two sorts of men. The most prevalent error arising from this fact has been the identification of Puritanism with evangelicalism in many accounts, though in histories written by Unitarian scholars the original doctrine has been almost as much distorted in the opposite direction.

Among the evangelicals the original doctrines were transformed or twisted into the new versions of Protestantism that spawned in the Great Awakening of the 1740s, in the succeeding revivals along the frontier and through the back country, in the centrifugal speculations of enraptured prophets and rabid sects in the nineteenth century. All these movements retained something of the theology or revived something of the intensity of spirit, but at the same time they threw aside so much of authentic Puritanism that there can be no doubt the founding fathers would vigorously have repudiated such progeny. They would have had no use, for instance, for the camp meeting and the revivalist orgy; "hitting the sawdust trail" would have been an action exceedingly distasteful to the most ardent among them. What we know as "fundamentalism" would have been completely antipathetic to them, for they never for one moment dreamed that the truth of scripture was to be maintained in spite of or against the evidences of reason, science, and learning. The sects that have arisen out of Puritanism have most strikingly betrayed their rebellion against the true spirit of their source by their attack upon the ideal of a learned ministry; Puritans considered religion a very complex, subtle, and highly intellectualized affair, and they trained their experts in theology with all the care we would lavish upon preparing men to be engineers or chemists. For the same reasons, Puritans would object strenuously to almost all recent attempts to "humanize" religion, to smooth over hard doctrines, to introduce sweetness and light at the cost of hard-headed realism and invincible logic. From their point of view, to bring Christ down to earth in such a fashion as is implied in statements we sometimes encounter — that He was the "first humanitarian" or that He would certainly endorse this or that political party — would seem to them frightful blasphemy. Puritanism was not only a religious creed, it was a philosophy and a metaphysic; it was an organization of man's whole life, emotional and intellectual, to a degree which has not been sustained by any denomination stemming from it. Yet because such creeds have sprung from

Puritanism, the Puritans are frequently praised or blamed for qualities which never belonged to them or for ideas which originated only among their successors and which they themselves would have disowned.

On the other hand, if the line of development from Puritanism tends in one direction to frontier revivalism and evangelicalism, another line leads as directly to a more philosophical, critical, and even skeptical point of view. Unitarianism is as much the child of Puritanism as Methodism. And if the one accretion has colored or distorted our conception of the original doctrine, the other has done so no less. Descendants of the Puritans who revolted against what they considered the tyranny and cruelty of Puritan theology, who substituted taste and reason for dogma and authority and found the emotional fervor of the evangelicals so much sound and fury, have been prone to idealize their ancestors into their own image. A few decades ago it had become very much the mode to praise the Puritans for virtues which they did not possess and which they would not have considered virtues at all. In the pages of liberal historians, and above all in the speeches of Fourth of July orators, the Puritans have been hymned as the pioneers of religious liberty, though nothing was ever farther from their designs; they have been hailed as the forerunners of democracy, though if they were, it was quite beside their intention; they have been invoked in justification for an economic philosophy of free competition and laissez-faire, though they themselves believed in government regulation of business, the fixing of just prices, and the curtailing of individual profits in the interests of the welfare of the whole.

The moral of these reflections may very well be that it is dangerous to read history backwards, to interpret something that was by what it ultimately became, particularly when it became several things. . . . The Puritans were not a bashful race, they could speak out and did; in their own words they have painted their own portraits, their majestic strength and their dignity, their humanity and solidity, more accurately than any admirer had been able to do; and also they have betrayed the motes and beams in their own eyes more clearly than any enemy has been able to point them out.

Puritanism began as an agitation within the Church of England in the latter half of the sixteenth century. It was a movement for reform of that institution, and at the time no more constituted a distinct sect or denomination than the advocates of an amendment to the Constitution of the United States constitute a separate nation. In the 1530s the Church of England broke with the pope of Rome. By the beginning of Elizabeth's reign it had proceeded a certain distance in this revolt, had become Protestant, had disestablished the monasteries and corrected many abuses. Puritanism was the belief that the reform should be continued, that more abuses remained to be corrected, that practices still survived from the days of popery which should be renounced, that the Church of England should be restored to the "purity" of the first-century church as established by Christ Himself. In the 1560s, when the advocates of purification first acquired the name of Puritans, no one, not even the most radical, knew exactly how far the process was to go or just what the ultimate goal would be;

down to the days of Cromwell there was never any agreement on this point, and in the end this failure of unanimity proved the undoing of English Puritanism. Many Puritans desired only that certain ceremonies be abolished or changed. Others wanted ministers to preach more sermons, make up their own prayers on the inspiration of the moment rather than read set forms out of a book. Others went further and proposed a revision of the whole form of ecclesiastical government. But whatever the shade or complexion of their Puritanism, Puritans were those who wanted to continue a movement which was already under way. Their opponents, whom we shall speak of as the Anglicans — though only for the sake of convenience, because there was at that time not the remotest thought on either side of an ultimate separation into distinct churches, and Puritans insisted they were as stoutly loyal to the established institution as any men in England — the Anglicans were those who felt that with the enthronement of Elizabeth and with the "Elizabethan Settlement" of the church, things had gone far enough. They wanted to call a halt, just where they were, and stabilize at that point.

Thus the issue between the two views, though large enough, still involved only a limited number of questions. On everything except matters upon which the Puritans wanted further reformation, there was essential agreement. The Puritans who settled New England were among the more radical — though by no means the most radical that the movement produced — and even before their migration in 1630 had gone to the lengths of formulating a concrete platform of church organization which they wished to see instituted in England in place of the episcopal system. Joining battle on this front gave a sufficiently extended line and provided a vast number of salients to fight over; the gulf between the belief of these Puritans and the majority in the Church of England grew so wide that at last there was no bridging it at all. But notwithstanding the depth of this divergence, the fact still remains that only certain specific questions were raised. If we take a comprehensive survey of the whole body of Puritan thought and belief as it existed in 1630 or 1640, if we make an exhaustive enumeration of ideas held by New England Puritans, we shall find that the vast majority of them were precisely those of their opponents. In other words, Puritanism was a movement toward certain ends within the culture and state of England in the late sixteenth and early seventeenth centuries; it centered about a number of concrete problems and advocated a particular program. Outside of that, it was part and parcel of the times, and its culture was simply the culture of England at that moment. It is necessary to belabor the point, because most accounts of Puritanism, emphasizing the controversial tenets, attribute everything that Puritans said or did to the fact that they were Puritans; their attitudes toward all sorts of things are pounced upon and exhibited as peculiarities of their sect, when as a matter of fact they were normal attitudes for the time. Of course, the Puritans acquired their special quality and their essential individuality from their stand on the points actually at issue, and our final conception of Puritanism must give these concerns all due importance. Yet if first of all we wish to

take Puritan culture as a whole, we shall find, let us say, that about 90 percent of the intellectual life, scientific knowledge, morality, manners and
customs, notions and prejudices, was that of all Englishmen. The other 10
percent, the relatively small number of ideas upon which there was dispute,
made all the difference between the Puritan and his fellow Englishmen,
made for him so much difference that he pulled up stakes in England,
which he loved, and migrated to a wilderness rather than submit them to
apparent defeat. Nevertheless, when we come to trace developments and
influences on subsequent American history and thought, we shall find that
the starting point of many ideas and practices is as apt to be found among
the 90 percent as among the 10. The task of defining Puritanism and giving
an account of its culture resolves itself, therefore, into isolating first of all
the larger features which were not particularly or necessarily Puritan at all,
the elements in the life and society which were products of the time and
place, of the background of English life and society rather than of the individual belief or peculiar creed of Puritanism.

Many of the major interests and preoccupations of the New England
Puritans belong to this list. They were just as patriotic as Englishmen who
remained at home. They hated Spain like poison, and France only a little
less. In their eyes, as in those of Anglicans, the most important issue in the
Western world was the struggle between Catholicism and Protestantism.
They were not unique or extreme in thinking that religion was the primary and all-engrossing business of man, or that all human thought and
action should tend to the glory of God. . . .

In its major aspects the religious creed of Puritanism was neither peculiar to the Puritans nor different from that of the Anglicans. Both were
essentially Protestant; both asserted that men were saved by their faith, not
by their deeds. The two sides could agree on the general statement that
Christians are bound to believe nothing but what the Gospel teaches, that
all traditions of men "contrary to the Word of God" are to be renounced
and abhorred. They both believed that the marks of a true church were
profession of the creed, use of Christ's sacraments, preaching of the word —
Anglican sermons being as long and often as dull as the Puritan — and
the union of men in profession and practice under regularly constituted
pastors. The Puritans always said that they could subscribe to the doctrinal
articles of the Church of England; even at the height of the controversy,
even after they had left England rather than put up with what they considered its abominations, they always took care to insist that the Church of
England was a "true" church, not Anti-Christ as was the Church of Rome,
that it contained many saints, and that men might find salvation within it.
Throughout the seventeenth century they read Anglican authors, quoted
them in their sermons, and even reprinted some of them in Boston.

The vast substratum of agreement which actually underlay the disagreement between Puritans and Anglicans is explained by the fact that they
were both the heirs of the Middle Ages. They still believed that all knowledge was one, that life was unified, that science, economics, political theory,
aesthetic standards, rhetoric and art, all were organized in a hierarchical

scale of values that tended upward to the end-all and be-all of creation, the glory of God. They both insisted that all human activity be regulated by that purpose. Consequently, even while fighting bitterly against each other, the Puritans and Anglicans stood shoulder to shoulder against what they called "enthusiasm." The leaders of the Puritan movement were trained at the universities, they were men of learning and scholars; no less than the Anglicans did they demand that religion be interpreted by study and logical exposition; they were both resolute against all pretenses to immediate revelation, against all ignorant men who claimed to receive personal instructions from God. They agreed on the essential Christian contention that though God may govern the world, He is not the world itself, and that though He instills His grace into men, He does not deify them or unite them to Himself in one personality. He converses with men only through His revealed word, the Bible. His will is to be studied in the operation of His providence as exhibited in the workings of the natural world, but He delivers no new commands or special revelations to the inward consciousness of men. The larger unanimity of the Puritans and the Anglicans reveals itself whenever either of them was called upon to confront enthusiasm [as seen in] . . . Governor John Winthrop's account of the so-called Antinomian affair, the crisis produced in the little colony by the teachings of Mistress Anne Hutchinson in 1636 and 1637. . . . Beneath the theological jargon in which the opinions of this lady appear we can see the substance of her contention, which was that she was in direct communication with the Godhead, and that she therefore was prepared to follow the promptings of the voice within against all the precepts of the Bible, the churches, reason, or the government of Massachusetts Bay. Winthrop relates how the magistrates and the ministers defended the community against this perversion of the doctrine of regeneration, but the tenor of his condemnation would have been duplicated practically word for word had Anne Hutchinson broached her theories in an Anglican community. The Anglicans fell in completely with the Puritans when both of them were confronted in the 1650s by the Quakers. All New England leaders saw in the Quaker doctrine of an inner light, accessible to all men and giving a perfect communication from God to their inmost spirits, just another form of Anne Hutchinson's blasphemy. John Norton declared that the "light of nature" itself taught us that "madmen acting according to their frantick passions are to be restrained with chaines, when they can not be restrained otherwise. . . ." Enthusiasts, whether Antinomian or Quaker, were proposing doctrines that threatened the unity of life by subduing the reason and the intellect to the passions and the emotions. Whatever their differences, Puritans and Anglicans were struggling to maintain a complete harmony of reason and faith, science and religion, earthly dominion and the government of God. When we immerse ourselves in the actual struggle, the difference between the Puritan and the Anglican may seem to us immense; but when we take the vantage point of subsequent history, and survey religious thought as a whole over the last three centuries, the two come very close together on essentials. Against all forms of chaotic

emotionalism, against all oversimplifications of theology, learning, philosophy, and science, against all materialism, positivism or mechanism, both
were endeavoring to uphold a symmetrical union of heart and head without impairment of either. By the beginning or middle of the next century
their successors, both in England and America, found themselves no
longer capable of sustaining this unity, and it has yet to be reachieved
today, if achieved again it ever can be. The greatness of the Puritans is not
so much that they conquered a wilderness, or that they carried a religion
into it, but that they carried a religion which, narrow and starved though it
may have been in some respects, deficient in sensuous richness or brilliant
color, was nevertheless indissolubly bound up with an ideal of culture and
learning. In contrast to all other pioneers, they made no concessions to
the forest, but in the midst of frontier conditions, in the very throes of
clearing the land and erecting shelters, they maintained schools and a college, a standard of scholarship and of competent writing, a class of men
devoted entirely to the life of the mind and of the soul.

Because the conflict between the Puritans and the Churchmen was as
much an intellectual and scholarly issue as it was emotional, it was in great
part a debate among pundits. This is not to say that passions were not
involved; certainly men took sides because of prejudice, interest, irrational
conviction, or for any of the motives that may incite the human race
to conflict. The disagreement finally was carried from the field of learned
controversy to the field of battle. There can be no doubt that many of the
people in England, or even in New England, became rabid partisans and
yet never acquired the erudition necessary to understand the intricate and
subtle arguments of their leaders. A great number, perhaps even a majority,
in both camps were probably not intelligent or learned enough to see
clearly the reasons for the cause they supported. . . .

The wonder is that by and large the populace did yield their judgments
to those who were supposed to know, respected learning and supported it,
sat patiently during two- and three-hour sermons while ministers expounded
the knottiest and most recondite of metaphysical texts. The testimony of
visitors, travelers, and memoirs agrees that during the Puritan age in New
England the common man, the farmer and merchant, was amazingly versed
in systematic divinity. A gathering of yeomen and "hired help" around the
kitchen fire of an evening produced long and unbelievably technical discussions of predestination, infant damnation, and the distinctions between
faith and works. In the first half of the seventeenth century the people had
not yet questioned the conception of religion as a difficult art in which the
authority of the skilled dialectician should prevail over the inclinations of
the merely devout. This ideal of subjection to qualified leadership was
social as well as intellectual. Very few Englishmen had yet broached the
notion that a lackey was as good as a lord, or that any Tom, Dick, or Harry,
simply because he was a good, honest man, could understand the Sermon
on the Mount as well as a master of arts from Oxford, Cambridge, or
Harvard. Professor Morison has shown that the life of the college in New
England was saved by the sacrifice of the yeomen farmers, who contributed

their pecks of wheat, wrung from a stony soil, taken from their none too opulent stores, to support teaching fellows and to assist poor scholars at Harvard College, in order that they and their children might still sit under a literate ministry "when our present Ministers shall lie in the Dust."

When we say the majority of the people in the early seventeenth century still acceded to the dictation of the learned in religion and the superior in society, we must also remark that the Puritan leaders were in grave danger of arousing a revolt against themselves by their very own doctrines. Puritans were attacking the sacerdotal and institutional bias which had survived in the Church of England; they were maintaining a theology that brought every man to a direct experience of the spirit and removed intermediaries between himself and the deity. Yet the authority of the infallible church and the power of the bishops had for centuries served to keep the people docile. Consequently when the Puritan leaders endeavored to remove the bishops and to deny that the church should stand between God and man, they ran the hazard of starting something among the people that might get out of hand. Just as the Puritan doctrine that men were saved by the infusion of God's grace could lead to the Antinomianism of Mrs. Hutchinson, and often did warrant the simple in concluding that if they had God's grace in them they needed to pay no heed to what a minister told them, so the Puritan contention that regenerate men were illuminated with divine truth might lead to the belief that true religion did not need the assistance of learning, books, arguments, logical demonstrations, or classical languages. There was always a possibility that Puritanism would raise up a fanatical anti-intellectualism, and against such a threat the Puritan ministers constantly braced themselves. It was no accident that the followers of Mrs. Hutchinson, who believed that men could receive all the necessary instructions from within, also attacked learning and education, and came near to wrecking not only the colony but the college as well. . . .

[T]he New England leaders were face to face with a problem as old as the history of the Christian church. Throughout the Middle Ages there had been such stirrings among the people as those to which Mrs. Hutchinson or the Fifth Monarchy Men gave voice. The great scholastic synthesis always remained incomprehensible to the vulgar, who demanded to be fed again and again with the sort of religious sustenance they craved. The Reformation drew upon these suppressed desires. Common men turned Protestant primarily because Protestantism offered them a religion which more effectively satisfied their spiritual hunger. Yet in Europe theologians and metaphysicians retained the leadership and kept Protestantism from becoming merely an emotional outburst. They supplied it with a theology which, though not so sophisticated as scholastic dogma, was still equipped with a logic and organon of rational demonstration. Though Protestantism can be viewed as a "liberation" of the common man, it was far from being a complete emancipation of the individual. It freed him from many intellectual restraints that had been imposed by the church, but it did not give him full liberty to think anything he pleased; socially it freed him from many exactions, but it did not permit him to abandon his traditional subjection to his social and ecclesiastical superiors. The original settlers of New England carried this Protestantism intact from Europe to America. Except for the small band that was driven into exile with Anne Hutchinson, and one or two other groups of visionaries who also were hustled across the borders into Rhode Island, the rank and file did follow their leaders, meekly and reverently. Captain Johnson[45] probably represents the average layman's loyalty to the clergy. The New England "theocracy" was simply a Protestant version of the European social ideal, and except for its Protestantism was thoroughly medieval in character.

It was only as the seventeenth century came to a close that the imported structure began to show the strain. In Europe social tradition had conspired with the ministers to check enthusiasts in religion and "levellers" in society; in England the authorities, whether Anglican or Puritan, royal or Cromwellian, were able to suppress the assault upon the scholarly and aristocratic ideal. In America the character of the people underwent a change; they moved further into the frontier, they became more absorbed in business and profits than in religion and salvation, their memories of English social stratification grew dim. A preacher before the General Court in 1705 bewailed the effects of the frontier in terms that have been echoed by "Easterners" for two hundred years and more; men were no longer living together, he said, in compact communities, under the tutelage of educated clergymen and under the discipline of an ordered society, but were taking themselves into remote corners "for worldly conveniences." "By that means [they] have seemed to bid defiance, not only to Religion, but to Civility it self: and such places thereby have become Nurseries of Ignorance, Profaneness and Atheism." In America the frontier conspired with the popular disposition to lessen the prestige of the cultured classes and to enhance the social power of those who wanted their religion in a more simple, downright and "democratic" form, who cared nothing for the refinements and subtleties of historic theology. Not until the decade of the Great Awakening did the popular tendency receive distinct articulation through leaders who openly renounced the older conception, but for half a century or more before 1740 its obstinate persistence can be traced in the condemnations of the ministers.

The Puritan leaders could withstand this rising tide of democracy only by such support as the government would give them — which became increasingly less after the new charter of 1692 took away from the saints all power to select their own governors and divorced the state and church — or else by the sheer force of their personalities. As early as the 1660s and '70s we can see them beginning to shift their attentions from mere exposition of the creed to greater and greater insistence upon committing power only to men of wisdom and knowledge. . . . By the beginning of the eighteenth century the task of buttressing the classified society, maintaining the rule of the well-trained and the culturally superior both in church and society seems to have

[45]Edward Johnson was a militia captain and author of a history of the Massachusetts colony, *Wonder Working Providence 1628–1651 of Scions Saviour in New England.* The book was written in 1650–1651.

become the predominant concern of the clergy. Sermon after sermon reveals that in their eyes the cause of learning and the cause of a hierarchical, differentiated social order were one and the same. . . . Leadership by the learned and dutiful subordination of the unlearned — as long as the original religious creed retained its hold upon the people these exhortations were heeded; in the eighteenth century, as it ceased to arouse their loyalties, they went seeking after gods that were utterly strange to Puritanism. They demanded fervent rather than learned ministers and asserted the equality of all men.

Thus Puritanism appears, from the social and economic point of view, to have been a philosophy of social stratification, placing the command in the hands of the properly qualified and demanding implicit obedience from the uneducated; from the religious point of view it was the dogged assertion of the unity of intellect and spirit in the face of a rising tide of democratic sentiment suspicious of the intellect and intoxicated with the spirit. It was autocratic, hierarchical, and authoritarian. It held that in the intellectual realm holy writ was to be expounded by right reason, that in the social realm the expounders of holy writ were to be the mentors of farmers and merchants. Yet in so far as Puritanism involved such ideals it was simply adapting to its own purposes and ideals of the age. Catholics in Spain and in Spanish America pursued the same objectives, and the Puritans were no more rigorous in their application of an autocratic standard than King Charles himself endeavored to be — and would have been had he not been balked in the attempt.

## DAVID D. HALL

# *from* Worlds of Wonder, Days of Judgment  [1989]

**DAVID D. HALL** (1936– ) has been the John A. Bartlett Professor of New England Church History at Harvard Divinity School since 1989. He has written widely on religion and culture, and his works include *Cultures of Print* (1996) and *The Colonial Book in the Atlantic World* (2000). He has also co-edited with Hugh Amory a collection of essays entitled *Lived Religion in America: Toward a History of Practice* (1997).

The people of seventeenth-century New England lived in a world that had not one but several different meanings. This book describes the cluster of those meanings that we designate as "religion" — the mentality of the supernatural, the symbolism of the church and sacraments, the ritual enclosing of sickness, death, and moral disobedience, the self-perception of "sinners" in the presence of a judging God. More exactly, this book is

David D. Hall, *Worlds of Wonder, Days of Judgment: Popular Religious Belief in Early New England* (New York: Knopf, 1989), 3–20. Copyright © 1989 by David D. Hall. Used by permission of Alfred A. Knopf, a division of Random House, Inc.

about religion as lay men and women knew and practiced it. Mine is a history of the religion of the people, or popular religion, in early New England. . . .

In describing the religion of the people, I hope to indicate some of the ways that culture works. We may think of culture as both ordered and dis-ordered, or, as I prefer to say, ambivalent. It has multiple dimensions; it presents us with choice even as it also limits or restrains the possibilities for meaning. What I attempt in this book is to sketch some of the possi-bilities that were present to the people of New England, and to suggest how they may have acted on them. . . . Above all, I have tried to deal with the vexing question of the relationship between the people and the clergy. At the center of this description of popular religion stands a political, social, and theological circumstance, the authority of the men who held office as religious teachers. In what ways was this authority effective? In what ways was it rejected or its consequences blunted?

To raise these questions is to invite definition of the term "popular religion." In borrowing this term from historians who have studied reli-gion and society in early modern Europe, I have come to realize that its meaning for my story must emerge from the circumstances of New England in the seventeenth century. These were not the circumstances to which Europeans were accustomed. The differences are great enough to force us to revise the very sense of "popular religion." . . .

Events that were commonplace in much of Europe were not re-created in New England. Nor was this accidental. The differences ran deep into the structure of society and the structure of religion. Six main circumstances deserve close attention: the role of the "folk," the geography of religion, the relationship between church and state, the appeal of "radical" religion, the appeal of "magic," and the sway of literacy.

For much of Christian Europe, it seems plausible to distinguish between two Christianities, the one that clerics taught, the other of the peasants or the lower social orders. The distinction rests on certain indisputable differ-ences: the language of the clergy was Latin, they subscribed to points of doctrine less well understood by laymen, and they practiced a demanding way of life. The distinction also flows from the perception that European peasants clung to a "folk" culture that resisted the encroachments of offi-cial Christianity. Referring to the Middle Ages, a French historian has insist-ed that the religion of the clerics "had incompletely penetrated among the common people." As he sees the situation of these people, "their religious life was also nourished on a multitude of beliefs and practices which, whether the legacy of age-old magic or the more recent products of a civi-lization still extremely fertile in myths, exerted a constant influence upon official doctrine." . . . We shall find that folk beliefs persisted in New England. Yet otherwise the situation was quite different, for the people who came to this region in the seventeenth century were not peasants but of "middling" status — yeomen, artisans, merchants, and housewives who knew how to articulate the principles of religion, and who shunned the "superstitions" of

Catholicism. Emigration simplified the cultural system by making it more uniform. We must start, therefore, by rejecting the conception of two separate religions, one rooted in folk ways of thinking, the other maintained by the clerics and their bourgeois allies.

In New England, too, space was much less consequential than in Europe. The significance of space was that religion varied with the distance between center and periphery. In outlying regions Christianity took on the character of "local" religion as distance turned into differences of style and understanding. This was true in part because so many of the clergy were but poorly educated, and because so many others chose to live outside their parish. Either circumstance enabled ordinary people to ignore the duties of religion and perhaps to remain ignorant. But space did not have the same meaning in New England. Here, *no minister held office unless he was in residence,* a rule (and practice) obligated by the "congregational" structure of the church. Here, there was no court or urban center to which the more ambitious clergy moved; the social and the spatial order of New England was radically decentralized. Dispersed throughout a hundred towns, the clergy helped maintain a common system. They had all been trained alike; they all thought alike.

A third point of difference concerns church and state. In most parts of Europe, church and state were closely allied. Every citizen was obliged to profess the religion of the king; everyone became a member of the church. The church itself had social functions to perform, and perhaps courts that imposed civil penalties; it owned vast properties, though also looking to the state for revenue. Such situations tended to arouse strong currents of anticlericalism, as in protests against tithes or in folk humor that mocked fat and overbearing clergy. In contrast to the normal European system, the colonists eliminated all church courts, abolished tithes, and made church membership voluntary. Here too, although the civil magistrates were quick to act against dissent, the system of control did not include an Inquisition or a central group of clergy who enforced conformity. Nor could "censure" by a church "degrade or depose any man from any Civil dignity, office or Authority." Cooperation was offset by independence, and the power of the clergy was defined as merely "spiritual." No longer agents of the civil state, and practicing, perforce, a life-style of asceticism, the New England clergy were less likely to arouse anticlericalism.

These clergy had their enemies. But we cannot define colonial popular religion as the worldview of those disaffected from official creeds. Somewhere in most European countries dissenters argued that Christianity promised universal redemption, that sin did not exist, that men possessed free will, that priests were superseded by new prophets, that the coming kingdom was at hand. Some of these beliefs were circulating in England in the fifteenth and sixteenth centuries, though they gained their widest hearing in the period of the English Civil War, when the weakness of the church made it safe to express "radical" ideas. The sects that came and went throughout this period all gained spokesmen in New England. Yet never in the colonies did such groups attract many converts; and never did

they speak for those resentful of their poverty. A few Baptists emerged in
the 1640s and again two decades later, enough to organize a congregation
of their own in 1665. Quaker missionaries worked hard after 1656 to gain
converts, but without much success. Even the most prominent of the New
England radicals, Samuel Gorton, was unable to recruit more than a handful of "Gortonists," and his group, which settled finally in Warwick, was
dying out by 1670. To equate any of these groups with popular religion is
to eliminate the majority of people; and it is the religion of that majority
that I want to describe.

Indifferent for the most part to the Quakers and the Baptists, ordinary
people had more sympathy for ideas originating in the occult sciences.
Many of the almanacs that every household used contained bits and pieces
of astrology. Some people practiced magic to defend themselves from
witchcraft, and some consulted fortune-tellers. It has been argued that
such "magical" ideas and practices provided an alternative to Christianity.
But when New England ministers lashed out at "superstitions," their anger
fell on an eclectic range of practices, from celebrating Christmas to nailing
up horseshoes. No war broke out between magic and religion, in part
because the clergy also were attracted to occult ideas; it was they who
wrote most of the almanacs, and in their response to the "wonder" they
relied on older lore as much as any layman. As I argue in detail in a succeeding chapter, we do better if we perceive an accommodation between
magic and religion than if we regard magic as somehow the substance of a
different tradition.

One other way of putting boundaries around popular religion has
been to propose that religion varies in accordance with the line that
divides those who read from those who share an "oral culture." Did literacy
have revolutionary consequences for one's worldview, or sustain other differentiating factors? Whatever may have been the case for early modern
Europe, the evidence is lacking from New England to uphold this argument. It seems likely that most people in New England learned to read as
children. Of no less importance is the fact that everyone had access to the
Bible in his native language, and to cheap books marketed especially for
lay readers. Always there were some who did not own a Bible or lacked
fluency in reading. But we can safely assume that most of the emigrants
to New England had broken through into the world of print — though
what this meant exactly will concern us in a moment.

All of these differences point to the influence of the Protestant Reformation in transforming the relationship between Christianity and the
people. This one reason, this one cause, is why New England was so different from Catholic France and Italy. . . .

When emigration to New England began, the new colony of Massachusetts attracted thousands of the godly who had previously accepted
the message and the life-style we think of as Puritanism. What these people
brought with them was also a deep revulsion against older customs and
beliefs. Long before the great migration to New England, reformers in
the sixteenth century had gone into churches to destroy statues and

stained glass. The same people had renounced the ritual calendar of saints' days and holy days. They rejected certain forms of play, as when men dressed up as animals or people danced around a maypole. This conscious attack on "pagan" ways and "superstitions" was occurring at the same time as the pace of social change was weakening folkways and ritual practices. The village feast, the pageants that once filled the streets of Coventry, the lore of fairies and of cunning folk — all these were being displaced in the sixteenth century by a sharper sense of how the pagan differed from the Christian, the holy from the secular.

This "disenchantment" of the world, or what Peter Burke has called the "reform" of traditional popular culture, was well advanced before the colonists set out to found New England. Occurring when it did, the process of emigration conveyed to America the substance of a transformed culture. Psalm-singing replaced ballads. Ritual was reorganized around the celebration of the Sabbath and of fast days. No town in New England had a maypole; no group celebrated Christmas or St. Valentine's Day, or staged a pre-Lenten carnival! New England almanacs used numbers for each month instead of names deemed "pagan." And in naming their children, parents largely restricted themselves to names that appeared in the Bible, preferring John, Joseph, Samuel, James, and Timothy for male children and Mary, Elizabeth, Sarah, Hannah, Abigail, Rebecca, and Ruth for females. . . .

The sum of all these differences was a transformation in the situation of religion and society. It was not the act of emigration or the "free aire of the new world" that caused this transformation. The impetus for change lay in two European movements, the Reformation and the steady dissolution of traditional society. What made New England special was that its founders were more Protestant than most, more ready to eliminate old customs and to liberalize the structure of the church. Some who stayed in England favored these reforms. But only in this region did a democratic and decentralized congregationalism prevail so completely. . . .

Let me return to the crucial question of the clergy and their role in shaping popular religion. They cannot be excluded from the story; they had too much in common with the people, and too prominent a part to play in teaching certain structures of belief. It is this commonness that complicates the meaning of popular religion. In what follows I modify two arguments that many others use in speaking of the people and their mental world. On the one hand I refuse to represent the clergy as so dominating in the churches that their way of thinking always prevailed. I acknowledge that the clergy were successful in persuading many of the colonists to adopt their understanding of religion as others by author. But the power of the clergy was too mediated to make them really dominant, and "domination" is a word that simply doesn't fit the pluralistic structure of New England towns and churches. On the other hand, I reject the argument that "popular religion" refers only to the ways in which lay men and women broke with what the clergy said. This happened in New England, as I demonstrate repeatedly. But it happened in conjunction with much sharing, and with a subtle process of *selection* between choices that the clergy helped articulate. It is an interesting and important irony that three great movements of lay protest were nurtured by some of the clergy; John Cotton and John Wheelwright took the side of "Antinomians" in the early stages of that controversy, John Davenport and others spoke out against the halfway covenant[46] of 1662, and the revivals of the 1740s involved Harvard and Yale graduates whose preaching played a major role in stirring up the New Light movement.[47] The process of selection was abetted by print culture; the books that people read, and especially the Bible, offered them conflicting messages. Yet here too the clergy figured as the writers of these books. Thus I find myself describing *mediations*: printers mediating what the clergy said, and vice versa, and the people bringing their needs to the meetinghouse. Where we find that people agreed with the clergy, this may simply mean that lay men and women exercised their freedom to accept the same ideas.

Hence my narrative unfolds as a tale of consensus and resistance, of common ground, but also differences. It did not take much time for a dialectic of resistance and cooperation to emerge. A crucial moment was the uprising of "Antinomians" in 1636 and 1637. Taking control of the Boston congregation, and threatening to dismiss a minister they did not like, lay men and women challenged the authority of the ministers as teachers of sound doctrine. Other groups would follow in defying the position of the ministers — Baptists, Gortonists, Quakers, Rogerenes. But we miss the real dynamics of the situation if we focus only on these radicals. Conflict was intrinsic to the congregational system despite agreement on its basic principles. Too much was vague, too much was open to interpretation. . . . Tension never vanished from this system, and long-nurtured anger exploded in the Great Awakening. Here it is enough to know that ministers and people worked uneasily together within a framework that empowered both. . . .

All this while I have been explaining why I am generously inclusive in my definition of "popular religion." I am also generous in defining what I mean by "the people" or the "colonists." Most certainly, the meaning of religion flows in part from social experience: social rank conditions how we understand the world. But it is another matter to discern specific ways in which this process worked. Did printers see things differently because of their work situation? Did shoemakers, or sailors, or chattel slaves on a plantation? Or, to speak more generally, did people of the "middling orders". . .

---

[46]The Halfway covenant was a way to extend church membership beyond those who had experienced saving grace to include, through baptism, the grandchildren of full church members, provided their parents agreed that they hoped to experience grace one day themselves and lead an outwardly godly life. These parents and children, although not full members of the church and permitted to take communion, would live under the church's discipline. The measure came at a time when few people were joining the church.

[47]The New Light movement, or the First Great Awakening, was a religious change among some Protestant congregants and ministers that encouraged an emotive and intense experience and discouraged formality in religious expression. It manifested itself first in the 1740s up and down the Eastern seaboard as itinerant colonial ministers and some from Great Britain, including George Whitefield and John Wesley, excited many listeners and divided many congregations into "awakened" and "old light" factions. Methodism (which developed from Anglicanism) and baptism, rooted in Calvinism, grew very rapidly after the Great Awakening.

support social and religious "discipline" because of their class needs? As it happens, I do not find this argument compelling. Sailors in New England do seem a rowdy lot, and merchants in such coastal towns as Boston and Salem were breaking free of Puritan asceticism. A more telling case is women. One clear pattern that emerges from the data on church membership is that wives and daughters were more likely to be members than husbands and sons. I have spoken of empowerment without observing that laywomen were denied the privilege of participating in church government. In the work of some historians there are promising suggestions of how women shaped religion to their needs, or found themselves the victims of its symbols. Where I can, I remark on the role of gender and of occupation. But in general, the mass of people in New England seem to have been relatively homogeneous in their social rank and practices; even those who worked as sailors were gradually absorbed within the system, and merchants intermarried with the ministers. Thus, to differentiate these people into groups each with a separate point of view seems less promising than to recognize the significance of family structure in the shaping of religious practice. My term "the people" does, however, always refer to lay men and women, as contrasted with the clergy, whom I mainly cite by name.

It is crucial that we not romanticize the people and their fascination with religion. Recalling the Connecticut farmers of his youth as they sat "stoically" in midwinter in an unheated meetinghouse, the nineteenth-century minister Horace Bushnell imagined them as

> men who have digestion for strong meat, and have no conception that trifles more delicate can be of any account to feed the system. . . . Under their hard . . . and stolid faces, great thoughts are brewing, and these keep them warm. Free-will, fixed fate, foreknowledge absolute, Trinity, redemption, special grace, eternity — give them anything high enough, and the tough muscle of their inward man will be climbing sturdily into it; and if they go away having something to think of, they have had a good day.

Bushnell's farmers relish the abstract logic of theology, the harsh truths of Calvinism. So, it sometimes seems, did many people in seventeenth-century England and New England — Cromwell's troopers in the English Civil War, those Roundheads who marched strictly to the rhythm of a well-regulated conscience; or else the men and women who courageously embarked in the *Mayflower.*

But we must keep this courage and commitment in perspective. Another man who knew firsthand the mental world of nineteenth-century farmers remembered things quite differently. G. Stanley Hall describes one branch of his family as believing in religion, "but always with moderation." What moderation meant was this:

> Most of them attended church more or less but few joined, or if they did they fell off later in life. In their maturer years my uncles almost never frequented public worship. They were not unfriendly to or critical of religion

but, as many expressions showed, considered it more manly . . . to stand
before the All-Father on their merits as livers of good lives than to be
saved by a vicarious atonement.

No Calvinists these farmers! Nor were they rigorously conscientious in the
duties of religion:

> In one church there was a long and bitter war of the more ardent element
> against the so-called "horse-shed class," composed of people who would
> spend the long intermission between the two services in the horse-shed
> talking of secular matters instead of attending Sunday School. To this class
> most of my male relatives here belonged, despite the criticisms of my
> father.

The truth this portrait captures outweighs, in my opinion, the ideal picture Bushnell paints. We have no way of knowing how many of the
colonists were devout Calvinists, for no one took a census of beliefs. Yet
common sense instructs us that religion (or the church) attracts not only
a committed core, but also others who, like "horse-shed" Christians, limit
their commitment. . . . From her childhood experiences as the daughter
of a New England minister, Harriet Beecher Stowe remembered that in
winters when the farm people were satisfied with their minister, they honored their contract to supply him with his firewood by bringing logs that
were "of the best: none of your old makeshifts, — loads made out with
crooked sticks and snapping chestnut logs, most noisy, and destructive to
good wives' aprons." I wish to insist, therefore, on acknowledging variety
and change, and accepting "horse-shed" Christians as part of my story. . . .

Some moved an even greater distance from the culture of the meetinghouse. A handful of persons may have questioned the very premises of
Christianity as it was ordinarily understood. Amid the witch trials at Salem
a man named William Barker declared that "the devil promeised that all
his people should live bravely that all persones should be equall; that
their should be no day of resurection or of judgement, and neither punishment nor shame for sin. . . ." In most European countries there were
regions where few clergy lived and where the church was weak. New
England, too, had its "dark corners of the land," the places or the groups
of people that were less affected by religion and less likely to want clergy.
The fishermen of Gloucester, Massachusetts, made life difficult for
Richard Blinman, who arrived as town minister in 1642. And, as told by
Cotton Mather, a minister in some unnamed coastal village urged on his
audience a more active practice of religion, lest otherwise they "contradict the main end of planting this wilderness!" Thereupon, a local resident cried out: "Sir, you think you are preaching to the people at the Bay;
our main end was to catch fish." . . .

What all this means is that in certain places and at certain times of life,
some of the colonists abstained from or practiced intermittently the
organized activities that help make up religion. Others may have mani-

fested their indifference by flouting moral rules, as some people do in every social system. But we must look more closely at these actions before we view them as signifying fundamental disaffection from religion. Young people settled down as they formed families of their own and brought their newborn children to be baptized. New towns acquired ministers, and some of those on the periphery at the beginning, like Marblehead, became more like the norm in later years. A handful of persons may have misbehaved persistently, but for others a premature pregnancy or attendance at a tavern was accidental and not a clue to a subversive politics. At another moment in the court proceedings at Salem, William Barker expressed a conventional repentance. No covert or consistent atheists can be detected in New England. . . .

Above all, my story is of people who had power to select among a range of meanings. Once more the key word is "ambivalence." I have suggested that lay people and the clergy shared some ways of thinking, and I make this point more strongly in describing the tradition of the "wonder." Yet when we come to matters such as baptism, the Lord's Supper, and the "practice of piety," the purpose of my narrative is to unfold different possibilities for meaning, and to argue that lay people sometimes distanced themselves from the message of the clergy. In general I describe a set of practices and situations that offered choice, that remained open-ended.

# 3 American Indians: New Worlds in the Atlantic World

"I am an *Indian*," wrote Virginia planter-historian Robert Beverley in his 1705 preface to his *The History and Present State of Virginia*, "and don't pretend to be exact in my language: But I hope the Plainness of my Dress, will give [the reader] the kinder Impressions of my Honesty, which is what I pretend to."[1] Beverley's appropriation of Indianness and his personal definition of it hints at some of the unique problems in tracking the historiography of American Indians. Historians of Indians, in addition to bringing to bear the weight of their various political agendas, have also often brought their own identities to studying indigenous peoples. Beverley was an unusual eighteenth-century observer-ethnographer in his relatively matter-of-fact, and even positive, description of the Powhatan of Virginia, but he was not unusual in reading them as a way to reflect aspects of himself, in this case his unadorned prose and person.

The difficulty for historians in writing about Indians without projecting onto them a dizzying variety of their own aspirations, fears, and odium has spawned a secondary historiography of its own, a history of how to explain European-American attitudes toward Indians. Gustav Jahoda's contribution, *Images of Savages: Ancient Roots of Modern Prejudices in Western Cultures* (New York, 1999), and Robert Berkhofer's *The White Man's Indian* (New York, 1978) are only two in a long procession of volumes probing the origins and development of Europeans' often toxic views of Native Americans. Very recently, this long-term problem has become a strength as historians have "contributed to making identity itself more problematic," because "Indians and Europeans were linked and mutually influential."[2] But for generations, the confusion between writer and subject figures prominently in studies of Native Americans.

In addition to the psychological difficulties historians have encountered in assessing the history of indigenous American people, there have been and continue to be formidable methodological problems in establishing even the most basic facts. Emotionally charged disputes over how many Native Americans lived in continental North America continue. Those who incline toward higher numbers see themselves not only as righting an incorrect perception but also as supplying potent evidence about the magnitude of the

---

[1]Robert Beverley, *The History and Present State of Virginia* (Charlottesville, Va., 1705), 9.
[2]Richard White, "Using the Past, History and Native America Studies," in Russell Thornton, ed., *Studying Native America: Problems and Prospects* (Madison, Wis., 1998), 231.

demographic disaster that began with Columbus's landing on San Salvador.[3] Much more than scholars in other fields, historians have had to look to archaeology, paleontology, and anthropology and await the establishment of fields like environmental history and biolinguistics in order to further their research. Even so, substantial questions remain.

How many Native Americans were there when the Spanish arrived? Was it European germs that were mainly responsible for the great population drops, or was colonization an important factor? How had their political and social organizations changed by the time the English arrived? How did Native American integration into the Atlantic market affect their internal economies and social orders? What control did the Indians have over these changes, and how welcome were they? What were pre-contact gender relations like, and how did they alter over time? How did slave raiding affect Native American societies? What was the relationship of Native Americans to their environment?

Contributing to our ignorance about many aspects of Indian history has been the fact that the Indian point of view was, for more than two centuries after Jamestown, of little concern to most historians. It was only with the Great Depression-era establishment of the precursors to the Indian Claims Commission, created to address complaints from Native Americans about land loss, that ethnography developed. Historians and anthropologists studied Native American cultures in order to establish Indian legal claims to land from which they had been dispossessed.[4] Anthropologists and historians both served as expert witnesses in these cases and, blending disciplines as ethnohistorians, founded their own society (The American Society for Ethnohistory) in 1954.[5] American Indian students in the 1960s demanded and got Native American studies departments first in Berkeley, UCLA, and the University of Minnesota. Faculty members and graduate students used the combined methods of anthropology and history to practice ethnohistory. Robert Berkhofer coined the term "the New Indian History" in 1971, which also marked the influence of the New Western history on the disciplines that made up ethnohistory. The New Indian History marked the "widespread

---

[3]See, for example, Wilbur Jacobs, "The Tip of an Iceberg: Pre-Columbian Indian Demography and Some Implications for Revisionism," in *The Fatal Confrontations: Historical Studies of American Indians, Environment, and Historians* (Albuquerque, N.M., 1996), 77–89, in which he describes the debate among early demographers, like James Mooney, positing a pre-contact population of 1 million Native Americans in North America and 8 to 14 million in the Western Hemisphere, versus later accounts revising that figure up to 10 million in North America and 100 million in the Western Hemisphere. See also Francis Jennings, *The Invasion of America: Indians, Colonialism, and the Cant of Conquest* (New York, 1975), 15–31, on the political meanings of the debate. See Noble David Cook, *Born to Die: Disease and the New World Conquest, 1492–1650* (New York, 1998), on individual episodes of plagues, and see Alfred Crosby, *The Columbian Exchange: Biological and Cultural Consequences of 1492* (Westport, Conn., 1972), 35–63, for a classic account of virgin soil epidemics in the New World.

[4]Christian McMillen, *Making Indian Law: The Hualapai Land Case and the Birth of Ethnohistory* (New Haven, Conn., 2007), 157.

[5]Thomas J. Pluckhahn and Robbie Ethridge, *Light on the Path: The Anthropology and History of the Southeastern Indians* (Tuscaloosa, Ala., 2006), 1.

adoption of historical discourse by anthropologists and the appropriation of ethnographic language and methods by historians."[6]

This sudden growth and enrichment of a field with imaginative and wide-ranging scholarship came about for many of the same reasons that pushed the growth of social history and the creation of new fields like women's history and African American history. Revulsion at American colonialism in Vietnam and at the nation's treatment of indigenous people overlapped. AIM, the American Indian Movement, initiated an era in 1969 in which activists went to the streets and to the courts to draw attention to their grievances and seek justice for centuries of racism, exploitation, and the resulting poverty, joblessness, and ill health and that were endemic on reservations.[7]

Indian historiography between Robert Beverley and the birth of ethnohistory had reflected the fears, desires, and projects of Euro-Americans far more than those of Native Americans. Puritan historians, who like Increase and Cotton Mather might also have been ministers, saw their world as one in which God repeatedly tested his chosen people. Indians constituted one of the greatest tests — as serious as witchcraft and a scourge inflicted upon the settlers to remind them to return to the paths of righteousness. God's favor in allowing his people to conquer both the Pequots in 1636 and the Wampanoags and their coalition in 1676 demonstrated both his love and forbearance toward his people and his frustration with them for frequently abandoning his way. The Puritans' conviction of their own superior claim to God's attention justified their occupation of Indian lands.

After the Revolution, historians had to assimilate local histories to a national purpose and deal, somehow, with the stunning contradiction between the young nation's declared promises of equality and freedom and its treatment of Native Americans, among others. In the first decade of the nineteenth century, Edmund Randolph, twice a member of the Continental Congress and governor of Virginia, wrote a history that ascribed to Virginia preeminence in the Revolution and in nation building. In his treatment of Indians, he took a number of positions, none of them new, that would be repeated throughout the nineteenth century to support the federal policy of displacing Indians and occupying their lands. In discussing Virginia's refusal to honor Cherokee land claims, Randolph wrote, "She [Virginia] supposed that it was no less absurd to recognize the extravagant hunting rights of savages than the idle assumption of the Pope to grant the Western world between two nations." White Americans had long insisted that to hold land legitimately, people had to farm it European style. Hence, Randolph wrote, while settlers had broken the law by settling beyond the proclamation line after the end of the Seven Years' War, they "had laid a stock of

---

[6]Melissa L. Meyer and Kerwin Lee Klein, "Native American Studies and the End of Ethnohistory," in Russell Thornton, ed., *Studying Native America: Problems and Prospects* (Madison, Wis., 1998), 185–86.
[7]For an account of AIM, see Paul Chaat Smith and Robert Allen Warrior, *Like a Hurricane: The Indian Movement from Alcatraz to Wounded Knee* (New York, 1996); for a contrasting evaluation, see White, "Using the Past."

merit in forming a barrier against the incursions of the Indians." Virginia therefore had to grant would-be settlers squatters' right to the "occupancy [of] the vacant western lands."[8] Randolph managed at the same time to sustain the contradictory myth that the lands Americans dispossessed the Indians of were empty.

One must keep in mind reading nineteenth-century historians that, from the time Randolph wrote his history until 1890, the U.S. government was almost continuously at war with Native Americans on some part of the continent. In 1839, George Bancroft published his *History of the United States*.[9] He discoursed on the "absence of all reflective consciousness, and of all logical analysis of ideas" in the savage mind. He picked up a colonial theme that would be repeated throughout the nineteenth century, that Indians had no religion. Practically, their mental and moral deficiencies meant that civilization would wipe out the Indians because they "could not change [their] habits."

All writers assumed that the Indian way of life was doomed, and most assumed that, along with their culture, Indians were doomed as well. For some, like the historian John Gorham Palfrey,[10] the demise of Indians and their way of life was no loss. For others, like the historian Francis Parkman, the presumed disappearance of Indians was a reason to memorialize their ways in prose. Parkman's major work, *The History of the Conspiracy of Pontiac and the War of the North American Tribes against the English Colonies*,[11] was in part a long excursus on why Indians were unable to survive in the Anglo-Saxon world of bustle and enterprise.

The first serious dissent, outside the Indian community, from the rightness and inevitability of the demise of Indians came from a New England poet and novelist, Helen Hunt Jackson, who had been deeply moved by the testimony of Standing Bear, a Ponca, who lectured on the tribulations suffered by his tribe when resisting removal from their home in Nebraska to a reservation in Oklahoma. In 1881, Jackson published *A Century of Dishonor*,[12] a compendium of the U.S. injustices toward various groups including the Cherokee, the Lakota, the Delaware, the Nez Percé, the Ute, and the Cheyenne. At her own expense, she sent a copy to each member of Congress. Subsequently appointed commissioner of Indian affairs by President Chester A. Arthur, she went on a fact-finding tour of California and used the material gathered for *Ramona*, a novel in which she dramatized in a tragic love story points she had made in nonfiction earlier. The two books created an alternative vision of

---

[8]Edmund Randolph, *History of Virginia* (Charlottesville, Va., 1970), 259. Randolph wrote the book after his retirement from public life in 1795, but it was not published in his lifetime (1753–1813) but was held by the Virginia Historical Society, where scholars consulted it.

[9]George Bancroft, *History of the United States: From the Discovery of the American Continent* (Boston, 1866), III, 302.

[10]John Gorham Palfrey, *History of New England* (Boston, 1865).

[11]Francis Parkman, *The History and the Conspiracy of Pontiac and the War of the North American Tribes against the English Colonies* (Boston, 1851).

[12]Helen Hunt Jackson, *A Century of Dishonor: A Sketch of the United States Government's Dealings with Some of the Indian Tribes* (New York, 1881).

Indians as victims rather than aggressors, if they didn't succeed in representing an Indian point of view.

By the beginning of the twentieth century, the population of Native American ethnic groups had fallen to their lowest numbers. They did seem to be vanishing. What disease, warfare, and despair had not already done, the Dawes Severalty Act of 1887 accelerated. This law prohibited the Indian practice of holding land in common and broke up most reservations into plots of 160 acres, selling to white settlers what was referred to as "surplus." (This was followed in 1903 by the court decision in *Lone Wolf v. Hitchcock* affirming that the federal government, not the Indians, ultimately decided whether Indians' land could be opened up for sale. The Kiowas in one generation went from a reservation of almost three million acres to one of about three thousand.)[13] The Dawes Act was meant to integrate Indians into the larger society, but the policy was a disaster for them.

In the late 1800s, Indians also sustained a concerted attack on their cultures and traditions. Reformers concerned with Indians wanted to wean them from the "blanket" — teach them to reject communalism and their native languages and customs. In this era, Indian children were placed in boarding schools, often very distant from their parents, to be immersed in American culture and alienated from their own.[14]

By the time Frederick Jackson Turner enunciated his famous frontier thesis in 1893, the last holdouts, the Lakota and the Apache, had been coerced onto reservations. Turner reflected the nation's sense that Indians had effectively disappeared by describing the land onto which settlers moved as empty. In his essay on the frontier, he noted that Indians had played a role in contributing to the martial spirit of the American pioneers who moved across the continent, settling its empty spaces. While he said almost nothing about Indians themselves, Turner posited that American men regressed into a kind of Indianness in settling new lands. However, these primitive settlements rapidly evolved into higher and more complex forms of society, recapitulating the growth of Western civilization. In Turner's model, life in the wilderness honed manliness, but for pioneers it was only a brief stop on the way to the final destination of higher civilization. Indians were both there and not there for Turner. Their presence was sufficiently threatening to evoke bravery among backwoodsmen; yet, somehow, the land the settlers farmed had been vacant. "So long as free land exists, the opportunity for a competency exists," explained Turner.[15]

At the same time Indians were disappearing from the national narrative, they were becoming the foundational subject of American anthropology. Turner's effort to write scientific history that progressed through stages was in step with work of the early anthropologist Lewis Henry Morgan, who had

---

[13]McMillen, *Making Indian Law*, xiv.

[14]For an excellent account, see David Wallace Adams, *Educated for Extinction: American Indians and the Boarding School Experience, 1875–1928* (Lawrence, Kans., 1995).

[15]Frederick Jackson Turner, "The Significance of the Frontier in American History," in *The Frontier in American History* (Tucson, Ariz., 1986).

traced the course of progress from barbarity to civilization. Morgan (1818–1881), his friend, the Swiss-born anthropologist Adolph Bandelier (1840–1914), and Henry Rowe Schoolcraft (1793–1864), an Indian agent, all published influential anthropological texts.[16] Morgan studied Iroquois kinship systems, branching out to other cultures including the Ojibwa and eventually concluding that all Native American societies were organized around kinship relations rather than property relations. To their credit, all three scholars studied Indian cultures as cultures, not simply as obstacles to the expansion of the nation, although in their parallel insistence on Indian savagery it was clear that the Indian and Indian culture should not and could not survive. Like the artist, George Catlin, who made numerous portraits of Native Americans in the 1830s, these anthropologists studied indigenous people to salvage a representation of their cultures from the destruction they all believed was imminent.[17] This gave their studies a certain urgency.

Native Americans numbered among the earliest anthropologists and included Arthur Parker, a Seneca;[18] James R. Murie, a Pawnee, educated at Hampton Institute, who became an ethnographer;[19] and Francis La Flesche, an Omaha who wrote extensively on Osage religion. Fluent in Osage, La Flesche had for sources the last remaining priests in the Mississippian tradition, heirs of the mound builders at Cahokia. His motivation was to expose the complexity and richness of Osage belief in order to contradict the stereotype of Indian religion as childlike or "murky," as Parkman described it. Whether other scholars and reformers were pro- or anti-Indian, they all, he felt, believed Indians incapable of thinking and speaking for themselves.[20]

The growth and excitement surrounding anthropology encouraged many young, aspiring intellectuals to enter the field, and by the 1920s Elsie Clews Parsons, Alfred L. Kroeber, Frank Speck, and John Swanton[21] had become

---

[16]Lewis Henry Morgan, *The League of the Ho-De-No-Sau-Nee, or Iroquois* (Rochester, N.Y., 1851, republished North Dighton, Mass., 1995) and *Ancient Society, or Researches in the Lines of Human Progress from Barbarism to Savagery to Civilization* (New York, 1877); for Adolph Bandelier, see, for example, *Final Report of Investigations among the Indians of the Southwestern U.S.* (Cambridge, Mass., 180–92), and *Documentary History of the Rio Grande Pueblos of New Mexico* (Santa Fe, N.M., 1910); for Henry Rowe Schoolcraft, see, for example, *Algic Researches* (New York, 1839), and *Notes on the Iroquois* (New York, 1846); for a discussion of his and Morgan's work and influence, see Roy Harvey Pearce, *Savagism and Civilization* (New York, 1953), 120–34.

[17]See George Catlin, *North American Indians*, edited and with an introduction by Peter Matthiessen (New York, 1989).

[18]Parker (1881–1955) was an archaeologist, historian, and folklorist and author of numerous books, particularly about the Seneca, including *The Code of Handsome Lake, the Seneca Prophet* (New York, 1913).

[19]See, for example, his publication with Alice Fletcher, *The Hako: Song, Pipe, and Unity in a Pawnee Calumet Ceremony* (Twenty-Second Annual Report for the Bureau of American Ethnography, Washington, D.C., 1904).

[20]See particularly Francis La Flesche, *The Osage and the Invisible World* (Norman, Okla., 1995).

[21]For examples of their work see Elsie Clews Parsons, ed., *American Indian Life* (Lincoln, Neb., and London, 1991) and *Fear and Conventionality* (New York and London, 1914); Alfred L. Kroeber, *The Arapaho* (New York, 1902) and *Anthropology* (New York, 1923); Frank Speck, *Beothuk and Micmac* (New York, 1922) and *Decorative Art and Basketry of the Cherokee* (Milwaukee, 1920); John Swanton, *Chickasaw Society and Religion* (Lincoln, Neb., 2006 [first published in 1928]) and *Contributions to the Ethnology of the Haida* (New York, 1975 [first published in 1905]).

scholars of Indian cultures. John Collier, a Progressive anthropologist, became dedicated to working for Indian reform after visiting the Taos pueblo and eventually got a position in Franklin Roosevelt's administration. He insisted that trying to extinguish Indian cultures was a mistake, that sending Indians away from the reservations to boarding schools and the Dawes Act were both disasters. He revolted from the Progressives' insistence on assimilation, and as Roosevelt's commissioner of Indian affairs, he worked to reverse the Dawes Act and the efforts to destroy Indian culture and institutions.[22] While some Indians approved of his initiatives, others opposed yet another Washington-directed program not shaped by and for each tribe.

During Collier's tenure as commissioner, Angie Debo, a Progressive Era professor of history at the University of Oklahoma, published *And Still the Waters Run* on the Choctaw, among the groups whom allotment had harmed the most dramatically.[23] She agreed with Collier about the importance of retaining Indian culture: "The policy of the United States in liquidating the institutions of the Five Tribes (The Creeks, Choctaws, Cherokees, Seminoles, and Chickasaws) was a gigantic blunder that ended a hopeful experiment in Indian development, destroyed a unique civilization, and degraded thousands of individuals."[24] Debo's book was published in 1940 to little initial notice, but another development linked it with the birth of the new discipline of ethnohistory.

The federal government, in setting up the Indian Claims Commission (ICC; finally completed in 1946, but started during the Great Depression), offered Indians the chance to sue to reclaim the value of lands wrongfully taken from them. Christian McMillen, in *Making Indian Law: The Hualapai Land Case and the Birth of Ethnohistory*, as the title suggests, dates the beginnings of ethnohistory to this case. The particular finding that initiated the turn to history was the court's announcement that Indian occupancy of land was "a fact to be determined as any other questions of fact."[25] Historians and anthropologists, who would be legal witnesses in claims suits, began researching the cultures and histories of the tribes in order to substantiate the claims they were making.

Despite Indian and scholarly resistance to the policy of integrating Indians into mainstream American society, and because so many Native Americans during World War II had been drawn off the reservations and into the services or other defense industry jobs, it seemed propitious to the Eisenhower administration to pursue a policy that came to be called "termination," aimed at ending reservations. Termination made an ideological fit with the consensus ideals of the 1950s, which posited a relatively seamless past with homogenous Americans united and progressing toward greater freedom and a

---

[22]John Collier, *Indians of the Americas: The Long Hope* (New York, 1947); Kenneth R. Philip, *John Collier's Crusade for Indian Reform, 1920–1954* (Tucson, Ariz., 1977).

[23]The Five Tribes were exempt from the Dawes Act, but the Curtis Act of 1898 abolished their tribal governments and forced allotment on them.

[24]Angie Debo, *And Still the Waters Run: The Betrayal of the Five Civilized Tribes* (Princeton, N.J., 1994), 483–84, 490.

[25]McMillen, *Making Indian Law*, xv, 187, ftn. 5.

higher standard of living. In 1954, Eisenhower signed a bill that gave the Menominee full control of their affairs and full citizenship. Proponents of termination saw it as a logical extension of the Dawes Act that had been wrongly, but understandably, interrupted because of the stress of the Great Depression. Disruption and misery produced by termination and relocation of Indians to cities were in part responsible for the development of the Indian rights movement of the 1960s and 1970s.

In the climate of postwar revulsion with Nazism, scholars of Indians, who almost by definition could not be consensus historians, not only looked at their subjects differently but also began to reevaluate themselves, their profession, and its responsibilities. Roy Harvey Pearce's *Savagism and Civilization*, published in 1953, studied literature about Native Americans in an attempt to understand the cultural ideas dominating scholarship about them. Pearce exposed the connections among ideas, information, and power and illuminated what had bedeviled studies of Indians from the start. "Studying the savage, trying to civilize him, destroying him, in the end they had only studied themselves, strengthened their own civilization."[26] Pearce was a professor of literature, and it took historians some years to recognize the significance of his work. Anthropologists, on the other hand, were more receptive to Pearce's interest in myth and symbol and in those days more actively concerned with the theoretical questions of where the scholar stands in relation to his subject.

A year after Pearce's book was published, scholars of Native Americans founded the journal *Ethnohistory*. This has been a central conduit of the new ideas and approaches toward Native American studies emerging from anthropologists, ethnographers, and historians as well. James Axtell, an early ethnohistorian, described the discipline as the use of both historical and ethnographical methods and materials to understand a culture and what causes it to change.[27] Both historians and ethnographers or anthropologists in the field were comfortable with a wide variety of methodological tools and shared the aim of putting Native American cultures at the center of their focus.

Joining with these ethnohistorians in the 1970s came historians who were practicing the New Western history. These scholars, like many of that generation, had a broad and inclusive idea about how to approach the history of the West. They identified new subjects, including Hispanics, women, African Americans, and Asians as well as Native Americans, without whose histories the West was incomplete.

Charles Hudson, author of *The Southeastern Indians*,[28] was among those who helped bring archaeology into the rich interdisciplinarity of Native American studies. For much of his career, Hudson worked to create bridges between the distant Mississippian Indian past of civilizations like those at

---

[26]Pearce, *Savagism*, xvii.

[27]James Axtell, "The Ethnohistory of Native America," in Donald L. Fixico, *Rethinking American Indian History* (Albuquerque, N.M., 1997), 4.

[28]Charles Hudson, *The Southeastern Indians* (Knoxville, Tenn., 1976).

Cahokia, for example, and those of the recent historical past like the Creek Confederacy. The early period was recoverable only through archaeology and only up until about the sixteenth century. A two-hundred year gap existed between the archaeological evidence and the eighteenth century, when Indian tribes had reconsolidated in modern groups like the Cherokees and could be tracked historically. Working on southeastern Indians, Hudson and historians like James Merrell[29] recognized the immense significance of the transformations that took place over those two centuries and helped integrate new methodology to explore them.[30]

Thus, 1970s scholars brought a wide range of methodologies as well as a shared desire to explore the role of Native Americans and their cultures in the history of the Americas. From anthropology and from the experience of ICC work, they brought a new sensitivity to the role of the observer in these endeavors. Four particularly significant volumes exemplify some of the concerns and methods of the new Indian historians. Vine Deloria Jr., a Standing Rock Sioux law student, published *Custer Died for Your Sins: An Indian Manifesto* in 1969, in which he satirized the work of anthropologists descending upon reservations each summer: "Their concern is not the ultimate policy that will affect the Indian people, but merely the creation of new slogans and doctrines by which they can climb the university totem pole." Deloria challenged non-Indian academics to reconsider their motives and methods for studying indigenous people. He saw the scholar, not the subject, empowered by knowledge about Indians. In Deloria's reading, the contemporary form of expropriation of Indian identity was no longer in the form of personal traits like valor or Robert Beverley's simplicity but in the form of information for careerists.[31]

The methodological sophistication of Anthony F. C. Wallace's *Death and Rebirth of the Seneca* (1969), which used history, anthropology, and psychoanalytic techniques to explore the transformation of Seneca culture from the colonial to the early national period, indicated the insights a multidisciplinary approach could produce. Through a probing study of Seneca lore concerning dreams, Wallace was able to explain how the group maintained its blend of fierce enmity toward foes and deep fellowship and the ethos of sharing among its members. His rich study of Handsome Lake's prophetic movement that combined elements of Iroquois culture as well as beliefs from the Protestant evangelical religion of the early nineteenth century has, since its publication, been a model for ethnohistorians.[32]

Gary Nash's groundbreaking *Red, White, and Black: The Peoples of Early America* (1974) placed Indians as major players in the colonial story. This inno-

---

[29]Hence the resonant and much acknowledged title of James Merrell's work on the Catawba, *The Indians' New World: Catawbas and Their Neighbors from European Contact through the Era of Removal* (Chapel Hill, N.C., 1989).

[30]Pluckhahn and Ethridge, *Light on the Path*, 1–25.

[31]Vine Deloria Jr., *Custer Died for Your Sins: An Indian Manifesto* (Norman, Okla., 1988), 94–95.

[32]Anthony F. C. Wallace, *Death and Rebirth of the Seneca* (New York, 1969).

vative synthesis of early American histories discarded the myth of the "discovery" of the continent and introduced readers to the variety of native people here when the European explorers arrived. "The history of the American peoples begins not in 1492, . . . but more than 30 centuries before the birth of Christ."[33]

Two years later, Francis Jennings's provocative *The Invasion of America* challenged more complacent interpretations of white-Indian relations. Commanding a wealth of detail, Jennings argued that land lust created the climate in which Puritans massacred Indians and called it God's will. Jennings relegated missionary efforts to the status of a hypocritical cover-up for Puritan expansion.[34]

A host of other works came pouring out: studies of individual groups, contact among Europeans and Native Americans, the effects and pace of market penetration on traditional groups, demography, Indian law, dispossession, and military methods, to mention only a few subjects.

Scholars in the last three decades have contributed substantially to understanding changing gender relations among Native Americans. Karen Anderson's study of the Huron conversion to Catholicism demonstrates how native women suffered important losses of power in converting to Christianity. James Ronda, on the other hand, in "Generations of Faith" has documented how, in a world where native culture is still viable, Christianity can be a source of solace and even empowerment for some women. Theda Perdue has traced many changes between the genders relating to religion, property, work, inheritance, and political participation in her study of Cherokee women up through removal. Sylvia Van Kirk has studied the Hudson's Bay Company through several generations, showing how a dependence on the skills and crafts of native wives gave way in the nineteenth century to the importation of British wives and increasingly racist attitudes toward natives and those of mixed racial heritage. Jean O'Brien's *Dispossession by Degrees* displays the parallel phenomena of Indian loss of land and changing demography in an Indian town in eighteenth-century Massachusetts. She shows how native adaptations to changing economic conditions scattered men and resulted in increasing invisibility for Natick Indians, predominantly women. O'Brien documents their persistence in the face of the myth of their extinction. Ann Marie Plane, in *Colonial Intimacies*, uses marriage as a way to investigate native and American cultures as they overlapped and altered each other until, after the Seven Years' War, Indian culture was irrevocably branded as inferior by the dominant culture.[35]

---

[33]Gary Nash, *Red, White, and Black: The Peoples of Early North America* (Englewood Cliffs, N.J., 1974).

[34]Jennings, *The Invasion of America.*

[35]Karen Anderson, *Chain Her by One Foot* (New York, 1991); James Ronda, "Generations of Faith: The Christian Indians of Martha's Vineyard," *William and Mary Quarterly*, 3rd Ser., 38 (1981): 369–94; Theda Perdue, *Cherokee Women: Gender and Culture Change, 1700–1835* (Lincoln, Neb., 1998); Sylvia Van Kirk, *Many Tender Ties: Women in Fur Trade Society, 1670–1870* (Norman, Okla., 1983); Jean O'Brien, *Dispossession by Degrees: Indian Land and Identity in Natick, Massachusetts, 1650–1790* (New York, 1997); Ann Marie Plane, *Colonial Intimacies: Indian Marriage in Early New England* (Ithaca, N.Y., 2000).

Richard White's *The Middle Ground*,[36] published in 1991, stands among the most influential books of recent decades. Imperial politics and rivalries among Europeans permitted Great Lakes Indians to force their French allies onto a "middle ground," where they created new, shared cultural meanings and forms of behavior. Justice, diplomacy, sexuality, and hospitality, among other experiences, came to be renegotiated and transformed as the French and their native allies worked out rules for cooperating and coexisting. Once the British had defeated the French, the Indians lost much of their power to participate in creating joint cultural practices. The American defeat of the British further weakened Indian power to shape politics and culture. Most scholars since White have found his concept of a middle ground strikingly useful in exploring the relationship between European and native societies.

Jill Lepore's influential *In the Name of War* shows that the New England colonists dominated the discourse of war by initiating a stream of sensationalized accounts of Indian ritual torture of captives. This propaganda effectively obscured English practices of indiscriminate killing, which, in the case of the Pequots in 1637, rose to genocide. Nevertheless, Europeans managed to propagate the idea of Indian war-making as unspeakably brutal, although, by comparison, it resulted in relatively few European deaths. Evan Haefeli and Kevin Sweeney's reconstruction of the 1704 raid on Deerfield, Massachusetts, provides the reader with an exhaustively researched example of French and Indian war-making. Their work offers an in-depth view of the pressures affecting the combatants and victims, a complex group including English, French, Abenaki, and Pennacook as well as Hurons and Mohawks, all transformed by a century of warfare. In their discussion of the communities from which the enemies emerged, Haefeli and Sweeney argue that the Indians were not powerful enough to produce a true middle ground, but they posit a more limited accommodation between individuals that lasted no longer than "the relationships that created it."[37]

Colin Calloway's *New Worlds for All*, excerpted below, reflects the recent emphases in Indian history on the continuing adaptability of native people and the increasingly lopsided impact of Indian and European cultures upon one another. The book takes its title from James Merrell's seminal work on the Catawba.[38] Calloway includes the transformed world of the citizens of the new United States in his survey of the new worlds produced by the Revolution. While not minimizing the disastrous consequences of contact, Calloway traces how native cultures adapted to European impositions, as well as how they selected and used some facets of the dominant culture while rejecting others.

In a recent work, Claudio Saunt places the eighteenth-century war between the British-allied Chickasaws and the French-allied Choctaws in the con-

---

[36]Richard White, *The Middle Ground: Indians, Empires, and Republics in the Great Lakes Region, 1650–1815* (New York, 1991).

[37]Jill Lepore, *The Name of War: King Philip's War and the Origins of American Identity* (New York, 1998); Evan Haefeli and Kevin Sweeney, *Captors and Captives: The 1704 French and Indian Raid on Deerfield* (Amherst, Mass., 2003), 4.

[38]Merrell, *The Indians' New World.*

text of a contemporary proxy war like the ones the United States and the Soviet Union fought in Angola and Afghanistan during the Cold War.[39] This parallel offers an alternative vision of the European-driven conflicts of the eighteenth century that engulfed many imperial native allies. It also rises to the challenge of recent historians to place Native American history in the Atlantic World, where it can be understood in its widest significance. As one historian has written, "Imagining Native American history in terms of world or global history makes it harder to subordinate cultural conflict and empire building to questions of national policy and character."[40] Saunt's article is included as the second reading below.

In recent years, scholars have advanced the historiography of identity formation and the emergence of racism by tracing the knotted relationship between African Americans and Native Americans and the particular intellectual and political conflicts and dynamics that encouraged racial thinking. In *History's Shadow*, Steven Conn argues that nineteenth-century historians' intense curiosity about Indians shaped both intellectual inquiry and mainstream history even as they wrote Indians out of that history. Maureen Konkle has studied nineteenth-century Indian thinkers who criticized Anglo-American policies and treaties while asserting their own political autonomy. She places these critics at the forefront of contemporary native challengers to U.S. domination of Indians.[41]

Alan Gallay's wide-ranging investigation of the slave trade in the South proves that "the trade in Indian slaves was at the center of the English empire's development in the American South." English colonists in South Carolina captured and bought Indian slaves, against the wishes of the proprietors, and sold those slaves in the Caribbean, where they purchased Africans to import to the continent. Gallay's narrative provides a tragic background for Claudio Saunt's several-generation study of a Creek family whose members married whites, Indians, and African Americans. Some held slaves; some intermarried with African Americans; some did both. Saunt tracks how the country's poisonous racial hierarchy infected this family, convincing one set of parents to reject their African American children.[42]

---

[39]Claudio Saunt, "'Our Indians': European Empires and the Native American South," in Jorge Cañizares-Esguerra and Erik Seeman, eds., *The Atlantic in Global History, 1500–2000* (Upper Saddle River, N.J., 2007).

[40]Meyer and Klein, "The End of Ethnohistory," 198; see also Richard White, "Using the Past," 230.

[41]Jack D. Forbes, *Africans and Native Americans: The Language of Race and the Evolution of Red-Black Peoples* (Urbana, Ill., 1993); Tiya Miles and Sharon P. Holland, *Crossing Waters, Crossing Worlds: The African Diaspora in Indian Country* (Durham, N.C., 2006); Steven Conn, *History's Shadow: Native Americans and Historical Consciousness in the Nineteenth Century* (Chicago, 2004); Maureen Konkle, *Writing Indian Nations: Native Intellectuals and the Politics of Historiography, 1827–1863* (Chapel Hill, N.C., 2004).

[42]Alan Gallay, *The Indian Slave Trade: The Rise of the English Empire in the American South, 1670–1717* (New Haven, Conn., 2002), 7. Claudio Saunt, *Black, White, and Indian: Race and the Unmaking of an American Family* (New York, 2005). See the exchange between Saunt and Theda Perdue on racial meaning among Native Americans in Theda Perdue, "Race and Culture: Writing the Ethnohistory of the Early South," *Ethnohistory* 51 (Fall 2004): 701–23; Claudio Saunt et al., "Rethinking Race and Culture in the Early South," *Ethnohistory* 53 (Spring 2006): 399–405; Theda Perdue, "A Reply to Claudio Saunt et al.," *Ethnohistory* 53 (Spring 2006): 406.

While Saunt provides an intimate view of the power of racism to distort family relationships, Colin Calloway's new work, *At the Scratch of a Pen*, identifies the Seven Years' War as the watershed after which race began to dominate Euro-American and Indian thinking about each other. In his brisk overview of the war and its aftermath, Calloway sees a blunt and indiscriminate racism filling in where the subtleties of the middle ground had suddenly eroded. Nancy Shoemaker, in *A Strange Likeness*, argues that Europeans and Native Americans shared broad intellectual skills and categories of knowledge, like land, the body, gender, and race, but that over time, despite similar abilities and concepts, conflict over land and ways of life pushed both increasingly to distinguish themselves from one another and exaggerate their differences. Like Calloway, she places the rise of racial thinking in the middle of the eighteenth century.[43]

It is ironic that a central problem facing many Indian groups today is establishing their legal identity as Indians in order to prosecute their various unfulfilled claims based on treaties with the United States. In a cultural context that has traditionally tried to wipe out most of the characteristics that count as "Indian," like language, religious traditions, and communal property, this tactic has proved anything but easy. Robert Beverley could assert that he was an Indian, but in 1978 a jury found that members of the Mashpee community on Cape Cod were not Indians, or anyway, not a tribe.[44] The claimants had several African American ancestors; many were Baptists; and they no longer spoke Mashpee. Given the pressures on indigenous peoples to convert to Christianity, to "give up the blanket," to join the economy as individual accumulators of property, and to sell whatever land they possessed, it is no longer entirely clear to an outsider what an Indian is, but our legal traditions are the ones that courts rely on to decide these questions. As historians take questions of Indian history and identity seriously, they raise a related question that has always been at the heart of our inability to see Indians for themselves: what is an American? In a partial answer, Claudio Saunt writes of the multiracial family he has chronicled, "with race, inequality, and conflict at the core of their story, the Graysons are truly American, and in one way or another, we all belong to their family."[45]

---

[43]Colin G. Calloway, *The Scratch of a Pen: 1763 and the Transformation of North America* (New York, 2006); Nancy Shoemaker, *A Strange Likeness: Becoming Red and White in Eighteenth-Century North America* (New York, 2004).

[44]Jack Campisi, *The Mashpee Indians: Tribe on Trial* (Syracuse, N.Y., 1991), 27–28, 59. A jury found in favor of the Mashpee in 2007.

[45]Saunt, *Black, White, and Indian*, 5.

COLIN G. CALLOWAY
*from* New Worlds for All    [1997]

**COLIN G. CALLOWAY** (1953– ) is professor of history and Native American studies at Dartmouth College. His books include *The Western Abenakis of Vermont, 1600–1800* (1990), *The American Revolution in Indian Country* (1995), *New Worlds for All* (1997), and *First Peoples: A Documentary Survey of American Indian History* (1999).

When Europeans first encountered Indian peoples, they saw no churches and little they recognized as organized worship. They met shamans and witnessed dances but dismissed Native American belief systems as primitive superstition or devil worship; Indian ceremonies struck them as heathen rituals. In the eyes of the Christian invaders, Indians had no real religion; converting them to Christianity would be a simple matter of filling a dark void with the light of the Gospel. Indian people, for their part, must have been mystified by the odd behavior of European "holy men," who came into their villages carrying Bibles and preaching about sin and damnation but who surely committed daily acts of sacrilege by failing to observe the rituals and proper behavior that maintained relationships between humans and spirits in the Indian world. Indian peoples responded to spirits and believed in the power of dreams to foretell the future and guide their lives. Father Jacques Frémin said the Senecas had "only one single divinity . . . the dream"; Jean de Brébeuf said dreams were "the principal God of the Hurons." Christians, too, believed in visions, but missionaries insisted that Indian people follow the injunctions of the Bible, not the messages in their dreams. In the new religious climate created by European invasion, many Indian people read the Bible and attended church services, but many continued to dream as well.

The soldiers of Christ were entering a world of deeply held religious beliefs every bit as complex and sophisticated as their own, but one they would rarely fathom or even try to understand. Native religions did not possess a specific theology; nor did they require that "believers" give verbal confessions of faith and live in obedience to a set of religious tenets stipulated by the church. Nevertheless, religion and ritual permeated the everyday lives of Indian peoples. European missionaries, convinced that there was only one true religion and it was theirs, tended to see things as black or white, good or evil. Indians who converted to Christianity must demonstrate unquestioning faith; Indians who resisted were clinging to heathen ways. For Christian missionaries, conversion was a simple matter:

Indian people who had been living in darkness and sin would receive the light and accept salvation. It proved to be not that simple. . . .

Indian religions tended to be much less exclusive and intolerant than Christianity, and Indian people often explored, considered, and incorporated elements of its teaching. Sometimes, Indians converted to Christianity and abandoned old beliefs. Often, old and new beliefs continued to exist side by side. Sometimes, Christianity itself changed as Indian people adopted it. They reshaped it to fit their notions of the world, eventually making it into an Indian as well as a European religion. Some Indians even used Christianity, and the missionaries who taught it to them, as a way of resisting white culture, of remaining Indian. . . .

The historical reputation of Christian missionaries has declined considerably in recent years. There was a time when, relying primarily on records written by missionaries and sharing their assumption that Christianity was synonymous with civilization, historians portrayed them as many missionaries thought of themselves. Courageous and selfless servants of Christ dedicated their lives to doing God's work and saving heathen souls. Indians gave up pagan ways, found contentment in their new lives, and experienced the joy that comes with the promise of everlasting life. Indian converts lived in peace and harmony with their priest or padre in idyllic mission communities within the sound of church bells.

Today, we are more inclined to question the missionaries' assumptions, finding their arrogance repellent and despising them as agents of cultural genocide. Indian people were wrenched from their homes and concentrated into mission villages, where they died of new diseases or had their traditional beliefs beaten out of them. Missionaries exploited their labor, stole their lands, and subjected them to sexual abuse. Oppression and chaos, not peace and harmony, characterized life in the missions. Christianity was a weapon of conquest, not a path to salvation.

Depending on time and place, circumstance and individual experience, one could provide examples to support any or all views of missionaries and their work. Indians were deeply spiritual people, but Europeans in those times, whatever we think of their assumptions and actions, were also spiritual, the products of powerful religious movements that enjoined them to go out and convert others.

For some Indian people, the missionaries brought them a new religion that changed their lives on earth and gave them reason to believe in eternal life in the hereafter. These individuals renounced their old ways and embraced the new, worked hard to make their mission villages into model Christian communities, and found meaning and hope in the church. . . .

Many more Indians kept the missionaries at arm's length, weighing their words but evading their evangelism by various strategies of passive resistance. "However much they are preached at," wrote a French officer in the Seven Years' War, "they listen very calmly & without ill-will, but they always return to their usual refrain, that they are not sufficiently intelligent to believe and follow what they are told, that their forefathers lived like them & that they adopt their way of life." The Indian custom of listening politely while missionaries regaled them with the word of God led many priests to misinterpret silence as tacit agreement and to see conversions where none occurred.

Other people did not listen quietly. They fought tooth and nail against the alien religion that threatened their world, resisting every effort to separate them from their cultural and spiritual roots, and saw missionaries as malevolent forces. The Reverend Samuel Kirkland encountered one Seneca in the 1760s who was of the "fixed opinion that my continuance there would be distructive to the nation, & finally over throw all the traditions & usages of their Forefathers & that there would not be a warrior remaining in their nation in the course of a few years." Another Seneca took a shot at the persistent missionary. . . .

Thousands of Indian people, however, selected a middle path of their own making. They heard the missionaries' message, asked questions, and found areas of common ground between old and new beliefs. According to David Weber, many of the Indians whom Spain claimed as converts "simply added Jesus, Mary, and Christian saints to their rich pantheons and welcomed the Franciscans into their communities as additional shamans." In a new world of suffering and uncertainty, people listened to preachers who assured them that terrestrial pain was temporary, life in paradise an eternity. Why not pray to the Christians' God? They had nothing to lose, so long as they did not abandon their own prayers, rituals, and beliefs. . . .

The collision and confluence of religious beliefs in North America did not occur in a vacuum. Indian people were dying of new diseases, succumbing to the inroads of alcohol, losing their economic independence, fighting new wars with deadly new weapons, struggling to hold on to their lands, and watching the physical world change around them. Converts most commonly came from communities that were falling apart. Christianity promised relief from the pain and suffering, but religious change also added to the turmoil.

Indian people and Christian missionaries shared areas of understanding. Both, for instance, attributed "natural" events to "supernatural" phenomena, although most Indian peoples saw no such arbitrary distinction between the two. At the same time, however, they saw their place in the world in radically different ways. For Christians, man was at the top of the hierarchy of creation and Europe at the pinnacle of civilization. Indian people shared their world with animals, plants, and their spirits. Where Europeans saw a religious void, Indian people had daily rituals and cycles of ceremonies that sustained life, propitiated spirits, and offered thanks, which helped maintain balance and order in the universe and gave meaning to the world. Missionaries who insisted that Indian people stop practicing such ceremonies were asking them to invite disaster.

Indian hunters often relied on the power of their dreams to help them locate their prey and foretell the kill. Hunting was a ceremonial activity as much as an economic necessity, since only if the proper rituals were observed would the animals consent to let themselves be taken, or agree to return. Traveling in the Carolina backcountry in 1701, John Lawson reported how the Indians he met carefully preserved and then burned the bones of the animals they killed, believing "that if they omitted that Custom, the Game would leave their Country, and they should not be able to maintain themselves by their Hunting." At a time when Indian people were becoming increasingly dependent on European trade goods, and commercial hunting to satisfy the demands of the European fur and deerskin trades threatened to undermine such ritual observances, European missionaries tried to sever Indians' ties to the animal world and to separate them from the world of dreams. . . .

As Carolyn Merchant points out, Christianity was altering the symbolic superstructure of the Indians' economy: "An ethic of moral obligation between human and God replaced the ethic of reciprocity between human and animal." God was above nature; the new religious teachings required no respect for animals and the natural world. Old hunting rituals continued, "but they ceased to function as a restraining environmental ethic." The way was open for Indian peoples to become commercial hunters, responding to the lure of the marketplace rather than listening to the spirits of the animals.

Farther west, on the northern shores of the Great Lakes in Ontario, Huron people also found ways to accommodate Christianity. The Hurons were trading partners of the French, and Jesuit priests were eager to carry the word of God to the Huron villages and establish a base for future missions. The Hurons were a people in crisis in the 1630s. Recurrent epidemics of disease cut Huron population in half between 1634 and 1640, but the mortality rate among children was much higher. Many Hurons blamed the Jesuits for the disaster: "With the Faith, the scourge of God came into the country," wrote Jesuit Father François Joseph Bressani, "and, in proportion as the one increased, the other smote them more severely." The Hurons believed that the Jesuits were sorcerers who, like shamans, could use their power for good or evil. But the need to maintain trading alliances with the French prevented them from exacting vengeance on the missionaries; indeed, the French would not sell guns to non-Christians in the first half of the seventeenth century, and many Hurons accepted baptism to secure firearms. Meanwhile, as traditional curing practices and ceremonies proved ineffective against the new killer diseases, Huron villages filled with the sick and dying. People looked in desperation for new answers or at least for some source of hope, and parents brought their children to the Jesuit fathers for baptism. The Jesuits recorded only twenty-two Huron baptisms in 1635, but baptisms increased dramatically as the Huron population plummeted. . . .

Only the Tahontaenrat Hurons survived as a group; the rest of the people scattered throughout the Great Lakes region. Many of them became incorporated into the villages of their Iroquois enemies; some survived at the mission town of Lorette on the St. Lawrence.

In New England, meanwhile, Indian peoples encountered a different brand of Christianity as English missionaries introduced them to the tenets of Puritanism. Puritan missionaries demanded what amounted to cultural suicide from their Indian converts, insisting that they live like their English neighbors if they intended to practice the Christian religion. Nevertheless, many Indian people accepted conversion as they sought spiritual meaning in an increasingly chaotic world. Thomas Mayhew Jr. began preaching to the Wampanoag Indians on Martha's Vineyard in the 1640s but with relatively little success. Then, epidemic diseases swept the island in 1643 and 1645. The shamans, the traditional spiritual leaders and healers, were unable to cure the sick. Scores of Indian people looked to Christianity to provide new explanations, if not new cures, and to fill a void left by the decline of traditional communal rituals. The Indians built their own church community and passed the Gospel from generation to generation.

But the Indian converts on Martha's Vineyard did not become English or cease being Indian. Some Indians who worshiped in Christian churches continued to live in wigwams. They made Christianity an Indian religion. Indian men served as preachers, pastors, and deacons; Indian women found that Christianity honored their traditional roles, offered them the opportunity to learn to read and write, and provided solace and support as their island society threatened to unravel amid alcoholism and violence. Christian Indians took Christian names, but they continued to be called by their Indian ones. A deacon named Paul, for instance, kept his Wampanoag name, Mashquattuhkooit. In time, some Christian Indian families began to use given names and surnames, in the European style. But the surnames were based on traditional names — the descendants of Hiacoomes, the first Indian convert on Martha's Vineyard, became known by the surname Coomes. . . .

On the mainland, John Eliot hoped to prevent any such "compromises." Eliot came to America in 1631, began to learn the Massachusett Indian language in 1643, and started preaching three years later. He compiled a dictionary and grammar of Massachusett and by 1663, with the assistance of Indian translators, had translated the entire Bible into Massachusett. For Eliot, enabling Indians to read the Bible was a vital first step on the road to "civilization." Eliot also established a total of fourteen "praying towns," model Christian communities where Indian converts lived quarantined from the negative influences of unconverted relatives or unsavory English characters. He laid down harsh penalties for Indians who disobeyed his rules. Men must work hard; women must learn to spin and weave. They must wear their hair English-style, stop using bear's grease as protection against mosquitoes, and give up plural wives. Discarded wives and children presumably suffered misery and poverty so that their now-monogamous ex-husbands and fathers could live Christian lives. Eliot's program promoted social revolution and cultural disintegration.

Not surprisingly, many Indian people refused to accept such an assault on their way of life. Indian communities that had not yet experienced devastation proved more resistant to Puritan teachings. At their height, Eliot's praying towns held only about eleven hundred people, and the extent of individual conversions among these people, and how many accepted Eliot's complete program of social change, remains uncertain. At Natick, Eliot's showpiece praying-town, some Indian converts were given a Christian funeral service, but were interred in traditional fashion with wampum, beads, and other earthly items. As Daniel Mandell notes, "The desire to maintain an Indian community in an English/Christian world extended even to the grave." . . .

For those who did accept Christianity, conversion may have meant something different from what it meant to Eliot. Massachusett Indians believed in a creator, but their world was inhabited by countless *mani-towuk*, spirits who directed the course of their daily lives. Adding God or Christ did not necessarily disrupt their worldview. . . .

Some people may have embraced Christianity as a way of fending off annihilation as the world crumbled about them. Missions offered Indian people a haven from some of the turmoil and provided them knowledge and skills to deal with the strange new world that was being created. Learning to read was a way of acquiring knowledge about the English as well as about God; it could be used to understand treaties, laws, and deeds in addition to the Bible. It may also have carried status and involved ritual and spiritual qualities of which Eliot would not have been aware. Some women may have been attracted to Christianity because it redefined gender roles or simply because they wanted to learn to spin. For all these people, conversion to Christianity had meaning; but that was not necessarily the same meaning that it had for Eliot.

However complete their conversion, the inhabitants of the praying-towns could not find shelter from the storms around them. During King Philip's War (1675–76), Indians from Natick supported the English, but the colonists viewed all Indians with fear and suspicion. Praying-town residents were rounded up and incarcerated on Deer Island in Boston Harbor. Eliot's mission program fell to pieces. . . .

Like Eliot in New England, Spanish missionaries in the South labored to save Indian souls with an assault on Indian culture that severed kinship relations, restricted sexual practices, altered settlement patterns, and promoted new divisions of labor. Jesuit Father Juan Rogel declared in 1570: "If we are to gather fruit, the Indians must join in and live in settlements and cultivate the soil." Spanish missionaries regarded resettling Indian people as peasants living in sedentary communities as a prerequisite to Christianity. Under the Spanish mission system, Indian people built the missions, raised and tended the crops and stock that fed the mission community, and performed the routine services that sustained the mission. But the reality the missions achieved rarely matched the goal they pursued. The Spanish missions also produced massive population decline, food shortages, increased demands for labor, and violence.

At its height in the mid-seventeenth century, the Spanish mission system in the colony of La Florida included seventy friars in forty missions stretching from St. Augustine to the coast of South Carolina in the north and the Apalachicola River near present-day Tallahassee in the west. . . .

But Indians resented and resisted Franciscan efforts. Guale Indians rebelled against their missionaries in 1597; Christian Apalachees revolted in 1638 and 1647; Timucuans, in 1656. British and Indian raids from the north at the beginning of the eighteenth century effectively brought the mission system to an end. The net result of Spanish missionary efforts in the area was abandoned missions, fragmented communities, and refugee converts huddled around St. Augustine.

Following Juan de Oñate's colonizing expedition into New Mexico in 1598, Spanish Franciscan missionaries established themselves in almost every pueblo along the Rio Grande. The Spanish Crown saw missions as a line of defense, protecting the colony from Indian enemies and European rivals. The Pueblos may have seen them in somewhat similar terms: the missions could stand against Apache enemies and against potentially aggressive Spanish soldiers and colonists. But Spanish priests not only invaded kivas (underground ceremonial chambers), they desecrated kachina masks and tried to suppress Native rituals and sexual practices. Many Pueblos refused to accept a new faith that threatened their social and spiritual order; others continued to practice their ancestral ways behind closed doors or, more accurately, in underground kivas. Some fled west to the Hopis and other more distant Pueblos; others retaliated in periodic outbreaks of violence. Drought, falling populations, and increasing Navajo and Apache raids indicated that the new religion was not a source of powerful spiritual protection, and that people should return to their ancient ways, if they ever had left them. In 1680, Popé, a Tewa medicine man from San Juan, synchronized an uprising of the different Pueblos that drove out the Spaniards for a dozen years. The Indians killed and mutilated many of the friars who had been trying to stamp out their religion and desecrated the alien paraphernalia of Catholicism.

The Spaniards returned, but they had learned from the experience. Where their predecessors had tried to eradicate all Native rituals, friars now more often turned a blind eye to such practices — a shift, as historian John Kessel describes it, "from crusading intolerance to pragmatic accommodation." Indian people meanwhile became resigned to the Spaniards and adopted more subtle tactics of resistance. When Diego de Vargas returned on his campaign of reconquest in 1692, Luis, a Picuri Pueblo leader, appeared before him dressed in animal skins and wearing a band of palm shell around his head; but he also wore a rosary round his neck and carried a silver cross, an Agnus Dei, and a cloth printed with the image of Our Lady of Guadeloupe. A century of contact with Spanish missionaries had left its imprint. Many Pueblos accepted the outward forms of Hispanic Christianity while keeping the friars away from clan, kiva, and kachina, the things that constituted the core of their religion and their Pueblo identity. Many Pueblos became nominally Catholic, attending mass and observing Christian holidays, but they continued to practice traditional rituals and kept their worldview intact. . . .

The Hopis were more insulated than other Pueblos from Spanish crusading. Their villages sat atop isolated mesas in northern Arizona, and they were better able to keep Spanish priests at arm's length. Hopi religious leaders not only resisted those Spanish missionaries who made the trek to their villages, they even on occasion debated and denounced the padres in public confrontations. . . .

The Franciscan friar Junípero Serra brought Catholicism to the Indians of California in 1769. Traveling north to the San Francisco Bay area, his expedition established the first Catholic mission at San Diego. Other missions followed until a chain of twenty-one missions stretched more than 650 miles. By 1800, Indian neophytes — as the converts were called — numbered some twenty thousand, testimony to the disintegration of Native societies under the hammerblows of new diseases as much as to the power of Christianity. But the fact that Indian neophytes adopted Christian symbols and stories did not necessarily mean they accepted conversion on Spanish terms. They may have seen in the pageantry and paraphernalia of Catholic services new sources of spiritual power which they could acquire without jeopardizing their old beliefs. Spanish missionaries congregated Indian peoples into new communities and used Indian labor to support the mission system while they themselves labored to save Indian souls. The friars segregated unmarried men and women into separate dormitories at night to enforce Catholic moral codes, imposed strict labor regimens, and resorted to whipping, branding, and solitary confinement to keep the Indians on the path to "civilization and salvation." . . .

Indian populations plummeted. Many Indians ran away from the missions; others turned to violence: several hundred Indians launched an unsuccessful attack on the San Diego mission in 1775.

Missionary efforts elsewhere met with limited success, although not always for the same reasons. Moravian missionaries won many converts among the Delaware Indians in Pennsylvania and Ohio in the eighteenth century, and some Delawares clearly embraced the Christian way of life that missionaries such as John Heckewelder and David Zeisberger brought them. But the Moravians and their converts were building peaceful mission havens in what was fast becoming a war zone. The colonial and revolutionary wars that raged in the Ohio Valley in the second half of the century disrupted the missionaries' work, dislocating their communities, and brought disaster to the converts. In 1782, American militiamen butchered ninety-six pacifist and unarmed Moravian Indians in their village at Gnadenhütten. The Moravians and their converts migrated to Canada in the years after the American Revolution. . . .

Converted and unconverted Indians alike noted differences between Christianity as preached and as practiced. Indians commonly countered missionary arguments by declaring, "We are better Christians than you." Those, like Occom, who converted during the Great Awakening found fault with the established church. Many Narragansetts converted to Christianity in the 1740s, embracing a religious movement that challenged the intellectual elitism of Puritanism. It more closely resembled their traditional religion, emphasizing visions, the spoken rather than the written word, and religious leadership based on a "calling" rather than on formal education. The Narragansetts built their own church and had Narragansett ministers. Samuel Niles, the first Narragansett minister, said that his people regarded educated ministers as "Thieves, Robbers, Pirates, etc. . . . They steal the word. God told the Prophets the words they Spoke: and these Ministers Steal that Word." . . .

Indians spread Christianity in less direct ways than operating as missionaries. Iroquois Indians who converted to Catholicism in the seventeenth century formed new mission communities at places like Caughnawaga near Montreal. In the early years of the nineteenth century, Iroquois from Caughnawaga migrated to the Rocky Mountain region to work in the fur trade as trappers and guides. Some of them intermarried with local Indian women and brought their Indian Catholicism to the tribes there.

Though many Indian people looked to Christianity for help in times of crisis, Christianity often generated additional crises and tensions in Indian communities. Rituals such as the Green Corn Ceremony united Indian communities, bringing people together in seasonal ceremonies of prayer, thanksgiving, and world renewal; Christian missionaries prohibited their converts from participating in such "pagan rituals," thereby severing ties of community and identity. Missionaries also attempted to set up new patterns of work and behavior between the sexes. In gender-egalitarian societies like the Hurons and the Montagnais, where women enjoyed an influence unknown in Europe, French missionaries tried to subordinate women, to reorder Indian society along more "civilized" lines.

Some communities split between traditional and Christian factions. The Hurons were bitterly factionalized by the time the Iroquois attacked them in 1648–49. Delawares who converted to the Moravian faith lived in separate villages from their unconverted relatives and sometimes experienced ridicule and resentment from them. Formerly viewed with respect by other Iroquois, Oneida headmen by 1772 felt "despised by our brethren, on account of our christian profession." Some opportunistic Indian leaders embraced Christianity to add spiritual sanction in their political challenge to established leaders. At Natick in the seventeenth century, Waban used Christianity as a core around which to organize a faction challenging the leadership of Cushamekin, which rested on more traditional spiritual foundations. Men like Waban employed the missionaries as allies to serve their own political interests.

Some communities split even further as factions formed around different denominations. In about 1700, the Christian Wampanoag community at Gay Head on Martha's Vineyard split into Baptist and Congregational churches. Most Mohawks became nominal Anglicans in the early eighteenth century; their relatives who accepted the Catholic faith moved away to form new communities near the French at St. Regis (present-day Akwesasne) and Caughnawaga. The surface harmony Richard Smith witnessed at Oquaga in 1769 concealed widening divisions between Anglican and Presbyterian factions within the community.

All across America, Christian and Indian peoples and elements mingled. In Quebec and northern New England, Abenaki Indians took French saints' names as surnames, wore crucifixes around their necks, spoke French, prayed to Catholic saints, and even hung wampum belts on Catholic statues. As did Spanish officers in the Southwest, French officers in the Northeast acted as godparents at baptisms of Abenaki children. Sebastian Rasles said the Abenakis' faith was "the bond that unites them to the French," and Abenakis themselves rejected English missionary efforts, asserting their loyalty to the French: "We have promised to be true to God in our Religion, and it is this we profess to stand by." But Abenakis also kept traditional rituals alive. When French priests frowned on dancing to drums, they danced to rattles instead.

The missionary experience also left an imprint on some missionaries, however. Men who went into Indian country to convert the "heathen" sometimes found themselves slowly being converted to an Indian way of life they were dedicated to destroy. . . .

As they did in China and Paraguay, Jesuit missionaries modified their practices to accommodate the culture of the native peoples whom they hoped to make into Catholics. They realized that their best strategy lay in first winning acceptance and support in the communities where they lived and preached, building on common ground and avoiding head-on confrontations with Native practices that did not clash openly with Christian teachings. They adapted their messages to suit Indian styles of oratory, looking for parallels in Indian belief systems and behaving as much as possible according to Native protocol. When Father Nau wanted to establish a mission among the Iroquois in 1735, he recognized that he would need to conform to Iroquois ways: he accepted adoption into the Bear clan, because, he explained, "a missionary would not be an acceptable person in the village were he not a member of the tribe."

Missionaries sought to discredit traditional spiritual leaders, yet took over many of their functions in Indian society — they dispensed advice, spoke in council, shared what they had, and ministered to the sick. Sebastian Rasles lived almost thirty years among the Abenaki Indians at Norridgewock in Maine. He dedicated himself to converting the Indians to Christianity and changing their way of life forever. It was, he wrote, "necessary to conform to their manners and customs, to the end that I might gain their confidence and win them to Jesus Christ." Yet, in a letter to his brother the year before he died, Rasles confided that the conversion process had been mutual: "As for what concerns me personally, I assure you that I see, that I hear, that I speak, only as a savage." The English hated Rasles, feared that he used his influence among the Indians to incite attacks on English settlements, and put a price on his head. In 1724, they raided Norridgewock, burned the village, killed Rasles, and mutilated his body.

David Brainerd, a young Presbyterian minister preaching to Indians along the Susquehanna River in the 1740s, found that their responses prompted him to question and reevaluate his mission. Munsee Indians rejected Christianity as a corrupting influence and told Brainerd they preferred to "live as their fathers lived and go where their fathers were when

they died." Delawares in western Pennsylvania seemed equally unrecep-
tive. The blank stares of the Indians whose souls he had set out to save
drove Brainerd into a critical period of soul searching, reassessing his
goals and even wondering about his God. More receptive Indian audiences brought a renewed commitment before Brainerd's early death from
tuberculosis, but the Indians he met clearly molded the young missionary's character and influenced "everything from his evangelistic method
to his psychological health." . . .

As James Axtell explains, the direction of religious change in North
America was "decidedly unilinear," largely because Indian religions, unlike
Christianity, were tolerant of other faiths. Indian religions were always on
the defensive, and any changes that occurred in colonial religion "were
minor and self-generated," not in response to Native pressures to convert.
Nevertheless, being on the defensive did not totally rob Indians of the initiative. Frequently, they used elements of Christianity for their own purposes: "By accepting the Christian priest as the functional equivalent of a
native shaman and by giving traditional meanings to Christian rites, dog-
mas, and deities," writes Axtell, "the Indians ensured the survival of native
culture by taking on the protective coloration of the invaders' culture."

Periodically, new religious movements developed in Indian country,
and messiahs preached a return to traditional ways of life. By the second
half of the eighteenth century, as Gregory Dowd has argued, Indian
peoples in the eastern woodlands who fought to preserve their remaining
lands from European and American expansion also struggled to recover
their world by restoring and reviving traditional rituals. Some messiahs
and prophets preached total rejection of the white man and his ways.
Indian people could become whole again only if they denounced alcohol,
trade goods, and Christianity. Others offered a more flexible approach.
In 1799, a Seneca Indian named Handsome Lake, who had given in to
alcoholism and despair as his world crumbled around him, experienced a
vision. He renounced alcohol and began to preach a program of social
reform and cultural rejuvenation, urging his people to abandon what was
evil but take what was best from white culture. He also offered them a
religion that blended elements of Christian teaching, possibly picked up
from neighboring Quakers, with traditional rituals such as the Green
Corn Ceremony and the Midwinter Ceremony. Handsome Lake revived
and restructured traditional religion for a new world. The Longhouse
religion, as it became known, thrived and spread and continues today.

Time and again in North America, Christian missionaries established a
foothold in Indian communities during a crisis, reaped a harvest of converts, and then were pushed back or held at arm's length as Indian
people kept or revived ancient beliefs. Indian people learned that the best
way to preserve their religious beliefs was to hide them from evangelizing
Europeans, a strategy that, ironically, often convinced outsiders that the
Indians' religion had died out. The result often lay somewhere between
total acceptance and total rejection. In southwestern pueblos, kivas still
exist alongside Catholic churches, and Indian people often participate in

Christian as well as traditional ceremonies. At Gay Head and Mashpee, in Massachusetts, where Indians became Christians as early as the seventeenth century, Native folk beliefs about ghosts, witches, and spirits survived into the twentieth century. In such instances, Christianity did not eradicate old beliefs; rather, it supplemented and even strengthened them, providing a new, broader spiritual basis. The new world that emerged was one in which Christian and traditional beliefs alike, sometimes separately and sometimes together, guided and gave meaning to people's lives.

## CLAUDIO SAUNT

# *from* "Our Indians": European Empires and the History of the Native American South    [2007]

CLAUDIO SAUNT (1967– ) is associate professor of history at the University of Georgia, where he teaches Native and Early American History. His works include *A New Order of Things: Property, Power, and the Transformation of the Creek Indians, 1733–1816* (1999) and *Black, White, and Indian: Race and the Unmaking of an American Family* (2005).

Atlantic World histories, like more familiar narratives of the rise of the nation-state, frequently seem to convey a sense of European omnipotence. Capitalism reaches across the Atlantic to engulf the Americas, Old World biota invade the New World and push out indigenous species, and historical narrative replaces oral traditions about the past. Searching the frayed edges of transatlantic empires, however, historians have located peripheral regions, variously described as frontiers, borderlands, or middle grounds, that lay just beyond the reach of imperial control. Once characterized as the proving grounds of empire, scholars now recognize that these regions were sites of negotiation and compromise, where Indians and colonists together forged new worlds.

In a 1999 article, Jeremy Adelman and Stephen Aron summed up recent literature on borderlands, the contested regions lying between empires. These regions, they observed, were characterized by "fluid and 'inclusive' intercultural frontiers." They were places of "mutual acculturation," "replete with ethnic mixing, syncretism, and cohabitation." Where borderlands existed, Adelman and Aron concluded, "Indian peoples deflected imperial powers from their original purposes and fashioned economic, diplomatic, and personal relations that rested, if not entirely

Claudio Saunt, "'Our Indians': European Empires and the History of the Native American South," in Jorge Cañizares-Esguerra and Eric R. Seeman, eds., *The Atlantic in Global History, 1500–2000* (Upper Saddle River, N.J.: Pearson/Prentice Hall, 2007). © 2007, pages 61–71. Reprinted by permission of Pearson Education, Inc., Upper Saddle River, N.J.

on Indian ground, at least on more common ground. Since Adelman and Aron's essay, the emphasis on "fluid" borderlands has shown no signs of waning. One historian describes the "relatively harmonious past" of the Deep South, where Indians and colonists participated in a system of "mutually beneficial economic interactions." Another writes about a "world of equals" in the Texas borderlands, where Indians and Europeans "brought together respective traditions of ceremony, gift giving, and protocol to forge new systems of diplomatic exchange with one another."

Paradoxically, this historiographical turn toward borderlands may in fact perpetuate rather than destabilize a Eurocentric perspective of the Atlantic World. Metaphorically, "middle ground" and "borderland" suggest a sense of in-betweenness, of negotiation and compromise, but literally they reflect the viewpoint of colonial ministers in Paris, Madrid, and London who eyed the possessions of their European rivals and dreamed of extending their territorial claims across Indian lands. To Native Americans, by contrast, middle grounds and borderlands were simply homelands. Narratives that foreground negotiation, compromise, and boundary crossing between races and cultures perhaps reflect more the emancipatory fantasies of twenty-first-century scholars than the lives of eighteenth-century Indians, whose nations were invaded and reduced, if not destroyed. Any account of Indians in this period must consider the imperial dimensions of the Atlantic World without resorting to older narratives that assumed that conquest was inevitable and total.

To understand the dynamics of regions that were, from different perspectives, both imperial borderlands and Indian homelands, a twentieth-century neologism may be helpful. Where European empires fought each other and Indian nations for Indian lands, they frequently did so by means of proxy warfare. Loosely defined, proxy wars are local or regional conflicts in which competing imperial states covertly invest. They are "large small wars," as two scholars said of the thirty-five-year civil war in Angola that began in the 1960s.

There are a number of obvious differences between the well-known proxy wars of the twentieth century in places such as Angola and Afghanistan and those in the eighteenth century in the Choctaw Nation, Iroquoia, and elsewhere, but there are a number of revealing similarities too. First, in the eighteenth-century Atlantic World, European empires exported their conflicts to other nations, and those conflicts were deeply imbricated in international imperial rivalry as well as in regional colonial ambitions. Second, imperial administrators displayed a deep contempt for the people who lived in battlegrounds, arrogantly and erroneously imagining that they could control the actions of local residents. Third, although administrators' fantasies of control were not in the least warranted, the guns, textiles, and other trading goods that they poured into battlegrounds in the interest of manipulating native peoples frequently had devastating consequences for indigenous communities, not unlike the effects that machine guns and mortars had more recently on Angolans and Afghanis. There is a significant disparity in the scale between eighteenth- and twentieth-century proxy wars, reflected in the deadliness of modern weapons and the tremendous reach of today's superpowers, yet the parallels remain compelling.

This chapter explores one European borderland and Indian homeland, the Choctaw Nation, where French and British empires fought a proxy war in the first half of the eighteenth century. It outlines how France and Britain exported their imperial rivalry to the Choctaw Nation. It explores the French administrators' fantasies of control over native peoples. And it concludes by arguing that the proxy war in the Choctaw Nation, though hardly controlled by French and British officers, nevertheless had devastating consequences for native peoples.

In the early eighteenth century, the lower South was shared by three large Indian nations. The Choctaw Nation in east-central Mississippi numbered about 17,000 people. On its northern border (present-day northern Mississippi), the Chickasaw Nation had 14,000 residents. And farther east, in present-day Alabama and western Georgia, the Creek Nation comprised 10,000 people. The European presence in the lower South remained negligible until 1670, when Britain established a settlement in Charleston. Some thirty years later, France established a competing colony along the Mississippi River. Separated by more than 600 miles and by the Choctaw, Chickasaw, and Creek nations, these two imperial outposts would spend the next sixty years struggling for control of the land lying between them. (Although Spain had settlements in present-day Florida, by the eighteenth century it was no longer able to mount a significant challenge to its imperial competitors.) For much of the time, France and Britain chose to fight by proxy rather than overtly.

The Choctaw and Chickasaw nations, with their relatively large populations and their strategic location, held the key to controlling access to the Mississippi River. In 1715, French colonists and their slaves numbered only 400, and even fifty years later, when the French abandoned their claim to the colony, their numbers would barely exceed 9,000. By making "striking comparisons" between the great numbers of people in France and the small numbers of Choctaws and Chickasaws in the South, Jean Baptist le Moyne de Bienville, the colony's governor from 1701 to 1713, tried to elide the power imbalance in Louisiana, but the fact remained, as the Indians pointed out to him in 1707, that "instead of increasing you are diminishing."

It should be noted that eighteenth-century states were far less cohesive than their twentieth-century counterparts. Dependent on slow-moving and unreliable ships, colonial officials sometimes received their orders months after they had been issued. Moreover, when it came to implementing Indian policy, traders played a critical role, and both French and British officials complained that these men had little allegiance to the crown. Britain faced the added disadvantage of managing affairs through several competing colonies. But the fact remains that French and British officials, schooled in the theory of mercantilism, believed they were engaged in a zero-sum game for control of the world's wealth. Even local traders, looking out for their own interests rather than those of the crown, spent a great deal of time trying to monopolize commerce for their own nation.

Despite the powerful presence of the Choctaws and Chickasaws, both France and Britain imagined that their true adversary for control of the lower South lay on the other side of the English Channel, not across the Atlantic Ocean. As one British agent put it, with the establishment of Louisiana, the "English American Empire" might become "unreasonably Crampt up." The key to thwarting the French colony, British officials believed, was the establishment of a western Indian trade. Carolina consequently organized an expedition in 1699 to forge commercial ties with Louisiana Indians and to claim the Mississippi region for the British crown, and that same year it began arming Indians against the rival colony. Friendly Indians, declared a Carolina governing committee, should be encouraged to make war "upon those Indians that are our and their Enemies." By offering high prices for enslaved Indians, Carolina and Virginia created a market that sent their native allies as far as east Texas in search of potential victims. Between 30,000 and 50,000 Indians were captured and sold into the British slave market between 1670 and 1750.

These actions did not go unnoticed in French Louisiana. "The English of Carolina are sparing nothing to have our Indians destroyed by theirs," Bienville wrote in 1709, using an expression of possession that became common among both French and British officials. By the end of Louisiana's first decade, it was clear to the governor that the Chickasaws would be "theirs." These people, whom the French could reach only with difficulty by ascending the winding path of the Tombigbee River, lay on a route frequently traveled by Carolina traders. As the Chickasaws expanded their relations with Carolina, Bienville announced that the more populous and more centrally located Choctaws were "the key to this country," an opinion that French officials would share for the next fifty years.

Like proxy wars in the twentieth century, the Choctaw–Chickasaw war was a regional conflict with connections to remote locales. The great distance between Paris and the lower South as well as the interest of French administrators in their far-flung colony is captured by the brief yet strongly worded comments left by Parisian officers in the margins of reports on Louisiana. "Last autumn, these savages killed two English," read one such report, to which a colonial minister noted in the margin, "*bon*." When French-allied Indians failed to attack the Chickasaws, another administrator wrote in the margin, "*tant pis*" ("too bad"). The King encouraged measures to have the Choctaws destroy the Chickasaws "as soon as possible," a more effusive marginal note explained in 1735, because if conflict with England became overt, the war with the Chickasaws would become especially costly. "I will spare no expense [ *Je n'épargnerai aucun soin*] to achieve the total defeat of the Chickasaws," Bienville wrote to the minister of the Marine soon afterward.

The imperial dimensions of the conflict were made real when Louisiana governors coordinated forces against the Chickasaw Nation with their ministerial counterparts in distant New France. In 1730, Governor Étienne Boucher de Périer (1726–1733) wrote to Governor Beauharnois in Quebec, requesting that Hurons, Iroquois, Miamis, and other northern Indians be sent against the Chickasaws. In that year, Hurons killed or captured some thirty Chickasaws. In later years, orders were relayed from New Orleans to Quebec to Fort Detroit to organize war parties against the Chickasaws. "The savages from the north are relentlessly harassing the Chickasaws," an officer reported from Mobile in 1738. Given the concerted French efforts spanning nearly half a century to set their Indian allies against the Chickasaws, it is not surprising that more than one Choctaw concluded that the French themselves should be doing the fighting. "For a number of years," one Choctaw reportedly said in 1745, they have fought the Chickasaws, who "never did anything to them except fail to be allied with the French."

French officers believed that with well-directed gifts, cleverly timed encouragements, and occasional threats they could manipulate Choctaws to conform to their strategic plans. They manifested a deep conviction in their own superiority. The Choctaws might "take a few scalps here and there," Périer wrote in 1731, but they would never be able to destroy a well-fortified nation such as the Chickasaws. By contrast, he wrote, "nothing is impossible for the well-led Frenchman," especially when "the glory of the King" was at stake. But French arrogance was undercut by two disastrous military campaigns in 1736 and 1740. In the first, Bienville, frustrated with the lack of progress against the Chickasaws, decided to organize two French forces to invade their homeland simultaneously. One, led by Martin d'Artaguette, would descend from Fort Illinois on the Mississippi River, while the other, commanded by Bienville himself, would ascend from Mobile.

Although Bienville was delayed by a lack of supplies for two months, d'Artaguette did not receive word until his party of 130 French soldiers, 38 Iroquois, and 190 Illinois and Miami Indians was already on the march. He decided not to turn back. When his troops arrived in the Chickasaw Nation in late March 1736, 400 to 500 warriors rushed over a nearby hill and pursued the panicked soldiers back to their camp. The Chickasaws killed d'Artaguette and forty other men and seized their supplies. When news filtered back that ten prisoners were burned alive, the French took consolation by reporting that their compatriots had sung bravely during their immolation. One officer explained, "That is the custom of the savages, who judge the valor of a warrior only by the strength or weakness of his voice at the moment when they have him killed." The stunning defeat, coupled with their painful adoption of Indian standards of valor, must have made colonists uncomfortable. Unwilling to attribute the rout to the skill of the Chickasaws, Bienville concluded that the English were to blame.

Bienville's belated foray into the Chickasaw Nation, two months after D'Artaguette's, fared no better. Numbering over 1,000 men, the expedition quickly got itself into trouble when French soldiers thoughtlessly set fire to several Chickasaw cabins providing cover from hostile gunfire. Forced into the open by the roaring flames, the soldiers were shot down by their own rear guard as well as by the Chickasaws. As their officers fell around them, the troops hurriedly took flight. Roughly eighty French soldiers were killed or wounded in the fighting, compared to perhaps twenty Chickasaws. Adding insult to injury, Bienville had to plead with his Choctaw allies to help carry the French wounded back to Mobile. A month later, Bienville humbly reported to the minister of the Marine that the campaign "occasioned the vacancy of several officers' positions." Once again, he attributed the defeat to the English: "What happened against my expectation was the assistance of the English, whom I did not think would take sides." Bienville also blamed the stature of his troops. Of fifty-two recent recruits, he wrote with dismay, only two were taller than five feet. Nevertheless, he recognized that this time he might not be able to avoid shouldering some of the responsibility. "Your silence, Monseigneur, regarding what I suggested about the cowardice of our soldiers," he wrote to the minister of the Marine, "leads me to believe that you are not well persuaded that it was the only cause of the poor success." This cowardice, he insisted, "was only too real and too public."

The 1736 expeditions did nothing to improve the image of the French in the minds of local Indians. Red Shoes, a noted Choctaw warrior, visited Mobile in May 1737 and told the commander that the French "know nothing about making war." They were unable to take even a small village of thirty or forty men, he observed, and in their failed attempt lost scores of soldiers without killing a single Chickasaw. French troops, encumbered by their heavy clothing, marched too slowly and too closely together, Red Shoes said, making it possible for the Chickasaws to fire blindly and still kill or wound several of them. Bernard Diron d'Artaguette, whose nephew had led the first expedition, listened to Red Shoes's humiliating reproach and responded as best he could: French soldiers had sacrificed themselves on the King's orders, he explained, to see if the Chickasaws were "true men" and if they, as "great warriors" merited a worthy attack. The Choctaws, he reported to the minister of the Marine, returned home impressed with the "great courage" and "obedience" of French soldiers, but his response could scarcely have soothed French doubts about their military prowess or bolstered the Indians' waning opinion of their neighbors. Bienville immediately began planning a 1740 campaign to redeem French honor.

This time Bienville intended to sail up the Mississippi and Wolf rivers, cross overland, and descend on the unwitting Chickasaws. The expedition, put into motion in the middle of 1739, ended in disaster because of a fatal oversight: there was no route from the Wolf River to the Chickasaw Nation that permitted a thousand French soldiers to pass with their artillery. Although by September the French troops were positioned on the Wolf River at Fort Assumption, not far from present-day Memphis, they could only bide their time while several parties desperately tried to discover a route that did not demand the construction of dozens of bridges or the fording of deep waters. Three months later, the number of Frenchmen, Indians, and slaves at Fort Assumption had risen to close to 3,000, but Bienville still had not discovered a road to the Chickasaw Nation. Winter set in, and the waters rose, flooding the lands and making overland routes even more impassable. In the cold weather, the army's horses and cattle, many of which had already drowned in the high waters, began to starve to death. Although it was clear by the end of the year that the entire campaign would have to be abandoned, Bienville maintained the charade until mid-February, when he finally called off the disastrous expedition. How disastrous is illustrated by the extraordinary cost to the French crown: over a million livres, more than three times the annual budget of the entire colony, expended on a war that Bienville abdicated before it began. Along with this immense sum, Louisiana lost 500 soldiers, who died of disease during the long, fruitless wait at Fort Assumption.

"Even if we did not get out of this fix as successfully as we had the right to expect we would," Bienville wrote, "the glory of the king's arms did not suffer." But no one shared his opinion, least of all the Choctaws. They wondered aloud why their allies had tried to carve out such a difficult route to the Chickasaws. They "have an infinite scorn for the French," reported one officer. Even as late as 1750, the expeditions of 1736 and 1740 were inspiring "such a great scorn for our inability to subdue the savages that they all boast of it." "I see it every day," wrote Governor Vaudreuil, "which pains and embarrasses me."

Considering these French military fiascos, it is hard to imagine how southern Indians could have been put at risk by a proxy war mounted by France and Britain. Indeed, the self-aggrandizing pronouncements of colonial officials must be read with skepticism. "At present, I am . . . the master of reestablishing the tranquility and peace of the colony," Bienville claimed in 1733, insisting that the Chickasaws were desperate to settle at all costs. Seven years later, after his embarrassing 1740 defeat, Bienville announced another truce with the Chickasaws. This time, however, even his inferiors reported (with some exaggeration) that the peace was a sham, agreed to by a single elderly Chickasaw and obeyed by no one. To sustain the pretense, Bienville ordered his officers to refrain from reporting on Indian affairs. It would be wrong to believe that Indians were merely victims in the French–English proxy war. But if they did not passively participate in their own destruction, as historians used to maintain, neither did they preserve "indomitable tribal independence in the face of relentless European intervention," as scholars more commonly assert today. Like the chaotic and dangerous worlds created by twentieth-century imperial rivalries in Angola, Afghanistan, and elsewhere, the French and British competition for the lower South destabilized the region and created a situation dominated by no one.

The impact of French interference in Choctaw affairs can be seen in three related arenas: the enrichment of Choctaw leaders through French presents, the introduction of firearms, and the creation of a scalp market. Although French trade with the Choctaws remained minimal, the governor of Louisiana annually awarded Choctaw leaders thousands of livres worth of cloth, guns, knives, and other items. The French were "masterly" at managing Indian affairs by the "great quantities of valuable goods they gave them with," observed one English competitor. In the early 1740s, these items averaged about 20,000 livres, rising to twice that amount by mid-decade. The goods were distributed to a little over 100 Choctaw leaders in the 1730s. Even if, in response to Choctaw demands, that number rose to 200 by the 1740s, it meant that each leader received 200 livres worth of commodities, the equivalent market value of fifty-four deerskins. By the measure of the Louisiana governor, who made 12,000 livres per year, this sum was not extraordinary, but for a common soldier, who made fifty-four livres, it was significant. More important, for Indians, the market value of fifty-four deerskins represented the profits of two years of hunting.

"The savages . . . learned from us to have true needs [*de vrais besoins*]," remarked Périer in 1731. Indians, he therefore concluded, could be manipulated with a plentiful supply of textiles and firearms. The truth was more complicated. "They are insolent," wrote one of Périer's fellow officers, "and one can say that they demand as tribute what we call presents." Whether textiles and guns were gift or tribute, the French distributed them to Choctaws inclined to kill Chickasaws and withheld them from those who were not. As a consequence, Choctaws always had to keep in mind the costs of opposing the French. When Alibamon Mingo agreed to the establishment of an English trading post in his town, he quickly realized that the disadvantages outweighed the benefits. "It turned me against the French leaders, who, to punish me," he explained, "deprived me for two years of the presents I was accustomed to receiving." This "disgrace," he continued, "made me lose all credit in the nation." Presents, concluded Governor Vaudreuil, "are indisputably the strongest ties that keep the Choctaws in our interest and the principal motive behind their actions."

Vaudreuil's dismissive assertion that the Choctaws were driven mainly by the desire for European goods flatly ignores the many other factors that influenced them: friendship; strategic considerations toward France, Britain, and Spain and toward other Indian nations; political competition within the Choctaw nation; and religious convictions. The French could not control the Choctaws merely by distributing textiles and firearms, but neither could the Choctaws control the effect of this new source of wealth flowing into their nation. The French first tried to channel goods through the great chief, an office created by them to facilitate the political manipulation of the Choctaw Nation. The great chief in turn redistributed the merchandise to the principal chiefs, who, according to French plans, were supposed to become beholden to their leader. Unfamiliar with such hierarchy, however, the principal chiefs successfully pressured the French to distribute goods more broadly.

The goods did not sow disorder because Choctaws abandoned their beliefs for the pursuit of wealth, as the French imagined. Rather, the stream of wealth traveled down traditional lines of distribution in such great quantities that the number of influential leaders multiplied without precedent. Customarily, Choctaw leaders redistributed goods to their extended families, sustaining a network of people who were beholden to them. With the practice of French gift giving, Bienville explained, "each of these chiefs, by means of the presents that he receives and that he knows how to distribute appropriately, forms a party that he employs independently of the great chief, who is now so only in name." The new sources of wealth in Louisiana and Carolina strengthened and enlarged these parties and introduced a heated competition between leaders for recognition from colonial authorities, as Red Shoes revealed. "I will be as faithful to the English as you want to be to the French," he challenged Alibamon Mingo, "and we will see whether my warriors or yours will return more satisfied with the presents they receive."

The presents also introduced another element of disorder into the nation. Common warriors watched the growing wealth and power of the principal chiefs with envy. Hoping to become chiefs themselves one day, they explained, they did not object to the gift-giving practices of the French. Nevertheless, "their needs were not any less great" than those of the chiefs, nor did they lack "a sound ambition [*une honnete ambition*]," both unfulfilled by French presents. "It was not surprising," the Choctaws therefore explained, "that they sought their advantage elsewhere," that is, in South Carolina. This dynamic was evidently at work in 1738 when Red Shoes convinced a large number of warriors to welcome the English into the nation. They did so, Alibamon Mingo explained, because "all of the warriors were very discontent after returning last winter from Mobile, where the presents were delivered to the chiefs, who shared them among themselves and their relatives." The result of French gift giving was a more turbulent Choctaw Nation that experienced social upheavals controlled by neither the French nor the Choctaws themselves.

Among the gifts distributed by the French were muskets, which led to an increase in violence in the lower South. Historians have questioned the prevalence of guns in the Choctaw Nation before the American Revolution. There have been virtually no archaeological excavations in the old Choctaw Nation to settle this question, but there is enough documentary evidence to suggest that firearms were more widespread in Choctaw communities than previously thought. The French clearly believed that their Indian allies were dependent on them for munitions, especially powder and lead, which were prohibitively difficult for the English to transport on horseback from South Carolina. Governor Vaudreuil even suspected that the Choctaws would abandon Louisiana entirely if it were not for their dependence on French ammunition and French alcohol. In fact, English-allied Indians occasionally found themselves without any ammunition, as one Choctaw warned they would in 1746. "They will completely lack munitions," he reportedly said, "unless they want to load their muskets with Limbourg [a textile] and other merchandise." He was proven right two years later when Red Shoes's English-allied followers desperately substituted pieces of hardwood knot and fire-dried oak for lead balls.

The importance and prevalence of firearms are best attested to not by the French but by the Choctaws themselves. In 1732, during a speech encouraging his men to go to war, the Choctaw great chief urged that "they had only to prepare their muskets and their war clubs to go take scalps." His reference suggests that guns already occupied a central place in Choctaw military campaigns. Indeed, Choctaws painted a bleak picture when they imagined what life would be like without firearms. In 1734, one Choctaw recalled when the British first began arming the Chickasaws, asserting, "Without M. de Bienville, our father who gave us muskets and munitions, we would no longer exist." At least one Choctaw considered the possibility of abandoning the French and "taking up the bow and arrow again," but others thought the prospect ruinous. The bow and arrow are a "pitiful resource for those who have a family to feed and support," said one Choctaw in 1748, "all the more because we have completely lost the ability to use them." Another, making the same point more forcefully, showed up with a bow and arrow at a debate about French alliance. He had just tried "his old weapons," he told this audience, but "he could no longer use them, having lost the ability." The Choctaws would be "miserable," he concluded, if the French abandoned them.

The Choctaw reliance on firearms, hastened by the violence unleashed by the French–English proxy war and encouraged by the French policy of supplying their Indian[s] with muskets, had two consequences. First, the Choctaws became dependent on a steady supply of weapons, severely limiting their ability to respond to the French and British invasion of their nation. Second, the violence in the Southeast became bloodier and deadlier. Musket balls pierced leather clothing, tore flesh, broke bones, and, if the victim survived, left irregular gashes that were more likely than arrow wounds to host fatal infections. The result was a Chickasaw population that, under sustained attack by French-armed Choctaws, plummeted by 50 percent between 1730 and 1760.

It is undeniable that the French–English proxy war made the Choctaw and Chickasaw nations more dangerous places to live. Periodically, to drive a wedge between their Indian allies and enemies, the French sponsored and hosted the burning alive of Chickasaw prisoners. One such fire occurred in October 1731 in New Orleans when Governor Périer sent three Chickasaw men to the flames despite pleas of clemency from Périer's Indian allies. "It will serve to enflame even more the war between the Choctaws and Chickasaws," he calculated. On another occasion, Périer reported that the Choctaws had burned to death twelve Chickasaws on the field of battle. He noted with satisfaction that "the war is more bitter than ever between these two nations" and suggested that the French should encourage "the Choctaws' fervor."

The role of the French in this upsurge in violence is visible in the transformation of scalping in the eighteenth century. Although likely an ancient practice among the Choctaws, scalping became both more frequent and commercially motivated as a result of the French–English proxy war. As early as 1708, the governor of Louisiana was encouraging Choctaws to bring him the scalps of English-allied Indians, and some time before 1721, the colony adopted an official policy of paying the Choctaws a gun, a pound of powder, and two pounds of bullets for each Chickasaw scalp in order to "encourage better the nation of the Choctaws to carry on vigorously the war against the Chickasaws." This bounty produced 400 scalps in a single winter, Bienville reported in 1723. When Choctaw ardor faded, French messengers appeared in the Choctaw Nation to reconfirm that Chickasaw scalps had a price, and when French governors wished to show special gratitude for a lock of enemy hair, they paid more "handsomely" than usual. No wonder Choctaws concluded that scalps were the "best gift" they could give the French governor. They would search out the Chickasaws "so as not to appear before him empty-handed," they announced to Bienville in 1736. The results of the French bounty on scalps are impressive: French governors collected at least 1,000 scalps in the twenty-year period beginning in 1732, averaging about fifty per year, and they likely received many more not accounted for in the official records. It is not clear what the French did with their gruesome purchases.

Before the arrival of the French, it is unlikely that there was an Indian market for scalps, for the practice of scalping seems to have been linked to rites of passage rather than to commerce. One eighteenth-century visitor recalled that among the neighboring Creeks, boys took their first scalps to establish their manhood. "When a young warrior brings back a scalp, for the first time," Louis Milfort explained, "the chiefs of the place where he lives assemble in the grand cabin to give him a name, and to take from him that of his mother." Later in life, men took scalps to establish their bravery and to rise in the estimation of their families and communities. James Adair noted an additional purpose for these "joyful trophies of a decisive victory." Mounted atop the houses of deceased family members, scalps marked the avenging of dead relatives and enabled their spirits to go to a place of rest. Although these uses persisted to the end of the eighteenth century, by the 1730s scalps had also become commodities. Responding to market incentive (albeit deceitfully), Choctaws adopted the practice of cutting enemy scalps into several pieces so as to receive more than one payment for a single scalp. "We paid them the price of ten scalps for a single enemy," Bienville complained. For a brief period, French officers closely inspected their grisly purchases, paying for pieces in proportion to the whole, but this cost-saving measure soon had to be abandoned when Choctaws objected to such market regulation.

The Chickasaws highlighted the disturbing logic of assigning a market value to a human scalp. One warrior asked, "What do the French claim to be doing? What use are our scalps to them to pay for them? . . . Do they find treasure in our scalps?" He knew the answer but wished to draw out the link between money and violence in the South. Another warrior looked forward to the time when the Choctaws would "tire of selling our scalps." But the Choctaws, the beneficiaries of this new market, said they would continue selling scalps until the French ceased paying for them. By mid-century, Indians far and wide associated the French with scalping. One Cherokee said he had "little Knowledge" of the French but heard that they raised a "constant Cry": "go kill and destroy, bring us plenty of Hair, plenty of Scalps."

Divided between the French and the English, the Choctaws fought a deadly civil war between 1748 and 1750. Governor Vaudreuil boasted that, because he was short of troops, he "made use of the eastern Choctaws" to destroy the English-allied Choctaws. The violence was extraordinary. French allies shot and eviscerated the captain of Boukfouka, stomping his intestines into the ground before pursuing and killing eighty of his followers. They exterminated Red Shoes's family, including his children, and they destroyed several towns entirely. Vaudreuil estimated that more than 800 English-allied warriors died in the conflict, or almost one out of every four Choctaw men. "I engaged them as much as I could to make war against their rebellious brothers . . . ," Vaudreuil boasted, "persuaded that while [the English] see a civil war among the Choctaws, they would not risk going there in significant numbers or with lots of merchandise." Purchasing hundreds of scalps and supplying firearms was costly, he admitted, but well worth the price.

By virtue of their numbers, political skill, and military acumen, Indians remained a significant presence in the lower South through the American Revolution. Nevertheless, describing the region as a borderland elides the destructive interference of France and Britain in the affairs of native nations. The analogy to twentieth-century proxy warfare captures the deadly influence of imperial powers as well as the chaotic and uncontrollable world that resulted. Regional conflicts and local communities in the lower South became part of a much larger hemispheric war between France and Britain. Although the number of French colonists in the region remained minimal, French officers, calling down Indian allies from the Great Lakes and ordering guns and munitions from across the Atlantic, drew on imperial networks that extended for thousands of miles. Choctaw warriors who carried muskets forged in France in place of their own hand-carved bows and arrows did not become the obedient foot soldiers of the French king. But neither did they remain immune from the rapid, unpredictable, and uncontrollable social transformations that were set off by the arrival of the French and English. As in Angola and Afghanistan in the twentieth century, the scale of geography in the lower South changed suddenly. Community rivalries, local economies, and regional conflicts all became international, immersed in networks of trade and warfare that encompassed millions of people and drew on vast amounts of capital. As the scale grew, so too did the order of violence. In the Atlantic World, it was sometimes a misfortune to have your homeland deemed a borderland.

# The Atlantic Slave Trade: Racism or Profit?

Tracing the slave trade has been one of historians' most difficult tasks for two kinds of reasons: political and methodological. Questions about slavery and the corresponding guilt of a slaveholding society are uniquely difficult to approach evenhandedly. Current concerns about race, poverty, and related issues influence historians' accounts of the slave trade, the origins of slavery, and slavery's economic contribution to the development of capitalism in the West. These accounts can fuel contemporary political arguments in ways the historians may not have anticipated or desired.

Why did Europeans enslave Africans? Did Europeans think blacks inferior and therefore deserved slavery? Or was it a purely economic decision? Did the profits from the slave trade create the capital that financed the industrial revolution in England, or was the trade marginal to the growth of the English economy? Did Africans profit in the trade, or were they simply victims of Europeans' exploitation? How many Africans were actually taken? How many did not survive the Middle Passage? From which ethnic groups did they come? Where did they end up? How did this affect their history in the New World? Was the trade abolished out of altruism or self-interest? These are just a few of the questions historians have asked in looking at the slave trade.

Further complicating the historian's task is the sheer difficulty of locating data about a multinational trade that lasted from the 1440s to the 1860s. It had a substantial illegal and therefore unrecorded component and included eight European nations or principalities, the North American colonies, a wide variety of African nations, the islands of the Caribbean, and Central and South America. Many questions could not even be posed, much less answered, until scholars began, in the early twentieth century, the painstaking process of building an empirical database about the capture and sale of Africans. The focus of the study has moved from England, the Caribbean islands, and the American colonies, usually under the rubric of mercantilism or the "triangular trade," and has gradually widened until it encompasses the economic, social, and political development of western Europe, the Caribbean, all the Americas, and Africa — the entire Atlantic World.

The study of the slave trade inaugurated discussion of an Atlantic World, that is, a region joined by commerce and by cultural interchange rather than defined more traditionally and rigidly by political and ethnic boundaries. Historians of the slave trade and its consequences brought the concept of the Atlantic World into being. As Alison Games wrote in 2006, "No other field has been so aggressively engaged for so many decades in pursuing an Atlantic vision and in framing the field as a whole."[1] Historians of empire and of colonialism have immeasurably broadened the field to treat multinational commerce, politics, and military conflicts. Ironically, however, in recent times they have often failed to integrate Africa and Africans as significant players in these events.[2] Focusing on what is sometimes called the Black Atlantic, this essay centers on the core of concerns that originally called forth the idea of the Atlantic World.

The earliest historians of the slave traffic were British abolitionists like Thomas Clarkson, who wrote in the decades around the American Revolution, at the height of the trade, when seventy-five thousand slaves were arriving in the New World every year. Because of their political aims, these writers tended to emphasize the tortures of the Middle Passage from Africa to the New World, exaggerating its already horrific conditions and leaving myths that subsequent historians have had to correct.[3] Up until the Civil War, American writers discussed the trade either to justify slavery as the rescue and redemption in Christianity of "heathen" Africans or to prove its immorality. In the decades after the Civil War, the topic rested while southern and northern whites made peace with one another, agreeing to shelve Reconstruction efforts to guarantee former slaves their rights as citizens.

The first professional American historian to delve into the international slave trade was W. E. B. Du Bois. Du Bois, who graduated from Fisk and got his doctorate from Harvard, explored the economics of slavery, countering the self-congratulatory histories that ascribed the regulation of the slave trade to ethical principles. In 1892, Du Bois read a paper on the North American slave trade to the American Historical Association. His account, drawn from British documents, looked for the motives behind the Anglo-American efforts to restrict the trade. He concluded that American attempts to regulate the slave trade before the Revolution derived from fear of the potentially rebellious slave population, not from moral qualms. Indeed, after the Revolution, South Carolina, which had lost about twenty-five thousand slaves during the conflict, began purchasing slaves with renewed enthusiasm.

Du Bois laid out many of the terms of debate for subsequent historians of slavery and reflected the Progressive thinking of his day. "Here was a rich new land, the wealth of which was to be had in return for ordinary manual labor. Had the country been conceived of as existing primarily for the benefit of its actual inhabitants, it might have waited for natural increase or immigration to supply the needed hands. Both Europe and the earlier colonists themselves regarded this land as existing chiefly for the benefit of

---

[1]Alison Games, "Atlantic History: Definitions, Challenges, and Opportunities," *American Historical Review* ( June 2006): 741–57, 743; see also Jorge Cañizares-Esguerra, "Entangled Histories: Borderland Historiographies in New Clothes?" *American Historical Review* 112 ( June 2007): 794, ftn. 19.

[2]Robin Law and Kristin Mann, "West Africa in the Atlantic Community: The Case of the Slave Coast," *William and Mary Quarterly*, 3rd Ser., 56 (April 1999): 308.

[3]Herbert Klein, *The Atlantic Slave Trade* (New York, 1999), xviii.

Europe, and designed to be exploited, as rapidly and ruthlessly as possible, of the boundless wealth of its resources. This was the primary excuse for the rise of the African slave-trade to America."[4]

The next historian to explore the trade was the son of a plantation owner, Ulrich B. Phillips, who like Du Bois was interested in the economics of the trade and of slavery itself, but whose underlying ethical ideas about race and slavery were decisively different.[5] Phillips, surveying contemporary race relations, found them fundamentally good despite some momentary "asperities." They were good because they duplicated the harmonious relations of the plantation, where white planters tactfully and affectionately managed their happy-go-lucky slaves, who manifested unthinking loyalty to whatever white man took charge. This was a remarkable finding shortly after a period marked by white disenfranchisement of blacks, the imposition of Jim Crow, and persistent lynchings, including the murder of black soldiers returning from service in World War I.[6]

Phillips, like Du Bois, thought the slave trade built up England's economic power, which was particularly visible in trading cities like Liverpool and Bristol. He also noted that the trade profited other European countries and "Yankees." He differed from Du Bois most starkly in arguing that slave owners themselves suffered from the system. The trade "immensely stimulated the production of the staple crops. On the other hand it kept the planters constantly in debt for their dearly bought labor, and it left a permanent and increasingly complex problem of racial adjustments."[7] In other words, planters (unlike slave traders) were not acting as economically rational men. Like Du Bois, Phillips compared the miseries of slaves with those of poor European immigrants, but unlike Du Bois, he asserted that poor Irish suffered more from the transatlantic journey. He quoted the South Carolinian slave owner Henry Laurens who protested that it made no economic sense for traders to mistreat slaves, since they had an investment in their well-being.[8]

Phillips saw northern abolitionism as hypocritical and derived from the North's particular economic conditions. In the South, he argued, one could not treat slavery as a theory; it was an overwhelming fact. "The negroes of the rice coast were so outnumbering and so crude," Phillips wrote, "that an agitation applying the doctrine of inherent liberty and equality to them could only have had the effect of discrediting the doctrine itself."[9]

Phillips's racial attitudes reflected those of many white people of the period. His contempt for Africa encouraged him to see Africans as both the instigators of the slave trade and so incompetent that they gained little or nothing by it and destabilized their continent at the same time. "In the

---

[4]W. E. B. Du Bois, *The Suppression of the African Slave-Trade* (Baton Rouge, La., 1896, 1969), 194.

[5]Ulrich Bonnell Phillips, *American Negro Slavery: A Survey of the Supply, Employment and Control of Negro Labor as Determined by the Plantation Regime* (New York, 1918), viii–ix.

[6]For a good collection of essays on Phillips, see John David Smith and John C. Inscoe, eds., *Ulrich Bonnell Phillips: A Southern Historian and His Critics* (Athens, Ga., 1993).

[7]Phillips, *Slavery*, 44–45.

[8]Ibid., 36.

[9]Ibid., 125.

irony of fate those Africans who lent their hands to the looting got nothing but deceptive rewards, while the victims of rapine were quite possibly better off on the American plantations than the captors who remained in the African jungle."[10] Like Du Bois, he argued that Africans were enslaved because they were available when colonists needed labor, not because of racial prejudice. Slavery, however, did not cause whites to see blacks as inferior — for Phillips, they simply were inferior. In fact, in Phillips's view, slavery gave blacks' lives, which would otherwise have been chaotic and hence full of fear and misery, the gifts of order and security.

Du Bois and Phillips, like other historians in this period studying the colonial economy, looked at slavery as an aspect of the mercantile system that ordered economic relations between England and her colonies. Through mercantilism, England attempted to insure that the raw riches of its colonies would benefit exclusively the mother country. England insisted on the extraction and importation of colonial resources, which it used in manufacturing products, many of which were then exported to the colonies. It forbade the American colonies to trade with any country except England. In studying mercantilism, however, most historians touched only lightly on the slave trade. They usually ignored American participation and profits from the trade, locating it under the rubric "The Triangular Trade," whereby English traders took American rum to Africa in exchange for slaves, brought them back to the Caribbean for molasses, which they brought to the American colonies where it was made into rum. Most historians left aside the larger geopolitical concerns of Europe and Africa in this period, as well as the effects on the world economy of the exploitation of African labor and the resources of Caribbean islands and South and Central America. The main question the study of mercantilism raised for Americans was whether it benefited the colonies or stunted their economic development.

Nationalist historians like George Bancroft argued that the mercantile system kept the colonies' manufacturing capacities primitive and contributed to the grievances bringing on the Revolution. Later historians in the early and mid-twentieth century argued instead that mercantilism benefited the New World[11] and that colonies easily smuggled goods to countries that were officially prohibited as trading partners, particularly French- and Dutch-owned islands in the Caribbean. In either view, slavery was mostly incidental to the functioning of the society and the economic system. In Du Bois's reckoning, on the other hand, slavery crucially and prodigiously benefited both the colonies and the mother country. Although Phillips insisted that the slave trade profited England and the North more than the South, he nevertheless believed that conditions in the Deep South warranted a slave system to execute the backbreaking work of converting swampy acreage into producing plantations.

---

[10]Ibid., 44–45.

[11]Lawrence Gipson, *The British Empire before the American Revolution*, 15 vols. (Caldwell, Idaho, 1936–1970).

The study of slavery as a key to the economic connections among and growth of all the early modern nation-states picked up after the First World War. The imperialism of its combatants and its deathly consequences impelled a few historians to look more closely into the slave trade. Most notably, Elizabeth Donnan's massive *Documents Illustrative of the History of the Slave Trade to America*, published in the early years of the Great Depression, and the works of anthropologist Melville Herskovitz, initiated the study of the links between African cultures and the culture of American slaves. At approximately the same time, the French scholars Père Rinchon and Gaston Martin began gathering together archival evidence in France and Great Britain of the great demographic changes that the trade caused.[12]

In 1944, Eric Williams, a Trinidadian scholar and statesman, published *Capitalism and Slavery*, which enlarged on the themes Du Bois had first outlined, placing slavery in the context of worldwide — not simply triangular — economic forces. Williams had studied under Sir Reginald Coupland at Oxford, who wrote admiringly about the moral mission of English colonialism and lauded abolitionism as Great Britain's most dazzling display of its national virtue.[13] At the time Williams wrote *Capitalism and Slavery*, however, the West Indies were fighting against English imperialism. It was in part to bolster West Indian demands for self-government that Williams argued, even more explicitly than Du Bois had, that race had nothing to do with the enslavement of Africans; it was about British self-interest. Williams ridiculed British claims that a civilizing mission inspired their bringing Africans from Africa. Profits from slavery were always at the core of the trade.[14]

In a daring move, Williams argued that slavery had provided the capital for England's industrial revolution. He artfully evoked the growing prosperity of the slave-trading centers of Liverpool and Bristol. While some subsequent historians would disagree that the capital accumulated from the slave trade directly financed the industrial revolution, virtually all scholars acknowledge that Williams had opened up the study of the slave trade and provided questions for decades to come. Indeed in 1987, more than forty years after the publication of *Capitalism and Slavery*, scholars held a conference to debate once again the issues Williams raised. And in recent years, scholars blessed with extraordinary new sources on the trade continue to work with the issues Williams laid out.[15]

For many years, historians struggled over the issue of why Europeans chose Africans to enslave. Linked to that was the question of how profitable the trade was. In recent years, almost all historians have agreed with Williams

---

[12]For examples of some of these works, see Elizabeth Donnan, *Documents Illustrative of the History of the Slave Trade to America* (New York, 1965); Melville J. Herskovitz, *Acculturation: The Study of Cultural Contact* (Gloucester, Mass., 1953); Père Dieudonné Rinchon, *Pierre-Ignace-Lieven van Alstein, Capitaine Negrier, Gand 1733–Nantes 1793* (Dakar, 1964); Gaston Martin, *Abolition de L'esclavage (27 avril 1848)* (Paris, 1948).

[13]Sir Reginald Coupland, *The British Anti-Slavery Movement* (London, 1933).

[14]Eric Williams, *Capitalism and Slavery* (Chapel Hill, N.C., 1944).

[15]"New Perspectives on the Transatlantic Slave Trade," *William and Mary Quarterly*, 3rd Ser., 58 ( January 2001).

that, for a variety of reasons, Europeans chose Africans for convenience and profit, not because of their color. Racism did not precede slavery, but grew and flowered along with it as it was practiced in the Americas. Eric Williams saw nothing inherently preordained in the selection of Africans as slaves. As others would after him, he looked at the failed efforts to enslave Native Americans and at the system of indenture, which supplied limited labor needs but could not provide for the huge plantations that grew sugar in the Caribbean and rice and cotton in the American colonies. Williams stated bluntly, "Slavery was not born of racism; rather racism was the consequence of slavery. Unfree labor in the New World was brown, white, black, and yellow; Catholic, Protestant and pagan."[16] The determinants in singling out Africans were price, quality, and manageability. Indentured servants could escape and blend into the white populace, find their own land, and farm. Furthermore, they were expensive. Africans — slaves for life — cost the same as ten years' labor from indentured servants, were good workers, and could not escape easily or disappear once free. They were easy to distinguish in regions where black skin increasingly signified slave status.

In support of Williams's preponderant emphasis on the business of slavery and in sympathy with the post–World War II civil rights movement, American scholars, including Oscar and Mary Handlin and Kenneth Stampp, insisted that racism derived from slavery and that it was an acquired prejudice that grew with the material degradation of Africans in America.[17] Other scholars, however, were not satisfied with the material explanation for slavery. They explored the idea that racial prejudice made Europeans think that enslaving black people in perpetuity was their proper destiny. The study of racial ideology has produced a wealth of knowledge on the etiology of racism and its employment in service of political and economic goals.

In 1959, Carl Degler challenged Williams's view that the economics of slavery led to racism, asserting that whites believed themselves superior to blacks from the moment they arrived on this continent. The problem of racism, he claimed, was deeper and more complicated than Williams or his followers had recognized. Because Degler and his adversaries all argued from the same small collection of Chesapeake documents, however, the argument seemed to be going nowhere until Winthrop Jordan published *White over Black* in 1968. In this learned study of European attitudes toward blackness, Jordan demonstrated that racial prejudice preceded African slavery. Jordan argued that once enslaved, Negroes became more and more degraded in the eyes of whites, but the initial enslavement, he thought, had more to do with English racial attitudes than with simple greed.[18]

---

[16]Williams, *Slavery*, 7.

[17]Kenneth Stampp, *The Peculiar Institution: Slavery in the Antebellum South* (New York, 1956); Oscar and Mary Handlin, "Origins of the Southern Labor System," *William and Mary Quarterly*, 3rd Ser., VII (1950): 210–11.

[18]Carl Degler, "Slavery and the Generation of American Race Prejudice," *Comparative Studies in Society and History* II (1959–1960): 48–66; Stampp, *Peculiar Institution*; Winthrop Jordan, *White over Black: American Attitudes toward the Negro, 1550–1812* (Chapel Hill, N.C., 1968).

Almost simultaneously, Philip Curtin published *The Atlantic Slave Trade: A Census*, a work that widened yet again the horizon on which historians would consider the origin and development of slavery.[19] His study also provided the framework for conceiving of an Atlantic World as a historical unit of study in which scholars now locate early modern history populated by a widely diverse group of trading and military powers — sometimes allies and sometimes competitors in exploiting the riches of the New World. Curtin, while not specifically addressing the racism-or-slavery-first debate, heavily emphasized the economics of slavery. Curtin pointed out that the slave trade was an ancient, improvised, ad hoc affair that changed and adapted to circumstances and therefore required careful empirical study. He also noted that traditional national histories had always treated the slave trade as peripheral to "their social and political development," whereas, like Williams, Curtin saw the slave trade as having central significance.

Curtin posed — and at least tentatively answered — a number of absolutely basic questions about the trade. From which parts of Africa did slaves come? How many were taken? When? To what destinations were they carried? Consulting all the available published sources from the mid-1400s to the 1860s, Curtin estimated the total number of slaves transported at somewhere between 9.5 and 11 million Africans. Among other themes, Curtin touched on changing African demography, European economic interests, mortality in crossing the Atlantic, and the ethnic variations among slaves imported into America. Curtin's figures and his methods of arriving at them laid the foundation for a host of new studies corroborating and challenging his findings. The debate over these numbers was intense and bitter, showing how politically charged even the most "objective" data can appear. Historians could interpret low mortality numbers, for example, as an effort to minimize the brutality of the trade. Conversely, high transportation figures might seem to others to exaggerate the scope of the trade and its effect on Africa.[20]

Following on Curtin in 1972, Richard Dunn published a book that would take a while to catch the attention of American historians, but that exerted a strong influence on them once it did. *Sugar and Slaves*, a discussion of the British experience in the West Indies, expanded the horizons of American historians beyond the Chesapeake to antecedents in the English Caribbean and introduced the consumption of sugar into play as a serious issue. African slavery was established firmly in Barbados in the 1640s when planters replaced tobacco with sugar production and consolidated their small farms into large ones. "Sugar did have a truly revolutionary impact upon the European pattern of colonization in the Indies," he found. "All of the English and French islands inexorably followed the Barbadian example, changing from European peasant societies into slave-based plantation colonies."[21] Dunn's careful

---

[19]Philip Curtin, *The Atlantic Slave Trade: A Census* (New York, 1969).

[20]For challenges to Curtin, see Joseph Inikori and Stanley Engerman, eds., *The Atlantic Slave Trade: Effects on Economies, Societies, and Peoples in Africa, the Americas, and Europe* (Durham, N.C., 1992).

[21]Richard Dunn, *Sugar and Slaves: The Rise of the Planter Class in the English West Indies, 1624–1713* (New York, 1972), 20.

depiction of the rise of plantation agriculture in the West Indies invited American historians to include the Caribbean experience in studying American slavery.

Dunn's work was also a reminder of how dependent North American economic growth was on supplying the slave islands of the Caribbean. Most of the colonists' trade was with the West Indies. It was vital because the West Indians used every inch of land to grow sugar and imported all their cattle, a variety of vegetables, corn, wood for barrels and building, and other staples from the mainland colonies.

Dunn also offered a view of the origins of slavery that emphasized the unique New World environment. In *Sugar and Slaves,* Dunn depicted living "beyond the line," a contemporary phrase for a lawlessness that Europeans adopted living in what Dunn described as the far West of sixteenth- and seventeenth-century European civilization. "The . . . record plainly showed that Spaniards, Englishmen, Frenchmen, and Dutchmen who sojourned in the tropics . . . exploited their Indian and black slaves more shamelessly than was possible with the underprivileged laboring class in Western Europe."[22]

The influence of Dunn's work extended as far as Puritan studies. Karen Ordahl Kupperman traced the Puritans' settlement of Providence Island in the Caribbean and their effort to run a successful plantation. Her work shows that the Puritans' vaunted aversion to slavery seems to have been environmentally, rather than morally, determined.[23]

The conjunction of Curtin's work with Dunn's and innovative comparative studies, such as those collected in Herbert Klein's *The Middle Passage: Comparative Studies in the Atlantic Slave Trade,*[24] confirmed that the origins and economics of slavery would be studied in a broader and broader context. Klein's contributors studied the French slave trade with the Portuguese in Angola and Brazil and the English in Virginia and Jamaica. Similar collections looked at the Dutch and Spanish as well, and Hugh Thomas's massive 1997 volume *The Slave Trade* implicated the Danes, the Genoese, and the Germans in the trade, leaving little of the European world untouched by the legacy. Nor was it just the European world: in a 1990 work, Curtin pointed out that the Portuguese, the earliest Europeans to trade in African slaves, were originally looking for gold when they discovered an already established trade in slaves in West Africa. They began establishing sugar plantations on Madeira and then São Tomé in the Gulf of Guinea that would become models for later European plantations farther west. Luck, economic opportunism, and a tendency to follow preestablished patterns — not racism — were, in this view, important factors in determining the outlines of the slave trade and slavery.[25]

---

[22]Ibid., 12.

[23]Karen Ordahl Kupperman, "Errand to the Indies: Puritan Colonization from Providence Island through the Western Design," *William and Mary Quarterly,* 3rd Ser., 45 (1988): 70–99; see also Alison Games, *Migration and the Origins of the English Atlantic World* (Cambridge, Mass., 1999), for a recent study of the Providence Island experience in a broader context.

[24]Herbert Klein, *The Middle Passage: Comparative Studies in the Atlantic Slave Trade* (Princeton, N.J., 1978).

[25]Hugh Thomas, *The Slave Trade: The Story of the Atlantic Slave Trade: 1440–1870* (New York, 1997); Philip D. Curtin, *The Rise and Fall of the Plantation Complex* (New York, 1990), 24, 43.

In the 1970s and 1980s, most agreed that Williams overstated the theory that the profits from slavery accounted for England's early industrial revolution. They said that the colonial trade just was not very important and "did little to stimulate the economy as a whole. . . . The data suggest that 'the periphery was peripheral.'" What was important, economists averred, was the home market.[26] This view largely dominated until the 1990s, when the challenges began.

According to a collection edited by Barbara Solow in 1991, foreign trade had much to do with Europe and particularly England's economic development.[27] This collection of essays distinguished two, rather than one, Atlantic systems of commerce. The first, presided over by Spain and Portugal, acquired wealth for those countries but was not able to create "an expanding type of plantation economy" that characterized the second Atlantic system. This second system was responsible for the breakthrough into "the new era of international capitalism." It remained for the English, Dutch, and colonial American entrepreneurs to invent a new, ruthless world in which the market dominated all other considerations. And slavery created the wealth in products that contributed to making this happen. "It was black labour that grew the commodities that entered international trade. Sugar alone provided 60% of British America's exports to Britain before the Revolution. The exports of the British colonies in the West Indies and the American South were overwhelmingly slave produced; 78% of New England's exports and 42% of those of the Middle Colonies went to supply the slave plantations of the British West Indies before the Revolution." As Barbara Solow concluded, "It was the coerced labor of African slaves that allowed Europe to benefit so greatly from its conquests in the New World."[28] Slave labor and the extraordinary profits it produced demonstrated the desirability of pouring more and more of society's resources into the international trade.

The historian and economist Robin Blackburn found that the slave trade and New World slavery significantly helped to maintain the English economy steady even in wartime and sometimes powerfully boosted it during its years of remarkable development. He rejected Williams's claim that slavery funded the industrial revolution, but he argued the more limited case that "exchanges with the slave plantations helped British capitalism to make a break through to industrialism and global hegemony ahead of its rivals."[29]

In 2002, the economic historian Joseph Inikori published his findings in the meticulously researched and argued *Africans and the Industrial Revolution*

---

[26]John J. McCusker and Russell Menard, *The Economy of British America, 1607–1789* (Chapel Hill, N.C., 1985), 43; for an account of the historiography of this question, see Joseph Inikori, *Africans and the Industrial Revolution in England: A Study in International Trade and Economic Development* (Cambridge, 2002), 85–155.

[27]P. C. Emmer, "The Dutch and the Second Atlantic System," in Barbara Solow, ed., *Slavery and the Rise of the Atlantic System* (Cambridge, Mass., 1991), 77.

[28]Barbara Solow, "Slavery and Colonization," in Solow, *Slavery*, 20.

[29]Robin Blackburn, *The Making of New World Slavery: From the Baroque to the Modern, 1492–1800* (London, 1997).

*in England*, in which he refuted at length the thesis that foreign trade and slave labor were insignificant in England's industrial revolution. He argued that slave labor was of great importance, particularly to the completion of the process: "Increases in overseas sales accounted for more than half of the increments in British industrial output between 1700 and 1760." It was overseas trade that contributed in England to a rising population, rising wages, and a growing domestic market. The strengthening and growth of the home market produced a growing demand for slave-made commodities like sugar, coffee, and tobacco. These had been luxuries once, but their prices fell with production increases and the ruthless coercion of labor that was possible only on slave plantations "beyond the line." Inikori argued that "There can be little doubt, however, that ultimately the growth of Atlantic commerce was the central element which permitted the successful completion of the industrialization process in England. Similarly there can be little doubt that the labor of Africans and their descendants was what made possible the growth of Atlantic commerce during this period."[30]

In January 2001, the *William and Mary Quarterly* published a group of papers under the heading "New Perspectives on the Transatlantic Slave Trade" to mark the appearance of the Du Bois Institute slave trade dataset, available on a CD-ROM, that made available information about 27,233 Atlantic slave voyages, or about 70 percent of the total, transporting 11 million Africans, over 9 million of them to the Americas. This wealth of material produced articles on aspects of the slave trade that had previously been impossible to calculate. David Brion Davis, in a foreword to some of the first papers that derived from this rich new dataset, agreed with the general thrust of Inikori's economic findings that "It is now clear that the settlement and development of the New World were both economically and culturally dependent on the labor of millions of African slaves and their enslaved descendents."[31]

In his full-length study of the slave trade and the rise and decline of slavery, *Inhuman Bondage*, Davis went on to draw parallels between the early modern trade in Africans and contemporary global economic relations, remarking that the investors in both systems put money into distant colonial areas, finding places with extremely low labor costs in order to produce cheaply a product for a transatlantic market. "With respect to consumerism, it is now clear that slave-produced sugar, rum, coffee, tobacco and chocolate greatly altered the European diet . . . [and] these luxuries helped" create a consumer mentality among working people across England. Making the kind of connection that the concept of the Atlantic World facilitated, Davis also related the products of slavery and the coercion of slaves to the experience of wage laborers in England's industrial sector. Their acquisition of

---

[30]Inikori, *Africans and the Industrial Revolution*, 476–77, 481–83, 485–86.
[31]"New Perspectives on the Transatlantic Slave Trade," *William and Mary Quarterly*, 3rd Ser., 58 (January 2001); David Brion Davis and Robert P. Forbes "Foreword," 7–8.

cheap slave-produced goods, argued Davis, made them more pliant in adjusting to the new, unnatural, and exploitive system of industrial production.[32]

For decades, no one had questioned the "unqualified link between economic motivation and slavery" that Williams had posited. In 2000, David Eltis challenged this assumption and raised questions about slavery's profitability in *The Rise of African Slavery in America*, in which he argued that a culture of individualism and individual freedom among Northern Europeans kept them from enslaving other Europeans.[33] They chose Africans as sufficiently "other," although it would probably have been cheaper, in the long run, to enslave people close to or at home. They enslaved Africans not because of a racial prejudice, which, Eltis argued, emerged after slavery, but because slavery for Europeans had become "a fate worse than death" given the culture's devotion to individual rights.[34] Thus his primary argument placed culture above economics. Although Eltis believed that "market analysis nevertheless remains central to any understanding of the slave trade," he pointed to the sex ratio of slave cargoes as another aspect of the trade that was subject to cultural rather than strictly economic motives. The proportion of females to males was significantly higher among the coerced African migrants than among voluntary English ones, leading Eltis to conclude that the Africans forced the European traders to include more women slaves in their cargoes than they would have wished. In African societies, women had many more significant economic roles than did European women, who derived what status they had from their reproductive roles. African slave traders therefore considered women desirable slaves and, because they had power over the supply of slaves, were able to control to some degree the gender balance of the slave trade. Eltis asserted that this forced the English to change their thinking about gender and labor, at least the gender of Africans. They rapidly came to embrace the economic exploitation of enslaved women and put them into whip gangs doing agricultural work, for example. However, they refused to teach them skills as they did men, thus making another cultural decision, one that cost them economically.[35]

Eltis surveyed the evidence for the profitability of slavery, particularly the trade itself and the sugar industry, and found its impact on the English economy small and easily replaced by imagined alternative uses of resources. Given his findings and his contention that cheaper substitute forms of coerced labor were conceivable, he argued "the strongest and most interesting influence of race-based slavery in the Americas on Europe, as well as vice versa, may not have been economic at all, but rather ideological." The ideological outcome of race-based slavery and its abolition was the enduring association of the unique compatibility of free labor with capitalism, whereas in the early years of slavery both slave and free labor seemed equally

---

[32]David Brion Davis, *Inhuman Bondage: The Rise and Fall of Slavery in the New World* (New York, 2006), 878.
[33]David Eltis, *The Rise of African Slavery in the Americas* (New York, 2000), 58, 18, 23, 26, 29.
[34]Ibid., 71.
[35]Ibid., 99–101, 112, 113.

compatible with it. This was a strong legitimizing boost for capitalism, validating, as it did, the legal, if not material, equality between employer and employee.[36]

Seymour Drescher responded to Eltis in 2004 by arguing that the moral constraints on Europeans against enslaving one another did not prevent the atrocities of slave and death labor camps in World War II and had not been the primary cause for the enslavement of Africans in the early modern era either.[37] Although he praised Eltis for introducing noneconomic considerations into the debate over the slave trade and slavery, he contended that the transportation and security costs of enslaving other Europeans would have been economically prohibitive, not to mention the price in unending warfare among Europeans. Drescher concluded that Europeans made the most economically sound choices by supporting wage labor at home and coerced labor abroad. "Extending the zone of enslavement throughout Western Europe would, at a minimum, have raised transaction costs, disrupted law and order, reduced property rights in one's own person and created a reign of terror, at least for a significant minority, and perhaps for all of Western Europe's inhabitants."[38]

In 2005, Gwendolyn Midlo Hall took strong exception to Eltis's argument as "flattering to Europeans" by minimizing motives of exploitation and greed while elevating the idea of individual freedom. She also criticized Eltis for claiming that abolition came about because the late-eighteenth-century British decided to include Africans among the people who deserve self-ownership and individual rights. Instead, Hall insisted that resistance of enslaved people had caused the end of slavery.[39]

The challenging questions that Eric Williams posed over sixty years ago still form the core of vital questions about the origins and motives for the Atlantic slave trade. An excerpt from Williams's pathbreaking work is the first reading, followed by a selection from David Eltis's rejoinder. Williams's work, along with that of Philip Curtin, produced the Atlantic World framework that has encouraged a perspective on early modern Europe, Africa, and the Americas that has now grown well beyond its origins. Conceptualizing the Atlantic basin as an interconnected whole allows historians to study the mechanics and effects of this precursor to globalization and the first worldwide search for cheap labor. The origins of the slave trade, the kind and degree of cooperation between African traders and European traders, the role the slave trade played in the development of European capitalism, and the commensurate role it played in distorting African economies continue to engage scholars today and to require multinational study. These historical concerns further stimulated investigation into the reasons for the economic dominance

---

[36]Ibid., 265–75.
[37]Seymour Drescher, "White Atlantic? The Choice for African Slave Labor in the Plantation Americas," in *Slavery in the Development of the Americas* (Cambridge, 2004), 31–69.
[38]Ibid., 68.
[39]Gwendolyn Midlo Hall, *Slavery and African Ethnicities in the Americas: Restoring the Links* (Chapel Hill, N.C., 2005), 10.

of the West and for pervasive poverty in Africa. Like the study of slavery, the study of the slave trade and its implications and results is freighted with political and ethical significance; for scholars and students of these debates, the stakes could hardly be higher.

ERIC WILLIAMS

*from* Capitalism and Slavery　[1944]

ERIC WILLIAMS (1911–1981) was born in Trinidad and Tobago, where he did his undergraduate work. He received his doctorate in history from Oxford and taught at Howard University in the United States before returning to his country. He led Trinidad and Tobago to independence within the British Commonwealth in 1962 and served as both premier and prime minister. He began publishing in 1940 with "The Golden Age of the Slave System in Britain" and continued to write on education, politics, slavery, and the history of the Caribbean for the next four decades.

Slavery in the Caribbean has been too narrowly identified with the Negro. A racial twist has thereby been given to what is basically an economic phenomenon. Slavery was not born of racism: rather, racism was the consequence of slavery. Unfree labor in the New World was brown, white, black, and yellow; Catholic, Protestant and pagan.

The first instance of slave trading and slave labor developed in the New World involved, racially, not the Negro but the Indian. The Indians rapidly succumbed to the excessive labor demanded of them, the insufficient diet, the white man's diseases, and their inability to adjust themselves to the new way of life. Accustomed to a life of liberty, their constitution and temperament were ill-adapted to the rigors of plantation slavery. As Fernando Ortíz writes: "To subject the Indian to the mines, to their monotonous, insane and severe labor, without tribal sense, without religious ritual, . . . was like taking away from him the meaning of his life. . . . It was to enslave not only his muscles but also his collective spirit."

The visitor to Ciudad Trujillo, capital of the Dominican Republic (the present-day name of half of the island formerly called Hispaniola), will see a statue of Columbus, with the figure of an Indian woman gratefully writing (so reads the caption) the name of the Discoverer. The story is told, on the other hand, of the Indian chieftain, Hatuey, who, doomed to die for resisting the invaders, staunchly refused to accept the Christian faith as the gateway to salvation when he learned that his executioners, too, hoped to get to

Heaven. It is far more probable that Hatuey, rather than the anonymous woman, represented contemporary Indian opinion of their new overlords.

England and France, in their colonies, followed the Spanish practice of enslavement of the Indians. There was one conspicuous difference — the attempts of the Spanish Crown, however ineffective, to restrict Indian slavery to those who refused to accept Christianity and to the warlike Caribs on the specious plea that they were cannibals. From the standpoint of the British government Indian slavery, unlike later Negro slavery which involved vital imperial interests, was a purely colonial matter. As Lauber writes: "The home government was interested in colonial slave conditions and legislation only when the African slave trade was involved. . . . Since it (Indian slavery) was never sufficiently extensive to interfere with Negro slavery and the slave trade, it never received any attention from the home government, and so existed as legal because never declared illegal."

But Indian slavery never was extensive in the British dominions. Ballagh, writing of Virginia, says that popular sentiment had never "demanded the subjection of the Indian race *per se*, as was practically the case with the Negro in the first slave act of 1661, but only of a portion of it, and that admittedly a very small portion. . . . In the case of the Indian . . . slavery was viewed as of an occasional nature, a preventive penalty and not as a normal and permanent condition." In the New England colonies Indian slavery was unprofitable, for slavery of any kind was unprofitable because it was unsuited to the diversified agriculture of these colonies. In addition the Indian slave was inefficient. The Spaniards discovered that one Negro was worth four Indians. A prominent official in Hispaniola insisted in 1518 that "permission be given to bring Negroes, a race robust for labor, instead of natives, so weak that they can only be employed in tasks requiring little endurance, such as taking care of maize fields or farms." The future staples of the New World, sugar and cotton, required strength which the Indian lacked, and demanded the robust "cotton nigger" as sugar's need of strong mules produced in Louisiana the epithet "sugar mules." According to Lauber, "When compared with sums paid for Negroes at the same time and place the prices of Indian slaves are found to have been considerably lower."

The Indian reservoir, too, was limited, the African inexhaustible. Negroes therefore were stolen in Africa to work the lands stolen from the Indians in America. The voyages of Prince Henry the Navigator complemented those of Columbus, West African history became the complement of West Indian.

The immediate successor of the Indian, however, was not the Negro but the poor white. These white servants included a variety of types. Some were indentured servants, so called because, before departure from the homeland, they had signed a contract, indented by law, binding them to service for a stipulated time in return for their passage. Still others, known as "redemptioners," arranged with the captain of the ship to pay for their passage on arrival or within a specified time thereafter; if they did not, they were sold by the captain to the highest bidder. Others were convicts, sent out by the deliberate policy of the home government, to serve for a specified period.

This emigration was in tune with mercantilist theories of the day which strongly advocated putting the poor to industrious and useful labor and favored emigration, voluntary or involuntary, as relieving the poor rates and finding more profitable occupations abroad for idlers and vagrants at home. "Indentured servitude," writes C. M. Haar, "was called into existence by two different though complementary forces: there was both a positive attraction from the New World and a negative repulsion from the Old. In a state paper delivered to James I in 1606 Bacon emphasized that by emigration England would gain "a double commodity, in the avoidance of people here, and in making use of them there."

This temporary service at the outset denoted no inferiority or degradation. Many of the servants were manorial tenants fleeing from the irksome restrictions of feudalism, Irishmen seeking freedom from the oppression of landlords and bishops, Germans running away from the devastation of the Thirty Years' War. They transplanted in their hearts a burning desire for land, an ardent passion for independence. They came to the land of opportunity to be free men, their imaginations powerfully wrought upon by glowing and extravagant descriptions in the home country. It was only later when, in the words of Dr. Williamson, "all ideals of a decent colonial society, of a better and greater England overseas, were swamped in the pursuit of an immediate gain," that the introduction of disreputable elements became a general feature of indentured service.

A regular traffic developed in these indentured servants. Between 1654 and 1685 ten thousand sailed from Bristol alone, chiefly for the West Indies and Virginia. In 1683 white servants represented one-sixth of Virginia's population. Two-thirds of the immigrants to Pennsylvania during the eighteenth century were white servants; in four years 25,000 came to Philadelphia alone. It has been estimated that more than a quarter of a million persons were of this class during the colonial period, and that they probably constituted one-half of all English immigrants, the majority going to the middle colonies.

As commercial speculation entered the picture, abuses crept in. Kidnaping was encouraged to a great degree and became a regular business in such towns as London and Bristol. Adults would be plied with liquor, children enticed with sweetmeats. The kidnapers were called "spirits;" defined as "one that taketh upp men and women and children and sells them on a shipp to be conveyed beyond the sea." The captain of a ship trading to Jamaica would visit the Clerkenwell House of Correction, ply with drink the girls who had been imprisoned there as disorderly, and "invite" them to go to the West Indies. The temptations held out to the unwary and the credulous were so attractive that, as the mayor of Bristol complained, husbands were induced to forsake their wives, wives their husbands, and apprentices their masters, while wanted criminals found on the transport ships a refuge from the arms of the law. The wave of German immigration developed the "newlander," the labor agent of those days, who traveled up and down the Rhine Valley persuading the feudal peasants to sell their belongings and emigrate to America, receiving a commission for each emigrant.

Much has been written about the trickery these "newlanders" were not averse to employing. But whatever the deceptions practised, it remains true, as Friedrich Kapp has written, that "the real ground for the emigration fever lay in the unhealthy political and economic conditions. . . . The misery and oppression of the conditions of the little (German) states promoted emigration much more dangerously and continuously than the worst 'newlander.' "

Convicts provided another steady source of white labor. . . . Offences for which the punishment prescribed by law was transportation comprised the stealing of cloth, burning stacks of corn, the maiming and killing of cattle, hindering customs officers in the execution of their duty, and corrupt legal practices. Proposals made in 1664 would have banished to the colonies all vagrants, rogues and idlers, petty thieves, gipsies, and loose persons frequenting unlicensed brothels. A piteous petition in 1667 prayed for transportation instead of the death sentence for a wife convicted of stealing goods valued at three shillings and four pence. In 1745 transportation was the penalty for the theft of a silver spoon and a gold watch. One year after the emancipation of the Negro slaves, transportation was the penalty for trade union activity. It is difficult to resist the conclusion that there was some connection between the law and the labor needs of the plantations, and the marvel is that so few people ended up in the colonies overseas.

Benjamin Franklin opposed this "dumping upon the New World of the outcasts of the Old" as the most cruel insult ever offered by one nation to another, and asked, if England was justified in sending her convicts to the colonies, whether the latter were justified in sending to England their rattlesnakes in exchange? It is not clear why Franklin should have been so sensitive. Even if the convicts were hardened criminals, the great increase of indentured servants and free emigrants would have tended to render the convict influence innocuous, as increasing quantities of water poured in a glass containing poison. . . .

The political and civil disturbances in England between 1640 and 1740 augmented the supply of white servants. Political and religious nonconformists paid for their unorthodoxy by transportation, mostly to the sugar islands. Such was the fate of many of Cromwell's Irish prisoners, who were sent to the West Indies. So thoroughly was this policy pursued that an active verb was added to the English language — to "barbadoes" a person. Montserrat became largely an Irish colony, and the Irish brogue is still frequently heard today in many parts of the British West Indies. The Irish, however, were poor servants. They hated the English, were always ready to aid England's enemies, and in a revolt in the Leeward Islands in 1689 we can already see signs of that burning indignation which, according to Lecky, gave Washington some of his best soldiers. The vanquished in Cromwell's Scottish campaigns were treated like the Irish before them, and Scotsmen came to be regarded as "the general travaillers and soldiers in most foreign parts." Religious intolerance sent more workers to the plantations. In 1661 Quakers refusing to take the oath for the third time were to be transported; in 1664 transportation, to any plantation except

Virginia or New England, or a fine of one hundred pounds was decreed for the third offence for persons over sixteen assembling in groups of five or more under pretence of religion. . . .

The transportation of these white servants shows in its true light the horrors of the Middle Passage — not as something unusual or inhuman but as a part of the age. The emigrants were packed like herrings. According to Mittelberger, each servant was allowed about two feet in width and six feet in length in bed. The boats were small, the voyage long, the food, in the absence of refrigeration, bad, disease inevitable. A petition to Parliament in 1659 describes how seventy-two servants had been locked up below deck during the whole voyage of five and a half weeks, "amongst horses, that their souls, through heat and steam under the tropic, fainted in them." Inevitably abuses crept into the system and Fearon was shocked by "the horrible picture of human suffering which this living sepulchre" of an emigrant vessel in Philadelphia afforded. But conditions even for the free passengers were not much better in those days, and the comment of a Lady of Quality describing a voyage from Scotland to the West Indies on a ship full of indentured servants should banish any ideas that the horrors of the slave ship are to be accounted for by the fact that the victims were Negroes. "It is hardly possible," she writes, "to believe that human nature could be so depraved, as to treat fellow creatures in such a manner for so little gain."

The transportation of servants and convicts produced a powerful vested interest in England. When the Colonial Board was created in 1661, not the least important of its duties was the control of the trade in indentured servants. In 1664 a commission was appointed, headed by the King's brother, to examine and report upon the exportation of servants. In 1670 an act prohibiting the transportation of English prisoners overseas was rejected; another bill against the stealing of children came to nothing. In the transportation of felons, a whole hierarchy, from courtly secretaries and grave judges down to the jailors and turnkeys, insisted on having a share in the spoils. It has been suggested that it was humanity for his fellow countrymen and men of his own color which dictated the planter's preference for the Negro slave. Of this humanity there is not a trace in the records of the time, at least as far as the plantation colonies and commercial production were concerned. Attempts to register emigrant servants and regularize the procedure of transportation — thereby giving full legal recognition to the system — were evaded. The leading merchants and public officials were all involved in the practice. The penalty for man-stealing was exposure in the pillory, but no missiles from the spectators were tolerated. Such opposition as there was came from the masses. It was enough to point a finger at a woman in the streets of London and call her a "spirit" to start a riot. . . .

The status of these servants became progressively worse in the plantation colonies. Servitude, originally a free personal relation based on voluntary contract for a definite period of service, in lieu of transportation and maintenance, tended to pass into a property relation which asserted a control of varying extent over the bodies and liberties of the person during service as if he were a thing. Eddis, writing on the eve of the Revolution, found the servants groaning "beneath a worse than Egyptian bondage." In Maryland servitude developed into an institution approaching in some respects chattel slavery. Of Pennsylvania it has been said that "no matter how kindly they may have been treated in particular cases, or how voluntarily they may have entered into the relation, as a class and when once bound, indentured servants were temporarily chattels." On the sugar plantations of Barbados the servants spent their time "grinding at the mills and attending the furnaces, or digging in this scorching island; having nothing to feed on (notwithstanding their hard labour) but potatoe roots, nor to drink, but water with such roots washed in it, besides the bread and tears of their own afflictions; being bought and sold still from one planter to another, or attached as horses and beasts for the debts of their masters, being whipt at the whipping posts (as rogues,) for their masters' pleasure, and sleeping in sties worse than hogs in England. . . ." As Professor Harlow concludes, the weight of evidence proves incontestably that the conditions under which white labor was procured and utilized in Barbados were "persistently severe, occasionally dishonourable, and generally a disgrace to the English name.". . .

Defoe bluntly stated that the white servant was a slave. He was not. The servant's loss of liberty was of limited duration, the Negro was slave for life. The servant's status could not descend to his offspring, Negro children took the status of the mother. The master at no time had absolute control over the person and liberty of his servant as he had over his slave. The servant had rights, limited but recognized by law and inserted in a contract. He enjoyed, for instance, a limited right to property. In actual law the conception of the servant as a piece of property never went beyond that of personal estate and never reached the stage of a chattel or real estate. The laws in the colonies maintained this rigid distinction and visited cohabitation between the races with severe penalties. The servant could aspire, at the end of his term, to a plot of land, though, as Wertenbaker points out for Virginia, it was not a legal right, and conditions varied from colony to colony. The serf in Europe could therefore hope for an early freedom in America which villeinage could not afford. The freed servants became small yeomen farmers, settled in the back country, a democratic force in a society of large aristocratic plantation owners, and were the pioneers in westward expansion. That was why Jefferson in America, as Saco in Cuba, favored the introduction of European servants instead of African slaves — as tending to democracy rather than aristocracy.

The institution of white servitude, however, had grave disadvantages. Postlethwayt, a rigid mercantilist, argued that white laborers in the colonies would tend to create rivalry with the mother country in manufacturing. Better black slaves on plantations than white servants in industry, which would encourage aspirations to independence. The supply moreover was becoming increasingly difficult, and the need of the plantations outstripped the English convictions. In addition, merchants were involved in many vexatious and costly proceedings arising from people signifying their willingness to emigrate, accepting food and clothes in advance, and then suing for unlawful detention. Indentured servants were not forthcoming in sufficient quantities to replace those who had served their term. On the plantations, escape was easy for the white servant; less easy for the Negro who, if freed, tended, in self-defence, to stay in his locality where he was well known and less likely to be apprehended as a vagrant or runaway slave. The servant expected land at the end of his contract; the Negro, in a strange environment, conspicuous by his color and features, and ignorant of the white man's language and ways, could be kept permanently divorced from the land. Racial differences made it easier to justify and rationalize Negro slavery, to exact the mechanical obedience of a plough-ox or a cart-horse, to demand that resignation and that complete moral and intellectual subjection which alone make slave labor possible. Finally, and this was the decisive factor, the Negro slave was cheaper. The money which procured a white man's services for ten years could buy a Negro for life. As the governor of Barbados stated, the Barbadian planters found by experience that "three blacks work better and cheaper than one white man."

But the experience with white servitude had been invaluable. Kidnaping in Africa encountered no such difficulties as were encountered in England. Captains and ships had the experience of the one trade to guide them in the other. Bristol, the center of the servant trade, became one of the centers of the slave trade. Capital accumulated from the one financed the other. White servitude was the historic base upon which Negro slavery was constructed. The felon-drivers in the plantations became without effort slave-drivers. "In significant numbers," writes Professor Phillips, "the Africans were latecomers fitted into a system already developed."

Here, then, is the origin of Negro slavery. The reason was economic, not racial; it had to do not with the color of the laborer, but the cheapness of the labor. As compared with Indian and white labor, Negro slavery was eminently superior. "In each case," writes Bassett, discussing North Carolina, "it was a survival of the fittest. Both Indian slavery and white servitude were to go down before the black man's superior endurance, docility, and labor capacity. The features of the man, his hair, color and dentifrice, his "subhuman" characteristics so widely pleaded, were only the later rationalizations to justify a simple economic fact: that the colonies needed labor and resorted to Negro labor because it was cheapest and best. This was not a theory, it was a practical conclusion deduced from the personal experience of the planter. He would have gone to the moon, if necessary, for labor. Africa was nearer than the moon, nearer too than the more populous countries of India and China. But their turn was to come.

DAVID ELTIS

*from* Atlantic History in Global Perspective    [1999]

**DAVID ELTIS** (1950– ) is the Woodruff Professor of History at Emory University and has also taught at Harvard, Yale, and Oxford. His publications include *Routes to Slavery: Directions, Ethnicity, and Mortality in the Transatlantic Slave Trade, 1595–1867* (1997), *The Rise of African Slavery in the Americas* (2000), and *Coerced and Free Migration: Global Perspectives* (2002). He also helped produce the massive *The Transatlantic Slave Trade: A Database* on CD-ROM (1999).

From a global perspective, Atlantic history from the sixteenth century down to the mid-nineteenth century was rather unusual. The movement of human beings, initially perhaps by land out of Africa, and eventually via the Bering land bridge and the Indonesian archipelago to the farthest terra firma, began many millennia ago. Typically, however, whether it was the central Europeans who are thought to have settled in Asia three thousand years ago, or the Chinese who visited Africa in the fifteenth century, movement and settlement were not accompanied by continuing and intensive contact between the source society and the migrant society. In the early modern Atlantic, however, for the first time in human history there appeared an hemispheric "community." Community in the sense used here, means that everyone living in it had values which if they were not shared around the Atlantic were certainly reshaped in some way by others living in different parts of the Atlantic basins, and, as this suggests, where events in one small geographic area were likely to stimulate a reaction — and not necessarily just economic — thousands of miles away. The end result was, if not a single Atlantic society, a set of societies fundamentally different from what they would have been without participation in the new transatlantic network. . . . Atlantic integration . . . was a paradigm for the integration of the whole world after 1800, a sort of precursor of globalisation at the turn of the twenty-first century.

This phenomenon of integration is all the more striking when we consider the disparate elements drawn into the Atlantic community. Most work on Atlantic history has focussed on the North Atlantic, and to a lesser extent the white North Atlantic. Geography and winds ensured the existence of two largely exclusive Atlantic systems, north and south, which both the Portuguese, through the long domination of the Asiento, and the English, through their contacts with the Rio de la Plata and their efforts to supply slaves to Brazil attempted to merge. The northern system was the larger of the two, but black migrants, who dominated the human movements within both systems, were proportionately more important in the south, which accounted

David Eltis, "Atlantic History in Global Perspective," *Itinerario, Journal of European Overseas Expansion* 23 (1999): 141–56.

for over half of all Africans carried to the Americas. As this implies, the role of Africans in the shaping of the Atlantic world still needs more attention. This is more than a conventional plea to give a voice to the non-elite in constructing the past. Africans not only moved across the Atlantic in far greater numbers than Europeans, they also had a major influence over who entered the slave trade, which regions supplied slaves, and through prices, what slaves did when they arrived in the Americas. One further major implication is the still not widely recognised fact that integration ensured that the experiences of Europeans and Africans in the Americas were more similar than first appears, despite the dramatic differences in how the two groups travelled to the Americas and in the subsequent labour regime under which they worked.

It is important at the outset to revise the traditional picture of the Atlantic system arising from a marriage of the vast unexploited resources of the Americas, with the abundant reserves of labour of the Old World. It was not resources that drove the expansion of Europe to the New World, but technology. Most of the land and mineral resources, forestry and fish of the Americas were not windfall gains that immediately increased European well being, but rather small additions at the margin. Thus at the point of contact, New World land had little value. . . . The exploitation of the resources in the Americas became possible only with later development of technology, and in the case of some plantation products such as sugar, the brutal exploitation of one group of human beings (Africans) by another (Europeans) who did not see the exploited as fully human, or at least full citizens.

Nevertheless, Old World technology will only get us so far in understanding the Atlantic World in the aftermath of 1492. From the broadest perspective, interpretations of Atlantic history require the incorporation of geophysical, economic, ideological and cultural elements in the interaction of four continents over as many centuries. There have been many first rate studies of pairings of these continents and elements, but, except at the level of textbooks, little attempt to integrate all. Economic hues have dominated the largest canvases, and even those whose interests have lain elsewhere have acknowledged this primacy. How strange, then, that after five centuries of transatlantic trade, between eighty and ninety-five percent of the international trade of any nation which borders the Atlantic is with its immediate neighbours, not with transatlantic partners. This is as true of Mexico, the United States and Canada (despite their facing on to the Pacific as well as the Atlantic) as it is of Germany, France, The Netherlands and the United Kingdom. Most of Africa and Latin America, with the notable exception until very recently of Cuba, also fit this pattern. Indeed, most of Africa and the Americas (especially the Caribbean) in the last five centuries has experienced diminishing, not increasing, dependence on transatlantic markets for goods, capital and labour over time. After a massive switch to transatlantic trade in the century or so after transatlantic contact was first established, the normal trend thereafter for most societies was a long secular shift back toward intra-African or (intra-American) trade, and perhaps above all, a return to a focus on domestic sources of demand for goods and supplies of factors of production. In the sense that most economies around the Atlantic have become more developed over time and the more developed the economy, the more important is its domestic relative to its external markets, globalisation (and Atlantic history) are myths.

To make sense of Atlantic history we still have to break out of the materialist paradigm and focus on the cultural, not the economic, or, to put it another way, to make sense of the economic, scholars should re-examine cultural patterns. Despite (or perhaps because of) the preoccupation of Europeans with seeking to increase production wherever they managed to establish a "plantation" in seventeenth-century terms, five centuries of Atlantic history is more about the merging of cultural values, than of economic integration. In the two centuries after Columbian contact, differences in the ways individuals defined themselves, the values they held and above all how the societies in which they lived were organised were likely far greater than say differentials in living standards, or rates of capital accumulation among the societies around the Atlantic basins in which they lived.

It is not possible in a short essay to more than sketch some parts of the emergence of an Atlantic culture. The basic unit of the expansionist societies of Europe in the early modern period was, or became, the individual; the basic unit of the societies with which they came into contact in the extra-European Atlantic world was some corporate entity comprising groups of individuals. It is not that individuals in sixteenth-century Europe had more rights in relation to society than those in Africa and the pre-contact Americas, though this was probably true. Rather it is that property rights in particular, especially those in human labour, one's own and others, were vested in the individual in Europe rather than the group. Kinship structures in Africa and the Americas were extremely varied, but generally, status and rights in much of Africa and the pre-Columbian Americas derived not from autonomy and independence, but from full membership of a kin-group or some other corporate body. Such a group would make collective decisions and hold, again collectively, at least some of the property rights in persons which in the European Atlantic world would be held by individuals. Europeans might purchase property rights in others (slaves) outright, or they might enter the labour market themselves and temporarily trade some of their own rights in persons in return for wages, but in either case there was an individual owner of the rights in persons and a market transaction.

This leads to one of the major ideological differences between Europe and the rest of the Atlantic in 1500. To be a full citizen in much of the non-European world meant having more social bonds and less autonomy than would a marginal person without kinship ties. Freedom meant a belonging to, not separateness. By contrast, in Europe and the European Americas full citizenship meant freedom from such bonds, full ownership of property rights in oneself, and, before the eighteenth century at least, the ability to avoid hiring out these rights to others in return for wages. If, in the Western World, possessive individualism meant a recognition that one owns full rights in oneself and that one has the right in a market society to bargain away such rights, it might also mean the accumulation of rights in others in the hands of a few, as indeed happened in the slave societies of the European Atlantic. A market system per se, and the vesting of property rights in persons with an individual instead of the group, were perfectly consistent with both waged and slave systems. It was the concept of rights, including rights to the labour of oneself and others, being vested in the individual, that deserves the title "the peculiar institution" to a much greater degree than did slavery. Indeed, the idea that holding such rights should qualify one for full membership in society was extremely peculiar in relative global terms. Thus the implications for slavery of western concepts of freedom and a focus on individual rights are more ambivalent than appear if examined through a twentieth century lens. Likewise, possessive individualism could mean that individuals have the right to sell themselves to others. Until not very long ago the slave trade and slavery were as western as emerging parliamentary democracy. The really interesting question, touched on below, is why this did not continue, and, more specifically, who Europeans (Africans and Amerindians) deemed eligible for slavery and how this shifted over time. . . .

Once in the Americas, the slaves were incorporated into the most closed system of slavery that the world has known under the direct control of people who valued, or at least said they valued, freedom to an equally unprecedented degree. Yet in the course of three hundred fifty years [of] transatlantic slave trading, huge shifts occurred in the way Africans and Europeans saw themselves and others which fundamentally restructured the Atlantic community and, as shown below, the movement of peoples from the old World to the New.

On the African side, the slave trade encouraged an elementary pan-Africanism. There is a pattern to slave ship revolts and the European use of gromettoes (castle slaves) and guardians in forts and slave vessels which suggests that non-elite Africans began to think of themselves as part of a wider African group. Initially, this group might be say, Igbo, or Yoruba, and soon, in addition, blacks as opposed to whites. As a consequence, by the second half of the eighteenth century, slave ship revolts were more likely to be successful as Africans from different areas on the same vessel co-operated, and Europeans could no longer use African guardians on slave vessels. In effect, slaves came to recognise a common white enemy, and in the process modified their own identities.

This process of reformulating identity, at root a search for common bonds with others on the same side of the slave-free divide, went further and fastest in the Americas, especially in the Caribbean and South America. African nationalities sought out their own kind on seventeenth-century sugar plantations when establishing personal relationships and celebrating the rituals of life, sometimes with the help of slave owners. Even in the very earliest days there were no counterparts to gromettoes or to guardians in the plantation Americas whose sole function was to prevent rebellion among those of different ethnicity from themselves. The rebellions and conspiracies in

Barbados later in the seventeenth century show little sign of internecine strife. The Coromantines (from the Gold Coast), most of whom had been brought over as guardians on slave ships, had a prominent role in the Barbados slave conspiracy of 1675, but they were neither acting alone nor were they thwarted by non-Coromantines. The better known and documented slave conspiracy of 1692 contains no hint of ethnic divisions. In Jamaica, an open land frontier ensured a greater frequency of armed resistance and escape. There is almost a consensus among scholars that slaves from the Gold Coast were over-represented among the rebels, but seventeenth-century documents on Jamaican revolts contain almost no references to the African origins of rebels and none at all to inter-ethnic strife. As Gold Coast slaves were over-represented among the early Barbados and Jamaican slave populations, Coromantines might have a larger place in the records on rebellions for the simple reason that they had a larger place in islands' slave populations. Acceptance of newcomers into maroon communities, however, had much more to do with geopolitical realities and the survival of the community than with the African origins of newly escaped slaves. This emergence of black identity posited here is somewhat earlier than Michael Gomez has argued for in the case of slaves in the old south.

On the European side, there were, by the mid-eighteenth century, two conceptions of the insider/outsider division. In Europe itself, there was a slow move to more inclusive definitions, specifically including non-Europeans. The belief that members of one's own community were not appropriate subjects for enslavement was not confined to early modern Europe. Romans, Greeks, Islamic and indeed all other societies developed similar attitudes. But Europeans began to back this up with substantial resources after 1500. Spanish and Portuguese religious orders began working for the release of captives in the sixteenth century — the first such efforts on a large scale. Further north almost every coastal town in The Netherlands had a "slave fund" for redeeming Dutch sailors from the galleys of the Barbary States by the seventeenth century. European seafaring states signed a series of treaties with North African powers and the Ottoman Turks to safeguard ships and crew from capture and enslavement. Most provided for the issuing of safe-conduct passes to merchant ships. The irony that among the main beneficiaries of such arrangements were Dutch and English slave traders on their way to Africa appears to have escaped historians and then contemporaries, among them the Earl of Inchquin, who was held captive in Algiers before becoming Governor of the slave colony of Jamaica. When the passes proved ineffective and seamen were captured and enslaved, petitions to the British government seeking their release demanded action in the cause of "Christian charity and humanity" — long before abolitionists began to invoke similar principles. . . . The relevant question is at what point did "Christian charity and humanity" come to encompass those of African descent for enough people to make a difference?

The gradual removal of the barriers that kept non-Europeans from insider status in the European worldview was a very slow process, and as the modern world suggests, capable of reverse. It was shaped in part by the actions

of Africans and people of African descent over three centuries of plantation slavery and the slave trade. The interaction between slave rebellions
and the strategies of abolitionists in the final years of slavery in the British
Caribbean, and co-operation of a different kind in Brazil in the 1880s is
now well known. But long before this point the actions of slaves both in the
Americas and on board slave vessels kept the issue of slavery before growing numbers of literate Europeans. Judging from the frequency with which
they are reported, slave rebellions were a constant source of fascination to
readers of early newspapers, a disproportionate share of which were in
English on both sides of the Atlantic. English citizens moreover had an
extraordinary proclivity to migrate (and return), most of them before
1800 going to plantation regions forming part of the most integrated of all
eighteenth-century colonial systems. As early as 1700, "communication
and community" across the English Atlantic had attained a depth, richness
and reliability of contact unrivalled among European powers, and quite
unprecedented in the history of long-distance migration. . . .

   What is often forgotten is that the Atlantic slave systems were the only
ones in history where those ultimately responsible for the system — consumers of what the slaves produced and ultimate[ly] governors and pro-
tectors of the plantations — were not directly a part of the slave societies
themselves. A reformulation of identities by Europeans was much more likely
under these circumstances. This is not the place to reassess the origins of
abolitionism. The intention is to suggest only that the key counterpoint is
not slavery and abolition, but rather the enslavement of non-Europeans and
abolition, and that abolition was in part a function of shifting identities.

   Among those of European descent in the slaveholding Americas, the
move to a more inclusive conception — one at least that might include
blacks, as opposed to different kinds of whites — came to a complete halt.
On the other hand, divisions between Europeans had lessened substantially. Jews received rights in the slaveholding Americas before they
received them in Europe. The despised Irish had a meteoric and largely
unrecognised rise to respectability before the arrival of the famine
refugees recast their image. By the time of the 1727 census they had
become the largest slaveholders on the island of Montserrat. They came
to hold a disproportionate share of colonial offices in eighteenth-century
Jamaica, and probably Cuba, too. Almost every European colony in the
Americas with the exception of the Spanish came to contain large elements of populations from parts of Europe other than the respective
mother countries. These populations, including Jews, came to have full
de facto rights. The eighteenth-century proscriptions against Catholics in
the English case were largely ignored in the slave colonies. In bald terms,
the planters sought allies wherever they could find them. At the same
time the experience of slavery made the divide between Europeans (and
in some jurisdictions free coloureds), with African slaves close to absolute. Planter classes that did not make these adjustments in how they
defined themselves — in St Domingue for example — did not survive.

A second and quite different impact of European and African cultural constructs on the Atlantic World stemmed from gender. It is now clear that early modern migration from Europe was overwhelmingly dominated by males. The coerced counterpart from Africa had much higher proportions of females. These differences point to major differences in constructions of gender in Africa and Europe. Indeed, intriguing contrasts and similarities appear in the roles of women in the two sub-continents. Opportunity for females in English, Dutch, and eventually in North Atlantic society appear much greater in the reproductive than in the economic zone of gender relations. This is particularly the case if a global comparative perspective is adopted. The exceptional nature of early modern western European marriage patterns is now widely accepted. Compared to women in Asia and Africa, western European women married late, had considerable choice over marriage partner, and a large proportion of them never married at all. The nuclear family was much more common in Western Europe than anywhere in Africa, and kinship structures were much stronger in Africa than in Europe. Nevertheless the bulk of labour in both continents at this time was performed within the household, however defined. Women in Africa tilled the fields, produced cloth and had major roles in trade, all of which gave them value as wives. "Polygyny," according to Remi Clignet, "is most tenacious in cultures where economic rights to women can be acquired and have high value." African women were expected to perform a much wider range of occupations than in most other parts of the Old World. For one small community on the western Slave Coast, however, Sandra Greene has shown how the women's economic and reproductive functions varied over time in response to resource availability and an influx of migrants. But even when most restricted by male-dominated patrilineages, the women of Anlo had access to a wider range of skills, and a role in economic decision-making not to be found in most of early modern Western Europe.

In effect Europeans went to Africa to buy labour, which for them meant mainly males. Africans could no more conceive of selling males as Europeans would have conceived of selling females if Africans had sent vessels to Europe for similar purposes. When Africans offered females for sale, the gender pattern of the trade emerged as a compromise familiar to anyone who has participated in market activity. Africans sold more males and Europeans bought more females than they wished. Europeans put African females to work on the plantations, though they would not bend their conceptions of gender to provide African (much less European) women with the necessary training to carry out skilled occupations outside the household. It is striking that the labour source over which Europeans are traditionally supposed to have had the most power was the source that provided them with a smaller proportion of males than they were able to obtain (albeit as indentured servants) from their own societies. It is even more striking that there is no obvious economic explanation for the constructions of gender which underlay such preferences. In effect there were two broad constructions of gender, one African and one European, which clashed in the slave trade.

The above arguments have some interesting implications. One is that Europeans, and more particularly the English, failed to take advantage of three rather large economic opportunities. If they had emulated the sixteenth-century Russian aristocracy, created some ideological distance between the masses and themselves, and enslaved some elements of their own society, lower labour costs would have ensured faster development of the Americas, and higher exports and income levels on both sides of the Atlantic. For those who see European, in particular English, economic power built on overseas colonies, it might be argued that for the underpopulated tropical Americas at least, exploitation of the periphery and the transfer of surplus to the core would have been far more rapid with white slave labour. A second failure to maximise an economic advantage was that Europeans did not make use of European women as gang-labourers, or even, extensively, as field labourers of any kind. They compounded their economic irrationality by ignoring totally the cheaper supplies of skilled labour — coopers, carpenters, blacksmiths et cetera — that could have emerged from the ranks of European and African women. Again, this could have only accelerated the development of the Americas. Third, Europeans gradually widened their perception of what constituted an insider from the late eighteenth century to include transoceanic peoples. This in effect brought a very profitable institution to an end. The first "missed opportunity" created the Atlantic slave trade from Africa; the second increased the costs of skilled labour; the third ended not only the slave trade but slavery in the Americas as well. The broadest implication, however, is not just that economic interpretations of the rise and fall of African slavery in the Americas have shortcomings, but that in the end any narrow economic interpretation of history will not probe into the behaviour of people very deeply. At the very least, it will run the risk of missing the cultural parameters within which economic decisions are made.

In one sense the impact of economics is clear enough. Prior to 1800, coerced and non-coerced migrant streams alike gravitated toward export-producing regions. Peaks in overall arrivals coincided broadly with the peak years of exports. After 1800, as domestic economies in the Americas evolved and intra-American trade became more important, that link disappears. Nevertheless the effect of merging transatlantic values may be seen from the composition and pattern over time or migration and time nations responsible for it. . . . As noted above, possessive individualism was consistent with all labour regimes — a traffic in free labour, which was fairly small in the early period, an indentured servant trade, as well as a slave trade. The west's magnification of the rights of the individual coupled with settlements located thousands of miles from direct government control and the social pressures of Old World societies meant an increased freedom to exploit. On the non-European side, there appears to have been no ideology, value system or social structure that inhibited the selling of individuals out of a given society despite conceptions of ownership that differed radically from those dominant in Europe. As a consequence, the slave trade was the prevailing migration stream to the Americas for

250 years. Moreover, . . . slaves increased their share of total transatlantic migration steadily from Columbian contact through to the beginning of the nineteenth century. . . .

The two [migration] flows supplied labour for the Americas and together repeopled the two continents in the aftermath of the Amerindian demographic disaster (the latter reaching a peak — or alternatively, the Amerindian population reaching a nadir — in the late seventeenth century). For the first two centuries, the African and European streams went to the same part of the Americas. Except for a moderate specialisation in silver mines, the Spanish used slaves in a variety of occupations usually to be found in Spanish settlements. In Brazil and the British Caribbean, early migration from both Europe and Africa was overwhelmingly to the semitropical sugar and tobacco growing areas. It was not until after 1680 that the African and European migrant streams began to diverge into what many scholars take as the standard transatlantic migrant pattern — Europeans to the temperate areas of the Americas and Africans to the tropical, so that the two peoples not only left from different parts of the Old World, they arrived in different parts of the New.

Perhaps the first question to ask is why Europeans brought Africans to the Americas in the first instance — in other words why was there *transatlantic* slave trade from Africa? Sugar was well established in the Old World to the point that São Tomé supplied most sugar consumed in Europe as late as 1550. The sugar complex had emerged from the Mediterranean and headed toward tropical Africa via the Atlantic Islands in the century before this. When it settled in the Gulf of Guinea, it appeared to be pausing before the jump to the mainland. Instead, of course, the jump was the rather larger one to north-eastern Brazil, and despite the best efforts of the Dutch and the English (they actually shipped slave sugar makers east across the Atlantic to Africa to facilitate this process), sugar was never commercially grown on the mainland of West Africa. A major part of the explanation for this was the political and military power of West Africans (Portuguese Angola was never a potential site for plantations) which before the late nineteenth century made it impossible for Europeans to establish the control required for a plantation economy. Europeans wanted mines and plantations. Africans did not want to give up the sovereignty that this would have entailed, and they certainly had no interest in working voluntarily on such operations. Europeans failed completely to gain control or even access to the production of African gold. A Dutch observer reported the Africans in the vicinity of Elmina stating "the forts don't protect us — we protect the forts." Aided by the epidemiological factor (though there was certainly no shortage of English, Dutch and Portuguese prepared to go to the coast) Africans were able to resist European incursions. African resistance resulted in Europeans taking slaves away in ships as a second best alternative to working slaves on African plantations or mines. The slave trade was a function of African strength, not weakness. Moreover, as Stephen D. Behrendt, David Richardson and myself have argued elsewhere, the distribution of the slave trade on the African coast was determined by an apparently regionally determined pattern of resistance on the part of Africans themselves.

But once the wall of African resistance helped force the plantation complex across the Atlantic, it seems self-evident that the transatlantic demand for labour from the Old World was economic. What do non-economic values have to do with shaping this pattern? . . . The explanation for the racial exclusivity of labour regimes and the transatlantic flows that supplied the labour itself must have been that Europeans were prepared to enslave Africans or use black slaves that other Africans had deprived of their freedom, but were not prepared to subject other Europeans, even despised minorities such as Jews, Huguenots and Irish, to the same fate.

Second, why was the nation most closely associated with the development of the possessive individualism and deeply involved in discourse on individual liberty and the rights of Englishmen, also the leading slave trader? Between 1660 and 1807, covering the period when the slave trade was at its peak, and when the traffic was still legal for British citizens, the English carried fifty percent more slaves than the Portuguese and almost half of all the slaves taken to the Americas. British migration to the Americas has received much attention, but the British actually carried three Africans to the New World for every European down to the beginning of the nineteenth century. Portuguese domination of the trade was limited to the period before the English Caribbean converted to sugar production, and after the British withdrew from the transatlantic slave trade then sent out their cruisers to suppress it. . . . English domination of the supply of coerced labour and, together with France, domination of the coerced labour sector in the Americas, occurred partly, as already noted, because western concepts of freedom incorporated the freedom to exploit, especially in lands remote from the metropolitan centres of European expansion. This paradox was carried to the extreme in the British case where metropolitan control of the colonies was weakest, and domestic developments most conducive to both large-scale migration to the Americas and a preoccupation with the substance and ideology of possessive individualism. On the eastern side of the Atlantic, the latter underpinned the emergence of a nascent market in free labour, whereas in the Americas, it supported slavery. A market system per se, and the vesting of property rights in persons with an individual instead of the group, were perfectly consistent with both waged and slave systems. It was the northwestern Europeans in particular who were likely to impose slavery whenever they found themselves in transoceanic lands. The worst features of the gang labour system which was at the heart of the economic efficiency of slavery probably emerged first under the English. Yet over the preceding three centuries, it was the English in particular who had developed concepts of the modern liberal state (and notions of personal freedom) that have become central parts of the western cultural domination of the late twentieth-century world.

Third, . . . the extraordinary and rapid disappearance of the slave trade, both relative to non-coerced migration, and in absolute terms, . . . is very hard to explain using conventional notions of profit and loss and economic self-interest. In 1860, it was possible to buy a prime male slave for $30 in the River Congo and sell the same individual for over $1,000 in Cuba when the cost of ferrying a steerage passenger (always assigned more space than a slave, anyway) across the Atlantic had fallen to less than $20. Scholars who argue that the plantation sector was in decline and therefore slavery died because it was no longer profitable have generally not examined profits in the slave trade very closely. The slave trade was a bulwark of labour supply for planters, outside the US at least, and it continued to be profitable throughout the nineteenth century until, in fact, it was prevented from continuing. The slave trade was suppressed; it did not die a natural economic death. Nor, except possibly in the US, did it die because slave purchasers acquiesced in, much less actively sought, its termination. If it had not been suppressed, there was nothing in the pre-1820 patterns of migration . . . to suggest that the dominance of Africa in transatlantic migration streams would not have continued, or at least not have eroded completely. With slave prices at historic highs in the US, Brazil and Cuba alike in the mid nineteenth century, and steamship technology evolving rapidly, it is hard to believe that the transatlantic slave trade would not have far surpassed its late eighteenth-century peaks before 1900 and perhaps beyond.

Fourth, the gender composition of transatlantic migration is . . . now well known. Before the nineteenth century, European migrants were overwhelmingly male, perhaps four out of five prior to the family based migration of later years. In the African slave trade, gender ratios were almost balanced in the mid seventeenth century, and while there was a steady trend toward more males over the next two centuries, the male ratio never climbed much above seventy percent. Before 1800, probably six out of seven females crossing the Atlantic were African, not European. These ratios, as with the social constructs that shaped them, were not very obviously rooted in the economic self-interest of either Africans or Europeans.

In summary, Atlantic history has the potential for generating broad new insights but to make the most of its potential we have first, to look beyond the economic phenomena that have tended to preoccupy historians, and second, give fuller recognition to the fact that it was created by non-Europeans as well as Europeans. On the first of these, let me appear to double back on the message of many of the preceding pages by concluding with an economic historian's favourite ploy and ask the question what that World would have been like if economic rationality had dominated human behaviour to the point of shaping cultural attitudes and indeed all else besides. White slaves would have been cheaper than their black counterparts in most of the Americas, and as a result sugar production would have been greater than it was and prices of plantation produce lower. The Americas would have developed more rapidly than they did. The one exception to this would have been in South America, where there could have been little difference in the cost of bringing slaves from Europe on the one hand and from Africa on the other — assuming of course that whites were subject to the full rigours of a slave-ship transportation regime. The slave trade from Europe — still drawing on convicts, rebels, and prisoners of war — as

in Africa — would not have ended when it did. Among the many implications for the twentieth century is that any civil rights movements would
have been class-, rather than race-based, though it is not at all clear where a
reform movement of any kind would have originated. With large numbers
of white slaves as well as black stretching back over several centuries, relations between blacks and whites in the twentieth century would presumably
have borne no relationship to the historical reality. Perhaps we can say that
giving primacy to culture over economics would have made class an even
more dominant analytical category for twentieth-century historians and
social scientists, though within a Weberian rather than Marxist framework.
The point of such speculation, of course, is simply to highlight shaping
influences over human actions, European as well as non-European, in the
early modern Atlantic world that have received insufficient attention. If
economic rationality had had the importance that many scholars think,
then the world would have been a very different place. For historians that
should in itself be much less interesting than getting the priorities right for
an analysis of the early Modern Atlantic World. The expansion of the Old
World into the New resulted in violence, exploitation and unprecedented
economic growth (though not as much as there might have been), but it
was the merging and transference of values and cultures that made this
happen, not the resources of the New World, or the transfer of capital and
labour from the Old.

The American Revolution is the single most significant event in this country's history. Within twenty years — 1763 to 1783 — Americans declared their independence, waged a war of liberation, transformed colonies into states, and created a new nation. But scholars disagree about using the term *revolutionary* to describe how new or different these developments were. Some historians argue that the Revolution was solely aimed at achieving the limited goal of independence from Britain. Colonial society, they say, was democratic, and there was a consensus among Americans about keeping things as they were once the break with Britain had been accomplished. Others claim that the Revolution was accompanied by a violent social upheaval — a class conflict — as the radical lower classes sought to gain a greater degree of democracy in what had been a basically undemocratic society in the colonial era. The question is, then, was the Revolution revolutionary, or was it not?

Throughout most of the nineteenth century, scholars reflected one of the underlying assumptions of that era — that the main theme of American history was the quest for liberty. Within this context, the Revolution was inevitably viewed as a struggle of liberty versus tyranny between America and Britain.

George Bancroft, one of the outstanding exponents of this point of view, set forth his thesis in his ten-volume *History of the United States*, published between the 1830s and 1870s. To Bancroft, the Revolution represented one phase of a master plan by God for the march of all mankind toward a golden age of greater human freedom. The Revolution was "radical in its character," according to Bancroft, because it hastened the advance of human beings toward a millennium of "everlasting peace" and "universal brotherhood."[1]

In the nineteenth century, Americans desired a national historian who would narrate the Revolution as patriotic epic, and Bancroft fulfilled this longing. In addition, in a turbulent period divided by the bitter politics of the Jacksonian era and the brutality of the Civil War, Bancroft reminded Americans that they had once fought as a united people for beliefs they held in common.[2]

Around the turn of the twentieth century, a reaction set in against Bancroft's ultrapatriotic interpretation. With the growing rapprochement

---

[1]George Bancroft, *History of the United States of America*, 10 vols. (Boston, 1852), vol. 4, 12–13.
[2]Wesley F. Craven, "The Revolutionary Era," in John Higham, ed., *The Reconstruction of American History* (New York, 1962), 46–47.

between Britain and America, there was a tendency to view past relations between the two countries in a more favorable light. Populism and Progressivism, popular reactions against the concentration of power and wealth in the hands of a relatively small number of leaders in industrialized America, influenced some historians to view the Revolution as an uprising by the lower classes against the control of the upper classes. Two schools of professional historians working from the 1880s to the 1940s revised Bancroft's interpretation.

One group — the imperial school — believed that political and constitutional issues brought on the Revolution. The other — the Progressive historians — held that the primary causes were social and economic. While these two groups of historians disagreed with Bancroft on the precise causes and nature of the Revolution, they were often in agreement with his conclusion that the movement was, indeed, a revolutionary one.

The imperial school of historians headed by George L. Beer, Charles M. Andrews, and Lawrence H. Gipson set the Revolution in the broader context of the history of the British empire as a whole, whose colonial policies, they argued, were not as unjust as Bancroft had declared. Beer claimed that the colonists prospered under an enlightened system. Andrews, writing in the 1930s, saw benefits as well as burdens in Britain's Navigation Acts because of the protection provided for America's goods and ships. And Gipson claimed the British were justified in taxing the Americans and tightening the Navigation Acts after 1763, because largely British blood and money had been expended in defending the North American colonies in the "Great War for Empire," 1754–1763.

All three believed that constitutional issues lay at the bottom of the dispute. Andrews, for example, argued that the colonies kept moving steadily in the direction of greater self-government; the mother country toward greater control over the empire.[3] The disagreement, while constitutional in nature, was the very essence of revolution: a deep-seated conflict between two incompatible societies.

The Progressive historians, on the other hand, emphasized the growing economic split caused by the competition between the colonies and mother country. Progressive historians such as Carl L. Becker, Charles A. Beard, Arthur M. Schlesinger Sr., and J. Franklin Jameson stressed class conflict in colonial America in part because they saw their own era in terms of a struggle by the people to free themselves from the shackles of the large corporate monopolies and trusts. They insisted that political or constitutional ideas had an underlying economic basis.

Carl L. Becker, one of the first and most effective of the Progressive historians, took the position that the American Revolution should be considered not as one revolution but as two. The first was an external revolution — the

---

[3]Charles M. Andrews, "The American Revolution: An Interpretation," *American Historical Review* 31 ( January 1926): 231; George L. Beer, *The Commercial Policy of England toward the American Colonies* (New York, 1893); Lawrence Gipson, *The British Empire before the American Revolution*, 15 vols. (Caldwell, Idaho, 1936).

colonial rebellion against Britain — caused by a clash of economic interests between the colonies and mother country. The second was an internal revolution — a conflict among America's social classes — to determine who would rule once the British departed. In his first major study of the Revolution, *The History of Political Parties in the Province of New York, 1760–1776*, published in 1909, Becker summed up his thesis of a dual revolution in a memorable phrase. New York politics prior to the Revolution, he wrote, revolved around two questions — the "question of home rule" and the "question . . . of who should rule at home."[4]

Arthur M. Schlesinger's *The Colonial Merchants and the American Revolution, 1763–1776* (1918) continued in the vein of Charles A. Beard's famous *An Economic Interpretation of the Constitution*. Schlesinger noted that the usually conservative merchant class played a leading role in bringing on the Revolution. Why? Disenchantment of the merchants with British rule, said Schlesinger, arose from the economic reverses they suffered as a result of the strict policy of imperial control enacted by the mother country after the French and Indian War. Merchants' resistance against the mother country grew less intense after 1770, he noted, for fear of what might happen to their position and property if the more radical lower classes — "their natural enemies in society" — should gain the upper hand. The merchant class later became, in Schlesinger's words, "a potent factor in the conservative counterrevolution that led to the establishment of the United States Constitution."[5] To Schlesinger, the Constitution was the antithesis of the Revolution.

After World War II, however, a new group of scholars — the consensus historians — challenged the Progressives. The consensus historians, unlike the Progressives, believed that American society was essentially democratic in the colonial period. Most colonists possessed enough land to meet the necessary qualifications for voting. Colonial society was characterized by a high degree of social mobility. Thus the common man in the colonial era was satisfied with his lot in society and felt no urge to participate in class conflict in order to achieve a greater degree of democracy. Consensus scholars argued that Americans fought the Revolution to preserve a social order that was already democratic. When British reforms after 1763 threatened to upset the existing democratic social order in America, the colonists rose up in rebellion. In the struggle between the colonies and mother country, the Americans emerged as the "conservatives" because they were trying to keep matters as they were before 1763.

The consensus interpretation of the Revolution that arose after 1945 reflected the conservative climate of opinion that pervaded the United States after World War II. The Cold War made some Americans increasingly preoccupied with the problem of national security. Consensus historians led by Robert E. Brown and Daniel J. Boorstin played down any past differences

---

[4]Carl L. Becker, *The History of Political Parties in the Province of New York, 1760–1776* (Madison, Wis., 1909), 22.

[5]Arthur M. Schlesinger, *The Colonial Merchants and the American Revolution, 1763–1776* (New York, 1918), 606; Charles Beard, *An Economic Interpretation of the Constitution* (New York, 1925).

among Americans in order to present an image of a strong and united nation.

Daniel J. Boorstin argued that the Revolution was conservative on the imperial as well as the local level because Americans were fighting to retain traditional rights and liberties granted to them under the British constitution. In *The Genius of American Politics,* he argued that Americans resisted British changes after the Seven Years' War because they were contrary to the British constitution. In refusing to accept the principle of no taxation without representation, Boorstin wrote, the patriots were insisting upon an old liberty, not a new right.[6]

Edmund S. Morgan, the distinguished colonial historian, also drew on consensus themes — the agreement among Americans on principles, and the continuity of ideas — in his *Birth of the Republic 1763–1789.* From the time of the Stamp Act in 1765 to the writing of the Constitution in 1787, according to Morgan, the majority of Americans consistently sought to realize three principles: the protection of property and liberty; the achievement of human equality; and, after the break from Britain, a form of American nationalism that would embrace the ideas of both liberty and equality. Morgan concluded that the Progressive historians had grossly exaggerated the divisions among the American people during the Revolutionary era.[7]

In the 1960s, three groups challenged the consensus school. Certain intellectual historians saw the Revolution as a radical rather than a conservative movement. Neo-Progressive and New Left historians used different approaches to search for the social and economic origins of the revolutionary movement. And an interest in studies of the Loyalists provided a third perspective.

The trend toward greater emphasis upon intellectual history was in part a reaction against the Progressive scholars who had generally shown a profound distrust of ideas as determining forces in history. Strongly influenced by the thought of Freud and Marx, the Progressive historians looked upon ideas as emerging from material conditions or psychological predispositions that motivated human behavior. They thought historians should pursue the material basis for ideas rather than disembodied ideas themselves.

Bernard Bailyn was the foremost among post–World War II scholars who rejected this view and saw the Revolution as a radical intellectual movement. In *The Ideological Origins of the American Revolution,* Bailyn took the position that ideas expressed in pamphlet literature before the Revolution constituted its major determinants.[8] Bailyn argued that an elaborate theory of politics lay at the heart of the American revolutionary ideology — an ideology that came to be called republicanism and whose roots could be traced back to the antiauthoritarian or opposition Whig Party tradition in England. Man had a natural lust for power, this theory held, and power by its very

---

[6]Daniel J. Boorstin, "The American Revolution: Revolution without Dogma," in *The Genius of American Politics* (Chicago, 1953), 66–98.
[7]Edmund S. Morgan, *The Birth of the Republic 1763–1789* (Chicago, 1956), 163.
[8]Bernard Bailyn, *The Ideological Origins of the American Revolution* (Cambridge, Mass., 1967).

nature was a corrupting force and could be attained only by depriving others of their liberty. To protect liberty against the corrupting force of power, all elements of the body politic had to be balanced off against each other in order to prevent one from gaining dominance over the others. The best solution was a balanced constitution, but the malignant influence of power was such that no system of government whatsoever could be safe or stable for very long.

The colonists, according to Bailyn, were convinced that there was a sinister plot against liberty in both England and America. In England, it was the king's ministers who were conspiring against liberty. They usurped the prerogatives of the crown, systematically encroached upon the independence of the Commons, and upset the balance of the British constitution in their corrupt drive for power, wealth, and luxuries. Americans believed the conspiracy had succeeded in England and that America represented the last bastion for the defense of English liberties and the freedom of all mankind.

Bailyn took issue with the Progressive historians who declared that the patriot leaders were indulging in mere rhetoric when they employed such words as *conspiracy, corruption,* and *slavery.* The colonists meant what they said; the fear of conspiracy against constitutional authority was built into the very structure of politics, and these words represented "real fears, real anxieties, [and] a sense of real danger."[9]

Gordon S. Wood extended this argument in *The Creation of the American Republic, 1776–1787,* which explained how the colonists' antiauthoritarian tradition was transformed after independence into a distinctive American republican ideology. His and Bailyn's works, written in the 1960s, gave rise to what came to be called the "republican synthesis" and, coupled with J. G. A. Pocock's *The Machiavellian Moment,* published in the 1970s, claimed that this republican ideology dominated the political culture throughout the whole sweep of American history from the 1760s to the Civil War. The republican synthesis moved John Locke's thought on natural rights from the center of revolutionary thought and replaced it with the republican ideals of citizens acting with disinterested virtue for the common good. Those upholding the republican synthesis relied heavily on the classical republican tradition, which emphasized citizenship and public participation and had roots stretching back to antiquity and the Renaissance. Pocock, in fact, declared the Revolution to be "the last great act of the Renaissance." Ideas of republicanism proved to be the most widely accepted interpretation in the voluminous literature written from the mid-1960s to the mid-1980s.[10]

Alongside these historians of the republican synthesis emerged a group who thought it useful to see the Revolution in a comparative context. The outstanding comparative historian was Robert R. Palmer, who concluded

---

[9]Ibid., ix.

[10]Gordon S. Wood, *The Creation of the American Republic, 1776–1787* (Chapel Hill, N.C., 1969), and J. G. A. Pocock, *The Machiavellian Moment: Florentine Political Thought and the Atlantic Republican Tradition* (Princeton, N.J., 1975). For the Pocock quotation, see "Virtue and Commerce in the Eighteenth Century," *Journal of Interdisciplinary History* 3 (1972): 12.

that the period from the American Revolution in 1776 to the European revolutions in 1848 constituted a series of democratic revolutions. He saw the
American Revolution, then, as part of the process of democratization that
was taking place throughout the entire Western world at that time. In his
magisterial two-volume work, *The Age of the Democratic Revolution*, published in
the late 1950s and early 1960s, Palmer was able to gain new insights into the
process of revolution by resorting to the method of comparative history.[11]

Meanwhile, a reaction to the republican synthesis was setting in in the
1970s and 1980s from a variety of groups. Bailyn, who had revised the neoconservatives by making the Revolution seem radical again, was subjected to revisionist assaults, as were Wood and Pocock. Bailyn was criticized because he
seemed to suggest that there was an ideological consensus among American
Whigs and that they all held the same republican ideas in common. Other
scholars quickly pointed out there were other ideologies at work — evangelical Protestantism, class-based perspectives, or different political orientations —
and that America's political culture was diverse. Supporters of the republican
synthesis were criticized, moreover, for omitting a discussion of the various
theories of political economy, including Lockean liberalism, that were so
important to those of the Revolutionary generation.[12]

Rhys Isaac, for example, undermined the idea of an ideological consensus by analyzing different powerful religious ideologies at work before, during, and after the Revolution. Focusing on prerevolutionary Virginia as a
case study, Isaac showed that deep ideological differences existed between
the Anglicans and Baptists. Deploying the imaginative techniques of cultural anthropologists, Isaac identified two contrasting religious subcultures: the
tradition-oriented Anglican gentry who represented the established order
and the humble evangelical Baptists who challenged the ruling Anglican
establishment. His work did more than destroy the idea of a possible ideological consensus; it showed that by omitting much serious discussion of religious beliefs, Bailyn and Wood had overlooked the important role religion
played in the formation of political beliefs during the Revolution.[13]

T. H. Breen in *Tobacco Culture* (1985), another cultural analysis, analyzed
the mental world of the Tidewater planters, arguing that they constructed
an idiosyncratic culture based on their ability to grow excellent tobacco.
During the decade-long depression in tobacco prices that preceded the
Revolution, this world fell apart as London creditors pressured growers.
Planters became revolutionaries as their British factors destroyed their sense

---

[11]Robert R. Palmer, *The Age of the Democratic Revolution*, 2 vols. (Princeton, N.J., 1959 and
1964).

[12]For an attack on the idea of an ideological consensus, see some of the essays in Alfred F.
Young, ed., *The American Revolution: Explorations in the History of American Radicalism* (DeKalb,
Ill., 1976). For two books that take up the issue of whether liberalism or republicanism was
dominant in the Revolutionary era, see Joyce Appleby, *Capitalism and a New Social Order* (New
York, 1984), and Lance Banning, *The Jeffersonian Persuasion: Evolution of a Party Ideology* (Ithaca,
N.Y., 1978). For discussions of the important role of political economy in the Revolutionary
and post-Revolutionary period, see the Appleby book and Drew R. McCoy, *The Elusive Republic: Political Economy in Jeffersonian America* (Chapel Hill, N.C., 1980).

[13]Rhys Isaac, *Transformation of Virginia, 1740–1790* (Chapel Hill, N.C., 1982).

of self-worth that derived from being "crop masters" — a nonmarket conceit, but one that could be confirmed only by market success. In Breen's work, ideas, culture, and economics blended unexpectedly to produce one particular group of revolutionaries.[14]

A group of New Left historians emerging in the 1960s blended with the neo-Progressive historians and challenged the ideological interpretation of the Revolution. The neo-Progressive and New Left historians were influenced not only by the earlier Progressive historians, but also by the social and political concerns of the times in which they lived. These scholars brought to the study of the Revolution a renewed awareness of the existence of minorities and the disadvantaged in American history. The protest movements in the 1960s and 1970s made these scholars sensitive to the claims of social groups who historically had been oppressed. The chief sources of the revolutionary movement, they argued, were to be found in the profound economic and social dislocations within eighteenth-century America. The tensions generated by such changes led to social unrest and protest on the part of the lower social orders during the Revolution. The neo-Progressive historians portrayed the Revolution as a democratic movement stimulated in part by these growing social inequalities and aimed at broadening participation in American political life.

The leading neo-Progressive historian to inherit the mantle of Beard was Merrill Jensen, who viewed the Revolution in terms of conflict — particularly political and economic clashes both between the colonies and mother country and within the colonies themselves.[15] (Gary B. Nash's 1990 book recounting the failure of abolitionism during the revolutionary period began as lectures in honor of Jensen.[16]) On the whole, the neo-Progressives were not successful in linking the widening economic inequalities directly to the Revolution itself, but they successfully challenged the notion of widespread ideological agreement among the colonists.

Gary B. Nash, a historian in the neo-Progressive/New Left tradition, discussed in his *Urban Crucible* an ideology found among laboring class and artisan groups on the eve of the Revolution that had not been treated by either Bailyn or Wood. Viewing the lives of urban dwellers in Boston, New York, and Philadelphia from the 1680s to the Revolution, Nash concluded that social changes had turned these seaport communities into "crucibles of revolutionary agitation." The increasing poverty and the narrowing of economic opportunities resulted in resentment and rising class consciousness among segments of the artisan class.[17]

---

[14]T. H. Breen, *Tobacco Culture: The Mentality of the Great Tidewater Planters on the Eve of Revolution* (Princeton, N.J., 1985).

[15]Merrill Jensen, *The Founding of a Nation* (New York, 1968) and *The American Revolution within America* (New York, 1974). For Jensen's students, see Jackson Turner Main, *The Sovereign States, 1775–1783* (New York, 1973), as but one example among many.

[16]Gary B. Nash, *Race and Revolution* (Madison, Wis., 1990).

[17]Gary B. Nash, *Urban Crucible: The Northern Seaports and the Origins of the American Revolution* (Cambridge, 1979).

Among the most important books by members of the New Left to challenge the consensus historians and adherents of the "republican synthesis" was a collection of essays, edited by Alfred F. Young, entitled *The American Revolution: Explorations in the History of American Radicalism*, published in 1976. Many scholars in this volume took issue with Bailyn's interpretation in particular. They rejected the idea of an ideological consensus and the notion of the Revolution as mainly ideological in its origins. Some pictured the Revolution as a social movement — an internal struggle within the colonies — caused in part by class antagonisms. Others, however, held that the Revolution was ideological in nature, but not as presented by Bailyn. They saw serious differences in ideology among local Whig leaders and the middle and lower orders of society who were patriots but held different political beliefs. The volume also contained essays about widely diverse effects of the Revolution on blacks, women, and Native Americans.[18]

The New Left historian Edward Countryman went farther than Merrill Jensen in tracing the Revolution to a distinct drive for democracy. Countryman concluded that the radical leaders of New York carried through a revolutionary redefinition of politics and society in the late 1770s. Using a sophisticated quantitative analysis, he revealed how the unruly crowds of the prerevolutionary period evolved into the popularly based committees of correspondence of the independence movement. His study showed also how closely economic issues — taxes, price controls, and monetary policies —were linked not only to clashing interest groups but also to conflicting visions of what republican society and government ought to be. Countryman's depiction of the collapse of the old elite order in New York after the war began undermined any idea of continuing the old consensus approach for that state.[19]

A third challenge to the consensus interpretation came from the historians who studied the Loyalists. The consensus historians had traced a line of continuity in political and constitutional principles from the late colonial era through the writing of state constitutions to the Constitution in 1787. Given the premise of a conservative Revolution, the consensus could not fit the Loyalists comfortably within their interpretation. How could conservatives like the Loyalists oppose a conservative Revolution? For this reason, the neoconservatives either failed to mention the Loyalists or made only superficial references to them.[20]

---

[18]Young, ed., *The American Revolution.*

[19]Edward Countryman, *A People in Revolution: The American Revolution and Political Society in New York, 1760–1790* (Baltimore, 1981).

[20]Daniel J. Boorstin, in *The Americans: The Colonial Experience* (New York, 1958); *The Americans: The National Experience* (New York, 1965); and "The American Revolution: Revolution without Dogma," in *The Genius of American Politics* (Chicago, 1953), 66–98, does not discuss the Loyalists. Louis Hartz, in *The Liberal Tradition in America* (New York, 1955), 58, and Clinton Rossiter, in *Seedtime of the Republic* (New York, 1953), 3, 155, 319, 322, 340, 349, say very little. Edmund S. Morgan, in *Birth of the Republic, 1763–1789* (Chicago, 1977 ed.), 99, 119–20, made only a slight mention, but Benjamin F. Wright, in *Consensus and Continuity, 1776–1787* (Boston, 1958), hardly accounted for the Loyalists at all.

From the 1960s to 1990, however, interest in the Loyalists revived. The most important work to appear during the 1960s was William H. Nelson's *The American Tory*. Although Nelson's book was a form of intellectual history, it also reflected the contemporary tendencies to concentrate on social history and to use concepts drawn from other academic disciplines. Nelson presented the arresting hypothesis that the Loyalists constituted a collection of isolated "cultural minorities" — social groups who had never been assimilated into American society. These cultural enclaves, therefore, looked to Britain for protection against the threatening Whig majorities that surrounded them. Nelson applied the sociological tool of negative reference group theory toward these ethnic minorities, who included Quakers and German Pietists in the middle colonies and certain racial minorities — slaves and certain Indian tribes.[21] Mary Beth Norton followed the fortunes of the Loyalists after their exile in England, finding them feeling ill at ease and out of place in English society. Once again, the negative reference group theory proved useful.[22]

Innovative historians in the 1970s and 1980s brought several major new approaches to the study of the Revolution. The new social historians included among their ranks those who saw the Revolution through community studies or the eyes of forgotten Americans. Others explored the Revolution from a psychological point of view. And yet another group of new military historians looked at the military as a microcosm of colonial society and studied the dynamics between it and the civilian world.

The new social historians were united loosely by their desire to examine America's social structure and its changes over time. They often directed their attention to small communities. Their work in many instances was characterized by quantitative techniques and research in nontraditional sources like wills, deeds, and tax lists to get at the lives of the inarticulate masses who left few personal memoirs. By employing such records, they hoped to re-create the universe in which ordinary citizens lived. Like the New Left historians, they sometimes were interested in specific socially or politically disadvantaged groups: the poor, blacks, and women. And like the new intellectual historians, they followed changes in the attitudes and behavior of groups over long periods of time.

Robert Gross's *The Minutemen and Their World* analyzed Concord, Massachusetts. Much of Gross's work was quantitative; he reconstructed the life of the community not from traditional literary sources but from church records, wills, deeds, petitions, tax lists, and minutes of town meetings. Rather than making sweeping statements about the Revolution as a broad social movement, Gross demonstrated how the events affected the lives of individuals

---

[21]William H. Nelson, *The American Tory* (New York, 1961). Another important work was Wallace Brown, *The King's Friends* (Providence, 1965), v, 250, 257–58, 261–67. Work that treated the Loyalists throughout the original thirteen states was Robert Calhoun, *The Loyalists in Revolutionary America, 1760–1781* (New York, 1973). One especially insightful biography of a Loyalist, among many, was Bernard Bailyn, *The Ordeal of Thomas Hutchinson* (Cambridge, Mass., 1974).

[22]Mary Beth Norton, *The British-Americans: The Loyalist Exiles in England, 1774–1789* (Boston, 1972).

within a single town. His conclusion was conservative — that the towns-people had gone to war not to promote social change, but to stop it. Ironically, the results of the Revolution opened the way to unintended innovations that profoundly altered Concord's way of life.[23]

The new social historians, among many others, paid more attention to certain social and racial groups such as blacks, women, and Indians to exam-ine how they were affected by the Revolution. Donald L. Robinson in *Slavery in the Structure of American Politics, 1765–1820* dealt with the institution of slavery over a long period of time. Edmund S. Morgan, more than a new social historian and no longer a consensus historian, produced the most search-ing study, *American Slavery, American Freedom,* dealing with the paradox of how slavery and freedom developed side by side in the colonies.[24]

The study of slavery and the Revolution has expanded rapidly. More and more scholars agree that it was central to the colonial experience and ex-planatory of much that followed. Sylvia Frey in *Water from the Rock* recreated the experiences of slaves during the Revolution and the ways in which both sides used them for their own political and military ends. Simon Schama in the gripping *Rough Crossings* (2006) argued that seeing the Revolution from the standpoint of slaves makes the British the more revolutionary of the two opponents. While ambivalent and very imperfect allies to enslaved people, the British did offer some opportunities for liberation, and the grow-ing British abolitionist movement worked for the welfare of slaves and for-mer slaves.[25]

Gary B. Nash's *Race and Revolution* looked at northerners' responsibility for failing to secure the abolition of slavery nationwide at the time of the Revolution. And recently, his *Forgotten Fifth,* analyzing the writings of disap-pointed free blacks in the postrevolutionary era, details the ways in which their condition as citizens dramatically worsened after the war to which they had contributed so much.[26]

In addition, there is a growing body of literature on the black founders, members of the revolutionary generation who embraced the ideals of the Revolution and gave them meaning in the context of black life in the New World. James Forten, the Reverend Richard Allen, Lemuel Haynes, and Paul Cuffe, among others, laid the groundwork for black abolitionism and created many of the black associations and institutions that shaped collec-tive black life in the nineteenth century. The ambitious Black Antislavery Writings (1760–1829) Project in Detroit has plans to collect and publish texts by black authors from the Revolutionary era on topics relating to race, slavery, and African American identity.[27]

---

[23]Robert Gross, *The Minutemen and Their World* (New York, 1976).

[24]Donald L. Robinson, *Slavery in the Structure of American Politics, 1765–1820* (New York, 1971); Edmund S. Morgan, *American Slavery, American Freedom* (New York, 1975).

[25]Sylvia Frey, *Water from the Rock* (Princeton, N.J., 1991); Simon Schama, *Rough Crossings: Britain, the Slaves, and the American Revolution* (New York, 2006).

[26]Nash, *Race and Revolution* and *The Forgotten Fifth: African Americans in the Age of Revolution* (Cambridge, Mass., 2007).

[27]Richard S. Newman and Roy E. Finkenbine, "Black Founders in the New Republic: Intro-duction," *William and Mary Quarterly*, 3rd Ser., 64 (January 2007): 83–94.

Mary Beth Norton and Linda K. Kerber looked at women in the Revolution and postrevolutionary period, finding the outlines of a role for them in the early republic as "republican mothers" or mothers of the virtuous citizens the new nation needed to maintain its purity in a corrupt world. This interpretation has been useful in linking women to the national body politic. Joan Hoff Wilson, on the other hand, found that the Revolution itself meant no change in the lives of women.[28] While the Revolution's positive political results for women are generally agreed not to have developed before the mid-nineteenth century, historians have researched and described women's participation in the Revolution as spinners of homespun, boycotters of English goods, and food rioters seeking a moral economy.[29]

Carol Berkin's *Revolutionary Mothers* synthesizes much material on women's various roles in the conflict, giving a brisk overview of the experiences of African Americans, Native Americans, elite Whigs, camp followers, and Loyalists. The book reminds readers that this was no quaint conflict, but a long, violent war with all that entails, including devastated farms and countrysides, rapes, family separations, death, and pervasive fear. Alfred Young offered perhaps the most unusual angle on women's participation in *Masquerade*, the biography of Deborah Sampson, who served undetected for eighteen months as a man in the Continental army. She spent most of her time in the dangerous Hudson Valley after the fall of Yorktown but before peace came officially. Through Sampson's experiences, Young offered a view of Revolutionary-era religious and social turmoil as well as a close look at the duties, risks, and living conditions of average soldiers. His haunting portrait of Sampson's postwar ill health and poverty and decades of appeals for veterans' benefits make this simultaneously a remarkable work of biography and community study.[30]

The new social history, which later merged with the new political history as it tried to connect social and cultural phenomena with politics, encouraged studies of Indians and the Revolution. Barbara Graymont's *The Iroquois in the American Revolution* was among the first full-scale ethnohistories of Indian participation in the war.[31] Gregory Evans Dowd, Richard White, and James Merrell have discussed the Revolution's effects on certain Indian groups, and in 1995 Colin Calloway published *The American Revolution in Indian Country*, a broad and ambitious look at the Revolution as it played out

---

[28]Linda Kerber, *Women of the Republic: Intellect and Ideology in Revolutionary America* (Chapel Hill, N.C., 1980); Mary Beth Norton, *Liberty's Daughters: The Revolutionary Experience of American Women, 1750–1800* (Boston, 1980); Joan Hoff Wilson, "The Illusion of Change: Women and the Revolution," in Young, ed., *The American Revolution.*

[29]Ronald Hoffman and Peter J. Albert, eds., *Women in the Age of the American Revolution* (Charlottesville, Va., 1989); Barbara Clark Smith, "Food Rioters and the American Revolution," *William and Mary Quarterly*, 3rd Ser., LI (1994): 3–38; for two historians who find the Revolution more influential earlier, see Susan Branson, *These Fiery Frenchified Dames: Women and Politics in Early National Philadelphia* (Philadelphia, 2001), and Catherine Allgor, *Parlor Politics: In Which the Ladies of Washington Help Build a City and a Government* (Charlottesville, Va., 2000).

[30]Carol Berkin, *Revolutionary Mothers: Women in the Struggle for America's Independence* (New York, 2005); Alfred F. Young, *Masquerade: The Life and Times of Deborah Sampson, Continental Soldier* (New York, 2004).

[31]Barbara Graymont, *The Iroquois in the American Revolution* (Syracuse, N.Y., 1972).

in various Indian communities. Alan Taylor's *The Divided Ground*, a dual biography of Joseph Brandt, the Mohawk leader, and his one-time friend Samuel Kirkland, paints a cultural landscape of the Revolutionary era in the northern borderlands. Brandt struggled to protect the Iroquois from land-hungry and violent Americans, while Kirkland promoted their conversion to Christianity and dispossession.[32]

Some of the new social historians working in the tumultuous 1970s and extending into the 1990s explored the nature of the Revolution in psychological terms. These scholars made use of psychohistory — a subdiscipline that had recently come into prominence. They suggested the Americans may have been caught up in a serious identity crisis as a people on the eve of the Revolution. Such historians saw Americans as profoundly conflicted toward the mother country. Colonial society underwent a process of Anglicization in the eighteenth century, and according to this hypothesis, Americans became more self-consciously English. On the one hand, they admired the mother country so much that they imitated British ways. On the other, they resented the idea of emulating the British because they were seeking to establish a separate sense of American identity. Jack P. Greene, John M. Murrin, and Robert M. Weir, among others, treated the theme of an identity crisis.[33]

One of the most interesting and complex attempts at psychohistory was Jay Fliegelman's *Prodigals and Pilgrims*, published in the early 1980s. Fliegelman postulated the rise of an antipatriarchal movement in Britain, France, and America during the Revolutionary era. Involved in this movement were new noncoercive assumptions regarding the rights of children and the duties of parents. The aim of the movement was to try to perfect and improve the purely voluntary contractual relationship existing between the two genera-

---

[32]Gregory Evans Dowd, *A Spirited Resistance: The North American Indian Struggle for Unity, 1745–1815* (Baltimore, 1992); Richard White, *The Middle Ground: Indians, Empire and Republics in the Great Lakes Region, 1640–1815* (Cambridge, 1991); James Merrell, *The Indians' New World: Catawbas and Their Neighbors from European Contact through the Era of Removal* (Chapel Hill, N.C., 1989); Colin Calloway, *The American Revolution in Indian Country: Crisis and Diversity in Native American Communities* (New York, 1995); Alan Taylor, *The Divided Ground: Indians, Settlers, and the Northern Borderland of the American Revolution* (New York, 2006).

[33]Jack P. Greene, "Search for Identity: An Interpretation of the Meaning of Selected Patterns of Social Response in Eighteenth-Century America," *Journal of Social History* 3 (1980): 189–220; John M. Murrin, "The Legal Transformation: The Bench and Bar of Eighteenth-Century Massachusetts," in Stanley N. Katz, ed., *Colonial America: Essays in Politics and Development* (Boston, 1971); Jack P. Greene, "An Uneasy Connection: An Analysis of the Pre-Conditions of the American Revolution," in Stephen G. Kurtz and James H. Hutson, eds., *Essays on the American Revolution* (Chapel Hill, N.C., 1973); Rowland Berthoff and John M. Murrin, "Feudalism, Communalism, and the Yeoman Freeholder: The American Revolution Considered as a Social Accident," in Kurtz and Hutson, eds., *Essays*, 256–88; and Robert M. Weir, "Who Shall Rule at Home: The American Revolution as a Crisis of Legitimacy for the Colonial Elite," *Journal of Interdisciplinary History* 6 (1976): 679–700. See also Winthrop D. Jordan, "Familial Politics: Thomas Paine and the Killing of the King, 1776," *Journal of American History* 60 (1973): 249–308; Edwin G. Burrows and Michael Wallace, "The American Revolution: The Ideology and Psychology of National Liberation," *Perspectives in American History* 6 (1972): 167–306; and Bruce Mazlish, "Leadership in the American Revolution: The Psychological Dimension," in Elizabeth H. Kagan, comp., *Leadership in the American Revolution* (Washington, D.C., 1974).

tions. Prolonged submission to parental rule was to give way. The young were to be properly prepared to take their place in the world — a world assumed to be filled with great temptations and corruption — and to be released freely from the family, without rancor and with no expectations of continuing gratitude. It was within this frame of reference, Fliegelman argued, that the dispute between Britain and America should be cast. By discussing political issues in such terms, Fliegelman related the public discourse to private attitudes regarding patriarchy, authority, and child rearing and uncovered an important strain of thought that illuminated, if it did not fully explain, the imperial crisis in a strikingly different way.[34]

Another innovation that social historians brought about in historiography of the Revolution was recasting military history as social history. The new military historians broke away from the old-fashioned drum-and-trumpet narrative approach to war and wedded military and social history. They removed military history from the narrow confines of the battlefield and placed it within a much broader context — that of the relationship between warfare and society as a whole.

Many new military historians believed that the way a nation waged war shed important light on the values held by its people. John Shy, in a book of brilliant essays, maintained that the pattern of military events during the Revolutionary War helped shape the way the American people came to view themselves and their relationship to the rest of the world. To Shy, the war was not an instrument of policy or a sequence of military operations solely, but rather a social process of education.[35]

Another leader in the field, Don Higginbotham, analyzed the ideas, attitudes, and traditions that helped determine how the war was fought. He showed how the armies were projections of the societies from which they sprang: the Continental army beginning as citizen-soldier amateurs, while the British forces were composed of professional fighting men led by aristocratic officers.[36]

Charles Royster's *A Revolutionary People at War* probed the American character and employed the Continental army as a touchstone to reveal the complex views that the army and society had of each other. He dismissed the materialistic interpretation of many recent studies that concluded men were motivated to enter the service for reasons of self-interest. In a subtle and imaginative analysis, Royster showed how the early people's army gave way increasingly to a more European-style professional army — though one

---

[34]Jay Fliegelman, *Prodigals and Pilgrims: The American Revolution against Patriarchal Authority, 1750–1800* (Cambridge, Mass., 1982).

[35]John Shy, *A People Numerous and Armed: Reflections on the Military Struggle for American Independence* (New York, 1976), 224. For the British army in America before the Revolution and the colonists' reaction to its presence, see Shy's *Toward Lexington: The Role of the British Army in the American Revolution* (Princeton, N.J., 1965).

[36]Don Higginbotham, *The War of American Independence* (New York, 1971). For a fine set of selected essays, see also Don Higginbotham, ed., *Reconsideration on the Revolutionary War* (Westport, Conn., 1978), one of which deals with the issue of the militia's use in conventional warfare. See also Caroline Cox, *A Proper Sense of Honor: Service and Sacrifice in George Washington's Army* (Chapel Hill, N.C., 2004).

that never lost the force of revolutionary ideals. Once independence was achieved, the belief grew that victory had been won by a virtuous people, not simply by the army. The American people thus reclaimed the war from the army and ungratefully shunted the army aside, leaving behind an ambiguous military legacy.[37]

While the New Left and the new social historians, including the new military historians and the psychohistorians, had provided insightful case studies and insights into the Revolution, the problem of a general synthesis remained. In 1991, Gordon Wood picked up the challenge and published *The Radicalism of the American Revolution*, in which he argued, as the title suggests, that the Revolution ushered in a new American no longer hampered by habits of deference, feelings of inferiority, or hesitations about economic advancement. This new man (and he was male) felt himself to be anyone's equal and quickly exchanged his republican insistence on suppressing his self-interest for the common good for a more liberal focus on his individual rights and economic well-being.[38]

Wood quickly drew fire for his interpretation. At a forum sponsored by the *William and Mary Quarterly*, Joyce Appleby, Michel Zuckerman, and Barbara Smith attacked Wood for disregarding the various groups new social historians had painfully recovered and leaving the struggling poor, enslaved and free blacks, and women out of his sweeping conclusions. Inclusion of these groups, they argued, would have altered his conclusions and made class conflict and the struggle for power more central to the founding of America. They found him emphasizing ideas at the expense of material realities. They also attacked him for what they saw as his abandonment of the republican ideal in his earlier *The Creation of the American Republic* and praise, instead, of liberal consensus. In the words of Barbara Smith, Wood celebrated "a lack of public life, [and] the transformation of people into consumers rather than public persons."[39]

Wood, like Bailyn before him, insisted on the Revolution's radical transformation of ideas about property, work, and the self. Property no longer meant simply land; it also meant personal wealth "dynamic, fluid, and evanescent . . . which," he claimed, unlike land, "could not create personal authority or identity." Work, not leisure, suddenly defined Americans, and, most important, the Revolution gave Americans a sense of equality and "self-worth."[40]

As this debate continued, historians tried to understand what seemed in retrospect like a republican juggernaut that unfairly displaced many other elements and ideologies that contributed to the Revolution. In 1992, Daniel Rodgers suggested that republicanism had been a useful concept partly due to its elasticity and vagueness. He contended that historians had needed

---

[37]Charles Royster, *A Revolutionary People at War: The Continental Army and the American Character, 1775–1783* (Chapel Hill, N.C., 1979). See also Royster's *Light-Horse Harry Lee and the Legacy of the American Revolution* (New York, 1981).

[38]Gordon S. Wood, *The Radicalism of the American Revolution* (New York, 1991).

[39]Forum, "How Revolutionary Was the Revolution? A Discussion of Gordon S. Wood's *The Radicalism of the American Revolution*," *William and Mary Quarterly*, 3rd Ser., XLI (1992): 691.

[40]Ibid., 711, 710.

it to be more useful and explanatory than it really could be. He noted that for New Left historians it had been a stand-in for an antimarket mentality. They had seen it as a respectably radical and thoroughly American set of ideas that seemed to suggest virtue among laboring people in a way that embracing liberal ideas about rights and self-interest never could. As Gordon Wood put it in 1998, "Suddenly, the left had something in the American political tradition to appeal to other than the rapacious, money-making justifications of liberal capitalism."[41] And for materialists in general, it seemed to define an ideology that somehow came from a material base, even though that base was never specified. For historians of women like Mary Beth Norton and Linda Kerber, who posited republican motherhood, republicanism had offered women an ill-defined but important link to the body politic. Rodgers wrote that its success as a tool "stands as a measure . . . of how deeply responsive the interpretive disciplines are, not to evidence . . . but to their interpretive problematics."[42] Having seemed to explain everything, republicanism's utility was circumscribed.

In the wake of what many historians found to be the declining possibilities of republicanism as a lens, Timothy Breen made two important interventions. He moved to restore the philosophy of John Locke to a place of importance in the minds of American colonists. Taking the view that colonial America must be seen in its relationship with Great Britain, Breen argued that England's growing chauvinism and nationalism made colonists aware that they were not considered Englishmen. This repudiation made them find Locke's emphasis on the natural rights of all men congenial to their purposes — more so than an appeal to the rights of Englishmen. It also explains the overdetermined nature of their outraged response to Great Britain's provocative policies in the years before the Revolution. They felt the sting not only of extra taxes and the burdens of maintaining the British military presence, but also the humiliation of rejection from participation in an Englishness they believed they shared. Breen concluded his essay noting that "It was not until after the Revolution, when Americans confronted the exclusionary and racist logic of their own nationalism, that ordinary men and women had reason to be thankful that whatever their country had become, it had commenced as a society committed to rights and equality, radical concepts then and now." While he revised Bailyn and Wood and challenged the republican synthesis in his emphasis on Locke, Breen concurred with Wood's conclusion that the Revolution provided the ideology that would eventually serve all Americans fighting to be included in the Declaration's promise of equality and rights. While Breen's revision returned to an earlier view of the ideological origins of the Revolution, nevertheless he agreed with Bailyn, Wood, and, in a modulated way, Bancroft, that the Revolution had, in the long run, radical results.[43] His essay is excerpted below.

---

[41]Gordon Wood, Preface to the 1998 edition of *Creation of the American Republic* (Chapel Hill, N.C., 1998), vi.

[42]Daniel Rodgers, "Republicanism: The Career of a Concept," *Journal of American History,* 79 ( June 1992): 38.

[43]T. H. Breen, "Ideology and Nationalism on the Eve of the American Revolution: Revisions Once More in Need of Revising," *Journal of American History* 84 ( June 1997): 13–39.

In 2004, Breen published *The Marketplace of Revolution,* in which he offered a provocative new exploration of the dual themes of consumption and citizenship, which some historians have argued are incompatible with one another. Breen described prerevolutionary political mobilization in the colonies as emerging due to the colonists' shared experience as consumers of the goods of the British empire. For Breen, there was no inherent contradiction between consuming and participating in politics. On the contrary, Breen saw widespread consumption politicizing the issue of choice in the marketplace (the pursuit of happiness) and turning it from a luxury to a right. This thesis mobilized republicanism to explain widespread boycotting, with liberalism growing alongside consumer savvy.[44]

Recently, Peter C. Messer has followed versions of republicanism through the early American historians who elaborated them. Republicanism in this view was a homegrown affair, shaped more by the Scottish moral philosophers than by Locke, and filtered through daily provincial experience. It included faith in continuing improvement, imperial corruption, and colonial virtue and commitment to securing "the foundations of every day life." Messer's republicanism changed and adapted in the hands of historians whose goal was to use it to provide a template for the past on which to build a uniquely American future. David Ramsay, whose *History of the United States* was published in 1816 and 1817, described a republicanism that had become comfortable with order, empire, property and profits, slavery, and Indian dispossession. By this period, republicanism did not require a politically active electorate, but rather people pursuing their own interests. Messer's view showed republicanism growing alongside liberalism.[45]

Popular writers as well as academics have found great public enthusiasm in the last decade for studies of the founders. Works have proliferated that violate the priorities of the new political historians — whose work goes, as one of their titles, *Beyond the Founders,* indicates — and that aim to balance the emphasis on the elites of the 1770s and 1780s with work on the activities of the unsung. Conversely, Bernard Bailyn's *To Begin the World Anew* celebrated John Adams, Thomas Jefferson, and Benjamin Franklin as "truly creative people." Similarly, Gordon Wood began *Revolutionary Characters* by calling the founders "an extraordinary elite, their achievements scarcely matched by those of any other generation." He defended them against attacks of racism, sexism, and elitism. And John Ferling's study of the war with sketches of the revolutionaries shares a celebratory tone with these volumes.[46]

---

[44]T. H. Breen, *The Marketplace of Revolution: How Consumer Politics Shaped American Independence* (New York, 2004); Wood, *Creation,* xi.

[45]Peter C. Messer, *Stories of Independence: Identity, Ideology, and History in Eighteenth-Century America* (DeKalb, Ill., 2005), 73, 170, 176; David Ramsay, *History of the United States from Their First Settlement as English Colonies, in 1607, to the Year 1808* (Philadelphia, 1816).

[46]David Waldstreicher, Jeffrey L. Pasley, Andrew Robertson, *Beyond the Founders: New Approaches to the Political History of the Early American Republic* (Chapel Hill, N.C., 2004). Bernard Bailyn, *To Begin the World Anew: The Genius and Ambiguities of the American Founders* (New York, 2003), 98; Gordon Wood, *Revolutionary Characters: What Made the Founders Different* (New York, 2000), 9, 27, 34; John Ferling, *A Leap in the Dark: The Struggle to Create the American Republic* (New York, 2003).

But none of these works integrates the findings of historians of women, blacks, Native Americans, and the poor. At the same time that interest in the founders is high, so there is considerable interest among historians in the activities and hopes of the oppressed for a democratic revolution. New political historians like David Waldstreicher, Terry Bouton, and Woody Holton have extended the work on social historians to politics and culture, trying to connect conventional politics with other activities that, when investigated, can reveal political messages. Woody Holton's *Forced Founders* argues for the sometimes indirect but powerful effects that Indians, slaves, and debtors had on encouraging the elite to break with Great Britain. Michael McDonnell's work, particularly "Class War? Class Struggles during the American Revolution in Virginia," details the drawn out and fierce contest between rich and poor over who was actually going to fight the war in that colony.[47]

Gary Nash in *The Unknown American Revolution* (excerpted below) has synthesized the stories of the Revolution as it involved the men and women who did most of the fighting and sustained most of the losses: the poor, slaves, and Native Americans. It was not the experience of consumption that mobilized these unknown men and women, but the experience of political exclusion, poverty, exploitation, and dispossession of their lands. The Great Awakening brought many of them together and encouraged them to challenge established authority. The high-handed policies of the British and colonial elites politicized others, and for yet others motivation came from enslavement or persecution at the hands of white settlers. In this view, at the end of the war, when poor soldiers, black and white, briefly turned against the Congress that refused to pay them fairly for their years of service, the forces were already gathering that would prevent the war from effecting enough change to reach those who needed it most.[48]

Many years ago, R. R. Palmer initiated comparative work on the Revolutionary era, and it has continued. In 1988, Patrice Higonnet, a historian of France, published *Sister Republics*, which compared the intellectual and ideological trajectories deriving from the American and French revolutions, finding more political consensus and continuity in the United States despite greater levels of inequality. In France, on the other hand, he contended that there had been less stability and more open conflict over class than in the United States. Nevertheless, Higonnet added, the French worker, while not necessarily benefiting greatly from France's politicized class struggles,

---

[47]David Waldstreicher, *Runaway America: Benjamin Franklin, Slavery, and the American Revolution* (New York, 2004); Terry Bouton, *Taming Democracy: "The People," the Founders, and the Troubled Ending of the American Revolution* (New York, 2007); Woody Holton, *Forced Founders: Indians, Debtors, Slaves, and the Making of the American Revolution in Virginia* (Chapel Hill, N.C., 1999); Michael McDonnell, "Class War? Class Struggles during the American Revolution in Virginia," *William and Mary Quarterly*, 3rd Ser., 63 (April 2006): 305, 344.

[48]Gary Nash, *The Unknown American Revolution: The Unruly Birth of Democracy and the Struggle to Create America* (New York, 2005).

has never been as invisible or as despairing of inclusion as African American members of the American working class have been.[49]

Lester D. Langley took a hemispheric approach in 1996, studying the American Revolution, the Haitian Revolution, and the Latin American wars for independence in the late eighteenth and early nineteenth centuries. He found that the American Revolution produced an inspiring ideology on which to base nationalism and further democratic change, although the Revolution itself resulted only in political rights for free white men. For this reason, he described it as a revolution from above. The Haitian Revolution instead freed the island from French control and simultaneously slavery, and newly freed men created a state for the first time. Langley called this a revolution from below. The Latin American rebellions, instead, were revolutions denied as they aimed to change government without changing the social and economic structures that supported the ruling class. In his analysis, Langley emphasizes the chaos of revolutionary violence, the "infuriating complications generated by" the conflict between "liberating ideas and traditional customs," and the social explosivity of meanings of race. Revolutions in the New World had an added charge of unpredictability that Langley argued historians have neglected.[50]

In summary it should be noted that historians who have addressed themselves to the question of whether the Revolution was revolutionary or not must answer a number of related questions. Was American society truly democratic during the colonial period? Or was American society undemocratic during the colonial era, thus resulting in a dual revolution: a struggle to see who would rule at home as well as a fight for home rule? What was the true nature of the Revolution? Was there a radical ideological change in the ideas that most Americans held regarding their image of themselves and of their institutions? Or did most of the changes take place within the political and social sphere rather than in the world of ideas? Was the "republican synthesis," with its emphasis on republican ideology, a convincing interpretation of this cataclysmic event? What were the results of the Revolution for women? For slavery? For Native Americans? For the poor? What motivated men to go off to fight in the Revolutionary War — was it materialism or idealism? The answers to these questions will determine the answer to the broader question of just how revolutionary was the American Revolution.

---

[49]Patrice Higonnet, *Sister Republics: The Origins of French and American Republicanism* (Cambridge, Mass., and London, 1988).

[50]Lester D. Langley, *The Americas in the Age of Revolution: 1750–1850* (New Haven, Conn., 1996), 1–10.

## T. H. BREEN

## *from* Ideology and Nationalism on the Eve of the American Revolution    [1997]

**T. H. BREEN** (1942– ) is the William Smith Mason Professor of American History at Northwestern University. He is the author of *The Character of the Good
Ruler* (1974), *Shaping Southern Society* (1980), *Puritans and Adventurers* (1980),
and *Tobacco Culture* (1985).

Over the last four decades historians of eighteenth-century England
reworked the entire field. . . . The newer literature . . . draws attention
back to Great Britain, to a highly commercial, modernizing North Atlantic
world, and to a shifting relation between an expansive metropolitan state
and a loosely integrated group of American colonies. More to the point,
this scholarship invites juxtaposition of two separate topics, each of which
alone has generated a rich and impressive literature, but that when
brought together hold out the promise of a greatly revised interpretation
of the coming of the American Revolution. First, the recent work fundamentally recasts how we think about the origins and development of
American nationalism. And second, it provides new insights into the character of popular political ideology on the eve of independence, suggesting
why the natural rights liberalism associated with John Locke had broader
emotional appeal during this period than did classical republicanism or
civic humanism. . . .

   Whereas we once concentrated on elite political life, on the activities
of unstable factions in court and Parliament, we now read of the development and maturation of an impressive fiscal-military state. No doubt, a
good many fox-hunting country gentlemen will survive. The monarch will
surely remain a key political figure. But those characters must now share
the historical stage with an articulate and powerful middle class. Instead
of tracing the genealogies of the members of parliament, English historians
examine topics such as the establishment of a vibrant consumer economy,
the creation of a complex state bureaucracy, the rise of manufacturing
towns and commercial ports, and the development of genuine ideological
differences within the political community. Dynamism, growth, and modernity suddenly seem apposite terms to describe this not-so-traditional
England of the late eighteenth century.

   We should remember that colonial Americans viewed those striking
developments from afar. . . . The colonists experienced the transformation of mid-eighteenth-century England in gross outline, but for all of
that, the impact of those changes on their sense of identity within the

T. H. Breen, "Ideology and Nationalism on the Eve of the American Revolution: Revisions *Once
More* in Need of Revising," *Journal of American History* 84 ( June 1997). Reprinted with the permission of the *Journal of American History*. Permission granted by Copyright Clearance Center.

empire was real and substantial. Four new elements in particular influenced how the colonists imagined themselves within the Anglo-American world: the developing military strength of Great Britain, the spread of a consumer-oriented economy, the creation of a self-conscious middle-class culture, and, most significant for our purposes, the stirrings of a heightened sense of British national identity.

Recent English historiography reminds us of something that probably should have been obvious all along: the British not only waged almost constant warfare against France and Spain throughout the world but also usually emerged victorious. In other words, they were remarkably good at it. . . . Unlike their continental adversaries, the British had learned how to pay for large-scale war without bankrupting its citizens and, thereby, without sparking the kind of internal unrest that frequently destabilized other ancien régime monarchies. . . . British rulers discovered the secret of fighting on credit; along with innovative banking and financial institutions, legions of new bureaucrats (tax collectors and inspectors) appeared throughout the country, persons who served as constant reminders of what Joanna Innes has termed "an impressively powerful central state apparatus."

A second element powerfully shaping the eighteenth-century colonial world was the rapid development of a new consumer marketplace. A flood of exports linked ordinary people living on the periphery of empire to an exciting metropolitan society. Few people understood the cultural, and therefore the political, impact of the burgeoning consumer trade better than did Benjamin Franklin. In his *The Interest of Great Britain Considered* (1760), he observed that the vast quantities of British imports had the capacity to influence how colonists imagined themselves within a larger empire. Sounding much like a twentieth-century anthropologist, Franklin announced that Americans "must 'know,' must 'think,' and must 'care,' about the country they chiefly trade with." . . .

Prosperous English men and women, much like their American counterparts, bought what they had seen advertised in an expanding commercial press. And, significantly, people of more modest means also participated in that vibrant marketplace. . . .

Colonial Americans . . . too had tasted luxury and increasingly called it happiness. On the eve of independence one American clergyman even went so far as to insist that civil rulers had an obligation to defend subjects "in the quiet and peaceable enjoyment of their persons and properties, i.e. their persons and worldly goods and estates, &c. together with all their just advantages and opportunities of *getting more worldly goods and estates*, &c. by labour, industry, trade, manufactures, &c."

A third element in the rapidly changing world of the midcentury colonists would almost certainly have been the activities of a new social group in Great Britain, the so-called middle class. . . . While no one denies the existence of other middle classes in the development of other nations, British-historians make a strong and well-documented case for the invention of a distinct middle class in Georgian England. Educated, professional, and prosperous people with no claim to aristocracy established, for the first time, what Langford terms a "polite and commercial" society. "English society was given a basic fluidity of status," explain Lawrence Stone and Jeanne C. Fawtier Stone, "by the vigour, wealth, and numerical strength of the 'middle sort,' mostly rural but also urban, whose emergence between 1660 and 1800 is perhaps the most important feature of the age." This burgeoning middle group industriously copied the manners of its betters, fashioning self in ever more colorful and elaborate ways, celebrating consumer fads, purchasing the novels now marketed in large volume, and populating the spas and resort towns; perhaps most remarkable, even as it redefined the character of English popular culture, the new middle class never seriously challenged the traditional landed oligarchy for the right to rule the nation. It was those men and women who entertained visiting Americans, English families headed by lawyers, merchants, and doctors, who regularly proclaimed that the freest nation in the world was also the most prosperous. For the colonists, it was an exciting and convincing display.

These economic, cultural, and social transformations fed what for the midcentury American colonists would certainly have been the fourth and most striking feature of the age, the birth of a powerfully self-confident British nationalism. . . . Some time during the 1740s English men and women of all social classes began to express a sentiment that might be described variously as a dramatic surge of national consciousness, a rise of aggressive patriotism, or a greatly heightened articulation of national identity. To be sure, during the period of the Armada English people took intense pride in the defeat of the hated Spanish, and distinguished Elizabethan writers celebrated their Englishness. But the Georgian experience was quite different. Even if the eighteenth-century development represents an intensification of an imaginative project with ancient roots, it nevertheless involved a much broader percentage of the population. It was now sustained by a new commercial press that brought stories about the empire to urban coffeehouses and country taverns. . . .

If the social sources of a heightened sense of national identity are in doubt no one questions the character of the swelling patriotic movement. Ordinary people — laboring men and women as well as members of a self-confident middling group — who bellowed out the words to the newly composed "Rule Britannia" and who responded positively to the emotional appeal of "God Save the King" gave voice to the common aspirations of a militantly Protestant culture. Or, stated negatively, they proclaimed their utter contempt for Catholicism and their rejection of everything associated with contemporary France. . . . In time, . . . even members of the traditional ruling class came to appreciate the symbolic value of John Bull in mobilizing a population in support of war and monarchy. For most English people the expression of national identity seems to have been quite genuine. Indeed, by noisy participation in patriotic rituals, the middling and working classes thrust themselves into a public sphere of national politics. As Roy Porter reminds us, "English patriotism during the Georgian century should not be passed off as nothing but hegemonic social control, the conspiratorial ideological imprint of the ruling order; rather it signified a positive and critical articulation of the political voice of the middle class." . . .

Georgian historians have paid considerably less attention to the darker face of national identity: its powerfully exclusionary tendencies and its propensity to reduce the "other," however defined, to second-rate status. . . .

For persons of Celtic background, for example, the rise of "British" nationalism at midcentury drew attention to their own marginality. . . . As P. J. Marshall remarks, British nationalism had an extremely adverse impact on men and women who did not happen to live "at home." According to Marshall, "The eighteenth-century experience . . . revealed that 'imagined communities' of Britishness were parochial. English people could perhaps envisage a common community with the Welsh and, often with much difficulty, with the Scots, but they failed to incorporate the Irish or colonial Americans into their idea of nation." . . .

At midcentury, therefore, colonial Americans confronted what must have seemed a radically "new" British consciousness. It radiated outward from the metropolitan center, providing officials of a powerful, prosperous, and dynamic state with an effective vocabulary for mobilizing popular patriotism. It was in this fluid, unstable context that colonists on the periphery attempted to construct their own imagined identity within the empire. Although the process of defining identity had begun as soon as European settlers arrived in the New World, the conversation across the Atlantic Ocean changed dramatically at midcentury. Americans found that they were not dealing with the same nation that their parents or grandparents had known. Confronted with a sudden intensification of British nationalism, the colonists' initial impulse was to join the chorus, protesting their true "Britishness," their unquestioned loyalty to king and constitution, and their deep antipathy to France and Catholicism. As one American pamphleteer proudly announced, "Britain seems now to have attained to a degree of wealth, power, and eminence, which half a century ago, the most sanguine of her patriots could hardly have made the object of their warmest wishes."

With due respect to Edmund Burke — and to the many colonial historians who have echoed the phrase — "salutary neglect" fails utterly to describe the complexity of the changing American situation. Although the number of crown officials in the colonies was always small, Britain aggressively intruded into the colonial world of the mid-eighteenth century: the metropolitan center spoke insistently through the flow of consumer goods that transformed the American marketplace, through the regulars who came to fight the French and Indians along the northern frontier, through celebrity itinerants such as George Whitefield, who brought English evangelical rhetoric to anxious American dissenters, and, for most literate colonists, through a commercial press that depicted the mother country in most alluring terms, indeed, as the most polite and progressive society the world had ever seen.

This revised perspective on eighteenth-century Britain, one that focuses on the dynamic character of the metropolitan center, has major implications for how we think of the colonies within the empire. First, the new literature suggests that we should situate the American experience firmly within a broad comparative framework, within an Atlantic empire that included Scotland as well as Ireland. People living in all three regions suddenly found themselves at midcentury confronting an England different from any that they had previously known. While London piped the tune, the outlying provinces and colonies accommodated themselves as best they could to England's heightened sense of national purpose. In each area the relationship raised hard questions. Did being "British" mean that one was also "English," or that people who did not happen to live in England could confidently claim equality with the English within a larger empire? Although each region brought different resources and perceptions to the conversation, we should appreciate that Scots, Irish, and Americans were in fact engaged in a common interpretive project, and however we choose to view the coming of the American Revolution, we should pay close attention to what recent historians of Scotland and Ireland have discovered about the construction of eighteenth-century imperial identities. . . .

However much midcentury Americans knew about the politics of contemporary Scotland and Ireland, they too found themselves struggling to comprehend the demands of a powerfully self-confident imperial state. We must pay close attention here to chronology, to the different phases in a developing conversation with England as the colonist moved from accommodation to resistance, from claims of Britishness to independence.

Like the Scots, the Americans initially attempted to demonstrate, often in shrill patriotic rhetoric, their loyalty to almost everything associated with Great Britain. Before the 1760s they assumed that popular British nationalism was essentially an inclusive category and that by fighting the French in Canada and by regularly proclaiming their support of the British constitution, they merited equal standing with other British subjects who happened to live on the other side of the Atlantic. The colonists were slow to appreciate the growing conflict between nation and empire, between Englishness and Britishness. Like the Irish, they conflated those categories within a general discourse of "imperial" identity.

A narration of the construction of identity *within the British Empire* properly begins in the 1740s. European settlers of an earlier period had, of course, struggled with some of the same issues, alternately celebrating and lamenting the development of cultural difference. But whatever the roots of the challenge, dramatic changes in English society, several of which we have already examined, forced provincial Americans for the first time to confront the full meaning of "Britishness" in their lives. The response was generally enthusiastic. . . . They believed that the English accepted them as full partners in the British Empire, allies in the continuing wars against France, devout defenders of Protestantism, and eager participants in an expanding world of commerce. Insomuch as Americans during this period spoke the language of national identity, as opposed to that of different regions and localities, they did so as imperial patriots, as people whose sense of self was intimately bound up with the success and prosperity of Great Britain. . . .

Consider a single example of this midcentury imperial patriotism. In 1764 the editor of the newly founded *New-Hampshire Gazette* lectured his readers on the social function of newspapers. "By this Means," he rhapsodized, "the spirited *Englishman,* the mountainous *Welshman,* the brave *Scotchman,* and *Irishman,* and the loyal *American,* may be firmly united and mutually RESOLVED to guard the glorious Throne of BRITANNIA. . . . Thus Harmony may be happily restored, Civil War disappointed, and each agree to embrace, as *British Brothers,* in defending the Common Cause."

Many other Americans shared the New England editor's assumptions about the inclusive character of the British; imperial identity. Some of them were quite distinguished. Appearing before the Committee of the Whole House of Commons in 1766, Benjamin Franklin argued for unity within the empire. When a member of Parliament pointedly asked him whether expanding the frontiers of the British Empire in North America was not in fact just "an American interest," Franklin shot back, "Not particularly, but conjointly a British and an American interest." The Reverend Jeremy Belknap, a talented historian and the founder of the Massachusetts Historical Society, also captured the spirit of eighteenth-century colonial nationalism. Like Franklin, Belknap assumed that England and America were equals. The success of one contributed directly to the success of the other. Both found fulfillment in their common Britishness. According to Belknap, the brilliant leadership of William Pitt during the Seven Years' War "had attached us more firmly than ever, to the kingdom of Britain. We were proud of our connection with a nation whose flag was triumphant in every quarter of the globe. . . . We were fond of repeating every plaudit, which the ardent affection of the British nation bestowed on a young monarch [George III], rising to 'glory in the name of Briton.' " . . .

In point of fact, however, the Americans were not really *"British Brothers."* As became increasingly and distressingly obvious during the run-up to independence, heightened British nationalism was actually English nationalism writ large. . . . To be sure, categories lower than free white colonists existed in this midcentury status hierarchy, but for the Americans such unflattering distinctions hardly mattered.

"We won't be their Negroes," snarled a young John Adams in 1765, writing as "Humphry Ploughjogger" in the *Boston Gazette.* Adams crudely insisted that Providence had never intended the American colonists "for Negroes . . . and therefore never intended us for slaves. . . . I say we are as handsome as old English folks, and so should be as free." Ploughjogger's

shrill, uncomfortably racist response to the Stamp Act revealed the shock
of rejection. The source of anger was not so much parliamentary taxation
without representation as it was the sudden realization that the British
really regarded white colonial Americans as second-class beings, indeed,
as persons so inferior from the metropolitan perspective that they somehow deserved a lesser measure of freedom.

The substance, if not the tone, of Ploughjogger's bitter complaint
echoed throughout the colonial press on the eve of revolution. To be
sure, the popular print materials contained other themes — religious and
constitutional arguments, for example — but in many cases, the raw emotional energy of the performance came from the American writers'
abrupt discovery of inequality. Like the anonymous writer of a piece that
appeared in the *Maryland Gazette* — actually an essay originally published
in a Boston journal — colonists throughout America found themselves
asking the embarrassing question, "Are not the People of *America*, BRITISH
Subjects? Are they not *Englishmen?*"

That the response to such questions was now in doubt became an issue
of general public concern. Consider the defensive, pathetic, frequently
querulous attempts by American writers during this period to demonstrate self-worth in relation to the men and women who happened to live
in Great Britain. The Reverend Samuel Sherwood of Connecticut protested
that colonists were "not an inferior species of animals, made the beast of
burden to a lawless, corrupt administration." Other Americans heard similar tales of alleged colonial inferiority. James Otis Jr., the fiery Boston
lawyer who protested the constitutionality of the Stamp Act, responded
with heavy-handed irony. "Are the inhabitants of British America," he
asked rhetorically, "all a parcel of transported thieves, robbers, and rebels,
or descended from such? Are the colonists blasted lepers, whose company
would infect the whole House of Commons?" The answer was more problematic than Otis would have liked. Arthur Lee encountered similar difficulty during a heated debate with "Mr. Adam Smith." The son of a
wealthy Chesapeake tobacco planter, Lee insisted that, whatever the great
economist might think, the original founders of Virginia had been "distinguished, even in Britain, for rank, for fortune, and for abilities." And
yet, as Lee remarked with obvious resentment, despite superior family
background, the Virginians of his own generation "are treated, not as the
fellow-subjects but as the servants of Britain."

As Adams well understood when he wrote as Ploughjogger, the simple
New England farmer, ordinary Americans were not particularly interested
in crafting a separate identity, at least not in the mid-1760s. It was the
English who had projected a sense of difference and inferiority upon the
colonists. In other words, "American" as a descriptive category seems in
this highly charged context to have been an external construction, a term
in some measure intended to be "humiliating and debasing." In an exhaustive survey of the contents of all colonial newspapers during the period
immediately preceding national independence, Richard L. Merritt discovered that "available evidence indicates that Englishmen began to identify

the colonial population as 'American' persistently after 1763 — a decade before Americans themselves did so." The full implications of Merritt's pioneering work have largely gone unappreciated. Indeed, it was not until quite recently that P. J. Marshall again reminded us that "the rise of the concept of 'American' owed quite a lot to British usage." The exclusionary rhetoric broadcast from the metropolitan center was a new development, a surprising and unsettling challenge to the assumptions of equality that had energized colonial nationalism until the Stamp Act crisis; since it came after an intense burst of imperial loyalty during the Seven Years' War, the colonists felt badly betrayed. . . .

Shifting constructions of identity within the empire involved more than simple miscommunication. England's assertion of its own Englishness shocked Americans, and the element of surprise helps to account for the strikingly emotional character of colonial political writing. Indeed, if one attempts to explain the coming of revolution as a lawyer-like analysis of taxation without representation or as an enlightened constitutional debate over parliamentary sovereignty, one will almost certainly fail to comprehend the shrill, even paranoid, tone of public discourse in the colonies.

Other historians have addressed this curious problem. In *The Ideological Origins of the American Revolution*, for example, Bernard Bailyn analyzed the disjuncture between popular rhetoric and statutory reality. The American reaction to various parliamentary regulations seemed to him far more rancorous than one might have predicted on the basis of actual levels of taxation. Bailyn concluded that over the course of the eighteenth century Americans had borrowed a highly inflammatory strand of English political discourse, one that warned incessantly against corruption and conspiracy, the loss of civic virtue, and a restoration of Stuart despotism. When Parliament attempted to tax the colonists without representation, Americans assumed the worst. Events appeared to be fulfilling their ideological nightmares. And in this situation, they employed a strident "country" language employed originally by English politicians critical of "court" corruption to translate imperial regulatory policy into a dangerous plot against provincial liberty and property.

While that interpretation of the apparently irrational political rhetoric of the colonists is entirely plausible, it does not seem sufficient to account for the sudden sense of personal humiliation. The extraordinary bitterness and acrimony of colonial rhetoric requires us to consider the popular fear that the English were systematically relegating Americans to second-class standing within the empire. To be sure, the colonists may have found in the borrowed "country" rhetoric a persuasive language in which to express their emotional pain. That is certainly part of the story. What we tend to forget, however, is that they also complained that their "*British Brothers*" had begun treating them like "negroes," a charge that cannot be easily explained as an American echo of English political opposition.

The racism that accompanied fear of exclusion appeared in the writings of several distinguished colonial patriots. Like John Adams, these were men who demonstrated that they could communicate successfully to a growing audience of unhappy Americans. Few were better at it than James Otis Jr. During the 1760s, he publicly lectured an imagined representative of English society: "You think most if not all the Colonists are Negroes and Mulattoes — You are wretchedly mistaken — Ninety nine in a hundred in the more northern Colonies are white, and there is as good blood flowing in their veins, save the royal blood, as any in the three kingdoms." And Daniel Dulany, a well-educated Maryland lawyer, sounded a lot like "Ploughjogger" when he protested in 1765 against how English officials regularly characterized American colonists. "What a strange animal must a North American appear to be," this enlightened gentleman explained in one of the most reprinted political pamphlets written before the Revolution, "from these representations to the generality of English readers, who have never had an opportunity to admire that he may be neither black nor tawny, may speak the English language, and in other respects seem, for all the world, like one of them!" . . .

Within this radically evolving imperial framework, the Stamp Act seemed an especially poignant reminder for the Americans of their new second-class status. . . .

As the constitutional crisis with Parliament evolved and as the possibilities for political reconciliation became less promising, the American sense of humiliation slowly transformed itself into bemused reflection on having been pushed out of an empire that once seemed to guarantee liberty and prosperity. Even at the moment of independence, the colonists still could not quite explain why the ministers of George III had decided systematically to dishonor a proud people. "Had our petitions and prayers been properly regarded," the Reverend Henry Cumings preached in 1781 at the site of the Battle of Lexington, "and moderate pacific measures pursued, we should have entertained no thoughts of revolt." This was hardly an expression of the kind of self-confident patriotism that one might have expected in that situation. But Cumings played on the theme of rejection. "It was far from our intention or inclination to separate ourselves from Great-Britain; and that we had it not even in contemplation to set up for independency; but on the contrary, earnestly wished to remain connected with her, until she had deprived us of all hopes of preserving such a connection, upon any better terms than unconditional submission." . . .

If assertion of English national superiority forced colonists to imagine themselves as a separate people, it also profoundly affected the substance of American political ideology. During the 1760s the colonists took up the language of natural rights liberalism with unprecedented fervor. That they did so is not exactly a momentous discovery. In recent years, however, historians of political thought have discounted the so-called Lockean tradition in prerevolutionary America. According to Bernard Bailyn, for example, the liberal discourse of this period lacked persuasive impact. "We know now," Bailyn insisted, "that Enlightenment ideas, while they form the deep background and give a general coloration to the liberal beliefs of the time, were not the ideas that directly shaped the Americans' responses to particular events." To some extent, Bailyn had a point. An earlier generation of historians had treated natural rights claims as sacrosanct principles, as self-evident and timeless truths whose popularity required no social explanation. When the case for Lockean ideas was stated in such reverent terms, it was very hard to understand why ordinary men and women might have found the natural rights argument so emotionally compelling, indeed, why they would have risked their lives on the field of battle for such beliefs. . . .

The explanation for the popularity of natural rights arguments in late colonial America now seems clear. Within an empire strained by the heightened nationalist sentiment of the metropolitan center, natural rights acquired unusual persuasive force. Threatened from the outside by a self-confident military power, one that seemed intent on marginalizing the colonists within the empire, Americans countered with the universalist vocabulary of natural rights, in other words, with a language of political resistance that stressed a bundle of God-given rights as "prior to and independent of the claims of political authority." The Locke of the *Second Treatise* seemed to the Americans to embody common sense precisely because he abstracted consideration of human rights and equality from the traditional rhetoric of British history. He liberated the theory of politics from the constraints of time and custom, from purely English precedent. As Ian Shapiro, a historian of political thought, explains, "Locke shifted the basis of antiabsolutist conceptions of political legitimacy away from history and toward a moral justification based on an appeal to reason." Those who still maintain that the republican ideology described in such detail in J. G. A. Pocock's *The Machiavellian Moment* would have served the colonists just as well are hard pressed to explain how a fundamentally historical justification for the Ancient Constitution spoke effectively to the problem of preserving timeless human rights.

However logical championing natural rights liberalism may have been, it was for the colonists a profoundly defensive move. Americans invoked "transhistorical arguments of natural equity and human liberty" because, in the words of one student of Anglo-Irish patriotism, "they did not have much of a historical leg to stand on." In their recent study entitled *Colonial Identity in the Atlantic World*, Nicholas Canny and Anthony Pagden came to a strikingly similar conclusion. The eighteenth-century Americans, they declared, "could only make their demands in terms either of claims of some set of political traditions that they shared with the metropolitan culture or, as most were ultimately to do, of claims of a body of natural rights shared by all men everywhere." What that suggests is that American liberalism may have owed much of its initial popularity to its effectiveness as a rhetorical strategy, as the political language of a colonial people who had not yet invented a nation and, therefore, who had not yet constructed a common history.

Everywhere in the public political debates, one encounters the language of rights and equality. Arguments for the dominance of a particular political discourse during any period, of course, are bound to be somewhat impressionistic. Although we can appreciate the echoes of classical republican thought and the inspiration of evangelical Protestantism, we most frequently encounter an angry, shrill, often nervous insistence on natural rights. During the 1760s and early 1770s, colonial writers repeatedly invoked the authority of John Locke, and even when the name of the great philosopher did not appear, his ideas still powerfully informed popular public consciousness. The appeal to natural rights sounded not only in the labored pamphlets that learned university-trained lawyers seem to have written for other learned lawyers but also in the more popular journals and sermons. Throughout prerevolutionary America, men and women responded to what they perceived as English arrogance with a truculent cry: we are as good as any English person. . . .

Natural rights liberalism was so pervasive that a colonial town meeting could quickly transform itself into a public seminar on Lockean philosophy. On November 20, 1772, the Boston Town Meeting charged a committee of twenty-one persons "to state the Rights of the Colonists, and of this Province in particular, as Men, as Christians, and as Subjects." In due time the committee report received the approval of Boston freeholders and other inhabitants. They agreed that "All Men have a Right to remain in a State of Nature as long as they please." No government could compel the subject to surrender his rights. On that central point the authors specifically cited Locke. From him, the Boston committee had learned that "The *natural* Liberty of Man is to be free from any superior Power on Earth, and not to be under the Will or legislative Authority of Man; but only to have the Law of Nature as his Rule." And finally, in a statement clearly intended to mobilize broad popular support, the authors of the report insisted that "All Persons born in the British American Colonies, are by the Laws of God and Nature . . . entitled, to all the natural, essential, inherent, and inseparable Rights, Liberties and Privileges of Subjects born in Great-Britain, or within the Realm." Whatever else this document may contain, its character does not seem particularly religious, nor, for that matter, the stuff of classic civic humanism. Like so many other Americans of this period, the members of the Boston committee demanded inclusion within an empire that seemed to have become increasingly exclusive; they understood instinctively that historical arguments drawn from a shared British past would not have much purchase against the claims of a nationalizing mother country.

A newly aggressive English state forced the Americans to leap out of history and to defend colonial and human equality on the basis of timeless natural rights. English national sentiment did not transform Americans into natural rights liberals, but it was a necessary catalyst. . . . By situating our interpretation of the run-up to revolution in the recent historiography of eighteenth-century England — we discover why the forgotten "Ploughjoggers" of colonial America were so angry and defensive, colonial liberals so fearful of rejection, and, above all, a people so profoundly confused by changing perceptions of identity within the British Empire. It was not until after the Revolution, when Americans confronted the exclusionary and racist logic of their own nationalism, that ordinary men and women had reason to be thankful that whatever their country had become, it had commenced as a society committed to rights and equality, radical concepts then and now.

GARY B. NASH

*from* The Unknown American Revolution     **[2005]**

**GARY B. NASH** (1933– ) is professor emeritus of history at the University of California, Los Angeles, and Director of the National Center for History in the Schools. He is the author of *Quakers and Politics* (1968), *Red, White, and Black* (1974), *The Urban Crucible* (1979), and *The Forgotten Fifth: African Americans in the Age of Revolution* (2006), and coauthor of *History on Trial* (1998).

"Who shall write the history of the American Revolution? Who can write it? Who will ever be able to write it?" Thus wrote John Adams in 1815 to Thomas Jefferson, his old enemy but by this time his septuagenarian friend. "Nobody," Jefferson replied from Monticello, "except merely its external facts. . . . The life and soul of history must be forever unknown."

Not so. For more than two centuries historians have written about the American Revolution, striving to capture the "life and soul" of which Jefferson spoke. We now possess a rich and multistranded tapestry of the Revolution, filled with engaging biographies, local narratives, weighty explorations of America's greatest explosion of political thinking, annals of military tactics and strategies, discussions of religious, economic, and diplomatic aspects of what was then called the "glorious cause," and more. Indeed we now have possession of far more than the "external facts."

Yet the great men — the founding fathers — of the revolutionary era dominate the reigning master narrative. Notwithstanding generations of prodigious scholarship, we have not appreciated the lives and labors, the sacrifices and struggles, the glorious messiness, the hopes and fears of diverse groups that fought in the longest and most disruptive war in our history with visions of launching a new age filling their heads. Little is known, for example, of Thomas Peters, an African-born slave who made his personal declaration of independence in early 1776, fought for the freedom of African Americans, led former slaves to Nova Scotia after the war, and completed a pilgrimage for unalienable rights by shepherding them back to Africa to participate in the founding of Sierra Leone. Why are the history books virtually silent on Dragging Canoe, the Cherokee warrior who made the American Revolution into a two-decade life-sapping fight for his people's life, liberty, and pursuit of happiness? We cannot capture the "life and soul" of the Revolution without paying close attention to the wartime experiences and agendas for change that engrossed backcountry farmers, urban craftsmen, deep-blue mariners, female camp followers and food rioters — those ordinary people who did most of the protesting, most of the fighting, most of the dying, and most of the dreaming about how a victorious America might satisfy the yearnings of all its peoples.

In this book the reader will find, I hope, an antidote for historical amnesia. To this day, the public remembers the Revolution mostly in its enshrined, mythic form. This is peculiar in a democratic society because the sacralized story of the founding fathers, the men of marble, mostly concerns the uppermost slice of American revolutionary society. That is what has lodged in our minds, and this is the fable that millions of people in other countries know about the American Revolution. . . .

This book presents a people's revolution, an upheaval among the most heterogeneous people to be found anywhere along the Atlantic littoral in the eighteenth century. The book's thrust is to complicate the well-established core narrative by putting before the reader bold figures, ideas, and movements, highlighting the true radicalism of the American Revolution that was indispensable to the origins, conduct, character, and outcome of the world-shaking event.

By "radicalism" I mean advocating wholesale change and sharp transformation rooted in a kind of dream life of a better future imagined by those who felt most dissatisfied with the conditions they experienced as the quarrel with Great Britain unfolded. For a reformed America they looked toward a redistribution of political, social, and religious power; the discarding of old institutions and the creation of new ones; the overthrowing of ingrained patterns of conservative, elitist thought; the leveling of society so that top and bottom were not widely separated; the end of the nightmare of slavery and the genocidal intentions of land-crazed frontiersmen; the hope of women of achieving a public voice. This radicalism directed itself at destabilizing a society where the white male elite prized stability because it upheld their close grip on political, economic, religious, sexual, and social power. This radicalism, therefore, was usually connected to a multifaceted campaign to democratize society, to recast the social system, to achieve dreams with deep biblical and historical roots, to put "power in the people," as the first articles of government in Quaker New Jersey expressed it a century before the American Revolution.

The pages that follow mostly view the American Revolution through the eyes of those *not* in positions of power and privilege, though the iconic founding fathers are assuredly part of the story. In reality, those in the nether strata of colonial society and those outside "respectable" society were *most* of the people of revolutionary America. Without their ideas, dreams, and blood sacrifices, the American Revolution would never have occurred, would never have followed the course that we can now comprehend, and would never have reverberated around the world among oppressed people down to the present day. Disinterring these long-forgotten figures from history's cemetery, along with their aspirations and demands, along with the events and dramatic moments in which they figured so importantly, is offered as an antidote to the art of forgetting.

Many of the figures we will encounter were from the middle and lower ranks of American society, and many of them did not have pale complexions. From these ranks, few heroes have emerged to enter the national pantheon. For the most part, they remain anonymous. Partly this is because they faded in and out of the picture, rarely achieving the tenure and status of men such as John Adams and John Hancock of Boston, Robert Morris and Benjamin Franklin of Philadelphia, Alexander Hamilton and John Jay of New York, or Thomas Jefferson, Patrick Henry, and George Washington of Virginia, all of whom remained on the scene from the Revolution's beginning to the very end. But, although they never rose to the top of society, where they could trumpet their own achievements and claim their place in the pages of history, many other men and women counted greatly at the time. "Lived inequalities," writes the Haitian philosopher-historian Michel-Rolph Trouillot, "yield unequal historical power." The shortness of their lives also explains the anonymity of ordinary people. It is safer to conduct a revolution from the legislative chamber than fight for it on the battlefield, healthier to be free than enslaved, and one is more likely to reach old age with money than with crumbs.

Even a casual reading of the reflections of those who occupy our national pantheon shows that these founders were far from reverent in their views of one another, and far from agreed on how to tell the story of the nation's birth. They thought the story would be messy, ambiguous, and complicated because they had experienced the Revolution in just these ways — as a seismic eruption from the hands of an internally divided people, two decades of problems that sometimes seemed insoluble, a gnawing fear that the course of the Revolution was contradicting its bedrock principles, and firsthand knowledge of the shameful behavior that was interlaced with heroic self-sacrifice during the long travail. . . .

While those atop the social pyramid couldn't agree on how to parcel out credit for the outcome of the American Revolution, or even to tell the story honestly, a few of them industriously published histories they hoped would serve to instruct the generations to come. In this effort, they were forerunners of a true people's history of the Revolution because they understood how crucial the rank and file of American society were to the outcome. For example, David Ramsay, transplanted from Pennsylvania to South Carolina, where he served as a delegate to the Continental Congress, organized his *The History of the American Revolution* around the key notion that "The great bulk of those, who were the active instruments of carrying on the revolution, were self-made, industrious men. These who by their own exertions, had established or laid a foundation for establishing *personal independence*, were most generally trusted, and most successfully employed in establishing that of their country." Ramsay also appreciated, even if in muted tones, the centrality of black and Native Americans to the Revolution. Publishing his account just a year after the ratification of the Constitution, Ramsay implored the new American generation — in two pages of advice at the end of his book — to "let the hapless African sleep undisturbed on his native shore and give over wishing for the extermination of the ancient proprietors of this land." . . .

Mercy Otis Warren, wife and sister of two important Massachusetts patriots, also hoped that the readers of her *History of the Rise, Progress, and Termination of the American Revolution* (published in 1805) would find moral lessons in her three-volume account; and she harbored no doubts that this obliged her to dwell on the bitter as well as the sweet, the ordinary as well as the great. Giving considerable play to women's importance in the Revolution, she wrote in detail about how ordinary Massachusetts plowmen and leather-apron men rose up in 1774 in "one of the most extraordinary eras in the history of man" — one that "led to that most alarming experiment of leveling of all ranks and destroying all subordination." Indeed, Warren gave *too much* importance to lesser people and not nearly enough to John Adams, husband of her good friend Abigail — or so John told her. Adams was furious at her history. Putting the writing of his autobiography aside, he wrote ten long letters telling her why. Yet Warren's was one of the accounts that, in paying attention to common people, anticipated Ralph Waldo Emerson's plea four decades later in his famous essay entitled "The American Scholar," where he urged those who would truly know their history to understand "the near, the low, the common."

After the last of the revolutionary generation was in their graves, some began to worry that forward-looking Americans, many of them plunging west, were losing all memory of the American Revolution. Philadelphia's John Fanning Watson in 1825 urged the newborn Historical Society of Pennsylvania "to rescue from oblivion the facts of personal prowess, achievements, or sufferings by officers and soldiers of the Revolutionary war" and to record "the recitals of many brave men now going down to the tomb." Watson was passionately interested in the "great" men of the Revolution but also the "many privates 'unknown to fame' peculiarly distinguished by their actions," for example, Zenas Macumber, a private in Washington's bodyguard who had served through the entire war and survived seventeen wounds.

Watson's fellow amateur historian Benson Lossing, orphaned at eleven and apprenticed to a watchmaker at fourteen in Poughkeepsie, New York, walked eight thousand miles in his midthirties to commune "with men of every social and intellectual grade" and sketch every part of the American landscape involved in the Revolutionary War for a hefty two-volume *Pictorial Field-Book of the American Revolution* (1850, 1852). While detailing every major battle of the Revolution, Lossing sprinkled his military history with vignettes about ordinary people: the poor shoemaker George Robert Twelves Hewes, who participated in the Boston Tea Party; the hardscrabble North Carolina farmers living in a region barren of printing presses, newspapers, and schools, who assembled to elect representatives from their militia companies who passed the Mecklenburg Resolutions that all but announced independence in May 1775, far ahead of the rest of the country; a frontier woman who beat off an Indian attack; and Pompey, the slave in the Hudson River valley who led General Anthony Wayne and his men "through the narrow defiles, over rough crags, and across deep morasses in single file" to storm the British fortress at Stony Point in July 1779.

Two years before the public saw Lossing's first volume of the *Pictorial Field-Book*, the granddaughter of a revolutionary soldier, Elizabeth Ellet, published *The Women of the American Revolution*, two volumes that sketched the lives of sixty women "who bore their part in the Revolution." In 1850, she followed with *The Domestic History of the American Revolution*. Prominent women had their place — Abigail Adams, Martha Washington, and Mercy Otis Warren, for example. But most vignettes related the "actions and sufferings" of unheralded women such as sixteen-year-old Dicey Langston, who in the dead of night stealthily moved through woods, forded unbridged creeks, and slogged through marshes to deliver news of Loyalist troops on the march to her brother's patriot camp in backcountry South Carolina. Many of the stories passed down from her remain unknown today.

Contemporaneous with these scribes of revolutionary heroes large and small were radical activists not only interested in ordinary people as agents of revolutionary change but worried about the conservative, reverent, tragedy-free core narrative being peddled in schoolbooks and popular histories by a genteel band of white male writers. Among the first to deplore this was a man remembered by virtually no American today. Born of obscure parents in 1822 near Philadelphia, George Lippard in his early twenties flashed across the literary sky like a meteor. A callow, crusading journalist, he took up labor's cause during the latter stages of the severe depression of 1837–1844. Sharpening his skills as a writer for the penny newspaper *Spirit of the Times*, whose motto was "Democratic and Fearless," Lippard turned into a "literary volcano constantly erupting with hot rage against America's ruling class." His *Quaker City, or, the Monks of Monk Hall* became a best seller in 1844. A muckraker before the term was coined, Lippard described Philadelphia as a stomach-turning subversion of American democracy and an insult to the old ideal of the City of Brotherly Love. Philadelphia's venerated leaders, charged Lippard, displayed a "callow indifference to the poor" that was "equaled only by their private venality and licentiousness." The book made him the most widely read author in the nation. His sales far exceeded those of Nathaniel Hawthorne, Herman Melville, Henry David Thoreau, Ralph Waldo Emerson, or Washington Irving; in fact, Lippard's books sold more than those of all the authors of the transcendentalist school put together.

In 1846, Lippard began churning out legends of the American Revolution, and this is where he becomes relevant to the concerns of this book. Writing at a frantic pace, he freshened the public's memory of local battles at Germantown and Brandywine, British victories that paved the way for the enemy occupation of Philadelphia in September 1777. Mixing hair-raising descriptions of the terrors of war with florid portraits of American battlefield heroism, Lippard presented the Revolution as a poor man's war, one that he hoped would provide inspiration for mid-nineteenth century labor reformers whom he admired and promoted. His stories in *Washington and His Generals; or Legends of the American Revolution* (1847) and *Washington and His Men* (1849) gave Washington his due, but it was the common man on the battlefield who was the true hero. "Let me make a frank confession," Lippard told the City Institute in 1852, after millions had read his books. "I have been led astray. I have looked upon effigies and . . . bowed down to uniforms and done reverence to epaulettes. . . . Gilt and paint and spangles have for ages commanded reverence, while men made in the image of God have died in the ditch." Lippard got more particular: "The General who receives all the glory of the battles said to have been fought under his eye, who is worshiped in poetry and history, received in every city which he may enter by hundreds of thousands, who makes the heavens ring with his name; this General then is not *the* hero. No; the hero is the private soldier, who stands upon the battle field; . . . the poor soldier . . . whose skull bleaches in the sands, while the general whose glory the volunteer helped to win is warm and comfortable upon his mimic throne." Lippard cautioned his audience to "worship the hero . . . [and] reverence the heroic; but have a care that you are not swindled by a bastard heroism; be very careful of the sham hero."

Lippard gave polite history a bad name; but the public loved him. He became their cultural arbiter and provided their understanding of the American Revolution. In a separate book, *Thomas Paine, Author-Soldier* (1852), Lippard helped restore Paine's reputation, which had gone into deep eclipse after Paine's attack on Christianity in *The Age of Reason*, written in the heat of the French Revolution. *The Age of Reason* left Paine an unattractive figure in polite circles and deeply offended churchgoing people. Yet Lippard's interest in Paine led to new editions of the revolutionary radical's many works, because Lippard rescued him as the unswerving herald of democracy who had more to say to the struggling mid-nineteenth century urban masses than all the revolutionary generals and statesmen. A year after Lippard's death in 1854, at age thirty-two, the Friends of Universal Liberty and Freedom, Emancipation and General Ruction celebrated "St. Thomas" Paine's birthday in Philadelphia. . . .

Lippard often dissolved the line between fiction and history in his revolutionary tales. Having Paine convert to Christianity on his deathbed or having the traitor Benedict Arnold don his old Continental army uniform and recant in his dying moments were examples of the liberties he took. The story of the muscular Black Sampson of the "Oath-Bound Five," who avenged the British murder of his white mistress by plunging into the Battle of Brandywine against the redcoats with Debbil, his ferocious dog, was pure fiction. So were other tales he told, though the historical events of which these vignettes were a part were accurate. Philadelphia's *Saturday Evening Post* charged that Lippard had "taken the liberty to palter with and corrupt the pages of history." Lippard retreated not an inch. He countered that in the hands of genteel historians, "The thing which generally

passes for History is the most impudent, swaggering bully, the most grace-
less braggart, the most reckless equivocator that ever staggered forth on
the great stage of the world." He embellished, he admitted. But a legend
from his hand, he explained, was "one of those heart-warm stories, which,
quivering in rude, earnest language from the lips of a spectator of a battle, or the survivor of some event of olden time, fill up the cold outlines
of history, and clothe the skeleton with flesh and blood, give it eyes and
tongue, force it at once to look into our eyes and talk with us!"

Even as Lippard was publishing his first stories about the poor man's
American Revolution, radical abolitionists were taking up the same cause.
But they were particularly concerned about how the contributions of free
black people, and some slaves, were fading away. John Greenleaf Whittier,
poet laureate of the abolitionist movement, took up his pen in dismay
and anger after hearing July 4 orations in the nation's capital. Writing in
1847 in Washington, D.C.'s *National Era*, an antislavery newspaper, he
expostulated on how "the return of the Festival of our National Independence has called our attention to a matter which has been very carefully
kept out of sight by orators and toast-drinkers." Why, asked Whittier, does
"a whole nation [do] honor to the memories of one class of its defenders,
to the total neglect of another class, who had the misfortune to be of
darker complexion?" For a half century, Whittier charged, "certain historical facts . . . have been quietly elbowed aside," that are of "the services
and sufferings of the colored soldiers of the Revolution." "They have no
historian," he continued. "With here and there an exception, they all
passed away, and only some faint tradition of their campaigns under
Washington and Greene and Lafayette, and of their cruisings under Decatur
and Barry, lingers among their descendants." . . .

The current generation of historians — a diverse group that looks
more truly American than any preceding one — has scoured the records
and posed new questions to take to the sources. In the last few decades a
remarkable flowering of an American history sensitive to gender, race,
religion, and class, which is to say a democratized history, is giving us an
alternative, long-forgotten American Revolution. "Each generation," the
English historian Christopher Hill told us several decades ago, "rescues a
new area from what its predecessors arrogantly and snobbishly dismissed
as 'the lunatic fringe.'" But "it is no longer necessary to apologize pro-
fusely for taking the common people of the past on their own terms and
trying to understand them," Hill advises. This book responds to this advice.

The aim of this book is to capture the revolutionary involvement of *all*
the component parts of some three million wildly diverse people living
east of the Mississippi River. I could not have attempted such a study without
changes in the historical profession over the past few decades — something
akin to a tectonic plate shift. Clio, the muse of history, is hardly recognizable today in comparison to her visage of 1960. The emergence of a profession of historians of widely different backgrounds has redistributed historical property, and the American Revolution is now becoming the property of the many rather than the few. Even the best-remembered heroes

are now seen with all their ambiguities, contradictions, and flaws. For example, it is no longer unpatriotic to read of Washington and Jefferson's tortured relationship to slavery, always mentioned in past biographies but usually soft-pedaled and marginalized. Now one can choose from a stack of books with enticing titles on the founding fathers and slavery such as William Wiencek's *An Imperfect God: George Washington, His Slaves, and the Creation of America*; Lucia C. Stanton's *Free Some Day: The African American Families of Monticello*; or David Waldstreicher's *Runaway America: Benjamin Franklin, Slavery, and the American Revolution.*

When historians fix their gaze downward or write a warts-and-all American history, they often offend people who cherish what they remember as a more coherent, worshipful, and supposedly annealing rendition of the past. In the history wars of the 1990s, many conservative-culture warriors called historians offering new interpretations of the American Revolution — or any other part of American history — "history bandits," "history pirates," or, sneeringly, "revisionists" intent on kidnapping history with no respect for a dignified rendition of the past. Yet the explosion of historical knowledge has invigorated history and increased its popularity. People who discover in accounts of the past figures like themselves — in color or class, religion, sex, or social situation — naturally find history more satisfying than when it is organized around a triumphalist version of the past in which the occupants of the national pantheon, representing a very narrow slice of society, get most of the play. Narratives of glory will always have a market, and some people will always prefer an uncomplicated, single-message history. But empathy with less than oversized figures, as much in history as in literature, has a market as well.

Unsurprisingly, those of the old school do not like to hear the question "whose history?" It is unsettling for them to see the intellectual property of the American Revolution, once firmly in the hands of a smaller and more homogeneous historians' guild, taken out of their safe boxes, put on the table, and redivided. Yet what could be more democratic than to reopen questions about the Revolution's sources, conduct, and results? And what is the lasting value of a "coherent" history if coherence is obtained by eliminating the jagged edges, where much of the vitality of the people is to be found? How can we expect people to think of the American Revolution as their own when they see no trace of their forebears in it? Historian Roger Wilkins writes: "Tales of the republic's founding — mythic national memories used to bind us together — are often told in ways that exclude and diminish all of us" (and thus, it might be added, keep us divided). In propagating this kind of simplified history "we ensure that our future will be rent along the same jagged seams that wound us so grievously today. There is much pain and loss in our national history, which contains powerful echoes of the pain and loss many of us feel in our daily lives."

A history of inclusion has another claim to make. Only a history that gives play to all the constituent parts of society can overcome the defeatist notion that the past was inevitably determined. Historical inevitability is a winner's story, excusing mistakes of the past and relegating the loser's story to a footnote. Is it not fitting in an open and generally optimistic society that we should portray a wide range of individuals who did not see themselves as puppets dancing on the strings of the supposed leaders? If the history we are making today is subject to human will, or what historians call human agency, then yesterday's history must have been fluid and unpredictable rather than moving along some predetermined course. If history did not unfold inevitably in the American Revolution, then surely a great many people must have been significant actors in its unfolding. Conscious of a complex past, readers today can embrace the idea that they, too, can contribute to a different future. Honest history can impart a sense of how the lone individual counts, how the possibilities of choice are infinite, how human capacity for both good and evil is ever present, and how dreams of a better society are in the hands of the dispossessed as much as in the possession of the putative brokers of our society's future.

# The Constitution: Conflict or Consensus?

The Constitution remains one of the most controversial documents in all of American history. Generations of Supreme Court justices have re-interpreted the document according to their own predilections when handing down constitutional decisions. Presidents and political parties in power traditionally have viewed the Constitution in the light of their own interests, pursuits, and philosophies of government; historians have presented conflicting interpretations of the Constitution and of the intentions of its framers. This changing outlook of historians has tended to coincide with changes in the intellectual climate of opinion within America.

From the Convention of 1787 to the close of the Civil War, the Constitution was considered a controversial document by historians because of the questions it raised about two opposing doctrines: states' rights versus national sovereignty, or a strict versus a loose construction of the Constitution. The outcome of the Civil War seemed to settle the issue in favor of the national theory of the Constitution.

Since the Civil War, however, six distinct groups of historians have arisen to offer differing interpretations of the constitutional period. The first, the nationalist school, emerged in the 1870s and 1880s; it approached the Constitution influenced by the intense nationalism marking American society in the Gilded Age. Around the turn of the century, there appeared the Progressive school that viewed the document and its framing in light of the Populist-Progressive reform movements of the 1890s and early 1900s. Charles A. Beard, the leading Progressive scholar, saw the Constitution as a document that was intended to protect private property and that reflected the interests of privileged groups in postrevolutionary America. Since World War II, three groups of historians — the consensus, the new intellectual historians, and the neo-Progressives — arose either to revise or to refine the Beardian interpretation. Then in the 1990s, another group arose, the new political historians who defined politics broadly to include conventional politics but also cultural manifestations with political meaning, and who studied a range of groups and offered perspectives on those "other founders" affected by the Constitution but left out of deliberations about it.[1]

---

[1]Saul Cornell, *The Other Founders: Antifederalism and the Dissenting Tradition in America, 1788–1828* (Chapel Hill, N.C., 1999); Jeffrey Pasley, Andrew Robertson, and David Waldstreicher, *Beyond the Founders: New Approaches to the Political History of the Early American Republic* (Chapel Hill, N.C., 2004).

George Bancroft and John Fiske best represented the nationalist school, which developed in the decades after the Civil War. Both believed in the racial superiority of white Anglo-Saxon Protestant peoples. They subscribed to the idea that the orderly progress of mankind toward greater personal liberty in modern times was due largely to the preeminent political ability of Anglo-Saxon peoples to build strong and stable national states. According to these two writers, America's democratic institutions could be traced all the way back to the ancient political practices of Teutonic tribes in the forests of Germany. The Constitution, in their eyes, represented the high point in world history in the efforts of human beings to civilize and govern themselves.

Bancroft visualized the years 1782 to 1788 as a single period, with the ratification of the Constitution as the climax of the Revolution itself.[2] The Articles of Confederation, ratified in 1781, were too weak to cope with external threats from Britain and Spain and internal problems such as Shays's Rebellion. The American people demanded a new and better instrument of government. Since America was divinely ordained to create the first perfect republic on earth, according to Bancroft, the Constitution symbolized the crowning success of the movement for a more popular government that had started with the Revolution.

Around the turn of the twentieth century, the Populist and Progressive reform movements brought about a marked change in attitudes toward the Constitution. Progressive reformers, concerned with the problems that had arisen from increasing industrialization, became convinced that unless the imbalance in wealth and political power in American society could be redressed, democracy in the United States was doomed. In response, state governments in the 1890s and early 1900s began regulating various aspects of the economy. Congress at the same time was making efforts to regulate certain industries like the railroads and to break up monopolies and trusts. To check the growing maldistribution of wealth, the state and federal governments passed income tax measures. When the Supreme Court declared much of this state and national legislation unconstitutional, however, many persons began to view the Constitution as an undemocratic document whose purpose was to protect the rich and powerful and to frustrate the democratic aspirations of the people.

To Progressive historians, conservatives wrote a reactionary Constitution at the 1787 convention to thwart the radicals who held visions of completely reforming American society. These scholars pointed to the undemocratic features of the Constitution — the system of checks and balances, the difficulty of adopting amendments, and the idea of judicial veto — which made majority rule all but impossible. Unlike the nationalist historians who had seen the Constitution as a forward step for democracy, the Progressive historians saw it as a setback in the movement for popular government.

---

[2]George Bancroft, *History of the Formation of the Constitution of the United States of America,* 2 vols. (New York, 1882). The glowing praise of John Fiske in *The Critical Period of American History, 1783–1789* (New York, 1888), 223, is typical of this period.

Many writers of the Progressive school reflected a major trend in historical circles at the time — the tendency toward an economic interpretation of history. The Progressive interpretation of the Constitution was based upon class conflict along economic lines — a point of view that had grown out of Carl Becker's interpretation of the American Revolution as a dual revolution posing the questions of home rule and who would rule at home. In the internal class struggle that took place, the lower classes — made up of small farmers in the interior and workingmen along the eastern seaboard towns — gained dominance over the upper classes — composed of merchants, financiers, and manufacturers. Once the lower classes were in control, the Progressive version continued, they proceeded to democratize American society by writing radical state constitutions and the Articles of Confederation. They set up democratic governments, which passed cheap paper money legislation, debtor laws, and measures that favored the small farmers.

Members of the upper classes whose economic stake was in personal property — holdings in money and public securities or investments in manufacturing, shipping, and commerce — became particularly alarmed because the democratic governments seemed to be discriminating against their kind of property and in favor of those who owned land and real estate. It was they who conspired to undermine the democratic Articles of Confederation and instituted instead the more conservative Constitution.

Charles A. Beard expressed this Progressive point of view most ably in *An Economic Interpretation of the Constitution*, published in 1913. The key to Beard's pathbreaking study was a person-by-person examination of the economic holdings and status of the framers of the Constitution. Using U.S. Treasury records, Beard was able to show that most of these men held public securities, a form of personal property that would increase dramatically in value if a new Constitution were written to strengthen the government and thus improve the nation's credit standing. Beard concluded, "The movement for the Constitution of the United States was originated and carried through principally by four groups of personalty interests which had been adversely affected under the Articles of Confederation: money, public securities, manufactures, and trade and shipping."[3] Those opposed were mostly small farmers and workingmen so far in debt that they could not qualify to vote for delegates to the Constitutional Convention.

Beard's book was perhaps the most influential work in American history of all time. Vernon L. Parrington's *Main Currents in American Thought*, published in 1927, and Louis M. Hacker's *Triumph of American Capitalism*, which appeared in 1940, echoed Beard's point of view. Textbooks in history and political science repeated Beard's thesis verbatim. Today's constitutional scholars still contend with Beard's ideas. Almost all interpretations of the Constitution written since Beard's book have been forced into a pro- or anti-Beard position. Until World War II, Beard, though often contested, reigned.

---

[3]Charles A. Beard, *An Economic Interpretation of the Constitution of the United States*, rev. ed. (New York, 1935), 324.

Since World War II, however, historians have launched strong challenges at Beard's interpretation. Although they often disagreed in their interpretations of the Constitution, they all agreed that Beard's study did not offer a satisfactory explanation of the document. The first of these, the consensus historians, rejected two of Beard's basic assumptions. First, they viewed the Constitution as evidence of a consensus rather than a class conflict among the American people. Second, they believed that the revolutionary and constitutional periods represented a line of continuous growth; they dismissed Beard's idea of a period of radical revolution followed by one of conservative reaction.

These two themes were reflected in the suggestive title — *Consensus and Continuity, 1776–1787* — of a book written by Benjamin F. Wright in 1958. Wright, a political scientist, viewed the Constitution as a political, not an economic, document. The most striking characteristic of the delegates at the Constitutional Convention, he claimed, was the broad agreement among them regarding what they considered to be the essentials of good government, including such basic issues as representation, fixed elections, a written constitution that is a supreme law and contains an amendment clause, separation of powers and checks and balances, a bicameral legislature, a single executive, and a separate court system. These principles could not have been taken for granted in any other country in the eighteenth century. The extent of this basic agreement better indicates the thought of Americans in 1787 than do the disputes over matters of detail or those based largely upon sectional disagreement or upon the size of the states.[4]

Wright showed also an essential continuity between the Revolution and the constitutional periods so far as men and ideas were concerned. The same men who held responsible public offices in 1787 held them in 1776. Wright noted, moreover, that the political ideas of the Revolution were expressed best in the state constitutions, which were, in many instances, framed by the very same men who had written and signed the Declaration of Independence. How could the constitutional period be considered a reaction to the Revolution? For Wright, as for most consensus historians, the Constitution was seen as the fulfillment of the Revolution.

Robert E. Brown in his study *Charles Beard and the Constitution*, published in 1956, challenged Beard's evidence.[5] He showed that Beard had consulted Treasury records dated several years after the Constitutional Convention in order to substantiate the point that the founding fathers had held public securities at the time they framed the document. Brown's study also challenged one of Beard's underlying assumptions that the "propertyless masses" of small farmers and workingmen were unable to participate in the political process. American society in the 1780s, according to Brown, was basically democratic because the majority of people were small farmers who owned enough land to qualify for the right to vote. To Brown, then, the Constitution

---

[4]Benjamin F. Wright, *Consensus and Continuity, 1776–1787* (Boston, 1958), 36.
[5]Robert E. Brown, *Charles Beard and the Constitution: A Critical Analysis of "An Economic Interpretation of the Constitution"* (New York, 1956).

represented the wishes of a democratically minded middle class rather than those of an aristocratically minded upper class. Brown did not find class conflict.

Most historians in the post–World War II period agreed with Wright and Brown. Their attitude toward the framers of the Constitution was far more favorable than that of the previous generation. Constitutional historians such as Henry Steele Commager declared that the Constitution was primarily a political document focusing mainly on the problem of federalism, not an economic document.[6] Many historians praised the constitutional period as a constructive era rather than a destructive age in which a propertied minority robbed the majority of the American people of their rights. These historians were reflecting a response to the challenges of communism abroad. To bolster America's position as preeminent leader of the free world, historians sought to show that the United States had been a strong and united country throughout its history and one free from class-based oppression.

Another challenge to the Beardian interpretation came from a generation of new intellectual historians whose work first appeared in the mid-1950s. These historians emphasized ideas. This renewed interest in ideas as an explanation of the Revolutionary era led scholars like Bernard Bailyn, Gordon Wood, Douglass Adair, and Cecelia Kenyon to view the confederation period and the writing of the Constitution within the broad framework of America's intellectual inheritance from Europe. Scholars like Caroline Robbins and Bernard Bailyn, writing in the 1960s, demonstrated the importance of British antiauthoritarian thought and how it influenced the formulation of America's republican ideology.[7]

One major problem facing the founding fathers was how to erect a republic whose representatives were elected by the people and, at the same time, to prevent the formation of a majority faction that might undermine the government. Republican governments in the past had inevitably succumbed to the tyranny of a majority faction. Douglass Adair, one of the new intellectual historians, wrote an article pointing out that James Madison's thoughts on the subject — contrary to Beard's economic interpretation — could be traced back to Hume.[8] America's enormous size and the multiplicity of factions and interests arising from that size, Madison had said, would make it less likely that this country would suffer the fate of earlier republics. The existence of so many diverse interests would make it difficult, if not impossible, for factions to reconcile their differences and to come together to form a majority faction.

Cecelia Kenyon took issue with Beard's view of the debate between the Federalists, who supported the Constitution, and the Antifederalists, who

---

[6]Henry Steel Commager and Allan Nevins, *America, the Story of a Free People* (New York, 1942).

[7]Bernard Bailyn, *The Ideological Origins of the American Revolution* (Cambridge, Mass., 1967); Caroline Robbins, *The Eighteenth-Century Commonwealthman; Studies in the Transmission, Development, and Circumstances of English Thought from the Restoration of Charles II until the War with the Thirteen Colonies* (Cambridge, Mass., 1959).

[8]Douglass Adair, 'That Politics May Be Reduced to a Science': David Hume, James Madison, and the Tenth Federalist," *Huntington Library Quarterly* 20 (1957): 343–60.

opposed it. Beard had portrayed the Antifederalists as majority-minded democrats, but Kenyon argued that the Antifederalists were as much anti-majoritarians as the Federalists and shared a common Whig mistrust of governmental power — legislative as well as executive. The Antifederalists believed, however, citing the French philosopher Montesquieu, that a successful republic must be geographically small and composed of a homogeneous population. What really distinguished the Antifederalists from the Federalists, Kenyon concluded, was their lack of faith in the ability of Americans to create and sustain a republic continental in size.[9]

The single most important work representing the point of view of these intellectual historians was *The Creation of the American Republic, 1776–1787* by Gordon S. Wood, published in 1969. A student of Bailyn, Wood explicitly connected the conceptual scheme of the American patriots to the classical republican tradition that existed in England. Wood portrayed American leaders as idealists at the start of the Revolution — men who dreamed of setting up a utopian commonwealth along lines English thinkers had earlier set forth. It was a radical ideology with moral implications. Revolutionary leaders, believing there was a direct relationship between the type of government a nation had and the character of its people, hoped that a republican government would morally regenerate the American people and thereby enable them to sustain a republic of continuing virtue.

Events of the late 1770s and early 1780s dashed these high hopes. The Revolution unleashed democratic forces that accelerated the breakdown of the existing hierarchy. What emerged in the 1780s was a society characterized by excessive egalitarianism, a contempt for the law by state legislatures bent on abusing their supremacy, oppression of minorities by the majority, and an increasing love of luxury that undermined the people's virtue. The 1780s were a "critical period" in moral terms, Wood said, because they shattered the dreams American leaders had in 1776 of creating a republican government along traditional lines.

The writing of the Constitution, then, was an attempt to save the Revolution from possible failure by restraining some of its democratic excesses. To Wood, the Constitution developed into a struggle between forward-looking Federalists and old-fashioned Antifederalists. Instead of the old idea of mixed government, in which the Antifederalists believed, the Federalists proposed that sovereignty resided in the people rather than in any single branch. Hence government should be divided into separate parts, not because each part represented a different social constituency, as the Antifederalists supposed, but simply because it would serve as a check upon the other branches of government. Every branch of government, in effect, represented the people. The result was the creation of a governmental system that was more modern, more realistic about political behavior, and that marked, according to Wood, the

---

[9]Cecelia M. Kenyon, "Men of Little Faith: The Antifederalists on the Nature of Representative Government," *William and Mary Quarterly*, 3rd Ser., 12 (1955): 3–43.

"end of classical politics in America."[10] The Federalists, troubled by the need to slow disorder in America during the confederation period, clung to a notion of political representation that emphasized deference and an elitist conception of republicanism. Wood's book dominated much of the profession for a decade and a half after its publication in 1969. The first selection in this chapter is from Wood's volume.

It remained for J. G. A. Pocock in 1975 to round out what came to be called "the republican synthesis." This synthesis, which encompassed both the Revolution and the Constitution, incorporated the writings of Bailyn and Wood. Pocock demonstrated how republican ideas distilled from the philosophers of ancient Greece and Rome, Renaissance Italian writers like Machiavelli, seventeenth-century republicans such as Harrington, and eighteenth-century English "country party" authors contributed to the American intellectual outlook.[11]

Embodied in this ideology was a constellation of ideas: the view of an inherent republican character in the American people; their desire for virtue; their fear of tyranny, corruption, and luxury; and particularly their dread of power. British policies intensifying these beliefs helped bring on the Revolution. Experience under the Articles of Confederation gave Americans a new perspective on them and led to the writing of the Constitution. This idealist approach was obviously at odds with the old Progressive interpretation that had downplayed the role of ideas.[12]

From the mid-1960s, beginning with the publication of Bailyn's book, until about the mid-1980s, the slowly emerging republican synthesis exercised a strong sway over the profession. But before, during, and after the bicentennial of the Constitution, the synthesis came under increasing criticism. It is impossible to summarize the vast literature appearing during the bicentennial, but at least three major trends were discernible. First, there were the battles over the republican synthesis and its alleged shortcomings: its overemphasis of ideology and its deemphasis of economic interests, its slighting of other important intellectual influences besides classical republicanism (including classical liberalism, Scottish common sense philosophy, and English common law), its failure to address ideas and practices regarding the political economy, and its omission of religion as a meaningful force in shaping political ideology. Second, there appeared a discernible trend away from the preoccupation with ideology toward a more integrative

---

[10]Gordon S. Wood, *The Creation of the American Republic, 1776–1787* (Chapel Hill, N.C., 1969, 1998), 606.

[11]Robert Shalhope, "Toward a Republican Synthesis: The Emergence of an Understanding of Republicanism in American Historiography," *William and Mary Quarterly*, 3rd Ser., 29 (1972): 49–80, and "Republicanism and Early American Historiography," *William and Mary Quarterly*, 3rd Ser., 39 (1982): 334–56. For Pocock's works, see *The Machiavellian Moment* (Princeton, N.J., 1975), *Politics, Language, and Time* (New York, 1960), and *The Ancient Constitution and the Feudal Law* (Cambridge, 1957).

[12]Gordon Wood in a penetrating essay in the mid-1960s himself called for a synthesis of the idealist and Progressive historiographical traditions, but they continued on their separate paths. See Wood, "Rhetoric and Reality in the American Revolution," *William and Mary Quarterly*, 3rd Ser., 23 (1966): 3–32.

approach that incorporated institutional, intellectual, social, cultural, and economic history as well as ideology into a broadly defined new political history. Third, there was a considerable amount of writing about the framing of the Constitution by scholars in other disciplines—political scientists, law professors, and legal theorists.[13]

Many of the criticisms of the republican synthesis were highlighted in a symposium held on Wood's book in 1987. Ruth Bloch was critical of Wood's contention that classical republicanism had ended by 1790; she noted that Pocock, Lance Banning, John Murrin, and Drew McCoy had all demonstrated that this concept had continuing vitality beyond that decade. Edward Countryman criticized Wood for writing his book as though a single intelligence lay behind the quotations he employed to draw the composite portraits of the Federalists and Antifederalists rather than focusing on single individuals and their distinctive intellectual positions. John Patrick Diggins took exception to the picture of consensus politics he felt was portrayed in Wood's description of the period. John Howe concluded that Wood had not emphasized enough the role of either religious beliefs or views on political economy in forming political convictions in the constitutional era.[14]

Wood defended his position on two grounds. First, he claimed that many of his critics had assumed a different role for ideas in human experience than he had intended. Their assumptions were that there is "a sharp separation between beliefs and behavior, between ideas and actions, [and] between culture and society." Wood, on the other hand, believed that "all human behavior can only be understood and explained, indeed can only exist, in terms of the meanings it has. Ideology creates behavior." Second, in response to those who argued that classical republicanism may have played less a part in late-eighteenth-century thought and action, Wood responded that republicanism and liberalism were historical constructs created by scholars. In the preface to his 1998 edition of the *Creation of the American Republic, 1776–1787,* Wood argued that historians, eager to label and explain, have wielded the concepts in too mechanical a fashion — republican and liberal traditions coexisted comfortably in the minds of eighteenth-century Americans. In the end and despite Wood's defense, it was clear that in the future the republican synthesis would have to address itself to certain issues

---

[13]The best historiographical essay on writings in the bicentennial was Peter Onuf's "Reflections on the Founding: Constitutional Historiography in Bicentennial Perspective," *William and Mary Quarterly,* 3rd Ser., 46 (1989): 341–75, a piece that not only reviews the literature but also contains many original insights. See also Richard Bernstein, "Charting the Bicentennial," *Columbia Law Review* 87 (1987): 1565–624, and Jack P. Greene, *A Bicentennial Bookshelf: Historians Analyze the Constitution Era* (Philadelphia, 1986). For a work that shows the popular neglect of the Constitution and its meaning, see Michael Kammen, *A Machine That Would Go of Itself: The Constitution in American Culture* (New York, 1986).

[14]"*The Creation of the American Republic, 1776–1787*: A Symposium of Views and Reviews," *William and Mary Quarterly,* 3rd Ser., 44 (1987): 550–657. Other critics included Jackson Turner Main, opposing the notion that ideas were the only motive of the framers, and Gary Nash, objecting to the omission of social groups like artisans, women, and blacks.

he had either omitted or deemphasized: the political economy, religion, those left out of citizenship, and interests such as sectionalism.[15]

A major debate sparked by Wood's book during the bicentennial was whether the Constitution had indeed marked "the end of classical politics in America." Some scholars held that classical republicanism was supplanted by another tradition — liberalism — either before, during, or after the adoption of the Constitution. This shift was said to signal the transition from premodern to modern America. Under classical republicanism, citizens presumably had followed the precepts of civic humanism within a premodern society: the pursuit of the public good, the upholding of virtue, and the hatred of luxury and corruption. With liberalism there appeared instead the pursuit of self-interest, a sense of personal acquisitiveness, and greater individual striving and competitiveness — in short, the attributes of modern America. The debate, which reflected contemporary political differences between scholars who worried about the advent of capitalism and those who favored it, focused on the relative intensity of the two outlooks, which became dominant, and at what time. By the end of the 1980s, it was generally agreed that both were present in the new Republic, that both were very influential, and that neither tradition appeared to have had undisputed primacy during the decades of the 1780s or 1790s.[16]

Another controversy over Wood's book arose over which intellectual traditions besides republicanism and liberalism had influenced America during the constitutional period. Garry Wills in *Explaining America: The Federalist* made a case for David Hume and the Scottish moral philosophers. The writings of Sacvan Bercovitch and others on Puritanism and Alan Heimert and Rhys Isaac on evangelical Protestantism demonstrated the importance of religion to America's political culture in that period. Forrest McDonald showed in an insightful way the bearing that certain English and European traditions had upon the framing of the Constitution. Wood, to be sure, had acknowledged certain of these intellectual traditions, as well as the role of religion, but had not given them sufficient attention, according to his critics.[17]

Historians, including Wood, also contended with controversies from scholars in other disciplines who were writing about the Constitution. One such challenge came from political scientists and legal theorists who did not accept the historians' methodologies. This was particularly true of the followers of the political theorist Leo Strauss. The Straussians, as they were called, condemned

---

[15]Ibid., 628, 631, 634; quotation from 631; Wood, *The Creation of the American Republic, 1776–1787*, 1998 ed., Preface.

[16]Lance Banning, "Quid Transit? Paradigms and Process in the Transformation of Republican Ideas," *Reviews in American History* 17 (1989): 199; Wood, *Creation*, 1998, Preface.

[17]Garry Wills, *Explaining America: The Federalist* (New York, 1981); Sacvan Bercovitch, *American Jeremiad* (Madison, Wis., 1978); Alan Heimert, *Religion and the American Mind: From the Great Awakening to the Revolution* (Cambridge, 1966); Rhys Isaac, *Transformation of Virginia, 1740–1790* (Chapel Hill, N.C., 1982); Forrest McDonald, *Novus Ordo Seclorum: The Intellectual Origin of the Constitution* (Lawrence, Kans., 1985); and Isaac Kramnick, "'The Great National Discussion': The Discourse of Politics in 1787," *William and Mary Quarterly*, 3rd. Ser., 45 (1988): 3–22.

historicism, which located ideas in their time and context and employed a conservative and ahistorical interpretation that was based on timeless truths and that was hostile to what they considered to be the historians' preoccupation with contextual problems, which gave ideas a relativistic cast. Historians, despite their disagreements with Straussians, found them useful for making all scholars more aware of the intellectual complexities involved in evaluating the constitutional period.[18]

Yet another challenge to historians came from present-minded members of the Reagan administration — such as Edwin Meese, the U.S. attorney general — who claimed that the Supreme Court should show greater respect for the "original intent" of the framers. Meese and other conservative public officials argued that if judges could freely ignore the intentions of both the framers and later legislators, they could substitute their own preferences or values for the decisions of popularly elected officials. Jack Rakove, in an article written in 1986, replied that the relationship between the meaning of the Constitution and the actual intentions of its framers could never be taken for granted; for a variety of reasons, it was often too difficult to discern or pinpoint.[19]

As a result of the writings of the new intellectual historians and other scholars during the bicentennial, the challenges to the republican synthesis, and the intrusion of contemporary politics into an academic debate, the constitutional period and early national era both became exciting and creative areas of American historical scholarship. What has been called recently "founders chic" meant that scholars and other writers found wide audiences for studies of the framers.

With the help of these fresh perspectives, scholars were able to create a new periodization that revolutionized American historiography. Although they disagreed on just when the transition from premodern to modern America took place, the new intellectual historians and others had raised and tried to answer one of the most pressing questions in our nation's history: just when did modern America emerge, and what were the forces that led to that emergence?[20]

Meanwhile, the neo-Progressive scholars, the third group writing since World War II, saw modern America emerging in early and ongoing struggles over economic questions. They continued to refine the old Progressive interpretation as an alternative to the republican synthesis. This grouping lumps together historians who often disagreed as much with one another as they did with certain findings of the older Progressive school. The one character-

---

[18]See Gordon S. Wood, "The Fundamentalists and the Constitution," *New York Review of Books* 35 (February 18, 1988): 33–40.

[19]Jack Rakove, "Mr. Meese, Meet Mr. Madison," *Atlantic* 258 (December 1986): 77–86.

[20]In tracing the evolution of republican ideology, several biographical studies showed that republicanism meant different things to different men. See, for example, Gerald Stourzh, *Alexander Hamilton and the Idea of Republican Government* (Stanford, Calif., 1970); John Howe, *The Changing Political Thought of John Adams* (Princeton, N.J., 1966); George Athan Billias, *Elbridge Gerry, Founding Father and Republican Statesman* (New York, 1976); and Pauline Maier, *The Old Revolutionaries: Political Lives in the Age of Samuel Adams* (New York, 1980).

istic they held in common was their belief that economic and social forces were the crucial determinants in the positions men took for or against the Constitution. Some neo-Progressives agreed with Beard in stressing class conflict, while others pictured divisions along more pluralistic lines.

The most prominent neo-Progressive scholar was Merrill Jensen. In two major works — *The Articles of Confederation* (1940) and *The New Nation* (1950) — Jensen rewrote the history of the period from 1774 to 1789 in terms of a socioeconomic division between two well-defined groups: the Nationalists, or conservative creditors and merchants who favored strengthening the central government, and the Federalists, radical agrarian democrats who controlled the state legislatures. The latter supported state sovereignty, of course, and favored rural and debtor interests.

The struggle between these two groups defined the entire Revolutionary era, according to Jensen. During the early 1770s, the radical agrarian democrats led the fight against both Britain and the entrenched colonial commercial aristocrats, achieving self-government with the Articles of Confederation. In the 1780s, they became apathetic, failing to maintain their political organizations. The commercial elite used this opportunity to mount a conservative counterrevolution. They wrote the Constitution in order to create a strong central government that would protect their political and commercial interests. Thus Jensen, like Beard, pictured American society split into polarized groups throughout the period and viewed the Constitution as a repudiation of the Revolution. Jensen charged Nationalists with deliberately undermining a government that might have served the United States well.[21]

Neo-Progressive Forrest McDonald tested Beard's famous study by redoing his work and reanalyzing the economic interests of the delegates at both the federal and state constitutional conventions. He concluded that Beard's use of polarized categories — lower classes versus upper classes, real property versus personalty, creditors versus debtors, and commercial versus agricultural interests — to explain the framing and ratification of the Constitution simply did not work. McDonald found pluralistic rather than polarized political and economic interests at work on the local, state, and regional levels. The Antifederalists, for example, held much more wealth than Beard realized.[22]

By the end of the 1980s, most scholars found the debate over economic interests and the Constitution along Beardian lines unrewarding. Scholarly interests had shifted to an analysis of the American political economy as a whole, or to the links among politics, society, and economics. With the appearance of the new social historians and historians who studied culture

---

[21]Jensen continued the neo-Progressive tradition in the documentary history of the ratification of the Constitution, which he was in charge of editing until his death in 1980. Merrill Jensen et al., eds., *The Documentary History of the Ratification of the Constitution*, 15 vols. to date (Madison, Wis., 1976– ); see also Jackson Turner Main, *The Antifederalists* (Chapel Hill, N.C., 1961) and *Political Parties before the Constitution* (Chapel Hill, N.C., 1973), and E. James Ferguson, *The Power of the Purse: A History of American Public Finance* (Chapel Hill, N.C., 1961).

[22]Forrest McDonald, *We the People: The Economic Origins of the Constitution* (Chicago, 1958) and *E Pluribus Unum* (Boston, 1965).

as a stand-in for politics, scholars paid more attention to the social bases of the Federalists and Antifederalists and less to their economic holdings in securities.

In political science, practitioners had analyzed documents like *The Federalist Papers* in terms of general ideas, whereas more recent scholars explored conceptual changes in the political language of such documents within more specific contexts. Some political scientists in departments of government continued the older tradition of analyzing certain constitutional ideas — federalism, sovereignty, separation of powers, and judicial review — though they often failed to connect these ideas with specific historical events. For historians, context was the order of the day.[23]

A recent work in this line of research is David Brian Robertson's *The Constitution and American Destiny*. Robertson, a political scientist, thoughtfully investigated the Constitution as the solution to political problems, an instrument conceived of by people who practiced politics. While Robertson insisted that the framers did not write the Constitution to further their own interests, overall they devised it to make the country sufficiently stable to encourage commercial growth and to accommodate its "emerging democracy." Robertson showed how the widely diverse interests of the regions and the states as well as the requirements of representative government forced the founders to create a political instrument that would be extremely hard to coordinate to produce "satisfactory public policy." It would be easier to get elected than to dominate the government. Robertson's careful reconstruction of the political ideas and desires that created the Constitution reveals much about its origins, capabilities, and weaknesses.[24]

Two major historiographical controversies about the constitutional period emerged prominently during the post–World War II era. One was the question on which scholars remained divided: just how critical was the so-called critical period? John Fiske, back in the 1880s, had done the labeling, but Merrill Jensen, writing in the 1950s, concluded that the picture was a mixed one — progress in certain areas and backsliding in others. Forrest McDonald, writing in the 1960s, ridiculed the idea of a critical period, and Michael Lienesch, in an article in 1980, charged that the Federalists created the myth of the critical period to make certain the Constitution would be written and ratified. Herbert Storing, who published in 1981 his superb edition of Antifederalist writings, found the crisis to be real and acute. Even

---

[23]See also Martin Diamond, "Democracy and *The Federalist*: A Reconsideration of the Framers' Intent," *American Political Science Review* 53 (1959): 53–61; Terence Ball and J. G. A. Pocock, eds., *Conceptual Change and the Constitution* (Lawrence, Kans., 1988); and Patrice Higonnet, *Sister Republics* (Cambridge, Mass., 1988). For the older tradition of scholars in departments of government and law schools interested mainly in constitutional ideas in terms of political theory, see Andrew C. McLaughlin, *A Constitutional History of the United States* (New York, 1955); Edwin Corwin, "Progress of Constitutional Theory between the Declaration of Independence and the Meeting of the Philadelphia Convention," *American Historical Review* 30 (1925): 511–36. For a work by a historian who posits the continuing constitutional dilemma of reconciling the claims of "center" and "periphery" within an extended imperial model and the independent American polity, see Jack P. Greene, *Peripheries and Center* (Athens, Ga., 1986).

[24]David Brian Robertson, *The Constitution and America's Destiny* (New York, 2005).

the Antifederalists conceded that conditions were bad. Richard B. Morris, writing in 1987, agreed that the postwar years were very critical indeed. To Gordon Wood, the critical period was mainly a moral crisis rather than a political and economic one: American elites faced a moral dilemma in trying to create a republican government — one premised on the notion of a virtuous people — with an American public that these leaders considered not virtuous. Recently, Woody Holton found the crisis quite real and people divided as to its solutions. In his view, we have heard only one of the two sides offering a cure for an acute crisis. In short, the historiographical controversy has yet to be settled satisfactorily.[25]

A second theme that became more pronounced during the period was the sectional basis of politics that influenced the creation of the Constitution. H. James Henderson, in the mid-1970s, produced the most exhaustive account of politics during the confederation to appear since Jensen's work in the 1950s. Employing a voting-bloc analysis of the members of the Continental Congress, Henderson described the parties within that body as sectional in nature, with various sections becoming dominant at different times. New England radicals controlled the Congress from 1776 to 1779, but from 1780 to 1783 the middle-state nationalists prevailed. After 1783, there existed a period of three-way sectional tension — among the New England, middle, and southern states — that was partly alleviated by the adoption of the Constitution. Although the three sections pulled and tugged in different directions, they were united in their belief in a republican ideology. Henderson's ideological-sectional interpretation was distinctly at odds with Jensen's neo-Progressive interpretation.[26]

Sectionalism likewise played an important part in Peter Onuf's important work, *Origins of the Federal Republic,* published in 1983. Onuf demonstrated that the thinking of the founders about an American union was profoundly shaped by the experience of interstate conflict, the difficulties of defining congressional authority, and the promotion of national interests under the confederation. New York's northeastern counties, Pennsylvania's Wyoming Valley, and the trans-Ohio region all either sought to become separate states (as in the case of the New York counties that became Vermont) or were the source of a quarrel over conflicting western land claims (as, for example, Connecticut's invasion of Pennsylvania's Wyoming Valley). Only the

---

[25]Merrill Jensen, *The New Nation* (New York, 1950), passim; McDonald, *E Pluribus Unum,* 154; Michael Lienesch, "The Constitutional Tradition: History, Political Action, and Progress in American Political Thought, 1787–1793," *Journal of Politics* 42 (1980): 13; Herbert Storing, ed., *The Complete Anti-Federalist,* 7 vols. (Chicago, 1981), vol. 1, 26; Richard B. Morris, *The Forging of the Union, 1781–1789* (New York, 1987); Wood, *The Creation of the American Republic, 1776–1787,* 1969 edition, 393–429; Woody Holton, "Did Democracy Cause the Recession That Led to the Constitution?" *Journal of American History* 92 (September 2005): 442–69.

[26]H. James Henderson, *Party Politics in the Continental Congress* (New York, 1974). For sectional tensions during the period, see also William Crosskey and William Jeffrey Jr., *Politics and the Constitution in the History of the United States,* 3 vols. (Chicago, 1953–1980), which argues that Madison and some of the other principal framers deliberately sought to create a government with a broad grant of power under the commerce clause. See also Jack N. Rakove's brilliant *The Beginnings of National Politics* (New York, 1979).

newly formed Congress, Onuf argued, could settle such overriding issues. The states had come to recognize that a central authority was needed to resolve these problems. Thus, instead of the orthodox story that pictured the new federal government and the states locked in a power struggle over sovereignty, Onuf showed there was an expansion of central authority and reinforcement of state sovereignty simultaneously. Recently, Saul Cornell, studying the Antifederalist tradition of dissent, has found that that body of thought split apart in 1828 over sectional issues. Sectionalism as an interpretive principle in the writing of the Constitution had come into its own after years of relative neglect.[27]

The most recent significant historical work has been in two major areas. First, new political historians merged with social historians have deepened our understanding of the groups that the Constitution marginalized — blacks, women, and Indians — how they expressed their concerns, and how those did not mesh with the concerns of other groups. Second, intellectual historians worked to integrate political, economic, and biographical insights. They struggled with two large themes: first, an emphasis on understanding the original meanings of the Constitution as it was written, debated, and implemented rather than as a set of abstract ideas, and second, healing what they saw as an artificial breach between republicanism and liberalism.

In a collection of essays published in 1992, a variety of scholars made a case for a new, hybrid liberal republicanism, or a republicanism that was modern rather than frightened and backward-looking. Liberal republicanism, which these scholars claimed characterized both the revolutionaries and the framers, "accepted self preservation and self-interest as fundamental to human nature." Furthermore, liberal republicanism saw the protection of natural rights and the acquisition of property and its protection as the proper purposes of government. Contributor John Murrin argued that the Constitution was a device for establishing republican government over liberal Americans. Jean Yarborough argued that framers saw commerce as producing its own virtues. Since they did not consider these sufficient to sustain a nation's virtue, they also looked to religion, although they remained silent about this in the Constitution. The states, which shared sovereignty with the national government — indeed, as Peter Onuf argued, which depended upon the national government for their sovereignty — were to be responsible for morality and religion.[28]

Bernard Bailyn offered another assessment of the blend of liberalism with republicanism in his 1990 essay "The Ideological Fulfillment of the

[27]Peter Onuf, *The Origins of the Federal Republic* (Philadelphia, 1983); Saul Cornell, *The Other Founders: Antifederalism and the Dissenting Tradition in America, 1788–1828* (Chapel Hill, N.C., 1999).

[28]Herman Belz, Ronald Hoffman, and Peter J. Albert, eds., *To Form a More Perfect Union: The Critical Ideas of the Constitution* (Charlottesville, Va., 1992), xii; Onuf, *The Origins of the Federal Republic*; see also his *Statehood and Union* (Bloomington, Ind., 1987); Joseph Davis, *Sectionalism in American Politics: 1774–1787* (Madison, Wis., 1977); and Drew R. McCoy, "James Madison and Visions of American Nationality in the Confederation Period: A Regional Perspective," in Richard Beeman and Edward C. Carter II, eds., *Beyond Confederation: Origins of the Constitution and American National Identity* (Chapel Hill, N.C., 1987), 226–58.

American Revolution: A Commentary on the Constitution." The essay shows how the Federalists were able to devise arguments to refute long-standing republican fears such as that of a standing army and of acquisitiveness.[29] Recently, Peter C. Messer has advanced the bridge-building between republicanism and liberalism with his view of republicanism as an evolving construction by eighteenth-century American historians wishing to produce a manual for republican citizens. Each elaborated a past that was to be a guide for behavior in a virtuous republic.[30]

In the last twenty years, there has been a great revival of interest in Antifederalists, in those left out of the Constitution, and in Charles Beard's work. Discontent with current American politics and a dramatic increase in the growth of inequality between the very rich and the rest of the population has led to a recrudescence of curiosity about the roles of dissent and economic conflict in our founding. Looking for those left out of the Constitution, Carroll Smith-Rosenberg in 1992 used the magazine rhetoric of the eighteenth century to compose a portrait of the "subjectivity" or the identity of the male American citizen whom the Revolution and the Constitution had constructed. She found strains of liberal and republican rhetoric overlapping to create a figure who took his definition largely from his differences from stereotyped characteristics of females, Africans, and Indians.

Gary B. Nash, in *Race and Revolution*, saw northerners as equally responsible, if not more so, than southerners for the constitutional stamp of approval on slavery. Paul Finkelman allied himself with abolitionist William Lloyd Garrison in seeing the Constitution as a covenant with slaveholders to protect the institution of slavery, although he disagreed with Garrison who thought that antislavery activists should not engage in politics. *Slavery and the Founders* explored the ways in which slavery and the intention to exclude blacks from political rights distorted American society from its origins. Wide scholarly interest in slavery and the black founders testifies to the growing significance of race and bondage in discussions of the Constitution (see Chapter 4).[31]

Saul Cornell's *The Other Founders* traced the evolution of Antifederalist dissent from 1788 until 1828, defining the early national "oppositional constitutionalism" that became a "defining characteristic of American political culture." Cornell's study argued against Richard Hofstadter's claim that the nation's political legacy is "essentially liberal and democratic." His evidence indicated that disagreement and tension were present in the early Republic

---

[29]Bernard Bailyn, *Faces of the Revolution: Personalities and Theme in the Struggle for American Independence* (New York, 1992).

[30]Peter C. Messer, *Stories of Independence: Identity, Ideology, and History in Eighteenth-Century America* (DeKalb, Ill., 2005).

[31]Carroll Smith-Rosenberg, "Dis-Covering the Subject of the 'Great Constitutional Discussion,' 1786–1789," *Journal of American History* 79 (1992): 841–73; Gary B. Nash, *Race and Revolution* (Madison, Wis., 1990); Paul Finkelman, *Slavery and the Founders: Race and Liberty in the Age of Jefferson* (Armonk, N.Y., 2001); Richard Newman, "Protest in Black and White," in Pasley et al., eds., *Beyond the Founders*. Akhil Reed Amar, *America's Constitution: A Biography* (New York, 2005), also sees slavery as very important in the Constitution, but otherwise tends to agree with Wood about its democratic tendencies.

and have been an important element in our politics ever since. Other historians working on the Antifederalists have greatly refined our understanding of the makeup and beliefs of this complex and shifting group.[32]

The new political historians whose goal is to integrate politics with social and cultural history have reenergized the debate over Beard. Woody Holton (excerpted below) has reconstructed the chain of economic hardships in the 1780s and the debate over them, showing that the causal links that Beard looked for were there but were more indirect than he thought. In Holton's dialectical view, the 1780s represented a crisis for farmers and other taxpayers who were assessed with record levies and required to pay them in scarce specie in order to pay interest to bondholders, many of whom were speculators and had bought discounted bonds. The crisis was analogous to that of many developing countries during and after the structural adjustment programs of the 1980s in which the World Bank favored creditors and forced countries to cut back on social services for the general population in an effort to make the countries inviting for investment. According to Holton's study, the founders wanted to create an environment that would encourage further investment. That meant transferring wealth from the working farmers to those who would use the money to invest and start up new ventures. Historians have explained and largely validated the Federalist argument that state legislatures were behaving irresponsibly by printing money and offering debt relief, but have given little or no voice to the farmers and debtors who were affected by these measures and who argued in favor of increasing the state debt relief measures that were inadequate to help many of them keep their farms. Holton sees this as a complex kind of class conflict in which not everyone necessarily pushed for his own class interest, but which posed Americans the stark problem: "which segment of society should bear the burden of reviving the economy . . . which classes should sacrifice for the good of the whole."[33]

In conclusion, the globalizing view of history has reached constitutional studies. Mary Bilder's *The Transatlantic Constitution* showed how Rhode Island's state law developed in conversation with English litigants, lawyers, legislators, and other practitioners of common law, and how these shared assumptions helped the new Republic accept federalism and judicial review as altered but recognizable aspects of a system they were long used to and found legitimate. Bernard Bailyn, in a recent collection of essays, discussed the varied responses to the Constitution in Europe and in South America, ranging from German praise to the bafflement of many South Americans

---

[32]Cornell, *The Other Founders*, 14, 19, 305; David J. Siemers, *Ratifying the Republic: Antifederalists and Federalists in Constitutional Time* (Stanford, Calif., 2002); Richard Hofstadter, *The American Political Tradition and the Men Who Made It* (New York, 1948).

[33]Woody Holton, "'From the Labours of Others': The War Bonds Controversy and the Origins of the Constitution in New England," *William and Mary Quarterly*, 3rd Ser., 61 (April 2004): 271–316, and "Did Democracy Cause the Recession?" *Journal of American History* 92 (September 2005): 442–69. See also Terry Bouton, *Taming Democracy: "The People," the Founders, and the Troubled Ending of the American Revolution* (New York, 2007). Shlomo Slonim's *Framers' Construction/Beardian Deconstruction: Essays on the Constitutional Design of 1787* (New York, 2001) is a soundly anti-Beard set of essays.

like Simon Bolivar.[34] And George Billias, one of the originators of *Interpretations of American History*, will soon publish *Heard Round the World: American Constitutionalism Abroad, 1776–1989, A Global Perspective.*

Were the proponents of the republican synthesis correct in believing that Americans shared a basic ideological consensus? Or was this a generalization that failed to describe the diverse people of the new nation? History students continue to come to grips with the problem of evaluating the Constitution and the developments that led to its writing and ratification. Was the Constitution a fulfillment or a repudiation of the ideals of the Revolution expressed in the Declaration of Independence? What was the nature of the Constitution, and in what ways did its framing reflect the developments in political thought during the 1780s? Were the differences that divided those who favored and those who opposed the Constitution based more on ideology or on interests? Was the Constitution, as Beard and some neo-Progressive historians argued, an undemocratic document — the work of a political and propertied minority who drafted it as an instrument to suit their own purposes? Were the Antifederalists tradition-minded classical republicans or enterprising protoliberals who glimpsed the future of America as Wood suggested? Asking these questions can help us decide how much the Constitution reflected political and economic conflict or consensus.

---

[34]Mary Sarah Bilder, *The Transatlantic Constitution: Colonial Legal Culture and the Empire* (Cambridge, Mass., 2004), 1, 7, 11, 186; Bernard Bailyn, *To Begin the World Anew: The Genius and Ambiguities of the American Founding* (New York, 2003), 143, 145, 148.


## GORDON S. WOOD

# *from* The Creation of the American Republic, 1776–1787   [1969]

**GORDON S. WOOD** (1933– ) is Alva O. Way University Professor and Professor of History at Brown University. He is the author of *The Creation of the American Republic, 1776–1787* (1969), which won the John H. Dunning Prize of the American Historical Association, and *The Radicalism of the American Revolution* (1991).

---

The division over the Constitution in 1787–1788 is not easily analyzed. It is difficult, as historians have recently demonstrated, to equate the supporters or opponents of the Constitution with particular economic groupings. The Antifederalist politicians in the ratifying conventions often possessed

---

wealth, including public securities, equal to that of the Federalists. While the relative youth of the Federalist leaders, compared to the ages of the prominent Antifederalists, was important, especially in accounting for the Federalists' ability to think freshly and creatively about politics, it can hardly be used to explain the division throughout the country. Moreover, the concern of the 1780s with America's moral character was not confined to the proponents of the Constitution. That rabid republican and Antifederalist, Benjamin Austin, was as convinced as any Federalist that "the luxurious living of all ranks and degrees" was "the principal cause of all the evils we now experience." Some leading Antifederalist intellectuals expressed as much fear of "the injustice, folly, and wickedness of the State Legislatures" and of "the usurpation and tyranny of the majority" against the minority as did Madison. In the Philadelphia Convention both Mason and Elbridge Gerry, later prominent Antifederalists, admitted "the danger of the levelling spirit": flowing from "the excess of democracy" in the American republic. There were many diverse reasons in each state why men supported or opposed the Constitution that cut through any sort of class division. The Constitution was a single issue in a complicated situation, and its acceptance or rejection in many states was often dictated by peculiar circumstances — the prevalence of Indians, the desire for western lands, the special interests of commerce — that defy generalization. Nevertheless, despite all of this confusion and complexity, the struggle over the Constitution, as the debate if nothing else makes clear, can best be understood as a social one. Whatever the particular constituency of the antagonists may have been, men in 1787–1788 talked as if they were representing distinct and opposing social elements. Both the proponents and opponents of the Constitution focused throughout the debates on an essential point of political sociology that ultimately must be used to distinguish a Federalist from an Antifederalist. The quarrel was fundamentally one between aristocracy and democracy. . . .

The disorganization and inertia of the Antifederalists, especially in contrast with the energy and effectiveness of the Federalists, has been repeatedly emphasized. The opponents of the Constitution lacked both coordination and unified leadership; "their principles" wrote Oliver Ellsworth, "are totally opposite to each other, and their objections discordant and irreconcilable." The Federalist victory, it appears, was actually more of an Antifederalist default. . . .

But the Antifederalists were not simply poorer politicians than the Federalists; they were actually different kinds of politicians. Too many of them were state-centered men with local interests and loyalties only, politicians without influence and connections, and ultimately politicians without social and intellectual confidence. In South Carolina the upcountry opponents of the Constitution shied from debate and when they did occasionally rise to speak apologized effusively for their inability to say what they felt had to be said, thus leaving most of the opposition to the Constitution to be voiced by Rawlins Lowndes, a low-country planter who scarcely represented their interests and soon retired from the struggle.

Elsewhere, in New Hampshire, Connecticut, Massachusetts, Pennsylvania, and North Carolina, the situation was similar: the Federalists had the bulk of talent and influence on their side "together with all the Speakers in the State great and small." In convention after convention the Anti-federalists, as in Connecticut, tried to speak but "they were browbeaten by many of those Cicero'es as they think themselves and others of Superior rank." "The presses are in a great measure secured to *their* side," the Antifederalists complained with justice: out of a hundred or more news-papers printed in the late eighties only a dozen supported the Anti-federalists, as editors, "afraid to offend the great men, or Merchants, who could work their ruin," closed their columns to the opposition. The Anti-federalists were not so much beaten as overawed. . . .

[F]ear of a plot by men who "talk so finely and gloss over matters so smoothly" ran through the Antifederalist mind. Because the many "new men" of the 1780s, men like Melancthon Smith and Abraham Yates of New York or John Smilie and William Findley of Pennsylvania, had bypassed the social hierarchy in their rise to political leadership, they lacked those attributes of social distinction and dignity that went beyond mere wealth. Since these kinds of men were never assimilated to the gen-tlemanly cast of the Livingstons or the Morrises, they, like Americans ear-lier in confrontation with the British court, tended to view with suspicion and hostility the high-flying world of style and connections that they were barred by their language and tastes, if by nothing else, from sharing in. In the minds of these socially inferior politicians the movement for the strengthening of the central government could only be a "conspiracy" "planned and set to work" by a few aristocrats, who were at first, said Abraham Yates, no larger in number in any one state than the cabal which sought to undermine English liberty at the beginning of the eigh-teenth century. Since men like Yates could not quite comprehend what they were sure were the inner maneuverings of the elite, they were con-vinced that in the aristocrats' program, "what was their view in the begin-ning" or how "far it was Intended to be carried Must be Collected from facts that Afterwards have happened." Like American Whigs in the sixties and seventies forced to delve into the dark and complicated workings of English court politics, they could judge motives and plans "but by the Event." And they could only conclude that the events of the eighties, "the treasury, the Cincinnati, and other public creditors, with all their con-comitants," were "somehow or other, . . . inseparably connected," were all parts of a grand design "concerted by a few *tyrants*" to undo the Revo-lution and to establish an aristocracy in order "to lord it over the rest of their fellow citizens, to trample the poorer part of the people under their feet, that they may be rendered their servants and slaves." In this cli-mate all the major issues of the Confederation period — the impost, com-mutation, and the return of the Loyalists — possessed a political and social significance that transcended economic concerns. All seemed to be devices by which a ruling few, like the ministers of the English Crown, would attach a corps of pensioners and dependents to the government and spread their influence and connections throughout the states in order "to dissolve our present Happy and Benevolent Constitution and to erect on the Ruins, a proper Aristocracy."

Nothing was more characteristic of Antifederalist thinking than this obsession with aristocracy. Although to a European, American society may have appeared remarkably egalitarian, to many Americans, especially to those who aspired to places of consequence but were made to feel their inferiority in innumerable, often subtle, ways, American society was distinguished by its inequality. . . . In all communities "even in those of the most democratic kind," wrote George Clinton (whose "family and connections" in the minds of those like Philip Schuyler did not "entitle him to so distinguished a predominance" as the governorship of New York), there were pressures — "superior talents, fortunes and public employments" — demarcating an aristocracy whose influence was difficult to resist.

Such influence was difficult to resist because, to the continual annoyance of the Antifederalists, the great body of the people willingly submitted to it. The "authority of names" and "the influence of the great" among ordinary people were too evident to be denied. "Will any one say that there does not exist in this country the pride of family, of wealth, of talents, and that they do not command influence and respect among the common people?" "The people are too apt to yield an implicit assent to the opinions of those characters whose abilities are held in the highest esteem, and to those in whose integrity and patriotism they can confide; not considering that the love of domination is generally in proportion to talents, abilities and superior requirements." Because of this habit of deference in the people, it was "in the power of the enlightened and aspiring few, if they should combine, at any time to destroy the best establishments, and even make the people the instruments of their own subjugation." Hence, the Antifederalist-minded declared, the people must be awakened to the consequences of their self-ensnarement; they must be warned over and over by the popular tribunes, by "those who are competent to the task of developing the principles of government," of the dangers involved in paying obeisance to those who they thought were their superiors. The people must "not be permitted to consider themselves as a grovelling, distinct species, uninterested in the general welfare."

Such constant admonitions to the people of the perils flowing from their too easy deference to the "*natural aristocracy*" were necessary because the Antifederalists were convinced that these "men that had been delicately bred, and who were in affluent circumstances," these "men of the most exalted rank in life," were by their very conspicuousness irreparably cut off from the great body of the people and hence could never share in its concerns nor look after its interests. It was not that these "certain men exalted above the rest" were necessarily "destitute of morality or virtue" or that they were inherently different from other men. "The same passions and prejudices govern all men." It was only that circumstances in their particular environment had made them different. There was "a charm in politicks"; men in high office become habituated with power, "grow fond of it, and are loath to resign it"; "they feel themselves flattered and elevated," enthralled by the attractions of high living, and thus they easily forget the interests of the common people, from which many of them once sprang. By dwelling so vividly on the allurements of prestige and power, by emphasizing again and again how the "human soul is affected by wealth, in all its faculties, . . . by its present interest, by its expectations, and by its fears," these ambitious Antifederalist politicians may have revealed as much about themselves as they did about the "aristocratic" elite they sought to displace. Yet at the same time by such language they contributed to a new appreciation of the nature of society.

In these repeated attacks on deference and the capacity of a conspicuous few to speak for the whole society — which was to become in time the distinguishing feature of American democratic politics — the Antifederalists struck at the roots of the traditional conception of political society. If the natural elite, whether its distinctions were ascribed or acquired, was not in any organic way connected to the "feelings, circumstances, and interests" of the people and was incapable of feeling "sympathetically the wants of the people," then it followed that only ordinary men, men not distinguished by the characteristics of aristocratic wealth and taste, men "in middling circumstances" untempted by the attractions of a cosmopolitan world and thus "more temperate, of better morals, and less ambitious, than the great," could be trusted to speak for the great body of the people, for those who were coming more and more to be referred to as "the middling and lower classes of people." The differentiating influence of the environment was such that men in various ranks and classes now seemed to be broken apart from one another, separated by their peculiar circumstances into distinct, unconnected, and often incompatible interests. With their indictment of aristocracy the Antifederalists were saying, whether they realized it or not, that the people of America even in their several states were not homogeneous entities each with a basic similarity of interest for which an empathic elite could speak. Society was not an organic hierarchy composed of ranks and degrees indissolubly linked one to another; rather it was a heterogeneous mixture of "many different classes or orders of people, Merchants, Farmers, Planter Mechanics and Gentry or wealthy Men." In such a society men from one class or group, however educated and respectable they may have been, could never be acquainted with the "*Situation* and Wants" of those of another class or group. Lawyers and planters could never be "adequate judges of tradesmen concerns." If men were truly to represent the people in government, it was not enough for them to be for the people; they had to be actually of the people. "Farmers, traders and mechanics . . . all ought to have a competent number of their best informed members in the legislature."

Thus the Antifederalists were not only directly challenging the conventional belief that only a gentlemanly few, even though now in America naturally and not artificially qualified, were best equipped through learning and experience to represent and to govern the society, but they were as well indirectly denying the assumption of organic social homogeneity

on which republicanism rested. Without fully comprehending the consequences of their arguments the Antifederalists were destroying the great
chain of being, thus undermining the social basis of republicanism and
shattering that unity and harmony of social and political authority which
the eighteenth century generally and indeed most revolutionary leaders
had considered essential to the maintenance of order.

Confronted with such a fundamental challenge the Federalists initially
backed away. They had no desire to argue the merits of the Constitution
in terms of social implications and were understandably reluctant to open
up the character of American society as the central issue of the debate.
But in the end they could not resist defending those beliefs in elitism that
lay at the heart of their conception of politics and of their constitutional
program. All of the Federalists' desires to establish a strong and respectable nation in the world, all of their plans to create a flourishing commercial economy, in short, all of what the Federalists wanted out of the
new central government seemed in the final analysis dependent upon the
prerequisite maintenance of aristocratic politics. . . .

The course of the debates over the Constitution seemed to confirm what
the Federalists had believed all along. Antifederalism represented the climax of a "war" that was, in the words of Theodore Sedgwick, being "levied
on the virtue, property, and distinctions in the community." The opponents
of the Constitution, despite some, "particularly in Virginia," who were operating "from the most honorable and patriotic motives," were essentially
identical with those who were responsible for the evils the states were suffering from in the eighties — "narrowminded politicians . . . under the
influence of local views." "Whilst many *ostensible* reasons are assigned" for
the Antifederalists' opposition, charged Washington, "the real ones are
concealed behind the Curtains, because they are not of a nature to appear
in open day." "The real object of all their zeal in opposing the system,"
agreed Madison, was to maintain "the supremacy of the State Legislatures,"
with all that meant in the printing of money and the violation of contracts.
The Antifederalists or those for whom the Antifederalists spoke, whether
their spokesmen realized it or not, were "none but the horse-jockey, the
mushroom merchant, the running and dishonest speculator," those "who
owe the most and have the least to pay," those "whose dependence and
expectations are upon changes in government, and distracted times," men
of "desperate Circumstances," those "in Every State" who "have Debts to
pay, Interests to support or Fortunes to make," those, in short, who "wish
for scrambling Times." Apart from a few of their intellectual leaders the
Antifederalists were thought to be an ill-bred lot: "Their education has
been rather indifferent — they have been accustomed to think on the small
scale." They were often blustering demagogues trying to push their way
into office — "men of much self-importance and supposed skill in politics,
who are not of sufficient consequence to obtain public employment."
Hence they were considered to be jealous and mistrustful of "everyone in
the higher offices of society," unable to bear to see others possessing "that
fancied blessing, to which, alas! they must themselves aspire in vain." In the

Federalist mind therefore the struggle over the Constitution was not one between kinds of wealth or property, or one between commercial or non-commercial elements of the population, but rather represented a broad social division between those who believed in the right of a natural aristocracy to speak for the people and those who did not.

Against this threat from the licentious the Federalists pictured themselves as the defenders of the worthy, of those whom they called "the better sort of people," those, said John Jay, "who are orderly and industrious, who are content with their situations and not uneasy in their circumstances." Because the Federalists were fearful that republican equality was becoming "that *perfect equality* which deadens the motives of industry and places Demerit on a Footing with Virtue," they were obsessed with the need to insure that the proper amount of inequality and natural distinctions be recognized. . . . Robert Morris, for example, was convinced there were social differences — even in Pennsylvania. "What!" he exclaimed in scornful amazement at John Smilie's argument that a republic admitted of no social superiorities. "Is it insisted that there is no distinction of character?" Respectability, said Morris with conviction, was not confined to property. "Surely persons possessed of knowledge, judgment, information, integrity, and having extensive connections, are not to be classed with persons void of reputation or character."

In refuting the Antifederalists' contention "that all classes of citizens should have some of their own number in the representative body, in order that their feelings and interests may be the better understood and attended to," Hamilton in *The Federalist*, Number 35, put into words the Federalists' often unspoken and vaguely held assumption about the organic and the hierarchical nature of society. Such explicit class or occupational representation as the Antifederalists advocated, wrote Hamilton, was not only impractical but unnecessary, since the society was not as fragmented or heterogeneous as the Antifederalists implied. The various groups in the landed interest, for example, were "perfectly united, from the wealthiest landlord down to the poorest tenant," and this "common interest may always be reckoned upon as the surest bond of sympathy" linking the landed representative, however rich, to his constituents. In a like way, the members of the commercial community were "immediately connected" and most naturally represented by the merchants. "Mechanics and manufacturers will always be inclined, with few exceptions, to give their votes to merchants, in preference to persons of their own professions or trades. . . . They know that the merchant is their natural patron and friend; and . . . they are sensible that their habits in life have not been such as to give them those acquired endowments, without which in a deliberative assembly, the greatest natural abilities, are for the most part useless." However much many Federalists may have doubted the substance of Hamilton's analysis of American society, they could not doubt the truth of his conclusion. That the people were represented better by one of the natural aristocracy "whose situation leads to extensive inquiry and information" than by one "whose observation does not travel beyond the circle of his neighbors and acquaintances" was the defining element of the Federalist philosophy.

It was not simply the number of public securities, or credit outstanding, or the number of ships, or the amount of money possessed that made a man think of himself as one of the natural elite. It was much more subtle than the mere possession of wealth: it was a deeper social feeling, a sense of being socially established, of possessing attributes — family, education, and refinement — that others lacked, above all, of being accepted by and being able to move easily among those who considered themselves to be the respectable and cultivated. It is perhaps anachronistic to describe this social sense as a class interest, for it often transcended immediate political or economic concerns, and, as Hamilton's argument indicates, was designed to cut through narrow occupational categories. The Republicans of Philadelphia for example, repeatedly denied that they represented an aristocracy with a united class interest. "We are of different occupations; of different sects of religion; and have different views of life. No factions or private system can comprehend us all." Yet with all their assertions of diversified interests the Republicans were not without a social consciousness in their quarrel with the supporters of the Pennsylvania Constitution. If there were any of us ambitious for power, their apology continued, then there would be no need to change the Constitution, for we surely could attain power under the present Constitution. "We have already seen how easy the task is for *any character* to rise into power and consequence under it. And there are some of us, who think not so meanly of ourselves, as to dread any rivalship from those who are now in office."

In 1787 this kind of elitist social consciousness was brought into play as perhaps never before in eighteenth-century America, as gentlemen up and down the continent submerged their sectional and economic differences in the face of what seemed to be a threat to the very foundations of society. Despite his earlier opposition to the Order of the Cincinnati, Theodore Sedgwick, like other frightened New Englanders, now welcomed the organization as a source of strength in the battle for the Constitution. The fear of social disruption that had run through much of the writing of the eighties was brought to a head to eclipse all other fears. Although state politics in the eighties remains to be analyzed, the evidence from Federalist correspondence indicates clearly a belief that never had there occurred "so great a change in the opinion of the best people" as was occurring in the last few years of the decade. The Federalists were astonished at the outpouring in 1787 of influential and respectable people who had earlier remained quiescent. Too many of "the better sort of people," it was repeatedly said, had withdrawn at the end of the war "from the theatre of public action, to scenes of retirement and ease," and thus "demagogues of desperate fortunes, mere adventurers in fraud, were left to act unopposed." After all, it was explained, "when the wicked rise, men hide themselves." Even the problems of Massachusetts in 1786, noted General Benjamin Lincoln, the repressor of the Shaysites, were not caused by the rebels, but by the laxity of "the good people of the state." But the lesson of this laxity was rapidly being learned. Everywhere, it seemed, men of virtue, good sense, and property, "almost the whole body of our enlighten'd and leading characters in every state," were awakened in support of stronger government. "The scum which was thrown upon the surface by the fermentation of the war is daily sinking," Benjamin Rush told Richard Price in 1786, "while a pure spirit is occupying its place." "Men are brought into action who had consigned themselves to an eve of rest," Edward Carrington wrote to Jefferson in June 1787, "and the Convention, as a Beacon, is rousing the attention of the Empire." The Antifederalists could only stand amazed at this "weight of talents" being gathered in support of the Constitution. "What must the individual be who could thus oppose them united?"

Still, in the face of this preponderance of wealth and respectability in support of the Constitution, what remains extraordinary about 1787–1788 is not the weakness and disunity but the political strength of Antifederalism. That large numbers of Americans could actually reject a plan of government created by a body "composed of the first characters in the Continent" and backed by Washington and nearly the whole of the natural aristocracy of the country said more about the changing character of American politics and society in the eighties than did the Constitution's eventual acceptance. It was indeed a portent of what was to come. . . .

If the new national government was to promote the common good as forcefully as any state government, and if, as the Federalists believed, a major source of the vices of the eighties lay in the abuse of state power, then there was something apparently contradictory about the new federal Constitution, which after all represented not a weakening of the dangerous power of republican government but rather a strengthening of it. "The complaints against the separate governments, even by the friends of the new plan," remarked the Antifederalist James Winthrop, "are not that they have not power enough, but that they are disposed to make a bad use of what power they have." Surely, concluded Winthrop, the Federalists were reasoning badly "when they purpose to set up a government possess'd of much more extensive powers . . . and subject to much smaller checks" than the existing state governments possessed and were subject to. Madison for one was quite aware of the pointedness of this objection. "It may be asked," he said, "how private rights will be more secure under the Guardianship of the General Government than under the State Governments, since they are both founded in the republican principle which refers the ultimate decision to the will of the majority." What, in other words, was different about the new federal Constitution that would enable it to mitigate the effects of tyrannical majorities? What would keep the new federal government from succumbing to the same pressures that had beset the state governments? The answer the Federalists gave to these questions unmistakably reveals the social bias underlying both their fears of the unrestrained state legislatures and their expectations for their federal remedy. For all of their desires to avoid intricate examination of a delicate social structure, the Federalists' program itself demanded that the discussion of the Constitution would be in essentially social terms.

The Federalists were not as much opposed to the governmental power of the states as to the character of the people who were wielding it. The constitutions of most of the states were not really at fault. Massachusetts after all possessed a nearly perfect constitution. What actually bothered the Federalists was the sort of people who had been able to gain positions of authority in the state governments, particularly in the state legislatures. Much of the quarrel with the viciousness, instability, and injustice of the various state governments was at bottom social. "For," as John Dickinson emphasized, "*the government will partake of the qualities of those whose authority is prevalent.*" The political and social structures were intimately related. "People once respected their governors, their senators, their judges and their clergy; they reposed confidence in them; their laws were obeyed, and the states were happy in tranquility." But in the eighties the authority of government had drastically declined because "men of sense and property have lost much of their influence by the popular spirit of the war." "That exact order, and due subordination, that is essentially necessary in all well appointed governments, and which constitutes the real happiness and well being of society" had been deranged by "men of no genius or abilities" who had tried to run "the machine of government." Since "it cannot be expected that things will go well, when persons of vicious principles, and loose morals are in authority," it was the large number of obscure, ignorant, and unruly men occupying the state legislatures, and not the structure of the governments, that was the real cause of the evils so much complained of.

The Federalist image of the Constitution as a sort of "philosopher's stone" was indeed appropriate: it was a device intended to transmute base materials into gold and thereby prolong the life of the republic. Patrick Henry acutely perceived what the Federalists were driving at. "The Constitution," he said in the Virginia Convention, "reflects in the most degrading and mortifying manner on the virtue, integrity, and wisdom of the state legislatures; it presupposes that the chosen few who go to Congress will have more upright hearts, and more enlightened minds, than those who are members of the individual legislatures." The new Constitution was structurally no different from the constitutions of some of the states. Yet the powers of the new central government were not as threatening as the powers of the state governments precisely because the Federalists believed different kinds of persons would hold them. They anticipated that somehow the new government would be staffed largely by "the worthy," the natural social aristocracy of the country. "After all," said Pelatiah Webster, putting his finger on the crux of the Federalists' argument, "the grand secret of forming a good government, is, to put good men into the administration: for wild, vicious, or idle men, will ever make a bad government, let its principles be ever so good." . . .

In short, through the artificial contrivance of the Constitution overlying an expanded society, the Federalists meant to restore and to prolong

the traditional kind of elitist influence in politics that social developments, especially since the Revolution, were undermining. As the defenders if not always the perpetrators of these developments — the "disorder"
of the 1780s — the Antifederalists could scarcely have missed the social
implications of the Federalist program. The Constitution was intrinsically
an aristocratic document designed to check the democratic tendencies of
the period, and as such it dictated the character of the Antifederalist
response. It was therefore inevitable that the Antifederalists should have
charged that the new government was "dangerously adapted to the purposes of an immediate *aristocratic tyranny*." In state after state the Antifederalists reduced the issue to those social terms predetermined by the
Federalists themselves: the Constitution was a plan intended to "raise the
fortunes and respectability of the *well-born few*, and oppress the plebians";
it was "a continental exertion of the *well-born* of America to obtain that
darling domination, which they have not been able to accomplish in their
respective states"; it "will lead to an aristocratical government, and establish tyranny over us." Whatever their own particular social standing, the
Antifederalist spokesmen spread the warning that the new government
either would be "in practice a *permanent* ARISTOCRACY" or would soon
"degenerate to a complete Aristocracy." . . .

Aristocratic principles were in fact "interwoven" in the very fabric of
the proposed government. If a government was "so constituted as to
admit but few to exercise the powers of it," then it would "according to
the natural course of things" end up in the hands of "the natural aristocracy." It went almost without saying that the awesome president and the
exalted Senate, "a compound of *monarchy* and *aristocracy*," would be dangerously far removed from the people. But even the House of Representatives, the very body that "should be a true picture of the people, possess a
knowledge of their circumstances and their wants, sympathize in all their
distresses, and disposed to seek their true interest," was without "a tinc-
ture of democracy." Since it could never collect "the interests, feelings,
and opinions of three or four millions of people," it was better understood as "an Assistant Aristocratical Branch" to the Senate than as a real
representation of the people. When the number of representatives was
"so small, the office will be highly elevated and distinguished; the style in
which the members live will probably be high; circumstances of this kind
will render the place of a representative not a desirable one to sensible,
substantial men, who have been used to walk in the plain and frugal
paths of life." While the ordinary people in extensive electoral districts of
thirty thousand inhabitants would remain "divided," those few extraordinary men with "conspicuous military, popular, civil or legal talents" could
more easily form broader associations to dominate elections; they had
family and other connections to "unite their interests." If only a half-
dozen congressmen were to be selected to represent a large state, then
rarely, argued the Antifederalists in terms that were essentially no different from those used by the Federalists in the Constitution's defense,
would persons from "the great body of the people, the middle and lower

classes," be elected to the House of Representatives. "The Station is too high and exalted to be filled but [by] the *first* Men in the State in point of Fortune and Influence. In fact no order or class of the people will be represented in the House of Representatives called the Democratic Branch but the rich and wealthy." The Antifederalists thus came to oppose the new national government for the same reason the Federalists favored it: because its very structure and detachment from the people would work to exclude any kind of actual and local interest representation and prevent those who were not rich, well born, or prominent from exercising political power. Both sides fully appreciated the central issue the Constitution posed and grappled with it throughout the debates: Whether a professedly popular government should actually be in the hands of, rather than simply derived from, common ordinary people.

Out of the division in 1787–1788 over this issue, an issue which was as conspicuously social as any in American history, the Antifederalists emerged as the spokesmen for the growing American antagonism to aristocracy and as the defenders of the most intimate participation in politics of the widest variety of people possible. It was not from lack of vision that the Antifederalists feared the new government. Although their viewpoint was intensely localist, it was grounded in as perceptive an understanding of the social basis of American politics as that of the Federalists. Most of the Antifederalists were majoritarians with respect to the state legislatures but not with respect to the national legislature, because they presumed as well as the Federalists did that different sorts of people from those who sat in the state assemblies would occupy the Congress. Whatever else may be said about the Antifederalists, their populism cannot be impugned. They were true champions of the most extreme kind of democratic and egalitarian politics expressed in the revolutionary era. Convinced that "it has been the principal care of free governments to guard against the encroachments of the great," the Antifederalists believed that popular government itself, as defined by the principles of 1776, was endangered by the new national government. If the Revolution had been a transfer of power from the few to the many, then the federal Constitution clearly represented an abnegation of the Revolution. For, as Richard Henry Lee wrote in his *Letters from the Federal Farmer,* "every man of reflection must see, that the change now proposed, is a transfer of power from the many to the few."

Although Lee's analysis contained the essential truth, the Federalist program was not quite so simply summed up. It was true that through the new Constitution the Federalists hoped to resist and eventually to avert what they saw to be the rapid decline of the influence and authority of the natural aristocracy in America. At the very time that the organic conception of society that made elite rule comprehensible was finally and avowedly dissolving, and the members of the elite were developing distinct professional, social, or economic interests, the Federalists found elite rule more imperative than ever before. To the Federalists the greatest dangers to republicanism were flowing not, as the old Whigs had thought, from the rulers or from any distinctive minority in the community, but from the widespread participation of the people in the government. It now seemed increasingly evident that if the public good not only of the United States as a whole but even of the separate states were to be truly perceived and promoted, the American people must abandon their revolutionary reliance on their representative state legislatures and place their confidence in the highmindedness of the natural leaders of the society, which ideally everyone had the opportunity of becoming. Since the Federalists presumed that only such a self-conscious elite could transcend the many narrow and contradictory interests inevitable in any society, however small, the measure of a good government became its capacity for insuring the predominance of these kinds of natural leaders who knew better than the people as a whole what was good for the society.

The result was an amazing display of confidence in constitutionalism, in the efficacy of institutional devices for solving social and political problems. Through the proper arrangement of new institutional structures the Federalists aimed to turn the political and social developments that were weakening the place of "the better sort of people" in government back upon themselves and to make these developments the very source of the perpetuation of the natural aristocracy's dominance of politics. Thus the Federalists did not directly reject democratic politics as it had manifested itself in the 1780s; rather they attempted to adjust to this politics in order to control and mitigate its effects. In short they offered the country an elitist theory of democracy. They did not see themselves as repudiating either the Revolution or popular government, but saw themselves as saving both from their excesses. If the Constitution were not established, they told themselves and the country over and over, then republicanism was doomed, the grand experiment was over, and a division of the confederacy, monarch, or worse would result.

Despite all the examples of popular vice in the eighties, the Federalist confidence in the people remained strong. The letters of "Caesar," with their frank and violent denigration of the people, were anomalies in the Federalist literature. The Federalists had by no means lost faith in the people, at least in the people's ability to discern their true leaders. In fact many of the social elite who comprised the Federalist leadership were confident of popular election if the constituency could be made broad enough, and crass electioneering be curbed, so that the people's choice would be undisturbed by ambitious demagogues. "For if not blind to their own interest, they choose men of the first character for wisdom and integrity." Despite prodding by so-called designing and unprincipled men, the bulk of the people remained deferential to the established social leadership — for some aspiring politicians frustratingly so. Even if they had wanted to, the Federalists could not turn their backs on republicanism. For it was evident to even the most pessimistic "that no other form would be reconcilable with the genius of the people of America; with the fundamental principles of the Revolution; or with that honorable determination which animates every votary of freedom, to rest all

our political experiments on the capacity of mankind for self-government."
Whatever government the Federalists established had to be "strictly republican" and "deducible from the only source of just authority — the People."

## Woody Holton

## *from* Did Democracy Cause the Recession That Led to the Constitution?   [2005]

**WOODY HOLTON** (1959– ) is an associate professor of history at the University
of Richmond. He is the author of *Forced Founders: Indians, Debtors, Slaves,
and the Making of the American Revolution in Virginia* (1999), as well as *Unruly
Americans and the Origins of the Constitution* (2007).

The supporters of the United States Constitution touted it as, among
many other things, the only solution to a terrible economic slump. Nearly
all free Americans believed much of the responsibility for the recession of
the 1780s lay with the thirteen state legislatures. Yet not everyone was of
the same mind about what the assemblies, which controlled debtor-creditor
relations, the money supply, and the collection of "Continental" as well as
state taxes under the Articles of Confederation (1781–1789), had done
wrong. The Federalists believed the lower houses of the legislatures —
which in most states were annually elected and essentially omnipotent —
had damaged the economy by caving in to taxpayers' and debtors'
demands for release from their legal obligations. They claimed relief legislation was unjust both to government bondholders (the primary recipients of tax money) and to private creditors — and that it had provoked
them to stop supplying the capital and credit that were the lifeblood of
the American economy. For them, one of the most attractive features of
the proposed Constitution was its abolition of relief. . . .

Scholars who embrace the Federalists' analysis of the financial crisis of
the 1780s often forget that thousands of Americans wrote pamphlets,
newspaper essays, petitions, private letters, and legislative speeches setting
forth their own, very different diagnoses and remedies. Although the
authors of these alternative analyses heartily concurred in the Framers'
claim that the state legislators had wrecked the economy, they did not
agree that the assemblies had provided too much relief to debtors and
taxpayers. They instead contended that the representatives had driven
the nation into recession by conveying too much money, too quickly,
from debtors and taxpayers to private creditors and investors in government bonds. That transfer of wealth had in their view depleted capital

Woody Holton, "Did Democracy Cause the Recession That Led to the Constitution?" *Journal
of American History* 92 (September 2005): 442–67. Permission granted by Copyright Clearance
Center.

stocks and, more important, eroded farmers' ability to perform the hard
work needed to pull the economy out of recession.

Americans who thus contested the Framers' diagnosis of the nation's
economic ills also denied that the only remedy was to shift some of the
states' most important duties to a new national government that would be
less responsive to popular influence. If those critics were correct, if the
state assemblies could have ended the recession simply by conveying less
property from debtors and taxpayers to government bondholders and private creditors, then we will need to stop exhibiting the 1780s as evidence
that popular rule inherently endangers the economy. . . .

Although until recently historians describing the economic origins of the
United States Constitution tended to focus on private debt, today more and
more scholars contend that the Constitution was also rooted in a struggle
between taxpayers and investors in government bonds. Between the
Yorktown victory of 1781 and the federal assumption of state debts in 1790,
Americans were hit with taxes that averaged three or four times those of
the colonial era. The principal purpose of the levies was to pay interest on
state and federal government securities, many of them bought up by speculators. In the mid-1780s, most states earmarked at least two-thirds of their
tax revenue for foreign and domestic holders of the war bonds. The tax
burden was magnified by a shortage of circulating coin. During the struggle
against the British, creditors had generally been required to accept paper
money from their debtors, but by the end of the war most assemblies were
permitting creditors to demand gold and silver. . . . The currency shortage
also magnified the burden of private debt. In 1785, four years after the
South Carolina assembly voted to require that debts be paid in gold or silver, a newspaper writer who took the name Americanus said he had seen
debtors forced to "give up £50" worth of property "to pay £10." "Who will
call this *Justice?*" he asked. Thus what was true of taxation was also true of
the money supply: in perhaps the two most important areas of peacetime
governmental action, most of the newly independent states adopted harsher
policies than the colonial governments they had replaced. . . .

Taxpayers, debtors, and their supporters proposed numerous remedies
for the mid-1780s economic pinch, from tax abatements to legislation
allowing farmers to pay their debts in several annual installments instead
of all at once. Thousands of petitioners and newspaper essayists proposed
that every war bond that had been bought by a speculator be redeemed
at its market price — roughly the price at which it had changed hands —
rather than at the price printed on its face. . . .

Since many Americans believed the fundamental problem with the
economy was the shortage of circulating currency, one of the most popular relief proposals was to issue paper money. . . . Many wanted the state
legislatures to revive the colonial practice of establishing public loan
offices where farmers could mortgage their land and obtain loans at a low
interest rate (and without becoming dependent upon wealthy neighbors).
Most paper money advocates were also trying to ease their tax burden.

Recall that the states were levying heavy taxes for the benefit of the bond speculators. If the states paid the bondholders paper instead of hard money, they would not have to extract scarce gold and silver from taxpayers, who could thereby keep their farms. Some writers proposed a more radical step: Bondholders should be forced to exchange their bonds for paper money, which did not pay interest. . . . Historians who depict paper money solely as a panacea for private debt have contributed to a process whereby Americans have forgotten that the movement for the Constitution, which barred the state governments from emitting paper money, grew partly out of a struggle over how much property the government should convey from taxpayers to bondholders.

Some of the most prominent men in America were appalled by the debt- and tax-abatement measures of the 1780s, and much of the popularity of the Constitution can be traced to its clauses prohibiting state-level relief legislation and transferring responsibility for collecting continental taxes to the federal government. . . . Why were the Framers so bent on rescuing both public and private creditors from perceived injustice? The answer was simple, Charles A. Beard declared in 1913. Many of the federal convention delegates had themselves lent large sums to private citizens, to Congress, or to one of the state governments (or they had bought up other people's bonds), and they and the other holders of "personalty" wanted their money. The Constitution had an obvious charm for creditors and bondholders. Yet thousands of Americans who did not belong to either of those groups joined them in celebrating the abolition of relief. Why? Today most students of the origins of the Constitution concur in Gordon S. Wood's assessment that the Framers were elitists who saw relief legislation as alarming mostly because it showed that the plebian-dominated state assemblies had departed from virtue — a problem they solved by writing the Constitution, "intrinsically an aristocratic document." Although Wood thus makes a persuasive case that the Framers hated tax and debt relief because they were elitists, it also seems clear that they were elitists (or, more precisely, that their habitual elitism was inflamed) at least in part because they hated relief. They believed the assemblymen's solicitude for taxpayers and debtors had destroyed Americans' collective credit rating.

The scholarly neglect of the desire to attract investment that motivated the Framers to oppose debt relief is surprising in light of the ample historiographical attention devoted to the Constitution's other expected economic benefits. Empowering Congress to bar foreign ships and goods from United States harbors would enable American diplomats to pry foreign (especially British) ports open to American commerce. National taxes would permit the federal government to protect American vessels in the Mediterranean Sea from the Barbary corsairs and western settlers from the Indians. By knocking down tariff barriers among the states, the Constitution would create a vast free-trade zone.

Yet none of those anticipated economic benefits of the Constitution looms as large in documents from the 1780s as the enticements it was expected to offer investors. Federalists claimed the Constitution would solve most of the problems farmers had spent the 1780s grumbling about, starting with their most vexing concern, the currency shortage. What was "necessary, in order to call forth the specie [gold and silver] that is accumulated and retained by men of affluence," the North Hampton, New Hampshire, minister Benjamin Thurston declared in a December 1786 speech, was for Americans to "renounce all ideas of introducing paper money" or other legislative relief. The moment the well-to-do stopped worrying about assemblymen allowing their debtors to repay them using "old horses," it was widely believed, they would take their gold and silver out of their strongboxes and put it in circulation. Abolishing relief would even eliminate a great anomaly of the 1780s: Cautious American investors, reversing the natural flow of capital from the Old World to the New, had sent their money to Europe for safekeeping.

The monetary famine was not the only threat, for European merchants were growing more and more reluctant to ship cargoes to Americans on credit. . . . This was not mere rhetoric. Louis Guillaume Otto, comte de Mosloy, the French chargé d'affaires in the United States, observed in May 1786 that American credit had "considerably suffered by the jolt given to it by several laws prejudicial to foreign creditors." American wholesalers were in turn starting to demand that their own customers, generally retail merchants, pay cash on delivery. They too feared that public officials might someday come between them and their delinquent debtors' property. . . .

The ban on debtor relief inscribed in the Constitution was widely celebrated during the ratification debate — for instance, by all three authors of the *Federalist Papers*. . . .

The authors of the *Federalist Papers* were not the only advocates for the Constitution who believed it would recruit capital and thereby revive the economy. In November 1787, A True Friend reminded his fellow Virginians that under British rule, "We could pass no act tending to hurt, or annihilate the rights and interests of British creditors; consequently they did not fear to advance considerable sums. . . . Those services and advances, though so dearly bought, were however indispensible." But now Virginians were "deprived of the assistance, advances and credit, which the metropolis, used to sell us so dear, and which all nations would be so eager to offer us were they to . . . find in America, the punctuality and security, which alone gain credit and support confidence." What stood in the way of restoring Americans' collective credit rating? "As long as the law will subsist in Virginia that the creditor cannot seize, lay attachment and sell the land of his debtor, at the epoch the debt fall due, it is as [if] we had nothing" to mortgage, he said, and "as long as it will be by the tediousness of the courts of justice almost impossible to force the debtor, we shall not find money lenders." Other Virginia Federalists offered similar visions of the Constitution's ability to attract investment from overseas. Meanwhile their counterparts in Massachusetts were making a slightly different case, asserting that their own state abounded in private reserves of gold and silver that would be lent out as soon as relief was abolished. "You may as well expect to turn a stream up hill, as try to hire a Dollar of our rich men, so long as the Government remains in its present deplorable situation," one Massachusetts Federalist declared in October 1787. Ratification would give "the wealthy" confidence "in the honour and justice of the govern-ment," another Bay State writer declared a month later. It would be the signal for the well-to-do to begin "*loaning* the surplus of their riches upon reasonable terms." Predictions like these echoed through other states as well. . . .

Most historians of the Constitution endorse the Framers' analysis of the economic and political crises of the 1780s. Edmund S. Morgan of Yale Uni-versity denounces the "legislative tyranny" of the period. Gordon S. Wood of Brown University writes that "paper money acts, stay laws, and other forms of debtor relief legislation hurt various creditor groups in the society and violated individual property rights." Bernard Bailyn of Harvard Uni-versity asserts that by the time James Madison defended the Constitution in the *Federalist Papers,* "he had observed the evil effects of legislative majori-ties within some of the states over the previous five years. Again and again minority property rights had been overwhelmed by populist majorities." Scholars who do not explicitly endorse the Framers' analysis of the crisis of the 1780s accord it tacit support by not explicating any other. Yet during the founding era, numerous Americans differed with the Framers about both the causes of the economic ills of the 1780s and the remedies. Unlike Charles Beard and the "neo-Progressive" historians such as Merrill Jensen, nearly every freeman who lived through the 1780s agreed that the economy was in trouble during the postwar years and that the state assemblies deserved much of the blame. Yet many Americans dissented from the Framers' con-viction that the legislators' error had been to grant debtors and taxpayers too much relief. They were happy to acknowledge that the nation needed a currency, investment capital, and the labor of American farmers, but they contended that prospects would brighten in all three sectors if the legislatures would only adopt more, not less, tax and debt relief.

The opponents of the record-high taxes of the 1780s rejected the claim that rigorous tax collection would expand the money supply. Indeed, they considered heavy taxation the chief culprit in draining the countryside of its gold and silver. They described a process whereby coins were collected from taxpayers and turned over to bondholders, who then shipped them to Britain in exchange for manufactured goods. In Virginia in fall 1787, a newspaper writer named Plain Reason blamed the "decay of specie in this country" on "the consumption of the greater part" of it "by the non-productive speculators, in European articles." . . .

Bond speculation also damaged the economy, some argued, by luring away capital that might otherwise have been invested productively. Plain Reason claimed that in Virginia "a great proportion of the specie" was "circulating in the traffick of military certificates," soaking up "funds, that would have gone to improve a farm, and increase the wealth of the state."

Since "nobody will, if he can avoid it, otherwise employ his money," Plain Reason contended, bond speculation was a major reason for "the languid state of agriculture." In September 1786 a farmers' convention in Worcester County, Massachusetts, demanded fiscal reforms that would "induce the man of wealth to deposit that wealth in the lands and products of his country, rather than in speculations of publick securities. . . .

In 1790 Congress would adopt Hamilton's proposal for eliminating government bonds as an "object of . . . speculation." It would levy sufficient taxes to pay regular interest on the bonds, raising their market price to parity with their face value. During the 1780s, however, many Americans had favored scaling the bonds down or redeeming them with paper money, measures that would not only take the profit out of bond speculation but also have another, profounder, effect, they argued. Relieving the plight of both taxpayers and debtors would restore their ability to realize their productive potential. They believed the state legislatures had imposed fiscal and monetary regimes so harsh as to reduce American farmers' harvests, for instance, forcing debtors and taxpayers to give up their tools and livestock. . . . A New Jerseyan who took the name Willing to Learn declared at the end of 1785 that if the government were to intervene — say, by printing paper money — farmers would be able to "save their estates" and remain "useful members of the community."

As important as livestock and tools were to the labor process, the most crucial element was the farmer himself, and many contended that aggressive tax and debt collection often prevented rural Americans from working. So scarce was money in the New Jersey countryside, Willing to Learn claimed in 1786, that artisans spent nearly as much time dunning their customers as they did laboring at their benches. If paper money were printed, the artisan could easily settle old scores and get back to work. . . . A Rhode Island writer identified a different way the currency shortage wasted time. Artisans often had to receive their wages in commodities such as tea and salt. Thus "a labourer after his day's work is done, must spend another in bartering away his tea or salt, into three or four articles more suitable."

Still more work hours were squandered when the debt- or tax-collection process ended in court. "The waste of time attending law suits . . . oppress[es] industry," A Husbandman told readers of the *Maryland Journal* on June 6, 1786. . . .

The most dramatic way to stop a debtor or taxpayer from working was to imprison him. When debtors were "thrown into Gaols," the town of Cumberland, Rhode Island, pointed out in February 1786, it was not only "their families" that were "deprived of the advantages of their labors," but the whole "society." . . .

Thus fiscal and monetary austerity reduced farmers' output by robbing them of both their tools and their time. These problems, themselves grave, also wrought secondary damage that was even more harmful to the nation's productive capacity, many Americans believed. If farmers' distress was not alleviated, they said, word would get back to Europe, discouraging would-be immigrants from crossing the Atlantic Ocean. . . .

During the 1780s a remarkable number of petitioners and essayists described themselves or other Americans using variants of the word "discouraged." For instance, A Citizen of Connecticut said the currency shortage "discourage[d]" farmers "from making any attempts towards extricating themselves; who otherwise would act with spirit and vigor."

Since aggressive debt and tax collection had "dispirited" farmers and "rendered [them] in some measure useless to Society," relieving their distress would revive their spirits, enabling them to make greater contributions both to their families and to the nation. In April 1787 a Marylander proposed that the state government replace its two hundred thousand pounds' worth of interest-bearing bonds with paper money, which did not pay interest. This proposal for "lessening the public debt" would allow the assembly to slash the state property tax (which had been levied "chiefly for the purpose of paying the interest on these certificates"), "thus animating the hopes of a desponding people.". . .

Americans who favored tax and debt relief affirmed that what made the loss of farmers' tools and time — and the consequent damage to both immigration and inspiration — so disastrous for the economy was that farmers' labor was the foundation of the nation's wealth. . . .

Although the most damning indictment of the legislatures' harsh fiscal and monetary policies was that they had reduced farmers' output, relief advocates did not neglect the consumption side of the ledger. They rejected their opponents' claim that farmers and their families had provoked the economic crisis by spending beyond their means. "When we complain of our taxes," one Massachusetts writer said in summer 1787, protax essayists "tell us of our fine feathers and dinners, and other extravagance; but for my part, I see no more of these things now, than I did before the war." Not farmers but speculators were indulging in excess consumption, this writer declared: "Feathers, feasts, and coaches, are the exclusive pleasures and privileges of men who draw from 20 to 60 per cent, from their country." . . .

Today it is a commonplace among economists that excessive taxation or overly restrictive monetary policies — or a combination of the two — can throw an economy into recession. That was essentially what the champions of tax and debt relief were saying, but they rarely used such abstract language. For them the matter was more personal. In their eyes, high taxes and currency deflation had led the wealthy to stop making productive investments and in many cases to stop producing. Even more important, the assemblies had prevented farmers and artisans from working at their full potential. Those were the fetters dragging the economy down. . . .

Debate over state-level fiscal and monetary policies . . . divided Americans on the eve of the Constitutional Convention. Is it appropriate to describe that debate as a class conflict? It cannot be confidently affirmed that the two principal sides represented conflicting classes: the authors of many fiscal and monetary treatises will forever remain unknown, and others sometimes took positions that ran counter to their own immediate self-interest. And yet the debate was a class conflict in a different sense. It hinged upon which segment of society should bear the burden of reviving the economy. Although the advocates for leniency and austerity both believed their plans would ultimately benefit every free American, the most candid champions of each approach acknowledged that it might force some segments of society to suffer for the good of the whole. . . .

The debate over which classes should sacrifice for the good of the whole was largely a disagreement about what to do on the frequent occasions when the two imperatives for economic renewal — attracting capital and encouraging labor — clashed. Some Americans believed the single best way to end the recession was to remove all restraints on productive labor — even at the risk of scaring off potential investors. Although their opponents shared their desperate desire to end the recession, they also sought boisterous growth, and they would achieve it by attracting capital — even at the risk of discouraging labor. Historians have long debated early American farmers' attitude toward capitalism. Farm families may be defined as anticapitalist in the sense that when their most prominent countrymen called on them to sacrifice property and personal liberty on behalf of the crusade to attract capital, most of them declined. When modern historians uncritically adopt the Framers' assumptions that the farmers were simply short-sighted, they forget two truths: First, that few of the men who called on farmers to accept sacrifice were proposing to join them in it, and, second, that farmers and their supporters seem to have sincerely believed that it was not capital that held the key to economic revival. It was labor.

The competing economic strategies advanced in the 1780s were rooted in conflicting assessments of popular virtue. Madison and other prominent Federalists believed the 1780s offered farmers a grim lesson about the limits of their own capacity for self-rule. According to this viewpoint, the authors of the Revolution-era state constitutions had placed too much faith in ordinary Americans' ability and willingness to act wisely and justly. . . . Yet many Americans . . . denied that the 1780s had taught any such lesson. Although they agreed that the state legislatures had mismanaged the economy, they traced this failure to elite, not popular, misrule. Consequently, they disputed the Federalists' assertion that the only way out of the economic bind was to embrace the restraints on popular influence embodied in the Constitution.

The contest between the elitist and populist political dispositions thus paralleled the dispute over whether the saviors of the economy were going to be moneyed men (who would invest in America as soon as they could do so safely) or ordinary farmers (who required only the removal of their fiscal and monetary shackles to become prodigiously productive). In politics as in economics, the question was whether redemption was going to come from above or below.

# 7

# Jacksonian Democracy: How Democratic?

To many historians, the election of Andrew Jackson as president in 1828 represents a turning point in American history. Prior to Jackson's election, the men who occupied the presidency had come from either Virginia or Massachusetts; they were closely identified with an aristocratic elite that seemed far removed from the great mass of Americans. Andrew Jackson, on the other hand, seemed to symbolize the common man rather than the aristocrat. Jackson's status as a self-made man and military hero made his election seem like the ultimate triumph of democracy in American society.

Although historians for many years accepted the relationship between Jackson and political democracy, they disagreed sharply over the precise nature of what came to be known as Jacksonian democracy. Indeed, the period from 1828 to 1840 became one of the most controversial eras in American history insofar as scholars were concerned. Americans had long attempted to define the unique characteristics that separated them from the rest of the world — a quest that inevitably led to an extended discussion of democracy and its meaning. Historians were no exception to this rule and much of their writing revolved around a historical examination of the nature and development of democracy in America. Because Andrew Jackson and democratic politics seemed so closely related, both topics became the subject of innumerable books and articles.[1]

Like that of Jefferson before him and other political leaders after him, Jackson's historical reputation has changed markedly from time to time. The earliest evaluations of his presidential career tended to be highly critical and hostile in tone. James Parton, Jackson's first serious biographer, freely admitted that Old Hickory was indeed the idol of the American people. Yet his portrait of Jackson was anything but flattering.[2]

Parton's criticisms were echoed even more strongly by other nineteenth-century writers, including Hermann E. von Holst, William Graham Sumner, and James Schouler.[3] These writers agreed that Jackson was illiterate, uned-

---

[1] For a significant analysis of the early historiography of Jacksonian democracy, see Charles G. Sellers Jr., "Andrew Jackson versus the Historians," *Mississippi Valley Historical Review* 44 (March 1958): 615–34.

[2] James Parton, *Life of Andrew Jackson*, 3 vols. (New York, 1861), vol. 3, 694.

[3] Hermann E. von Holst, *The Constitutional and Political History of the United States*, 8 vols. (Chicago, 1876–1892); William Graham Sumner, *Andrew Jackson* (Boston, 1899); James Schouler, *History of the United States of America under the Constitution*, 7 vols. (New York, 1880–1913).

ucated, uninformed, and emotional, and that his actions were motivated by a desire to dominate merely for the sake of power. In short, his election as president in 1828 was considered to be a mortal blow to cherished American ideals. "His ignorance," wrote Parton, "was as a wall around him — high, impenetrable. He was imprisoned in his ignorance, and sometimes raged round his little, dim enclosure like a tiger in his den."[4]

The hostility of these historians toward Jackson, oddly enough, did not arise from the fact that their own political ideology and preferences differed sharply from those held by Old Hickory. Indeed, most of them were nineteenth-century economic liberals who staunchly championed laissez-faire principles, condemned governmental intervention in the economy, and supported a sound currency. In this respect, they were in general agreement with many of Jackson's policies, including his attack on the Second Bank of the United States and his hard-money views. Moreover, they approved of his forceful and assertive nationalism — particularly his bold stand during the South Carolina nullification controversy.

What these nineteenth-century scholars found most deplorable about Jackson's presidency, however, was the fact that the democratization of American politics had resulted in the exclusion from high public office of those individuals and groups that had been traditionally accustomed to holding the reins of power. The older political leaders were being replaced by the wrong sort of men — men who pandered to the desires of the mob and acted according to political expediency rather than to the principles of justice. "The undeniable and sadly plain fact," wrote von Holst, "is that since that time the people have begun to exchange the leadership of a small number of statesmen and politicians of a higher order for the rule of an ever increasing crowd of politicians of high and low degree, down even to the pot-house politician and the common thief, . . . politics became a profession in which mediocrity — on an ever descending scale — dominated, and moral laxity became the rule, if not a requisite."[5] Von Holst's words were echoed by other writers. Since Jackson, Parton charged, "the public affairs of the United States have been conducted with a stupidity which has excited the wonder of mankind."[6]

Most of these nineteenth-century scholars had come from eastern, middle-class, patrician families that had enjoyed social and political leadership for well over a century. Viewing themselves as an elite that monopolized the ability to govern wisely, they were especially resentful of the democratization of American politics. In their eyes, Jacksonian democracy was the movement that had resulted in their own loss of status and power. They condemned Jackson for supposedly beginning the process of corrupting an ideal state of affairs. The interests of the masses could best be looked after by an incorruptible aristocracy devoted to the welfare of the nation. Their historical

---

[4]Parton, *Life of Andrew Jackson*, vol. 3, 699.
[5]von Holst, *The Constitutional and Political History of the United States*, vol. 2, 77.
[6]Parton, *Life of Andrew Jackson*, vol. 3, 700.

writings represented a Federalist-Whig-Republican point of view, and they were in most respects highly critical of Jackson.

By the beginning of the twentieth century, the eastern patricians no longer dominated historical writing. Younger scholars, many of whom came from different parts of the country and did not hold elitist views, began writing history. They saw in their discipline a means of both illuminating contemporary problems and providing guidelines for future action. Believers in democracy, they tended to favor leaders and movements that had contributed to the growing democratization of the American people and their institutions. Unlike the patricians, they did not write about American history in terms of decline from some supposed earlier golden age. On the contrary, they wrote American history in terms of protracted conflict between the people and the special interests, between the forces of democracy and the aristocracy. These historians, most of whom were part of the Progressive school of American historiography, began to break with the views of the older patrician school, and they set the stage for a radical reevaluation of Jackson.

The changing attitude toward Andrew Jackson first became evident in the writings of Frederick Jackson Turner, one of the earliest of the great Progressive historians. Just as Parton and other patrician historians leaned toward aristocracy, so Turner leaned toward democracy. For Turner, Andrew Jackson was in some ways the logical culmination of the triumph of democratic values in the United States. "On the whole," Turner wrote, "it must be said that Jackson's Presidency was more representative of the America of his time than would have been that of any of his rivals. The instincts of the American people in supporting him conformed to the general drift of the tendencies of this New World democracy."[7]

From the turn of the century until the end of World War II, the Progressive school interpretation of Jacksonian democracy remained dominant among American historians. In numerous books and articles, scholars contributed to the growing identification of the triumph of political democracy with the accession of Jackson to the presidency. Even the supposed introduction of the spoils system — a development that patrician historians had regarded as an unmitigated disaster — began to be studied in a new light. The spoils system, Progressive historians emphasized, was both a reflection and a result of democracy. Prior to Jackson, a small elite who had regarded government as their own private preserve had monopolized public office. But the introduction of universal manhood suffrage and the emergence of a broad-based two-party system destroyed that monopoly and threw open governmental office to all persons regardless of their class or background. The spoils system, then, was the democratic alternative to an elitist monopoly — the logical consequence of democracy — even though they recognized that it could be susceptible to abuse.

---

[7]Frederick Jackson Turner, *The United States, 1830–1850: The Nation and Its Sections* (New York, 1935), 28.

In 1945, Arthur M. Schlesinger Jr. published his Pulitzer Prize–winning study, *The Age of Jackson.* This book became the starting point for historiographical controversy and scholars, generally speaking, fell into either the pro- or the anti-Schlesinger camp. So great was the impact of the book that much of the current debate over Jacksonian democracy still dates from the publication of *The Age of Jackson.*

Schlesinger succeeded in sharpening in a brilliant manner the Progressive interpretation of the Jacksonian era. Most Progressive historians depicted the major struggle of this era as a sectional conflict among the democratic West, the capitalist Northeast, and the aristocratic slave-owning South. Schlesinger, on the other hand, minimized sectional conflict as the key to understanding American politics during the 1830s. "It seems clear now," he argued, "that more can be understood about Jacksonian democracy if it is regarded as a problem not of sections but of classes."[8] In his eyes, Jacksonian energy came from noncapitalists, farmers, and workingmen who were reacting to the economic hardships of the period as well as to the domination of business interests seeking to extend their control over the economy. Where Turner and other sectional historians had emphasized the support that Jackson drew from the West, Schlesinger argued that the eastern urban working class had played the more important role.

Schlesinger's interpretation of Jacksonian democracy in terms of class conflict was set within a broader framework of his understanding of American history as a whole. The Jacksonian era, Schlesinger maintained, was simply one phase in the continual conflict between liberalism and conservatism in America. American democracy, he wrote, had always accepted the idea of an enduring struggle among competing groups for control of the state. Such a struggle was one of the guarantees of liberty, for it prevented the domination of the government by any single group.[9]

Schlesinger's approach to Jackson and his followers was highly favorable: Jackson's attack on the Second Bank of the United States was justified because the bank was completely independent of popular control and actually symbolized the alliance between the federal government and the business community. Jacksonian democracy could only be understood and interpreted within the liberal reformist tradition.

Within two years of the publication of *The Age of Jackson,* a number of scholars expressed their dissent in no uncertain terms. While few of these critics could agree on an alternative hypothesis, they concurred that Schlesinger's democratic and class conflict hypothesis was not substantiated by the facts. The result was an extended debate that continues today among American historians over the problem of explaining the nature and significance of Jacksonian democracy.

Generally speaking, Schlesinger's critics fell into two general schools. The first, known as the entrepreneurial school, maintained that Jackson did not

---

[8]Arthur M. Schlesinger Jr., *The Age of Jackson* (Boston, 1945), 263.
[9]Ibid., 505.

represent the great masses of people attempting to curb the power and authority of the business community. On the contrary, the Jacksonians themselves were middle-class entrepreneurs and businessmen seeking to free
themselves from the restraining hand of government and to embark on ventures that would bring them immediate wealth. The second tradition in American historiography that emerged after 1945 went even further and denied
the existence of a movement known as Jacksonian democracy. The political struggles of the 1830s, argued some of these historians, revolved around
local issues and a desire for public office; no ideological divisions whatsoever were involved.

In a series of articles and then in a Pulitzer Prize–winning book, Bray Hammond, a scholarly official of the Federal Reserve Board, took to task Schlesinger's interpretation of the Second Bank of the United States. Hammond
denied Schlesinger's contention that the bank was "the keystone in the alliance between the government and the business community."[10] He argued
instead that this institution performed the role of a central bank — that is,
it was a responsible regulatory agency with the function of preventing disastrous periodic economic crises by pursuing sound monetary and fiscal
policies. However, within the Democratic Party, Hammond wrote, a rising
group of entrepreneurs resented the obstacles that prevented them from
embarking on speculative ventures that would bring them quick wealth. They
resented particularly the Second Bank of the United States, in part because
its sound monetary policy hampered their speculative enterprises.

In Andrew Jackson, according to Hammond, these rising entrepreneurs
found their champion. Jackson, who never clearly comprehended the issues
involved, was persuaded that the bank was destroying economic opportunity.
Hence he destroyed the bank. But that greatly diminished the power of the
federal government to regulate the economy through fiscal and economic
policy. Consequently American society throughout the nineteenth century
was subjected to the extreme ups and downs of the business cycle. The price
of industrialization during the nineteenth century, Hammond concluded,
was much greater than it might have been had the bank been able to continue its regulatory activities.[11]

Contrary to Schlesinger, Hammond and other historians of the entrepreneurial school saw Jackson and his followers as expectant capitalists seeking
to free themselves from government restraint. By emphasizing the middle-
class sources of Jacksonian democracy, the entrepreneurial historians were,
in effect, denying that the movement was in the American liberal tradition.
Instead of championing the cause of the people, Jackson was upholding the
cause of liberal capitalism.

Richard Hofstadter echoed aspects of Hammond's entrepreneurial approach, as both saw in Jackson a pro-business president. In *The American Political Tradition and the Men Who Made It*, Hofstadter entitled one of his chapters

---

[10]Hammond's most extended discussion of Jacksonian democracy appeared in his *Banks
and Politics in America: From the Revolution to the Civil War* (Princeton, N.J., 1957), 286 ff.
[11]Ibid., 76.

"Andrew Jackson and the Rise of Liberal Capitalism." The Jacksonian move-ment, he emphasized, was "a phase in the expansion of liberated capitalism" and "was closely linked to the ambitions of the small capitalist." To Hofstadter, the popular hatred of privilege and the dominant laissez-faire ideology cre-ated an unfortunate mythology that defined democracy as a weak central government that permitted powerful economic interests a disproportion-ate share of influence in questions involving national policy.[12]

Consensus historians after 1945 rejected a class analysis of history and emphasized a basic consensus that supposedly united all Americans. In the United States, these historians argued, politics never revolved around ideo-logical and class conflicts precisely because Americans shared a common outlook founded on Lockean middle-class liberalism. Reacting to the external challenge posed to American institutions by the Soviet Union in particular and Marxism in general, the work of these historians reflected the emphasis on national unity so characteristic of the postwar era. The rejection of a class interpretation of Jacksonian politics was reinforced by the work of historians who were influenced by the quantitative studies undertaken in other social science disciplines, especially political science, and who analyzed party strug-gles through the aggregate voting behavior of large numbers of individuals. Their statistical findings raised some questions about the validity of an inter-pretation that relied on a simple class division and the platforms and state-ments of parties and leaders.

Some historians, influenced by work done in the social and behavioral sciences, sought to apply concepts from these disciplines, particularly psy-chology. Historians had long been interested in understanding the personal motivation and behavior of reformers, and several scholars determined that the Jacksonians could only be understood in terms of status insecurity. Jacksonians engaged in various reform efforts not from their ideology but rather from their anxiety over their status in society. Reform gave them an alternative outlet for self-expression. From the psychological point of view, Jacksonians resorted to reform activities because of their inability to adjust to the changing ways of American society. Reform calmed their fears regard-ing their own status insecurity.

The most sophisticated example of the psychological interpretation of Jacksonian democracy was Marvin Meyers's prize-winning book *The Jacksonian Persuasion*. Meyers argued that the Jacksonians wanted to preserve the virtues of a simple agrarian republic without having to sacrifice the rewards and conveniences already evident by the 1830s. The Jacksonians were unprepared for all the changes that were undermining traditional values. Their response was a crusade to try to restore the virtues of the simple agrarian republic that had supposedly existed about the time of the American Revolution. The enemy, according to Jackson and his followers, was best personified by the Second Bank of the United States, for this institution did not create true wealth, but

---

[12]Richard Hofstadter, *The American Political Tradition and the Men Who Made It* (New York, 1948), 55–63.

merely represented a "*paper* money power, the *corporate* money power — i.e., concentrations of wealth arising suddenly from financial manipulation and special privilege." Because the bank was corrupting the plain republican order that they held so dear, the Jacksonians decided to cut out this source of corruption in the body politic. Herein, Meyers concluded, lay a paradox. The Jacksonians believed that in attacking the bank they were destroying an institution that menaced their idealized agrarian republic; in reality, they were destroying a regulatory institution, thereby paving the way for the triumph of laissez-faire capitalism.[13] Meyers's synthesis reduced the Jacksonian movement to a set of psychological adjustments; one could not understand Jackson and his followers as part of a long and viable political tradition. Class conflicts became competition for status and position by certain groups within society.

Within the next two decades, another group of scholars denied that Jacksonian democracy, as an organized movement or even a concept, ever existed. They argued instead that American historians who had utilized the concept had been influenced by their commitment to a democratic ideology. Such a commitment had led these historians to read their own values back into the past, thereby making Andrew Jackson a symbolic champion of the people in what they saw as a perennial struggle against the business class and other special interests. An examination of the sources, these historians emphasized, would completely discredit the Progressive school's interpretation of Jacksonian democracy.

But if Andrew Jackson was neither the champion of the people nor even the representative of the emerging laissez-faire capitalism, then how could the politics of the 1830s be interpreted? In answering this question, these historians tended to borrow heavily from the behavioral sciences and to use quantitative techniques in order to demonstrate that the American people were not divided along class and ideological lines. In parallel thinking, Robert E. Brown and other colonial historians had argued that seventeenth- and eighteenth-century America was already a middle-class democratic society. If American society was obviously democratic by the 1820s, Jackson could hardly be considered within a democratic reformist tradition.

Thus Richard P. McCormick, in several studies of voting behavior during the Jacksonian era, challenged the thesis that an unprecedented upsurge in voting had been responsible for Jackson's victories in 1828 and 1832. Indeed, McCormick argued, the real upsurge in voter participation came after Jackson was out of office in 1840. The growth of what he called the second American party system (to distinguish it from the Federalist and Jeffersonian party system) was not precipitated by ideological or class issues. It originated rather in the successive presidential contests between 1824 and 1840. "It did not emerge," McCormick wrote, "from cleavages within Congress, nor from any polarization of attitudes on specific public issues. . . . The second party system did not spring into existence at any one time. . . . The most influential factor determining when alignments appeared within a particular region was the regional identifications of the presidential candidates." Subsequently,

---

[13]Marvin Meyers, *The Jacksonian Persuasion: Politics and Belief* (Stanford, Calif., 1957).

McCormick defined what he called the "Presidential Game," a theory about the methods of selecting the president, the implications of which were that Jacksonian democracy, in terms of a distinct ideological party apparatus, never existed.[14]

Others insisted that the age of Jackson was simply too heterogeneous and defied simple labeling. In a study of the distribution of wealth during this era, Edward Pessen emphasized the theme of inequality rather than equality. Wealth, rather than being widely distributed, was becoming ever more concentrated, and the nation's social structure more rigid and less fluid. Those who succeeded were generally born into affluent families. If society was becoming more unequal, Pessen asked, how could historians continue to equate the age of Jackson with egalitarianism?[15]

In an equally significant work, Lee Benson shifted the focus from political parties to the electorate. Rejecting a socioeconomic approach, Benson was among the earliest historians to emphasize the role of national origins and religion as among the most important determinants of voting behavior. He attempted to demonstrate that voting behavior was due in large measure to basic differences in religious values and worldviews. Jacksonian democracy, he concluded, was a fiction created by American historians, and in *The Concept of Jacksonian Democracy: New York as a Test Case* he attempted to prove the validity of the proposition that since the 1820s "ethnic and religious differences have tended to be *relatively* the most important sources of political differences." In succeeding years, others followed Benson's lead in developing an ethnocultural interpretation of American politics, thus vitiating the reality of Jacksonian democracy as a conceptual construct.[16]

---

[14]Richard P. McCormick, *The Second American Party System: Party Formation in the Jacksonian Era* (Chapel Hill, N.C., 1966), 13. See also McCormick's two articles, "New Perspectives on Jacksonian Politics," *American Historical Review* 65 (January 1960): 288–301, and "Suffrage Classes and Party Alignments: A Study in Voter Behavior," *Mississippi Valley Historical Review* 46 (December 1959): 397–410; Richard P. McCormick, *The Presidential Game: The Origins of American Presidential Politics* (New York, 1982).

[15]Edward Pessen, "The Egalitarian Myth and the American Social Reality: Wealth, Mobility, and Equality in the 'Era of the Common Man,'" *American Historical Review* 76 (October 1971): 989–1034, and *Jacksonian America: Society, Personality and Politics* (Homewood, Ill., 1969), 350–51. Surprisingly enough, New Left scholars have all but ignored the Jacksonian era. One exception is Michael A. Lebowitz, "The Jacksonians: Paradox Lost?" in *Towards a New Past: Dissenting Essays in American History*, ed. Barton J. Bernstein (New York, 1968), 65–89.

[16]Lee Benson, *The Concept of Jacksonian Democracy: New York as a Test Case* (Princeton, N.J., 1961). For a more recent discussion of the Jacksonian period by Benson, see his essay "Middle Period Historiography: What Is to Be Done," in *American History: Retrospect and Prospect*, ed. George A. Billias and Gerald N. Grob (New York, 1971), 154–90. For a perceptive discussion of the ethnocultural approach to nineteenth-century American political history, see Richard L. McCormick, "Ethno-Cultural Interpretations of Nineteenth-Century American Voting Behavior," *Political Science Quarterly* 89 (June 1974): 351–77. Benson insisted that the program of the Jacksonian party — which included states' rights, a strong executive leadership, freedom of conscience, and the idea of representative government — could hardly be equated with democracy. Such a program, he suggested, was the negation of the democratic and humanitarian movements that emerged during the nineteenth century. As an alternative hypothesis, Benson suggested that the era be named the "Age of Egalitarianism." Ideological changes, a phenomenal growth of the nation, and a high rate of physical mobility all combined to increase sharply the opportunities available to Americans and hence produced a more egalitarian society by 1860.

The new political historians have increasingly rejected simple dualisms and explanations. As Ronald P. Formisano noted in a review of the literature, Whigs and Democrats *did* diverge in their conception of the individual, society, and the relationship between government and the economy, but the patterns of divergence were complex rather than simple. "It is unlikely, however," he noted, "that parties in this period will be fitted to a liberal-conservative schema or that Jackson and his opponents will be divided again into radical democrats and aristocrats. No single ideological scheme will do to order the political, social, and cultural conflicts of that world."[17]

In a similar vein, some scholars have insisted that the consequences of actions by such political leaders as Andrew Jackson have been exaggerated. In an important study of the Jacksonian economy and the cycle of inflation, crisis, and deflation, Peter Temin maintained that the role of Jackson was far less than contemporaries believed; historians also erred in making Jackson a prime mover on the economic scene. Despite the criticisms of the very concept of Jacksonian democracy, the conviction that there were significant ideological and programmatic differences between parties has persisted. The Whigs, according to Lawrence F. Kohl, represented the emerging commercial society; the Democrats were unalterably opposed. Others emphasize the Whig commitment to entrepreneurial values, as compared with their opponent's faith in equality.[18]

In *Chants Democratic*, Sean Wilentz employed insights from the new social history to demonstrate that working-class political movements in New York City during the 1830s were class-based and directed against an emerging capitalism. Wilentz was also aware of the elements that impeded the unity of workers, including nativism, sex, and race. In effect, his book represented an effort to synthesize several older historiographical traditions that emphasized class and conflict with some of the insights of the new social history.[19]

Since the 1980s, two important schools of historians have been working on the Jackson era. The new historians of political culture have studied the ways in which Democrats and Whigs mobilized voters, how capitalism affected this process, and how the political activism of women influenced party and extra-party politics. These historians look at traditional Jacksonian politics, ideology, voting, and the role of the economy in new and subtle ways, exploring, among other things, gender, antiparty feeling, and degrees of confidence in or alienation from the centers of economic dynamism. A second group beginning in about 1990 opened a profound debate over the role of race in dividing Americans of the 1830s and 1840s, treating the fight over Jackson's removal of the southeastern Indians and the Democrats' support of slavery.

---

[17]Ronald P. Formisano, "Toward a Reorientation of Jacksonian Politics: A Review of the Literature, 1959–1975," *Journal of American History* 63 ( June 1975): 64. See also Formisano's *The Transformation of Popular Culture: Massachusetts Parties, 1790s–1840s* (New York, 1983).

[18]Peter Temin, *The Jacksonian Economy* (New York, 1969), 176; Lawrence F. Kohl, *The Politics of Individualism: Parties and the American Character in the Jacksonian Era* (New York, 1989); Daniel W. Howe, *The Political Culture of the American Whigs* (Chicago, 1979); John Ashworth, *"Agrarians" and "Aristocrats": Party Political Ideology in the United States, 1837–1846* (London, 1983).

[19]Sean Wilentz, *Chants Democratic: New York City and the Rise of the American Working Class, 1788–1850* (New York, 1984); see also Wilentz, "On Class and Politics in Jacksonian America," *Reviews in American History* 10 (December 1982): 45–63.

In 1982, Edward Pessen, an old and new historian of political culture, refurbished his 1969 argument that the eras of Thomas Jefferson and Andrew Jackson had many similarities, including growing economic inequality, the practice of distributing political spoils, and increasing democratization of the vote, but the election of elites to office. In his view, political elites mobilized mass support, but both parties were "hoaxes," and the few governed the masses, regardless of which party was in power.[20]

Pessen argued that conflict was submerged in the consensus among elites to manage the economy to their advantage. Michael J. Connolly in *Capitalism, Politics, and Railroads in Jacksonian New England* instead uncovered a broad consensus among Americans about the market economy, but differences about the degree of involvement that communities and citizens wanted. Studying the debates over plans for a railroad connection between northeastern Massachusetts and southeastern New Hampshire, Connolly discovered that radical Jacksonians saw the railroad as a tool of distant capitalists to rob them of their economic livelihoods, while more conservative Jacksonians, more integrated into the market, welcomed the railroad and the enhanced profits they imagined enjoying because of it.[21]

Political historians continued to ask what constitutes political activity and how people choose their affiliations. In two significant essays, Ronald Formisano looked beyond voting to the broader political culture to understand what made people ally with a particular party and what mobilized their passions. In "The Party Period Revisited," he questioned the sanctity of the Five Party System scheme and suggested that the Second Party System perhaps was not as significant in channeling popular activism as it has been seen. He incorporated some of the new scholarship from constitutional studies on antipartyism as well as the large body of literature on women's reform activities, such as abolitionist work, suffrage, and temperance, to show the vitality of nonparty political activity.[22]

In a subsequent study, Formisano looked at political culture, rather than just voting patterns, to understand better the pivotal election of 1840 in which Whigs took the presidency from the Democrats for the first time. He questioned explanations of the high voter turnout for that election as having been caused by the bad economic conditions following the panic of 1837. He particularly challenged the historian of the Whig Party, Michael Holt, who asserted that the Whigs won because they offered a comprehensible and appealing program on banks, railroads, and corporation rights to stabilize the economy. Formisano instead argued that in 1840, Whigs passionately repudiated Jackson's treatment of Indians and his perceived irreligion. They mobilized to vote against the Democrats' welcome of the Irish and Catholics

---

[20]Edward Pessen, "The Beleaguered Myth of Antebellum Egalitarianism: Cliometrics and Surmise to the Rescue," *Social Science History* 6 (Winter 1982): 111–28.

[21]Michael J. Connolly, *Capitalism, Politics, and Railroads in Jacksonian New England* (Columbia, Mo., 2003); see also Reeve Huston, "The Parties and 'The People': The New York Anti-Rent Wars and the Contours of Jacksonian Politics," *Journal of the Early Republic* 20 (Summer 2000): 241–71.

[22]Ronald Formisano, "The 'Party Period' Revisited," *Journal of American History* 86 (June 1999): 93–120.

in general along with their covert rejection of temperance. The Whigs warmly embraced Harrison's piety. Evangelical Whig womanhood featured importantly in this election, complete with aprons and handkerchiefs bearing Harrison's image.[23]

Catherine Allgor's *Parlor Politics* looked at the political culture of the early Republic as elite Washington women practiced it from Washington through Jackson's presidencies. Allgor analyzed gossip and gender to probe Jackson's failed plan to force Peggy Eaton with her scandalous reputation into the social circle of his cabinet ministers and their wives. Allgor's focus on elite women's parallel political world provides a significant perspective on Jacksonian democratization.[24]

Glen Altschuler and Stuart Blumin queried the notion of an enlarged and empowered Jacksonian electorate in an article followed by their longer analysis, *Rude Republic*. Pursuing themes that Michael McGerr and William E. Gienapp had explored concerning professional politicians' efforts to mold public opinion and the elite control of policy and elective offices, they asked whether Jacksonian politics had been as vibrant as many historians had painted it or if a substantial portion of the populace was disengaged and apathetic, whether or not it participated in elections. Did voting actually mean significant political engagement? And if it did, voting peaked in electing a Whig, not a Democrat.[25]

Gerald Leonard explored an aspect of Altschuler and Blumin's study: antiparty feeling. He found in the broad antipathy to parties the origins of the Democratic Party, which claimed not to be a party but the bearer of the undivided popular sovereignty that derived from the Constitution. Leonard argued that Hofstadter and other historians were wrong to see the early Democratic Party as representing a broad political consensus as it does today. Agreeing with Andrew Robertson (see Chapter 5) that American Party politics developed along differing interpretations of the Constitution, Leonard looked for the origin of parties in views of the Constitution rather than in economic interest groups or cultural associations. Jacksonian Democrats did not emerge from a particular socioeconomic base but claimed themselves as the legitimate nonpartisan expression of the will of the people. The Democrats went back to the Antifederalists for their principles. They were strict

[23]Ronald Formisano, "The New Political History and the Election of 1840," *Journal of Interdisciplinary History* 23 (Spring 1993): 661–82; Michael Holt, *The Rise and Fall of the Whig Party* (New York, 1999).

[24]Catherine Allgor, *Parlor Politics: In Which the Ladies of Washington Help Build a City and a Government* (Charlottesville, Va., 2000).

[25]Glenn Altschuler and Stuart Blumin, "Limits of Political Engagement in Antebellum America: A New Look at the Golden Age of Participatory Democracy," *Journal of American History* 84 (September 1997): 855–85, and *Rude Republic: Americans and Their Politics in the Nineteenth Century* (Princeton, N.J., 2000); Michael McGerr, *The Decline of Popular Politics: The American North, 1865–1928* (New York, 1986); William E. Gienapp, "'Politics Seem to Enter Everything,' Political Culture in the North, 1840–1860," in *Essays on American Antebellum Politics: The American North*, ed. Steven Maizlish and John J. Kushman (College Station, Tex., 1982); Norma Basch, "A Challenge to the Story of Popular Politics," *Journal of American History* 84 (December 1997): 900–903.

constructionists because Hamilton's implied powers could also centralize wealth and power, creating political dependency among the poor. Thus, the Democrats incorporated the widespread antebellum antiparty sentiment and channeled it, paradoxically, into a party, but one that claimed it was not really a party, but rather the legitimate will of the people. Supporting Formisano's thesis of the weakness of the Second Party System, Leonard points to the breakdown of the Second Party System and the war as proof that the Democrats failed to establish themselves as the true channel of the will of the people. It would not be until after the Civil War that the United States would achieve a functioning two-party system.[26]

Harry Watson in his acclaimed synthesis, *Liberty and Power*, disagreed that there was no difference between the parties and argued that the Jacksonian era did produce a profound transformation in American politics. The dramatic expansion of the American economy at the end of the War of 1812 prompted a significant debate about the new Republic's direction and the dimensions and control of its political economy. Parties were not hoaxes but drew numerous people into political activity. Watson acknowledged that while Jacksonian democracy liberated ordinary white men from traditional restraints and gave them more rights, men of color were losing rights: "Many historians would argue that these two processes were deeply intertwined."[27] Indeed, he was alert to the emerging debate over race in Jacksonian democracy.

In his most recent volume, *Andrew Jackson and His Indian Wars*, Robert V. Remini, the renowned author of a multivolume biography of Jackson and subscriber to the traditional view that Jacksonian politics represented an expanded democracy, took on directly one of the two subjects that have only recently started to become central to the study of Jackson: Indian policy and slavery. The work of scholars of Native Americans, like Joel Martin, Claudio Saunt, and Anthony F. C. Wallace, who had explored Jackson's relations with the southeastern Indians, began to acquire more prominence in assessments of Jackson. Scholars critical of Jackson pointed to his intervention in the Creeks' civil war and the punitive treaty he imposed afterward, taking 23 million acres of Creek land from both his Native American enemies and his allies. Scholars studying his removal of the Cherokees have pointed out its ghastly human costs and linked the outrage over it to the origins of the abolition movement, seeing in anti-removal activity the philosophical basis for the anti-slavery reformers' rejection of colonization.[28]

---

[26]Gerald Leonard, *The Invention of Party Politics: Federalism, Popular Sovereignty, and Constitutional Development in Jacksonian Illinois* (Chapel Hill, N.C., 2002).

[27]Harry Watson, *Liberty and Power: The Politics of Jacksonian America* (New York, 1990), 13.

[28]Robert V. Remini, *Andrew Jackson and the Course of the American Empire, 1767–1821* (New York, 1977); *Andrew Jackson and the Course of American Freedom, 1822–1832* (New York, 1981); *Andrew Jackson and the Course of American Democracy, 1833–1845* (New York, 1984); *Andrew Jackson and His Indian Wars* (New York, 2001); Mary Hershberger, "Mobilizing Women, Anticipating Abolition: The Struggle against Indian Removal in the 1830s," *Journal of American History* 86 (June 1999); Anthony F. C. Wallace, *The Long, Bitter Trail: Andrew Jackson and the Indian* (New York, 1993); Michael Paul Rogin, *Fathers and Children: Andrew Jackson and the Subjugation of the American Indian* (New York, 1975); Andrew Burstein, *The Passions of Andrew Jackson* (New York, 2003); Gerard Magliocca, *Andrew Jackson and the Constitution: The Rise and Fall of Generational Regimes* (Lawrence, Kans., 2007).

Jackson defenders, like Remini and Sean Wilentz in his 2005 biography of Jackson, have argued that Jackson had no particular animus against Native Americans, but sincerely believed that they would be better off away from white settlers and that previous presidents hypocritically offered assimilation as a way to integrate Indians in society without any real faith in its possibilities. John Buchanan saw Jackson's assault against the Creeks and Seminoles as deriving from concern over the weakness of the southwestern boundary of the new United States.[29]

Jackson's critics point out that he came into office set on removal above all other programs, that he and his close friend and negotiator John Coffee profited substantially from the Creek cession, and that he was committed to states' rights only when it suited his purposes: he permitted Georgia to do its worst against the Cherokees while he stared down South Carolina when it passed nullification legislation. More vociferous Jackson critics saw him as an inveterate Indian hater, an Indian killer intent on genocide. This debate, only recently near the center of assessments of Jackson, has provoked strong feelings and language on both sides.

The other disagreement that has penetrated as deeply into the discussion of Jacksonian politics is over the role of racism and slavery in Jacksonian democracy. Alexander Saxton's *The Rise and Fall of the White Republic*, a meticulously researched study, argued that Jacksonian democracy was constructed on an ideology of racial exclusivity and that excluding and dehumanizing blacks was inextricable from the expansion of white egalitarian politics. This study extended Saxton's exploration of the role of anti-Chinese sentiment in solidifying white workers' political consciousness and programs in mid-century California to the role of anti-black racism in constructing a white democratic nationalism. Building on Saxton's work, David Roediger's influential *Wages of Whiteness* enumerated the benefits laborers enjoyed by being white and the consolidation of these rewards in the post–Civil War period. At the same time, Saxton's and Roediger's works also initiated the growing field of whiteness studies.[30]

Working within Saxton's and Roediger's framework, Anthony Gronowicz wrote that Wilentz and others ignored the role antebellum workers played in disseminating racism. Lacy K. Ford Jr. (excerpted below) has shown how the South arrived at a new, "modern" understanding of race in the 1830s that denied "the viability of a biracial republic, [doubted] the efficacy of efforts to promote respectability and social uplift among people of color, and conceded only a measure of white responsibility for the well-being of an allegedly 'inferior' race."[31]

---

[29]Sean Wilentz, *Andrew Jackson* (New York, 2005); see also John Buchanan, *Jackson's Way: Andrew Jackson and the People of the Western Waters* (New York, 2001); H. W. Brands, *Andrew Jackson: His Life and Times* (New York, 2005).

[30]Alexander Saxton, *The Rise and Fall of the White Republic: Class Politics and Mass Culture in Nineteenth-Century America* (New York, 1990), and *The Indispensable Enemy: Labor and the Anti-Chinese Movement in California* (Berkeley, Calif., 1971); David Roediger, *The Wages of Whiteness: Race and the Making of the American Working Class* (London, 1991).

[31]Anthony Gronowicz, *Race and Class Politics in New York City before the Civil War* (Boston, 1998); Lacy K. Ford Jr., "Making the 'White Man's Country' White: Race, Slavery, and State Building in the Jacksonian South," *Journal of the Early Republic* 19 (Winter 1999): 713–37.

Sean Wilentz, in his massive study of democracy from Jefferson to Lincoln that synthesizes the new scholarship in a neo-Schlesinger interpretation, responded that Saxton and others had failed to distinguish the difference between the Democratic Party and Jacksonian democracy, and further that they had ascribed ideas and policies that were true of the highly polarized 1850s to the Democrats of the 1830s and 1840s, who had more varied views. Wilentz (whose work is included below) pointed to Democratic antislavery beliefs that emerged from a fear for white civil rights generated by mob attacks on abolitionists and the violation of their free speech rights. Jacksonians, he argued, wished to avoid public discussions of slavery to preserve the Union. Jonathan Earle enlarged on this line of debate in his study of three antislavery Jacksonians and aligned his interpretations with Schlesinger's. Earle saw the contribution of dissident Democrats to nonevangelical antislavery thought as crucial to creating an antislavery base to be mobilized through politics, not morals.[32]

Wilentz saw the Democrats' commitment to sectional harmony that kept them supporting the gag rule and attacks on abolitionists' speech rights as a decision that would cost them the party itself. The ironic tragedy of the Democrats was that by opening up politics to "new forms of agitation over precisely the issue they and the Whig leadership had tried so hard to suppress . . . [they would] ignite a democratic revolution more profound than anything discernible amid the torchlight furies of the Log Cabin campaign." Thus, he implied, the Republican Party, emancipation, and the Fourteenth and Fifteenth Amendments were direct descendants of Jacksonian liberal democracy.[33]

Considering the ways in which historians have approached the Jacksonian era, is it possible to offer any judgment about their relative worth? Was the Progressive school correct in arguing that Jackson and his followers represented the people in their struggle against privilege and vested interests, and that the movement was one phase in the continuing conflict for political, social, and economic democracy? Or were entrepreneurial historians right to stress the identification of the Jacksonians with laissez-faire capitalism? Were both partially right and wrong, as some recent historians have insisted? Was national politics simply a struggle between competing electoral machines? Did voter preferences reflect ethnic and cultural rather than class differences? Or was class the most significant element even though modified by ethnic and religious elements? Were citizens, even those who voted, actually engaged in politics or alienated by the manipulations of party elites? Did the Democratic Party develop precisely because it claimed not to be a party? Was Jacksonian democracy created and solidified through the exclusion of blacks from political voice? Was it the confiscation of Indian land that gave economic independence to white men the glue that held Jacksonian Democrats together? Despite the Democrats' racist policies, did the Jacksonians provide a basis for what is democratic about the United States today? Is Jacksonian

---

[32]Sean Wilentz, *The Rise of American Democracy: Jefferson to Lincoln* (New York, 2005); Jonathan Earle, *Jacksonian Antislavery and the Politics of Free Soil, 1824–1854* (Chapel Hill, N.C., 2004).
[33]Wilentz, *Rise of American Democracy*, 518.

democracy a meaningful designation for this important era of American history, and if so, what, exactly, is that meaning?

## SEAN WILENTZ

## *from* Slavery, Antislavery, and Jacksonian Democracy   [1996]

**SEAN WILENTZ** (1935– ) is the Dayton-Stockton Professor of History at Princeton University and the author of numerous books and articles, including *Chants Democratic: New York City and the Rise of the American Working Class, 1788–1850* (1984) and *The Rise of American Democracy: Jefferson to Lincoln* (2005). He is also co-editor, with Greil Marcus, of *The Rose and the Briar: Death, Love and Liberty in the American Ballad* (2005).

Although the time is fast growing distant, it was once relatively simple to admire the Jacksonian Democrats. Indeed, over the first half of the twentieth century, the Jacksonians' reputation rose to levels that few political parties in our history have ever enjoyed. Progressive-era academics and intellectuals, in rebellion against the genteel tradition, praised Jackson and his party as pioneers of a democratic agrarianism that had gone on to give the country some of its better moments. Historians who came of age in the 1920s read of the Jacksonians as the intrepid foes of American plutocracy, as described in the influential works of Charles and Mary Beard and of Vernon L. Parrington.

After the crash of 1929, the Jacksonians' standing soared even higher. Amid the turmoil of the Great Depression and the New Deal, the Jacksonian Democrats began to look like the spiritual forerunners of the modern reformist Democratic party — the party, supposedly, of the forgotten, downtrodden farmer and workingman. Historians of diverse temperaments and backgrounds — Yankee patricians, big-city cosmopolitans, southern liberals, midwestern neo-Populists — all found reasons to honor the Jacksonian heritage. As if to make matters official, President Roosevelt joined in the eulogies, gratefully looking back to Jackson's presidency — "the struggles he went through, the enemies he encountered, the defeats he suffered and the victories he won" — for inspiration and guidance.

The second half of this century has been far less kind to Jackson's legacy. Soon after the publication in 1945 of the celebratory *Age of Jackson* by Arthur M. Schlesinger Jr., the Jacksonians began falling victim to what C. Vann Woodward later described as a "disenchantment of the intellectual

Sean Wilentz, "Slavery, Antislavery, and Jacksonian Democracy," in *The Market Revolution in America: Social, Political, and Religious Expressions, 1800–1880*, ed. Melvyn Stokes and Stephen Conway (Richmond: University Press of Virginia, 1996), 202–24. © 1996 University of Virginia Press.

with the masses" — a disenchantment, Woodward added, that was already "well under way in the forties." The devastation wrought by German Nazism and Soviet Communism undermined what had once been a reflexive identification by liberal intellectuals with mass-based political movements. The worrisome rampages of Senator Joseph McCarthy in the early 1950s only deepened intellectuals' misgivings about democratic excesses. By the early 1960s, the Jacksonians were appearing in history books as unheroic ancestors of the demagogues of modern times — as rabble-rousing, self-interested, backward-looking pols whose populist rhetoric was just so much claptrap. By contrast, the Whigs, cast by earlier historians as conservative, monied manipulators, began receiving sympathetic treatment as the high-minded, activist, positive liberals of their day.

The later 1960s and 1970s brought yet another turn in historiographical fashion, but little in the way of a reprieve for the Jacksonians. The rise of the civil rights movement and the agitation against the war in Vietnam shattered the ironic liberal consensus mood of the postwar years, particularly among younger scholars. A spirit of revolution, cultural and political, gripped the campuses and produced fresh enthusiasm for the history of popular movements and the oppressed — workers, slaves, American Indians, women. People once dismissed as marginal to American history suddenly became the new historians' major preoccupations. The result might be described (following Woodward) as a reenchantment of the intellectual with the masses.

Unlike their Progressive and New Deal predecessors, however, the new social and radical historians tended to regard the traditional Democratic party with suspicion, even contempt. Outrage at the Johnson administration's Vietnam policies contributed to the anti-Democratic mood. Thereafter, the final breakup of the one-party Democratic South and the subsequent sectional realignment of American politics reminded historians that the Democracy of F.D.R. had been the party of southern segregation as well as the party of liberal reform. And looking further back in time, Jackson's Democratic party appeared to have been the party of slavery, white racism, and imperial-minded manifest destiny — hardly something to inspire up-and-coming young historians. Ever since, the Jacksonians' reputation has languished, mainly because of their record on slavery and race. Today, even those historians who are inclined to sympathize with the Jacksonian Democrats feel compelled to confess, as Harry L. Watson has written, that "racism and support for slavery were . . . logical aspects of Democratic Party ideology."

Recent revisionist scholarship has not completely repudiated the Jacksonian heritage. One of the harsher studies, for example, allows that Jackson and his supporters "asserted the political, civil and moral equality of white male citizens" and "rejected the concept of class hierarchy as applicable to the American nation" — all praiseworthy goals. But the key qualifying words in these assessments are *white* and *male*. Interpreted within the revisionist grid of race, gender, and class, the Jacksonians were at best only one-third admirable — and regarding race, they were repugnant.

Jacksonian Democrats, recent works observe, consistently opposed political efforts to tamper with southern slavery and led legislative and judicial efforts to restrict northern free blacks' political and legal rights. Even more than the Whigs (who, overall, were not exactly enlightened on racial matters), the Democrats appealed to the voters with racist slurs, portraying blacks as the subhuman enemies of white men's equal rights and as allies of the crypto-aristocratic money power. To the extent that the Jacksonians were democrats, we are told, they were herrenvolk (that is, master race) democrats whose flattery of the white male masses was explicitly anti-Negro and often explicitly proslavery.

Some of the anti-Jacksonian studies have concentrated on Old Hickory's elevated political standing in the South and on the Democratic party's emergence as a sentinel of the slaveholders' interests. Progressive-era historians, following Frederick Jackson Turner, described Jacksonianism as basically a western frontier movement; New Deal historians, led by Schlesinger, reinterpreted it as a class movement shaped by eastern workers and radicals; today, it is more common to see Jacksonianism portrayed as a southern movement that protected and accelerated the spread of the South's peculiar institution. According to an influential article by Richard H. Brown, the Jacksonian Democratic party was conceived in the aftermath of the Missouri crisis as a guarantor of slaveholders' rights. Building on Brown's contentions, Michael Paul Rogin has described Jackson as a symbol of a "southern majority" position in national affairs, fusing nationalism and support for territorial expansion with support for slavery.

Over the past few years, critics attuned to multiculturalism have expanded this line of argument by shifting attention northward, chastising northern Jacksonians and workers for their racist, proslavery views and asserting that racial identity politics allied the northern and southern wings of the Democratic party. David Roediger, for example, has claimed that white racism permeated the emerging northern working class of the Jacksonian era. With their denunciations of wage labor as "white slavery," Roediger believes, pro-Jacksonian workers and labor leaders drew upon racial as well as class antagonisms, fashioning an ideology of "whiteness" that "at times strongly supported the slavery of Blacks." In a broader consideration of the period, Alexander Saxton has claimed that both the party managers and the rank and file of the northern Democracy were committed to white supremacy and to the preservation of southern slavery — remaining firm in their conviction "that plantation slavery provided the only sure means for quarantining Africans in America."

No fair-minded assessment of Jacksonian politics can dismiss these interpretations out of hand. Democratic aversion to abolitionists and blacks, the insistence by party leaders that the slavery issue be kept out of national affairs, the proslavery leanings of some Jacksonian labor leaders — these matters were all well established in the historical record long before the latest round of academic revisionism began. At times, to be sure, the revisionists may be too quick to detect proslavery motives in every effort by northern Jacksonians to accommodate the South. As John McFaul has pointed out, fear for the fate of the Union — and for the fate of the Democratic party — was the chief factor behind most northern Jacksonian pronouncements about slavery, not active support for slavery as an institution. But in retrospect, whether it was predicated on principle or expediency, the Jacksonian leadership's record on slavery and on attendant racial issues was shabby at best and shameful at worst.

The danger, however, is that, in correcting the pro-Jacksonian writings of earlier generations, current historians have gone too far in the other direction. The old image of the Jacksonians may have exaggerated their liberal egalitarianism; the new image, however, threatens to turn white supremacy into an essential feature of Jacksonian politics, as if racism and proslavery were inevitable ingredients of early nineteenth-century American democratic thought. In what has become a trend toward seeing much of American political history in racial terms, the Jacksonians as a group may well come to be seen as the precursors not of Franklin Roosevelt, but of George C. Wallace and David Duke. Such a jaundiced view, however, not only confuses the expediency of some Jacksonian leaders with race hatred. It also slights those Jacksonians who, as early as the 1830s, took principled stands against slavery and against the racism that justified slavery. It ignores the vital contributions these antislavery Jacksonians made toward enlarging the antislavery cause. It suggests that the Jacksonians left behind a single odious legacy on slavery and race, when in fact their legacy was much more complex.

Part of the problem stems from a common tendency to blur the differences between the Democratic party and the Jacksonian Democracy. It is quite true that, in the 1850s, the party that Jackson helped to found became the primary national political instrument of what its opponents labeled the slave power. Southern defections to the Democrats had created what came to be known as the solid South; and in the North, a long string of doughface presidents and would-be presidents, from Franklin Pierce to Stephen A. Douglas, boasted of their impeccable Jacksonian credentials. In the 1830s and 1840s, however, Jacksonian attitudes toward slavery were less uniform. Southern planters, for example, gravitated to the Whigs, not the Democrats, in the mid-1830s. And over the next twenty years, as the planters switched their allegiances to the Democrats, many once-stalwart northern Jacksonians rejected the party, repelled by its increasingly prosouthern, proslavery stance. "All democracy left the democratic party," the veteran Massachusetts labor Jacksonian Frederick Robinson later recalled, "and every true democrat that was too intelligent to be cheated by a name, deserted its ranks." As early as 1846, sectional antagonisms had fractured the original Jacksonian coalition; by the time of the massive defections that accompanied the Kansas-Nebraska controversy, Jacksonian Democracy was dead and buried.

With a few exceptions, notably Richard Sewell, current scholars have tried to explain away these events (and sustain the herrenvolk view of Jacksonianism) by attacking the antislavery Democrats as racists. Unlike the sincere abolitionists (so the argument goes), antislavery Jacksonians had no intention of interfering with slavery where it already existed. Indeed, as far as *southern* slavery was concerned, the supposedly antislavery Jacksonians were actually *proslavery* men who feared that emancipation would cause untold thousands of undesirable blacks to emigrate to the North. The dissidents (it is alleged) were chiefly interested in barring blacks from the western territories and in restricting blacks' rights in the free states. Accordingly, beginning in the mid-1840s, they undertook political efforts to halt slavery's spread. At all costs, Alexander Saxton writes, the antislavery Jacksonians insisted "that the entry of Africans, slave or free, into the promised land of the West had to be prevented." Securing that aim required breaking with those Democrats who favored or who tolerated slavery's westward expansion.

There is an ample supply of quotations from antislavery Jacksonians that lend plausibility to these contentions. The Democratic antislavery leader David Wilmot, a favorite target of recent historians, often remarked that he undertook his antislavery efforts on behalf of the white man, not the black man, in order to "preserve to free white labor a fair country, a rich inheritance" in the West. (Wilmot was even more direct in private: "By God, sir," he exclaimed to one associate, "men born and nursed by white women are not going to be ruled by men who were brought up on the milk of some damn Negro wench!") Other antislavery Democrats, wary of appearing overly solicitous of blacks, carefully framed their rhetoric in self-interested terms, claiming that "the question is not, whether black men are to be made free, but whether we white men are to remain free." Some antislavery Democrats, notably the leading lights of New York's Barnburner faction, joined with conservative Democrats in efforts to restrict northern blacks' political and civil rights. And overall, antislavery Democrats were much more prone to resort to racist appeals than antislavery Whigs.

Still, even a brief review of the political and ideological origins of Jacksonian antislavery shows that the racialist interpretation is greatly exaggerated. It was, of course, perfectly possible for antislavery Democrats also to be racists. (Most of them, like most white Americans of the early nineteenth century, almost certainly were, to one degree or another.) But it does not necessarily follow that dissident Democrats opposed slavery *because* they were racists. Although racial anxieties and territorial ambitions swayed some Jacksonian dissidents, other concerns — economic, political, and constitutional — loomed much larger in the antislavery Jacksonians' writings and speeches. These concerns were rooted in egalitarian Jacksonian principles about political democracy and economic justice, not in doctrines of white supremacy. Out of their Jacksonianism, the dissident Democrats forged a democratic antislavery appeal that, at bottom, opposed the perpetuation of slavery in any form, and in any part of the country. That democratic appeal proved of crucial importance to the rise of antislavery as a northern mass political movement.

Jacksonian dissent over slavery began in the 1830s, not the 1840s, and it grew from controversies over abolitionism, not over slavery in the territories.

As soon as the American Antislavery Society and its allies began agitating for immediatist abolitionism, mainstream Jacksonian leaders, North and South, opposed them bitterly — by supporting a ban on abolitionist mailings to the South, by applauding mob attacks on abolitionist meetings and newspaper offices, and by voting for the gag rule that tabled abolitionist petitions to the House of Representatives. The abolition movement, Jacksonian leaders proclaimed, amounted to a conservative plot designed to distract attention from the crucial banking and currency questions and to drive a wedge between northern and southern Democrats. Worse, some northern labor Jacksonians claimed, the abolitionists wanted to free the slaves in order to dispatch them to the North, where their presence would depress the wages and the status of white workingmen.

The Jacksonians (it is important to note) were not alone in condemning the abolition movement. Among the most outspoken, violent, and negrophobic of the antiabolitionists were some leading northern Whigs and ultraconservative Democrats. In New York City, it was not the Jacksonians, but the antiadministration editors James Watson Webb and William Leete Stone who whipped up racist mobs to attack abolitionist meetings and black neighborhoods. Whig gentlemen of property and standing stirred antiabolitionist violence in other cities as well. And still elsewhere, individual Whig politicians joined with Democrats in promoting the repression. The "hard" antiabolitionist racism that Saxton has ascribed to the Jacksonians was also ubiquitous among their Whig opponents.

Northern Jacksonians, meanwhile, did not universally support their party leaders' antiabolitionist campaign. Some of the more prominent dissenting Democrats endorsed abolitionism outright, among them Amasa Walker, James G. Birney, and (in time) William Leggett. (Likewise, some of the abolitionists, notably Gamaliel Bailey, held strongly pro-Jacksonian views on issues other than slavery.) Other dissident Democrats limited themselves to attacks on slavery, the antiabolitionists, or both. Collectively, however, they established the political and intellectual basis for what would become an irrepressible antislavery division in northern Democratic ranks.

In Massachusetts, the future governor Marcus Morton pronounced slavery "the greatest curse and most portentous evil which a righteous God ever inflicted upon a nation." In New York City, hard-money, prolabor Jacksonian radicals led by Leggett and George Henry Evans lambasted the antiabolitionist mobs and (in Leggett's case) broke with the Jackson and Van Buren administrations over their antiabolitionist policies. In Ohio, the Democratic lawyer and ex-slaveholder Birney began contacting friends about the possibility of forming an independent antislavery political party. In Washington, D.C., Birney's fellow Ohioan, the hard-money Democrat Thomas Morris, took the floor of the U.S. Senate to defend the abolitionists and attack the gag rule — the only senator, of either party, who did so.

Studies of the abolitionist rank and file of the 1830s suggest that these early antislavery Jacksonians helped gain the movement a significant portion of its support. But, lacking anything resembling an independent institutional vehicle, the Democratic dissidents were vulnerable to reprisals from national and state party managers, and the crackdowns quickly followed. Leggett, cut off from party patronage in 1835, was narrowly defeated three years later in a bid for a Democratic congressional nomination, largely because of his antislavery views. Party chieftains castigated other dissenting Democratic editors and lauded mob assaults against them as (in Silas Wright's words) "evidences of the correct state of public opinion." In 1838, Ohio's Democratic legislators denied Thomas Morris reelection to the United States Senate, despite an overwhelming show of support for Morris at the polls. Antislavery, it seemed, was Jacksonian heresy, at least as far as the party's leadership was concerned.

Had the antislavery Democrats and Democratic sympathizers stopped there (or had they converted to the Whig party), they might deserve to be remembered as some historians have described them — as scattered minor exceptions who proved the rule about prosouthern herrenvolk Jacksonianism. Instead, they stuck by both their antislavery politics and their Jacksonian principles, echoing Leggett's remarks that antislavery was "a glorious, and necessary part of democracy" and charging that it was the party regulars, not themselves, who had "deserted the democratic party." The most determined of them became schismatics, joining with abolitionists and antislavery Whigs in the Liberty party in the hope that independent political action might force the Democracy to come to its senses.

Until 1845, the Jacksonian breakaways managed to convince only a tiny sliver of the northern Democratic electorate to abandon its party loyalties. Still, their efforts sustained a fledgling political antislavery movement with marked Jacksonian accents. In Ohio, the hard-money abolitionist Gamaliel Bailey overcame his suspicions of third-party politics, endorsed the Liberty party (and its presidential candidate, his old associate Birney), and went on to become perhaps the most influential antislavery advocate in the West. Thomas Morris also joined the party (and ran for vice president on the Liberty ticket in 1844). In time, the ex-Whig and Democratic sympathizer Salmon P. Chase — who became more closely attached to radical Jacksonian economic ideas the more that he agitated against slavery — emerged as another party stalwart. William Leggett's untimely death in 1839 robbed northeastern antislavery Democrats of their most eloquent voice, but other dissident editors, including William Chaplain of Albany, attempted to fill the void.

Throughout the North (but especially in the western states), antislavery men appealed directly to Jacksonian Democrats, charging that slavery had created "an overwhelming political monopoly" — an insidious force that, in league with the Yankee "aristocracy," had "mobbed, cheated, and gagged" its critics and intended to reduce the "white laborers of the North and South . . . to the condition of serfs." Liberty party campaigners announced that they intended to create a "True Democratic Party," dedicated to the proposition (as one party newspaper exclaimed) that "no man can be a democrat, who is not an abolitionist." And although much remains to be learned about the party's slender political base, studies of western New York and Massachusetts suggest that the Liberty men were especially effective in attracting votes from pockets of antislavery artisans, workers, and nominal Democrats. . . .

Thereafter, amid the political struggles over Texas annexation and the Mexican War, many more Democrats reached the same conclusion — and the antislavery Jacksonians vastly augmented their following. In 1845, when New Hampshire's Democratic managers attempted to read the antiannexationist John P. Hale out of the party, an alliance of so-called Independent Democrats, Liberty men, and antislavery Whigs reelected Hale to Congress and captured control of the state government. Along with the simmering battles between the antislavery Barnburners and the conservative Hunkers in New York, the Hale insurgency persuaded some antislavery leaders that the Democratic party could at last be turned into a national union of antislavery forces. . . .

At the heart of the Democrats' antislavery beliefs was their fear and resentment of the "slave power" — a term that Morris and other antislavery Jacksonians helped to popularize nearly twenty years before it became a rhetorical staple of the Republican party. Especially to radical, hard-money Democrats, the Jacksonians' raison d'être had been to resist the money power — the interlocking set of monied individuals and institutions, exemplified by the Second Bank of the United States, that supposedly exploited the nation's honorable farmers and workingmen. By the mid-1830s, hard-money Jacksonians were sure that Jackson and his administration had the money power on the run — only to discover, Morris observed, that another enemy, slavery, was in league with the Yankee plutocrats. "The slave power of the South and the banking power of the North . . . are now uniting to rule the country," Morris told the Senate. "The cotton bale and the bank note have formed an alliance; the credit system with slave labor. These two congenial spirits have at last met and embraced each other, both looking to the same object — to live upon the unrequited labor of others — and have now erected for themselves a common platform . . . on which they can meet, and bid defiance, as they hope, to free principles and free labor." Whereas orthodox Jacksonians described the slaveholding planters as honorable producers, antislavery Jacksonians ranked the slaveholders among the oppressive aristocrats who had scant respect for ordinary men's rights and liberties. Tied as they were to their southern creditors, northern capitalists would allow no interference with slavery's prosperity and expansion; southern slaveholders, in turn, would undercut *all* workingmen's dignity and equal rights by attempting to stigmatize labor as an estate fit only for slaves. . . .

In order to preserve the balance of power between the blighted South and the industrious North, the dissidents held, the slave power set its sights on "crippling the energies of the latter." To achieve these economic ends (antislavery Jacksonians argued), the slave power had to secure command of the nation's politics. And, much as orthodox Jacksonians saw political corruption at the root of the money power's ascendancy, so the dissenting Democrats believed that the slave power's success required curtailing the equal rights of white freemen. . . . Undaunted southern slaveholders, however, had managed to win control of federal patronage and to gain the upper hand in Congress, and when these measures failed to silence their critics, the slaveholders and their northern friends fought back with mobs, gag rules, and other assaults on the citizenry's democratic privileges. . . . Antislavery Democrats simply claimed that the slaveholders and their allies would stop at nothing to preserve and extend the peculiar institution — including limiting the freedoms of speech and debate in ways, one Michigan paper charged, that "tyrannically subverted the constitutional liberties of more than 12,000,000 of nominal American freemen."

Had they stuck only to their attacks on slavery's backwardness and political perfidies, the dissenting Democrats might have avoided any moral reckoning with slavery. Yet, even as they declaimed in favor of white men's equal rights, they made it clear that their basic objection was to the institution of slavery and not merely to its effects on nonslaves. "The oppression which our fathers suffered from Great Britain," Leggett asserted, "was nothing in comparison with that which the negroes experience at the hands of the slaveholders." Slavery, he continued, defied "the great fundamental maxim of democratic faith . . . the natural equality of mankind." . . . Through the late 1840s, antislavery Democrats repeated unambiguously that they were fighting slavery as well as the slave power — that the buying and selling of human beings was, as one Barnburner paper put it, "a great moral and political evil." "We hold that slavery is an evil, a deep, detestable, and damnable evil, an evil in all its aspects," the Democratic Cleveland *Plain Dealer* declared in 1848, "an evil to the blacks and an evil to the whites . . . an evil that stares you in the face from uncultivated fields, and howls in your ears with its horrid din of clanking chains and fetters, and the groans of wretched bondsmen."

Opposing Negro slavery did not, by any means, imply support for making either freeborn blacks or ex-slaves the social and political equals of whites. Yet, as early as the 1830s, at least some influential dissenting Jacksonians did support black equality as well as black freedom, and they took issue with their negrophobic antislavery allies. Leggett, for example, argued that the United States would be truly democratic only when the "enfranchised spirit" of the ex-slave could "roam on the illimitable plain of equal liberty." Ten years later, the Jacksonian sympathizer Gamaliel Bailey declared that the Free Soilers, in fighting for the True Democracy, were "opposed to the spirit of caste, whether its elemental idea be a difference of color, birth, or conditions." Although the intellectual center of gravity among antislavery Democrats was more conservative on racial matters, at least some of them believed that "the antipathy of race" and "the prejudices of color" (along with "the tyranny of capital" and "the pride of birth") were aristocratic enormities.

But wherever they found themselves along the spectrum of racialist thinking, antislavery Democrats insisted on the basic humanity of blacks and rejected racist arguments justifying slavery. In doing so, they also turned

Jacksonian principles regarding labor's rights into a central feature of their antislavery arguments. . . .

As good Jacksonians, the antislavery Democrats believed in strict construction of the United States Constitution. By any such construction, the federal government had no power to interfere with slavery in those states where slavery already existed. Yet this did not render the Constitution a proslavery document in the dissident Democrats' eyes (as it did for both Garrisonian abolitionists and proslavery partisans). The founding fathers, Leggett argued, considered slavery "the direst curse inflicted upon our country," and hoped that it would one day be erased "and the poor bondsman restored to the condition of equal freedom for which God and nature designed him." And although the delegates at Philadelphia had wound up giving covert recognition to slavery in the Constitution, it was a "great mistake" to assume that they left "the power of the southern states over slavery *and all its incidents* undiminished." . . .

The antislavery Democrats, by helping to force the slavery issue to the center of politics, certainly played an important part in bringing about these revolutionary events. They did so in line with what they thought was their unswerving devotion to Jacksonian principles — opposition to the money power and its slave power ally, protection of white men's equal political rights, support for the rights of all producers (black and white) to the fruits of their toil, strict construction of the Constitution, and adherence to the founding fathers' antislavery intentions. . . .

The antislavery Jacksonians' achievements hardly vindicate the entire Jacksonian movement, or even most of it. Nor, looking back, were the antislavery Jacksonians always admirable, especially on the question of black political rights (although some important figures, like William Leggett, were more admirable than others). Nevertheless, it is important to recognize that the antislavery Democrats provided an alternative view of where Jacksonians ought to stand regarding slavery and the racism that justified slavery. That alternative eventually caused the vast majority of antislavery men to abandon the Democratic party — but not to abandon their Jacksonian ideals. It was the Democracy, the antislavery leader Preston King later remarked, that had "changed its members, its principles, its purposes, its character." Antislavery Jacksonians, by their own lights, had kept the faith.

LACY K. FORD JR.

## *from* Making the "White Man's Country" White: Race, Slavery, and State-Building in the Jacksonian South   [1999]

**LACY K. FORD JR.** is professor of history at the University of South Carolina. He is the author of more than a dozen articles in addition to *The Origins of Southern Radicalism: The South Carolina Upcountry, 1800–1860* (1988).

The coming of racial modernity in the South, which by the 1830s held more than ninety percent of the nation's African Americans and virtually all its slaves, looms as an especially inviting area of inquiry. Moreover, as scholars have explored "whiteness" as a national phenomena rather than as the source of southern exceptionalism, they have implicitly challenged southern historians to review and perhaps recast their understanding of precisely how the Old South became a white man's country. In response to these twin challenges, this essay will attempt to explain the triumph of racial modernity in the South of the 1830s by focusing on the political process through which race or "whiteness" became codified, formally and informally, as the defining characteristic of antebellum southern society. Put differently, it will describe how shapers of the Old South's Jacksonian political tradition ventured to make what U. B. Phillips later called "the white man's country" white.

A peculiar combination of economic circumstance and political ideology shaped the Jacksonian South's reconsideration of race and slavery. Contrasting subregional political economies, together with patterns of racial demography associated with these different political economies, ensured that questions relating to slavery and race were framed in different ways in different parts of the South. Central among these many internal variations in the Old South's political economy lay the growing contrast between the Upper South and the Lower South. Between 1800 and 1830, much of the Lower South swirled into the vortex of an economic transformation that Ira Berlin has aptly labeled the "cotton revolution." The "cotton revolution" pulled slavery and plantation agriculture from its comparatively limited tidewater and alluvial strongholds and spread them across a vast plain of black and brown loam soils and through lush river valleys that became the Old South's rich Black Belt. It also promoted staple growing among the region's yeomen and helped spur the expansion of the cash economy in the red clay upland portions of the Old South. The process of cultivating cotton and complementary foodstuffs required

"Making the 'White Man's Country' White: Race, Slavery, and State-Building in the Jacksonian South," *Journal of the Early Republic* 19(4), Special Issue on Racial Consciousness and Nation-Building in the Early Republic (Winter 1999): 713–37. Reprinted with permission of the University of Pennsylvania Press.

steady attention for much of the growing season, making slave labor, with its high ratio of fixed to marginal costs, a highly profitable system. To a large extent, the cotton revolution transformed the Lower South into a true slaveholding region rather than a region characterized by important slaveholding enclaves known for their production of rice, sugar, and sea-island cotton. By doing so, it accelerated the movement of population, both slave and free, from long-settled regions to the frontier of the Old Southwest.

In the Upper South, however, during the same three decades, the once dominant staple, tobacco, whose success had sustained first Chesapeake and later Piedmont demand for slave labor, fell into comparative decline. Alternative cash crops, including grains such as wheat and oats, emerged, but they required substantially less labor than tobacco, except during harvest. With sharp peaks and valleys in the demand for labor, grain cultivation rendered slavery, with its high fixed costs for labor, inefficient and financially unattractive. Thus, although some areas within the Upper South remained heavily dependent on slave labor, the future prospects for the region's slave-labor economy appeared problematic.

By the early 1830s, an ominous antislavery challenge to the slaveholding social order of both the Upper and Lower South appeared from several different quarters. In 1827 the American Colonization Society first requested public funds from Congress; two years later, militant free black David Walker published an appeal for slaves to rebel against their masters; and in 1831, William Lloyd Garrison ushered in a new era of abolition propaganda with *The Liberator*, a publication dedicated to "immediate" emancipation and effusive in its moral chastisement of slaveholders. But no event focused southern attention on slavery and related issues as intensely as did the bloody if ultimately unsuccessful slave uprising led by Nat Turner in August 1831. Turner's rampage across a small swath of Virginia's lower Tidewater spread fear, rumor, and recrimination across the Old Dominion and sent waves of anxiety through the white population in other areas of the South. . . .

The timing and particular conjunction of these events prompted not simply a short-term return of vigilance against slave rebellion, but also serious reconsideration of public policy toward slavery and the region's free black population precisely at the moment when mounting pressure from white egalitarians spurred most southern states to consider sweeping democratic revision of their existing state constitutions, thus giving southern constitution makers a chance to write a new racial order into fundamental law at their early convenience.

The Jacksonian South's political discussion of race and slavery revealed a variety of racial attitudes and ideologies ranging from exclusion and marginalization at one end of the spectrum to complete subordination of African Americans at the other end, with a bewildering array of selectively cobbled together variations on either the exclusion or the subordination themes, or both, lying in between. Full-voiced advocates of exclusion sought either to remove African Americans from southern society altogether, or, more realistically, minimize the role of blacks, slave and free, in the civic, social, and economic life of the South, much as had been done in northern society following the postrevolutionary emancipations. To implement their strategy, southern exclusionists advocated pushing free blacks further toward the margins of society and taking some cautious first steps toward putting slavery on the road to ultimate extinction. Thus they favored colonization because it reduced the free black population in the near term and established a working mechanism to facilitate gradual emancipation on a larger scale in the future. In essence, exclusionists wanted to "whiten" their society by reducing the size and diminishing the importance of the region's African-American population.

In contrast, champions of subordination recognized that the southern staple economy depended so heavily on slave labor that the region could not thrive without it. Subordinationists accepted racially justified slavery as a necessary labor system, and some argued affirmatively that the region's reliance on slaves for menial labor strengthened the virtues of independence and equality among whites. Viewing slavery as at least essential, arguably beneficial, and, in all likelihood perpetual, subordinationists sought to render white dominance of blacks as complete and thorough as possible.*

But if the ideological poles of the southern Jacksonian debate over race and slavery seemed well-defined, the actual terms and issues of the discussions varied widely across the region. In the Upper South, the debate occasionally focused on the future of slavery itself, and almost without exception, addressed the problematic role free blacks played in a slaveholding society. As a whole, the Upper South remained committed to a conception of slavery as a necessary (but possibly temporary) evil — an evil that could be at odds with the ideals of white independence and equality over the long term. Thus the arguments over race in the Upper South often centered on how the region might "whiten" itself, either through gradual emancipation and colonization of slaves, the colonization of free blacks, a gradual shift to free white labor facilitated by the sale of slaves to the cotton growing areas of the Deep South, or some combination of these approaches. By contrast, in a heuristic "Middle South" of Tennessee and North Carolina, even though few saw slavery as a positive good, sentiment favoring emancipation on any terms nevertheless declined. In these states, the discussion of race centered on whether or not free people of color should have a political voice. In the Middle South, Whiggish

---

*My choice of terms requires some clarification. I have used the term "exclusion" to refer to the idea that African Americans, whether slave or free, should be either removed from American society or, failing that, pushed to its social, political, and economic margins. Thus it was an ideology of exclusion and/or marginalization. I have used the term "subordination" to refer to the idea that slaves were simply too numerous and their labor too valuable to the South to consider exclusion a viable option. Thus long-term southern dependence on slave labor must be accepted and measures taken to guarantee white domination and black subordination in a biracial, slaveholding society in which slavery was justified largely on racial grounds. Clearly exclusionists saw marginalization as a way of subordinating blacks who remained in their society, and just as clearly subordinationists wanted to exclude both slaves and free blacks from the realm of political and social equality.

paternalists defended the idea of promoting uplift and respectability among free blacks, while subordinationists championed disfranchisement.

In the Lower South, the case for slavery as a positive good remained in its infancy at the beginning of the Jacksonian era, and some of the peculiar institution's defenders still called it a necessary evil. But the "evils" of slavery were less and less often proclaimed openly, and public policy treated slavery as if it were a permanent institution, or one likely to thrive for as long as white southerners could imagine. Indeed, most Lower South political leaders considered slavery essential to the region's staple economy, which, despite fits and starts in the international market and vulnerability to unpredictable credit crunches, remained the bellwether of the region's prosperity. In the cotton South, the Jacksonian debate over race centered more on the prevention of insurrections, tighter regulation or removal of free blacks, and the desirability of regulating or even eliminating the interstate slave trade. Together, these three subregional debates constituted the larger Jacksonian South's attempt to define "racial modernity" and render it tangible in their political arrangements.

Upper South sentiment in favor of gradual emancipation, though always conditional, retained significant strength throughout the Jacksonian era. In the pensive months following Nat Turner's rebellion in the late summer of 1831, Virginia actively reconsidered its policy toward slavery and the free black population within its borders. Long time advocates of both gradual emancipation and colonization found full voice. Virginian John Marshall, the venerable Chief Justice of the United States Supreme Court, believed that the "removal of our free colored population" had emerged as a "common object" in postinsurrection Virginia and expressed a fervent hope that the legislature would seize upon "the excitement produced by the late insurrection" to pass sweeping legislation facilitating colonization. . . .

Arguing an exclusionist position, Virginia's critics of slavery generally cited the harm the institution inflicted on white society, whether in retarding individual opportunity for ordinary whites, dragging the whole society down in comparison with the dynamic free labor society further north, or simply exposing whites to the horrors of insurrection and perhaps racial warfare. Virginia exclusionists believed that slavery bred personal arrogance and economic backwardness, and hindered the advancement of whites. During a heated debate over the issue in the Virginia House of Delegates 1831–32 session, Shenandoah Valley representative Samuel McDowell Moore blamed slavery for demoralizing the state's poorer whites, who, he insisted, viewed labor "as a mask of servitude." Another Valley delegate, Charles J. Faulkner, echoed Moore's sentiments, explaining that the "independent yeomanry" west of the Blue Ridge feared losing its vitality to the "slothful and degraded African." Slaveholder and colonization advocate Thomas Marshall carried the curse of blackness argument even further, contending that both slavery and a large free black population "banishes the yeomanry of the country . . . until the whole country will be inundated by one black wave, covering its whole extent, with a few white faces here and there floating on the surface."

As a rule, proslavery Virginians admitted the evils of the institution but argued that, for all its faults, slavery remained essential for maintaining racial control and ensuring the availability of an adequate agricultural labor supply. . . . Amid rumblings from Southside slaveholders about separation from the antislavery western portion of the state, the 1832 Virginia legislature rejected immediate emancipation as "inexpedient" by a vote of 73 to 58, but they endorsed the idea of emancipation at some undetermined future time by a vote of 67 to 60.

After the legislative debate concluded, Thomas R. Dew, a young professor at William and Mary College, denounced "every plan of emancipation and deportation" that the legislature had considered as "utterly impracticable." Yet Dew predicted that slavery was headed toward "ultimate extinction" through the decline of tobacco as a staple and the steady flow of slaves to the newer cotton states of the Southwest. As slavery waned, Dew envisioned a new type of economic development for Virginia, driven by transportation improvements and the growth of towns, attracting "capitalists and free labourers of the north," and producing the consequent rise of manufacturing. Dew also believed that, despite their post-Southampton hesitancy, Alabama, Mississippi, and Louisiana would open their borders to additional slave labor and serve as an "absorbent" for Virginia's "excess" slave population. Focusing on race as the basis of slavery in Virginia, Dew insisted that emancipation without removal was unthinkable since white society could neither absorb nor uplift a free colored population. "[T]he emancipated black carries a mark which no time can erase," Dew maintained; "he forever wears the indelible symbol of his inferior condition: the Ethiopian can not change his skin, nor the Leopard his spots." The young Virginia ideologist nimbly advanced a market-driven exclusionist argument for noninterference with slavery, emphasizing racial differences as permanent and insurmountable obstacles to the successful uplift of blacks, whether slave or free.

Countering Dew, American Colonization Society supporter Jesse Burton Harrison, a native Virginian who moved to New Orleans to further his legal career, warned against the continued presence of "a distinct race of people within our bosom . . . soon to be more numerous than ourselves, exposed to every temptation . . . to become our deadliest foe." Also an exclusionist, Harrison admitted that his concerns about slavery were "founded but little on the miseries of the blacks" but instead "almost exclusively to the injuries slavery inflicts on the whites." Slavery degraded labor, Harrison contended, and created among whites "a disposition to look on all manual labor as menial and degrading." Slavery slowed the growth of manufacturing by retarding the "rearing of a large class of skillful mechanics." Slavery also discouraged immigration. With its slave-based staple economy stagnant, Virginia lagged behind much of the nation in wealth and population growth, and, Harrison insisted, as Virginia grew "blacker" such economic backwardness would only worsen. . . .

In sum, the Jacksonian debate over slavery and race in the Upper South raged between, on the one hand, committed exclusionists who lacked the political muscle they needed to succeed, and, on the other, apologetic but uncompromising subordinationists. Given the Upper South's large slave population, exclusion loomed a daunting task, and even its advocates recognized that it could be accomplished only gradually and with respect for the rights (including financial compensation) of slaveholders. But the putative defenders of slavery in the Upper South, tentative subordinationists if subordinationists at all, accepted many of the basic propositions advanced by the exclusionists. . . . Though heated at times, the Jacksonian era debate over slavery and the status of free blacks yielded little more than a reluctant acceptance of the status quo in the Upper South.

By contrast, few in the Lower South doubted that slavery was anything but the single best passport to wealth and prosperity. Virtually no public figure in the Lower South seriously advocated or favored emancipation of any kind, including gradual and fully compensated emancipation. Even though many slaveholders and Jacksonian politicians in the Lower South still acknowledged that slavery was an evil, proposals for colonization of free blacks and small numbers of slaves voluntarily manumitted by their masters were crafted chiefly to strengthen the institution and better maintain public safety rather than as a modest first step toward a more sweeping emancipation. Ironically, exclusion as an ideology of racial control enjoyed currency in the Lower South during the Jacksonian era but as an approach to the "problem" of the region's substantial Native-American population. . . . A large majority of whites in the Lower South showed a singular determination to guarantee that their "white man's country" was not red, even when tribes like the Cherokees appeared to be strong supporters of slavery. . . .

[The] prolonged controversy over the slave trade revealed the fundamental contradictions and concerns of the cotton South during the Jacksonian era. Even as many Lower South whites yearned for enough slaves to bring cotton riches to themselves and their fellow citizens, they also fretted over the drain of capital to the Upper South and, more importantly, over the potential dangers of a large black population. As a result, they pondered ways to modulate their region's ever-volatile racial demographics. Within the emerging subordinationist consensus in the Lower South remained very substantial room for maneuver and internal disagreement; only external challenge inspired unified denunciation.

If the debate in the Upper South indicated that the momentum given the exclusion argument by the circumstances of the early 1830s could not overcome the power of entrenched proslavery interests, the experience of the Lower South suggested that even where subordination reigned, hegemonic issues related to slavery and race still held significant divisive potential, a potential that both Jacksonian era parties in the region feared and manipulated over the next two decades. But in the Middle South, exclusionists and subordinationists of varying stripes debated an issue central to defining the relationship of race and citizenship: the question of free black suffrage.

A vigorous debate erupted over free black voting at the Tennessee constitutional convention of 1834. Tennessee's original 1796 constitution granted the suffrage to all "freemen" who met minimal freehold or residency requirements, and thus permitted a rather small number of free blacks who were freeholders or long time residents of a particular county to vote. In 1834, however, egalitarian reformers who pushed hard for the extension of suffrage to all whites also complained bitterly about the state's practice of allowing propertied free black men, otherwise considered "outside the social compact," to vote. Contending that white Tennesseans "reprobate and abhor" black voting, western delegate G. W. L. Marr declared that the "political fabric of Tennessee denied citizenship to all people of color, slave or free," and argued that the "supposed claim" of free blacks "to exercise the great right of free suffrage" should be "prohibited." Marr insisted that the United States Constitution's phrase "We, the People" meant "we the free white people of the United States and the free white people only." . . . Ultimately . . . the convention disfranchised all free blacks, including freeholders, by a vote of 33 to 23.

The question of voting rights for free blacks proved even more contentious when debated at North Carolina's constitutional convention of 1835. The use of the term "freeman" in the suffrage clause of North Carolina's constitution of 1776 opened the door to voting rights for free blacks who met the constitution's freehold or taxpaying requirements. Eligible free blacks voted regularly and with comparatively little controversy in most locales during the first three decades of the nineteenth century. When the convention met in Raleigh in June 1835, however, James Bryan of Carteret County led a charge for the disfranchisement of free blacks, baldly declaring that the United States was "a nation of white people — its offices, honors, dignities, and privileges, are alone open to, and to be enjoyed by, the white people." Nathaniel Macon, the venerable former speaker of the United States House, agreed, insisting that free blacks were "no part of the then political family" in 1776 and that free black suffrage in North Carolina rested on a flawed interpretation of the state's old constitution. Treading carefully around the state's racial sensibilities, defenders of free black suffrage argued that respectable free blacks served as a valuable buffer between whites and slaves. . . . Presenting a consistent Whig ideology for protecting property and promoting uplift, jurist William Gaston, the most respected figure at the convention other than Macon, offered an eloquent defense of free black suffrage. "Let them know they are a part of the body politic," Gaston pleaded, "and they will feel an attachment to the form of government and have a fixed interest in the prosperity of the community, and will exercise an important influence over the slaves." Judge Joseph Daniel of Halifax, an eastern district with the largest free black population in the state, proposed raising the property and taxpaying requirement for free-black voting to a freehold of $250. Such a substantial property requirement would allow "all colored men of good character and industrious habits" to vote and thus "conciliate the most respectable portion of the colored population" by giving them "a standing distinct from the slave population." . . . Prominent Whig planter John Morehead also warned that disfranchising free blacks might "close the door entirely against this unfortunate class of our population," and hence encourage them to "light up the torch of commotion among our slaves."

Leading a spirited attack on the "respectability" argument advanced by Daniel, Gaston, and Morehead, eastern delegate Jesse Wilson opposed any compromise based on property-holding or character in favor of a sweeping disfranchisement of all free blacks. "Color is a barrier which ought not to be broken between the classes," Wilson argued. "If you make it your business to elevate the condition of the blacks," he contended, "in the same proportion . . . you degrade that of poorer whites." Piedmont delegate Hugh McQueen concurred, arguing that "white portion of the population of this country constitutes the proper depository of political power" and complaining that "the exercise of the right of suffrage by free blacks was repugnant to public feeling in the State."

After vigorous debate, the North Carolina convention approved a constitutional provision depriving all free persons of color by the relatively narrow margin of 67–62. A strong sectional component appeared in the voting. Seventeen of the twenty-five counties whose delegates voted against disfranchisement lay in the Piedmont and mountain regions, while nineteen of the twenty-six counties whose delegates voted entirely in favor of disfranchisement lay in the heavily slaveholding East. There was also a crude relationship between party alignment and convention votes on the black disfranchisement. The heavily Whig Piedmont and mountain regions tended to oppose disfranchisement and the generally Democratic East tended to favor it. With the constitutional decisions of Tennessee and North Carolina in 1834 and 1835, the last vestiges of political rights for people of color disappeared from all parts of the future Confederacy. The southern body politic had become an exclusively white preserve. . . .

In sum, racial modernism in the Jacksonian South wore several faces, all of them forbidding to blacks and supportive of white supremacy in some form. In nearly all of its southern guises, however, racial modernism viewed race as biologically determined and looked no further than skin color for the determination of racial categories. Except for paternalists increasingly on the defensive, character, reputation, and property made less difference than skin color in the public life of the Old South. Some diehard conservatives, like Virginia's William Colquohoun, openly scoffed at the supposed triumph of such *herrenvolk* egalitarianism, ridiculing the notion that the "mere animal man, because he happens to wear a white skin" was entitled to full and exclusive privileges of citizenship. But across the Jacksonian South as a whole, such occasional conservative laments proved no match for the racial *esprit* and entitlement expressed and claimed in a young Mississippian's enthusiastic declaration upon coming of age that he was "*free, white, and twenty-one.*"

Thus in the Jacksonian South, as in the rest of Jacksonian America, the reconsideration of race produced an accommodation that enshrined whiteness as the standard measure of citizenship and racial entitlement. Proof of personal independence and public virtue deemed essential to republican citizenship no longer rested in the ownership of productive property, but instead hinged simply on "whiteness." To be sure, shared racism hardly united the Jacksonian South any more than it united the Jacksonian North. In the Upper South, belief in the permanent racial inferiority of nonwhites created a strong and continuing preference for racial exclusion, for a "whiter" society, one less dependent on slavery and characterized by a dwindling black population. Whites in the Lower South generally accepted slavery as an institution essential to the region's continued prosperity and agreed that the thorough subordination of blacks best served their society's interests. But even the cotton South's apparent consensus left considerable room for disagreement among whites over the status of free blacks, the regulation of the domestic slave trade, and the preferred racial balance of the population.

Yet despite these on-going disagreements, the Old South's contested decisions to emphasize whiteness at the expense of wealth, property, and character, choices most explicitly debated in the Middle South, revealed an important aspect of the great accommodation that held planter and plain folk in delicate political equipoise throughout the late antebellum era. However scornful of such claims in private, the slaveholding elite had to accept white equality, the spirit of *herrenvolk* democracy, in the public realm to ensure white solidarity in the coming stand against antislavery. Reluctant egalitarians to be sure, perhaps even hypocritical ones, the slaveholding elite of the Old South accepted the public creed of white equality as the price of broad support for slavery. At the same time, common whites found in the privileges of whiteness a social entitlement and a source of leverage they could employ with great effect in political debate. Lacking wealth but boasting numbers, white egalitarians used the ideological imperative of whiteness to wrest meaningful political concessions, if not outright control, from wealthy elites at key moments. Put another way, common whites in the Jacksonian South defined their whiteness as "property," as evidence of the requisite independence and virtue, and thus forged a southern *herrenvolk* republicanism, much in the same way that artisans and journeymen defined their skill as a sort of surrogate property and used it to forge artisanal republicanism in the urban North during the same era. In turn, by accepting, even tacitly, the legitimacy of slavery and the material inequalities it sustained, white egalitarians left the wealth and economic power of the planter elite secure.

Thus the triumph of whiteness allocated valuable privileges, including voting and legal equality, solely on the basis of skin color, or at least on cultural perceptions and definitions of skin color, leaving race rather than class the key social divide in the public realm. And that sense of white racial entitlement has proven tenacious indeed, surviving not only the collapse of slavery in the 1860s, but also (albeit in altered and sometimes disguised form) the dismantling of segregation a century later. By linking "whiteness" so closely to the prerogatives and rights of citizenship and political participation, the Jacksonian construction of racial modernity defined not merely the South but the entire American nation-state as a "white man's country." Thus racial modernity shaped a powerful national self-definition which would grudgingly sacrifice its gender dimension well before the Civil Rights Movement of the mid-twentieth century mounted a successful challenge to the claims for "whiteness" that lay at its very core.

# Antebellum Reform: Evolving Causes and Strategies

The reform movements that swept across America during the first half of the nineteenth century took a variety of forms. The most famous was the antislavery crusade, but others included movements to improve the condition of people afflicted with blindness, intemperance, deafness, insanity, and poverty. Some of these reform movements were intended to help individuals and groups powerless to change their condition; others were even more ambitious, aiming to end war, remake society through utopian communities, establish greater equality between the sexes, and found a free system of universal education. There were clear global dimensions to reform as well. Many of the movements had parallels in Great Britain, and more and more historians are beginning to work on abolition in an international context.

If it is difficult to characterize reform, it is equally difficult to categorize the ideologies of the reformers. Some saw social evils arising out of improvident and immoral behavior on the part of the individual. Others believed that an imperfect environment was at fault and that a meaningful solution to the problem at hand involved structural changes in American society. Some viewed reform as diminishing class rivalries and antagonisms, thereby preserving a fundamentally good and moral social order; others saw reform in more radical terms and urged fundamental changes in the structure of society. Similarly, there was little agreement about the use of the state to effect reform; some regarded state intervention as an absolute necessity, while others felt that reform efforts should be confined to private endeavors.

Although reform movements were heterogeneous in nature, there were a few themes common to them all. The reformers were optimists. In their eyes, no problem was so difficult that it could not be solved; no evil was so extreme as to be ineradicable; no person was so sinful as to be unredeemable. Second, a large number of them had been influenced by the revivals of the Second Great Awakening. Although often disinterested in and even hostile to disputes about fine points of belief, most were evangelical Christians motivated by a firm sense of responsibility to God for their fellow man. Third, most reformers believed that science and reason complemented rather than contradicted religious faith. Indeed, reason and science provided the means of fulfilling the moral and religious obligations that bound all individuals. Finally, most reformers recognized the complexity and interdependence of society.

Many of the intended beneficiaries of reform, it should be noted, included a disproportionately high percentage of the poor and helpless. Slaves, for example, needed allies to bring about their own liberation. The mentally ill, orphans, drunkards, and convicts could not agitate for the establishment or improvement of institutions that would benefit them. At the same time, reformers had to have both time and a sufficient income to pursue social activism. Reform movements, therefore, drew much of their inspiration and personnel from the ranks of the middle class and the well-to-do.

Reformers found it difficult to deal with an individual problem without bringing under scrutiny broader institutional structures. As a result, reformers — particularly in antislavery and women's rights — typically developed moral judgments about the basic arrangements of American society, judgments likely to engender conflict.

Just as Americans between 1800 and 1860 argued and fought over various visions of what constituted a just and moral society, so historians have argued over the nature, sources, and intentions of reformers. The result has been a wide range of interpretations of the many reform movements that developed during the first half of the nineteenth century, interpretations that reflect the personal values and the cultural context of the historians writing about the problem.

The first generations of students of reform were Progressives who looked on it favorably, except for abolitionists. At the turn of the century, when Ulrich Phillips's view of slavery as benign prevailed, most white historians saw abolitionists as fanatics and agreed with antebellum southerners that they stirred up the Civil War needlessly.

The negative view of abolitionists among mainstream historians prevailed until racial prejudice began to erode. With the civil rights movement and the advent of social history and New Left scholarship, historians looked much more favorably on the abolitionists, but more critically upon reform as a whole, which some scholars saw as ineffective and failing to challenge the real problems of advancing capitalism and others saw as efforts by the middle class to control the lower class. In 1975, David Brion Davis, influenced by the New Left, altered the study of reform dramatically by pointing out the ways in which abolitionism helped to solidify the ideology supporting the advent of capitalism. At about the same time, scholars of women's history and black history began to explore the contributions of women and African Americans to reform, and recently historians have looked at abolition's international scope as Black Atlantic studies have fed studies of emancipation.

The special calling of historians is to track and explain change, so reformers have always had unique appeal as a subject. "In that time, if ever in American history," wrote the Progressive historian Alice F. Tyler in her comprehensive study of antebellum reform, "the spirit of man seemed free and the individual could assert his independence of choice in matters of faith and theory. . . . The idea of progress . . . was at the same time a challenge to traditional beliefs and institutions and an impetus to experimentation with new theories and humanitarian reforms."[1] The origins of reform, she argued, were to be found in the interaction of Enlightenment rationalism, religious revivalism, transcendentalism, and the democratization of society that resulted from the frontier experience.

Although most Progressive accounts were favorably disposed toward antebellum reform, they were often critical of specific movements. The temperance crusade, they believed, was led by narrow-minded and bigoted individuals seeking to impose their own moral code upon the rest of the people. Indeed, Tyler, in her generally sympathetic survey of reform, noted that in back of the temperance crusade "lay the danger, ever present in a democracy, of the infringement by a majority of the rights of a minority and the further dangers inherent in the use of force to settle a moral issue." Equally distasteful to historians was the strong current of nativism — a movement that took a marked anti-Catholic turn during and after the arrival of thousands of Irish and German immigrants beginning in the 1830s, and that entered politics in the form of the Know-Nothing or Native American Party during the 1850s. Most scholars found it difficult to reconcile this movement and its accompanying intolerance with the general current of reform.[2]

Much the same pattern was true of abolitionism. Virtually no scholar defended slavery, yet a large number were extraordinarily critical of the abolitionist movement because of its inflexibility and zealotry. Southerners flatly laid the blame for the Civil War at the doorstep of the abolitionists. Some even charged that the intolerance and fanaticism of the abolitionists had aborted a moderate and sensible emancipation movement that had been under way in the South.

The southern view of abolitionism by the early part of the twentieth century had become the dominant tradition in American historiography. One reason for this was that a significant number of scholars came from the South. In his discussion of the causes of the Civil War, Frank L. Owsley condemned the abolitionists in unequivocal terms. "One has to seek in the unrestrained and furious invective of the present totalitarians," he stated, "to find a near parallel to the language that the abolitionists and their political fellow travelers used in denouncing the South and its way of life. Indeed, as far as I have been able to ascertain, neither Dr. Goebbels . . . nor Stalin's propaganda agents have as yet been able to plumb the depths of vulgarity and obscenity reached and maintained by . . . Stephen Foster, Wendell Phillips, Charles Sumner, and other abolitionists of note."[3]

Historians reflected some of the general apathy — even hostility — toward the plight of black Americans that was characteristic of the first three or so

[1]Alice Felt Tyler, *Freedom's Ferment: Phases of American Social History from the Colonial Period to the Outbreak of the Civil War* (Minneapolis, 1944), 1.

[2]Ibid., 359. See especially Ray Allen Billington, *The Protestant Crusade, 1800–1860: A Study of the Origins of American Nativism* (New York, 1938).

[3]Frank L. Owsley, "The Fundamental Cause of the Civil War: Egocentric Sectionalism," *Journal of Southern History* 7 (February 1941): 16–17.

decades of the twentieth century. A few scholars also noted that not all abolitionists were committed to the proposition that blacks and whites were equal. Consequently they alleged that abolitionists were "insincere" and "hypocritical." Since they routinely excluded black reformers from their studies, there was no inconsistency in calling the abolitionists insincere.[4]

Scholars using insights borrowed from the social and behavioral sciences to inquire into the motives of reformers provided further ways to denigrate the abolitionists. Interpreting fanaticism in psychiatric terms could reduce abolitionism to pathology. Hazel Wolf, for example, described the behavior of individual abolitionists as obsessive and paranoiac in nature. All of them, she wrote, were "eagerly bidding for a martyr's crown."[5] David Donald, in an essay that became a classic after its publication in 1956, used social psychology and status anxiety to explain the behavior of the abolitionists as a reform group. They were born to lead in a world that was modernizing so fast that their leadership was in jeopardy, so "agitation allowed the only chance for personal and social self-fulfillment." Donald described them as complacent about capitalism, but unhappy with the transfer of power to slave owners and textile manufacturers. "An attack on slavery was their best, if quite unconscious, attack upon the new industrial system."[6]

While the majority of historians were unfriendly in their treatment of the abolitionists, there were rare exceptions by scholars of the black experience like Carter Woodson and Dorothy and Charles Wesley who wrote biographies of black abolitionists, but more important collected and preserved the speeches, writings, and proceedings of meetings of black abolitionists.[7] And older and more favorable views held by some northern writers in the 1860s and 1870s did not completely disappear. Indeed, by the late 1930s — especially as racist theory was beginning to be discredited — a change in the portrait of abolitionism began to appear. Dwight L. Dumond, for example, showed considerable sympathy for the abolitionists in his study of the origins of the Civil War in 1939.[8] The broadening of the civil rights movement and the struggle for equality in the 1950s and 1960s further shifted the framework of the debate, for it was difficult, if not impossible, for historians to avoid dealing with the tragedy of black-white relationships in America. By the 1960s, a significant number of historians sympathized with

[4]For example, Gilbert H. Barnes argued that abolitionists, influenced by evangelical religion, were more interested in rebuking slave owners than in freeing slaves. See *The Antislavery Impulse, 1830–1844* (New York, 1933), 25.

[5]Hazel C. Wolf, *On Freedom's Altar: The Martyr Complex in the Abolition Movement* (Madison, Wis., 1952), 4.

[6]David Donald, *Lincoln Reconsidered: Essays on the Civil War Era* (New York, 1956), 33–34. For a critique of Donald's thesis, see Robert A. Skotheim, "A Note on Historical Method: David Donald's 'Toward a Reconsideration of Abolitionists,'" *Journal of Southern History* 25 (August 1959): 356–65.

[7]Manisha Sinha, "Coming of Age: The Historiography of Black Abolitionism," in *Prophets of Protest: Reconsidering the History of American Abolitionism*, ed. Patrick McCarthy and John Stauffer (New York, 2006).

[8]Dwight L. Dumond, *Antislavery Origins of the Civil War in the United States* (Ann Arbor, Mich., 1939).

the abolitionists, and their approach became dominant. In a major study on antislavery in 1961, Dumond began by stating his own viewpoint: "The course of the men and women who dedicated their lives to arresting the spread of slavery was marvelously direct and straightforward. They denounced it as a sin which could only be remedied by unconditional repentance and retributive justice. . . . These people were neither fanatics nor incendiaries. . . . They precipitated an intellectual and moral crusade for social reform, for the rescue of a noble people, for the redemption of democracy."[9]

To Merle Curti, a scholar writing within the Progressive tradition of American history in the early 1940s, the roots of reform were to be found in a complex combination of Enlightenment beliefs — faith in reason, natural law, and the idea of progress — and a liberal humanitarian religion that assumed the goodness of humans and the perfectibility of the individual. Two other intellectual trends also played a role in stimulating reform: romanticism, with its enthusiasm for the individual without reference to status; and utilitarianism, which insisted that all institutions be judged by standards of social utility rather than tradition or custom.[10]

In addition to the publication of numerous favorable biographies of abolitionists, there was a new tendency to write about the movement in friendly, even glowing, terms. One book of essays by various authorities in 1965 explicitly rejected earlier views of abolitionism as a movement of maladjusted and evil fanatics. Indeed, in the concluding essay, Howard Zinn argued that abolitionist radicalism was highly constructive when compared with the extreme inhumanity of slavery.[11] Similarly, Donald G. Mathews, who analyzed the arguments and rhetoric of the abolitionists, concluded that they were neither irrational nor fanatic. The abolitionists as agitators were not attempting to change the values of Americans — rather they were trying to extend them to human beings who were generally considered to be outside of society. Nor were the men and women who spent much of their lives fighting against slavery guilty of oversimplification, according to Mathews. The absolute power of whites over blacks corrupted not only individuals, but the South as a section as well as the entire nation. Mathews's interpretation reflects the more sympathetic views of abolitionism characteristic of historical literature during the last few decades.[12]

These assessments, while providing useful intellectual background to the reformers, seemed to offer no new views on the subject. They also ignored the work of African American historians like Benjamin Quarles who had been writing about black abolitionists since the 1930s, along with a few other scholars including Herbert Aptheker, Philip Foner, Howard Bell, and Dorothy

---

[9]Dwight L. Dumond, *Antislavery: The Crusade for Freedom in America* (Ann Arbor, Mich., 1961), 417–51, v.

[10]Merle Curti, *The Growth of American Thought*, 3rd ed. (New York, 1964), especially Chapter 15. The first edition of this book appeared in 1943.

[11]Howard Zinn, "SNCC: The New Abolitionists," in *The Antislavery Vanguard: New Essays on the Abolitionists*, ed. Martin Duberman (Princeton, N.J., 1965), 417–51.

[12]Donald G. Mathews, "The Abolitionist on Slavery: The Critique behind the Social Movement," *Journal of Southern History* 23 (May 1967): 163–82.

Sterling. Their scholarship did more than document the presence and importance of black abolitionists in the antebellum movement; it pointed, for example, to the importance African American reformers gave to Revolutionary ideology. But it remained ignored, and did not, therefore, exert valuable influence on the debates about the origins, methods, and motives of reformers.[13]

In 1959, in his controversial study *Slavery*, Stanley M. Elkins offered what he thought was a view without moral evaluation as well as a major reinterpretation of reformers in general. Instead of judging their movement, Elkins, drawing on social psychology, looked at their world and their worldview. To Elkins, the most distinctive feature of American society in the early nineteenth century was the general breakdown of a number of key social institutions. The older establishments that had stood for order and stability — the church, the bar, the Federalist Party, the eastern merchant aristocracy — had been stripped of their power by the 1830s and replaced by an almost mystical faith in the individual. With formal institutions losing their influence, a new kind of reformer emerged who did not rely upon such agencies to bring about social change. When abolitionists sought to abolish slavery, they did not feel impelled to discuss institutional arrangements in their proposed solutions to the problem. Protest, therefore, occurred in an institutional vacuum, and reformers were never called upon to test their ideas. Out of Elkins's interpretation emerged a more generalized description of the abstract and moral nature of American reform and its failure to come to grips with concrete and specific problems. Subsequent scholars have attributed very different — and positive — meanings to the institutional vacuum that Elkins described.[14]

In an article published in 1965, John L. Thomas attempted to synthesize many of the diverse and even conflicting interpretations of antebellum reform. Beginning with a romantic faith in perfectibility and confined to religious institutions, wrote Thomas, reform quickly overflowed its specific limits and spread across society and politics. Defining social sin as the sum total of individual sin, reformers worked to reeducate individuals. Reform therefore involved a broad moral crusade — but with a strong anti-institutional bias since it was based on the concept of the free and regenerate individual. In an important sense, Thomas agreed with Elkins. Even the communitarian experiments, Thomas noted, were anti-institutional solutions, for they involved an abandonment of political and religious institutions in favor of an ideal society giving full rein to the free individual.[15]

---

[13]Sinha, "Coming of Age," 29–31.

[14]Stanley M. Elkins, *Slavery: A Problem in American Institutional and Intellectual Life* (Chicago, 1959), 140–222. Several historians, on the other hand, have argued that reformers and abolitionists were shrewd strategic thinkers. See in particular Aileen S. Kraditor, *Means and Ends in American Abolitionism: Garrison and His Critics on Strategy and Tactics, 1834–1850* (New York, 1969), and James M. McPherson, *The Struggle for Equality: Abolitionists and the Negro in the Civil War and Reconstruction* (Princeton, N.J., 1964).

[15]John L. Thomas, "Romantic Reform in America, 1815–1865," *American Quarterly* 17 (Winter 1965): 656–81; see also Robert H. Walker's three-stage typology of reform: *Reform in America: The Continuing Frontier* (Lexington, Ky., 1985). In *American Reformers, 1815–1860* (New York, 1978), Ronald G. Walters explored social and cultural conditions that permitted reformers to perceive reality as they did.

Elkins's focus on anti-institutionalism as well as the dramatic protests of the 1960s helped spur the development of new themes among historians studying pre–Civil War reform. Influenced by the New Left and the new social history, scholars explored new facets of antebellum reform in their examination of the legacy of unsolved problems in American society. An initial phase of studying the social control aspect of reform gave way to a more complex exploration of the relations among the reform movements and the emerging classes of the new capitalist order.

In the early 1970s, historians began to suggest that the motivation behind the actions of many reformers, either consciously or unconsciously, was to impose some form of social control over those whom they were ostensibly trying to help. This interpretation arose in part from the understanding that the reformers were active at the same moment that class formation was taking place, and historians, particularly those influenced by the New Left, looked to the largely middle-class reformers for class conflict and class interest. The continued exclusion of African Americans from discussions of reform facilitated this trend.

Religious benevolence — clearly a major theme in mid-nineteenth-century America — also underwent a sharp reevaluation. Clifford S. Griffin, a new social historian, noting the phenomenal increase in the number of national societies established for such benevolent purposes as education, conversion, temperance, peace, antislavery, moral reform, and the dissemination of the Bible, saw in them more than merely the disinterested exercise of charitable impulses. As more and more people confronted political and social upheavals of the early national period, and immigration shattered the homogeneity of American society, many turned to evangelical Protestantism as the only social force capable of restoring "stability and order, sobriety and safety." Both clergymen and laymen turned to new, national, voluntary societies to promote religious benevolence and charity. Most of the leaders of these societies were relatively well-to-do and viewed religious benevolence as a means of social control. "Religion and morality, as dispensed by the benevolent societies throughout the seemingly chaotic nation," argued Griffin, "became a means of establishing secular order."[16]

In a similar vein, Michael Katz, another historian influenced by the New Left, was critical of those historians who had interpreted the educational reform movement as merely an outgrowth of mid-nineteenth-century humanitarian zeal and the extension of political democracy. "Very simply," he wrote, "the extension and reform of education in the mid-nineteenth century [was] . . . the attempt of a coalition of the social leaders, status-anxious parents, and status-hungry educators to impose educational innovation, each for their own reasons, upon a reluctant community."[17] Those community

---

[16]Clifford S. Griffin, *Their Brothers' Keepers: Moral Stewardship in the United States, 1800–1855* (New Brunswick, N.J., 1960), x–xiii. Some historians have modified the social control interpretation of benevolence by emphasizing that the effort to establish a general standard of right conduct is characteristic of many groups. See Paul Boyer, *Urban Masses and Moral Order in America, 1820–1920* (Cambridge, Mass., 1978).

[17]Michael B. Katz, *The Irony of Early School Reform: Educational Innovation in Mid-Nineteenth-Century Massachusetts* (Cambridge, Mass., 1968), 218.

leaders promoting education sought a school system that would harmonize America's economic growth with a business-oriented value system to prevent the violent consequences that had accompanied the rise of industrialism in England.[18]

The themes of social control and imposition of reform were not confined to religious benevolence or education. Joseph R. Gusfield, a sociologist by profession, analyzed the temperance movement in much the same manner as Donald, Griffin, and Katz viewed their reform movements. Gusfield argued that cultural groups act to preserve, defend, and enhance the dominance and prestige of their own style of living. During the federal era, temperance attracted a declining social elite bent on retaining its power and leadership. This elite "sought to make Americans into a clean, sober, godly, and decorous people" — a people that reflected their own values. By the 1840s, those who favored temperance saw the curtailment of the use of liquor as a means "of solving the problems presented by an immigrant, urban poor whose culture clashed with American Protestantism." Similarly, David J. Rothman insisted that fear of social disorder in the early nineteenth century led elite groups to espouse institutional solutions in the hope of controlling deviant behavior by predominantly lower-class groups. Prisons, mental hospitals, and almshouses, he observed, were not the fruits of benevolent reform; they reflected rather a desire to control and to change behavior through the application of institutional solutions.[19]

Students of abolitionism, influenced by the new social and intellectual history of the 1960s and 1970s, tended to reject the social control argument and instead wondered about a number of other concerns, like the social and cultural context of the movement and the concern of individual abolitionists with self-realization. In 1976, for example, Ronald G. Walters published a study of antislavery after 1830 that emphasized the abolitionists' immersion in, not alienation from, such values of their culture as devotion to family, hard work, and adherence to the Constitution. The activists' deep belief in commonly held antebellum values encouraged them to see slavery as rupturing their dearest ideals. Three years later Lewis Perry and Michael Fellman brought out a collection of essays representative of this trend. This work, together with several others, dealt with the desire of abolitionists to create a universe of free and autonomous individuals, each able to realize his own destiny, free from social constraints. And in 1982, Lawrence J. Friedman

---

[18]For an interpretation that similarly stressed education for the new industrial society, see David Nasaw, *Schooled to Order: A Social History of Public Schooling in the United States* (New York, 1979).

[19]Joseph R. Gusfield, *Symbolic Crusade: Status Politics and the American Temperance Movement* (Urbana, Ill., 1963), 5–6, and David J. Rothman, *The Discovery of the Asylum: Social Order and Disorder in the New Republic* (Boston, 1971). For a somewhat different interpretation from Rothman's, see Gerald N. Grob, *Mental Institutions in America: Social Policy to 1875* (New York, 1973), and Nancy Tomes, *A Generous Confidence: Thomas Story Kirkbride and the Art of Asylum-Keeping, 1840–1883* (New York, 1984). For an effort to synthesize all of the nineteenth century within a quasi-Marxian model that emphasizes a two-class system, see Michael B. Katz, Michael J. Doucet, and Mark J. Stern, *The Social Organization of Early Industrial Capitalism* (Cambridge, Mass., 1982).

attempted to depict the experiences of abolitionists from their youthful beginnings to their later careers, starting with inner psychology and moving outward to immersion in social and political conflicts.[20]

Meanwhile, some scholars pursued the relationship of abolitionism and developing capitalism, but rejected overt self-interest and social control as too reductive. Perhaps the most important step in finding the connections between the two trends came with David Brion Davis's *The Problem of Slavery in the Age of Revolution, 1770–1823.* Davis explored in detail the various antislavery ideologies available in the late eighteenth century. He posed the question, why was it not until the emergence of a capitalist order that a powerful abolitionist movement was able to excite the revulsion of people toward an institution that had existed throughout history? Davis's wide-ranging argument rescued abolitionists from being portrayed as self-interested, market-driven hypocrites, but retained the link between antislavery and capitalism. His argument, highly simplified, was that antislavery was able to grow powerful at a moment in which the new capitalist relations of employer and contractual wage earner or "free laborer" benefited from a flattering contrast with the evils of slavery.[21]

At more or less the same time, Paul Johnson in *A Shopkeeper's Millennium* made the case that participation in evangelical religion for employers and ambitious laborers provided a stamp of powerful moral credibility for these new contractual relations in a world that was rapidly losing its old hierarchical controls. These views of religion and slavery posited a framework in which people made choices within moral systems they understood, but their actions also served different aims from those they could have understood at the time.[22]

Steven Mintz, surveying all mid-nineteenth-century reform in *Moralists and Modernizers,* argued that reform arose in a moment of growing laissez-faire in which reformers shared fears of capitalist development and believed in the need for a wide array of internal controls to guard against the system's obvious excesses. "Antebellum reformers played a critical role in establishing minimum standards of human dignity and decency, imposing limits of exploitation, and creating modern institutions to rescue and rehabilitate

---

[20]Ronald G. Walters, *The Antislavery Appeal: American Abolitionism after 1830* (Baltimore, 1976); Lewis Perry and Michael Fellman, eds., *Antislavery Reconsidered: New Perspectives on the Abolitionists* (Baton Rouge, La., 1979); Peter F. Walker, *Moral Choices: Memory, Desire, and Imagination in Nineteenth-Century American Abolition* (Baton Rouge, La., 1978); Lewis Perry, *Childhood, Marriage, and Reform: Henry Clarke Wright, 1797–1870* (Chicago, 1980); Lawrence J. Friedman, *Gregarious Saints: Self and Community in American Abolitionism, 1830–1870* (New York, 1982). See also John R. McKivigan, *The War against Proslavery Religion: Abolitionism and Northern Churches, 1830–1865* (Ithaca, N.Y., 1984), and James H. Moorhead, *American Apocalypse: Yankee Protestants and the Civil War, 1860–1869* (New Haven, Conn., 1978).

[21]David Brion Davis, *The Problem of Slavery in the Age of Revolution, 1770–1823* (Ithaca, N.Y., 1975). In 1985, Thomas Haskell linked humanitarianism to capitalism through how it extended participants' appreciation of chains of consequences and hence the potential range of their empathy; Thomas Haskell, "Capitalism and the Origins of the Humanitarian Sensibility," *Journal of American History* 90 (April and June 1985).

[22]Paul E. Johnson, *A Shopkeeper's Millennium: Society and Revivals in Rochester, New York, 1815–1837* (New York, 1978).

the victims of social change." Mintz presented the reformers fully, their good intentions intertwined with repression and paternalism. He studied them in the larger framework of capitalism and found continuity between them and liberals, embodying tolerance and respect for the opinions of others. While Stanley Elkins had seen reformers behave irresponsibly due to their lack of institutional attachments, Mintz saw them trying to fill the vacuum left by laissez-faire government and capitalism.[23]

While a more sophisticated view of reform and modernization was developing, reflecting the decline in the power of nation-states and, in that vacuum, the rise of human rights organizations and nongovernmental organizations, the new social history encouraged the study of reformers previously neglected because of gender or race. Vincent Harding, in *There Is a River*, argued for the unflagging persistence and leadership of black abolitionists in the antislavery struggle. He pointed to the participation of slaves and free blacks together in the movement and argued that Frederick Douglass and other black abolitionists were wrong to rest their hopes on the good intentions of white reformers.[24]

Manisha Sinha, in her study of the historiography of black abolitionism, placed Benjamin Quarles as the "progenitor of modern black abolitionist historiography" and his *Black Abolitionists* (1969) as the most important work in the field.[25] Given the fact that abolition studies heretofore had all but ignored the presence of black abolitionists, Quarles insisted upon their presence and significance in abolitionism since its beginnings, but also demonstrated their role as creators of their own liberation, not the passive recipients of white concern. This idea is central to African American history today and reflects the influence of the work of scholars of the African diaspora and the Black Atlantic. This view informs Joseph Miller's essay, in which he argues that it was the active resistance to slavery by slaves themselves, particularly in America, that caused abolition in the West, not the actions of white reformers. Quarles's other important contribution was to link the activities of black abolitionists to the ideals of the Revolution, an idea that subsequent historians have adopted and that provides a contrast to the nearly exclusive focus on religion that previously dominated abolition studies.[26]

---

[23]Steven Mintz, *Moralists and Modernizers: America's Pre–Civil War Reformers* (Baltimore, 1995), xviii.

[24]Vincent Harding, *There Is a River: The Black Struggle for Freedom in America* (New York, 1981); Anne Firor Scott, *Natural Allies: Women's Associations in American History* (Urbana, Ill., 1991), 13–14, 46; see, for example, Nell Irvin Painter, *Sojourner Truth: A Life, a Symbol* (New York, 1996); Marilyn Richardson, ed., *Maria W. Stewart: America's First Black Woman Political Writer: Essays and Speeches* (Bloomington, Ind., 1987); Frederick Blue, *No Taint of Compromise: Crusaders in Antislavery Politics* (Baton Rouge, La., 2005); Richard S. Newman, *The Transformation of American Abolitionism: Fighting Slavery in the Early Republic* (Chapel Hill, N.C., 2003); Jonathan Earle, "The Making of the North's 'Stark Mad Abolitionists': Anti-Slavery Conversion in the United States, 1824–1854," *Slavery and Abolition* 25 (December 2004): 59–75. See also John Q. Quist, *Restless Visionaries: The Social Roots of Antebellum Reform in Alabama and Michigan* (Baton Rouge, La., 1998), for a comparative study of the origins of reform in a northern and southern community.

[25]Sinha, "Coming of Age," 29–31, 34–35.

[26]Ibid., 31–33; Joseph C. Miller, "The Abolition of the Slave Trade and Slavery: Historical Foundations," in *From Chains to Bonds: The Slave Trade Revisited*, ed. Doudou Diene (Paris, 2001).

Just as the civil rights movement created a climate sympathetic to abolitionists, so the women's movement helped to transform the ways in which historians interpreted earlier efforts to further social change. Women's participation in the reform movements was vigorous, and scholarship about female reform documented the high percentage of women in movements from abolitionism to Bible societies, the establishment of Sunday schools, sexual reform, temperance, and suffrage. Research on women abolitionists has demonstrated that it was black women in Salem, Massachusetts, who founded the first antislavery society in the nation. One strain of gender historiography spotlighted the empowerment women felt, the networks they created, the isolation they overcame, and the challenges they issued to male domination. Carroll Smith-Rosenberg's 1971 article, "The Beauty, the Beast and the Militant Woman," is a good example of how a primary focus on gender has emphasized women's struggle with men and has tended to sideline issues of class and racial conflict with other women.[27]

Soon, however, scholars like Christine Stansell complicated the gender picture by pointing to class conflict and the effort of middle-class women to enforce their standards of motherhood and comportment on working-class women as the price of aid. Mary Ryan's *The Cradle of the Middle Class* studied women's role in creating a middle class in Utica, New York. Ryan emphasized the formation of a new class identity out of traditional religious materials, not class conflict or efforts to control the working class so much as the development of traits useful to a new bourgeoisie. Nancy Hewitt, in her study of reform in nearby Rochester, New York, emphasized striations in the emerging middle class itself. Anne Firor Scott in *Natural Allies* described the myriad benevolent associations that sprang up across the country from 1800 on and analyzed their evolution into the widespread activism of the antebellum and, eventually, the Progressive period. She found reformist energy coming from a variety of backgrounds, including groups without an evangelical foundation. As to social control, "the evidence does not support any simple hypothesis." Reformers divided up the world in many ways, economic class not being a particularly significant marker. Scott concluded that "There is a difference, too, between trying to promote social order by keeping people 'in their place,' as the phrase went, and trying to help them develop characteristics that — if accomplished — might admit them to the middle class."[28]

In another challenge to the view of middle-class women's commitment to social control, Carolyn J. Lawes's study of Worcester, Massachusetts, contended that women in that community over time organized across class lines.

---

[27]Carroll Smith-Rosenberg, "The Beauty, the Beast and the Militant Woman: A Case Study in Sex Roles and Social Stress in Jacksonian America," *American Quarterly* 23 (October 1971): 562–84.

[28]Christine Stansell, *City of Women: Sex and Class in New York, 1789–1860* (New York, 1986); Mary Ryan, *Cradle of the Middle Class: The Family in Oneida County, New York, 1790–1865* (New York, 1981); Nancy Hewitt, *Women's Activism and Social Change, Rochester, New York, 1822–1872* (Ithaca, N.Y., 1984); Anne Firor Scott, *Natural Allies: Women's Associations in American History* (Urbana, Ill., 1991), 4.

They perceived the volatile economic condition of the antebellum Republic and the unpredictability of health as capable of damaging rich and poor alike.[29]

After Eleanor Flexner's unsurpassed survey of the women's suffrage movement was published in 1959, little was written until Ellen Carol DuBois's *Feminism and Suffrage*, in which she argued for a new interpretation of the relationship between abolitionism and feminism. The assumption had been that women saw their own subordination through identification with slaves, and that this mobilized them. DuBois argued that they understood their subjugation perfectly well, but needed to learn organizing skills and free themselves from intellectual and moral dependence on the clergy before they could start their own movement.[30]

Lori D. Ginzberg (excerpted below) studied the institutionalization of this initially spontaneous women's movement and its costs. In the 1830s, women emphasized moral suasion in fighting for a wide array of feminist reforms including suffrage. Moral suasion's failure to eradicate social evils led them to focus on politics and institutional change by the 1850s. Ironically, this shift tended to narrow the goals of feminist activism, ending in a concentration on the vote at the expense of other, more wide-ranging and radical aims. Ginzberg's study indicated a shift in studying reform toward politics and away from religion.[31]

Amy Dru Stanley looked at the abolitionists' constant focus on the enslaved and violated female body as the symbol of all that was wrong with slavery. That, she believed, led women to a new understanding of gender differences and the individual rights of women. By emphasizing the figure of the female slave, for whom slavery meant the loss of control not only of her labor but of her sexuality, and arguing for a form of possessive individualism for both men and women, abolitionists contradicted contemporary middle-class notions of the completely different natures and rights of men and women.[32]

Mary Hershberger linked the movement protesting the removal of the so-called Five Civilized Tribes (see the first reading below) to the energizing

---

[29]Carolyn J. Lawes, *Women and Reform in a New England Community, 1815–1860* (Lexington, Ky., 2000), 3–6. See also Sandra Haarsager, *Organized Womanhood: Cultural Politics in the Pacific Northwest, 1840–1920* (Norman, Okla., 1997), and Julie Roy Jeffrey, *The Great Silent Army of Abolitionism: Ordinary Women in the Antislavery Movement* (Chapel Hill, N.C., 1998).

[30]Ellen Carol DuBois, *Feminism and Suffrage: The Emergence of an Independent Women's Movement in America, 1848–1869* (Ithaca, N.Y., 1978). See also Kathryn Kish Sklar's excellent summary of the relationship of women abolitionists with suffrage, *Women's Rights Emerges within the Antislavery Movement, 1830–1870: A Brief History with Documents* (New York, 2000); Eleanor Flexner, *Century of Struggle: The Women's Rights Movement in the United States* (Cambridge, Mass., 1959).

[31]Lori D. Ginzberg, *Women and the Work of Benevolence: Morality, Politics, and Class in the Nineteenth-Century United States* (New Haven, Conn., 1990). See also Suzanne Marilley, *Woman Suffrage and the Origins of Liberal Feminism in the United States, 1820–1920* (Cambridge, Mass., 1996), and Rosalyn Terborg-Penn, *African American Women in the Struggle for the Vote, 1850–1920* (Bloomington, Ind., 1998).

[32]Amy Dru Stanley, "'The Right to Possess All the Faculties That God Has Given': Possessive Individualism, Slave Women, and Abolitionist Thought," in *Moral Problems in American Life: New Perspectives on Cultural History*, ed. Karen Halttunen and Lewis Perry (Ithaca, N.Y., 1998).

and radicalizing of the antislavery movement and the mobilization of women to the antislavery cause. Hershberger traced women's involvement in anti-removal activity through their support of missionary associations ministering to various Indian groups. Opposition to removal soon led these reformers to reject the colonization of former slaves in Africa, which they saw as analogous, and mobilized and radicalized the first cohort of antislavery activists. Hershberger credits Jackson with enlarging democracy not directly, but through the protest he provoked: "his determination to carry out Indian removal generated the deepest political movement that the country had yet witnessed."[33]

In recent years, studies of reform, particularly abolition, have acquired generally positive energy from historians of the Black Atlantic, by fields external to history like sociology and political science looking for the origins of human rights work[34] and a reevaluation of politics in the face of the rise of politicized religion. Steven Mintz and John Stauffer in *The Problem of Evil: Slavery, Freedom, and the Ambiguities of American Reform* reflected this new atmosphere, asserting that "studying moral questions and problems of evil was the most important task historians could perform."[35] In studying abolition, these scholars were not just looking for heroes and heroines, they were also studying the "ambiguities" of the reformers and their positions, retrieving stories of resisting evil intertwined with contradictory ideas and behavior, stories with heroism and human frailty.

Some scholars have focused on the structures of reform, its rhetoric, methodologies, politics, degree of success, and legacy for democratic institutions. T. Gregory Garvey, pursuing some of the questions Mintz and Stauffer's study raised, used abolition and women's rights to look at the modes of public discourse that they generated for expressing and dealing with divisive matters. He charted the growth of a secular rhetoric of advocacy that developed for mediating contentious issues that the political system could not handle. He argued that the emergence of these tactics and modes of discussion were "part of a broad structural change in American society" and marked a great expansion of the role of popular debate in a society that was convinced that politics was a place for insincerity and manipulation, while extrapolitical organizations and people could legitimately claim sincerity. Like Elkins, Garvey studied the institutional void, but unlike him he found creativity not irresponsibility. Garvey did not see the developments he studied as part of Mintz and Stauffer's "liberal tradition," but offered his work, instead, as a study of the "structure of debate" that took place in "a new sphere of

---

[33]Mary Hershberger, "Mobilizing Women, Anticipating Abolition: The Struggle against Indian Removal in the 1830s," *Journal of American History* 85 (June 1999): 15–40.

[34]See, for example, Margaret Keck and Kathryn Sikkink, *Activists beyond Borders: Advocacy Networks in International Politics* (Ithaca, N.Y., 1998).

[35]Steven Mintz and John Stauffer, *The Problem of Evil: Slavery, Freedom, and the Ambiguities of American Reform* (Amherst, Mass., 2007), 1.

activism that remains central to the means through which Americans mediate social conflict."[36]

A number of scholars have given politics a positive role in the antislavery struggle, including Frederick Blue, Richard S. Newman, and Jonathan Earle. *Beyond Garrison: Antislavery and Social Reform*, Bruce Laurie's meticulous study of the politics of abolition in Massachusetts, ceded no moral high ground to Garrisonians as it demonstrated the surprising vitality of antislavery among Massachusetts nativists as well as the remarkable strength of working-class support for abolition in that state. Tracing antislavery sentiment from the Liberty Party, through the Free-Soil Party, to the Know-Nothings, to the Republicans, Laurie argued that politics was as effective if not more so than moral suasion. Acting in the political rather than the reform arena did not mean insincerity, unseemly compromises, or wavering commitment to the cause. In particular, Laurie contended that Garrison brought his followers to inaction through endless self-scrutiny and no practical program for change, while political antislavery galvanized a grassroots movement of laborers as well as members of the middle class to action.[37]

The other major stream of abolitionist thought comes from scholars attentive to developments in the field of Black Atlantic studies for whom abolition, particularly British abolition, has long been a central concern and who have seen it, along with the cessation of the slave trade, in an international context. The initiation of the journal *Slavery and Abolition* in 1980 gave scholars an interdisciplinary and international forum in which to consider these issues.

The recent inclusion of radical black abolitionist thought in the early republican intellectual reform mix has linked American abolition with developments in Black Atlantic historiography because African American abolitionists conceived of their struggle in international terms. Manisha Sinha, in an article discussing Revolutionary-era black radicals, wrote, "Their notion of revolution was transnational and expansive, transcending the narrow and largely uncritical celebration of the American Revolution."[38] David Brion Davis has also pointed out the acute awareness of American abolitionists, white and black, of their British predecessors in the struggle.[39] Historians of West Africa during the slave trade have uncovered ongoing violent resistance to the forced migration. David Richardson, for example, documented revolts on shipboard along the coast of West Africa that were sufficient to increase substantially the cost of the trade and reduce its volume by as much

---

[36]T. Gregory Garvey, *Creating the Culture of Reform in Antebellum America* (Athens, Ga., 2006), 1, 2, 9–10; Leo Hirrel, *Children of Wrath: New School Calvinism and Antebellum Reform* (Lexington, Ky., 1998).

[37]Blue, *No Taint of Compromise*; Newman, *The Transformation of American Abolitionism*; Earle, "The Making of the North's 'Stark Mad Abolitionists,'" 59–75; Bruce Laurie, *Beyond Garrison: Antislavery and Social Reform* (New York, 2005). See also Quist, *Restless Visionaries.*

[38]Manisha Sinha, "To 'Cast Just Obliquy' on Oppressors: Black Radicalism in the Age of Revolution," *William and Mary Quarterly* 64 (January 2007): 149–60.

[39]David Brion Davis, *Inhuman Bondage: The Rise and Fall of Slavery in the New World* (New York, 2006), 259–60.

as one-tenth. Sylviane Diouf edited a volume of essays each delineating an aspect of African resistance to the trade.[40] As yet there has been no attempt to synthesize this body of knowledge or even to integrate the historiography of black and white American abolitionists.[41]

There are still wide gaps in our knowledge about who, exactly, the re-formers were and what motives they had for their work. How did they view themselves? How did they view those they were trying to change? How do we evaluate their legacy? There also remains much to learn about the links among reform movements, about the degree of community between white and black reformers, about the influence of international events like British abolition and the revolution in Haiti. As the protest movements of the 1960s and 1970s continue to influence our society, historians will continue to look for parallels and explanations capable of telling us more about the origins, dynamics, and failures of the American impulse to improve.

---

[40]David Richardson, "Shipboard Revolts, African Authority, and the Atlantic Slave Trade," *William and Mary Quarterly* 58 ( January 2001): 69–92. Sylviane Diouf, *Fighting the Slave Trade: West African Strategies* (Athens, Ohio, 2003).

[41]See Joseph C. Miller, "The Abolition of the Slave Trade and Slavery: Historical Founda-tions," in *From Chains to Bonds*, ed. Doudou Diene, 173, 178, for a discussion of how slave resist-ance, not reformers, caused abolition.

## MARY HERSHBERGER

# *from* Mobilizing Women, Anticipating Abolition: The Struggle against Indian Removal in the 1830s [1999]

**MARY HERSHBERGER** teaches at Capital University in Ohio. She is the author of *Traveling to Vietnam: American Peace Activists and the War* (1998) and *Jane Fonda's War: A Political Biography of an Antiwar Icon* (2005).

Andrew Jackson's request to Congress in December 1829 for federal monies to remove Southeast Indians beyond the Mississippi River generated the most intense public opposition that the United States had witnessed. In six short months, removal opponents launched massive petition drives that called on Congress to defeat removal and to uphold Indian rights to property. To block removal, Catharine Beecher and Lydia Sigourney organized the first national women's petition campaign and flooded Congress with antiremoval petitions, making a bold claim for women's place in national political discourse. The experience of opposing removal

---

Mary Hershberger, "Mobilizing Women, Anticipating Abolition: The Struggle against Indian Removal in the 1830s," *Journal of American History* 86 ( June 1999): 15–40. Permission granted by Copyright Clearance Center.

prompted some reformers to rethink their position on abolition and to reject African colonization in favor of immediatism.

The strength of antiremoval forces stunned Martin Van Buren who, writing of the events over twenty years later, portrayed the government's side as besieged from all quarters and stated flatly that "a more persevering opposition to a public measure had scarcely ever been made." Though Jackson's former vice president consistently defended removal, he believed that the issue of Indian removal "unlike histories of many great questions which agitate the public mind in their day will in all probability endure . . . as long as the government itself, and will in time occupy the minds and feelings of our people." It was an issue, Van Buren concluded, in which the nation was responsible "to the opinion of the great family of nations, as it involves the course we have pursued and shall pursue towards a people comparatively weak." . . .

President Jackson's proposed legislation to move the Southeast Indians across the Mississippi was not new. The heart of Indian land policy had always been nothing less than massive Indian land cessions to white markets, and treaties were the preferred weapons of transfer. The removal crisis of Jackson's administration was precipitated by the Georgia Compact of 1802 between the national government and Georgia (an agreement to which no Indian group was party), which provided that Georgia would relinquish all claims to western lands in return for Washington's assuming the costs of moving Indians off land that Georgia claimed "as soon as the same can be peaceably obtained on reasonable terms." Between 1802 and 1819, federal treaties with the southern Indians transferred 20 million acres of land to white settlers, a greater expansion of the territory open to slaveholding than the Missouri Compromise had provided. By 1819 only 5 million acres of land were left to the Cherokee, and when they refused to cede any more land, Georgia officials called on the federal government to remove the Indians by force, if necessary. For years the federal government resisted those demands, but Jackson's election brought, for the first time, an executive who wholeheartedly favored such removal.

President Jackson offered two rationales for Indian removal: one, that having an independent Indian nation residing within the borders of any state was an intolerable situation, and two, that for their own survival, southeastern Indians had to move across the Mississippi away from white encroachment. Jackson and other removal proponents insisted that should the southern Indians remain east of the Mississippi, they would shortly become "extinct" as whites steadily invaded their land and destroyed Indian life and culture. Moving the Indians west, Jackson argued, would solve both of those difficulties and preserve the Indians. Critics pointed out that the removal solution conveniently increased vast and valuable acreage for white settlers and that land transfer was the real goal, humanitarian concerns to halt Indian "extinction" notwithstanding.

Andrew Jackson's pursuit of Indian removal took by surprise many Americans who had believed that under presidents James Monroe and John Quincy Adams the federal government's Indian policy was becoming more, rather than less, beneficent. The dismay aroused by President Jackson's position was followed by shock at the speed with which Georgia legislators moved to reap the benefits of his election. Indian removal by force, if necessary, simultaneously dispossessed Indians and increased demand for slave labor in the seized territory. As such, it involved the political issues of the day that roiled American politics most: relations with Indians, relations with Africans, states' rights, and the potential growth of the system of slave labor. That American reform organizations, originally formed to improve the American character through voluntary moral persuasion, organized a powerful challenge to Jackson's removal goals was not coincidental. As a proposed federal action, Indian removal symbolized to them a rupture in the national fabric, a portentous triumph of the market values of aggressive acquisitiveness that placed a monetary value on everything and encouraged human exploitation for commercial gain. "How long shall it be that a Christian people . . . shall stand balancing the considerations of profit and loss on a national question of justice and benevolence?" asked the young theological student George Cheever in response to Andrew Jackson's removal bill. Benevolence involved a search for the general good, for principles of universal application, a willingness to sacrifice for the benefit of those in need. Indian removal appeared to Cheever the direct opposite — an unrestrained striving for individual gain at the expense of the less fortunate. If Indian removal was a striking example of commercial injustice, equally so was its consequence — millions of additional acres for an intensified slave labor system that carried those market values to their destructive end. It is not surprising that throughout the 1820s and into the following decade, issues of Indian policy and Indian removal received more attention in the nation's periodicals than did issues of tariffs and the Bank of the United States.

Opposition to removal can be measured through the new denomination-based periodicals of the 1820s and 1830s, which developed an early and decisive stance against removal. These religious organs were by far the most widely circulated of all periodicals at the time, enjoying a readership far larger and more diverse than that of the traditional party and secular periodicals, whose circulations rarely exceeded 1,500 copies and whose audiences were primarily male and elite. At a time when the esteemed *North American Review* had a circulation of only 3,000, thirty religious periodicals reported subscription lists of 3,000 or more, with fifteen of those having over 5,000 subscribers each. The Methodist *Christian Advocate and Journal* had a subscription list of 25,000, the Presbyterian *New York Observer* over 6,000, the American Board of Commissioners for Foreign Missions (Congregational) *Missionary Herald* 14,000, the *Religious Intelligencer* 5,000, *Zion's Herald* 6,000, and the Congregational *Boston Recorder* over 5,000. Arthur Tappan's evangelical *New York Journal of Commerce* far outsold every other newspaper in New York. All of these periodicals opposed removal on grounds that it violated legal treaties and that the southern Indians' practices of agriculture and commerce had made them virtually indistinguishable from the white farmers of Georgia. When southern officials portrayed Southeast Indians as nomadic hunters who could not make their land productive, these papers responded by characterizing removal proponents as motivated primarily by greed, favoring removal because of the considerable Indian assets it transferred, at little cost, to whites.

Another indicator of deep dissent from Indian removal was the organized opposition of women in towns and communities across the nation. Denied political standing by the nation's founders, women in the new republic had developed the concept of republican motherhood, which implied that women's interests could diverge from those of the male electorate and recognized women's role in promoting public virtue. Republican motherhood sanctioned women's petitions on widows' pensions and employment and on behalf of the needy in their communities. In these experiences, women made themselves subjects in the early republic, a status removed from full citizenship but one that laid on women an obligation to act as moral guardians of the nation's virtue, a duty that required a public presence and public activities. To achieve these ends, women created their own organizations and societies to improve social life and alleviate the harsher consequences of the market economy for urban and rural life.

The new denomination-based newspapers undermined traditional political hierarchies in their pages by according women's work a status equal to men's public activities. They printed side by side accounts of women's benevolent activities, men's political campaigns and elections, articles on the health of women and children, marriage announcements, details of legislative activity, reports of mission achievements. In the new newspapers, the sharp partisanship that characterized the traditional political press was absent. That absence implicitly de-emphasized the importance of a formal politics that excluded women while it justified women's public work on behalf of others within civic society.

Many women's charitable organizations made their priority the missions and schools for American Indians in the American South and the Northeast, and their philanthropy was markedly personal; they corresponded regularly with missionaries and Indian students at the mission schools and spoke of them as personal friends. . . . Women organized collections of foodstuffs, fabric, writing materials, books, and money to educate Indian youths, whose names and life stories they knew, and to support the missionaries who taught them. During the 1820s, women regularly sponsored Indian youth and community leaders from the Southeast as they toured northern areas and spoke to overflow public crowds about the schools and agricultural progress in their communities. In 1824, when Georgia representatives opposed federal appropriations of money for schools and agriculture in Cherokee territory, arguing that the Cherokees were becoming "extinct" anyway and had hardly any schools and even less agriculture, denominational periodicals ran lengthy responses from southern Indians and printed tables detailing the number of Cherokee schools and scholars, their extensive agriculture and commerce. Furthermore, they pointed out, the history of white dealings with Indian tribes contained many "blots on the character of our ancestors and of our nation." In this climate, the *Missionary Herald* found it instructive to print an account of the 1782 massacre by a white mob of over ninety Moravian Indians at Gnadenhutten.

By 1830, the benevolent community, imbued with a vision of a nation governed by universal principles of justice, aided by mission reports throughout the religious periodicals that stressed the perspective of the Indians, and benefitting from the inclusion of women's concerns and work, had developed a clear position against the coerced removal of southern Indians that was forcefully expressed in the widely circulated religious press. Opponents of removal believed that Americans had made an implicit promise to the Indians: If they adopted European agricultural practices, they would be granted the same rights and privileges as white settlers. The Cherokees' success in mastering European techniques and culture, along with the enormity of the Cherokee removal, the organized and articulate opposition of the Cherokee themselves, and the fact that removal would open vast new areas to the slave labor system, made this case appear unique to antiremovalists. Each time that the state of Georgia wrested new land concessions from the Cherokee or demanded federal aid in forcing their removal, protest increased. Readers of the denomination papers read regular reports such as the *Boston Recorder*'s account of a cession of Cherokee territory in 1824 that quoted an elderly Indian as saying that he was "afraid of the white people and distressed for his children lest they be driven from the earth. . . . White people kill my people and no notice is taken of it." The *Missionary Herald* printed a Cherokee woman's lengthy protest against land expropriation, which concluded that "white people seem to aim at our destruction. . . . This grieves me more than I can tell . . . we shall be driven away from the land of our fathers, which is as dear to us as our lives." The *Religious Intelligencer* went beyond merely defending the Indians to placing them in a superior moral position:

> Were any arguments necessary to prove the doctrine of total depravity, we
> might among other proofs, refer to the treatment which some of the Indian
> Tribes receive from the whites. . . . White men make inroads into the
> Indian Territories, destroy their game, and steal their furs. If the natives,
> indignant at such outrages, make any resistance, we immediately find arti-
> cles in newspapers, headed with "*Indian Barbarities, Murders, &c. &c.!!*"

When Georgia surveyors marked out Cherokee lands for distribution to white farmers in 1829, religious periodicals attacked state officials. The *Journal of Commerce* said that the proceedings "awaken our indignation and lead us almost to wish that the Cherokees had the power to vindicate their rights and chastise their oppressors." The *Missionary Herald* declared that Georgia state officials were engaged in a massive land grab and told its readers that "now is the time when every Christian, every philanthropist and every patriot in the United States ought to be exerting themselves to save a persecuted and defenceless people from ruin." The *Hamilton* [Ohio] *Intelligencer* asserted that the Indians were "the living monuments of the white man's wrongs."

After Jackson's election in 1828, Georgia legislators added, by fiat, Cherokee lands to the northwestern counties of Georgia, forbade Cherokee gold mining, nullified all Cherokee laws, and prohibited Indians from testifying against whites in court. Alabama and Mississippi quickly followed suit. For men and women attentive to Indian issues, the time was short. The president-elect would be inaugurated in March 1829, and a new Congress would convene the following December. Denominational periodicals already carried antiremoval sentiments, and voluntary reform associations provided an organizational network for opposing the legislation. The first attacks on removal came from these quarters, and they initially followed the established boundaries of political tradition: Public meetings were called on the issue, petitions drawn up, and pamphlets printed.

This early opposition came from every region of the country: from the South, even from Georgia itself; from the Northwest, throughout Ohio and the city of Pittsburgh; from the New England states; and from northeastern cities, including Boston, New York, and Philadelphia. It particularly captured the imagination and fervor of the nation's young adults, the second generation of reformers. When Angelina Grimké left Charleston for Philadelphia in 1829, before she became a Quaker or an abolitionist, the strongest political references in her letters back home were sharp objections to the Indian Removal Bill. Likewise, the only political references in the letters of young Harriet Beecher are enthusiastic reports of her work in the women's petition campaign to oppose Indian removal. George Cheever, a future leader in the abolitionist movement and a student at Andover Seminary during the removal crisis, led antiremoval efforts there, organizing public meetings and petitions and even taking on Lewis Cass, governor of the territory of Michigan and a strong proponent of Indian removal. "Nothing can save us," Cheever wrote in castigating Cass's defense of Indian removal, "unless the public mind be universally aroused from its lethargy, and an appeal made, so loud, simultaneous, and decisive, as shall astonish the world at the power of moral feeling in the heart of the country, and cause the most inveterate and bold supporters of national iniquity to tremble." . . .

As the campaign against removal spread, Jeremiah Evarts, a lawyer and commissioner of the American Board of Commissioners for Foreign Missions, pulled removal opponents' broad arguments into a legal treatise known as *The "William Penn" Essays*. The essays offered detailed information on the past treaties between the Southeast Indians and the United States that had established the Indians as legal possessors of their then remaining lands. Evarts argued eloquently that forced removal would constitute a grave legal breach, and his appeal for justice found a ready audience. The mass public bought, read, and discussed the Penn essays, which were reprinted in more than a hundred newspapers and published as pamphlets that blanketed the country. They were, according to a contemporary, read by more than half a million people during the summer of 1829.

Even before the Indian Removal Act was introduced in Congress in 1830, petition drives against it spread throughout the nation, and the religious periodicals uniformly endorsed them, reporting on local petition efforts and reprinting a steady stream of newspaper accounts of petition campaigns in other areas. In Washington, Pittsburgh, Boston, Hartford, Philadelphia, New York, and towns in the Midwest and South, opponents called public meetings and drew up petitions to defeat the removal bill. The petitions poured into Washington. "Having nearly exhausted my stock of memorials, I must ask for more," a professor at Amherst College wrote on February 20, 1830, "I should want 15 or 20 copies more, at least." College presidents exhorted students to send petitions to Congress; at other colleges, students led the opposition. In some cities, mayors chaired the public meetings called to draw up petitions. In New York City two thousand people gathered in the Masonic Hall to draw up a petition against removal. A Pennsylvania representative noted in disbelief that in his notably quiet district, people were holding large and enthusiastic public meetings to petition Congress on the bill. In Brown County along the Ohio River just east of Cincinnati, over two hundred men signed a petition calling the removal act "cruel, unjust, and disgraceful." At a meeting in Boston to consider a petition to Congress on Sunday mails, the petitioners also drew up one on Indian removal and sent it to Congress. In Tallmadge, Ohio, over one hundred men signed petitions opposing Indian removal. "The tables of the members (of Congress) are covered with pamphlets devoted to the discussions of the Indian question," the congressional correspondent for the *Journal of Commerce* wrote in late March. "There is a mighty movement in the land on this subject." The *Christian Watchman*, the largest-circulation Baptist periodical, declared that "it must be gratifying to every citizen who loves equal and exact justice to notice the feeling which is now excited in the community in relation to the rights of the Aborigines of this country."

Popular opposition to Jackson's removal bill overwhelmed traditional forms of political participation. The massive outpouring of pamphlets and petitions itself was unprecedented. The demand for Jeremiah Evarts's Penn essays was so great that they were more widely distributed and read in the summer of 1829 than any political pamphlet since Thomas Paine's *Common Sense*. Not only did men send an unprecedented number of petitions, women began to draw up and circulate their own petitions opposing removal, the first time that they did so on a national political issue. Ultimately, some opponents of removal went to prison rather than comply with Georgia's removal laws. The political crisis that the popular political activism created resulted in two Supreme Court decisions against the administration's position on removal, decisions that an embattled and defiant president ignored.

To defeat removal, Catharine Beecher initiated the first national petition drive by women. During the summer of 1829, she heard Jeremiah Evarts speak in Boston on the prospect of Indian removal. He asked her, Beecher recalled in her memoirs, published in the 1870s, to do what she could to avert the tragedy. When Beecher returned to the Hartford Female Seminary, where she was director, she called together some friends, including Lydia Sigourney, a popular writer and poet, to discuss the impending removal bill. The women immediately resolved to draw up a petition opposing removal and to send copies to female acquaintances throughout the country.

A national women's petition drive was unprecedented, and the Hartford group decided to conceal its own role in organizing it. In her memoirs, Beecher did not indicate why she opted for anonymity. It was not because she hoped that the public would assume the petition was organized by men, for the circular asserted that it was prepared and sent solely by women. Perhaps she feared personal condemnation. If so, she was certainly vindicated, for removal proponents in Congress seized the women's circular as a point of attack on removal opponents. In any case, the requirements for organizing a petition campaign anonymously impeded it; Beecher even felt compelled to swear the printer to secrecy. To compile their mailing list, the Hartford women relied on the network of benevolent women's associations, drawing up names and addresses of their friends and acquaintances throughout cities across the nation. It was remarkable, Beecher said, how many names they collected in this first step. Sending out the circular from Hartford would risk exposing their involvement, so Beecher arranged to have all of the petitions sent on the same day from four different cities, but none from Hartford itself. Each recipient was asked to send copies of the circular to friends, or to draw up her own petition, and to assemble public meetings on behalf of the Cherokees, gathering as many signatures as possible to sway the representatives in Congress. Through it all, they were asked to pray "for the intervention of the National Government to protect the Indians." The Hartford women maintained their secrecy so completely that they began to be solicited to sign copies of their own petition.

The Ladies' Circular, as it came to be called, addressed itself first to "benevolent ladies of the United States" and urged them to combine piety and politics by using both "prayers and exertions to avert the calamity of removal." It depicted the Indians of the United States as "saviors" of the Europeans in times past, supplying their necessities in crucial periods and, by now, as "fitted by native talents" as any other American for intellectual and refined pursuits. Legal treaties guaranteed the southern Indians their lands, the circular argued, and Beecher inserted parts of past treaties to prove the point. The claims that Georgia made on the Cherokee rose primarily from acquisitive, not legal, motives, the circular said: "the lands of this people are *claimed* to be embraced within the limits of some of our southern states, and as they are fertile and valuable they are demanded by the whites as their own possessions, and efforts are making to dispossess the Indians of their native soil."

The circular then appealed directly to women to join the political struggle against removal. "Have not the females of this country some duties devolving upon them in relation to this helpless race?" it asked. Indeed, the circular asserted, women should exercise the same benevolent influence in alleviating the plight of the Indians as they already did in aiding the needy in their own communities. Benevolent women could exert legislative pressure in this instance because the Indians needed it — that itself represented a moral imperative. Beyond that, the circular drew on a biblical model for dealing with a people in crisis, the account of Esther, who approached the king to plead for her people's existence. Women, the circular argued:

> are protected from the blinding influence of party spirit, and the asperities of political violence. They have nothing to do with any struggle for power, nor any right to dictate the decisions of those that rule over them. But they may *feel* for the distressed; they may stretch out the supplicating hand for them, and by their prayers strive to avert the calamities that are impending over them. It may be, that female petitioners can lawfully be heard, even by the highest rulers of our land. . . . It may be this will be *forbidden*; yet we still remember the Jewish princess who, being sent to supplicate for a nation's life, was thus reproved for hesitating even when *death* stared her in the way: "If thou altogether hold thy peace at this time, then shall deliverance arise from another place; but thou and thy father's house shall be destroyed. And who knoweth whether thou art come to the kingdom for such a time as this?"

The circular urged haste, "A *few weeks* must decide this interesting and important question, and after that time sympathy and regret will be in vain." It asserted its female authorship and called all women to action: "This communication was written and sent abroad solely by the female hand. Let every woman who peruses it, exert that influence in society which falls within her lawful province, and endeavour by every suitable expedient to interest the feelings of her friends, relatives, and acquaintances, in behalf of this people, that are ready to perish."

The result of their petition efforts, Beecher wrote, "exceeded our most sanguine expectations." The women who received the Hartford petitions called public meetings against removal where they drew up their own petitions for signatures, and they set out to enlist friends and neighbors in the campaign. The petition campaign spurred other political activities; some women organized the Ladies Association for Supplicating Justice and Mercy Toward the Indians, which met regularly to send antiremoval petitions to Congress. Petitions signed by hundreds of women began pouring into Congress, a feat that many newspapers noted with astonishment. The largest single petition came from Pittsburgh, where 670 women signed and sent it to the Senate. In organizing to defeat removal, many women viewed themselves as continuing work to which they had long been accustomed. For twenty years they had donated money and materials for Indian schools. In their periodicals they read regular reports from Indian missions that provided an Indian perspective on removal. Women were familiar with local petitioning for the welfare of specific individuals and groups; they had grown accustomed to seeing women's concerns given equal status in their periodicals; they felt a sense of mission as guardians of national virtue. Allocating federal funds to force Indian removal threatened Indians whom they had heard speak in their churches and homes, whose writings they had read in their periodicals, and who appeared fully deserving of legal protection.

The circular succeeded in deluging Congress with women's petitions, but fear of being found out took its toll on Catharine Beecher. She frequently found herself in conversations that turned to the question of the circular's author, and she had, she said, "many narrow escapes from falsehood in efforts to preserve our secret." When someone asked her once who she supposed wrote the circular, she replied that, though some attributed it to Lydia Sigourney, she thought it was not like Sigourney's writing style but more like that of a man whom Beecher named, thereby "escaping" without revealing her own authorship but directly contradicting the circular itself, which flatly declared its female origin. In writing of the campaign years later, she said that "not at all aware of the consequences of this additional excitement, I suddenly found myself utterly prostrated and unable to perform any school duty without extreme pain and such confusion of thought as seemed like approaching insanity." She went to recover at the home of friends, leaving others, including her sister Harriet, to carry out her duties at the Hartford Female Seminary. Harriet thrived in her new responsibilities, sending enthusiastic letters to Catharine about the work involving the circular. "Last night we teachers sat up till eleven o'clock finishing our Cherokee letters," she wrote, adding that speculation still abounded about the likely author. The success of the circular, and her knowledge that it was written by her older sister, inspired the future author of *Uncle Tom's Cabin* to write that "the excitement, I hope, is but just begun. So 'great effects come from little causes.'"

The women's petition campaign drew criticism from some antiremovalists and from congressional Democrats, with one crucial difference: objections from the former were muted and temporary, while the latter offered harsh and persistent criticism. Some editors of denomination periodicals initially expressed dismay at women's political petitions to Congress, but they also printed the circular in their newspapers, thereby spreading public awareness of the campaign and increasing its success. Among antiremovalists, objections to the Ladies' Circular were undercut by the realization that it represented a new source of political assistance. Henry Clay, for example, noted the practical advantage of using women's political organizing in defeating removal when he pointed out to Jeremiah Evarts that "the female sex is generally on [the Indians'] side, and a cooperation between that and the clergy would have a powerful, if not decisive, influence." . . .

In contrast, congressional Democrats subjected the women's petitions to unalloyed criticism, castigating antiremoval men for failing to keep their women out of political debate and faulting the petitions for undermining political order and the norms of chivalry. They scorned women for taking up congressional time with their petitions and depicted the benevolent men who supported women's political activity as effeminate. Thomas Hart Benton, chairman of the Senate Committee on Indian Affairs, summed up Democratic sentiments when he mockingly described a "vision" he had of the antiremovalists, both men and women marching under a single banner, the females, he said, having "earned the place by the part they are acting in the public meetings for the instruction of Congress on the subject of these Georgia Indians." . . .

Andrew Jackson had placed Indian removal at the top of his policy priorities, and the storm of opposition it created seemed to baffle the president, who tried, unsuccessfully, to counter the organized opposition by manufacturing an alternative base of benevolent support for removal. Thomas McKenney, head of the Indian Office in the War Department, formed what he called the Indian Board for the Emigration, Preservation, and Improvement of the Aborigines of America and set out to recruit religious figures to promote removal. He hoped to duplicate the antiremovalists' tactics by organizing public meetings, drawing up a public petition for removal, and publishing proremoval pamphlets. But the Indian Board generated scant support beyond McKenney's office, and it soon collapsed. Another administration effort cultivated Isaac McCoy, a former Baptist missionary who supported removal. Although McCoy had gone on the government payroll in 1828 as a surveyor of Indian lands, the Jackson administration used his former status as a Baptist missionary to claim that removal had Baptist support. McCoy was not representative of the Baptist mission board's position, and tensions between him and that board grew more pronounced as the removal crisis intensified. In 1830 the Baptist board flatly refused to endorse McCoy's petition favoring removal. The Baptist *Christian Watchman* subsequently printed on its front page a stinging criticism of McCoy's efforts to put the Baptist stamp of approval on removal. Because of McCoy, the article said, it was now necessary "to correct the false impression that is now going on in the public mind that the Baptists are engaged with the Georgians or others in removing the Indians *against their will.*" Baptists were completely opposed to removal efforts, the article said, and for good measure the editor signed the writer's name as "Veritas." McCoy later began his own separate Baptist Mission Board, which was supported by the Southern Baptist churches after the split over slavery in the 1840s.

Opposition to the removal bill made its passage more difficult than Jackson had envisioned. The Senate passed the bill by a vote of 28 to 19 on April 24, 1830. The House margin on May 26 was narrower: 102 to 97. Southern representatives, their numbers swelled by the three-fifths clause, voted heavily in favor of the bill; representatives from the rest of the country voted two to one against it. The House vote was so close that Jackson held his veto of the Maysville Road project in check, fearing that if aid to the road were vetoed first, Congress would reject Indian removal. When the veto came down immediately after the removal act passed the House, congressional opponents tried to retrieve the bill before it reached the president's desk, hoping that Congress could reconsider it, but it was beyond their legislative reach.

The Cherokees immediately appealed to the Supreme Court to strike down Georgia's attempt to legislate for them. Spirited public meetings continued, petitions poured once again into Congress, and periodicals carried lengthy articles defending Cherokee rights. In March 1831, in *Cherokee Nation v. Georgia*, the Supreme Court concurred that the laws of the state of Georgia could have no force over the Cherokee, who were protected by federal treaties that gave them full rights to their lands. Though the Court also acknowledged that the legal status of the Cherokee placed them outside its jurisdiction, opponents of removal were cheered by its endorsement of their position. The president remained determined to coerce Indian removal, and he responded by defiantly withdrawing federal troops from Georgia, leaving no buffer between the Cherokee and the state, which moved immediately to force the Indians out.

The Georgia legislature then passed a law aimed at missionaries in Cherokee territory, requiring that all white men living within the now-appropriated Cherokee lands apply for, and receive, licenses from the state of Georgia or face prison. Applying for the license included swearing an oath of allegiance to all of Georgia's laws, and most of the missionaries refused to do so. In repeated incidents over a dozen missionaries were chained and marched to prisons where they were unsuccessfully pressured to sign documents promising to leave Georgia. Female missionaries were not included in the legislation, and as the male missionaries were arrested over the next months, they took over the running of mission operations. The denomination periodicals covered these events with outraged astonishment, printing dispatches from the missionaries describing their repeated and lengthy detainment and harassment by Georgia state officials in violation of civil and criminal laws. . . .

When the Jackson administration ignored Georgia's actions, officials there brought charges against the missionaries for refusing to apply for the newly required license. In September 1831 a Georgia jury convicted eleven of the missionaries on this charge. They were sentenced to expulsion or four years' hard labor in the penitentiary. Nine were expelled, but two, Samuel Worcester and Elizur Butler, elected to serve their terms and appeal to the United States Supreme Court. They were marched in chains to the state penitentiary in Milledgeville. As their appeal wound its way through the court system, petitions pleading for legislative redress for the missionaries poured into Congress. The Supreme Court's decision, *Worcester v. Georgia*, came down in early 1832, ruling that, based on previous treaties, the Cherokee nation was a "distinct community" over which the laws of Georgia were null and void and ordered that the missionaries be released.

The court's decision granted the opponents of the removal bill one brief euphoric moment of victory. Arthur Tappan carried the news directly from Washington to Boston where, one observer said, "no event since the organization of the government, except perhaps the treaty of peace, has created a livelier sensation of joy . . . than this decision of the Supreme Court." In Boston, Lyman Beecher heard the news of the Court's decision from Elias Boudinot, the Cherokee editor of the *Cherokee Phoenix*, who was then on a lecture tour in the Northeast. When Beecher heard the news, Boudinot said, he "jumped up, clapped his hands, took hold of my hand and said 'God be praised,' and rushed out to tell his family." At that moment Boudinot believed that the Court's decision "creates a new era on the Indian question." But it soon became clear that the ruling would never be enforced. Georgia threatened violent resistance if blocked and refused to release Worcester and Butler. After Andrew Jackson was reelected that year, the state of Georgia expelled the two missionaries.

The deep divisions over removal touched even the vice president's family. Martin Van Buren recalled that his own niece, whom he admired, fiercely denounced him for his role in removal. During the 1832 election season, when he was a guest in her house, she told him sharply that she earnestly hoped that he and Jackson would lose the election because "such a result ought to follow such acts!" Though the Indians were finally removed, Van Buren wrote, it was a hard struggle because opponents of Indian removal received what he called a "full and unfair measure of cooperation" from "the Press, the Courts of law and last, tho' far from the least in power and influence, the Church." . . .

In looking back on the passage of the removal bill, Van Buren gave generous credit to the president that he had served under. "It was his judgment, his experience, his indomitable vigor and unrestrained activity that secured success. There was no measure in the whole course of his administration of which he was more exclusively the author than this. His was the hand, mind, and spirit that controlled throughout." But the former president also concluded that the widespread and fierce opposition to the Indian Removal Act and the success of its opponents in portraying removal as unjust had forever diminished Jackson's legislative victory. Van Buren lamented that "the credit which has been awarded to him for the effective aid he rendered to his country by his policy in respect to Indian affairs and by the success with which it was executed has fallen far short of his desserts." . . .

Antiremovalists failed to defeat the removal bill, but the experience provided reform women with political skills valuable in subsequent anti-slavery and woman suffrage campaigns. Writing antiremoval petitions and gathering signatures for them required attention to legal details and skill in defining public issues in compelling and persuasive language. Petitioning provided women with a means of measuring support in their communities, opportunities to educate other women on issues, and a sense of achieving concrete results. It could also be discouraging. Catharine Beecher's writings contain no response to the congressional attacks on the Ladies' Circular, but her unsettling experience in that endeavor seems to have contributed to the end of both her work at the Hartford Seminary and her advocacy of women's political petitioning. In 1837, after Congress had responded to the flood of petitions on slavery by passing the Pinckney gag rule, Beecher wrote a lengthy treatise on the role of women in the antislavery struggle, and she dealt with the issue of women's petitions in a manner that recalled Thomas Hart Benton's attacks on her petition campaign:

> If petitions from females will operate to exasperate; if they will be deemed obtrusive, indecorous, and unwise, by those to whom they are addressed; if they will increase, rather than diminish the evil which it is wished to remove; if they will be the opening wedge, that will tend eventually to bring females as petitioners and partisans into every political measure that may tend to injure and oppress their sex, in various parts of the nation, and under the various public measures that may hereafter be enforced, then it is neither appropriate nor wise, nor right, for a woman to petition for the relief of oppressed females.

The case of Esther, Beecher concluded, was a suitable precedent only when a woman was faced literally with the destruction of herself and her nation; when death was imminent, "then she may safely follow such an example." But when a woman was asked to join an abolition society or put her name on a petition to Congress, "the case of Queen Esther is not at all to be regarded as a suitable example for imitation." In this country, Beecher went on, "petitions to congress, in reference to the official duties of legislators, seem, *in all cases*, to fall entirely without the sphere of female duty." Women's responsibility, she said, was to induce men to petition for just legislation. Beecher's breakdown over the stress of the petition campaign marked a retreat from political activity. She became a critic of both immediatism and women's political rights.

If the experience of mass political petitioning ultimately made Beecher opt for traditional politics, it had a different effect on others. For example, from the time of her marriage in 1819, Lydia Sigourney had published all her writings anonymously because her husband did not want her to use her name in her writings. In 1832, after her considerable efforts in the antiremoval campaign, Sigourney's writings began appearing under her own name despite her husband's objections. Angelina Grimké, who was captivated by the women's petition campaign, subsequently adopted the position that women had the right to petition Congress on all issues. "The fact that women are denied the right of voting for members of Congress, is but a poor reason why they should also be deprived of the right of petition. If their numbers are counted to swell the number of representatives in our State and National legislation, the *very least* that can be done is to give them the right of petition in all cases whatsoever; and without any abridgement," Grimké declared in a public reply to Beecher's argument against women's right to petition.

Experience in opposing Indian removal also dampened support for African colonization. Before 1830, colonization efforts received broad political support and colonization societies raised large sums. As the debate over

Indian removal intensified, colonization supporters who opposed removal grew discomfited by the strong similarities between the two issues, discovering that they opposed removal in one case but supported it in the other. If he worked for African colonization while opposing Indian removal, an uncomfortable rationalizer wrote in late 1829, it was only because colonization was, in part, "a remuneration of past injury." Delineating differences between the two removals could not obscure their similarities, and ultimately the experience of opposing Indian removal prompted some reformers to rethink their stand on slavery, rejecting African colonization in favor of immediatism and embarking on a determined campaign to stop what they feared would be a second removal injustice.

Most of the immediatist leaders of the 1830s had been colonizationists during the 1820s. They had also been antiremovalists at the turn of the decade. Roberts Vaux, Angelina Grimké, Theodore Weld, Beriah Green, Charles Storrs, Elizur Wright Jr., Lydia Maria Child, Arthur Tappan, Benjamin Lundy, and James Birney, among many others, supported colonization efforts during the 1820s, but all of them opposed removal and later became outspoken immediatists. William Lloyd Garrison delivered a supportive Fourth of July colonization address in 1829, but by January 1831 he had made what he called a "full and unequivocal recantation" of the "pernicious doctrine of *gradual* abolition."

Historical explanations for the remarkable surge of a new abolitionism after 1830 have usually centered on three factors: the abolitionists' sense of social displacement, their ethical commitment to the oppressed, or their religious beliefs. Some of the most prominent abolitionist leaders also drew explicit parallels between their opposition to Indian removal and their opposition to colonization. At the very time when Garrison delivered the Fourth of July colonization address in Boston's Park Street Church in 1829, he began to denounce removal in harsh terms. As coeditor, with Benjamin Lundy, of the *Genius of Universal Emancipation*, Garrison regularly printed strong denunciations of removal in the paper, often including excerpts from the *Cherokee Phoenix* and the *Savannah Mercury*. When Jackson brought in federal government troops to help Georgia dispossess Indians, the *Genius* declared that forcible removal "would brand this country with eternal infamy," and Garrison declared that "we are a nation of tyrants, and the bent of our legislation is oppressive. God of heaven! When shall equity prevail on the earth and the rights of thy creatures be protected from domestic invasion?" In December 1829 the *Genius* printed Jackson's annual message in its entirety and urged readers to pay especial attention to the portion that related to the Cherokee. . . .

Garrison then used the removal act to denounce colonization directly. In 1832, when he published *Thoughts on African Colonization*, his powerful attack on the American Colonization Society, Garrison devoted half of that argument to describing Negro rejection of colonization and chose a comparison that many of his fellow reformers would instantly understand: "they are as unanimously opposed to a removal to Africa, as the Cherokees from the council-fires and graves of their fathers," he asserted.

The *Liberator* continued to carry the latest news on the removal crisis, and for years Garrison distributed pamphlets on what his children called the "wrongs of the red man."

The prominent abolitionist James Birney also linked African colonization to Indian removal. When Birney, who had provided legal services to the Cherokee during the 1820s, resigned as vice-president of the Colonization Society of Kentucky, he wrote a widely distributed open letter explaining his new opposition to colonization as stemming from its parallels with the recent removal act. Birney pointed out to his readers "the very great resemblance this case bears in its most prominent features to that of the Indians who have been moved upon, in nearly the same measure to 'consent' to leave their lands within the limits of several of the states." Slaves often were freed only on the condition they go to Liberia, he said, and sometimes consent was gained by unfair pressures, often the same kind of consent that he had seen extorted from the Indians. . . .

Another prominent abolitionist, Elizur Wright Jr., also supported the American Colonization Society through 1829, when he presented its Fourth of July fund-raising address in his hometown. That fall Wright helped lead opposition to removal at Western Reserve College, where he was a professor of mathematics. After the removal bill passed, he publicly repudiated colonization and funneled his energies into the American Anti-Slavery Society, becoming its secretary for domestic correspondence. Wright charged that colonization to Liberia merely repeated in Africa the same pattern that had been followed with American Indians, and he set out to convert others to immediatism. His colleagues at Western Reserve College, Beriah Green and Charles Storrs, were also antiremovalists who went from that cause directly into immediatism. After Theodore Weld spent several weeks at Western Reserve College in October 1832, he likewise abandoned colonization for immediatism. . . .

George Cheever, the student at Andover Seminary who led the antiremoval campaign there, well expressed the passion that antiremovalists carried with them into radical abolition. "The passage of the Indian bill has disgraced us as a people, has wounded our national honor, and exposed us to the merited reproach of all civilized communities in the world," he concluded when the bill passed. "We would rather have a civil war, were there no other alternative, than avoid it by taking shelter in crime," Cheever said later of his opposition to Indian removal. "We would take up arms for the Indians in such a war," he went on, anticipating sentiments that many abolitionists later expressed in opposition to slavery. The Ladies' Circular had similarly raised the prospect of a civil war over the removal issue, saying that the president had the power "to command *the whole military force of our nation* to protect and sustain the Indian in his rights."

Protesting Indian removal encouraged antiremovalists to challenge slavery directly. The antislavery upsurge in the early 1830s benefitted from the deep disappointment of antiremovalists who vowed not to repeat that process by removing Africans through colonization policies, and to defeat the Democratic party — the party of removal — on slavery. The Indian

Removal Act made abolitionists bolder in acting against slavery and more determined to achieve their goals.

Whether Andrew Jackson's presidency fostered an increase in democratic participation may be debated, but credit for an enlarged democracy may accrue to him by default, for his determination to carry out Indian removal generated the deepest political movement that the country had yet witnessed. It also ushered in a new age of popular politics that saw energized antiremovalists transfer their techniques of removal protest to the struggle against slavery: massive and continuous pamphleting and petitioning by both women and men, persistent reports in periodicals that sought to present slavery from the perspective of the slave, and a willingness to challenge laws that they believed were deeply unjust.

## LORI D. GINZBERG

# *from* "Moral Suasion Is Moral Balderdash": Women, Politics, and Social Activism in the 1850s   [1986]

**LORI D. GINZBERG** (1957– ) is assistant professor of history and women's studies at Pennsylvania State University. She is the author of *Women and the Work of Benevolence: Morality, Politics, and Class in the Nineteenth Century United States* (1990).

As a result of the Second Great Awakening of the 1820s and early 1830s, a millennial spirit pervaded efforts at transforming United States society. Abolitionists, vegetarians, temperance activists, and crusaders against "male lust" — "ultraists" in nineteenth-century terms — sought not merely social change but spiritual transformation, the moral regeneration of the world. That evangelical impulse, as numerous historians have argued, provided the framework in which radical social change was articulated in the antebellum period. American middle-class radicalism in the 1830s and 1840s evolved in a religious context, one in which the regeneration of individuals would precede — and assure — the salvation of society.

Women played a central role both in the ideology and in the means of the proposed national transformation. Viewed as inherently moral, women were to instruct by example and to participate in movements for social, or moral, change. Moral suasion, the chosen means for those who sought nothing less than the transformation of the public soul, conformed both to women's supposed qualities and to the nature of their access to those in power.

Lori D. Ginzberg, "'Moral Suasion Is Moral Balderdash': Women, Politics, and Social Activism in the 1850s," *Journal of American History* 73 (December 1986). Permission granted by Copyright Clearance Center.

For a brief period in the 1830s, ultraist women called on men to adhere to a single — "female" — standard of behavior in the interest of social change. Being voteless and, in theory, nonpartisan was part of the radical vision, and votelessness was a choice made with pride. "Far be it from me to encourage women to vote," declared Lucretia Mott in an early speech asserting women's right to do so, "or to take an active part in politics in the present state of our government. . . . Would that man, too, would have no participation in a government recognizing the life-taking principle." "As to [women's] ever becoming partisans, i.e., sacrificing principles to power or interest," wrote Angelina Grimké, "I reprobate this under all circumstances, and in *both* sexes." Access to the political process itself — long assumed by relatively elite and conservative women who petitioned legislators for legal changes, state funds, and corporate status for their organizations — represented to more radical activists the privileges of class, the advocacy of a traditional cause, and narrowness of vision. For ultraists, the adoption of "practical" means for change represented a retreat from principle, from the ideal of an aggressively Christian and implicitly "female" identity that would be shared by all. To those who believed that governments were ineffective at implementing fundamental change, "moral" power was the only kind worth exerting.

By the late 1840s, however, all but a few of the most "ultra" of reformers agreed that moral suasion had failed to transform society. Increasingly, reformers turned to electoral means and to institutional settings through which to consolidate the work of the previous decades. For women, who had been at the heart of the earlier movements, the shifting context of reform was especially momentous.

Two trends in the 1850s helped redefine both the rhetorical and the actual association of women with benevolent change. First, women reformers faced a narrowing definition of political action that emphasized electoral activity rather than the traditional forms of lobbying in which women had participated. As moral suasion became a less convincing call to action, ultraist women's influence in benevolent movements declined. Women became less prominent in a number of activities, such as petitioning, in which they had participated fully in the earlier decades. Voteless, women discovered that benevolent work's growing dependence on electoral means had by the 1850s rendered "female" means for change less effective and thus less popular.

At the same time, more conservative benevolent activists increasingly sought to alleviate social and moral conditions by founding benevolent institutions, often in close alliance with men. Earlier, women had refused male offers of organizational "assistance": When an 1803 legislative committee suggested that the "ladies" of the Boston Female Asylum permit male trustees to control their funds, the female managers "firmly opposed" the attempt to limit their autonomy, and the suggestion was withdrawn, apparently with little dispute. But in 1849, for example, the American Female Guardian Society engaged an advisory board composed of men. Conservative women's new reliance on male advisers suggests that they

too were finding traditional female avenues to political and economic favors
inadequate.

Both trends affected reformers' commitment to broad social change,
for the narrower focus on elections and on institutions corresponded to a
declining faith in the moral transformation of American society. To many
women in the "utilitarian" 1850s, who came to accept both the brick and
stone of institutionalized benevolence and the new emphasis on electoral
results, movements that called on slave-owners to free the slaves, drunkards to reject liquor, and seducers to protect the innocent had, quite simply,
failed. Substantial changes in the work of activists across the benevolent
spectrum signified a more limited, if perhaps more realistic, vision of the
possibilities for social change, as benevolent activists sought to restrain
the sins they had been unable to eradicate.

The changing nature of politics itself made the commitment to a nonvoting position increasingly anachronistic. Political parties organized
unprecedented numbers of voters in the antebellum decades, and voters
behaved as if voting mattered. Interest in presidential politics in particular increased greatly. The growing prestige of the vote is seen in the rising
percentage of eligible voters who actually bothered to cast ballots. Fewer
than 30 percent of adult white males, an unusually small percentage, voted
in the presidential election of 1824; in 1828 more than 57 percent did.
Voter turnout continued to rise dramatically. In 1840 more than 80 percent
of eligible voters, which by then included virtually all white men, went to
the polls. Only once more in the antebellum period did the percentage
of voters casting ballots in a presidential election top 80 percent (81.2 percent in 1860), but only once did it fall below 70 percent (69.6 percent in
1852). Increased voter participation was even more pronounced in some
northeastern states.

The editors of the *History of Woman Suffrage* recognized that a significant
change in the popular perception of elections occurred in 1840, when
women began to attend "political meetings, as with the introduction of
moral questions into legislation, they had manifested an increasing interest in government." In keeping with the growing concern for electoral
politics, activist movements increasingly framed their conception of social
change in terms of electoral means and goals. The 1850s witnessed a
burst of legislative activity on the part of women; hundreds and thousands
demanded their civil and political rights and joined men in appealing for
laws against alcohol, for removal of politicians and judges, and for corporate charters and funds for their organizations. Women's interest in legislation introduced them to a wider range of political issues. As one writer
for the *Lily* commented sarcastically, "The women of Seneca Falls have so
far dared to outstep their sphere as to go by scores and hundreds to the
political meetings recently held to discuss the constitutionality of the
Canal Bill, and to pass upon the conduct of the resigning Senators! And
what is more strange still, the men consented to it. . . . Yes, our ladies
have mingled at political meetings with the 'low rabble' who go to the polls."
The *Una* published regular and varied reports from a correspondent in

the visitors' gallery of the United States Senate. In 1854, for the benefit of its largely female readership, the paper added a column entitled "Acts of Legislatures."

Gradually ultraists among both sexes, including the most unyielding of "nonvoters," shifted their enthusiasm to elections in the decade or so before the Civil War. "I am rejoiced to say that Henry is heart and soul in the Republican movement," wrote Elizabeth Cady Stanton to Susan B. Anthony, adding that she herself had "attended all the Republican meetings." Such intense interest in electoral politics characterized the decade that Martha Coffin Wright feared for the attendance at the 1856 Woman's Rights Convention: "[The] engrossing subject of the coming elections," she wrote worriedly to Anthony, "will distract somewhat from the interest of anything not strictly political." Reformers' growing dependence on and interest in electoral politics underscored the powerlessness of a nonvoting position.

The temperance movement provides perhaps the best example of the decidedly "partisan political turn" taken by reformers in the late 1840s and the 1850s. Ironically, the shift toward electoral politics coincided with the entrance of significant numbers of women into temperance work and with the beginning of a long history of viewing temperance as a woman's issue. Its timing suggests that temperance women might have early become convinced of their own growing need for the ballot. Those women most identified with antebellum temperance — Mary C. Vaughan, Amelia Bloomer, and Susan B. Anthony — turned quickly to the emerging woman's movement's demand for suffrage for a new source of authority.

The *Lily*, Amelia Bloomer's paper, most self-consciously reflected the connection between the temperance movement of the 1850s and women's emerging recognition of the value of suffrage. "We have not much faith in moral suasion for the rumseller," the paper admitted in its third issue, as it advocated legislative solutions to problems associated with drunkenness. Over time, contributors — including the vociferous, although not typical, Elizabeth Cady Stanton — demanded that women have a share in the making of laws to restrict the sale of liquor and to permit wives to divorce intemperate men. The paper's tone broke sharply from that of the previous decade, when reformers had encouraged petitioning as a "moral" tool. "Why shall [women] be left only the poor resource of petition?" wondered one article. "For even petitions, when they are from women, without the elective franchise to give them backbone, are of but little consequence."

Because of the temperance movement's outspokenness about the importance of electoral politics, temperance women were indeed relatively willing to express what Amelia Bloomer called "a strong woman's-rights sentiment." In Buffalo, New York, she wrote, "all feel that the only way in which women can do anything effectually in this cause is through the ballotbox, and they feel themselves fettered by being denied the right to thus speak their sentiments in a manner that could not be misunderstood." As early as 1846 "fourteen hundred women from Monroe County [New York] 'bemoaned their lack of the ballot,' and 'petitioned voters to safeguard their welfare at the polls' by voting for candidates opposed to the liquor traffic." Indeed, it was through frustration with temperance men and the "senseless, hopeless work that man points out for woman to do" that Susan B. Anthony became a supporter of woman suffrage.

Many benevolent women, still convinced that the broadest possible social change would be achieved by "female" means, were dismayed by the trend toward electoral means and eschewed the demand for woman suffrage. Only a few women, such as Elizabeth Cady Stanton, had always been aware of the dual nature of moral suasion, its power and its weakness, and had labeled "nonpolitical" means a screen set up by conservative men who smugly advised more radical women to "'pray over it.'" More had doubted whether the vote was a tool that could advance a moral cause: "It is with reluctance that I make the demand for the political rights of women," admitted Lucretia Mott. Even as they moved into suffrage activity, some women continued to insist that only in moral suasion lay the possibilities for a major social transformation and for an enlarged female influence. By the 1850s, however, the radical possibilities of that analysis, like the evangelical fervor that had nurtured it, had been exhausted, and some advocates of social change looked more to the ballot for assistance.

Those who turned to electoral means and goals continued to express ambivalence about partisanship, that buzzword of moral compromise. Within the antislavery movement, for example, even abolitionists who embraced the idea of a third party worried over what partisanship would do to their souls. Women, who did not benefit directly from political victory, sought to take the moral high ground in the electoral contest. Antoinette Brown, who "like her father, was a 'voting abolitionist'" and who had campaigned actively for Gerrit Smith's election to Congress, told Lucy Stone that she "should hate to sink so low as to become a common vulgar politician. Let me first be a [nonvoting] Garrisonian ten times over. I say, Lucy, I pray you won't get converted to such politics as the world at large advocates." Brown had reason to worry; conversions to "such politics as the world at large advocates" were becoming more frequent every day. . . .

That transition was reflected in the work of individual women who consolidated decades-old benevolent organizations in new settings that signified both stability and more limited goals. For example, Abby Hopper Gibbons, abolitionist, prison reformer, and frequent and effective lobbyist, increasingly turned to institutional contexts in which to achieve her benevolent ends. In 1854, following a dispute with male colleagues over conflicting prerogatives, the Female Department of the Prison Association of New York, with Gibbons as president, formed an independent Women's Prison Association and Home. At the same time, Gibbons became president of the Industrial School for German girls, under the auspices of the Children's Aid Society of New York. Virtually all of her work in the 1850s was geared toward building and promoting those institutions. Gibbons was unusual in that she maintained contact with abolitionist and woman's rights circles. Her almost exclusive focus on institutional and legislative means, however, was characteristic of the time.

Even activists who united for the purpose of lobbying for legislation occasionally ended up building institutions. In January 1847 a group of women, leading ultraists such as Lucretia Mott, Abby Kimber Burleigh, Mary Grew, and Sarah Pugh among them, organized in Philadelphia to petition the state legislature for the abolition of capital punishment. After sending off almost twelve thousand signatures a mere six weeks later, the women eagerly applauded the suggestion made by one of their number that they "open a house for the reformation, employment, and instruction of females, who had led immoral lives." By October they had formulated a plan for the new undertaking, purchased a building, recruited 346 women as members, and opened a house of industry. By the following April they had acquired an act of incorporation and a $1,300 mortgage and were on their way to becoming a respected, established institution in the city. In 1854, as evidence of that status, the Pennsylvania legislature granted the Rosine Association an annual appropriation of $3,000.

More conservative and elite women avoided the questionable connotations of aiming their efforts at prostitutes and pursued the tradition of aiding the "worthy poor." Still they, like members of the Rosine Association, focused on establishing institutions. By mid-decade, industrial schools and houses of industry had sprouted throughout urban areas. The American Female Guardian Society (AFGS) alone sponsored a number of industrial schools in New York City and elsewhere in addition to its Home for the Friendless and House of Industry. Numerous older institutions celebrated their growth and stability by moving into larger buildings in the 1850s. The New Haven Orphan Asylum did so in 1853. The AFGS dedicated its first building in 1848 and opened a larger one in 1857. Sketches of those imposing structures constitute the frontispiece of many an annual report, capturing in a picture a changing intellectual and physical environment that the women saw little need to explain. . . .

Both the trend toward electoral means and that toward institutional structures tended to weaken women's overall position in benevolent movements and to narrow the goals of social activism. The rhetorical evidence of women's displacement is clear: Rarely does a student of the 1850s come across calls to men to adopt the standard set by "female" virtues and female votelessness. Even for women working in all or predominantly female institutions, the change in rhetoric signaled an altered context — a waning of authority based on the special morality of "female" values. Indeed, "female" virtue was coming to be seen as just that: an exclusively female quality to be applied within those settings that continued to be dominated by women rather than to be inculcated in the world at large. The prestige of female influence, so celebrated in the form of moral suasion a decade earlier, was seriously threatened at the same time that the focus on elections and on institutions narrowed the goals of benevolence itself. Increasingly those who had once called for the regeneration of the world through "female" virtues relied on asylums and on laws as pragmatic steps to a more limited transformation.

As the goals that activist women sought became more frequently confined to legislation and the issues that absorbed the nation increasingly focused on elections and on the federal government, some women came to feel acutely the limitations of their disfranchisement. The fact that activists recognized voting as an essential tool suggests a new interpretation of the call for woman suffrage made by a small group of women in 1848. The changing political context of the era, rather than simply a sudden awareness of the injustices of women's status, was central to women's demand for the ballot.

The most forward-looking movement of the day, the emerging woman's rights movements, constituted a wholly new route for women, one that advanced explicitly electoral rather than "moral" means for effecting social change. Women active in the movement understood the limitations placed on their work by the ideology of benevolent womanhood and by the strategy of moral suasion. At the same time, woman's rights activists engaged in a rhetorical displacement of "female" virtues: They demanded, in essence, that women's status be raised to a level of equality with men rather than that men should aspire to the standard supposedly set by women. Determined to use the essential tools of electoral change, they adopted a political rather than a moral definition of status. For them, the growing centrality of electoral politics underscored the irony of extolling the virtues of a nonvoting stance. Female influence seemed to have lost its power of persuasion. . . .

The Civil War and the immediate postwar decades would make even clearer how benevolence itself had changed. As their work in the 1850s anticipated, reformers became political activists in a secular society. The women who reached adulthood in the 1850s, launched their careers during the Civil War, and worked on postwar charity boards and committees composed of elite women and men virtually never used the imagery of gender in their public work. Indeed, the founders of postwar charity undermined those traditional images in their very dependence on the wartime principles of efficiency, order, and unsentimental discipline. The State Charities Aid Association of New York, for example, founded by Louisa Lee Schuyler, stressed its freedom from "weak or sickly sentimentality" so closely associated with "a gathering of sympathetic women." Benevolent workers had become liberals who, according to David Montgomery, "sought to bring under the sway of science the management of the social order itself." In close alliance with state governments, they set about creating institutional settings for the "social welfare" programs that would be the focus of a later generation.

By the postwar period the genteel Protestant reformers of antislavery heritage were no longer on the radical cutting edge of United States society. Organizations such as Josephine Shaw Lowell's Charity Organization Society, with its emphasis on science and business principles, helped recast

benevolent discourse from a radical call for the moral transformation of
society into a conservative defense of the class privilege of benevolent
leaders. "Outraged respectability" found an outlet in the new journal the
*Nation*, which, although founded by abolitionists James Miller McKim and
William Lloyd Garrison, Jr., "opposed nearly all the political economic
movements of that period." One of the *Nation*'s primary goals was to find
"means of checking the popular passions, which it felt were largely manifestations of ignorance and sin" and which were increasingly defined in
class terms.

Workers' and farmers' organizations came to represent the radical voice
of United States society after the Civil War. Laying claim to the utopianism
that the middle class had rejected, they often adopted the ideals of earlier
reformers. "[T]he Christian perfectionism of pre–Civil War evangelical
and reform movements," asserts Herbert G. Gutman, "lingered on among
many discontented postbellum workers." Middle-class liberals, in contrast,
found themselves defending a distasteful "procorporation credo." Depres-
sions, strikes, corruption, and noticeably greater extremes of wealth — all
played a role in transforming the context in which middle-class Protestants
had once sought a grand moral change in society. Slavery no longer provided an issue around which ultraists could rally their moral forces. Battles
between classes and regions cornered the middle class in a defense of
privilege based on a growing conviction of human nature's imperfectability.
Even the demand for woman suffrage was losing its radical associations as
more conservative women became convinced of the value of the vote in
their own work. The 1870s and 1880s were a conservative time, as the
middle class engaged in a backlash against both prewar utopianism and
the radical possibilities of abolition. "Many persons who have been
Radicals all their lives," wrote the *Nation*'s editor E. L. Godkin in 1871,
"are in doubt whether to be Radical any longer.". . .

The ideology of women's unique moral calling thus seemed to have lost
its radical potential as a means of social change. Virtue itself came to be
treated as solely, even biologically, women's responsibility, rather than as a
model to which men should aspire. The belief that human perfectibility
was possible through female benevolence was as anachronistic in the postwar decades as the utopian impulse that had inspired it. Not until the
Progressive decades would elite Protestant women such as Grace Hoadley
Dodge and Jane Addams again infuse social reform with the rhetoric of
female virtue and moral righteousness.

The reemergence of a radical voice among middle-class Protestants in
the late 1880s suggests the cyclical nature of the history of social reform
in the United States. Commonly, reform activity has moved from an agita-
tional focus on the transformation of individuals to an emphasis on electoral and institutional solutions. For example, ultraist reform in the 1830s
emerged in part as a reaction against the conservative political tactics of
the Benevolent Empire, only to return to political strategies in the 1850s
with the decline of moral suasion. Certainly the woman suffrage movement abandoned its concern for broad social change to campaign for suf-

frage alone. Mainstream suffragists defended their increasingly racist rhetoric and rigid class and ethnic bias on the basis of the difficulty of achieving their exclusively legislative goal.

Similarly, the Progressive movement of the turn of this century, the civil rights movement of the 1950s and 1960s, and the women's movement of the 1960s and 1970s experienced a shift in focus as each moved from an effort to achieve what might loosely be called a moral transformation to a narrower concentration on electoral politics. To the extent that those movements have been absorbed into the electoral process at the expense of other forms of action, they may have both limited their vision of social change and isolated less powerful groups within them.

That is not to say that a vision of social change that proscribes electoral politics — such as that advanced by many ultraists in the 1830s — can necessarily be productive of change in other political contexts. The belief that only in moral change lay the broadest female power, for example, is far less convincing in our own time than it was in the 1830s, when the power of government and other institutions was far less pervasive and the rigidity of class boundaries less daunting. Reformers' adoption of electoral means and goals, however, though it has seemed to democratize the holding of political power, has involved tradeoffs: As the history of benevolent reform during the 1850s illustrates, electoral politics has tended to isolate groups with limited access to those in authority, to redefine the nature of social reform, and to limit the vision of reformers themselves.

# Slave Culture: African or American?

After decades of academic silence on the topic of slavery, many scholars now place it at the very heart of the nation's development. Interest in slave life is even more recent. As historian Nathan Huggins has written, "The social death implicit in slavery and racial caste was carried over into the writing of American history until the 1960s. Black historians aside, American history almost universally was written as if blacks did not exist and their experience was of no consequence."[1]

But since the civil rights movement, research on slave culture has attracted an ever increasing number of scholars and is one of the richest fields of historical studies today. The evolution of the debates over slave culture, its existence, its roots, and its accomplishments is to a substantial degree intertwined with the ongoing debate over race relations in the United States. The debates involve ideas about race, the degree and kind of resistance to slavery, the existence of autonomous black life and culture distinct from the impress of white institutions, the profile of the black family and the meanings attaching to it, the causes and cures for black poverty, the role of Africa in the imagination and culture of African Americans, and North American slaves' transnational connections. These questions have taken the study of slavery from a U.S. context to become part of the new field of the Black Atlantic that views the early modern and modern world from the standpoint of the African diaspora and the movement of people and ideas resulting from the international slave trade. There are few areas of investigation so morally charged, so loaded with contemporary significance, and so bound up with a transnational perspective on our history. Taking a position on the nature of slave culture inevitably entails a vision of black life today as well as a vision of the relationship of African Americans to people of African descent in the New World, to Africans and Africa, and to the way cultures develop and change.

One significant strand in the historiography of slave culture has connected the degree of autonomy slaves were able to retain with the degree to which they were able to use their African past as a source for cultural creation and continuity. Slave studies began around the turn of the twentieth century with Ulrich Phillips, a southern apologist with racist views who argued that slaves had a fair degree of autonomy, but no connection with Africa, a place he believed they were fortunate to have left. This view stood until the early

---

[1]Nathan Irvin Huggins, *Black Odyssey: The African American Ordeal in Slavery* (New York, 1977, 1990), xvii.

1960s when Stanley Elkins argued that the experience of slavery obliterated any connection with a usable past.[2] The 1970s saw an outpouring of scholarship refuting this view. Historians searched for links with Africa among other evidences of an autonomous culture. This quest became more sophisticated, using techniques from anthropology, linguistics, and archaeology to prove that West Africans not only brought their culture with them, but also transferred elements of it to the surrounding white community. Increasingly, contemporary scholars have managed to do what earlier historians believed impossible — to trace the American fate of various West African ethnic groups. Current scholars may differ on the degree to which Africa shaped the American black experience, but few deny its significance completely. Indeed, many historians regard ignoring the African background of slave culture a glaring scholarly omission.

Ulrich B. Phillips, son of a plantation owner, set the tone of early slave studies. He desired to put a humane face on slavery and slaveholders in *American Negro Slavery*, published in 1918 (see Chapter 4). He portrayed slavery as a benign institution, not very profitable and something of a burden to slave owners who were responsible for looking after their charges.[3]

Despite, or because of, his racist view, Phillips's work inspired other historians. Among them were the African American historians W. E. B. Du Bois and John Hope Franklin, who challenged different aspects of Phillips's work, and in 1945 the Marxist scholar Herbert Aptheker, who published a slim collection of essays attacking Phillips and his views, particularly the idea that blacks submitted easily to slavery.[4]

Aptheker's *Essays in the History of the American Negro* listed numerous instances of resistance to slavery. Aptheker also restored blacks to their rightful place as Union soldiers, 200,000 strong, and as leaders and forceful participants in the abolitionist movement, whom historians had seen until then as dangerous (white) fanatics or liberal (white) reformers.

Despite Aptheker's work, Phillips's account remained the more widely accepted version of slavery. No full-scale treatment of the subject appeared until Kenneth Stampp, in 1956, published *The Peculiar Institution: Slavery in the Antebellum South*. Stampp's interest in showing that the Civil War was fought over slavery led him to study slavery itself. He researched *The Peculiar Institution* in archives that were still largely segregated during the volatile years surrounding the *Brown v. Topeka Board of Education* decision and its immediate aftermath.[5]

Stampp reversed Phillips's findings and, backed by meticulous archival research, asserted that slavery was an institution both of great severity and

---

[2]Ulrich B. Phillips, *American Negro Slavery* (New York, 1918); Stanley Elkins, *Slavery: A Problem in Institutional and Intellectual Life* (Chicago, 1959).

[3]Phillips, *American Negro Slavery*.

[4]Herbert Aptheker, *Essays in the History of the American Negro* (New York, 1945); for just two examples, see W. E. B. Du Bois, *Black Reconstruction: An Essay toward a History of the Part Which Black Folk Played in the Attempt to Reconstruct Democracy in America, 1860–1880* (New York, 1935), and John Hope Franklin, *From Slavery to Freedom: A History of Negro Americans* (New York, 1956).

[5]Kenneth Stampp, *The Peculiar Institution: Slavery in the Ante-Bellum South* (New York, 1956).

profitability. To Stampp, race was without significance: "[S]laves were merely ordinary human beings."[6] These findings found a receptive audience in the postwar years of renewed civil rights activism. However new his racial views, Stampp, like many others who came after him, followed Phillips's outline for the debate. Did planters treat slaves well or badly? What was the extent of paternalism on plantations? Was there a slave culture? If so, were its elements African or American? While Phillips had seen African Americans as imitating white culture, Stampp saw them suspended between the two, unable to use the past fruitfully and not yet able to create their own traditions. Influenced by the African American sociologist E. Franklin Frazier's *The Negro Family in the United States*, Stampp portrayed the slave family as too fragile to provide much respite from the rigors of slave life and as fundamentally matriarchal such that men contributed little or nothing of importance and in which even mothers could barely cook, clothe, or take care of their children.[7]

Phillips insisted that slaves were able to carve out a space for themselves and were able to negotiate the system of slavery so that owners simply could not exercise anything like total control. This was an aspect of his effort to give slavery a benign profile. Subsequent historians like Stampp, however, developed a theme of black helplessness and familial destruction in a well-intentioned attempt to prove that slavery was devoid of black complicity.

Just three years later, Stanley Elkins suggested in *Slavery: A Problem in American Institutional and Intellectual Life* that slavery had been a system of such complete and effective coercion that it reduced slaves to psychological helplessness. Elkins, using social psychology to make his argument, had been influenced by Frank Tannenbaum's classic comparative work *Slave and Citizen*. Tannenbaum maintained that slavery in Iberian colonies had been a looser system than in the United States, more subject to the moderating influences of the Catholic Church and feudal loyalties. Elkins, like Tannenbaum, insisted that slavery in the United States had been a total system analogous to the concentration camps of World War II, producing radically dependent and foolish "Sambos" or damaged people capable of little in the way of resistance or creativity. Elkins criticized Stampp and the anthropological scholarship on which he relied for focusing on "examples of Negro courage, Negro rebelliousness, Negro hatred for the slave system, and so on — all of the characteristics one might expect of white men who knew nothing of what it meant to be reared in slavery."[8]

Elkins's thesis and E. Franklin Frazier's *Black Bourgeoisie: The Rise of a New Middle Class*, which elaborated on the theme of a damaging matriarchy, provided fuel for Daniel Patrick Moynihan's *The Negro Family: The Case for National Action*, published in 1965. Ironically, he intended his study to be a liberal

---

[6]Robert Abzug and Stephen Maizlish, eds., *New Perspectives on Race and Slavery in America: Essays in Honor of Kenneth Stampp* (Lexington, Ky., 1986), 1–3.

[7]E. Franklin Frazier, *The Negro Family in the United States* (Chicago, 1939); Kenneth M. Stampp, "The Daily Life of the Southern Slave," in *Key Issues in the Afro-American Experience*, ed. Nathan Huggins, Martin Kilson, and Daniel Fox (New York, 1971), 116–37.

[8]Elkins, *Slavery*, 23; Frank Tannenbaum, *Slave and Citizen: The Negro in the Americas* (New York, 1946); E. Franklin Frazier, *Black Bourgeoisie: The Rise of a New Middle Class* (New York, 1957).

call for programs to ameliorate the poverty of urban ghetto life. Moynihan described what he saw as the "tangle of pathology" of matriarchal families that stemmed from slavery and subsequent white supremacist policies. The mother-dominated family "seriously retards the progress of the group as a whole, and imposes a crushing burden on the Negro male and, in consequence, on a great many negro women as well."[9]

Elkins's book and Moynihan's *Report* produced an extraordinary outpouring of criticism. Calling black women, arguably the least powerful members of American society, matriarchs and placing the burden of black family pathology on their already overburdened shoulders as they struggled to raise children in ghettos ravaged by unemployment and poverty was simply too much, however good Moynihan's objectives. Ironically, this debate was partly responsible for mobilizing historians to research and revive Phillips's depiction of a lively and to some degree autonomous slave culture.

Since the 1970s, no historian has claimed that slaves were rendered incapable of creating a world of their own or that they did not resist the conditions of slavery. In the process of re-creating aspects of slave initiative and creativity, historians have spent considerable time on slave family life and religion. For the first time, historians asked about the precise relationship of the slave culture to the dominant culture and under what conditions it flourished or withered.

Elkins as well as E. Franklin Frazier had argued that slaves arrived traumatized by the horrors of capture and the Middle Passage and were sold without regard to their ethnicity. These experiences and subsequent sales meant that they retained little or nothing of their African past. Stampp's work also insisted on the extinction of any trace of African culture. Other historians would argue that African culture and religion played a role in the lives of slaves and were a source of inspiration for an Afro-American culture. This argument has its roots in the work of the anthropologist Melville Herskovitz, who had tracked down material "survivals" from Africa, such as musical instruments.[10]

Historians responded to Moynihan and Elkins with massive evidence detailing resilience, vitality, cultural coherence, and the presence of Africa in slave communities. Eugene Genovese, in *Roll, Jordan, Roll: The World the Slaves Made* (1972), initiated the first historical effort to look at slave life from the point of view of slaves. Genovese essentially adopted Phillips's concept of paternalism, agreeing with Phillips that it allowed slaves a certain negotiating room, including the ability to force planters into accepting compromises with regard to the speed and conditions of their work. While Phillips had been interested in exonerating owners by emphasizing their paternalistic concerns, Genovese was interested in demonstrating that paternalism provided slaves with a substantial margin — contrary to Elkins — in which to

---

[9]Daniel Patrick Moynihan, *The Negro Family: The Case for National Action* (Washington, D.C., 1965); Lee Rainwater and William Yancey, *The Moynihan Report and the Politics of Controversy* (Cambridge, Mass., 1967), 29.

[10]See, for example, Melville Herskovitz, *The American Negro: A Study in Racial Crossing* (Bloomington, Ind., 1956).

maneuver and create relationships and rituals to serve their social and cultural needs.[11]

Although some criticized him for ignorance of Africa, Genovese asserted the African basis of aspects of slave culture. He believed that Herskovitz had overstated his case for "survivals," but Frazier had similarly overstated his against the possibilities of African influences. "Black America's tie," he wrote, "with an African tradition . . . helped shape a culture entirely its own."[12] He used evidence from anthropologists and archaeologists in describing African origins of a variety of burial customs and religious and magical beliefs. For contemporary scholars of black culture, Genovese's view of the importance of paternalism compromised the independence he claimed for slave culture, yet Genovese was the first since W. E. B. Du Bois, in another context, to argue that the influences of culture went both ways, and that when whites and blacks interacted, the former did not merely impose their culture on the latter.[13]

In the same year that Genovese's volume was published, the economic historians Robert Fogel and Stanley Engerman published *Time on the Cross*, a book as controversial as Elkins's had been. They used a quantitative approach to aspects of slavery to determine how profitable it was and how brutal. While their focus was not slave culture, they did try to describe the plantation atmosphere in which culture might or might not develop. For many, their methodology — estimating the number of whippings on a plantation and the calories in a slave's diet — seemed inappropriate and offensive. That Fogel and Engerman's conclusions showed that slavery was a mild and profitable system of coerced labor, offering a range of worker incentives and promotions, seemed to many further evidence that their project was ill conceived. Herbert Gutman and Roger Ransom and Richard Sutch showed that Engerman and Fogel's arguments were flawed by over-reliance on their economic model rather than substantial research and that they grossly underestimated punishments on plantations while overestimating planters' incentives to keep slaves healthy and motivated. Critics also argued that counting whippings did nothing to explain their psychological effects or to contribute to a genuine assessment of the severity of slavery — that "cliometry" was the wrong tool for evaluating slavery. Despite, or rather because of its critics, however, *Time on the Cross*, like Elkins's *Slavery*, provoked many responses that have enlarged our understanding of living conditions of slaves. And it emphasized the importance of understanding how work shaped slave culture.[14]

John Blassingame wrote *The Slave Community: Plantation Life in the Antebellum South* to refute Elkins's thesis. He distinguished slave life in the quarters

[11]Eugene D. Genovese, *Roll, Jordan, Roll: The World the Slaves Made* (New York, 1974), 3–7.

[12]Ibid., 210; Michael A. Gomez, *Exchanging Our Country Marks: The Transformation of African Identities in the Colonial and Antebellum South* (Chapel Hill, N.C., 1998), 248–49.

[13]W. E. B. Du Bois, *The Souls of Black Folk*, ed. David Blight and Robert Gooding-Williams (1903; reprinted Boston, 1997).

[14]Peter J. Parish, *Slavery: History and Historians* (New York, 1989), 32–37; Robert W. Fogel and Stanley L. Engerman, *Time on the Cross: The Economics of American Negro Slavery* (Boston, 1974); Herbert Gutman, *The Black Family in Slavery and Freedom, 1750–1925* (New York, 1976); Roger L. Ransom and Richard Sutch, *One Kind of Freedom: The Economic Consequences of Emancipation* (New York, 1977).

as the primary environment and slave life in contact with whites and during work as a secondary environment, which he argued "was far less important in determining his personality. . . . The more [he was] immune from the control of whites, the more the slave gained in personal autonomy."[15] He insisted that slavery and plantation life had not undermined the slave's ability to invent a life for himself out of a rich past and a meager present. As to African influence, it was "much more resistant to the bludgeon that was slavery than historians have hitherto suspected." Scholars have questioned how light the influence of the work environment could have been on slaves whose lives were determined by the work they did. And women have challenged Blassingame's unswerving focus on males. But Blassingame's conclusions about Africa, ongoing slave resistance, and the complexity of slave culture stand.

Herbert Gutman's *The Black Family in Slavery and Freedom, 1750–1925*, published in 1976, was another early and forceful response to the Elkins-Moynihan theses. He also criticized Genovese's emphasis on paternalism for shifting the focus from the development of an Afro-American culture to overemphasizing white influence. Gutman's work detailed the remarkable stability of slave marriages under the assaults of slavery and the persistent and poignant efforts of former slaves during Reconstruction to find spouses and children who had been sold away or had disappeared during the war. Gutman revealed a strong knowledge of and preference among slaves for exogamy, which contrasted sharply with the frequency of first-cousin marriages among planters. In a similar vein, Gutman traced naming patterns among slave parents to African customs, demonstrating both the efforts of slaves to hold their families together and the long shadow African ways cast in the formation of kin ties in the New World.[16]

Gutman's findings attracted some criticism from scholars who were afraid it was too rosy a picture of people living under a terrible regime. On the one hand, sociologist Orlando Patterson, in his wide-ranging exploration of slave systems throughout world history, found that slave owners *aspired* to accomplish what Elkins insisted they did accomplish — the destruction of the slave's individuality and sense of self-respect — but that by and large they failed. He agreed with Genovese and Gutman that the search for dignity and honor was omnipresent in slave communities, rendered more urgent because those were precisely what slave owners tried to monopolize. On the other hand, he disagreed with Gutman's reading of some of his particular evidence, for example, that most slaves managed to choose a surname other than their owners' and rejected their masters' overbearing intimacy to establish a degree of autonomy. Patterson found that most slaves had their owners' surnames after all and that those changed if they changed owners.[17]

---

[15]John Blassingame, *The Slave Community: Plantation Life in the Antebellum South* (New York, 1972), 105, 106. Blassingame revised his book to present a fuller picture of slave culture in a second edition.

[16]Herbert Gutman, *The Black Family in Slavery and Freedom, 1750–1925* (New York, 1976).

[17]Orlando Patterson, *Slavery and Social Death: A Comparative Study* (Cambridge, Mass., 1982), 56.

Although most scholarship on slavery would be of narrower scope than Gutman's or Genovese's and would consist of investigations of communities at particular times, the discovery of autonomous cultures and African influence would continue. Among the foremost of these was Charles Joyner's *Down by the Riverside*, a study of Waccamaw Neck, All Saints Parish, in South Carolina, one of the richest rice-growing communities in America and source of a large number of South Carolina's secessionist leaders. South Carolina had the highest population of blacks in the country, and in Lower All Saints Parish the ratio was nine blacks to one white. Joyner meticulously recreated the work habits of residents of Waccamaw Neck and their West African roots. He explained the invention and use of the Waccamaw Neck residents' Gullah language, made up of English and West African words, primarily Wolof but also Igbo, Ewe, Mandinke, and Yoruba. Gullah was a creole language that had a completely different grammar from English and a distinctive vocabulary and form, evolving over the late eighteenth and the nineteenth centuries. In Joyner's view of Waccamaw Neck just before the Civil War, the slaves had created "Out of African traditions as well as American circumstances . . . a new language, a new religion — indeed, a new culture — that not only allowed them to endure the collective tragedy of slavery, but to bequeath a notable and enduring heritage to generations to come."[18] Erskine Clarke's prize-winning family biography, *Dwelling Place: A Plantation Epic*, traces the lives of the intertwined families of Charles Colcock Jones of Liberty County, Georgia, and Lizzie Jones, head of a large clan of Gullah-speaking slaves. This study would not be possible without scholarship that has re-created the low-country world of eastern Georgia and South Carolina.[19]

As a result of studies like Joyner's, few scholars today examine pre–Civil War life without some attention to African pasts. This is true for works as different as Margaret Washington Creel's study of slave religion among the Gullahs, W. Jeffrey Bolster's *Black Jacks: African American Seamen in the Age of Sail*, in which he probed West African sailing and navigational experience to introduce African American mariners, and *The Sounds of Slavery*, an imaginative study of the music and rhetorical skills and the practices of slavery, by Shane and Graham White.[20]

The possibilities for exploring slave culture more broadly also grew from the expansion of social history to include the history of women. In 1984, Deborah Gray White published *Ar'n't I a Woman?* the first challenge to the male bias in the historiography of slavery. White's argument was twofold — not only had historians left women out of their accounts of slavery, but when they included them, it was as matriarchs or helpless dependents. In her first chapter, she discussed two destructive stereotypes that derived from the slave trade and slavery: black women as promiscuous and black women as mam-

---

[18]Charles Joyner, *Down by the Riverside: A South Carolina Slave Community* (Urbana and Chicago, 1984), 196–224, 242.

[19]Erskine Clarke, *Dwelling Place: A Plantation Epic* (New Haven, Conn., 2005).

[20]Margaret Washington Creel, *"A Peculiar People": Slave Religion and Community-Culture among the Gullahs* (New York, 1988); W. Jeffrey Bolster, *Black Jacks: African American Seamen in the Age of Sail* (Cambridge, Mass., 1997); Shane White and Graham White, *The Sounds of Slavery: Discovering African American History through Songs, Sermons, and Speech* (Boston, 2005).

mies. Providing a new perspective on destructive old clichés, she found continuity between West African marriage traditions and slave families, particularly in the strength of mother-child relationships and in the tracing of matrilineal ties. She also established the existence of a strong female network, which helped account for numerous examples of strong and resilient slave women. White's study led the way for others that explored female experience as workers, mothers, wives, girls, and players in the plantation struggles for slave survival. In this, she and others enlarged definitions of resistance to slavery.[21]

Feminist criticism has also contributed forcefully to the idea that race, like gender, is socially constructed. In this view, as Kenneth Stampp posited, in and of itself race has no meaning; its meanings accrue from ideas the powerful attach to it. A dominant group gives racial characteristics social meaning when it is in their interest. Edmund Morgan identified the phenomenon in the Chesapeake when elite Virginians deliberately stigmatized blackness as a way to consolidate their bonds with poor whites. Kathleen Brown, updating Morgan in *Good Wives, Anxious Patriarchs, and Nasty Wenches,* placed the social construction of gender and race at the heart of political relations in early Virginia. Whereas Edmund Morgan saw the development of racist legislation after Bacon's Rebellion as a way to secure the loyalty of poor white farmers to wealthy white planters against the black "other," Brown saw a more complex construction, not only of the male black other, but the extremely other black female. Building on White's point that black women are doubly vulnerable to stereotyping, Brown depicted African women as powerfully objectified by their defeminization as well as their degraded status, secured through new legal and social meanings given to (white, English) womanliness. The spread of gentility for white women, defined by their freedom from agricultural work, furthered the degradation of black women who labored in the fields.[22]

Brenda Stevenson's thickly detailed study of Loudoun County, Virginia, in the antebellum years focused on the devastation caused by constructions of gender for both black and white women. But she also investigated the more literal and horrific devastation that the active and expanding internal slave trade caused slave women of the Upper South, sundering one in three marriages and leaving increasing numbers of slave children without either parent to look after them. Stephanie Camp's study of plantation women's resistance to slavery explores private acts and veiled defiance, bringing out into the open acts of opposition that were never intended to be fully revealed.[23]

---

[21]Deborah Gray White, *Ar'n't I a Woman?: Female Slaves in the Plantation South* (New York, 1984), 23, 27–61, 91–141. For example, Brenda Stevenson, *Life in Black and White: Family and Community in the Slave South* (New York, 1996); Marie Jenkins Schwartz, *Born in Bondage: Growing Up Enslaved in the Antebellum South* (Cambridge, Mass., 2000); *Birthing a Slave: Motherhood and Medicine in the Antebellum South* (Cambridge, Mass., 2006); Emily West, *Chains of Love: Slave Couples in Antebellum South Carolina* (Urbana, Ill., 2004).

[22]Kathleen M. Brown, *Good Wives, Anxious Patriarchs, and Nasty Wenches: Gender, Race, and Power in Colonial Virginia* (Chapel Hill, N.C., 1996).

[23]Stevenson, *Life in Black and White;* Stephanie Camp, *Closer to Freedom: Enslaved Women and Everyday Resistance in the Plantation South* (Chapel Hill, N.C., 2004).

Scholars continued to develop the links between the growing knowledge about African roots in slave culture to a militant contemporary black consciousness. George Rawick, Sterling Stuckey, and Lawrence Levine have all emphasized the autonomous growth of black culture. Rawick and Stuckey looked for the African dimensions of black nationalism. Stuckey wrote of the "centrality of the ancestral past to the African in America."[24] This claim was directly related to his account of the varieties of resistance of African Americans to the oppression of whites. Lawrence Levine, author of *Black Culture, Black Consciousness: Afro-American Folk Thought from Slavery to Freedom* (1977), focused on African traditions, folktales, and beliefs at the center of his study of storytelling, music, and other aspects of Afro-American culture. In emphasizing African origins of slave music, Levine created a new understanding of resistance to include spirituality among African American Christians. Levine saw an uncolonized imagination as essential to resistance.[25] The sacred worldview of slaves, Levine argued, invested all natural things with spiritual life. Slaves thus possessed a radically different attitude toward the environment and living creatures than their owners (not to mention their historians).

Levine, like Genovese, emphasized that slave religion was the all-important center of black resistance, the heart of African American vitality, and the spiritual fuel that helped them endure their daily lives. The distinguished historian of southern religion, John Boles, however, has argued that scholars may have exaggerated the degree of autonomy blacks experienced in practicing their religion. Instead, Boles stressed the degree to which black Christians adopted white values. John Blassingame has agreed, seeing the church more as a force for Americanizing slaves than as a site of cultural resistance. The debate over the degree of religious autonomy slaves experienced is crucial to estimating how effectively they were able to establish positive, alternative ways of constructing their world.[26]

Sylvia Frey and Betty Wood steeped their account of black experience of the First and particularly the Second Great Awakening in West African traditions. In their view, slaves adopted Christianity in part because it fit into West African ideas about the deities, the universe, and rebirth. Slaves brought a tradition of exuberant and ecstatic worship to Christianity that contributed uniquely to evangelical culture and became reflected in white patterns of worship.[27]

---

[24]Sterling Stuckey, *Slave Culture: Nationalist Theory and the Foundations of Black America* (New York, 1987), 43, quoted in Parish, *Slavery*, 77; George Rawick, *From Sundown to Sunup: The Making of the Black Community* (Westport, Conn., 1972).

[25]Lawrence Levine, "Slave Songs and the Slave Consciousness," in *American Negro Slavery*, ed. Allen Weinstein and Frank Otto Gatell (New York, 1973), 177, and *Black Culture, Black Consciousness: Afro-American Folk Thought from Slavery to Freedom* (New York, 1977).

[26]Parish, *Slavery*, 83–84; John Boles, *Masters and Slaves in the House of the Lord: Race and Religion in the American South, 1740–1870* (Lexington, Ky., 1988); Blassingame, *Slave Community*.

[27]Sylvia Frey and Betty Wood, *Come Shouting to Zion: African American Protestantism in the American South and British Caribbean to 1830* (Chapel Hill, N.C., 1998).

In contrast, Albert J. Raboteau, in *Slave Religion: The "Invisible Institution" in the Antebellum South,* also looked at eighteenth-century African American culture and cosmology and argued that a variety of factors "tended to inhibit the survival of African culture and religion in the United States." What remained was to be found in spirituals, the ring shout, and folk beliefs. In studying black religion, Raboteau emphasized less the autonomy and Africanness of worship than the search for and insistence upon equality within Christianity. In his account, slaves turned not to traditional African sources of wisdom and solace but to Christianity for a useful and restorative understanding of daily life. And, although some scholars have criticized him for underestimating the significance of the African past in his search, others have sustained his findings.[28]

In recent years, scholarship on slavery has grown at an accelerated pace. Peter Wood, in *Black Majority: Negroes in Colonial South Carolina from 1670 through the Stono Rebellion,* published in 1974, was among the earliest to open up this field. By seeing the antebellum period as the defining moment of slavery, scholars had overlooked important differences in agriculture, the structure and pace of labor, and slave life. Wood also pioneered in revealing the great diversity among slave cultures regionally and temporally. He plumbed West African and eighteenth-century colonial sources in discussing slavery in South Carolina. Since then, many historians have looked at the institution in the seventeenth and eighteenth centuries, which brought them into direct contact with Africa and Africans. Wood's groundbreaking study traced the partial immunity of many Africans to the worst effects of malaria, which unfortunately made them desirable as workers, particularly to rice planters who wanted workers to toil in hot, insect-infested bogs day after day. Wood argued that these planters actively sought slaves from West African regions with knowledge of rice cultivation. (This was an early contradiction of prevalent ideas that ethnicity did not correlate with colonial slave selection.) Wood also noted direct African carryovers, like the guinea fowl, guinea corn, and the use of drinking gourds, and the most important carryover of all — the large percentage of Angolans who participated in the Stono Rebellion. Wood's scholarship on both Africa and colonial America inspired scholars to investigate less timidly the specific African roots of African American practices, beliefs, and traditions and to imagine pre–Civil War America as a dynamic mixture of these influences.[29]

Mechal Sobel made imaginative use of West African philosophy in *The World They Made Together* (1978), an innovative view of the eighteenth-century

---

[28]Albert J. Raboteau, *Slave Religion: The "Invisible Institution" in the Antebellum South* (New York, 1978), 92; Timothy J. Fulop and Albert J. Raboteau, *African American Religion: Interpretative Essays in History and Culture* (New York, 1997), 14–15; Creel, "Peculiar People," 6–7, Intro., ftn. 9; Albert J. Raboteau, "The Slave Church in the Era of the American Revolution," in *Slavery and Freedom in the Age of the American Revolution,* ed. Ronald Hoffman and Ira Berlin (Urbana and Chicago, 1983), 205–6.

[29]John K. Thornton, "The African Dimensions of the Stono Rebellion," *American Historical Review* 96 (October 1991): 101–13; Peter Wood, *Black Majority: Negroes in Colonial South Carolina from 1670 through the Stono Rebellion* (New York, 1974).

Chesapeake. Although noting African influences, she set in relief those beliefs of blacks and whites in the Chesapeake that overlapped: beliefs about time, work, space, architecture, and the universe. She placed them in the early Baptist context where blacks experienced a measure of equality. While some scholars disagreed with her conclusion that whites and blacks formed something that could be truly called a community, her study of early interracial Baptist congregations was of great importance in integrating African and Western thought. And she reasserted the important theme that African and white colonial cultures interpenetrated one another and that mutual shaping took place.[30]

Gwendolyn Midlo Hall, an influential scholar of Africans in America, studied eighteenth-century Louisiana, where she found an unusual ethnically unified African community. By 1731, the French had imported into Louisiana about six thousand Africans, a large proportion of whom were Bambara (or Bamana, as Hall claims is correct) from what is today Senegal. The French had traded extensively with the Bambara/Bamana in Africa, whose military traditions were so strong that the word *Bambara*, all along the western coast of Africa, came to mean slave soldier. Bambara/Bamana words made their way into French as their navigating skills, recipes, and other contributions poured into Louisiana culture. The unusual demography in Louisiana allowed Hall to find numerous correspondences between African and New World customs and practices. She has since created a database containing all the information she mined in her study of Louisiana slaves.[31]

In Hall's most recent, ambitious work, she set out to identify and link particular groups in Africa with people of African descent in the New World. She wrote, "African ethnicities were not nearly as fragmented by the transatlantic slave trade as scholars . . . have long believed." Her book detailed the ways particular groups of Africans retained and insisted upon their ethnic identities and contributed to forming new cultures in the Americas. She notes, for example, the large percentage of voyages leaving from Senegambia and Sierra Leone (rice-cultivating regions) to rice-growing regions in the South: South Carolina and Georgia.[32]

Michael Gomez's *Exchanging Our Country Marks* makes the broadest claims for the role of ethnicity in how Africans became Afro-Americans. Gomez (a sample of whose work appears below) argues from extensive research on various African ethnic groups that these identifications and the specific abilities attaching to them were initially the way planters created occupational hierarchies within the slave community. Over time, ethnically motivated hier-

[30]Mechal Sobel, *The World They Made Together: Black and White Values in Eighteenth-Century Virginia* (Princeton, N.J., 1978); see also her *Trabelin' On: The Slave Journey to an Afro-Baptist Faith* (Westport, Conn., 1979).
[31]Gwendolyn Midlo Hall, *Africans in Colonial Louisiana: The Development of an Afro-Creole Culture in the Eighteenth Century* (Baton Rouge, La., 1992), and *Slavery and African Ethnicities in the Americas: Restoring the Links* (Chapel Hill, N.C., 2005), xix.
[32]Hall, *Slavery and African Ethnicities*, xvii, 28, xv, 67; see Sylviane A. Diouf, *Dreams of Africa in Alabama: The Slave Ship Clotilda and the Story of the Last Africans Brought to America* (New York, 2007), for an account of the last slaves smuggled into the United States in 1860.

archies gave way to occupational and color hierarchies as those who had inherited skills and mulatto slaves usually found themselves doing the most desirable work. In this original work, Gomez, following the work of Sterling Stuckey and Lawrence Levine, has used folktales to identify the period when ethnic divisions among slaves gave way to a shared sense of themselves as united by race.[33]

Building on the work of Hall and Gomez, Walter C. Rucker argued that enslaved men and women began the process of becoming Africans (as opposed to Mandigoes or Igbos, for example) in the act of resistance. His study of slave revolts in three regions shows how the resistors' shared ethnic heritage bonded and emboldened them and underlay the emergence of their New World identity as "Africans," forged in their common struggle.[34] Rucker has argued that enslaved "Coromantees" (a people from the present-day area of Ghana), for example, through resistance came to see themselves as Africans, and through further resistance, over time, came to identify as African Americans.

An ever-larger number of scholars place slavery at the very center of our development as a nation: economically, politically, and socially. This has prompted studies of the impact of the Revolution on slavery and vice versa. Scholars have traced both the Revolution's successes and its failures to the fault lines that led to the Civil War. The Revolution, historians realized, hastened slavery's demise in the North while setting it on the road to expansion, not extinction, in the South. As David Brion Davis has explained, the Revolution removed the British effort to control westward expansion. At the same time, it fueled northern artisans' hatred of any form of bound labor. Hence, the forces of slave expansion and free labor ideology unleashed by the Revolution were responsible for deepening the already evident divisions in the country.[35]

Of very great significance in inciting resistance among slaves, the Revolution provided black people with the ideal of equality to which they continued to hold their country accountable after the brief rush of postrevolutionary manumissions had ceased.[36] Historian Benjamin Quarles quoted Virginian St. George Tucker's observation that blacks who went to fight for the British to get their freedom in exchange for Revolutionary military service thought of freedom as a good, but blacks who joined Gabriel Prosser's rebellion in 1800 thought of freedom as a right. Quarles concluded, "To a degree approaching unanimity, [blacks] clothed the War for Independence with meaning and a significance transcending their own day and time. . . . To

---

[33]Gomez, *Exchanging Our Country Marks,* and "African Identity and Slavery in the Americas," *Radical History Review* 75 (Fall 1999): 111–20.

[34]Walter C. Rucker, *"The River Flows On": Black Resistance, Culture, and Identity Formation in Early America* (Baton Rouge, La., 2006), 6–7.

[35]David Brion Davis, "American Slavery and the American Revolution," in *Slavery and Freedom,* ed. Hoffman and Berlin, 271.

[36]See Michael L. Nicholls, "'The Squint of Freedom': African-American Freedom Suits in Post-Revolutionary Virginia," *Slavery and Abolition* 20 (August 1999): 47–62.

them the full worth of the American Revolution lay ahead."[37] Gary Nash's *The Forgotten Fifth* exposes the rapidly shrinking hopes of several free African American thinkers in the postrevolutionary period to exercise their rights as citizens fully.[38]

Two immensely important studies by Ira Berlin and Philip Morgan place the eighteenth century at the heart of any understanding of North American slavery. These massive syntheses chart slavery's changes. Berlin's *Many Thousands Gone* introduced an all-but-unknown first generation of enslaved Africans, a sophisticated multilingual group with experience in international trade and inhabitants of West Africa but also of the Atlantic World. Berlin explains how race and slavery were both transformed in the antebellum years. Racism grew in the North to bolster the rights and prerogatives of the common man who understood the value of "whiteness" in a society that consigned its most servile labor to blacks. In the South, racism grew to gird up planter control of the new, more taxing system of slavery rapidly expanding in the black belt where short staple cotton and sugar grew. "The cotton revolution — like the earlier tobacco and rice revolutions — eroded the traditional constraints on the master's power. . . . Planters used the new demands of cotton cultivation to revoke the long-established prerogatives, strip slaves of skills, and ratchet up the level of exploitation."[39]

Morgan's decades' long research and comparative approach to the cultures of Chesapeake and low-country slavery distinguished the ways in which the demographic results of the international slave trade and the demands of particular crops shaped the lives of the cultivators. Morgan's focus on demography, labor, family structure, and slave life privileged the New World experience, particularly among second-generation slaves, as the most important force in creating an Afro-American culture. Creoles, according to Morgan, worked hard to create a new culture less inflected by African ethnicities than by New World experience (see below). As Morgan wrote, historians should give weight to "heterogeneity . . . fluid boundaries . . . precarious and permeable zones of interactions . . . hybrid societies" and resist the tendency to emphasize cultural homogeneity and the "dominance of particular African coastal regions or ethnicities in most American settings."[40]

---

[37]Benjamin Quarles, "The Revolutionary War as a Black Declaration of Independence," in *Slavery and Freedom*, ed., Hoffman and Berlin, 294, 301; see also Sylvia Frey, *Water from the Rock: Black Resistance in a Revolutionary Age* (Princeton, N.J., 1991).

[38]Gary Nash, *The Forgotten Fifth: African Americans in the Age of Revolution* (Cambridge, Mass., 2006).

[39]David Roediger, *The Wages of Whiteness: Race and the Making of the American Working Class* (New York, 1991); Ira Berlin, *Many Thousands Gone: The First Two Centuries of Slavery in North America* (Cambridge, Mass., 1998), 363–64; Philip Morgan, *Slave Counterpoint: Black Culture in the Eighteenth-Century Chesapeake and Lowcountry* (Chapel Hill, N.C., 1998).

[40]Philip Morgan, "The Cultural Implications of the Atlantic Slave Trade: African Regional Origins, American Destinations and New World Developments," *Slavery and Abolition* 18 (April 1997): 123–45, 142; Ira Berlin and Philip Morgan, eds., *Cultivation and Culture: Labor and the Shaping of Slave Life in the Americas* (Charlottesville, Va., 1993); see Richard Follett, *The Sugar Masters: Planters and Slaves in Louisiana's Cane World, 1820–1860* (Baton Rouge, La., 2005), and Judith Carney, *Black Rice: The African Origins of Rice Cultivation in the Americas* (Cambridge, Mass., 2001), for examples of this area of research.

*Slave Country*, Adam Rothman's important and wide-ranging work, uses an international political and economic perspective to understand the unexpectedly rapid and thorough postrevolutionary expansion of slavery from the area Morgan investigated to the southwest. In Rothman's account, the Napoleonic Wars, the War of 1812, and the revolution in Saint Domingue (Haiti) shaped U.S. markets, provided Andrew Jackson with the opportunity to strip the Creek Indians of 23 million acres of land, and built up a growing sugar industry with sugar planters and enslaved workers fleeing Haiti to populate the new Deep South with market-driven farmers, hungry for profits.[41] Rothman's work incorporates the kind of ethnic research that scholars like Gwendolyn Midlo Hall are doing as well as another important new area of inquiry: the internal slave trade.

Recently, several scholars have explored the institution most destructive to slave culture, the internal slave trade. Michael Tadman, Walter Johnson, and Stephen Deyle show conclusively that the tentacles of the trade extended into every part of the South and linked the South with the global market.[42] These studies locate slavery at the center of the nation's expanding commitment to world capitalism. Tadman's careful reconstruction of the trade, the number of traders, the number of slaves traded, the money involved, and the geography transformed changes forever the image defenders of slavery — and even Harriet Beecher Stowe — painted of the trader as rare, unwelcome, and uncouth. Slave traders and their preference for cash deals were welcome all over the South; some were bankers, others merchants. They facilitated the movement, Tadman estimates, of a million people of African descent in the years 1790 to 1860 from the Upper South to the Lower South. Walter Johnson's wrenching *Soul by Soul* looks instead at the personal and collective meanings of the trade that he describes elsewhere as "a history of subjection that in demographic scale, cultural impact, and sheer psychological terror ranks as one of the most obscene in human history." And Steven Deyle puts (astronomical) numbers on the U.S. commitment to slavery. He estimates the country's investment in slave property at $3 billion, or three times as much as the nation had put into manufacturing and seven times the amount of all currency in circulation.[43]

Slavery, in the eyes of its historians, carries as much if not more significance in our growth as any other American institution. Scholars today not only assume a slave culture but also assume some degree of its African characteristics. Understanding Africa and Africanness, like considering the entire Atlantic World, has become integral to most historians of the Afro-American

---

[41]Adam Rothman, *Slave Country: American Expansion and the Origins of the Deep South* (Cambridge, Mass., 2005).

[42]Michael Tadman, *Speculators and Slaves: Masters, Traders, and Slaves in the Old South* (Madison, Wis., 1989); Walter Johnson, *Soul by Soul: Life Inside the Antebellum Slave Market* (Cambridge, Mass., 2000); Steven Deyle, *Carry Me Back: The Domestic Slave Trade in American Life* (New York, 2005). Jonathan Martin's *Divided Mastery: Slave Hiring in the American South* (Cambridge, Mass., 2004) details the hiring-out practices, another somewhat lesser form of disruption of slave life.

[43]Walter Johnson, ed., *The Chattel Principle: Internal Slave Trades in the Americas* (New Haven, Conn., 2004), 6, 17, quoting from Steven Deyle's essay in that volume, "The Domestic Slave Trade in America: The Lifeblood of the Southern Slave System," 91–116.

experience. The debate has proceeded well beyond the either-or phase and has become one about how to understand processes of mutually interpenetrating cultures, how the generational experience of slaves altered them and their culture, and how people of differing ethnicities came to become African and then African Americans.

Scholars today investigate not only African origins and cultures but also the transnational connections among slaves in North America and those in the Caribbean, Canada, and elsewhere. Jeffrey Kerr-Ritchie has written about the rise of black militias here and in Canada in the antebellum period, especially in the violent 1850s. One of his purposes is "to reveal the limitations of nationalist narratives by seeking out connections among people of African descent as well as the ways in which individuals and organizations provide alternative means for comparison."[44] Kerr-Ritchie numbers among a group of historians working to place the study of slavery into a transnational context and to invite a broader, more comparative approach. Claude Clegg's *The Price of Liberty*, on the creation of Liberia, broadens the discussion of American slave culture and its effects on shaping a distant part of the Black Atlantic.[45]

Other important studies of slavery reach in new directions. First, Alan Gallay has demonstrated the importance of the trade in Indian slaves to the early development of South Carolina. Settlers, against the wishes of the colony's proprietors, enslaved and sold Indians in the West Indies in exchange for Africans to build their colony and grow their crops (see Chapter 3). Second, James Brooks's work on the Southwest borderlands re-creates the conditions of Indian slavery there and the enthusiastic participation of the Spanish. And Juliana Barr studies the French, Spanish, and Indian men who commodified and enslaved Indian women and their political and economic goals.[46] These studies (including Claudio Saunt's; see Chapter 3) point to new comparative directions and studies of transnational slave systems along with the cultural and economic pressures that make them similar and distinguish them. Dylan C. Penningroth has made a beginning in this direction with "The Claims of Slaves and Ex-Slaves to Family and Property," in which he compares slavery, kinship, and the shape of property disputes in the United States with those systems among the Asante in what is now Ghana.[47]

Finally, James and Lois Horton's collection, *Slavery and Public History: The Tough Stuff of American Memory*, offers the wisdom of a number of great historians on why it is crucial never to forget our nation's history of slavery

---

[44]Jeffrey Kerr-Ritchie, "Rehearsal for War: Black Militias in the Atlantic World," *Slavery and Abolition* 26 (April 2005): 1–14. See also David Cecelski, *The Waterman's Song: Slavery and Freedom in Maritime North Carolina* (Chapel Hill, N.C., 2001).

[45]Claude Clegg III, *The Price of Liberty: African Americans and the Making of Liberia* (Chapel Hill, N.C., 2004).

[46]Alan Gallay, *The Indian Slave Trade: The Rise of the English Empire in the American South, 1670–1717* (New Haven, Conn., 2002); James Brooks, *Captives and Cousins: Slavery, Kinship, and Community in the Southwest Borderlands* (Chapel Hill, N.C., 2002); Juliana Barr, "From Captives to Slaves: Commodifying Indian Women in the Borderlands," *Journal of American History* 92 (June 2005): 19–46.

[47]Dylan C. Penningroth, "The Claims of Slaves and Ex-Slaves to Family and Property: A Transatlantic Comparison," *American Historical Review* 112 (October 2007): 1039–69.

and to remember it accurately. False beliefs, often still taught in southern schools — like, for example, the notion that the Civil War was not fought over slavery, or that slavery was a benign institution, or that many African Americans fought willingly for the Confederacy — make meaningless the 250, or 400 depending on who's counting, years of suffering of Americans of African descent. It also trivializes the Civil War and the 600,000 who died fighting, and obscures from us the ease with which we can collaborate in harming others. Frederick Douglass said the history of African Americans could be "traced like that of a wounded man through a crowd by the blood."[48] Painful as remembering is, he believed that only by recognizing and incorporating the memory of slavery as it truly was could the nation begin to create a hopeful future for all Americans. We still have a way to go, despite the patient and painful truth-seeking of the historians represented here.

---

[48]David Blight, "If You Don't Tell It Like It Was, It Can Never Be as It Ought to Be," in *Slavery and Public History: The Tough Stuff of American Memory*, ed. James Horton and Lois Horton (New York, 2006), 28–29.

## PHILIP D. MORGAN
### *from* Slave Counterpoint    [1998]

**PHILIP D. MORGAN** (1949– ) teaches history at Johns Hopkins University. He is the author of *Slave Counterpoint: Black Culture in the Eighteenth-Century Chesapeake and Lowcountry* (1998), as well as editor of many volumes including *Arming Slaves: From Classical Times to the Modern Age* with Christopher L. Brown (2006) and *The Slaves' Economy: Independent Production by Slaves in the Americas* (1995) with Ira Berlin.

The mind-numbing trauma of the Middle Passage defies easy comprehension. Some newcomers recalled a recent branding on board ship. The memory of so many days at sea undoubtedly explains the description that some Africans gave of their master's residence as being near the "Big Water" or "great water." One newcomer, arriving at Charleston, was unable to stand after his long confinement. "It was more than a week after I left the ship," he noted, "before I could straighten my limbs." Other new arrivals, hardly able to speak any English, could yet identify the name of their ship's captain or the merchant who had handled their sale — another indication of the indelible impression that the Middle Passage and the auction block made on their minds. Yet others succumbed to utter

---

Philip Morgan, *Slave Counterpoint: Black Culture in the Eighteenth-Century Chesapeake and Lowcountry* (Chapel Hill, N.C., 1998), 445–64. Published for the Omohundro Institute of Early American History and Culture. Copyright © 1998 by the University of North Carolina Press. Used by permission of the publisher.

despair and committed suicide. One "poor pining creature hanged herself with a piece of a small Vine," another with a small piece of cord.

If they lived long enough to be purchased, Africans underwent a period
of painful adjustment. Some plainly did not wish to adjust, perhaps returning to the site of their sale in a forlorn attempt to find a return passage.
Indeed, some Africans explicitly spoke of returning home — and acted
on their words. In Virginia, a thirty-year-old African made at least "three
attempts, as he said, to get to his country," and two recent immigrants
joined other slaves near Petersburg, "being persuaded that they could
find the Way back to their own Country." In South Carolina, five "Angolans"
pursued "an East course as long as they could, thinking to return to their
own country that way." Another group of five — four men and a woman —
commandeered a small paddling canoe on the Ogeechee River. The men
soon put the woman ashore, telling "her they intended to go to look for
their own country, and that the boat was not big enough to carry her with
them."

Disoriented and alienated, many Africans yet demonstrated a significant measure of camaraderie. Most cooperated when they ran away. If
runaway advertisements are a reliable guide, just over half the African
fugitives in Virginia and South Carolina ran away in pairs or in larger
groups. In Virginia, the typical African fugitive ran away, at best, with one
other African; in South Carolina, exactly half the Africans who ran away
together left in groups of three or more, and bands of six, seven, or eight
fugitives were fairly common. Evading capture was also somewhat easier
in South Carolina than in Virginia. In South Carolina, four "Senegambians"
remained at large for at least ten months in 1754; in 1773, after about a
year in the colony, a number of Africans belonging to William Flud had
absconded twice and seem to have spent as much time off as on his Santee
plantation. Conversely, the African fugitive in Virginia faced a much bleaker
existence, as is suggested by Robert "King" Carter's optimism concerning
a recently captured "new negro woman." Now that "she hath tasted of the
hardship of the woods," he predicted, "she will go near to stay at home
where she can have her belly full." A single, isolated African fugitive, far
more common in Virginia than in South Carolina, had a hard time scav-
enging off the land.

Sometimes Africans from the same coastal region or of a similar ethnic
background collaborated. In Virginia, two "Senegambians" ran away from
their Hanover County master in 1745, and two "Ibos" quit the service of
their King William County master in 1773. In South Carolina, the ethnic
collaborations were more spectacular. In 1761, seven "Coromantees" and
a "Calabar" ran away from an estate in Prince William Parish; eight years
later, five recent immigrants "of Angola country" absconded from their
Welch Tract residence. Overall, a quarter of the runaway groups advertised
in colonial South Carolina newspapers consisted of Africans who shared
regional origins. Perhaps most remarkable, in South Carolina, Africans of
similar ethnicity established or renewed ties with one another even when
they lived on separate plantations. In 1775, an African fugitive who had

"been many years in the province" apparently headed toward a plantation "where he *frequently* used to visit a countryman of his." A decade later, two recent immigrants escaped in a four-oared boat along with "two new negroes (countrymen of theirs)" resident on a neighboring plantation. In 1807, a runaway "Mandingo" slave was "supposed to be secreted by some of his country people" on another plantation. It was not easy to maintain ethnic ties across plantation boundaries, but it was certainly not impossible — at least in the Lowcountry.

Over time, however, Africans from one ethnic group increasingly cooperated with those of another ethnic group. From the 1730s to the 1770s, runaway groups composed of a single African ethnicity declined from a third to a quarter of all groups, whereas those formed by individuals of different African origins rose from 3 to 13 percent. In 1770, the warden of the workhouse reported the capture of two women who called themselves Binsaw and Cumba, one a "Mondingo," the other a "Congo," and two men from the "Malimbo" and "Kishey" country, respectively. The following year, an African couple ran away, with their one-year-old infant: the husband was from Angola, the wife from Calabar. By necessity or choice, Africans increasingly associated with members of other ethnic groups.

Another association that became important to Africans in the New World was that among shipmates. A number of runaway groups consisting of slaves described as "lately come in the country" or "lately imported" or simply as "new" likely comprised former shipmates. In Virginia, concrete evidence of the shipmate bond is rare. A good example, however, concerns a few of the 240 Africans imported in the snow *Yanimarew* in the summer of 1770. One month after being purchased and taken to Amherst County, Charles ran away. Meanwhile, in Richmond, three men from the same ship fled their master. They apparently sought out the companionship of their former shipmates (perhaps Charles was among them), for their master reported, "It is imagined that they were seen some time ago (along with three others of the same cargo) on Chickahominy, and it is supposed they are still lurking about the skirts of that swamp." But the sale of Africans individually or in small groups to dispersed plantations throughout the Chesapeake made the maintenance of shipmate ties difficult.

In South Carolina, shipmates had an easier time maintaining contact. Some ran away from the same plantation, such as three Senegambians who eloped three weeks after disembarking the *Princess Carolina*, or the four Angolans, part of a complement of 360 slaves shipped in the *Shepherd*, who returned to the site of their sale two months after their purchase. Shipmates separated from one another also renewed contact. Thus, in 1774, two young men from the Grain Coast ran off with "five or six wenches of the same cargo" belonging to a neighboring plantation, and, eleven years later, Robin ran away to a shipyard because it employed some slaves "purchased out of the same ship" as himself. Two shipmates brought to the Charleston workhouse in 1759 identified their master and then declared that he owned "a negro wench named Betty and that she came out of the same ship with them." In 1774, Homidy, a "Guinea negro," and Polidore, a "Congo," absconded from their Goose Creek plantation; their master thought they would stick together because "both came here in one ship about 18 months ago." This ready recognition of the shipmate tie suggests its importance.

Very occasionally, African kin ties, usually between siblings, survived the Middle Passage. Three slaves from Angola who ran away from a Wando Neck plantation in 1734 included two brothers; in 1779, two African runaways, one aged about twenty-five and the other twenty-three, were brothers who belonged to the same planter and had worked at the same jobs (first on a schooner and then in a rum distillery); and, six years later, two Senegambian brothers ran away together. One runaway group reveals that even generational ties sometimes remained intact. Two Africans lodged in the New Bern jail in 1767 said they were father and son; the father, aged forty-five, spoke "broken English," whereas his young son spoke "better English."

Some Africans made a greater commitment to long-term cooperation when they attempted to establish an autonomous *maroon* (from *cimarrón*, meaning escaped or runaway, in a New World context) settlement. In the Chesapeake, African numbers were never overwhelming, whites predominated, and the topography was not particularly conducive to maroon settlements. In the early eighteenth century, Africans attempted to establish a few settlements on the frontier, but they were short-lived. In the Lowcountry, more Africans, a black majority, and extensive swamplands were greater encouragements to maroon bands. Furthermore, the proximity of Spanish Florida provided a ready sanctuary for Lowcountry fugitives. In 1738, a large contingent — perhaps seventy slaves — fled from South Carolina to Saint Augustine, attracted no doubt by the founding of a new frontier town named Gracia Real de Santa Teresa de Mose populated by freed slaves. A small but steady stream of Lowcountry slaves aimed their flight for Saint Augustine. By what they took with them, a number of African runaway groups in South Carolina indicate that they had independence firmly in mind. Carrying axes, hoes, and blankets, a number of African groups revealed a determination to cope with their new environment.

Some of these Lowcountry groups established settled camps. A vivid account of an expedition mounted against a band of Savannah River maroons in November 1765 provides a graphic description of a quasi-permanent settlement. The expedition first encountered a large canoe that, according to their guide, was manned by the maroons' "head or leading man." They then encountered three blacks who took to the swamp. Proceeding at least four miles through a swamp in which they were often up to their waists in water and mud, they came to the "town," where

they discovered two Negroes on a Scaffold one Beating a Drum and the other hoisting Colours, but on their resoluteing coming up they Jump'd off the scaffold and betook themselves to flight after discharging their guns without doing them any mischief, that on their arrival at the Town which was then totally deserted they found it a square consisting of four

Houses 17 feet long and 14 feet wide, that the kettles were upon the fire boiling rice and about 15 bushels of rough rice, Blanketts, Potts, Pails, Shoes, Axes, and many other tools all which together with the Town they set fire to.

The military organization of this township, together with its regular lay-out and signs of residential stability, make it a notable example of *marronage* in mainland British America. . . .

In the Chesapeake, the vast majority of Africans neither fled with ship-mates nor attempted to set up independent communities, and they left little trace. Their "invisibility" is easily explained. Africans were a minority of Virginia slaves by the early eighteenth century, and their proportion declined markedly throughout the century. Slaveholdings were generally small, and the occasional large plantation often garnered a number of Africans, so most recent immigrants would be fortunate indeed to end up sharing the same residence. Even on a large estate, the overwhelming majority of immigrants lived on quarters with numerous native adults and children.

African names soon disappeared in Virginia. According to a study of slave names in Middlesex County in the late seventeenth and early eigh-teenth centuries, fewer than 5 percent of slaves had African names. The proportion throughout Virginia declined rapidly thereafter. Rare indeed were the two plantations in mid-eighteenth-century Goochland County that listed eleven African names in all ( Jolloff, Quaw, Fatima, Congo, Cudgo, Shantee, Cudjee, Bussee, Jallapa, Jubah, and Abanah); if all of these individuals were Africans, they accounted for about a third of the adult slaves on each estate. Ethnic designations as well as African names were sparse. In 1782, "Ebo" Billy and Billy "Congo" belonged to William Daingerfield, but they were heavily outnumbered by the other 140 Dain-gerfield slaves who betrayed no African antecedents in their names. African names were also infrequent among Virginia slave runaways. In 1767, a run-away from Lunenburg County preferred to be known as Fooser; four years later an African runaway from Williamsburg went by the name of Quomony; and, as late as 1790, an African resident of Surry County was known as Mungo. Perhaps more telling, however, was the "outlandish" slave who, like these others, retained his African name but compromised with Anglo-American expectations. He sometimes called "himself John Quash."

On Lowcountry plantations, the African presence was more notable. In 1778, the thirty-four slave men resident on Elias Ball's Comingtee planta-tion were equally divided between native-born and African-born. The three oldest men were from Angola, all estimated at age fifty-five, whereas another fourteen from "Gambia" predominated among men in their early thirties and forties. The youngest African was only twenty-seven, whereas all men in their late teens and early twenties were creoles. If authority followed age, then these African men should have been dispro-portionately influential. Thirty years later, Colonel Stapleton of Saint Helena Island owned 112 slaves. Three Africans—seventy-nine-year-old

Sambo, a former gardener, eighty-year-old Dorinda, "a cripple crawling upon hands and knees," and fifty-year-old Dido from "Moroco" — were no doubt survivors from the eighteenth-century era of African immigration. Another twenty-seven Africans — a quarter of the total complement and fully half of the prime slaves (aged twenty to fifty) — were recent immigrants, survivors of the last great flourish of the African slave trade into Carolina. Almost all of these newcomers were in their twenties; two were brothers; a remarkable number (twenty in all) had paired off in marriage; four of these couples had produced at least one child; only one African man had found a creole wife; five men and one woman were single. These Africans, perhaps in large part because of the demographic structure of this plantation, looked inward for their most important social ties.

On these and other Lowcountry plantations, African names were more common among creoles than among recent immigrants. At Comingtee, only one African man (Quash) but two creoles (Quau and Quaco) had African names. Similarly, creoles with African names (Coomba, Dembo, and Minda) outnumbered Africans with homeland names (Mamoody and Sambo) on Colonel Stapleton's plantation. Of the 208 slaves belonging to the estate of Daniel Huger, 10 percent of the 96 adults, 13 percent of the 27 boys and girls (many if not most of whom must have been creoles), and 15 percent of the 85 children (almost certainly all creoles) had African names. The pattern seems clear: although some African immigrants were able to retain their names, more often they bequeathed homeland names to their children in an effort to honor tradition and family ties.

Throughout the eighteenth century, Africans in South Carolina maintained symbolic ties to their native country through their naming patterns. At midcentury, about one in five slaves belonging to Benjamin De St. Julien, to Elisha Ball, and to Benjamin Godin had African names. Although no late-eighteenth-century estate matched these levels, at least one in ten slaves on plantations belonging to Daniel Huger, to Thomas Elliott, and to George Austin had an African name. Moreover, not just the number but the range of African names was impressive in South Carolina. In Virginia, the standard African names — Cudjo, Cuffee, Quamina, Quash, Sambo — predominated, whereas in South Carolina they were joined by more unusual names, such as Balipho, Bendar, Dubau, Fulladi, Moosa, Noko, Okree, Sogo, Yanki, and Yarrow. Furthermore, African ethnic or regional designations — Jack Gambia or John Gola, for instance — were more than occasional on some South Carolina plantations: 10 of 148 slaves belonging to Noah Serre conveyed their ethnic identity in their names, as did 5 of 83 belonging to Joshua Grimball.

Perhaps most significant, many Africans in South Carolina continued to use a "country name" *after* their masters had christened them. This evidence obviously complicates patterns of naming based on lists drawn up by masters. Even the most Anglicized list of names could conceal the continued use of African names among the slaves. In some cases, as Peter Wood has pointed out, African and Anglo-American names coexisted because they sounded alike. Alexander Wood reported that his slave went "by the Name of Cooper Joe or Cudjoe"; a recent African immigrant brought to the Charleston workhouse gave his name as "Tom or Tomboe." But since most African and Anglo-American names were not readily convertible, a newcomer often had to struggle to retain a homeland name. A surprising number were successful. Thus, two Angolan slaves named after the biblical heroes Moses and Sampson continued to be known as Monvigo and Goma. Bristol held to his African name Cuffee, John to Footabea, London to Appee, March to Arrow, and Charlestown to Tamoo. One slave woman's retention of an African name led to much confusion when she became part of a marriage settlement. Her former overseer testified that the slave named both Affey and Occoe was indeed one and the same person. He recalled that the slave's owners "oftner called her by [the name Affey] than by the Name of Occoe." More significant, perhaps, is that Occoe, like many another slave, ensured that whites knew the name she presumably preferred.

The most dramatic example of African self-identification occurred during the Stono Rebellion. The instigators were twenty "Angolan" slaves — from the Kongo kingdom. Perhaps, as John Thornton has suggested, former soldiers provided the nucleus of the rebels. Their seizure of a supply of guns, which they seem to have handled adroitly, suggests prior experience with weapons. Their marching under banners to the accompaniment of drums is also reminiscent of African practices. Finally, when the rebels "set to dancing," they were not necessarily acting shortsightedly but, rather, engaging in a form of military exercise, much like drill in Europe. For Kongo soldiers, "dancing was a form of training to quicken reflexes and develop parrying skills." In Kongo, dancing a war dance was virtually synonymous with declaring war.

In the long run, however, Africans, even in the Lowcountry, were aliens in a strange land. Many found themselves completely isolated. One "Angolan" man, found on the high seas off the coast of South Carolina, lay "in a small canoe half-full of water in a wretched helpless condition"; another recent immigrant, hauled out of a swamp after swimming across the Santee River, was "almost perished with hunger, very much crippled in his feet and legs"; an elderly Angolan arrived at the workhouse in tattered rags, saying he had been in the woods for two years; and the Cherokees captured a runaway who spoke very little English, though he had been absent "two summers," who reported that his companion had "died in the woods by eating a snake." The sense of bewilderment and frustration at not being able to communicate with fellow slaves or whites is personified by an African "of the Horobania country" who, when asked to report his own or his master's name, could only mouth "a word like Fisher, which cannot be understood, whether he means that for his own or his master's name"; he languished in the Cheraws district jail for well over a year.

Africans in the Chesapeake were even more alienated. None was more so than the African, recently imported, who "taking Notice of his Master's giving another Correction for a Misdemeanor, went to a Grindstone, and making a Knife sharp cut his own Throat, and died on the spot." The typical experience for the eighteenth-century African in Virginia must have been rather like that recounted by Olaudah Equiano, who spoke eloquently of his sense of isolation on arrival in the colony:

> We were landed up a river a good way from the sea, about Virginia coun-t[r]y, where we saw few or none of our native Africans, and not one soul who could talk to me. I was a few weeks weeding grass, and gathering stones in a plantation; and at last all my companions were distributed dif-ferent ways, and only myself was left. I was now exceedingly miserable, and thought myself worse off than any of the rest of my companions; for they could talk to each other, but I had no person to speak to that I could understand.

Equiano might have been mistaken only in his assumption that his fellow Africans had companions with whom to talk. More than likely, they did not.

But Equiano never forgot Africa, as he later vividly recollected in his autobiography. The pool of homeland memories was always deeper than surface appearances might suggest. These remembrances might amount to nothing more than a reminder of an important event. In South Carolina, Malinke Ben had a large scar on his left arm produced by a knife, Toby a blotch on his right cheek from a dog bite, Anthony a hole near his eye from a bullet, and a "Jalunka" (Dyalonke) slave a great bump in the small of his back, the result of a fall. All remembered receiving these wounds in their "own country." In Virginia, Charles had a couple of broken front teeth, which he said "was done by a Cow in his Country." As insignificant as these connections to a homeland might seem in themselves, they were reminders of a valued past. These, and many other memories, were a resource on which Lowcountry and Chesapeake slaves could draw.

Homeland divisions continued in the New World. Differences among Africans were particularly noticeable and persistent in the Lowcountry. In 1740, Alexander Garden observed the "many various Ages, Nations, Lan-guages" within the "Whole Body of Slaves." Differences were known to produce hostilities. Some Lowcountry Africans bore palpable reminders of homeland conflict: Jack had a "large blotch under his lower lip, occa-sioned by fighting in his own country," and Joe had a great scar in the small of his back, the result of a knifing in Africa. James Barclay's experi-ences on a South Carolina rice plantation in the 1770s indicate that African memories were not short-lived. "There are some provinces from whence they are brought," Barclay observed, "whereof the people have a violent antipathy to one another, and [when] they are brought over here, the same antipathy subsists." In particular, Barclay continued, "those of Gully or Gulli [Angola] and Iba [Igbos] are the chief. The one will say to the other, 'You be Gulli Niga, what be the use of you, you be good for noth-ing.' The other will reply 'You be Iba Niga; Iba Niga great 'askal [rascal].'"

Even in the late eighteenth century, the deep strains that divided African from African were evident, as an exchange between the traveler William Attmore and a slave immigrant illustrates:

ATTMORE, How came you brought from yr. Country.

POLYDORE, I went with many more to attack a town, where they were too strong for us, they killed a great many, and took 140 of us prisoners, and sold us —

ATTMORE, Had you not better have left them alone and remained in peace at home?

POLYDORE, No — My Nation always fight that Nation —

ATTMORE, And what would [you] do if you return'd to your Country now, wou'd you be quiet?

POLYDORE, No — I go there, and fight 'em worse than ever.

Apparently, absence had not made the heart grow fonder.

In the Chesapeake, conflict among Africans was less evident and confined to the early eighteenth century. African marriage customs provided a source of tension on Edmund Jenings's Selsdon quarter in King William County. In 1712, Roger hanged himself in an old tobacco house for "not any Reason," an uncomprehending master observed, except his "being hindred from keeping other negroes mens wifes beside his owne." After about 1740, however, the tidewater received few Africans, and the piedmont, the destination of most Africans for the next thirty years, dispersed its African influx widely. As a result, Africans rarely generated the numbers sufficient to maintain homeland rivalries and antipathies.

As Africans became less numerous in both regional populations, their differences must have seemed increasingly incongruous, even irrelevant. This process occurred earlier in Virginia than in South Carolina. But, from the first, many Africans in both regions dramatically overcame ethnic differences by cooperating in maroon bands, by running away together, by marrying. An even more notable social bond that emerged among Africans was the tie between shipmates. Whether the shipmate attachment became as significant a principle of social organization in North America as in other parts of the New World — where it extended beyond the original tie to encompass the children of shipmates — is unlikely, but its existence is a testament to the creativeness and cooperativeness of Africans in the New World. Last, perhaps the most important way differences among Africans became irrelevant was the necessity for extensive contact with creoles.

## Creoles and Africans

Creoles and Africans did not always get along. An occasional glimpse can be caught of tensions between native and newcomer in the early Chesapeake. In 1728, Robert "King" Carter, aware of "a great many new hands" in his gangs, warned his overseers to take particular care that the "old hands," no doubt largely native-born, did not abuse the immigrants. One African who arrived in the Chesapeake at about this time needed no such protection. He "always expressed great contempt for his fellow slaves." He viewed them, "as he said, a mean and vulgar race." Africans did not always defer to creoles. Conversely, a child of African parents might feel embarrassment at his origins. In the narrative of his life, David George, who was born in Virginia, mentioned the names of his parents — John and Judith — but precious little else, except to point out that they "had not the fear of God before their eyes." With this note of disapproval, George preferred to draw a veil over their lives.

Tensions among creoles and Africans persisted longer in the Lowcountry than in the Chesapeake. In the beginning, the African majority was more powerful. Thus, in 1710, the Reverend James Gignilliat reported that, when a slave was baptized, all the other slaves, predominantly Africans, "do laugh at 'em and render 'em worse and worse." Thirty years later, the Reverend Lewis Jones found that the seed of Christianity "Sown in the young Ones," or native born, "seems to be Choak'd by their conversation with the Elder uninstructed Negroes," or Africans. But creoles soon dominated in the Lowcountry as in the Chesapeake, and, inevitably, the objects of laughter began to shift. At midcentury, Scipio, an accomplished waterman, boasted of his ability to "go before Gentleman, for he had waited before on his Master in the Council Chamber, and was used to it" and described one of his crew members as "a Fool" who "did not know how to Talk before White People." By the early nineteenth century, creoles could adopt a less strident, more condescending tone when referring to those less conversant with white ways than themselves. A traveler overheard a native black Carolinian "observe, on seeing a drove of newly imported negroes going out of Charleston to a plantation in the country — 'Ah! dey be poor devils, me fetch ten of dem, if massa swap.'" The self-confident creole took pity on the newcomers.

Continuing friction among Africans and creoles should not obscure how they learned to cooperate. In the Chesapeake, creoles were a majority on most plantations and neighborhoods by the early eighteenth century; they set the tone and tenor of slave life in the region remarkably early. Africans learned the ropes from them. Instructive is the pair of runaways who fled their Surry County home. Bristol, an "outlandish Fellow," ran away in the company of Bob, a ferryman, an "artful, designing, and exceedingly smooth tongued" mulatto who possessed "an immoderate Stock of Assurance." The master predicted that Bristol would "entirely submit to, and confide in, his Companion's Counsels." Similarly, even in a Maryland parish that in the late 1730s had seen an influx of Africans, the leader of the approximately two hundred slaves allegedly involved in a plot to kill all white men was a creole. . . .

Although the lessons largely flowed from creoles to Africans, the reverse also occurred. Charles Ball, born in Maryland about 1780, was fortunate enough to know his African grandfather, "old Ben," who had been brought to Calvert County a half-century earlier. Ball recalled that his father, after he had been forcibly separated from his wife (Ball's mother), consoled himself by spending "nearly all his leisure time with my grandfather, who claimed kindred with some royal family in Africa, and had been a great warrior in his native country." After his father fled to escape sale, Charles had only his grandfather to "claim kindred." He learned of his grandfather's "strange and peculiar notions of religion" and marveled at how, even at age eighty, the half-acre he cultivated on his own account produced "a large portion of his subsistence." Charles Ball's African grandfather became the significant other in his early life.

In Charleston, even the most sophisticated creole slaves lived cheek by jowl with Africans. Urban settings promoted acculturation, and, in Charleston more than anywhere else, creoles could congregate. But they rubbed shoulders with Africans. Creoles met African women in the marketplace, played the popular African dice game papaw, and saw "frequent" African-style funeral processions. They introduced Africans to the delights of grogshops, to Sunday recreations, and to work opportunities. They cooperated, as did Mulatto Betty and African Molly, two runaways, who were seen "lurking about town" together. Urban Africans adapted quickly. Titus was "very cunning and artful" — the standard description of a creole — even though he spoke "bad English." Perhaps he learned from his more acculturated acquaintances his ability to "pass for a fool."

Rural creoles in South Carolina associated closely with Africans at work, at home, in flight, even in dress. Creole Sampson labored alongside five other sawyers, all from Angola. Native-born Jack married Sapho "of the Guiney country." A creole family of husband, wife, and daughter ran away with a Calabar and an Angolan. Creoles were often the dominant partners. Native-born Red "persuaded" Isaac, an African, to run away. Peter of "Angola country" spoke very good English when he fled; one reason might have been his association with Jamaican-born Tom, who was "very sensible [and] artful." The master predicted that Peter would "accompany Tom wherever he goes"; and the duo ran away twice more that same year. Rumor had it that the native-born slave who persuaded twelve Angolan slaves to run away with him "was taking them back to their own country." This native leader knew what the newcomers wanted to hear. By example, if nothing else, creoles taught Africans to modify their appearance. Igbo Beckey assimilated to the point that she "look[ed] more like a country born" slave; "Angolan" Peter could "pass for country born."

Forcibly moved from the Chesapeake to the Lowcountry in about 1805, Charles Ball's contacts with Africans greatly expanded. Rather than his single grandfather, he now encountered "a great many African slaves," many newly arrived, with whom he became "intimately acquainted." Their range of religious beliefs impressed him: he met "Mohamadans," worshipers of many gods, and believers in witchcraft and conjuration. One of the "Mohamadans," who prayed "in a language I did not understand," told him an elaborate animal story featuring camels and lions, as a way to explain his own capture and transportation to North America. Ball recalled a weekend feast to celebrate "the laying by of the corn and cotton" at which the old folks "recited the stories of former times." Most of the tales concerned events in Africa "and were sufficiently fraught with demons, miracles, and murders, to fix the attention of many hearers."

Not all was harmonious. Ball met a former Maryland creole slave, like himself, who had been compelled to marry. Her husband was, in her condescending words, "a native of Africa, and still retains the manners and religion of his country." A priest in his former nation and the proud possessor of many wives, the immigrant had trouble adjusting to his lowly status in South Carolina and often maltreated his native-born wife. This troubled marriage symbolized what, for Ball, was the most significant division on his new South Carolina plantation: the rift of incomprehension between the African, "indignant" about enslavement, "revengeful" toward whites, uninterested in material comforts, and bent on returning to Africa after death, and the creole, who was "not so impatient of slavery" and whose "heart pants for no heaven beyond the waves of the ocean."

Yet Ball's close contacts with Africans, his respect for their religions, his recollection of their stories, his inclusion in their feasts, and particularly his account of how he entered into "the participation of the felicity of [this plantation] community" demonstrate that racial solidarity could overcome divisions between native and newcomer.

## Creoles

The emergence of a creole majority facilitated cohesiveness among slaves. Once sex ratios became more balanced, slaves found it much easier to find mates; a major source of tension was thereby greatly reduced. Similarly, once numbers of children and old people began to populate the slave quarters, the barracks atmosphere associated with concentrations of adult men dissipated. Furthermore, for all the pain that slavery entailed, creoles at least did not have to undergo the traumas of capture, enslavement, and overseas migration. They had a distinct advantage over Africans in growing up in their environment. They knew no other home. They were raised with whites and knew their ways.

No slave population in the plantation world of British North America was as familiar with white ways as that of the Chesapeake. In describing their creole slaves, Virginia masters employed a battery of flattering adjectives. Native-born slaves were brisk, lively, smart, sharp, sensible, shrewd, subtle, ingenious, and artful. Some slaves were even said to be "genteel." Creoles generally spoke fluently and were often described as smooth-tongued or fair-spoken. A few could read and write; one knew a number of "indecent and Sailor songs"; another spoke "Scotch and [sang] Scotch songs"; some loved cockfighting, cardplaying, and horse races, three notable regional pastimes; yet others grew fond of the major product of the region, so that one slave "always had a great Quid of Tobacco in his mouth," another was a great taker of snuff, and an elderly couple wore down their teeth by incessant pipe smoking. In short, many native-born slaves seemed thoroughly at home, which is not really surprising because they knew no other.

This is not to imply, of course, that Virginia creoles were passive and content with their lot. Indeed, their masters also exploited a rich vocabulary that bespoke a far more negative view of the native-born. All too often they described creoles as bold, audacious, impertinent, saucy, sly, knavish, cunning, crafty, insinuating, slippery, dissembling, and deceitful. Consider mulatto Argyle, resident in Hampton, who loved to drink, was "very bold in his Cups," but, even more ominously, was "dastardly when sober." Or sixteen-year-old George, born on Maryland's Eastern Shore, who was "very smart in Conversation, and an insinuating Rascal, as would appear from his cozening the Post Rider out of his Mail about 15 Miles" north of Urbanna. Or twenty-year-old Anthony, who was "very cunning and comical in his behavior," indicating perhaps an early attempt to use humor to dupe white folks. Thoroughly conversant with white mores, creoles proved extremely irritating to their masters. Creole slaves were more likely than Africans to subvert authority with stealth.

Perhaps the most common way in which Virginia creoles, like Africans, vexed their masters was to run away. Unlike Africans, however, creoles generally ran away alone. This was especially true in Virginia, where three-quarters of creole fugitives absconded singly. Creoles might have realized that a fugitive stood a better chance of escape by relying on his or her own resources, rather than by joining a more conspicuous group. The minority who engaged in cooperative action, however, sometimes combined resources in daring ways.

MICHAEL GOMEZ
# from African Identity and Slavery in the Americas [1999]

MICHAEL GOMEZ (1955– ) teaches in the History and Middle Eastern and Islamic Studies Departments at New York University. His works include *Exchanging Our Country Marks* (1998), *Reversing Sail: A History of the African Diaspora* (2005), and *Black Crescent: The Experience and Legacy of African Muslims in the Americas* (2005).

We will never know what we want to know about African enslavement in the Americas until we understand who the Africans were. New World slavery certainly qualifies as one of the most important chapters in the history of labor, and in truth informs (if not transforms) the meaning of labor in the Western Hemisphere in a fundamental way. Slavery has served and continues to serve as a measure by which workers assess the equity of wages, working conditions, benefits, and relations with management, so that slavery has been and continues to be the touchstone of American labor movements. Those movements began with Africans, forcibly removed

Michael Gomez, "African Identity and Slavery in the Americas," *Radical History Review* 75 (1999): 111–20. Copyright © 1999, MARHO: The Radical Historians Organization, Inc. All rights reserved. Used by permission of the publisher, Duke University Press.

to myriad circumstances in the West where they were called upon to provide every conceivable service in support of economies both within and
beyond colonial eras. The full response of Africans to their enslavement,
however, will never be appreciated if only interpreted through the lone
prism of labor. Africans were workers, but they were far more than that.
They had lived as members of specific societies in Africa, so that although
their lives were altered by enslavement, they continued to be informed
by both the African antecedent and by the unique combinations of their
distinctive backgrounds in the various locales of the Americas. Their
cultural and social provenances, therefore, become critical to grasping
the totality of their sojourn and its relation to corresponding experiences
elsewhere.

It may be that scholars of North American history are uncomfortable
with the idea of the enslaved as Africans. Based upon the voluminous literature on slavery concerning the nascent United States, there seems to
be a consensus and a decided preference for writing about Africans as
slaves. Leading authorities on slavery in North America produce with
impunity tome after tome, with little regard for the fact that their subjects
came out of specific social and political contexts, that they had collective
identities, and that they participated in recognizable cultures. In fact, it is
perfectly acceptable for scholars of North American slavery to have absolutely no background or training in African history and political economy.
It is not that the African background is beyond reach or unattainable. It
is not that the scholarship on Africa has not made substantial progress
over the last thirty years. Rather, this lamentable state of affairs is the con-
fluential consequence of at least two factors: an abysmally low level of
dialogue between Africanists and Americanists, and a lingering, arrogant
assumption in the academy that an appreciation of the African background is at best tangential to North American slavery, a view in part sustained by the mistaken argument that the relatively smaller importation
of Africans into North America vis-à-vis the Caribbean and South America
renders their origins unimportant. The objectification of the African therefore necessarily continues, notwithstanding protestations to the contrary.
Clearly, the status quo is egregious, intolerable, and no longer justifiable.
The day of the learned scholar of North American slavery, unlearned in
the histories and cultures of Africa, is mercifully coming to an end.

Recent work on the history of North American slavery demonstrates
both the necessity and the viability of envisioning the enslaved as Africans
in North America. A number of books and articles can be mentioned, but
there are three which are particularly noteworthy. Gwendolyn Midlo
Hall's study of Africans in colonial Louisiana demonstrates the potential
of applying a class analysis to workers who were simultaneously cultural
and sociopolitical agents. Margaret Washington's discussion of the Gullah
explores very specific linkages between the Georgia–South Carolina coast
and West Africa, and provides an example of effective scholarly method.
Sterling Stuckey's examination extends beyond slavery, but his point is that
the enslavement experience is crucial to understanding what follows. His

elaboration of ring ceremonies and the shout in particular is important, but more pertinent for the purposes of this essay is his success in identifying these rites with certain groups and territories within Africa. In all three studies, there is a clearly established pattern of moving the discourse from generalization to specification. We are no longer talking about "Africans" in abstraction; rather, the faces and perspectives of more precisely and carefully defined groups of Africans are materializing. In my own work, I have tried to extend the logical implications of these seminal studies.

While such efforts as the aforementioned are a beginning, they are only a beginning. There is so much more to be learned from approaching the enslaved as Africans with distinct heritages. Fortunately, the growth and expansion of the African Diaspora as a field of organized academic inquiry is providing a much-needed analytical context and stimulus for the study of Africans throughout the Americas, including North America. The concept of the African Diaspora allows scholars who have conventionally worked within territorially defined boundaries to begin transcending those circumscriptions and to initiate the process of reconfiguring the paradigms, working across disciplines and incorporating multiple methodologies. A knowledge of Africa becomes central to the enterprise, transforming it from mere variant on the theme of comparative inquiry to one in which a series of exchanges along cultural, political, and social lines are simultaneously negotiated between Africa and multiple sites within the Diaspora. In fact, the surge of intellectual activity in the African Diaspora is increasingly revealing just how retarded the scholarship on North American slavery really is. For example, it is practically a matter of course that the discussion of enslaved Africans in Latin America and the Caribbean is placed within the framework of specific provenance, and this has characterized the secondary literature for decades. While the background and accomplishments of Africans are not always highly esteemed, the fact that Africans are cultural agents is at least acknowledged. Insofar as the African presence is concerned, then, North Americanists have much to learn from their Latin Americanist and West Indianist colleagues.

A brief consideration of only a few examples of a vast literature will make the point. Perhaps the most obvious place to begin is with Brazil, where the discourse concerning the African presence during enslavement has seen its share of controversy. From the "benign" school best represented by Gilberto Freyre, and in particular his 1933 publication *Casa grande e senzala,* to the São Paulo school led by Emilia Viotti da Costa, Florestan Fernandes, and Fernando Henrique Cardoso, the debate centered on the severity of the institution and vacillated between placing an emphasis on the overall impact of slavery and the inner lives of the enslaved, polar positions successfully merged by Katia M. de Queirós Mattoso in 1979. But whatever the position taken, few such scholars have argued against seeing Africans as members of specific sociocultural groups, or what could be called in some cases ethnicities, and what in point of fact were called *nações* in Brazil. Africans were seen as members of varying *nações,* and whether the collective identity was imported from Africa or was assembled in Brazil is really a minor point. Africans responded to enslavement as members of *nações*, often rebelling on the basis of ethnicity and forming cooperative ventures such as the *irmandades* (brotherhoods) on that same premise. Indeed, it is customary to see in the literature whole chapters devoted to an examination of the *procedências africanas* (African origins) of black Brazilians, and the distinctions are often carried and made applicable throughout the body of the work. Nagôs (Yoruba), Minas, Haussás, Tapas or Nupês, Bornus, Fulás, Jejes, Mandingas or Mandingueiros, Congos, and Angolas, some of whom were Muslim while others remained faithful to uniquely African religions, very much inform the analysis; the fact that these terms at times refer to sociocultural groups and at other times to geographic locations does not obscure the fact that Africans in Brazil organized their lives around identities initially formed on African soil. It is not possible to discuss Africans in Brazil as constituting a single community without referring to their "procedêndias."

The case of Brazil presents few surprises, as the expectation of African continuities runs high. In fact, Brazil is often used to demonstrate how "unAfrican" North America was/is; this contention will be addressed later. At this point, it is sufficient to see that to be African in Brazil during (and often after) slavery was to live in close identification with and proximity to a proscribed community, at times in sympathy with others from Africa, but with the understanding that ethnic or cultural heterogeneity was to be maintained. These were choices made by Africans.

The non-Spanish speaking Caribbean provides interesting examples of ethnically-articulated African identities in patterns reminiscent of the Brazilian experience. Concerning Saint-Domingue, Gabriel Debien relates that of 14,167 named persons enslaved in 1796 and 1797, there were 6,188 of African origin, some of whom could be divided into the following categories: Congo (1,651), Nago (736), Arada (544), Igbo (519), Bambara (24), Hausa (124), "Senegals" (95), Susu (67), "Poulards" (26), Mandinka (26), "Malles" (3). Similar distinctions were made in Guadeloupe, Martinique, and Guiana by observers in the seventeenth and eighteenth centuries. David Barry Gaspar and Mavis Campbell have determined that Akan affiliation was crucial to certain developments in Antigua and Jamaica, respectively, while Michael Mullin has likewise emphasized the Akan element in revolts throughout the English colonies, particularly Jamaica. Some of the more fascinating work on ethnicity in the West Indies in fact postdates slavery proper, and concerns the importation of indentured laborers in nineteenth-century Trinidad. Maureen Warner-Lewis has compiled studies which take as their premise the perpetuation of African identity in Trinidad as a function of ethnicity, having interviewed informants from 1966–72 who even then claimed precise descent from Igbo, Kissi, Wolof, "Popo" (from Dahomey), and Akan forbears. The memory of the Hausa, the Mandinka, the Gurunsi (of Ghana), and even the Fulbe was yet alive among these descendants. But in particular, the Yoruba and Yoruba culture were recalled. As is the case with Brazil, there is a substantial secondary literature on the Caribbean for which the notion of African ethnicity is certainly familiar.

Spanish-speaking America conforms to the general pattern. This is expected in the instance of Cuba, where importation of Africans was substantial and protracted. To take only two examples of the literature, Fernando Ortiz's 1906 study of African culture in Cuba, as problematic as it is, pays particular attention to the *Lucumí* (Yoruba) contribution to "*brujería*" ("witchcraft") while also making references to a Muslim presence on the island. Esteban Montejo's famous autobiography reveals a wide range of cultural continuities with Africa, and makes the following observation: "On the sugar mills/plantations there were blacks of distinct nations. Each one had its characteristics. The Congos were black, although there were a lot of *jabaos* [of mixed white and black ancestry]. They were usually small boys. The Mandingas were of medium complexion. They were tall and very strong. As far as my mother was concerned they were bad influences and criminals. They always kept to themselves. The *gangas* [from Congo] were good people. They were short, with freckled faces. Many were living as runaways. The Carabalis were fierce like the Congos."

The skeptic would surmise that such categorizations based upon perceived ethnicity were largely derivative of the eighteenth and nineteenth centuries, after slaveholders had accumulated sufficient knowledge and experience to typecast various Africans and presumed to assign ethnic identities based upon phenotype and alleged ports of origin. There is no doubt that some Africans were given putative group names by slaveholders, and there is no question but that some were misidentified. But it must be remembered that fictive identity was a universal phenomenon formulated all over the world and during much of human history. This holds true for Africans as well, for whom the question of group identity did not begin on this side of the Atlantic, but in Africa itself. The vicissitudes of the slave trade, for example, necessitated frequent and significant population displacements all over West and West Central Africa. Persons taken as prisoners of war or by way of kidnaping may have eventually wound up in the Americas (or in the Islamic world), but as many never left African soil, they entered into a continuum of relations with the host society whereby the stranger gradually, often over generations, overcame her or his alien status and moved closer to the ideal of socially-sanctioned familial ties. In time, legal fiction invariably became social and cultural reality. Such historical verities should give pause, but should not deter us from recognizing group identity in Africa or Asia or Europe, and should not hinder the process in the Americas. Even so, there are even more compelling reasons to conclude that African ethnicity played a powerful role in the Americas.

Esteban Montejo recorded his Cuban memoirs in the late nineteenth century. However, some four hundred years earlier, in the fifteenth century, similar distinctions among Africans were already being made. To be sure, the Portuguese and Spanish had become acquainted with sub-Saharan

Africans via the Muslim occupation of Iberia beginning in the eighth century. By 1462 the Portuguese had come to know inhabitants of Senegambia better than others; interestingly the Portuguese did not call them Senegambians or "Senegals," but *negros de jalof*, a reference to the state of Jolof. By 1522, the Wolof of Senegambia were known as the "Gelofes" by the Spanish, and were fingered in Hispaniola as troublemakers along with Jews, Moors, Moriscos, and *ladinos* or acculturated blacks, such that a series of royal decrees were repeatedly issued to ban their importation into Hispaniola. In their place, the Spanish developed a preference for *negros bozales*, or non-Spanish speaking, recently-arrived Africans, as they were thought to be easier to control. By the middle of the sixteenth century, however, the Spanish had become much more familiar with Africans, and took some care in distinguishing enslaved "Gelofes" from the "Mandingas" in Mexico. By 1570 we have documents referring to the *castas de rios de Guinea*, or the "nations of the rivers of Guinea" as the land of the "Gelofes," "Biafras," and "Mandingos." By 1600, the *castas de Angola* were added and further divided into the "Loandas," "Benguelas," "Congos," and "Manicongos." For that same century, Gonzalo Aguirre Beltrán has produced documentation for some 501 enslaved persons in Mexico (out of a total of more than 20,569 Africans), who were placed into some twenty-nine categories, the latter a mixture of place names (e.g., "Guinea," Mozambique") and ethnic or group affiliations ("Zape," Mina," "Arara"). Clearly, the Spanish and Portuguese were learning rapidly.

As Colin Palmer points out, Mexico and Peru were the two largest slave importers in the sixteenth and seventeenth centuries. By the second half of the seventeenth century these importations were in sharp decline, but even so, some 200,000 Africans had labored in Mexico by 1827, the year of formal emancipation. Long before then, the view of Africans as members of particular *naciones*, like the Brazilian *nações*, was fully elaborated. The Sarakole, Mandinka, Susu, Mossi, Bambara, Fulbe (divided into the Fula and the Tukulor), and the Hausa are delineated as such in the primary documentation, and the secondary literature on Mexican slavery customarily includes a discussion of the *procedencia* (origin) of the Africans. As for Peru, Africans began trickling into the colony as early as 1529, initially to work the silver mines. Of 256 enslaved persons identified as Africans in Peru prior to 1560, 45 were Wolof, 40 "Biafras," 23 were "Bran," 15 were Mandinga, and 1 was Fulbe. In fact, during the sixteenth and seventeenth centuries the elaboration of African *naciones* included the following, again a mix of state designations, ports, and ethnic groupings: "Bran, Biafra, Berbesi, Jolofo, Mandinga, Nalu, Bañol, Casanga, Fula, Bioho, Guinea, Folupo, Soso, Balanta, Terranova, Zape, Cocoli, Bleblo, Arasa, Caravali, Mina, Lucumi, Congo, Mozambique, Anchico, Benguela, Angola, Alonga, Malemba, Mosanga." By 1640 there were perhaps thirty thousand Africans in all of Peru, and Lima's population was at least fifty percent African until that year. Miscegenation between Spanish men and African and Native American women was extensive, such that a popular saying was thought to encapsulate seventeenth-century Peruvian society:

"Él que no tiene de Inga tiene de Mandinga" (he who is not descended from an Inga [Inca] is descended from a Mandinga). Interestingly, Senegambians imported into Puerto Rico after 1680 would also be collectively referred to as "Mandingas."

It is in Santo Domingo, however, that some of the most fascinating data has been recovered. As Carlos Larrazabal Blanco observes, "from the first years of the foundation of the city of Santo Domingo [1496] there existed slaves. The [very] first slaves—whites, Berbers or blacks—must have been imported illegally." Later, by way of Cape Verde, came "jolofos, mandingas, branes, zapes, biafaras"; from São Tomé arrived "minas, popós, barbas, falás, araraes, lucumíes, carabalíes"; and from Luanda "congos y angolas." It was often the case in Santo Domingo, as was true elsewhere in the New World, that Africans either took or were given ethnic or place name designations as surnames. Thus we read of Pedro Angola, married to Victoriana Angola; Francisco Biáfra, the husband of Luisa Manicongo; Lucía Arará, the wife of Pedro Congo, and so on. There are numerous examples of this naming pattern.

As was the case throughout the Americas, such groupings were stereotyped as possessing distinguishing characteristics. Often the slaveholders rendered the assessment, but as was seen in the case of Esteban Montejo, Africans and their descendants also held certain views of other Africans. One eighteenth century depiction of the ethnic kaleidoscope in Santo Domingo seems to be a composite image incorporating both African and slaveholder perspectives, such that "the Senegalese are [seen as] insolent and thieves; the Fante as extremely proud and ready to commit suicide; the Arda women as always arguing and gossiping; the Igbo as difficult to manage and given to suicide when subjected to the least punishment or ridicule; the Congo as docile and happy, equally true of the Angolas and other Bantu blacks, with the exception of the Mondongos, who were feared among the same Africans." Reputations were not uniform throughout the Diaspora, however, as the following statement on Africans in Paraguay reveals: "With respect to races or ethnic groups, of the many Africans who were taken in the trade, the Senegalese were the easiest to discipline and the best suited for domestic work; the Bambara were famous for their love of thievery; the Arada were skillful in agriculture, but proud; the Congos were skillful fishermen, but of short stature and given to absconding; the Nagos, the most humane; the Mondongo, the cruelest; the Minas, the most determined, capricious, and given to desperation." Similar information exists for Uruguay, Venezuela, Chile and Costa Rica.

There are at least two lessons that can be extracted from the foregoing depictions: one, responses to enslavement were certainly informed by the cultural and social antecedent, but not to the extent that behavior was predictable, especially in light of divergent New World circumstances; and two, the veracity of these characterizations is not the real issue, but rather the likelihood that slaveholders made decisions regarding such matters as labor assignments and material treatment based upon such perceptions. Even social order within the enslaved community was probably affected by these appraisals: Esteban Montejo's mother, for example, was certainly influenced by them. But to the extent that there are glimmers of truth here, it is important to follow the leads back to the African antecedents and there discover as much as possible about the beliefs, aspirations, fears, and accomplishments of these enslaved persons. At least the Latin American and West Indian scholarship makes some attempt to achieve this, as it approaches the problem of African enslaved laborers with the understanding that they were persons extracted from distinctive communities in Africa and removed to places of perverse hostility and irrationality. Labor extractions followed spatial extractions; psychological dislocations necessarily flowed from displacements of another kind. The African response to regimes of exploitation was therefore complex and intricate.

Africans were often identified by their ethnicity, affixed as it was to their names. There is greater evidence for this in the Caribbean and South America than in North America, but the same pattern can be found in the latter. It is certainly possible to explain this as a putative process, but it could not have been purely so, as African agency was just as clearly a factor. The innovation was not in the concept of ethnicity or region of origin, but in making such a descriptor part of the personal name. As such, ethnicity became associated with the individual African. But beyond this we have the phenomenon of Africans gathering and organizing among themselves on the basis of ethnicity all over the New World, from the 1712 Slave Revolt in New York City (an Akan-led affair) to the 1739 Stono Rebellion in South Carolina (an Angolan/West Central African venture) to the 1835 Malê uprising in Bahia (with the Yoruba as the principals), to cite just a few examples. These moments of social segregation could not have been derivative of slaveholder misidentification. The cumulative evidence therefore leads to one conclusion: Africans in the New World were very much aware of who they had been in the Old, and engaged patterns of collective behavior that sought to recapture and reinforce Old World realities. The same Africans who arrived in the West Indies and South America also came to what would become the United States, albeit in different patterns of importation, carrying the same sense of collective identity. Scholars of North American slavery need to either reconsider the African antecedent as playing a major role in the histories and cultures of people of African descent and thereby retool, or they need to consider changing to a field of inquiry in which they can more accurately demonstrate their expertise.

# The Civil War: Repressible or Irrepressible?

**N**o event in American history has been studied more than the Civil War. Scarcely a year passes without the publication of a wave of books and articles dealing with the war and its causes and consequences. So widespread has been interest in the field that many organizations and journals have been founded expressly for the purpose of furthering additional research and stimulating popular and professional interest in this subject. The History Book Club sells more books on the Civil War than any other subject; Ken Burns's Civil War series on PBS was the most-watched television documentary of all time; Civil War enactments on battle sites from Pennsylvania to Georgia increase in number and popularity every year. Indeed, to refer to a "cult" of Civil War enthusiasts is not to exaggerate the intensity of interest in the subject.

Despite the vast body of published material dealing with the Civil War, dispute over its causes never ceases. "Historians, whatever their predispositions," noted a famous scholar more than sixty years ago, "assign to the Civil War causes ranging from one simple force or phenomenon to patterns so complex and manifold that they include, intricately interwoven, all the important movements, thoughts, and actions of the decades before 1861."[1] This comment is as true today as it was when first written. Disagreements among historians over what caused the Civil War, as well as what consequences proceeded from it, seem to be as sharp today as they were over a century ago. While Americans have debated the wisdom and meaning of every war in which they participated, the Civil War has undoubtedly been the most controversial of all.

One reason for the enduring interest in the Civil War undoubtedly lies in the fact that the conflict pitted Americans against Americans. No external foe, no set of factors beyond the control of Americans led to the cataclysm: the Civil War was our fratricidal tragedy. Both a symbolic and actual dividing line in American history, the Civil War bears a similar relationship to the American people as the French Revolution to the French, the English Civil War to the English, and the Russian Revolution to Russians. Questions involving vital national issues seem to be at stake in any interpretation of the event: the status of African Americans in our society; the sovereignty of the nation-state and the competing claims of "states' rights" and sectionalism; the contest

---

[1]Howard K. Beale, "What Historians Have Said about the Causes of the Civil War," in *Theory and Practice in Historical Study: A Report of the Committee on Historiography*, Social Science Research Council, Bulletin 54 (1946): 55.

between a society shaped by urbanization and advanced industrial capitalism and one shaped by agriculture; the meaning of those ideals of freedom
and democracy on which the nation was founded and the very viability of
a republic in a world of centralized nation-states.

A second reason for the depth and persistence of interest in the Civil
War is related to the first: the sheer level of violence unleashed by the war
is unprecedented in American history. The more than 600,000 who died in
the Civil War exceed the total American death count recorded in the Revolution, the War of 1812, the Mexican War, the Spanish-American War,
World Wars I and II, and the Korean War *combined*. A staggering *one out of
every four* Civil War combatants was killed. "Future years will never know the
seething hell" of that slaughter, Walt Whitman asserted at war's end. "Its
interior history will not only never be written," he went on to say, it "will
never even be suggested."[2] Moreover, unlike the American Revolution or
World War II — whose results few ever questioned — American historians
have never been unanimous about whether all the horror of the Civil War
was necessary or worthwhile. Fixing responsibility for so great a calamity upon
specific groups or institutions has therefore been a continuous — and continuously contentious — task.

In the three decades following the end of fighting in 1865, writers marked
out most of the lines of argument that would shape interpretations of the
war into the future. These lines separated those who saw one region or the
other as more responsible for causing the war; those who saw the war as avoidable or unavoidable; and those who saw slavery, as opposed to economic differences, as the cause of hostility between North and South. In the immediate
aftermath of the war, Northern writers portrayed Southern secessionists as
men dedicated to the advance of slavery, regardless of the harm to the rest
of the nation. The "slave power," wrote Henry Wilson in a famous book published in the 1870s, "after aggressive warfare of more than two generations
upon the vital and animating spirit of republican institutions, upon the cherished and hallowed sentiments of a Christian people, upon the enduring
interests and lasting renown of the Republic organized treasonable conspiracies, raised the standard of revolution, and plunged the nation into a bloody
contest for the preservation of its threatened life."[3] Thus, in the prevailing
Northern view, an aggressive conspiracy of slave owners forced the North to
defend the Union, the Constitution, and basic human rights. For Southern
writers, the war was not a moral conflict over slavery. Rather, the war resulted
from the unconstitutional and aggressive strategy of the North to use its growing economic power to reduce the southern states to political subservience.

---

[2]From Whitman's *Specimen Days and Collect* (1882), excerpted in *The Union in Crisis,
1850–1877*, ed. Robert W. Johannsen (Acton, Mass., 1999), 192–93. See Thomas J. Pressly,
*Americans Interpret Their Civil War* (Princeton, N.J., 1954), 321–23, on the persistence and
intensity of emotion in Civil War studies.

[3]Henry Wilson, *History of the Rise and Fall of the Slave Power in America*, 3 vols. (Boston,
1872–1877), vol. I, vi–vii.

The North's domineering attitude toward the South was based on its self-righteous sense of moral and cultural superiority. Convinced that their liberal, commercial values were the only basis for a modern civilization, Abraham Lincoln and the Republican Party deliberately provoked a conflict with the "backward" — but agriculturally rich — South. Like most partisans of the Union cause, partisans of the Confederacy saw the war as unavoidable — a noble, defensive struggle against an alien conspiracy.

While Northern and Southern partisans attacked each other, a third school of writers began to argue that the Civil War had in fact been needless or avoidable. These writers blamed the war on the failures of statesmen, both Northern and Southern. For example, former President James Buchanan — a Northern Democrat who imagined himself caught between rabid Northern Republicans and rabid Southern Democrats — argued in 1865 that the cause of the Civil War could be found in "the long, active, and persistent hostility of the Northern abolitionists, both in and out of Congress, against Southern slavery, until the final triumph of President Lincoln; and on the other hand, the corresponding antagonism and violence with which the advocates of slavery resisted these efforts, and vindicated its preservation and extension up till the period of secession."[4] Buchanan implied that, had Northerners controlled their abolitionist fanatics and had Southerners controlled their secessionist extremists, all the misery of the war might have been avoided. To put it another way, no substantive issue necessitated a resort to arms in 1861; the war had been brought on by the malice of a few and the folly and weakness of many more.

These three contemporaneous views of the causes of the Civil War set the terms for the historical debate into the twentieth century. Even historians who agreed on the relevant "facts" divided over their interpretation. Nevertheless, by the 1890s, a postwar generation of historians attempted the first serious explanations of the Civil War that were free from the bitterness of contemporary accounts. To them the Civil War was "history" rather than a part of current events. But it was not just historical distance that characterized the work of these scholars. They were influenced by the rising tide of American nationalism at the turn of the century. The phenomenal industrial growth of the United States in the decades after the Civil War had made the nation a world power.[5] Politicians, journalists, and intellectuals — including historians — increasingly turned their attention from the divisiveness of the past toward a newly nationalist future. Intent upon cementing the bonds of American nationality, they cast upon the Civil War a gaze that was if less partisan, also highly selective.

One of the first and most influential works of the nationalist school was James Ford Rhodes's multivolume history of the United States from 1850 to 1877. In many ways, Rhodes sounded like his Northern predecessors: slavery

---

[4] James Buchanan, *The Administration on the Eve of the Rebellion: A History of Four Years before the War* (London, 1865), iv.

[5] On industrialization, see Volume Two, Chapter 3.

was the basic cause of the war; the Southerners' claim that they had been persecuted was false; the South had fought the war to extend slavery, an inherently immoral institution. The Civil War, Rhodes concluded, involved an "irrepressible conflict" between North and South, and the South had been clearly in the wrong. Despite his obvious Northern sympathies, however, Rhodes modified considerably the Northern partisan approach to the South and its peculiar institution. Southerners were not monsters; they might very well have overseen the peaceful and gradual abolition of slavery, he argued, had it not been for the cotton gin. It was thus an unforeseen and fateful bit of technological progress that revived slavery by turning cotton into the economic backbone of the Southern economy. Moreover, both England and New England played an important role in the preservation of slavery, because their citizens regularly purchased slave-grown cotton without any moral compunction. Rhodes also distinguished between the institution of slavery and individual slave owners. He absolved the latter of guilt, insisting they deserved sympathy rather than censure because they had inherited a burdensome institution they could not fully control. Indeed, Rhodes found much to praise in Southern life: its gallantry, its concern for nonmaterial values, its respect for tradition. To Rhodes, therefore, the Civil War was a tragedy, the collision of impersonal forces beyond the control of individuals, most of whom were personally honorable and whose moral and cultural loyalties commanded respect. Finally, Rhodes concluded, the Civil War, like any other tragic conflict, had yielded an unforeseen and undeniable good: a modern, united, and powerful America.[6]

Rhodes's nationalist approach proved especially attractive to Southern scholars. For them, the causes of war were less important than its results: sectional reconciliation and the integration of the South into national life, including the blessings of industrialization and prosperity. Sympathetic to the South, these historians (including future president Woodrow Wilson) were nonetheless critical of slavery and secession. But their condemnation of slavery did not rest on a belief in racial equality. Instead, they blamed slavery for saddling the South with a backward economy and a hopelessly unproductive workforce, thereby retarding Southern progress in industrial, economic, social, and cultural matters. Because of slavery, they concluded, the South developed along lines increasingly different from the rest of the country and therefore remained outside the rising spirit of nineteenth-century nationalism. Given their sense of history as a chronicle of great nations moved by tragic destiny, nationalist historians often characterized the Civil War as an "irrepressible conflict." As one of them, Edward Channing, wrote, "two distinct social organizations had developed within the United States. . . . Southern society was based on the production of staple agricultural crops by slave labor. Northern society was bottomed on varied employments — agricultural, mechanical, and commercial — all carried on under the wage system. Two such diver-

---

[6] James Ford Rhodes, *History of the United States: From the Compromise of 1850 to the Final Restoration of Home Rule in the South in 1877*, 7 vols. (New York, 1893–1906).

gent forms of society could not continue indefinitely to live side by side within the walls of one government. . . . One or the other of these societies must perish, or both must secure complete equality."[7]

Most of the nationalist historians wrote approvingly of the outcomes of the Civil War. The growth of industrial capitalism proved to be an unambiguous good. A more integrated economy and a more powerful federal government promoted the flourishing of an expansive world power. The nationalist historians, that is, looked smilingly upon the nation that had emerged from the Union victory of 1865. Few took occasion to protest the abandonment of African Americans after Reconstruction or to assert egalitarian racial views of any kind. Being self-consciously modern scholars, they buttressed conventional prejudice with contemporary pseudoscientific findings about the supposed evolutionary differentiation of races. They therefore accepted the subordinate role of blacks in American society as a natural development.

By the early twentieth century, the nationalist school of Civil War historiography began to face a formidable challenge from the rising Progressive school. Like many of their reform-minded fellow citizens, Progressive historians condemned the ill social effects of industrialism, especially the increasing maldistribution of wealth and power in the United States.[8] Looking to the past to provide solutions to problems in the present, they found in American history a continuous cycle of struggle between democracy and aristocracy, between have-nots and haves, between "the people" and "the interests." Led by Charles A. Beard, these scholars emphasized not the development of a beneficent and unified nationalism, but the emergence of a turbulent democracy with alternating periods of reform and reaction generated by class conflict and other kinds of social antagonism.

Perhaps the most influential Progressive interpretation of the Civil War appeared in *The Rise of American Civilization*, which Beard wrote with his wife Mary in 1927. To the Beards, the 1861 secession crisis and the debates over slavery masked a much more deeply rooted conflict. Stripped of all nonessentials, the Civil War was, they insisted, "a social war, ending in the unquestioned establishment of a new power in the government, making vast changes in the arrangement of classes, in the accumulation and distribution of wealth, in the course of industrial development, and in the Constitution inherited from the Fathers. . . . In any event neither accident nor rhetoric should be allowed to obscure the . . . [revolutionary] character of that struggle. . . . [It was a] social cataclysm in which the capitalists, laborers, and farmers of the North and West drove from power in the national government the planting aristocracy of the South."[9]

Unlike the nationalist historians, the Progressives condemned the results of the Civil War in no uncertain terms. Its major result had been to install a gang of ruthless and self-aggrandizing capitalists into a position of dominance

---

[7]Edward Channing, *A History of the United States*, 6 vols. (New York, 1905–1925), vol. I, 3–4.
[8]See Volume Two, Chapter 6.
[9]Charles A. Beard and Mary R. Beard, *The Rise of American Civilization*, 2 vols. (New York, 1927), vol. II, 53–54.

over the American economy. To Progressive historian Matthew Josephson, the half century that followed the Civil War was the era of the "Robber Barons": "Under their hands the renovation of our economic life proceeded relentlessly. . . . To organize and exploit the resources of a nation upon a gigantic scale, to regiment its farmers and workers into harmonious corps of producers, and to do this only in the name of an uncontrolled appetite for private profit — here surely is the great inherent contradiction whence so much disaster, outrage and misery has flowed."[10]

While the Beardian economic interpretation of the Civil War grew in influence during the depression decade of the 1930s, a small group of Marxist historians began to move beyond the Beards in stressing the importance of economic causes of historical events. The Marxist periodization of American history followed the stages of capitalist development from self-sufficient agriculture, through commercial and industrial revolutions, and finally issuing in the inevitable proletarian revolution. The place of the Civil War within this framework was clear: it was indeed — as the Beards claimed — a "Second American Revolution." Unlike the Beards, however, Marxist historians did not condemn the results of war. The destruction of the slave power had been the necessary preparation for the triumph of the bourgeois capitalist class — which in its turn set the stage for the inevitable triumph of the proletariat. "The sectional nature of the conflict and the geographical division of the contending classes," wrote James S. Allen, "have obscured the essential revolutionary nature of the Civil War. But this conflict was basically a revolution of a bourgeois democratic character, in which the bourgeoisie was fighting for power against the landed aristocracy. . . . The destruction of the slave power was the basis for real national unity and the further development of capitalism, which would produce conditions most favorable for the growth of the labor movement."[11]

Even as the Progressive and Marxist economic interpretations flowered during the depression of the 1930s, two schools of historical scholarship emerged in sharp contrast to them. The first of these, a loosely defined and romantic assortment sometimes referred to as the Southern Agrarians, portrayed the Southern way of life as superior to the urbanized and industrialized condition of the rest of twentieth-century America. In their 1930 publication entitled *I'll Take My Stand*, they announced that Southerners would no longer tolerate the condescension of Northern critics and, further, that the nation desperately needed what the South could offer it — an alternative to the corrosive skepticism and materialism that were the fruits of liberal capitalist society. This sectional feeling was sharply mirrored in the work of three Southern historians, Ulrich B. Phillips, Charles W. Ramsdell, and Frank L. Owsley, who set out to renovate the prevailing historical portrait of the South. At the center of this revised story was the Civil War, and on that

---

[10]Matthew Josephson, *The Robber Barons: The Great American Capitalists 1861–1901* (New York, 1934), viii.

[11]James S. Allen, *Reconstruction: The Battle for Democracy, 1865–1876* (New York, 1937), 18, 26–28. The quotations are taken from the 1955 edition of this work.

ground the Southern historians did indeed "take their stand." Sounding remarkably like Confederate apologists of the 1860s and 1870s, these scholars idealized a land of chivalrous planters, genteel mistresses, and pathetically helpless and loyal slaves, all bound together with the threads of honor and tradition. At the same time, inevitably, they portrayed the North as nasty, brutish, and short on culture, except for the most debased commercial sort. In odd ways, the broad-brush Southern critique of modern bourgeois society echoed that of Marxists and Progressives. Like the Progressives, the Southern historians pictured nineteenth-century Northern industrialists as cynically exploiting abolitionist sentiments in pursuit of their own economic motives. And like Marxists, they found the politics and culture of modern America as bankrupt as the corporate economy that lay in ruins during the 1930s. If in denying that slavery caused the Civil War they sounded like Progressive or Marxist historians, however, the Southern apologists sounded quite otherwise in asserting the beneficence of Southern institutions, including slavery. The flavor of their racial animosities was unmistakable. The blacks of the South, one of them wrote, were "cannibals and barbarians."[12] Slavery was simply a system of racial discipline: necessary, albeit burdensome, and fully ethical.

The second school of Civil War historiography that flourished in the 1930s and 1940s, the so-called revisionist school, rejected all approaches, whether nationalist, Progressive, or Marxist, that proposed a fundamental confrontation — economic, social, or cultural — between North and South. The Civil War, even more than most wars, they insisted, was profoundly evil. Not only had it inflicted unspeakable suffering upon millions, but it had been avoidable. Genuine political alternatives had been available to political leaders in both sections. In refusing to choose those alternatives, the leaders bore the enormous moral burden of having sent hundreds of thousands to their deaths and of having impoverished millions. Such views gained credibility in the 1930s because an entire generation had been disillusioned with the results of World War I. Cynical about all patriotic appeals, the revisionist historians, like many of their contemporaries, determined to stay out of any future conflict caused by imperial arrogance, capitalist greed, or petty national rivalries. Thus, when revisionists turned their gaze upon the Civil War, they saw a catastrophe: a struggle that cost much, gained little, and had been fully avoidable.

The most mature formulation of the revisionist hypothesis came from the pens of Avery Craven and James G. Randall in the years just before Pearl Harbor. Both of these distinguished scholars believed that wars never attained the noble objectives for which they were supposedly fought, and both

---

[12]The quotation comes from Frank L. Owsley, "The Irrepressible Conflict," in Twelve Southerners, *I'll Take My Stand: The South and the Agrarian Tradition* (New York, 1930), 77–78; see also "The Fundamental Cause of the Civil War: Egocentric Sectionalism," *Journal of Southern History* 7 (February 1941): 3–18; Ulrich Bonnell Phillips, *Life and Labor in the Old South* (Boston, 1929); Charles Ramsdell, *Behind the Lines in the Southern Confederacy* (Baton Rouge, La., 1944); and essays by Owsley and Ramsdell in Edwin C. Rozwenc, ed., *The Causes of the Civil War* (Lexington, Mass., 1972).

equated war with pathological irrationalism. Given such assumptions they insisted that the Civil War had been a "repressible conflict" brought on by the political failure of the generation of the 1850s and 1860s.[13]

Craven argued that sectional differences — economic, social, political — could not explain the causes of the war; many countries with pronounced sectional dissimilarities had avoided civil strife. Nor was slavery the cause of the war. "If it had not become a symbol — first of sectional differences and then of southern depravity, or superiority, according to the point of view — it might have been faced as a national question and dealt with as successfully as the South American countries dealt with the same problem."[14] The war, Craven maintained, occurred because normal sectional differences — which could have been resolved through political means — were magnified and emotionalized until they could no longer be dealt with in rational terms. "For more than two decades these molders of public opinion steadily created the fiction of two distinct peoples contending for the right to preserve and expand their sacred cultures. . . . Opponents became devils in human form. Good men had no choice but to kill and to be killed."[15] To the men who erred so catastrophically, Randall gave the name "the blundering generation."[16]

Although the revisionist approach remained popular through the 1940s and into the 1950s,[17] historians began to attack its basic premises in sharp terms. Although wars could never be good in themselves, these scholars argued, sometimes avoiding war was a far greater evil. Pointing to World War II, Samuel Eliot Morison argued in his 1950 presidential address before the American Historical Association that "war does accomplish something, that war is better than servitude, that war has been an inescapable aspect of the human story."[18] Reflecting on the recent struggle against fascism — and the growing Cold War against communism — Morison and other scholars insisted that war was justified when it involved the defense of uncompromisable moral and ethical issues. Some historians drew inspiration from the prominent theologian Reinhold Niebuhr, who insisted that evil was an unavoidable part of reality and had to be taken into account in any adequate explanation of human experience. Finally, in the 1940s and early 1950s, growing demands by African Americans for equal rights contributed to a reevaluation of the causes of the Civil War. Taking civil rights seriously in post–World War II America reinforced the tendency to take slavery seriously as a cause of the Civil War.

---

[13]See Philip G. Auchampaugh, *James Buchanan and His Cabinet on the Eve of Secession* (Lancaster, Pa., 1926); George Fort Milton, *The Eve of Conflict: Stephen A. Douglas and the Needless War* (New York, 1934); and Gilbert H. Barnes, *The Antislavery Impulse, 1830–1844* (New York, 1933).

[14]Avery Craven, *The Repressible Conflict: 1830–1861* (Baton Rouge, La., 1939), 64.

[15]Avery Craven, *The Coming of the Civil War* (New York, 1942), 2.

[16]J. G. Randall, "The Blundering Generation," *Mississippi Valley Historical Review* 27 ( June 1940): 4–16.

[17]Two outstanding revisionist works published after the end of World War II are Roy F. Nichols, *The Disruption of American Democracy* (New York, 1948), and Kenneth M. Stampp, *And the War Came: The North and the Secession Crisis, 1860–1861* (Baton Rouge, La., 1950).

[18]Samuel Eliot Morison, "Faith of a Historian," *American Historical Review* 56 ( January 1951): 267.

In 1949, Arthur M. Schlesinger Jr. wrote one of the most cogent attacks on the revisionist historians. He asked one specific question: if the war could have been avoided, what course should American leaders have followed? None of the revisionists had ever spelled out a plausible scenario that might have avoided war. Schlesinger listed three possible alternatives: that the South might have abolished slavery by itself if left alone; that slavery would have died because it was economically unsound; or that the North might have offered some form of compensated emancipation. Finding all three answers inadequate, Schlesinger charged that revisionism "is connected with the modern tendency to seek in optimistic sentimentalism an escape from the severe demands of moral decision." The South, in defending its evil institution, had posed moral challenges too profound to be solved by political compromise. Only by ignoring the moral dimensions of humanity, he concluded, could historians ascribe the cause of the Civil War to mere blundering.[19]

At about the same time that Schlesinger was attacking the revisionists, another famous historian was trying to reconcile revisionist and nationalist approaches, while strongly rejecting the Progressives' economic interpretation. Allan Nevins's magisterial history of the United States from the 1840s through the 1860s, *Ordeal of the Union*, and his two-volume *The Emergence of Lincoln* sounded revisionist on the question of causation. The Civil War, wrote Nevins, "should have been avoidable." He went on, however, sounding like a nationalist, to say that "the problem of slavery *with its complementary problem of race-adjustment*" involved basic differences between North and South.[20] And finally, he returned to the revisionist argument that bad leadership — and, indeed, in his view, bad citizenship — caused the war. The first selection in this chapter, from Nevins's second volume on Lincoln, presents this argument.

By the 1960s, as the debate over the avoidability of the Civil War had become fairly static,[21] a new generation of historians pursued new approaches and asked new questions. The rise of the new political history (which emphasized the social basis of politics and employed quantitative techniques) led some scholars to minimize the significance of slavery in nineteenth-century American society. Sounding like neo-Progressives, the practitioners of this brand of history insisted that the behavior of Americans and their political parties in the two decades preceding the Civil War involved more than merely a reaction to slavery. Unlike the old Progressives, however, these new historians paid less attention to class conflict than to "ethnocultural" conflict. Antebellum politics revolved around conflicts between natives and immigrants, Protestants and Catholics, proponents and opponents of temperance.

---

[19]Arthur M. Schlesinger Jr., "The Causes of the Civil War: A Note on Historical Sentimentalism," *Partisan Review* 16 (October 1949): 969–81.

[20]Allan Nevins, *The Emergence of Lincoln*, vol. II (New York, 1950), 468; emphasis in the original. See also his *Ordeal of the Union*, 2 vols. (New York, 1947).

[21]Indeed, David Donald wrote in 1960 that historians were no longer concerned with the causes of the Civil War: "American Historians and the Causes of the Civil War," *South Atlantic Quarterly* 59 (Summer 1960): 351–55.

Passions fired by these causes were more significant than differences over slavery.[22] Broadly speaking, for these scholars, the Civil War became just one event within the larger and more important story of the modernization of American society.[23]

One of the most sophisticated of the new political historians was Michael F. Holt. Combining a behavioral with an ideological analysis, he conceded that the sectional conflict over slavery was relatively important to antebellum Americans. Nevertheless, he insisted, most of those Americans were more preoccupied with what they saw as the threat of corruption to the survival of republican institutions. The threat manifested itself in excessive individualism and urban vice. In response, many Americans decried extreme personal ambition, devotion to material success, and political and social contentiousness; they demanded a halt to massive immigration, which turned once homogeneous communities into boomtowns, and modest cities into alien and polyglot metropolises. Anti-Mason, anti-Catholic, and anti-immigrant movements, culminating in the Know-Nothing Party of the 1850s, arose to explain these disturbing changes and to propose ways of combating them. But the normal political process proved inadequate to the task of relieving so widespread and multidimensional a sense of social anxiety. When the second party system collapsed in the 1850s amid a sense of crisis that a once-republican "government was beyond control of the people, that it had become a threatening power dominated by some gigantic conspiracy," politicians north and south responded by scapegoating the other section: each became for the other the chief menace to republicanism. To prevent the triumph of the great "slave power conspiracy," or of the great "antislavery conspiracy," became a cause of supreme political and moral urgency. "The consequence was secession and a tragic Civil War."[24]

In Holt's version of the new political interpretation, analysis of ethnocultural conflict and the stresses of modernization were interwoven with the persistent view that slavery was somehow central to the coming of war. In a study of the ideology of the Republican Party, Eric Foner moved from the opposite pole but in the same direction. He began with the basic assumption that conflict over the expansion of slavery into the western territories caused the Civil War. In order to connect that issue with the whole range of social and cultural concerns that political historians had shown to be so important to nineteenth-century Americans, he explored the concept of free labor. Those who espoused the doctrines of free labor — most of whom eventually came together in the Republican Party in the late 1850s — believed in an open and mobile society that rewarded individual work. Whatever

---

[22]See the collected essays of Joel H. Silbey in *The Partisan Imperative: The Dynamics of American Politics before the Civil War* (New York, 1985); see also his *The Shrine of Party: Congressional Voting Behavior, 1841–1852* (Pittsburgh, 1967).

[23]See Eric Foner, "The Causes of the American Civil War: Recent Interpretations and New Directions," *Civil War History* 20 (September 1974): 194–214.

[24]Michael F. Holt, *The Political Crisis of the 1850s* (New York, 1978), and "An Elusive Synthesis: Northern Politics during the Civil War," in *Writing the Civil War: The Quest to Understand*, ed. James M. McPherson and William J. Cooper (Columbia, S.C., 1998), 112–34. See also Ronald P. Formisano, *The Birth of Mass Political Parties, Michigan, 1827–1861* (New York, 1971).

their other differences, Republicans were united in their conviction that slavery was incompatible with such a free-labor society and would sooner or later have to disappear. Most Northerners were willing to let it erode slowly in the Old South, but they refused to allow the "slave power" to expand any farther. To do so would not only threaten the material interests of small farmers and traders intent on winning the West for small-scale capitalist development; slavery's expansion would also threaten the very survival of the American experiment in constitutional republicanism.

Unlike Holt and the other historians who stressed ethnocultural conflict, Foner saw nativism as only one, and not the most important, among many issues contributing to the crisis of the Union.[25] In the half century following the adoption of the federal Constitution, he argued, the political system functioned "as a mechanism for relieving social tensions, ordering group conflict, and integrating the society." By the 1830s and 1840s new, more formalized party structures channeled voter participation in politics. In both North and South, the dynamics of party competition inadvertently gave rise to sectional agitators who increasingly forced public opinion — and hence government — to confront the issue of slavery. The result was a polarization of American politics along ideological lines and a growing inability of normal political institutions to resolve basic differences between North and South. In each section, an ideological coalition emerged that was antithetical to the idea of national unity on any terms other than its own. Slavery had indeed caused the Civil War, Foner concluded, because its expansion threatened the continued evolution of the society, culture, and political ideology of free labor. Only a country dominated by the North, the home of free labor, could accomplish the goal originally envisaged by the framers: the creation and preservation of a single nation founded on republican principles. Conversely, as William Barney has shown, Southerners believed that only if slavery guaranteed white men's democracy could the nation realize that same original goal.[26]

Against the proposition that the Civil War amounted to a fracturing within a common political culture, Manisha Sinha argues passionately that secession in South Carolina was a counterrevolution against the republican and democratic heritage. Slavery fouled and undermined the legacy, however imperfect, that proceeded from the founders through Jacksonian democracy and that threatened to inspire yeoman Southerners to cast their political lot with their free-labor brethren in the border and northern states.[27] Though Sinha's account forcefully demonstrates the exceptionality of the South

---

[25]Eric Foner, *Free Soil, Free Labor, Free Men: The Ideology of the Republican Party before the Civil War* (New York, 1970). For other views on the evolution of Northern politics, see James L. Huston, *The Panic of 1857 and the Coming of the Civil War* (Baton Rouge, La., 1987); Mark W. Summers, *The Plundering Generation: Corruption and the Crisis of the Union, 1849–1861* (New York, 1987); William E. Gienapp, *The Origins of the Republican Party, 1852–1856* (New York, 1987); Kenneth M. Stampp, *America in 1857: A Nation on the Brink* (New York, 1990); Jean H. Baker, *Affairs of Party: The Political Culture of Northern Democrats in the Mid-Nineteenth Century* (Ithaca, N.Y., 1983).

[26]William L. Barney, *The Road to Secession: A New Perspective on the Old South* (New York, 1972).

[27]Manisha Sinha, *The Counterrevolution of Slavery: Politics and Ideology in Antebellum South Carolina* (Chapel Hill, N.C., 2000).

Carolina aristocracy's worldview, it does not countervail the view held by
Barney and many others that a diverse South was far more committed to
white folk-democracy and republicanism than to an antimodern vision of
hierarchical society. David Brown and William W. Freehling also highlight
slaveholders' fear that free-labor Republicanism would spread to the South's
non-slaveholding classes.[28]

James Huston recently issued a powerful anti-Beardian interpretation of
the economic origins of the Civil War that puts slavery at the very center.
"The realignment of the 1850s was about slavery, the slave power, and protection of a free labor village society — not about economic issues of corporate capitalism or even about tariffs and banks. Republicans changed the
agenda of the country by altering the law of property rights in people. The
Thirteenth Amendment . . . was the massive agenda change of that realignment."[29] Huston goes on to claim that the weakness of reconstruction efforts,
and the relegation of the Fourteenth and Fifteenth Amendments to the status of dead letters, also reflected the centrality of the question of slave property to the political economy of the United States in the nineteenth century.
Once the Civil War had doomed property in persons, the commitment of
Republicans to broader freedom weakened because of disagreements, doubts,
and prejudices about the limits of both their nationalism and their liberalism. The work of these historians, and also of Richard Sewell and James
McPherson, has reset slavery firmly in the center of Civil War historiography.[30]
These historians also integrate elements of nationalist and Progressive approaches while decisively rejecting revisionist ones. That is, like the nationalists, they reaffirm the character of the Civil War as tragic but morally
unavoidable. Like the Progressives they acknowledge the economic divergence between North and South, even while insisting that a range of social,
cultural, and ideological differences moved millions toward a war that would
settle the issue between slave labor and free.

Other historians in the 1990s have explored several lines of social historical analysis that connect the Civil War with the intimate, small group, and
local history of the nineteenth century.[31] Women's history has significantly
enriched Civil War historiography in recent years.[32] In the past, women were

---

[28]David Brown, "Attacking Slavery from Within: The Making of *The Impending Crisis of the
South*," *Journal of Southern History* 70 (2004): 541–76; William W. Freehling, *The Road to Disunion, Volume II: Secessionists Triumphant, 1854–1861* (New York, 2007), Chapters 16 and 17. See
also John C. Inscoe and Robert C. Kenzer, eds., *Enemies of the Country: New Perspectives on Unionists in the Civil War South* (Athens, Ga., 2001).
[29]James L. Huston, *Calculating the Value of the Union: Slavery, Property Rights, and the Economic
Origins of the Civil War* (Chapel Hill, N.C., 2003), 234.
[30]See Richard H. Sewell, *A House Divided: Sectionalism and the Civil War, 1848–1865* (Baltimore, 1988); and James M. McPherson, *Ordeal by Fire: The Civil War and Reconstruction* (New
York, 1982), and *Battle Cry of Freedom: The Civil War Era* (New York, 1988).
[31]See, for example, the essays in Maris A. Vinovskis, ed., *Toward a Social History of the American Civil War: Exploratory Essays* (Cambridge, 1990).
[32]See Drew Gilpin Faust, " 'Ours as Well as That of the Men': Women and Gender in the
Civil War," in *Writing the Civil War*, McPherson and Cooper, ed., 228–40. A recent brisk summary
of the scholarship is David Williams, *A People's History of the Civil War: Struggles for the Meaning
of Freedom* (New York, 2005), Chapter 3, "The Women Rising." On women at or near the front,

either absent from Civil War history or appeared as stoic nurturers. Whether serving as nurses, fund-raisers, or domestic managers, their role was auxiliary to the main action and distinctly gender-bound. Eventually, feminist historians focused on the effects of the war on the trajectory of women's advancement in the late-nineteenth and early-twentieth centuries. Women's exertions in the war years contributed to the professionalization of nursing and other "helping" professions and ultimately strengthened women's claim to equal political rights.[33] Recently, historians have qualified this picture, noting that differences among women, especially in terms of race and class, sharply determined their Civil War experiences. For example, while many middle-class Northern white women made significant gains in their quest for social and political equality, Susan Lebsock shows that in one Southern town the war confirmed women's subordination and reinforced the racial divide between white and black women.[34] Historians Drew Gilpin Faust and LeeAnn Whites show the significant impact of women, and more broadly of the gender system, on the conduct and outcome of the war. In their accounts, men's failure to "protect" their women and women's unpreparedness for the roles of slave manager and plantation administrator created a climate of gendered hostility within families and communities, weakened the Confederate war effort, and speeded the dissolution of slavery.[35] And finally, with an even broader brush Anne C. Rose shows that Northern middle-class Americans could only understand the Civil War — its causes, experiences, and consequences — within the context of Victorian culture. She suggests that the religious values, gender codes, and family practices that were at the heart of that culture played a role in leading Americans to and through that transformative event.[36]

---

see Elizabeth D. Leonard, *All the Daring of the Soldier: Women of the Civil War Armies* (New York, 1999); De Anne Blanton, *They Fought Like Demons: Women Soldiers in the American Civil War* (Baton Rouge, La., 2002); Jane E. Schultz, *Women at the Front: Hospital Workers in Civil War America* (Chapel Hill, N.C., 2004); Nina Silber, *Daughters of the Union: Women Fight the Civil War* (Cambridge, Mass., 2005); Margaret S. Creighton, *The Colors of Courage: Gettysburg's Forgotten History* (New York, 2006); Richard Hall, *Women on the Civil War Battlefront* (Lawrence, Kans., 2006).

[33] Judith Giesberg, *Civil War Sisterhood: The U.S. Sanitary Commission and Women's Politics in Transition* (Boston, 2000).

[34] Susan Lebsock, *The Free Women of Petersburg: Status and Culture in a Southern Town, 1784–1860* (New York, 1984); see also George C. Rable, *Civil Wars: Women and the Crisis of Southern Nationalism* (Urbana, Ill., 1989); Jeanie Attie, *Patriotic Toil: Northern Women and the American Civil War* (Ithaca, N.Y., 1998); and Laura F. Edwards, *Scarlett Doesn't Live Here Anymore: Southern Women in the Civil War Era* (Urbana, Ill., 2000).

[35] Drew Gilpin Faust, *Mothers of Invention: Women of the Slaveholding South in the American Civil War* (Chapel Hill, N.C., 1996); LeeAnn Whites, *The Civil War as a Crisis in Gender: Augusta, Georgia, 1860–1890* (Athens, Ga., 1995).

[36] Anne C. Rose, *Victorian America and the Civil War* (Cambridge, 1992); Alice Fahs, in "The Feminized Civil War: Gender, Northern Popular Literature, and the Memory of War, 1861–1900," *Journal of American History* 85 (March 1999): 1461–94, and W. Fitzhugh Brundage, in *The Southern Past: A Clash of Race and Memory* (Cambridge, Mass., 2005), 12–54, show that despite defeat in the Civil War, Southern women "won the popular battle for its memory." See also Catherine Clinton, *The Other Civil War: American Women in the Nineteenth Century* (New York, 1984); LeeAnn Whites, *Gender Matters: Civil War, Reconstruction, and the Making of the New South* (New York, 2005).

Some of the most important advances in the social history of the Civil War have been made by historians of African Americans. For years, historians from W. E. B. Du Bois to Benjamin Quarles and John Hope Franklin have written of the experiences of slaves and free blacks in the Civil War era.[37] But only recently has the black contribution to Union victory and to slaves' self-emancipation received sustained attention.[38] Dudley Taylor Cornish and Joseph T. Glatthaar, among others, have demonstrated the decisive contribution of black soldiers to the Union victory.[39] More recently, Ira Berlin and a team of co-editors have made clear beyond a doubt that the preservation of the Union, the destruction of slavery, and the reconstitution of Southern society all depended crucially on the contributions of African Americans.[40]

Appreciation for the indispensable contribution of blacks to emancipation and military victory may have led some historians to exaggerate the power of efforts toward self-liberation and to obscure the military and, increasingly, the ideological commitment of Lincoln and other white Americans to the cause of emancipation. The debate on this question is wide-ranging, but may be sampled in the exchange between Barbara Fields and James McPherson.[41] For Fields, only desperate necessity and continual prodding from black Americans pushed Lincoln and his government toward emancipation; and Reconstruction after the war proved short-lived and ineffective precisely because the original commitment to freedom was weak. For McPherson, Lincoln's evolving moral commitment to emancipation embodies the "new birth of freedom" that was, in the end, the central meaning of the Civil War. Beyond this particular debate, a number of historians, McPherson and Edward Blum among them, have shown just how complex and enriching was the interaction of black and white Americans during the Civil War. As David Blight's study of the great black abolitionist Frederick Douglass and Garry Wills's recent meditation upon the significance of Lincoln's Gettysburg Address show in quite different ways that interaction was at the heart of the struggle to rede-

---

[37]W. E. B. Du Bois, *Black Reconstruction in America, 1860–1880* (New York, 1935); Benjamin Quarles, *The Negro in the Civil War* (Boston, 1953); John Hope Franklin, *The Emancipation Proclamation* (New York, 1963). See also Bell Irvin Wiley, *Southern Negroes, 1861–1865* (New Haven, Conn., 1938).

[38]A fine bibliographic essay is Peter Kolchin, "Slavery and Freedom in the Civil War South," in *Writing the Civil War,* McPherson and Cooper, ed., 241–60.

[39]Dudley Taylor Cornish, *The Sable Arm: Negro Troops in the Union Army, 1861–1865* (New York, 1956); Joseph T. Glatthaar, *Forged in Battle: The Civil War Alliance of Black Soldiers and White Officers* (New York, 1990), and "Black Glory: The African American Role in the Union Victory," in *Why the Confederacy Lost,* ed. Gabor S. Boritt (New York, 1992), 133–62. See also James M. McPherson, *The Negro's Civil War: How American Negroes Felt and Acted during the War for the Union* (New York, 1965).

[40]Ira Berlin et al., eds., *Freedom: A Documentary History of Emancipation, 1861–1867,* 4 vols. (Cambridge, 1985–1993), with further volumes forthcoming; a sample of their findings can be found in *Free at Last: A Documentary History of Slavery, Freedom, and the Civil War* (New York, 1992); and works cited in Kolchin, "Slavery and Freedom in the Civil War South." See also Catherine Clinton, *Harriet Tubman: The Road to Freedom* (New York, 2004).

[41]Barbara J. Fields, "Who Freed the Slaves?" in *The Civil War: An Illustrated History,* ed. Geoffrey C. Ward (New York, 1990), 178–81; James M. McPherson, "Who Freed the Slaves?" in *Reconstruction* 2 (1994): 35–40, reprinted in his *Drawn with the Sword: Reflections on the American Civil War* (New York, 1996), 192–207.

fine the American constitutional republic.[42] Nothing that came before escapes reinterpretation in light of the Civil War; nothing that has come after escapes its shaping influence. "The scale of the union's triumph and the sheer drama of emancipation," Eric Foner has declared, "fused nationalism, morality, and the language of freedom in an entirely new combination."[43]

One of the most promising developments in Civil War scholarship involves the deployment of comparative history. Historians of slavery have been prominent in this endeavor for years. Eugene Genovese, Peter Kolchin, and many others have rightly insisted that an international phenomenon of such scale and endurance can only be properly understood in comparative terms.[44] Similarly, a few historians of the Civil War have sought to compare the American road to emancipation with that of nations in the Caribbean and South America.[45] Among their most important findings are those of William Freehling, excerpted in this chapter. First, according to Freehling, the American experience was notably bloody; only a few nations abolished slavery as the result of a civil war. And second, the United States found itself ensnared in fratricidal struggle precisely because of its decentralized and quite exuberant mass political democracy; no central state or authority could decree or enforce emancipation on the self-governing societies of North America. Freehling makes clear just how intimately and fatally interwoven was slavery with the institutions and values of local democracy and small-scale capitalism.[46]

---

[42]David W. Blight, *Frederick Douglass' Civil War: Keeping Faith in Jubilee* (Baton Rouge, La., 1989); Garry Wills, *Lincoln at Gettysburg: The Words That Remade America* (New York, 1992). On Douglass, see also Waldo E. Martin Jr., *The Mind of Frederick Douglass* (Chapel Hill, N.C., 1984), and William S. McFeely, *Frederick Douglass* (New York, 1990). On Lincoln and the Union commitment to freedom, see LaWanda Cox, *Lincoln and Black Freedom: A Study in Presidential Leadership* (Columbia, S.C., 1981); James M. McPherson, *Abraham Lincoln and the Second American Revolution* (New York, 1991); William Lee Miller, *Lincoln's Virtues: An Ethical Biography* (New York, 2002), which contains an excellent bibliography; Doris Kearns Goodwin, *Team of Rivals: The Political Genius of Abraham Lincoln* (New York, 2005); Edward J. Blum, *Reforging the White Republic: Race, Religion, and American Nationalism, 1865–1898* (Baton Rouge, La., 2005), Chapter 2; Harry S. Stout, *Upon the Altar of the Nation: A Moral History of the American Civil War* (New York, 2006); and Brian R. Dirck, ed., *Lincoln Emancipated: The President and the Politics of Race* (DeKalb, Ill., 2007).

[43]Eric Foner, *The Story of American Freedom* (New York, 1998), 99.

[44]See Eugene D. Genovese, *From Rebellion to Revolution: Afro-American Slave Revolts in the Making of the Modern World* (Baton Rouge, La., 1979); *The World the Slaveholders Made: Two Essays in Interpretation* (New York, 1969); Genovese with Laura Foner, eds., *Slavery in the New World: A Reader in Comparative History* (Englewood Cliffs, N.J., 1969), and with Elizabeth Fox-Genovese, *Fruits of Merchant Capital: Slavery and Bourgeois Property in the Rise and Expansion of Capitalism* (New York, 1983). See also Peter Kolchin, *Unfree Labor: American Slavery and Russian Serfdom* (Cambridge, Mass., 1987), as well as his "Slavery and Freedom in the Civil War South," in *Writing the Civil War: The Quest to Understand*, ed. James M. McPherson and William J. Cooper Jr. (Columbia, S.C., 1998), 258–59. See also works discussed in Chapter 4.

[45]See, for example, George M. Fredrickson, *White Supremacy: A Comparative Study in American and South African History* (New York, 1981); Rebecca J. Scott, "Comparing Emancipations: A Review Essay," *Journal of Social History* 20 (Spring 1987): 565–83, and the early chapters of her brilliant *Degrees of Freedom: Louisiana and Cuba after Slavery* (Cambridge, Mass., 2005); Peter Kolchin, "Some Thoughts on Emancipation in Comparative Perspective: Russia and the United States South," *Slavery and Abolition* 21 (December 1990): 351–67; Robert E. May, *Manifest Destiny's Underworld: Filibustering in Antebellum America* (Chapel Hill, N.C., 2002), as well as his earlier *The Southern Dream of a Caribbean Empire, 1854–1861* (Athens, Ga., 1989).

[46]See also Barney, *Road to Secession*; and James Oakes, *The Ruling Race: A History of American Slaveholders* (New York, 1982).

Roughly 150 years after Fort Sumter, determining "the cause" of the Civil War seems as daunting a task as ever. Many of the same problems that confronted historians for nearly a century continue to confront the student today. Were North and South diverging into "two civilizations" and therefore heading toward irrepressible conflict? What role did social and economic differences play in the coming of the war? Did the extremism and folly of politicians and citizens turn a serious quarrel into an irresolvable one? How did religion, ethnicity, culture, and ideology shape political behavior on local, state, and national levels in the years leading up to the conflict? Did the comparatively violent and revolutionary character of America's Civil War reflect distinctive characteristics of its system of unfree labor, of its larger socioeconomic order, or of its political system?

Despite these unresolved questions — and similar ones that emerge in trying to decide on "the consequences" or "the meaning" of the Civil War — most historians seem to agree today that slavery was central to the crisis of the Union and the coming of the Civil War. More broadly, they agree that the Civil War was a momentous event — perhaps the most consequential event — in American history. Whatever else they believe to have profoundly shaped the nation's history in the last century and half, the Civil War almost certainly leads the list. In abolishing slavery and confirming once and for all the question of the integrity of the national republic and the dominance of industrial capitalism, the Civil War set the stage for all that has followed. Thus, although many questions remain, a few of the biggest seem for now to be settled.

## ALLAN NEVINS

## *from* The Emergence of Lincoln   [1950]

**ALLAN NEVINS** (1890–1971) was professor of history at Columbia University. He was one of the most prolific American historians of the twentieth century. In addition to his multivolume study of the Civil War era, he also wrote biographies of John D. Rockefeller and Henry Ford, among many other books.

Great and complex events have great and complex causes. Burke, in his *Reflections on the Revolution in France*, wrote that "a state without the means of some change is without the means of its conservation," and that a constant reconciliation of "the two principles of conservation and correction" is indispensable to healthy national growth. It is safe to say that every such revolutionary era as that on which the United States entered in 1860 finds its genesis in an inadequate adjustment of these two forces.

It is also safe to say that when a tragic national failure occurs, it is largely a failure of leadership. "Brains are of three orders," wrote Machiavelli, "those that understand of themselves, those that understand when another shows them, and those that understand neither by themselves nor by the showing of others." Ferment and change must steadily be controlled; the real must, as Bryce said, be kept resting on the ideal; and if disaster is to be avoided, wise leaders must help thoughtless men to understand, and direct the action of invincibly ignorant men. Necessary reforms may be obstructed in various ways; by sheer inertia, by tyranny and class selfishness, or by the application of compromise to basic principles — this last being in Lowell's view the main cause of the Civil War. Ordinarily the obstruction arises from a combination of all these elements. To explain the failure of American leadership in 1846–1861, and the revolution that ensued, is a baffling complicated problem.

Looking backward from the verge of war in March, 1861, Americans could survey a series of ill-fated decisions by their chosen agents. One unfortunate decision was embodied in Douglas's Kansas-Nebraska Act of 1854. Had an overwhelming majority of Americans been ready to accept the squatter sovereignty principle, this law might have proved a statesmanlike stroke; but it was so certain that powerful elements North and South would resist it to the last that it accentuated the strife and confusion. Another disastrous decision was made by Taney and his associates in the Dred Scott pronouncement of 1857. Still another was made by Buchanan when he weakly accepted the Lecompton Constitution and tried to force that fraudulent document through Congress. The Northern legislatures which passed Personal Liberty Acts made an unhappy decision. Most irresponsible, wanton, and disastrous of all was the decision of those Southern leaders who in 1858–1860 turned to the provocative demand for Congressional protection of slavery in all the Territories of the republic. Still other errors might be named. Obviously, however, it is the forces behind these decisions which demand our study; the waters pouring down the gorge, not the rocks which threw their spray into the air.

At this point we meet a confused clamor of voices as various students attempt an explanation of the tragic denouement of 1861. Some writers are as content with a simple explanation as Lord Clarendon was when he attributed the English Civil War to the desire of Parliament for an egregious domination of the government. The bloody conflict, declared James Ford Rhodes, had "a single cause, slavery." He was but echoing what Henry Wilson and other early historians had written, that the aggressions of the Slave Power offered the central explanation. That opinion had been challenged as early as 1861 by the London *Saturday Review*, which remarked that "slavery is but a surface question in American politics," and by such Southern propagandists as Yancey, who tried to popularize a commercial theory of the war, emphasizing a supposed Southern revolt against the tariff and other Yankee exactions. A later school of writers was to find the key to the tragedy in an inexorable conflict between the business-minded North and the agrarian-minded South, a thrusting industrialism colliding with a rather static agricultural society. Still another group of writers has accepted the theory that the war resulted from psychological causes. They declare that agitators, propagandists, and alarmists on both sides, exaggerating the real differences of interest, created a state of mind, a hysterical excitement, which made armed conflict inevitable.

At the very outset of the war Senator Mason of Virginia, writing to his daughter, asserted that two systems of society were in conflict; systems, he implied, as different as those of Carthage and Rome, Protestant Holland and Catholic Spain. That view, too, was later to be elaborated by a considerable school of writers. Two separate nations, they declared, had arisen within the United States in 1861, much as two separate nations had emerged within the first British Empire by 1776. Contrasting ways of life, rival group consciousness, divergent hopes and fears made a movement for separation logical; and the minority people, believing its peculiar civilization in danger of suppression, began a war for independence. We are told, indeed, that two types of nationalism came into conflict: a Northern nationalism which wished to preserve the unity of the whole republic, and a Southern nationalism intent on creating an entirely new republic.

It is evident that some of these explanations deal with merely superficial phenomena, and that others, when taken separately, represent but subsidiary elements in the play of forces. Slavery was a great fact; the demands of Northern industrialism constituted a great fact; sectional hysteria was a great fact. But do they not perhaps relate themselves to some profounder underlying cause? This question has inspired one student to suggest that "the confusion of a growing state" may offer the fundamental explanation of the drift to war; an unsatisfactory hypothesis, for westward growth, railroad growth, business growth, and cultural growth, however much attended with "confusion," were unifying factors, and it was not the new-made West but old-settled South Carolina which led in the schism.

One fact needs emphatic statement: of all the monistic explanations for the drift to war, that posited upon supposed economic causes is the flimsiest. This theory was sharply rejected at the time by so astute an observer as Alexander H. Stephens. South Carolina, he wrote his brother on New Year's Day, 1861, was seceding from a tariff "which is just what her own Senators and members in Congress made it." As for the charges of consolidation and despotism made by some Carolinians, he thought they arose from peevishness rather than a calm analysis of facts. "The truth is, the South, almost in mass, has voted, I think, for every measure of general legislation that has passed both houses and become law for the last ten years." The South, far from groaning under tyranny, had controlled the government almost from its beginning, and Stephens believed that its only real grievance lay in the Northern refusal to return fugitive slaves and to stop the antislavery agitation. "All other complaints are founded on threatened dangers which may never come, and which I feel very sure would be averted if the South would pursue a judicious and wise course." Stephens was right. It was true that the whole tendency of federal legislation from 1842 to 1860 was toward free trade; true that the tariff in force when secession began was largely Southern-made; true that it was the lowest tariff the country had known since 1816; true that it cost a nation of 30 million people but $60 million in indirect revenue; true that without secession no new tariff law, obnoxious to the Democratic party, could have passed before 1863 — if then.

In the official explanations which one Southern state after another published for its secession, economic grievances are either omitted entirely or given minor position. There were few such supposed grievances which the agricultural states of Illinois, Iowa, Indiana, Wisconsin, and Minnesota did not share with the South — and they never threatened to secede. Charles A. Beard finds the taproot of the war in the resistance of the planter interest to Northern demands enlarging the old Hamilton-Webster policy. The South was adamant in standing for "no high protective tariffs, no ship subsidies, no national banking and currency system; in short, none of the measures which business enterprise deemed essential to its progress." But the Republican platform in 1856 was silent on the tariff; in 1860 it carried a milk-and-water statement on the subject which western Republicans took, mild as it was, with a wry face; the incoming president was little interested in the tariff; and any harsh legislation was impossible. Ship subsidies were not an issue in the campaign of 1860. Neither were a national banking system and a national currency system. They were not mentioned in the Republican platform nor discussed by party debaters. The Pacific Railroad was advocated both by the Douglas Democrats and the Republicans; and it is noteworthy that Seward and Douglas were for building both a Northern and a Southern line. In short, the divisive economic issues are easily exaggerated. At the same time, the unifying economic factors were both numerous and powerful. North and South had economies which were largely complementary. It was no misfortune to the South that Massachusetts cotton mills wanted its staple, and that New York ironmasters like Hewitt were eager to sell rails dirt cheap to Southern railway builders; and sober businessmen on both sides, merchants, bankers, and manufacturers, were the men most anxious to keep the peace and hold the Union together.

We must seek further for an explanation; and in so doing, we must give special weight to the observations of penetrating leaders of the time, who knew at firsthand the spirit of the people. Henry J. Raymond, moderate editor of the *New York Times*, a sagacious man who disliked Northern abolitionists and Southern radicals, wrote in January 1860 an analysis of the impending conflict which attributed it to a competition for power.

> In every country there must be a just and equal balance of powers in the government, an equal distribution of the national forces. Each section and each interest must exercise its due share of influence and control. It is always more or less difficult to preserve their just equipoise, and the larger the country, and the more varied its great interests, the more difficult does the task become, and the greater the shock and disturbance caused by an attempt to adjust it when once disturbed. I believe I state

only what is generally conceded to be a fact, when I say that the growth of
the Northern States in population, in wealth, in all the elements of political influence and control, has been out of proportion to their political
influence in the Federal Councils. While the Southern States have less
than a third of the aggregate population of the Union, their interests have
influenced the policy of the government far more than the interests of
the Northern States. . . . Now the North, has made rapid advances within
the last five years, and it naturally claims a proportionate share of influence and power in the affairs of the Confederacy.

It is inevitable that this claim should be put forward, and it is also inevitable that it should be conceded. No party can long resist it; it overrides all
parties, and makes them the mere instruments of its will. It is quite as
strong today in the heart of the Democratic party of the North as in the
Republican ranks and any party which ignores it will lose its hold on the
public mind.

Why does the South resist this claim? Not because it is unjust in itself, but
because it has become involved with the question of slavery, and has
drawn so much of its vigor and vitality from that quarter, that it is almost
merged in that issue. The North bases its demand for increased power, in
a very great degree, on the action of the government in regard to slavery —
and the just and rightful ascendency of the North in the Federal councils
comes thus to be regarded as an element of danger to the institutions of
the Southern States.

In brief, Raymond, who held that slavery was a moral wrong, that its
economic and social tendencies were vicious, and that the time had come
to halt its growth with a view to its final eradication, believed that the contest was primarily one for power, and for the application of that power to
the slave system. With this opinion Alexander H. Stephens agreed. The
Georgian said he believed slavery both morally and politically right. In his
letter to Lincoln on December 30, 1860, he declared that the South did
not fear that the new Republican Administration would interfere directly
and immediately with slavery in the states. What Southerners did fear was
the ultimate result of the shift of power which had just occurred — in its
application to slavery:

Now this subject, which is confessedly on all sides outside of the constitutional action of the Government, so far as the States are concerned, is
made the "central idea" in the platform of principles announced by the
triumphant party. The leading object seems to be simply, and wantonly, if
you please, to put the institutions of nearly half the States under the ban
of public opinion and national condemnation. This, upon general principles, is quite enough of itself to arouse a spirit not only of general indignation, but of revolt on the part of the proscribed. Let me illustrate. It is
generally conceded by the Republicans even, that Congress cannot interfere with slavery in the States. It is equally conceded that Congress cannot
establish any form of religious worship. Now suppose that any one of the

present Christian churches or sects prevailed in all the Southern States, but had no existence in any one of the Northern States, — under such circumstances suppose the people of the Northern States should organize a political party, not upon a foreign or domestic policy, but with one leading idea of condemnation of the doctrines and tenets of that particular church, and with an avowed object of preventing its extension into the common Territories, even after the highest judicial tribunal of the land had decided they had no such constitutional power. And suppose that a party so organized should carry a Presidential election. Is it not apparent that a general feeling of resistance to the success, aims, and objects of such a party would necessarily and rightfully ensue?

Raymond and Stephens agreed that the two sections were competing for power; that a momentous transfer of power had just occurred; and that it held fateful consequences because it was involved with the issue of slavery, taking authority from a section which believed slavery moral and healthy, and giving it to a section which held slavery immoral and pernicious. To Stephens this transfer was ground for resuming the ultimate sovereignty of the states. Here we find a somewhat more complex statement of James Ford Rhodes's thesis that the central cause of the Civil War lay in slavery. Here, too, we revert to the assertions of Yancey and Lincoln that the vital conflict was between those who thought slavery right and those who thought it wrong. But this definition we can accept only if we probe a little deeper for a concept which both modifies and enlarges the basic source of perplexity and quarrel.

The main root of the conflict (and there were minor roots) was the problem of slavery *with its complementary problem of race adjustment*; the main source of the tragedy was the refusal of either section to face these conjoined problems squarely and pay the heavy costs of a peaceful settlement. Had it not been for the difference in race, the slavery issue would have presented no great difficulties. But as the racial gulf existed, the South inarticulately but clearly perceived that elimination of this issue would still leave it the terrible problem of the Negro. Those historians who write that if slavery had simply been left alone it would soon have withered overlook this heavy impediment. The South as a whole in 1846–1861 was not moving toward emancipation, but away from it. It was not relaxing the laws which guarded the system, but reinforcing them. It was not ameliorating slavery, but making it harsher and more implacable. The South was further from a just solution of the slavery problem in 1830 than it had been in 1789. It was further from a tenable solution in 1860 than it had been in 1830. Why was it going from bad to worse? Because Southern leaders refused to nerve their people to pay the heavy price of race adjustment. These leaders never made up their mind to deal with the problem as the progressive temper of civilization demanded. They would not adopt the new outlook which the upward march of mankind required because they saw that the gradual abolition of slavery would bring a measure of political privilege; that political privilege would usher in a measure of economic equality; that on the heels of economic equality would come a rising social status for the Negro. Southern leadership dared not ask the people to pay this price.

A heavy responsibility for the failure of America in this period rests with this Southern leadership, which lacked imagination, ability, and courage. But the North was by no means without its full share, for the North equally refused to give a constructive examination to the central question of slavery as linked with race adjustment. This was because of two principal reasons. Most abolitionists and many other sentimental-minded Northerners simply denied that the problem existed. Regarding all Negroes as white men with dark skins, whom a few years of schooling would bring abreast of the dominant race, they thought that no difficult adjustment was required. A much more numerous body of Northerners would have granted that a great and terrible task of race adjustment existed — but they were reluctant to help shoulder any part of it. Take a million or two million Negroes into the Northern States? Indiana, Illinois, and even Kansas were unwilling to take a single additional person of color. Pay tens of millions to help educate and elevate the colored population? Take even a first step by offering to pay the Southern slaveholders some recompense for a gradual liberation of their human property? No Northern politician dared ask his constituents to make so unpopular a sacrifice. The North, like the South, found it easier to drift blindly toward disaster.

The hope of solving the slavery problem without a civil war rested upon several interrelated factors, of which one merits special emphasis. We have said that the South as a whole was laboring to bolster and stiffen slavery — which was much to its discredit. But it is nevertheless true that slavery was dying all around the edges of its domain; it was steadily decaying in Delaware, Maryland, western Virginia, parts of Kentucky, and Missouri. Much of the harshness of Southern legislation in the period sprang from a sense that slavery was in danger from *internal* weaknesses. In no great time Delaware, Maryland, and Missouri were likely to enter the column of free states; and if they did, reducing the roster to twelve, the doom of the institution would be clearly written. Allied with this factor was the rapid comparative increase of Northern strength, and the steady knitting of economic, social, and moral ties between the North and West, leaving the South in a position of manifest inferiority. A Southern Confederacy had a fair fighting chance in 1861; by 1880 it would have had very little. If secession could have been postponed by two decades, natural forces might well have placed a solution full in sight. Then, too, the growing pressure of world sentiment must in time have produced its effect. But to point out these considerations is not to suggest that in 1861 a policy of procrastination and appeasement would have done anything but harm. All hope of bringing Southern majority sentiment to a better attitude would have been lost if Lincoln and his party had flinched on the basic issue of the restriction of slavery; for by the seventh decade of nineteenth-century history, the time had come when that demand had to be maintained.

While in indicting leadership we obviously indict the public behind the leaders, we must also lay some blame upon a political environment which gave leadership a poor chance. American parties, under the pressure of sectional feeling, worked badly. The government suffered greatly, moreover, from the lack of any adequate planning agency. Congress was not a truly deliberative body, and its committees had not yet learned to do long-range planning. The president might have formulated plans, but he never did. For one reason, no president between Polk and Lincoln had either the ability or the prestige required; for another reason, Fillmore, Pierce, and Buchanan all held that their duty was merely to execute the laws, not to initiate legislation. Had the country possessed a ministerial form of government, the Cabinet in leading the legislature would have been compelled to lay down a program of real scope concerning slavery. As it was, leadership in Washington was supplied only spasmodically by men like Clay, Douglas, and Crittenden.

And as we have noted, the rigidity of the American system was at this time a grave handicap. Twice, in the fall of 1854 and of 1858, the elections gave a stunning rebuke to the Administration. Under a ministerial system, the old government would probably have gone out and a new one have come in. In 1854, however, Pierce continued to carry on the old policies, and in 1858 Buchanan remained the drearily inept helmsman of the republic. Never in our history were bold, quick planning and a flexible administration of policy more needed; never was the failure to supply them more complete.

Still another element in the tragic chronicle of the time must be mentioned. Much that happens in human affairs is accidental. When a country is guided by true statesmen the role of accident is minimized; when it is not, unforeseen occurrences are numerous and dangerous. In the summer and fall of 1858, as we have seen, the revival of a conservative opposition party in the upper South, devoted to the Union, furnished a real gleam of hope. If this opposition had been given unity and determined leadership, if moderate Southerners had stood firm against the plot of Yancey and others to disrupt the Democratic Party, if Floyd had been vigilant enough to read the warning letter about John Brown and act on it, the situation might even then have been saved. Instead, John Brown's mad raid fell on public opinion like a thunderstroke, exasperating men everywhere and dividing North and South more tragically than ever. The last chance of persuading the South to submit to an essential step, the containment of slavery, was gone.

The war, when it came, was not primarily a conflict over state rights, although that issue had become involved in it. It was not primarily a war born of economic grievances, although many Southerners had been led to think that they were suffering, or would soon suffer, economic wrongs. It was not a war created by politicians and publicists who fomented hysteric excitement; for while hysteria was important, we have always to ask what basic reasons made possible the propaganda which aroused it. It was not primarily a war about slavery alone, although that institution seemed to many the grand cause. It was a war over slavery *and* the future position of the Negro race in North America. Was the Negro to be allowed, as a result of the shift of power signalized by Lincoln's election, to take the first step toward an ultimate position of general economic, political, and social equality with the white man? Or was he to be held immobile in a degraded, servile position, unchanging the next hundred years as it had remained essentially unchanged for the hundred years past? These questions were implicit in Lincoln's demand that slavery be placed in a position where the public mind could rest assured of its ultimate extinction.

Evasion by the South, evasion by the North, were no longer possible. The alternatives faced were an unpopular but curative adjustment of the situation by the opposed parties, or a war that would force an adjustment upon the loser. For Americans in 1861, as for many other peoples throughout history, war was easier than wisdom and courage.

## WILLIAM W. FREEHLING
### *from* Democracy and the Causes of the Civil War    [1994]

**WILLIAM FREEHLING** (1935– ) holds the Singletary Endowed Chair in the Humanities at the University of Kentucky. He is the author of *The Reintegration of American History* (1994) and *The Road to Disunion*, vol. I (1990) and vol. II (2007).

It is a telling historical irony that of all the New World slavocracies, only slaveholders in the United States lived in an advanced republic, and only the United States required a civil war between whites to abolish slavery for blacks. . . .

The southern slaveholders' unique acceptance of trial by warfare demanded unique self-confidence. Secession required both nerve and the perception of power. The Brazilian and Cuban slavocracies could have no such nerve in the 1870s and 1880s, after watching U.S. slaveholders go down in flames in the 1860s. Nor did their nondominant position in their respective political power structures embolden Cuban or Brazilian slaveholders with the illusion that they could win a civil war. . . .

The divergent U.S. and Latin American roads toward emancipation began with dissimilar colonial settlements. During the seventeenth century, England, the most republican of the European colonizing nations, sent to the North American mainland by far the largest percentage of nonslaveholding settlers to be found in any New World area containing large numbers of slaves. Because of that comparatively huge white republican population, the thirteen colonies had special leverage to resist English metropolitan impositions on colonial republicanism, and out of that resistance came the American Revolution and the first New World liberation from Old World control. With the establishment of the federal Union, the Revolutionaries encased one of the most extensive slaveholder regimes in the Americas inside the most republican nation in the New World. . . .

As the eighteenth century gave way to the nineteenth, an invention and a law pressed U.S. slavery toward tropical habitats. Eli Whitney's invention of the cotton gin in 1793 impelled the movement of slaveholders toward Lower South frontiers. Fourteen years later, in 1807, the federal government's closure of the African slave trade contracted the Cotton Kingdom's source of slaves. Unlike mid-nineteenth-century tropical developers in Cuba and Brazil, the two other large New World slavocracies, cotton planters could not legally buy slaves from Africa. But only U.S. slaveholders could purchase slaves from their own northerly, relatively nontropical areas, which had concurrently fallen into chronic economic recession.

A slave drain ensued, especially from the more northern South to the more southern South. Between 1790 and 1860, some 750,000 Middle and Border South slaves traveled downriver to the Cotton Kingdom. The Lower South, which had had 21 percent of U.S. slaves in 1790, had 59 percent in 1860. Maryland and Virginia, with 60 percent in 1790, had 18 percent in 1860. Thirty-seven percent of Lower South white families owned slaves in 1860, compared to only 12 percent in the Border South, down from 20 percent in 1790. . . .

With slavery swiftly concentrating southward and slowly fading northward, different social attitudes and political priorities developed. Lower South slaveholders came to call slavery a probably perpetual blessing, while Border South masters persistently called the institution a hopefully temporary evil. So too Lower South political warriors cared more about perpetuating slavery than the Union, while Border South leaders would compromise on slavery in order to save the Union. . . .

In the mid-nineteenth century, then, slaveholders overwhelmingly controlled the Lower South, which had been belatedly but massively developed. The slavocracy somewhat less solidly controlled the Middle and Border South, where percentages of slave owners were slowly dropping. But even in the Border South, vestiges (and sometimes defiant concentrations) of the old relatively nontropical slavocracy occasionally fought to salvage a fading system. The mature Slave South had a tropical base of states, containing large slave populations, and several layers of buffer zones to the north, with less tropical conditions and less proslavery commitments and fewer slaves in each successive tier above.

Yet despite this degree of geographic disunity, no other New World slavocracy could muster as united a front against worldwide antislavery currents. . . .

A more intense racism fueled the U.S. slaveholders' greater capacity to mobilize a united front. Because Latin American racial attitudes toward blacks were less hidebound than in the United States, greater tolerance for free-womb emancipation, for mulattoes, and for individual manumissions — and less willingness to fight a civil war over the issue — pervaded Latin American slavocracies. Because U.S. racism was so extreme, a more unified slaveholding class and more support from white nonslaveholders — and thus a greater capacity to fight a civil war — infused the Slave South.

Behind the more severe U.S. racism lay in part a different heterosexual situation, itself another result of the largest white migration to an important New World slavocracy. English colonists to the future United States migrated far more often in family groups and/or with equal numbers of unmarried males and females in the entourage than did colonists headed farther south, who more often sought their fortunes as unattached males, with only slaves available for sexual liaisons. More frequent and less taboo interracial sexual intimacies resulted south of British North America, which led to more mulattoes and less insistence that the world be rigidly separated into black and white. . . .

Some historians doubt that racism was more culturally deep-seated in the United States than south of the border. That position founders before the greater U.S. taboo surrounding miscegenation and the far greater desire to deport blacks from antebellum America than from any other New World slavocracy. . . . Uniquely in the United States, slaveholders had to mobilize nonslaveholders, and racism was their most potent weapon. . . .

The racial foundation of Southwide unity, however, was a two-edged sword. For racism to unite nonslaveholders and slaveholders, the black race had to be significantly present. With the slave drain to the Lower South and the movement of European whites to such northerly slave states as Maryland and Missouri, Border South blacks became steadily less visible. As for that highly visible group of blacks in northern Maryland and Delaware, the free blacks, their energetic labor and law-abiding deportment demonstrated that racial control hardly required slavery.

That conclusion had proved fatal to slavery in northern states where percentages of blacks had declined. . . . Mid-nineteenth-century Border South states were in no immediate danger of becoming a New York. . . . But given the Border South's waning percentage of blacks, its . . . manumissions, its propensity for thinking of slavery as a temporary evil, and its commitment to Union-saving compromises on the institution, could the Lower South rely on its northern hinterlands' future loyalty?

On the answer hung the Slave South's capacity to be that unique New World slave regime: the one that could defy an emancipating century rather than settle for a few more decades of slaveholder profits. . . . The Brazilian slavocracy could only postpone emancipation. . . . The Old South, in contrast, had various powers to command a majoritarian democracy despite its minority status — *if* all fifteen slave states hung together and the Border South did not go the way of New York. . . .

Numbers indicate how much was at stake in that *if*. The seven Lower South states of 1860 (South Carolina, Florida, Georgia, Alabama, Mississippi, Louisiana, and Texas, with 47 percent of their population enslaved) could not fight off the sixteen northern states (containing 61 percent of the American population) without the enthusiastic support of the four Middle South states (Virginia, North Carolina, Tennessee, and Arkansas, with 32 percent of their population enslaved) and the four Border South states (Maryland, Delaware, Kentucky, and Missouri, with 13 percent of their population enslaved). Those buffer areas above the Lower South could come under siege — the siege of democratic public opinion. Would the Border South remain foursquare behind slavery and the Lower South, even if the slavocracy's northern hinterlands came to possess scantier and scantier percentages of blacks?

That question transcended the Border South. The slaveholders' worst internal problem involved not a single localized place but a regionwide lopsided distribution of blacks. While the Border South was the most widespread locale with a relatively low percentage of slaves, some areas farther south also contained few blacks; and everywhere a paucity of slaves allowed more nonslaveholder hostility toward slaveholders. Wherever blacks were concentrated, whites drew together, however much the poor resented the rich, for lowly whites despised lowlier blacks even more than they resented lordly masters. But whenever blacks were scarce, race hatred intensified class hatred, for nonslaveholders preferred to have neither autocrats nor blacks around. A relatively slaveless situation, while most prevalent in the Border South, also predominated in western Virginia, in eastern Tennessee, and in piney woods and semimountainous areas of the Lower South. Here the Border South predicament came closer to home to worried Lower and Middle South slavocrats. Could upper-class ideology command lower-class loyalties in areas where no racial tensions united the whites? . . .

The North American dialogue about emancipation began with the foundation of U.S. republicanism, the Declaration of Independence. . . . Thomas Jefferson of Virginia, author of the Declaration and a large slaveholder, believed that all men would and should rise up against so antirepublican a horror as slavery. He thus feared that slave insurrection would disrupt white republics unless white republicans freed blacks. . . .

Yet if Jefferson called slavery antithetical to republicanism, he considered racism compatible with the Declaration of Independence. Whites and blacks, thought Jefferson, were innately different. Whites allegedly possessed a keener abstract intelligence; blacks, a keener sexual ardency. Ex-slaves, he further worried, would be eager for revenge and ex-masters determined to repress the avengers. If slaves were freed and remained in the United States, "deep-rooted prejudices entertained by the whites" and "ten thousand recollections by the blacks, of the injuries they have sustained" would "produce convulsions, which will probably never end but in the extermination of one or the other race."

Thus to preserve white republics, freed blacks had to be deported. The dangerous alternative was to keep blacks enslaved. Jefferson's conviction that emancipation must be conditional on removing blacks, the first thrust in the U.S. dialectic on abolition, was rare in Latin America. An insistence on race removal would have ill-suited Latin American nations, where individual bargains between masters and slaves slowly led to a third class of semifree blacks and a fourth class of free blacks. . . .

In the wake of Nat Turner's slave revolt, the most successful (although still abortive) slave uprising in the United States, Thomas Jefferson Randolph, Jefferson's favorite grandson, proposed to the Virginia legislature that slaves born after 1840 be freed on their eighteenth (women) and twenty-first (men) birthdays. Thus far Randolph's proposal was standard Latin American–style free-womb emancipation. But Randolph's bill added the condition, alien to Latin America, that the state must remove the freedmen to Africa. Randolph's speech for the historic proposal also featured the cynical prediction, more alien still south of the U.S. border, that many Virginia masters would sell slaves to the Lower South before emancipating birthdays. Thus, Randolph cheered, masters would profitably remove slaves from Virginia at no cost to state coffers.

Randolph's proposal led to a famous state crisis, for Virginia's largely nonslaveholding areas rallied behind Jefferson's grandson in defiance of slaveholding areas. Never before in the history of the Slave South, and never again until western Virginia seceded from Virginia during the Civil War, was the potentially dangerous antagonism between slaveless and slaveholding geographic zones more obvious, for here western Virginian nonslaveholders sought to impose emancipation on eastern Virginia planters. Earlier, eastern squires had built a bulwark against the nonslaveholder threat. They had insisted that slaveholders have more seats in the Virginia House of Delegates (lower house) than eastern Virginia's white numbers justified. The underrepresented western Virginians responded, like later Northerners, that the Slavepower thus enslaved *them.* These nonslaveholders preferred that all blacks depart the commonwealth. Then true white democracy would replace Slavepower dominion in Virginia. So western Virginians cheered Thomas Jefferson Randolph's black removal proposal.

After two weeks of debate, the Virginia House of Delegates rejected a variation of Randolph's proposal by a vote of 73–58. The margin against antislavery would have shriveled to one vote if the slaveholders had not held those extra legislative seats. The shaky anti-Randolph majority warned that even after masters had sold off some blacks, state-financed removal of other slaves would bankrupt the government. . . .

Thomas Jefferson had proposed a swifter way to deport blacks: a federal constitutional amendment that would authorize compulsory emancipation and colonization to be financed by federal land sales, a richer source of funds than state taxation. Throughout the nation, antislavery moderates perpetuated this scheme for liberating slaves while also whitening the republic. The persistent admirers of Jefferson's black removal plan included the Border South's favorite statesman, Henry Clay; the Republicans' favorite politician, Abraham Lincoln; and the North's favorite novelist, Harriet Beecher Stowe. A national volunteer organization, the American

Colonization Society, used private donations to establish a rather unstable African colony, Liberia, to receive American blacks. In those unusual days of a federal budgetary surplus, the national government had excess funds to help with the financing. But South Carolina threatened secession if Congress even discussed the possibility. So the debate stopped before much was said. . . .

The more republican U.S. slavocracy ironically outdid their less republican Latin American counterparts in eradicating antislavery opinion. . . .

Nor could Border South whites altogether deter their most threatening black dissenters — fugitive slaves. Group insurrectionists in the United States, though momentarily more terrifying than individual runaways, were less numerous. . . .

Thus fugitives achieved more than their own freedom in the seemingly apolitical act of running away from masters (and from millions of enslaved brethren). The runaways advanced the political process that led to war and emancipation. Particularly Border South fugitives illuminated the slavocracy's geographic area of weakness — an illumination that provoked border masters into initiating Union-shattering political controversies. The slaveholders' political answer to border fugitives lay in the national forum, for only national laws could consolidate the line between South and North, as well as the barrier between slavery and free democratic discourse.

The electoral numbers might seem to have forbidden slaveholders from wielding national governmental power to deter border fugitives or otherwise consolidate their outposts. During pre–Civil War controversies, around 70 percent of U.S. whites lived outside the Slave South, and around 70 percent of southern white families did not own slaves. In those overwhelming numbers lay the slaveholders' potential peril. But the democratic system, as ever both threatening and empowering for a besieged minority, long enabled the master class to protect its borderlands and dominate Yankee majorities.

The federal Constitution provided the minority's most obvious defensive weapon. Abolitionists often conceded that the Constitution protected slavery, not least because it authorized Congress to pass fugitive slave laws. The Constitution also contained many restrictions on majority antislavery action, including the ultimate one: a forbidding amendment process. Three-fourths of the states have to agree on a constitutional amendment before it becomes operative. . . .

This potential Border South problem illustrated the slaveholders' provokingly small margin for error. Totally to control 11/15 of slaveholders' territory and largely to control the other 4/15 of their world would have been a miracle in any other New World slaveholding regime. But U.S. slaveholders, unlike Latin American counterparts, were seeking to stonewall the Age of Emancipation; and the singular effort would fail if the slaveholders' large degree of control over their most vulnerable four states weakened. In part for that reason, southern extremists, including Calhoun, came to eschew the doctrine of federal hands off slavery and to urge that federal hands be heavily laid on, especially in the borderlands, to protect the slaveholders' interests there. National majorities must annex Texas on the Lower South's flank, admit Kansas on the Border South's edge, and ensure the return of fugitive slaves who escaped over any border.

Two more empowerments of the southern minority long enabled slaveholders to maneuver congressional majorities into fortifying southern outposts. First, the Constitution let the slaveholding states count three out of five slaves, in addition to all whites, when the number of southern congressmen and presidential electors was calculated. Thus in 1860 the Slave South, containing 30 percent of the nation's white citizens, had 36 percent of the nation's congressmen and presidential electors. That extra power (which had first prompted the coining of the word *Slavepower*) turned southern defeat into victory on key occasions, including the election of Virginia's Thomas Jefferson over Massachusetts's John Adams to the presidency in 1800, the Missouri Controversy, the Gag Rule Controversy, and the Kansas-Nebraska Controversy.

Second, national political parties gave a 30 percent popular minority with a 36 percent congressional minority the leverage to secure another 14 percent or more of congressional votes. Especially the dubiously titled Democratic Party became a bulwark of the slavocracy. . . . Jackson's egalitarianism, for white males only, won him huge majorities in the Lower South but progressively smaller majorities at every step northward and few majorities in New England. That voting distribution gave the Democratic Party a majority control in the nation and Southerners a majority control in the party. Thus when slavery controversies emerged in national politics, Southern Democrats could use the leverage of the nation's usually dominant party to demand that Northern Democrats help consolidate the slavocracy's frontiers.

Southern Democrats had to insist that Northern Democrats support the fullest proslavery protection. Southern Whigs also had to repel the Northern Whigs' slightest conditional antislavery overture. . . .

Ironically, northern extremists were southern extremists' best ally in these loyalty contests. Garrison's righteous denunciations, aimed at all who opposed unconditional emancipation, damned all Southerners, whether they hoped to remove or to retain slaves. Southern moderates, enraged at being called sinners, passionately joined proslavery extremists in resenting the slur on their honor. . . .

The Gag Rule Controversy, the first national slavery crisis after Garrison's emergence, introduced the deadly process. In 1835, antislavery zealots petitioned Congress to abolish slavery in Washington, D.C. The petitions inadvertently demonstrated that abolitionists constituted a fringe group outside the northern mainstream. Only a tiny fraction of Northerners signed the appeals, and a large number of signers were women, barred from the electorate.

Nevertheless, the petitioners reshaped national mainstream slavery politics. . . . That provocative response shook northern complacency about the slavery issue more than any abolitionist could.

The slaveholders' provocative demand was that petitions for congressional action against slavery must be barred from congressional deliberations. Antislavery must not be discussed in secret committees, much less publicly. . . . By attempting to gag congressional debate, Southerners tried to impose on the nation their regional version of republicanism: all ideas, *except* antislavery, were open to discussion.

Northerners responded that republicanism would lie in ruins unless *all* ideas could be debated. Representative republicanism especially would become a mockery, said Northerners, unless citizens could request that their representatives discuss whether slavery, an arguably antirepublican institution, should exist in the republic's capital city. The southern gag rule tactic, an irrelevant strategy in largely undemocratic Latin America, thus immediately produced the key non–Latin American question: Were slavery for blacks and democratic procedures for whites compatible? From that question, an otherwise rather isolated abolitionist movement would spread in the North, and the U.S. slavery controversy would assume its irrepressible — and non–Latin American — form. . . .

The most airtight of the Democratic Party's gag rules, passed in 1840, forbade the House of Representatives from receiving, much less considering, antislavery petitions. To the embarrassment of Southern Whigs, the Northern Whigs, led by Massachusetts's ex-President John Quincy Adams, refused to be gagged. Adams relentlessly attacked Northern Democrats as the Slavepower's slaves. The issue, he said, was not black slavery but white republicanism. The minority South must not rule the majority North. The slaveholding minority must not gag republican citizens. Northern Democrats must represent the majority North, sustain white men's democracy, and repeal the minority South's antidemocratic gag rule.

In December 1844, Northern Democrats finally acted to protect their home base. By voting down all gag rules, after eight years of caving in to ever-tighter gags, they signaled that the southern minority could push Northerners only so far. This denouement of the Gag Rule Controversy also signaled that northern and southern antiparty extremists had unintentionally collaborated to weaken their mutual foe: national party moderates. . . .

By demanding a gag on the discussion of that one issue, slaveholders had confirmed one aspect of the abolitionists' case: The preservation of southern-style black slavery meant the annihilation of northern-style white republicanism. These dynamics of northern consciousness raising ultimately forced those key northern appeasers, Northern Democrats, to join Northern Whigs and northern extremists in opposing all gags, just as the dynamics of southern consciousness raising forced southern moderates to join southern extremists in seeking ever-tighter gags. Then neither centrist national party could find a middle position between the two sections' different versions of republicanism. And in any democracy, the erosion of the vital center can be the first step toward civil war.

In 1844, an ominous second step was taken. Southern Democrats surrendered on the gag rules, partly to press Northern Democrats to support the annexation of the then-independent Republic of Texas . . . of whose population only 20 percent was enslaved in the early 1840s. That was a Border South percentage of slaves. But this time, the borderland with a low proportion of slaves abutted the slaveholders' southwestern flank, thick with slaves. . . . An annexed Texas, under U.S. control, would consolidate the Lower South frontier. . . .

A Southern Whig administration had proposed a border safeguard. But as usual, only the National Democratic Party could pass prosouthern legislation. Northern Whigs, as usual, denounced the southern proposal. Southern Democrats, however, induced reluctant Northern Democrats to replace the lukewarm annexationist New Yorker, Martin Van Buren, with the strongly annexationist Tennessean, James K. Polk, as the party's presidential candidate in 1844. After Polk won the election, Southern Democrats, now pressured by Southern Whigs to do still more for the South, successfully insisted that reluctant Northern Democrats not only admit Texas to the Union but also allow the annexed state, any time in the future, to divide itself into five slave states. Four years later, a resentful Van Buren bolted the Democratic Party, arguing that white men's majoritarian democracy must be protected from minority dictation. Van Buren ran for president on the Free-Soil ticket, hoping to stop slavery from spreading into federal territories.

At midcentury, while Van Buren sought to contain the Slavepower in the South, Southerners sought to stop the flight of slaves to the North. In 1850, border Southerners proposed a new fugitive slave law, especially designed to protect the South's northernmost hinterlands from northern slave raiders. The proposed law contained notorious antirepublican features. . . . Black fugitives were denied a jury trial. . . . Any nonslaveholder could be compelled to join a slave-chasing posse in the manner of a southern patrol — an outrageous requirement in the North.

In the face of the southern minority's latest attempt to impose on the nation southern-style republicanism, Northern Whigs again balked. But again Northern Democrats reluctantly acquiesced, and again the minority South, using the National Democratic Party as a congressional fulcrum, had gained protection of vulnerable frontiers. When Southerners subsequently attempted to extradite captured fugitives from the North, the new procedures returned the alleged slaves 90 percent of the time. But in the remaining cases, northern mobs blocked the return of the escapees. The well-publicized stories of rare fugitive slave rescues dramatized Garrison's most telling lesson: Southern-style power over blacks damaged northern-style republics for whites.

The Kansas-Nebraska Act of 1854 drove the lesson home. Once again a vulnerable slaveholders' hinterland, this time the Border South's Missouri, with only 10 percent of its population enslaved, demanded protection of its frontier. . . .

Before slaveholding citizens could come, Congress would have to repeal the Missouri Compromise of 1820, which had prohibited slavery in all Louisiana Purchase territories north of the 36°30´line. That man-made geographic boundary continued westward from the latitude of Missouri's southern border, thus barring slaveholders from living west of Missouri, once Congress allowed settlement there. Stephen A. Douglas, the Northern Democrats' leader in the post–Van Buren era, warned Southerners that repeal of the Missouri Compromise would raise "a hell of a storm." . . .

Douglas was as convinced as any Southerner that supposedly superior whites should evict supposedly inferior Native Americans from the West and that the enslavement of supposedly inferior blacks was no Northerner's moral business. Yet Southern Democrats had to pressure Douglas to be Douglas, for their shared program bore the taint of Slavepower domination. And this astute majoritarian politician did not want to be labeled a tool of the minority.

Nevertheless, he had to risk the noxious designation. What became known as *his* Kansas-Nebraska Act, passed by a Douglas-rallied National Democratic Party plus a majority of Southern Whigs, repealed the Missouri Compromise ban on slavery in Kansas Territory, located due west of Missouri, and in Nebraska Territory, located due north of Kansas. Any settler with any form of property could come to these two territories, declared the law, and the majority of settlers in each territory would decide which institutions should thereafter prevail. This most important of all mid-nineteenth-century American laws authorized slaveholding migrants to move to Kansas, seek to make it a slave state, and thus protect the Border South's western flank, just as Texas Annexation had fortified the Lower South's western frontier and the Fugitive Slave Law guarded the Border South's northern extremities. Douglas's law also invited the Democrats' northern opponents to claim that the Slavepower minority, in its anxiety to quarantine border slavery from neighboring democratic currents, had again bullied a congressional majority in the manner of an imperious dictator. . . .

In the next six years the northern majority would revoke the minority's domination of the republic, making problems inside the southern outposts more threatening. . . .

In post-1854 politics, the South's most vulnerable instrument was the national party. Long useful in passing the slaveholders' favorite legislation, it had lately buckled under the weight of the minority's attempts to seek ever-more domination over the majority. . . .

In the early 1850s, however the National Whig Party collapsed. Until the middle of the century, Lower South Whigs had hoped that Northern Whigs would relent on slavery-related matters. But after Northern Whigs said no to the Fugitive Slave Law, no to the Kansas-Nebraska Act, and, all too often, yes to the rescue of fugitive slaves, the Southern Democrats' charge rang all too true: Southerners who cooperated with Yankee Whigs might be secretly soft on slavery. After the Kansas-Nebraska Act, Whiggery lost all credibility in the Lower South.

Whiggery simultaneously lost some northern credibility. Old Whig rhetoric did not sufficiently convey many Yankees' twin indignations in 1854: hostility toward new immigrants and loathing for the Kansas-Nebraska Act. . . . A fusion of northern immigrants and southern slaveholders, many native Yankees thought, bid fair to destroy American republicanism, using as the agent of destruction the deplorably named Democratic Party.

A countervailing fusion swiftly transpired. Northern campaigns against immigrants and the Kansas-Nebraska Act, originally separate matters, partly funneled into one deliberately named *Republican* Party in time for the presidential election of 1856. The Republicans' first presidential campaign almost swept enough northern votes to win the White House, despite the lack of southern votes. Some Northerners especially welcomed most Republicans' secondary mission: to serve free laborers' economic interests. Republicans often saw southern and immigrant economic threats as similar. Impoverished immigrants could displace Yankee wage earners by accepting low wages, just as affluent slaveholders could displace Yankee farmers by making Kansas a slave territory. . . .

Republican rhetoric showed how much (and how little) William Lloyd Garrison had triumphed. Lincoln's mainstream rhetoric appropriated Garrison's extremist vocabulary about southern sinfulness, his conception that free-labor and slave-labor economies were antithetical, his demand for inclusion of blacks in the Declaration of Independence, his hopes for slavery's extinction, and his detestation of slaveholders' imperiousness. Still, Republicans' condemnation of the Slavepower's tyrannizing over whites, not Garrison's condemnation of slaveholders' tyrannizing over blacks, had been most responsible for spreading moral outrage about slaveholders from the northern extreme to the northern mainstream. The average Northerner rejected Slavepower imposition on *him*. But most Northerners were as fearful as ever that federally imposed abolition would break up the Union, jeopardize national commerce, and lead northern blacks to demand *their* egalitarian rights.

The Republicans' resulting caution outraged Garrison. He loathed Lincoln's political formula: Always emphasize containment of the Slavepower and occasionally add a vague hope of slavery's ultimate extinction. Garrison equally detested Lincoln's emphasis on the slow transformation of public opinion. . . .

The Southern Democratic majority on the U.S. Supreme Court provided the clearest protection for slaveholders' right to expand into the nation's territories. In its notorious Dred Scott decision (1857), the Court pronounced the Republican Party's containment program unconstitutional. Congress could not bar slavery from national territory, ruled the Court, for slaves were property and seizure of property violated the due process clause of the Constitution. Alarmed Republicans replied (and apparently believed) that a second Dred Scott decision would follow. Since citizens of one state had the rights and immunities of citizens of another state, the Court allegedly would next empower slaveholders to take (human) property into northern states!

If Republicans needed post–Dred Scott evidence that Southerners meant to extend slavery into northern latitudes, southern insistence on admitting Kansas as a slave state in 1857–58 seemed to provide it. The Kansas-Nebraska Act had allowed both Southerners and Northerners to come to the area, with the majority of settlers to decide on an eventual state's constitution and its labor arrangements. Three years later, when Kansans applied for admission to the Union as a state, northern settlers predominated. But the minority of southern settlers demanded admission as a slave state anyway, despite the majority of Kansans' frenzied objections. This time, Stephen A. Douglas defied the Southerners, for they were asking him to abjure his Popular Sovereignty principle that the majority of settlers should determine their own institutions. Despite Douglas's protests, the U.S. Senate voted 33–25 to admit Kansas as a slave state, with most Northern Democrats casting their usual prosouthern vote. The House then rejected a proslavery Kansas, 120–112.

Southerners, enraged at their first congressional loss on a major slavery issue since gag rule times, principally blamed the 40 percent of House Northern Democrats, admirers of Douglas, who had voted against them. Two years later, at the first of two 1860 Democratic National Conventions, Lower South Democrats insisted that the party platform contain anti-popular-sovereignty language on slaveholders' rights in the territories. Douglas and his supporters balked, just as Martin Van Buren had balked at southern control of the party during the Texas episode. But this time, when the key Northern Democrat said no to Slavepower rule, Lower South convention delegates walked out. At the subsequent Democratic convention, Northern Democrats barred those who had left from returning as accredited delegates.

With the split of the National Democratic Party, the minority South lost its long-standing leverage to secure majority laws protective of its hinterlands. The need never seemed greater. When the House of Representatives rejected a proslavery Kansas, six Upper South ex-Whigs voted with the North. Had they voted with the South, the slaveholders' 120–112 defeat would have been a 118–114 triumph. The episode again illuminated one reason for southern defensive maneuverers' frantic quality: Even a small amount of southern internal disunity could destroy slaveholders' national dominion. . . .

Other departures from proslavery solidarity arose. . . .

Antebellum Southerners intemperately clashed over the fastest rising Lower South political movement of the 1850s, the crusade to reopen the African slave trade. . . .

Reopening the African slave trade seemed to offer the most hopeful remedy yet for uncertain southern commitment. But hope swiftly gave way to a sinking realization: that instead of permanently fortifying a slightly shaky Border South, the proposed panacea drove the more northern and the more southern South further apart. Border South masters denied that slavery would be bolstered in their region if Lower South masters could buy cheap Africans. Instead, the more northern South would find its slaves devalued and its slave sales ended; and then its rationale for complicity in slavery would evaporate.

More ominous still for Lower South slaveholders who wished to import Africans in the 1850s, the Border South preference for exporting African Americans grew stronger. . . .

And in North Carolina, Hinton R. Helper's *Impending Crisis in the South: How to Meet It* was published in 1857. Helper urged the southern non-slaveholder majority to serve both its own economic interests and America's racial interests by deporting slaveholders' blacks. With this publication, the 1850s, not the 1830s, had become the Upper South's great age of dispute over removing slaves. . . .

Northern Republicans printed hundreds of thousands of copies of Helper's emancipation-by-removal scheme. Did Republicans, many Southerners wondered, thereby hope to provoke a southern white lower-class revolt against the slaveholding class? . . .

Lincoln . . . would have liked to build a national Whiggish party on this promising Border South foundation — a preference he later signaled by placing a couple of Border Southerners in his cabinet. But with no southern votes needed to gain the presidency, the biggest northern issue in the 1860 election remained the southern minority's domination of the white man's majoritarian republic. Upset over the recent southern triumph in the Dred Scott case and near-triumph on the Kansas issue, the majoritarian section now meant to rule like a majority. That determination could be seen in the Northern Democrats' rejection of the Lower South's demand for a proslavery platform at the party's conventions and in the northern electorate's sweeping affirmation of Lincoln's leading message: that the *Republican* Party must keep the South from destroying *republicanism.* Yet the question remained, after Lincoln's election in November 1860, would the southern minority now truly destroy the republic by withdrawing its consent to be ruled by the victorious majority?

Before southern secessionists could escape the northern majority, they had to win over their own majority. If some Southwide Gallup poll had inquired whether Southerners wished to secede immediately after Lincoln's election the secessionists' vote likely would have been down in the 25 percent range. . . . In late November 1860, only Mississippi and Florida probably would have affirmed the expediency of secession, and only South Carolina assuredly would have done so. . . .

Lincoln's party did not have a majority in the Senate or in the House or on the Supreme Court. If Lincoln nevertheless managed to act against slavery, the South could *then* secede. Why secede now over an uncertain northern menace, thereby subjecting slavery to certain menace in a civil war?

Secessionists retorted that a stealthy northern majority would initially let Southerners do the menacing. Southern politicians would form a wing of the Black Republican Party, dedicated to agitating against slavery, especially in the Border South. South Carolina patricians, the most avid secessionists, considered all agitating parties dangerous. . . . Patronage-hungry demagogues would stir up the masses and thus overwhelm disinterested paternalists.

In contrast, Lower South mainstream politicians beyond crusty South Carolina, having long happily participated in national parties, feared not democratic parties in general but a prospective Southern Republican Party in particular. They uneasily recalled Frank Blair's delivery of 10 percent of Missourians to Lincoln in the election of 1860, Delaware's 24 percent vote for Lincoln, the more northern South's Opposition Party's recent overtures to the Republicans, and Northern Republicans' publication of Helper's call for nonslaveholder war against slaveholders. They knew that Lincoln had patronage jobs at his disposal and that Border South leaders wanted them. They understood that Lincoln, like the Border South's hero, Henry Clay, carried on Thomas Jefferson's vision of emancipation with freedmen's removal financed by the federal government. Lincoln, in short, need not force abolition on the most northern South. He could instead encourage and bribe Border Southerners to agitate for their misty hope of, and his nebulous plan for, removing blacks from a whitened republic.

Nor, warned the secessionists, would Republican efforts for black removal be restricted to rallying a Border South *white* majority. Republicans would encourage slaves to flee the Border South. With white support melting away and black slaves running away, border slaveholders would dispatch their human property to Lower South slave markets. Then nothing could deter a Border South Republican Party. The Slave South, shrunk to eleven states or less and prevented from expanding into new territories, could only watch while northern free-labor states swelled from sixteen to thirty-three. In that forty-four-state Union, concluded secessionists, Republican emancipators would have the three-fourths majority to abolish slavery in eleven states by constitutional amendment. . . .

For the first time, many Lower South slaveholders felt powerless. . . . Their feeling of impotence rivaled that of Latin American colonists when European metropolitan centers abolished slavery and that of Brazilian coffee planters when sugar planters assaulted the institution. But if Lincoln's election seemed to revoke a democracy's unique invitation for slaveholders to control their fate, the U.S. republican system offered a final invitation for minority self-protection, unavailable in less democratic Latin America. The people of a single colony, the American Revolutionaries had declared, had a right to withdraw their consent to be governed. It was as if the Brazilian coffee provinces had a *right* to secede, which the sugar provinces might feel an obligation to defend.

A *right* of secession, held by a single one of the South's fifteen states! . . . But to force-feed secession to the antisecessionist majority, secessionists had to abort the southern Unionists' favorite idea: a regionwide southern convention, where a Southwide majority would veto immediate secession. Secessionists instead wanted the most secessionist state to call a convention to consider disunion. If the most secessionist state seceded, other southern state conventions would have to decide not whether secession was *expedient* but whether a seceded state could be denied its *right* of secession. Furthermore, other slave states might discern less expediency in remaining in the Union after several states with large slave populations had departed to form a proslavery confederacy. . . .

On December 20, 1860, the secessionists' stronghold, South Carolina, withdrew its consent to Union. South Carolina's neighbor, Georgia, was wary of secession. But with its neighbor out, could Georgia stay in? After a brilliant internal debate, Georgia decided, narrowly, to join South Carolina. And so it went, neighbor following neighbor, throughout the Cotton South. By the time Lincoln was inaugurated on March 4, 1861, the seven Lower South states had left the Union. But the eight Upper South states, containing the majority of southern whites, still opposed secession.

The balance of power changed in mid-April after the Civil War started. Now the more northern South had to decide not on secession per se but on whether to join a northern or a southern army. In making that decision, the Middle South affirmed that each state had the American right to withdraw its consent to be governed. These southern men in the middle also reaffirmed that Yankee extremists were more hateful than secessionist extremists. The Garrisonian insult, encompassing all Southerners who would not unconditionally and immediately emancipate, had long infuriated most Southerners. The Republican insult, encompassing all Southerners who sought to dominate or depart the Union, was equally enraging. To protect their self-respect and honor, Southerners usually felt compelled to unite against taunting Yankees. That duty had so often drawn together a region otherwise partially disunited. In April 1861, when Lincoln sent reinforcements to federal troops in Charleston's harbor, the old tribal fury swept the Middle South. By May 1861, eleven angry southern states had departed the Union. In that fury, parallel to Republican rage over an allegedly antirepublican Slavepower, lies the solution to the largest apparent puzzle about secession: why 260,000 men, whatever their initial preference for Union, died for the Confederacy.

# The Reconstruction Era: How Large Its Scope?

To students of American history, the Civil War years stand in sharp contrast to those of the Reconstruction era. The war years represented a period of heroism and idealism; out of the travail of conflict, there emerged a new American nation. Although the cost in lives and money was frightful, the divisions that had plagued Americans for over half a century were eliminated in the ordeal. Henceforth America would stand as a united country, cleansed of slavery, destined to take its rightful place as one of the leading nations in the world.

Reconstruction, on the other hand, had to address the problems of putting the nation back together again. The federal government had to bring back the South into the Union on terms that permitted reconciliation, protect newly freed slaves from the wrath of angry whites, and construct a biracial society of free people. The era was marked by conflict, brutality, and corruption, and historians have not agreed in evaluating the results. Three schools of thought about Reconstruction succeeded one another: the Dunning school, the Progressives, and the revisionists. A fourth that sees Reconstruction exceeding its traditional geographic and temporal boundaries is emerging.

The first dominant view of Reconstruction, called the Dunning school after its founder, emerged from the widespread racism of both North and South in the years after the Civil War. It was reinforced by the worldwide European imperialism of the late nineteenth century and the racist ideology that intensified to justify it. These historians saw Reconstruction as a disaster, giving rights to freed people who were unprepared for them and were vulnerable to corruption. The best thing about it was that it ended, and whites reestablished political control of the South.[1]

By the 1920s, American historiography had come under the influence of the Progressive, or new history, school. Growing out of the dissatisfaction with the older scientific school of historians that emphasized the collection of impartial empirical data and eschewed "subjective" interpretations, this school borrowed heavily from the new social sciences. These historians sought to explain historical change by isolating underlying economic and social forces that transformed institutions and structures. In place of tradition and stability, it emphasized change and conflict. Liberal and democratic in their

---

[1]For example, William A. Dunning, *Reconstruction: Political and Economic, 1865–1877* (New York, 1907), and John W. Burgess, *Reconstruction and the Constitution, 1866–1876* (New York, 1902).

orientation, Progressives maintained that economic issues were basic in shaping this era. The real conflict was not between North and South or white and black; it was between industrial capitalism and agrarianism, with the former ultimately emerging victorious. The question of the status of black people in American society was simply a facade for the more basic conflicts that lay hidden beneath the surface. Reconstruction, they concluded, was the first phase in the emergence of the United States as a leading industrial and capitalist nation.

The revisionists, although owing much to the Progressives, were influenced by the egalitarianism of the period following World War II and the idealism and optimism of the civil rights movement. Providing equal rights for blacks, revisionists maintained, was complicated by economic and other factors but was, nevertheless, a potent issue in its own right. In a real sense, the fundamental problem of Reconstruction was on what terms freed people would participate economically and politically in the nation. Even though the Radical Republicans ultimately failed in achieving equality for African Americans, they left an enduring legacy in the forms of the Fourteenth and Fifteenth Amendments. These amendments took on a new meaning as they gave legal sanction to civil rights after 1945. This is a broad school and includes social historians whose work has been to broaden history to include the poor, blacks, other minorities, and women. In the wake of Eric Foner's stunning, definitive revisionist synthesis, *Reconstruction: America's Unfinished Revolution, 1863–1877,* historians are not so much challenging his interpretation as broadening the field of Reconstruction studies to include questions of intellectual history, gender, and culture, as well as literally broadening the field forward and backward to include the Mexican-American War through the Gilded Age and territories beyond the South, even other post-emancipation societies.[2]

In the 1890s, led by Professor William A. Dunning of Columbia University, who founded the school of Reconstruction historiography that still bears his name, the historical profession set out to prove that the years following the Civil War were marked by tragedy because men of good will were momentarily thrust out of power by the forces of evil. In this period, in the words of one historian, "The Southern [white, it went without saying] people literally were put to the torture."[3]

Dunning school historians assumed first that the South should have been restored to the Union quickly and without penalty. Most Southerners, they asserted, had accepted their military defeat gracefully and were prepared to pledge their loyalty to the Union. Second, white Southerners should have had political and economic responsibility for the freedmen, who as former slaves and blacks could never be integrated into American society on

---

[2]Eric Foner, *Reconstruction: America's Unfinished Revolution, 1863–1877* (New York, 1988). For differing new perspectives, see Thomas J. Brown, ed., *Reconstructions: New Perspectives on Postbellum America* (New York, 2006), 6–8; and Rebecca J. Scott, *Degrees of Freedom: Louisiana and Cuba after Slavery* (Cambridge, Mass., 2005).

[3]Claude G. Bowers, *The Tragic Era: The Revolution after Lincoln* (Cambridge, Mass., 1929), v–vi.

an equal plane with whites. Behind these assumptions were many others about antebellum society, among them that slavery was benign, that slave-holders were kindly patriarchs protecting their faithful but ignorant slaves, and that slavery was not very profitable.

According to the Dunning school, the Radical carpetbagger state governments that came into power were totally incompetent — in part because they included illiterate blacks who were unprepared for the responsibilities of self-government. Still worse, these governments were extraordinarily expensive because they were corrupt. Most of them, indeed, left nothing but a legacy of huge debts.[4] The decent whites in the South united out of sheer desperation to force the carpetbaggers, scalawags, and blacks from power. In one state after another, Radical rule was eventually overthrown and good government restored. Thus the tragic era of Reconstruction came to an end.

For nearly three decades after the turn of the century, the Dunning point of view largely dominated in the academy, and it persisted into the 1960s in northern high schools. In 1942, Albert B. Moore, in his presidential address at the Southern Historical Association, argued that Reconstruction had the effect of converting the South into a colonial appendage of the North. Moore found the enfranchisement of blacks, which laid the basis for carpet-bag government, perhaps the most incredible event of an incredible era. The South, he concluded, was still paying for the wrongs of Reconstruction.[5]

In the late 1920s, however, historians influenced by Progressive thinking, particularly its emphasis on the importance of economic considerations, changed the interpretive framework of the Reconstruction era. In 1939, Francis B. Simkins, a distinguished Southern historian (who with Robert Woody published one of the first Progressive studies of Reconstruction in 1932), summed up some of the findings of the school. He emphasized many of Radical Reconstruction's constructive achievements. Simkins denied that the Radical program was radical; indeed, the Radical Republicans failed because they did not provide freedmen with a secure economic base. Past historians, he concluded, had given a distorted picture of Reconstruction because they had assumed that blacks were racially inferior. Only by abandoning their biases could historians contribute to a more accurate understanding of the past.[6]

While the Progressives often disagreed among themselves, there were common areas of agreement. For example, most viewed the problem of corruption in American society during these years as national rather than sectional in scope. To single out the South in this regard was patently unfair and

[4]E. Merton Coulter, *The South during Reconstruction, 1865–1877* (Baton Rouge, La., 1947), 148.

[5]Albert B. Moore, "One Hundred Years of Reconstruction of the South," *Journal of Southern History* 9 (May 1943): 153–65.

[6]Francis B. Simkins, "New Viewpoints of Southern Reconstruction," *Journal of Southern History* 5 (February 1939): 49–61; Francis B. Simkins and Robert Hilliard Woody, *South Carolina during Reconstruction* (Chapel Hill, N.C., 1932).

ahistorical.[7] Progressives also denied that the Radical governments in the South were always dishonest, incompetent, and inefficient. On the contrary, they claimed, such governments accomplished much of enduring value. The new Reconstruction constitutions, written by black and white Republicans, represented a vast improvement over the older ones, bringing about many long-needed and lasting social reforms, including state-supported school systems for both blacks and whites and a revision of the judicial system. Above all, these governments operated — at least in theory — on the premise that all men, white and black alike, were entitled to equal political and civil liberties.

Second, the Progressives drew a sharply different portrait of blacks during Reconstruction. They denied that corruption and violence in the postwar South resulted from black participation in government or that the freedmen were illiterate, naive, and inexperienced. In no Southern state, they pointed out, did blacks control both houses of the legislature. Moreover, there were no black governors and only one black state supreme court justice. Only two blacks were elected to the U.S. Senate and fifteen to the House of Representatives. These numbers hardly supported the charge that the supposed excesses of Reconstruction were due to activities of black Americans.

Indeed, the Progressives maintained that blacks, as a group, were quite capable of understanding their own interests without disregarding the legitimate interests of others. The freedmen were able to participate at least as intelligently as other groups in the American political process. As Vernon L. Wharton concluded in his pioneering study of the Negro in Mississippi after the Civil War, there was "little difference . . . in the administration of . . . counties [having blacks on boards of supervisors] and that of counties under Democratic control. . . . Altogether, as governments go, that supplied by the Negro and white Republicans in Mississippi between 1870 and 1876 was not a bad government. . . . With their white Republican colleagues, they gave to the state a government of greatly expanded functions at a cost that was low in comparison with that of almost any other state."[8]

Progressives refuted the Dunning school contention that state governments were controlled by evil, power-hungry, profit-seeking carpetbaggers and renegade scalawags who used black votes to maintain themselves in power. The stereotype of the carpetbagger and scalawag, according to Progressives, was highly inaccurate. Carpetbaggers, for example, migrated to the South for a variety of reasons — including the lure of economic opportunities as well as a desire to serve the former slaves in some humanitarian capacity. Among them were former Southern unionists and Whigs, lower-class

---

[7]For a progressive synthesis, see J. G. Randall and David Donald, *The Civil War and Reconstruction*, 2nd ed. (Boston, 1961). The first edition, written by Randall in 1937, was in the Dunning school tradition.

[8]Vernon L. Wharton, *The Negro in Mississippi, 1865–1890* (Chapel Hill, N.C., 1947), 172, 179–80. See also Willie Lee Rose, *Rehearsal for Reconstruction: The Port Royal Experiment* (New York, 1964), and Joel Williamson, *After Slavery: The Negro in South Carolina during Reconstruction, 1861–1877* (Chapel Hill, N.C., 1965).

whites who sought to use the Republican Party as the vehicle for confiscating the property of the planter aristocrats, and businessmen attracted by the promise of industrialization. The Radical governments, then, had a wide base of indigenous support in most Southern states.[9]

Finally, the Progressives rejected the charge that the Radical governments were extraordinarily expensive and corrupt, or that they had saddled the South with a large public debt. State expenditures did rise sharply after the war, but for good reasons. The war's destruction required an infusion of public funds. Deferring regular appropriations during the war years also meant that a backlog of legitimate projects had accumulated. Most important of all, the South for the first time had to build schools and provide other facilities and services for blacks and whites that did not exist before the 1860s and for which public funds had never been expended.

The Progressives also found that the rise in state debts, in some instances, was more apparent than real. Grants to railroad promoters, which in certain states accounted for a large proportion of the increase in the debt, were secured by a mortgage on the railroad property. Thus the rise in the debt was backed by sound collateral. The amount of the debt chargeable to theft, the Progressives maintained, was negligible. Indeed, the restoration governments, which were dominated by supposedly honest Southerners, proved to be far more corrupt than the governments controlled by the Radicals.

Progressives shared the conviction that economic forces related to the growth of an industrializing nation played a major role during this period. Beneath the political and racial antagonisms of this era, some Progressives argued, lay economic rivalries. Eager to gain an advantage over their competitors, many business interests used politics as the vehicle to further their economic ambitions — especially since the South, like the North and West, was ardently courting businessmen. The result was that economic rivalries were translated into political struggles.[10]

Progressives identified racism as important in party affiliation but otherwise subordinate to economics in determining the rise and fall of Reconstruction. During Reconstruction, many former Whigs joined the Republican Party because of its pro-business economic policies. These well-to-do conservatives, at first, were willing to ally with blacks and guarantee their civil and political rights in return for their support at the polls. Within the Democratic Party, however, Progressives argued that lower-class whites, fearful of competition from blacks, insisted on white supremacy. Conservatives found their

---

[9]See Otto H. Olsen, "Reconsidering the Scalawags," *Civil War History* 12 (December 1966): 304–20, and Allen W. Trelease, "Who Were the Scalawags?" *Journal of Southern History* 29 (November 1963): 445–68.

[10]Recent historians have once again begun to study the importance of economic factors and rivalries in Reconstruction. See Mark W. Summers, *Railroads, Reconstruction, and the Gospel of Prosperity: Aid under the Radical Republicans, 1867–1877* (Princeton, N.J., 1984), and Terry L. Seip, *The South Returns to Congress: Men, Economic Measures, and International Relationships, 1868–1879* (Baton Rouge, La., 1983). See also Mark Summers, *The Era of Good Stealings* (New York, 1993), which argues that there was no more corruption in the South than in the North.

affiliation with the Republican Party increasingly uncomfortable, and they slowly began to drift back into the Democratic Party.

This changed alignment left Southern blacks politically without white allies, which later made it easy to eliminate them from political life. This move came at a time when Northerners, tired of conflict and turmoil, became reconciled to the idea of letting the South work out its own destiny — even if it meant sacrificing black people. Northern businessmen likewise became convinced that only Southern conservatives could restore order and stability and thus create a favorable environment for investment. Elite Southern Democrats deliberately polarized politics along racial lines, disguising their desire to dominate the region economically through appeals to white racism.

The end of Reconstruction, according to the Progressives, accompanied the triumph of business values and industrial capitalism. When the contested presidential election of 1876 resulted in an apparent deadlock between Rutherford B. Hayes, the Republican candidate, and Samuel J. Tilden, his Democratic opponent, some prominent Republicans saw an opportunity to rebuild their party in the South upon a new basis. Instead of basing their party upon propertyless former slaves, they hoped to attract well-to-do former Whigs who had been forced into the Democratic Party to fight against Reconstruction governments. To accomplish this goal, a group of powerful Republican leaders began to work secretly to bring about a political realignment. If Southern Democratic congressmen would not stand in the way of Hayes's election and would also provide enough votes to permit the Republicans to organize the House of Representatives, these leaders were willing to promise the South federal subsidies — primarily for railroads — to name a Southerner as postmaster general, and to abandon Radical Reconstruction. The Compromise of 1877, as this political deal was called, was not fully carried out, but the broad outline prevailed.

Perhaps the most important and initially the most overlooked Progressive was W. E. B. Du Bois who published *Black Reconstruction, 1860–1880,* in 1935. Du Bois, like the other Progressives, claimed that economics, not race, shaped Reconstruction and black-white relations. In his passionately argued volume, he insisted that Reconstruction involved an effort to unite Northern workers with Southern blacks. The attempt failed because Southern conservatives employed racial animosities to fragment working-class unity and thus maintain their own class hegemony. Racism, in this view, was a tool that upper-class whites used to their advantage, not an inherent, unchanging characteristic of poor whites, as most historians portrayed it. For Du Bois, Reconstruction was a valiant but short-lived attempt to establish true democracy in the South, an opportunity quickly foreclosed.

The *Journal of American History* ignored the book, and most professional historians disparaged it. One complaint was that Du Bois had based his work on secondary sources, not archival materials. This was true, but it was also true that during Du Bois's research, most Southern archives were closed to blacks. When blacks were allowed in, they had to hide themselves from view of the white scholars. C. Vann Woodward was one of the few professional historians who recognized the value of Du Bois's work at the time. He wrote

Du Bois in 1938 of his "indebtedness for the insight which your admirable book, *Black Reconstruction*, has provided me."[11]

Woodward, the historian who propounded the thesis of the Compromise of 1877, concluded that the bargain "did not restore the old order in the South, nor did it restore the South to parity with other sections. It did assure the dominant whites political autonomy and nonintervention in matters of race policy and promised them a share in the blessings of the new economic order. In return the South became, in effect, a satellite of the dominant region. So long as the Conservative Redeemers held control they scotched any tendency of the South to combine forces with the internal enemies of the new economy — laborites, Western agrarians, reformers. Under the regime of the Redeemers the South became a bulwark instead of a menace to the new order."[12]

After the early 1950s, a new school of Reconstruction historiography called the revisionist school emerged. Many of these historians had been affected by the racial injustice that the civil rights movement demonstrated. Generally speaking, while the revisionists accepted many findings of the Progressives, they rejected the idea of interpreting Reconstruction in strictly economic terms. The Republican Party, the revisionists maintained, was not united on a pro-business economic program; it included individuals and groups holding quite different social and economic views. The revisionists saw the factor of race as an issue that had profound moral implications and was as much of a motivating factor — both positively and negatively — as economics. One of the unresolved dilemmas after the Civil War, they insisted, was the exact role that blacks were to play in American society.[13]

Within the Republican Party, a number of factions each offered their solution to this question. Andrew Johnson, who had been nominated as Lincoln's running mate in 1864 on a Union Party ticket despite his Democratic Party affiliation, spoke for the conservatives, for whom blacks were incapable of self-government. Consequently, he favored the white state governments in the South that came back into the Union shortly after the end of the war. He went along with the black codes passed by Southern whites whose aims were to make black freedom as much like slavery as possible. Radical Republicans fiercely opposed Johnson. While the Dunning school had painted the Radicals as vindictive hypocrites eager for power, and the Progressives saw them as representing the interests of the industrial Northeast, the revisionists saw many of them joining the Republican Party for antislavery rather than economic reasons. After the war, they wanted blacks to have the same rights as white Americans, which brought them into conflict with President Johnson. Taking advantage of Johnson's growing unpopularity and motivated

[11]W. E. B. Du Bois, *Black Reconstruction, 1860–1880* (New York, 1992; originally published 1935), x, xvi.

[12]C. Vann Woodward, *Reunion and Reaction: The Compromise of 1877 and the End of Reconstruction* (Boston, 1951), 246.

[13]Robert Sharkey, *Money, Class, and Party: An Economic Study of Civil War and Reconstruction* (Baltimore, 1959), and Irwin Unger, *The Greenback Era: A Social and Political History of American Finance, 1865–1879* (Princeton, N.J., 1964).

by idealism, the Radicals set out to remake Southern society by transferring political power from the planter class to the freedmen.[14]

In 1965, Kenneth M. Stampp published an important synthesis that emphasized the moral dimension of the Reconstruction years, arguing that the central question of the postwar period was the place of the freedmen in American society. To argue that the Radicals had invidious and selfish motives does them a severe injustice and results in a distorted picture of the Reconstruction era. The Radicals, according to the revisionists, ultimately failed in their objectives. Most Americans, harboring conscious and unconscious racial antipathies, were not willing to accept blacks as equals. By the 1870s, the North was prepared to abandon blacks to the white South for three reasons: a wish to return to the amicable prewar relations between the sections, a desire to promote industrial investment in the South, and a growing conviction that the cause of black Americans was not worth further strife. Reconstruction's tragedy was in ending short of achieving the major goal sought by the Radicals.

The struggle over Reconstruction, nevertheless, had not been in vain. In addition to the many achievements of the Radical governments, the Radicals had succeeded in securing the adoption of the Fourteenth and Fifteenth Amendments. These amendments, in Stampp's words, "which could have been adopted only under the conditions of radical Reconstruction, make the blunders of that era, tragic though they were, dwindle into insignificance. For if it was worth four years of civil war to save the Union, it was worth a few years of radical Reconstruction to give the American Negro the ultimate promise of equal civil and political rights."[15]

During and after the 1970s, revisionist scholarship began to take a more pessimistic turn, while interest in Reconstruction remained strong. Pervasive inequality and racial friction after the civil rights movement seemed to reflect mockingly the failure of post–Civil War Americans to ensure that blacks would be integrated into the social and political framework of the Union.[16] Revisionist scholars identified various reasons for the failure of Reconstruction, covering ground similar to that the Progressives had tilled. In his study of the Ku Klux Klan, Allen W. Trelease argued that Radical Reconstruction failed because the seeds of biracial democracy fell on barren soil in the South, and the federal government's artificial nurture was ephemeral and quickly discontinued. George C. Rable emphasized the counterrevolutionary guerrilla warfare employed by white Southerners concerned with the destruction of the Republican Party in the South. Michael Perman insisted that in the

---

[14]This point of view was best expressed by Howard K. Beale, one of the fathers of the revisionist school, in *The Critical Year: A Study of Andrew Johnson and Reconstruction* (New York, 1930); see James H. McPherson, *The Struggle for Equality: Abolitionists and the Negro in the Civil War and Reconstruction* (Princeton, N.J., 1964), and Hans L. Trefousse, *The Radical Republicans: Lincoln's Vanguard for Racial Justice* (New York, 1969).

[15]Kenneth M. Stampp, *The Era of Reconstruction, 1865–1877* (New York, 1965), 215.

[16]For a descriptive analysis of black Americans after slavery that does not deal with Reconstruction as a political event, see Leon F. Litwack's important *Been in the Storm So Long: The Aftermath of Slavery* (New York, 1979).

context of the political tensions that prevailed in the immediate postwar era, the very moderation that marked presidential and congressional Reconstruction was doomed to fail; only a coercive policy could have succeeded. In a subsequent work, Perman emphasized the ways in which the center in both the Republican and Democratic parties proved unable to hold together, thus permitting color to become the political line. And in a broad study of national politics, William Gillette observed that Reconstruction was so easily reversed because it had always been "fragmentary and fragile."[17]

Interest in Andrew Johnson persisted. Michael Les Benedict, for example, insisted that Johnson was impeached because he seemed to be violating the principle of the separation of powers and because he failed to carry out some key provisions in legislation pertaining to Reconstruction. Hans Trefousse emphasized the degree to which Johnson thwarted Radical policies and strengthened conservative forces, thereby facilitating the latter's eventual triumph in the 1870s. Of three other studies of Johnson, two (by Patrick W. Riddleberger and James E. Sefton) emphasized his commitment to sometimes incompatible principles that rendered him impotent, and one (by Albert Castel) accentuated the degree to which his inordinate ambition and desire for power helped to destroy him.[18]

Robert J. Kaczorowski synthesized many themes that have resonated throughout Reconstruction historiography through the 1980s. The Thirteenth and Fourteenth Amendments represented a revolutionary change in American federalism, for citizenship was no longer within state jurisdiction. Consequently, Congress had authority to protect all citizens in their enjoyment of rights. This congressional Radical Republican theory of constitutionalism, however, Kaczorowski argued, was altered during the 1870s by a Supreme Court bent on permitting partisans of states' rights in the South to reestablish their domination over former slaves.[19]

The first to use comparative history better to evaluate Reconstruction, George M. Fredrickson compared it with the experiences of Jamaica and South Africa. He concluded that white Southerners were less able than

---

[17]Allen W. Trelease, *White Terror: The Ku Klux Klan Conspiracy and Southern Reconstruction* (New York, 1971); George C. Rable, *But There Was No Peace: The Role of Violence in the Politics of Reconstruction* (Athens, Ga., 1984); Michael Perman, *Reunion without Compromise: The South and Reconstruction, 1865–1868* (Cambridge, 1973), and *The Road to Redemption: Southern Politics, 1869–1879* (Chapel Hill, N.C., 1984); William Gillette, *Retreat from Reconstruction, 1869–1879* (Baton Rouge, La., 1979), 380.

[18]Michael Les Benedict, *The Impeachment and Trial of Andrew Johnson* (New York, 1973); Hans L. Trefousse, *Impeachment of a President: Andrew Johnson, the Blacks, and Reconstruction* (Knoxville, Tenn., 1975); Patrick W. Riddleberger, *1866: The Critical Year Revisited* (Carbondale, Ill., 1979); James E. Sefton, *Andrew Johnson and the Uses of Constitutional Power* (Boston, 1980); Albert Castel, *The Presidency of Andrew Johnson* (Lawrence, Kans., 1979). See also the following works: Michael Les Benedict, *A Compromise of Principle: Congressional Republicans and Reconstruction, 1863–1869* (New York, 1974), and *The Fruits of Victory: Alternatives in Restoring the Union, 1865–1877* (Philadelphia, 1975); Dan T. Carter, *When the War Was Over: The Failure of Self-Reconstruction in the South, 1865–1867* (Baton Rouge, La., 1985); and Richard N. Current, *Those Terrible Carpetbaggers: A Reinterpretation* (New York, 1988).

[19]Robert J. Kaczorowski, "To Begin the Nation Anew: Congress, Citizenship, and Civil Rights after the Civil War," *American Historical Review* 92 (February 1987): 45–68.

Jamaicans or South Africans to make even a limited adjustment to the concept of equality, resulting in a racist order in the United States that was not exceeded until the formal adoption of apartheid in South Africa after 1948. Historians are just beginning to work comparatively again, a method that can powerfully illuminate the past by placing it in a broad perspective.[20]

At the same time that interest in national politics remained high, monographic studies dealing with single states continued to appear, identifying circumstances unique within the larger pattern of Reconstruction. Jonathan Wiener's study of postwar Alabama argued that Reconstruction might never have happened for all the difference it made in the lives of black people. White elites retained control of the land and forced blacks into a form of tenant serfdom in which they were little better off than in slavery. In a novel study of black political leadership in South Carolina that utilized quantitative techniques, Thomas Holt argued that black leaders were divided among themselves by education and prewar status; their divisions contributed to the fall of the Republican Party in the state. Holt's profile of black leadership demonstrated that most owned property and were literate, and 10 percent were professionally or college trained. Other scholars pursued this topic of diversity among politically and economically active blacks, such as John Rodrigue in his work on sugar growers in Louisiana.[21] And Barbara Fields, focusing on the changing economy in her study of Maryland, argued for eventual changes as the market slowly transformed the border state. But the racist fallout from slavery persisted with such intensity that change came painfully slowly when it came.[22]

The 1988 publication of Eric Foner's massive *Reconstruction: America's Unfinished Revolution, 1863–1877*, excerpted below, restored cohesion to a field long fragmented and summed it up definitively. Initially, he argued, Reconstruction was a Radical attempt to destroy the South's antebellum social structure. But by the 1870s, fear of class conflict in the North led that section's industrial leaders to evince greater sympathy for the white South. The result was a resurgence of white domination below the Mason-Dixon line. Like W. E. B. Du Bois, Foner centered much of his analysis on class and the political initiatives of newly freed black people. Unlike Du Bois, Foner

---

[20]George M. Frederickson, "After Emancipation: A Comparative Study of White Responses to the New Order of Race Relations in the American South, Jamaica and the Cape Colony of South Africa," in *What Was Freedom's Price?* ed. David G. Sansing (Jackson, Miss., 1978).

[21]Jonathan Wiener, *Social Origins of the New South: Alabama, 1860–1885* (Baton Rouge, La., 1978); John Rodrigue, "Black Agency after Slavery," in *Reconstructions*, ed. Brown, 40–65; John Rodrigue, *Reconstruction in the Cane Fields: From Slavery to Free Labor in Louisiana's Sugar Parishes, 1862–1880* (Baton Rouge, La., 2001); see also Mark Wetherington, *Plain Folk's Fight: The Civil War and Reconstruction in Piney Woods, Georgia* (Chapel Hill, N.C., 2005).

[22]Thomas Holt, *Black Over White: Negro Political Leadership in South Carolina during Reconstruction* (Urbana, Ill., 1977); Barbara Fields, *Slavery and Freedom on the Middle Ground, Maryland, during the Nineteenth Century* (New Haven, Conn., 1985). See also Jerrell H. Shofner, *Nor Is It Over Yet: Florida in the Era of Reconstruction, 1863–1877* (Gainesville, Fla., 1974); Joe Gray Taylor, *Louisiana Reconstructed, 1863–1877* (Baton Rouge, La., 1974); William C. Harris, *The Day of the Carpetbagger: Republican Reconstruction in Mississippi* (Baton Rouge, La., 1979); Ted Tunnell, *Crucible of Reconstruction: War, Radicalism and Race in Louisiana, 1862–1877* (Baton Rouge, La., 1984).

could and did make use of enormous archival material, providing his political and economic history with a deep base in vivid social history. Looking at the political and economic experience of freed people, Foner charted the demise by the 1870s of the free-labor ideology that had brought the Republican Party into existence. White concern to restrict the conditions of work and the political participation of blacks led to a virtual abandonment of the equal rights and free-labor ideology. Sharecropping emerged as the compromise between planters who dreamed of the days of gang slave labor and freed people who longed for land and economic and social self-sufficiency. Foner saw Reconstruction as a failure, but an immensely important one. Through the mechanisms of Radical Reconstruction, the joint activism of white and black Republicans had created, however fleetingly, an unprecedented, biracial democracy.

Foner's inquiries into the ideology of free labor and ideas of contract prompted various studies of those topics. Foner himself addressed the issue in "The Meaning of Freedom in the Age of Emancipation," as well as in the book that grew out of that article.[23] He wrote that "Reconstruction emerges as a decisive moment in fixing the dominant understanding of freedom as self-ownership and the right to compete in the labor market, rather than propertied independence." Subsequently, Foner expanded on the transformation during Reconstruction of the meaning of the Fourteenth Amendment. In his view, it came to mean the freedom to contract, not equality before the law. Legal scholar Peggy Cooper Davis came at the disappointment blacks experienced with postwar interpretations of the Fourteenth Amendment from a different tack. In *Neglected Stories: The Constitution and Family Values*, she re-created, through stories from slavery and Reconstruction, the problems the Fourteenth Amendment was attempting to address, particularly the complete absence of white respect for the rights of blacks to make and protect their families.[24]

Recent historians have not so much challenged Foner's synthesis as added new perspectives to it, among them gender, a broader geographic and temporal definition of the period, and a fresh look at African American political mobilization and activities.[25]

Several scholars have supplemented Foner's work with studies of women's activities and how constructions of gender contributed to the dynamics of Reconstruction. Nina Silber published *The Romance of Reunion* in 1992, a study of the way the South, while losing the war itself, managed to win the interpretation of it. In her analysis, in the face of rapid postwar industrialization and immigration, Northerners and Southerners looked to antebellum Southern myths of manliness and femininity to give order to a fragmenting

---

[23]Eric Foner, *Reconstruction: America's Unfinished Revolution, 1863–1877* (New York, 1988); Eric Foner, "The Meaning of Freedom in the Age of Emancipation," *Journal of American History* 81 (March 1995): 435–60; see also Eric Foner, *The Story of American Freedom* (New York, 2000).

[24]Peggy Cooper Davis, *Neglected Stories: The Constitution and Family Values* (New York, 1997).

[25]Brooks D. Simpson, *The Reconstruction Presidents* (Lawrence, Kans., 1998), ix; Michael Perman, *Struggle for Mastery: Disfranchisement in the South* (Chapel Hill, N.C., 2001); Nicholas Lemann, *Redemption: The Last Battle of the Civil War* (New York, 2006).

society. Romantic myths of prewar chivalry, delicate femininity, and interracial harmony blossomed in a period of labor agitation, the violent retaliation of industrialists, the arrivals of millions of foreign poor, and militant suffragist activity.[26]

In 1995, LeeAnn Whites interpreted the Civil War and Reconstruction through a crisis in gender in Augusta, Georgia. Whites studied the conflicts for Confederate women as the war took their men away and called upon them to increase their domestic activities to help supply the troops. Demobilization exacerbated the tension that even this circumscribed female empowerment had created between the sexes. In the aftermath of emancipation, white males could now legitimately dominate only their wives, who were less prepared to accept it. Women's associational life after the war to memorialize the Confederacy promised them a public role, but, with Reconstruction and redemption, men assumed these tasks and forced women back into domesticity. Drew Faust's study of elite Confederate women portrayed them as reluctantly and resentfully shouldering male responsibilities during the war, unwilling victims of a kind of liberation. They eagerly embraced the old arrangements when men returned home and rejected Northern ideas of women's emancipation. Jane Turner Censer instead detected enthusiasm for limited independence among younger postbellum women that would ultimately be crushed by the imposition of Jim Crow in the 1890s. In LeeAnn Whites's most recent collection of essays, she has worked to make gender visible and show its significance in shaping women's postwar role as restorers of white men's rightful position, as well as in justifying the racial violence that accompanied redemption in the name of controlling white women's sexuality.[27]

Laura Edwards's *Gendered Strife and Confusion*, a subtle study of gender in Granville County in postwar North Carolina, points out that domestic institutions, particularly marriage, and constructions of masculinity and femininity served new political and social uses because of the demise of slavery as a method of control. Appealing to constructions of maleness, femaleness, and family sanctity provided freed people and poor whites with some new options for themselves. Edwards also describes how conservative Democrats could and did use the tool of gender construction to bring about the expulsion of blacks from political life.[28]

Tera Hunter's *To 'Joy My Freedom* studied black women's lives in Atlanta after the war. In an innovative mix of social, urban, political, economic, and gender history, Hunter revealed women's widespread postwar labor agitation, particularly by African American laundresses, as well as the concerted

---

[26]Nina Silber, *The Romance of Reunion: Northerners and the South, 1865–1900* (Chapel Hill, N.C., 1993).

[27]LeeAnn Whites, *The Civil War as a Crisis in Gender: Augusta, Georgia, 1860–1890* (Athens, Ga., 1995); Drew Faust, *The Mothers of Invention: Women of the Slaveholding South in the American Civil War* (Chapel Hill, N.C., 1996); Jane Turner Censer, *The Reconstruction of White Southern Womanhood, 1865–1895* (Baton Rouge, La., 2003); LeeAnn Whites, *Gender Matters: Civil War, Reconstruction, and the Making of the New South* (New York, 2005).

[28]Laura Edwards, *Gendered Strife and Confusion: The Political Culture of Reconstruction* (Urbana, Ill., 1997).

action of the white community to break women's first strike in the South. She also showed how real estate developers and city officials planned the growth of Atlanta to be sure that urban blacks would get as few benefits, such as running water, as possible.[29]

In *Gendered Freedoms*, a study of the Mississippi Delta, Nancy Bercaw looked at African American women's wartime economic independence and postwar family tensions as planters, trying to curtail women's power, tried to enforce patriarchy on black families. Bercaw studied the changing strategies and ideologies of African American households, arguing that family form developed in accord with ideas about property rights and the meaning of free labor. The nuclear family, essential to cotton production, became dominant among rural people, while urban families often created other arrangements. The shape of black families was the result of negotiations among black men and women, but was also subject to unwelcome pressure from white planters.[30]

Contributing to scholarship on the direction of postwar women's reform, Carol Faulkner studied the women of the Freedmen's Aid Movement (*Women's Radical Reconstruction*), finding a significant continuation of the tradition of abolitionist-feminism, usually construed to have been fatally wounded by the postwar split in the suffrage movement. Faulkner's radical women who went south to serve the needs of free people preceded and prefigured the Progressives in seeing the federal government as the natural ally of the vulnerable and in trying to make the government accept that responsibility. Faulkner also found blindness among these women about their own biases. Consequently, some tried to coerce freed people into adopting middle-class habits and values.[31]

In 2003, Elliott West published a provocative essay, excerpted below, titled "Reconstructing Race." West called for a study of "greater Reconstruction" that would take a broader national perspective and include the West, and would begin as far back as the 1840s with the integration of this region into the expanding, industrializing nation. This approach would allow for exploration of parallel conflicts over the rights of people of Native American, Hispanic, Chinese, and African descent. Because of their "races," members of all groups were welcome in only low-status and low-paying jobs. The United States excluded some from the body politic and only included others on limited terms. "This greater Reconstruction was even more morally ambiguous

---

[29]Tera Hunter, *To 'Joy My Freedom, Southern Black Women's Lives and Labors after the Civil War* (Cambridge, Mass., 1997); see also Elsa Barkley Brown's "Negotiating and Transforming the Public Sphere: African American Political Life in the Transition from Slavery to Freedom," *Public Culture* 7 ( Fall 1994): 107–46.

[30]Nancy Bercaw, *Gendered Freedoms: Race, Rights, and the Politics of Household in the Delta, 1861–1875* (Gainesville, Fla., 2003). See also Amy Dru Stanley, *From Bondage to Contract: Wage Labor, Marriage, and the Market in the Age of Slave Emancipation* (New York, 1998), for an exploration of contract in an age of increasingly limited freedom for free people and workers; and Julie Saville's monograph on South Carolina free people contesting the notion of freedom as subjection to landowners and market values: Julie Saville, *The Work of Reconstruction: From Slave to Wage Laborer in South Carolina, 1860–1870* (New York, 1994).

[31]Carol Faulkner, *Women's Radical Reconstruction: The Freedmen's Aid Movement* (Philadelphia, 2004).

than the lesser one. It included not one war but three — the Mexican War, the Civil War, and the War Against Indian America — and while it saw the emancipation of one nonwhite people, it was equally concerned with dominating the others."[32]

Although West did not expand his themes into a book, Heather Cox Richardson has written about Reconstruction as a nationwide political negotiation lasting through the Gilded Age. In Richardson's view, this negotiation produced an American consensus uniting the political center that, she argues, still holds true and even explains the results of the 2004 presidential election. She identifies growing middle-class worry about "special interests" in the postwar nineteenth century, concerns that strikingly echo those of historians and journalists today explaining the decline of the New Deal Democratic consensus. (See Volume Two, Chapter 11.) In her view, Reconstruction failed nationally because the Northern middle class lost its enthusiasm for freed people as well as for Northern workers when it seemed to them that both groups were trying to use government for legislation to further their own welfare, instead of applying themselves to their work and trusting in the free-labor ideology to make them rise economically. In contrast to West, she underplays the significance of racism in favor of an increasingly outmoded middle-class belief in the free-labor promise.[33]

Picking up West's challenge to include the Chinese in the postwar national experience, Moon-Ho Jung's case study, *Coolies and Cane*, portrays the struggles of Chinese laborers in the Reconstruction of Louisiana's sugar industry. The immigrants' disputed and unstable identity as "coolies," or coerced Caribbean plantation laborers (shipped in U.S. boats) made them (the false) equivalent, in the eyes of many postwar white Americans, of emancipated slaves. This, in turn, was critical in persuading the general public to deny them the possibility of naturalized citizenship and, eventually, in excluding them in 1888. This carefully argued monograph expands the agony of Reconstruction to include "outlawing coolies at home," which "became an endless and indispensable exercise that resolved and reproduced contradictory aims — racial exclusion and legal inclusion, enslavement and emancipation, parochial nationalism and unbridled imperialism — of a nation deeply rooted in race, slavery, and empire."[34]

Rebecca Scott's *Degrees of Freedom* also looks to Louisiana, but farther afield to Cuba, another sugar growing region, to enlarge Reconstruction's scope. While slaves in Louisiana achieved freedom in 1865, Cuba underwent emancipation more gradually, pushed forward by a liberation struggle that combined the demand for freedom with the demand for independence from Spain, finally producing freedom in 1886 and liberation from Spain only

---

[32]Elliott West, "Reconstructing Race," *Western Historical Quarterly* 34 (Spring 2003): 11.

[33]Heather Cox Richardson, *The Death of Reconstruction: Race, Labor, and Politics in the Post–Civil War North, 1865–1901* (Cambridge, Mass., 2001), and *West from Appomattox: The Reconstruction of America after the Civil War* (New Haven, Conn., 2007); for a different interpretation of the postwar reshaping of classical liberal thought that evolved to protect capitalism, see Nancy Cohen, *The Reconstruction of American Liberalism, 1865–1914* (Chapel Hill, N.C., 2002).

[34]Moon-Ho Jung, *Coolies and Cane: Race, Labor, and Sugar in the Age of Emancipation* (Baltimore, 2006), 9.

when the United States invaded in 1898. Although Louisiana black and white laborers had some limited experience of working together to better their conditions, the Cuban working class had united in its idea of a nation, so racism, while present, never achieved the suffocating supremacy that it had in Louisiana "after forty years of struggle."[35] Scott teases out numerous insights on the consequences of the way freedom arrived in the southern United States and the limits that emerged on what it meant from comparing it to the more fluid and extended process of achieving and defining freedom in Cuba.[36]

Stephen Hahn's *A Nation under Our Feet: Black Political Struggles in the Rural South from Slavery to the Great Migration* made a sweeping and original contribution to the study of Reconstruction that evoked a neo-revisionist turn to culture in an effort to make politics more visible and more inclusive.[37] Hahn stretched the period of Reconstruction to include slavery, wartime, and the hard years after redemption in order to trace the creation and development of African American politics. In this groundbreaking study, Hahn not only enlarged the time frame, but also enlarged and enriched the definition of politics itself. He identified politics during slavery as growing from a nucleus of resistance to the potentially deadly personal dominance of the slave owner. He found extended kin systems, both blood and fictive, at the root of slave solidarities, with the wisest members of these solidarities, usually but not always men, emerging as leaders. Hahn's discussion of those years officially defined as Reconstruction pointed out the continuity from the antebellum years of violence as a southern companion to politics. After the war, white militias and terror groups emerged out of prewar slave patrols. Blacks readied themselves to participate in a politics that they learned to their sorrow would be "paramilitary."

Hahn's extraordinary ability to recognize political activity in unusual shapes and around nontraditional issues informs this important and imaginative volume. Its scope develops organically from Hahn's incisive investigation, beginning with the emergence of pre-political groups united by the experience of resistance and mutual aid. The politics become more visible as African Americans shake off slavery and reach for citizenship. When the government fails to protect the prerogatives of these new citizens, they reorganize to find a place where they hope to be able to practice a less desperate form of politics.

Edward J. Blum also looks to culture — in this case religion — for broad explanations for the postwar settlement. In *Reforging the White Republic*, Blum argues for the centrality of northern Protestantism as an active agent in removing blacks from the postwar reunification and permitting the white South to define the nation's attitude toward African Americans. He cites the

---

[35]Rebecca Scott, *Degrees of Freedom: Louisiana and Cuba after Slavery* (Cambridge, Mass., 2005), 262.

[36]For another comparative view by a long-time student of the era, see Stanley Engerman, *Slavery, Emancipation, and Freedom: Comparative Perspectives* (Baton Rouge, La., 2007).

[37]Stephen Hahn, *A Nation under Our Feet: Black Political Struggles in the Rural South from Slavery to the Great Migration* (Cambridge, Mass., 2003).

response to the yellow fever epidemic of 1878 of denying African Americans the medical care they needed; the WCTU's racial exclusivity, particularly under Frances Willard's leadership (Willard famously refused to condemn lynching) and its racist effect on the suffrage movement; and the great revivals led by Dwight Moody, encouraging a retreat from social reform movements, as important moments in uniting Northerners and Southerners in whiteness. Finally, he sees this flourishing nationalistic, militaristic Christianity as crucial for our acquisition of an overseas empire and devastating for "African Americans and people of color throughout the world."[38]

Through Reconstruction, historians continue to struggle with the most basic questions about the meanings of democracy, citizenship, and freedom in our country with its long and ignominious history of racial slavery. Reconstruction, longer or shorter, in the South, in the nation, or in the context of the wider world, forces us to confront the overturning of a courageous experiment in democracy. And its historiography tells us that for a century, many of us refused to see this experiment as anything but a travesty of misrule. Future studies will no doubt include more attempts to realize the nationwide impact of both Reconstruction and redemption, the former in explorations like Hahn's of the politics of the dispossessed that have not been visible to us before, and the latter in expansive works like the one Elliott West proposed that will let us see what our nineteenth-century nation-building cost the people who labored on its construction, the people who willingly sacrificed democracy for domination, and increasingly people in the rest of the world.

---

[38]Edward J. Blum, *Reforging the White Republic: Race, Religion, and American Nationalism, 1865–1898* (Baton Rouge, La., 2005), 18.

## Eric Foner

# *from* Reconstruction: America's Unfinished Revolution, 1863–1877　[1988]

**ERIC FONER** (1943– ) is the DeWitt Clinton Professor of History at Columbia University. He is the author of *Free Soil, Free Labor, Free Men* (1970), *Tom Paine and Revolutionary America* (1976), *Reconstruction: America's Unfinished Revolution*, winner of the Bancroft Prize and Francis Parkman Prize (1988), and *The Story of American Freedom* (1998).

Thus, in the words of W. E. B. Du Bois, "the slave went free; stood a brief moment in the sun; then moved back again toward slavery." The magnitude of the Redeemer counterrevolution underscored both the

---

Eric Foner, *Reconstruction: America's Unfinished Revolution, 1863–1877* (New York: Harper and Row, 1988). Copyright © by Eric Foner. Reprinted by permission of HarperCollins Publishers, Inc. Pages 602–12.

scope of the transformation Reconstruction had assayed and the consequences of its failure. To be sure, the era of emancipation and Republican rule did not lack enduring accomplishments. The tide of change rose and then receded, but it left behind an altered landscape. The freedmen's political and civil equality proved transitory, but the autonomous black family and a network of religious and social institutions survived the end of Reconstruction. Nor could the seeds of educational progress planted then be entirely uprooted. While wholly inadequate for pupils of both races, schooling under the Redeemers represented a distinct advance over the days when blacks were excluded altogether from a share in public services.

If blacks failed to achieve the economic independence envisioned in the aftermath of the Civil War, Reconstruction closed off even more oppressive alternatives than the Redeemers' New South. The post-Reconstruction labor system embodied neither a return to the closely supervised gang labor of antebellum days, nor the complete dispossession and immobilization of the black labor force and coercive apprenticeship systems envisioned by white Southerners in 1865 and 1866. Nor were blacks, as in twentieth-century South Africa, barred from citizenship, herded into labor reserves, or prohibited by law from moving from one part of the country to another. As illustrated by the small but growing number of black landowners, businessmen, and professionals, the doors of economic opportunity that had opened could never be completely closed. Without Reconstruction, moreover, it is difficult to imagine the establishment of a framework of legal rights enshrined in the Constitution that, while flagrantly violated after 1877, created a vehicle for future federal intervention in Southern affairs. As a result of this unprecedented redefinition of the American body politic, the South's racial system remained regional rather than national, an outcome of great importance when economic opportunities at last opened in the North.

Nonetheless, whether measured by the dreams inspired by emancipation or the more limited goals of securing blacks' rights as citizens and free laborers, and establishing an enduring Republican presence in the South, Reconstruction can only be judged a failure. Among the host of explanations for this outcome, a few seem especially significant. Events far beyond the control of Southern Republicans — the nature of the national credit and banking systems, the depression of the 1870s, the stagnation of world demand for cotton — severely limited the prospects for far-reaching economic change. The early rejection of federally sponsored land reform left in place a planter class far weaker and less affluent than before the war, but still able to bring its prestige and experience to bear against Reconstruction. Factionalism and corruption, although hardly confined to Southern Republicans, undermined their claim to legitimacy and made it difficult for them to respond effectively to attacks by resolute opponents. The failure to develop an effective long-term appeal to white voters made it increasingly difficult for Republicans to combat the racial politics of the Redeemers. None of these factors, however, would have proved decisive without the campaign of violence that turned the electoral tide in many parts of the South, and the weakening of Northern resolve, itself a consequence of social and political changes that undermined the free labor and egalitarian precepts at the heart of Reconstruction policy.

For historians, hindsight can be a treacherous ally. Enabling us to trace the hidden patterns of past events, it beguiles us with the mirage of inevitability, the assumption that different outcomes lay beyond the limits of the possible. Certainly, the history of other plantation societies offers little reason for optimism that emancipation could have given rise to a prosperous, egalitarian South, or even one that escaped a pattern of colonial underdevelopment. Nor do the prospects for the expansion of scalawag support — essential for Southern Republicanism's long-term survival — appear in retrospect to have been anything but bleak. Outside the mountains and other enclaves of wartime Unionism, the Civil War generation of white Southerners was always likely to view the Republican party as an alien embodiment of wartime defeat and black equality. And the nation lacked not simply the will but the modern bureaucratic machinery to oversee Southern affairs in any permanent way. Perhaps the remarkable thing about Reconstruction was not that it failed, but that it was attempted at all and survived as long as it did. Yet one can, I think, imagine alternative scenarios and modest successes: the Republican party establishing itself as a permanent fixture on the Southern landscape, the North summoning the resolve to insist that the Constitution must be respected. As the experiences of Readjuster Virginia and Populist-Republican North Carolina suggest, even Redemption did not entirely foreclose the possibility of biracial politics, thus raising the question of how Southern life might have been affected had Deep South blacks enjoyed genuine political freedoms when the Populist movement swept the white counties in the 1890s.

Here, however, we enter the realm of the purely speculative. What remains certain is that Reconstruction failed, and that for blacks its failure was a disaster whose magnitude cannot be obscured by the genuine accomplishments that did endure. For the nation as a whole, the collapse of Reconstruction was a tragedy that deeply affected the course of its future development. If racism contributed to the undoing of Reconstruction, by the same token Reconstruction's demise and the emergence of blacks as a disenfranchised class of dependent laborers greatly facilitated racism's further spread, until by the early twentieth century it had become more deeply embedded in the nation's culture and politics than at any time since the beginning of the antislavery crusade and perhaps in our entire history. The removal of a significant portion of the nation's laboring population from public life shifted the center of gravity of American politics to the right, complicating the tasks of reformers for generations to come. Long into the twentieth century, the South remained a one-party region under the control of a reactionary ruling elite who used the same violence and fraud that had helped defeat Reconstruction to stifle internal dissent. An enduring consequence of Reconstruction's failure, the Solid

South helped define the contours of American politics and weaken the prospects not simply of change in racial matters but of progressive legislation in many other realms.

The men and women who had spearheaded the effort to remake Southern society scattered down innumerable byways after the end of Reconstruction. Some relied on federal patronage to earn a livelihood. The unfortunate Marshall Twitchell, armless after his near-murder in 1876, was appointed U.S. consul at Kingston, Ontario, where he died in 1905. Some fifty relatives and friends of the Louisiana Returning Board that had helped make Hayes President received positions at the New Orleans Custom House, and Stephen Packard was awarded the consulship at Liverpool — compensation for surrendering his claim to the governorship. John Eaton, who coordinated freedmen's affairs for General Grant during the war and subsequently took an active role in Tennessee Reconstruction, served as federal commissioner of education from 1870 to 1886, and organized a public school system in Puerto Rico after the island's conquest in the Spanish-American War. Most carpetbaggers returned to the North, often finding there the financial success that had eluded them in the South. Davis Tillson, head of Georgia's Freedman's Bureau immediately after the war, earned a fortune in the Maine granite business. Former South Carolina Gov. Robert K. Scott returned to Napoleon, Ohio, where he became a successful real estate agent — "a most fitting occupation" in view of his involvement in land commission speculations. Less happy was the fate of his scalawag successor, Franklin J. Moses, Jr., who drifted north, served prison terms for petty crimes, and died in a Massachusetts rooming house in 1906.

Republican governors who had won reputations as moderates by courting white Democratic support and seeking to limit blacks' political influence found the Redeemer South remarkably forgiving. Henry C. Warmoth became a successful sugar planter and remained in Louisiana until his death in 1931. James L. Alcorn retired to his Mississippi plantation, "presiding over a Delta domain in a style befitting a prince" and holding various local offices. He remained a Republican, but told one Northern visitor that Democratic rule had produced "good fellowship" between the races. Even Rufus Bullock, who fled Georgia accused of every kind of venality, soon reentered Atlanta society, serving, among other things, as president of the city's chamber of commerce. Daniel H. Chamberlain left South Carolina in 1877 to launch a successful New York City law practice, but was well received on his numerous visits to the state. In retrospect, Chamberlain altered his opinion of Reconstruction: a "frightful experiment" that sought to "lift a backward or inferior race" to political equality, it had inevitably produced "shocking and unbearable misgovernment." "Governor Chamberlain," commented a Charleston newspaper, "has lived and learned."

Not all white Republicans, however, abandoned Reconstruction ideals. In 1890, a group of reformers, philanthropists, and religious leaders gathered at the Lake Mohonk Conference on the Negro Question, chaired by former President Hayes. Amid a chorus of advice that blacks eschew political involvement and concentrate on educational and economic progress and remedying their own character deficiencies, former North Carolina Judge Albion W. Tourgée, again living in the North, voiced the one discordant note. There was no "Negro problem," Tourgée observed, but rather a "white" one, since "the hate, the oppression, the injustice, are all on our side." The following year, Tourgée established the National Citizens' Rights Association, a short-lived forerunner of the National Association for the Advancement of Colored People, devoted to challenging the numerous injustices afflicting Southern blacks. Adelbert Ames, who left Mississippi in 1875 to join his father's Minnesota flour-milling business and who later settled in Massachusetts, continued to defend his Reconstruction record. In 1894 he chided Brown University President E. Benjamin Andrews for writing that Mississippi during his governorship had incurred a debt of $20 million. The actual figure, Ames pointed out, was less than 3 percent of that amount, and he found it difficult to understand how Andrews had made "a $19,500,000 error in a $20,000,000 statement." Ames lived to his ninety-eighth year, never abandoning the conviction that "caste is the curse of the world." Another Mississippi carpetbagger, Massachusetts-born teacher and legislator Henry Warren, published his autobiography in 1914, still hoping that one day, "possibly in the present century," America would live up to the ideal of "equal political rights for all without regard to race."

For some, the Reconstruction experience became a springboard to lifetimes of social reform. The white voters of Winn Parish in Louisiana's hill country expressed their enduring radicalism by supporting the Populists in the 1890s, Socialism in 1912, and later their native son Huey Long. Among the female veterans of freedmen's education, Cornelia Hancock founded Philadelphia's Children's Aid Society, Abby May became prominent in the Massachusetts women's suffrage movement, Ellen Collins turned her attention to New York City housing reform, and Josephine Shaw Lowell became a supporter of the labor movement and principal founder of New York's Consumer League. Louis F. Post, a New Jersey-born carpetbagger who took stenographic notes for South Carolina's legislature in the early 1870s, became a follower of Henry George, attended the founding meeting of the NAACP, and as Woodrow Wilson's Assistant Secretary of Labor, sought to mitigate the 1919 Red Scare and prevent the deportation of foreign-born radicals. And Texas scalawag editor Albert Parsons became a nationally known Chicago labor reformer and anarchist, whose speeches drew comparisons between the plight of Southern blacks and Northern industrial workers, and between the aristocracy resting on slavery the Civil War had destroyed and the new oligarchy based on the exploitation of industrial labor it had helped to create. Having survived the perils of Texas Reconstruction, Parsons met his death on the Illinois gallows after being wrongfully convicted of complicity in the Haymarket bombing of 1886.

Like their white counterparts, many black veterans of Reconstruction survived on federal patronage after the coming of "home rule." P. B. S.

Pinchback and Blanche K. Bruce held a series of such posts and later moved to Washington, D.C., where they entered the city's privileged black society. Richard T. Greener, during Reconstruction a professor at the University of South Carolina, combined a career in law, journalism, and education with various government appointments, including a stint as American commercial agent at Vladivostok. Long after the destruction of his low-country political machine by disenfranchisement, Robert Smalls served as customs collector for the port of Beaufort, dying there in 1915. Mifflin Gibbs held positions ranging from register of Little Rock's land office to American consul at Madagascar. Other black leaders left the political arena entirely to devote themselves to religious and educational work, emigration projects, or personal advancement. Robert G. Fitzgerald continued to teach in North Carolina until his death in 1919; Edward Shaw of Memphis concentrated on activities among black Masons and the AME Church; Richard H. Cain served as president of a black college in Waco, Texas; and Francis L. Cardozo went on to become principal of a Washington, D.C., high school. Aaron A. Bradley, the militant spokesman for Georgia's low-country freedmen, helped publicize the Kansas Exodus and died in St. Louis in 1881, while Henry M. Turner, ordained an AME bishop in 1880, emerged as the late nineteenth century's most prominent advocate of black emigration to Africa. Former Atlanta councilman William Finch prospered as a tailor. Alabama Congressman Jeremiah Haralson engaged in coal mining in Colorado, where he was reported "killed by wild beasts."

Other Reconstruction leaders found, in the words of a black lawyer, that "the tallest tree . . . suffers most in a storm." Former South Carolina Congressman and Lieut. Gov. Alonzo J. Ransier died in poverty in 1882, having been employed during his last years as a night watchman at the Charleston Custom House and as a city street sweeper. Robert B. Elliott, the state's most brilliant political organizer, found himself "utterly unable to earn a living owing to the severe ostracism and mean prejudice of my political opponents." He died in 1884 after moving to New Orleans and struggling to survive as a lawyer. James T. Rapier died penniless in 1883, having dispersed his considerable wealth among black schools, churches, and emigration organizations. Most local leaders sank into obscurity, disappearing entirely from the historical record. Although some of their children achieved distinction, none of Reconstruction's black officials created a family political dynasty — one indication of how Redemption aborted the development of the South's black political leadership. If their descendants moved ahead, it was through business, the arts, or the professions. T. Thomas Fortune, editor of the New York *Age*, was the son of Florida officeholder Emanuel Fortune; Harlem Renaissance writer Jean Toomer, the grandson of Pinchback; renowned jazz pianist Fletcher Henderson, the grandson of an official who had served in South Carolina's constitutional convention and legislature.

By the turn of the century, as soldiers from North and South joined to take up the "white man's burden" in the Spanish-American War, Reconstruction was widely viewed as little more than a regrettable detour on the road to reunion. To the bulk of the white South, it had become axiomatic that Reconstruction had been a time of "savage tyranny" that "accomplished not one useful result, and left behind it, not one pleasant recollection." Black suffrage, wrote Joseph Le Conte, who had fled South Carolina for a professorship at the University of California to avoid teaching black students, was now seen by "all thoughtful men" as "the greatest political crime ever perpetrated by any people." In more sober language, many Northerners, including surviving architects of Congressional policy, concurred in these judgments. "Years of thinking and observation" had convinced O. O. Howard "that the restoration of their lands to the planters provided for [a] future better for the negroes." John Sherman's recollections recorded a similar change of heart: "After this long lapse of time I am convinced that Mr. Johnson's scheme of reorganization was wise and judicious. . . . It is unfortunate that it had not the sanction of Congress."

This rewriting of Reconstruction's history was accorded scholarly legitimacy — to its everlasting shame — by the nation's fraternity of professional historians. Early in the twentieth century a group of young Southern scholars gathered at Columbia University to study the Reconstruction era under the guidance of Professors John W. Burgess and William A. Dunning. Blacks, their mentors taught, were "children" utterly incapable of appreciating the freedom that had been thrust upon them. The North did "a monstrous thing" in granting them suffrage, for "a black skin means membership in a race of men which has never of itself succeeded in subjecting passion to reason, has never, therefore, created any civilization of any kind." No political order could survive in the South unless founded on the principle of racial inequality. The students' works on individual Southern states echoed these sentiments. Reconstruction, concluded the study of North Carolina, was an attempt by "selfish politicians, backed by the federal government . . . to Africanize the State and deprive the people through misrule and oppression of most that life held dear." The views of the Dunning School shaped historical writing for generations, and achieved wide popularity through D. W. Griffith's film *Birth of a Nation* (which glorified the Ku Klux Klan and had its premiere at the White House during Woodrow Wilson's Presidency), James Ford Rhodes's popular multivolume chronicle of the Civil War era, and the national best-seller *The Tragic Era* by Claude G. Bowers. Southern whites, wrote Bowers, "literally were put to the torture" by "emissaries of hate" who inflamed "the negroes' egotism" and even inspired "lustful assaults" by blacks upon white womanhood.

Few interpretations of history have had such far-reaching consequences as this image of Reconstruction. As Francis B. Simkins, a South Carolina-born historian, noted during the 1930s, "the alleged horrors of Reconstruction" did much to freeze the mind of the white South in unalterable opposition to outside pressures for social change and to any thought of breaching Democratic ascendancy, eliminating segregation, or restoring suffrage to disenfranchised blacks. They also justified Northern indifference to the nullification of the Fourteenth and Fifteenth Amendments. Apart from a few white dissenters like Simkins, it was left to black writers to challenge the prevailing orthodoxy. In the early years of this century, none did so more tirelessly than former Mississippi Congressman John R. Lynch, then living in Chicago, who published a series of devastating critiques of the racial biases and historical errors of Rhodes and Bowers. "I do not hesitate to assert," he wrote, "that the Southern Reconstruction Governments were the best governments those States ever had." In 1917, Lynch voiced the hope that "a fair, just, and impartial historian will, some day, write a history covering the Reconstruction period, [giving] the actual facts of what took place."

Only in the family traditions and collective folk memories of the black community did a different version of Reconstruction survive. Growing up in the 1920s, Pauli Murray was "never allowed to forget" that she walked in "proud shoes" because her grandfather, Robert G. Fitzgerald, had "fought for freedom" in the Union Army and then enlisted as a teacher in the "second war" against the powerlessness and ignorance inherited from slavery. When the Works Progress Administration sent agents into the black belt during the Great Depression to interview former slaves, they found Reconstruction remembered for its disappointments and betrayals, but also as a time of hope, possibility, and accomplishment. Bitterness still lingered over the federal government's failure to distribute land or protect blacks' civil and political rights. "The Yankees helped free us, so they say," declared eighty-one-year-old former slave Thomas Hall, "but they let us be put back in slavery again." Yet coupled with this disillusionment were proud, vivid recollections of a time when "the colored-used to hold office." Some pulled from their shelves dusty scrapbooks of clippings from Reconstruction newspapers; others could still recount the names of local black leaders. "They made pretty fair officers," remarked one elderly freedman; "I thought them was good times in the country," said another. Younger blacks spoke of being taught by their parents "about the old times, mostly about the Reconstruction, and the Ku Klux." "I know folks think the books tell the truth, but they shore don't," one eighty-eight-year-old former slave told the WPA.

For some blacks, such memories helped to keep alive the aspirations of the Reconstruction era. "This here used to be a good county," said Arkansas freedman Boston Blackwell, "but I tell you it sure is tough now. I think it's wrong — exactly wrong that we can't vote now." "I does believe that the negro ought to be given more privileges in voting," echoed Taby Jones, born a slave in South Carolina in 1850, "because they went through the reconstruction period with banners flying." For others, Reconstruction inspired optimism that better times lay ahead. "The Bible says, 'What has been will be again'," said Alabama sharecropper Ned Cobb. Born in 1885, Cobb never cast a vote in his entire life, yet he never forgot that outsiders had once taken up the black cause — an indispensable source of hope for one conscious of his own weakness in the face of overwhelming and hostile local power. When radical Northerners ventured South in the 1930s to help organize black agricultural workers, Cobb seemed almost to have been waiting for them: "The whites came down to bring emancipation, and left before it was over. . . . Now they've come to finish the job." The legacy of Reconstruction affected the 1930s revival of black militancy in

other ways as well. Two leaders of the Alabama Share Croppers Union,
Ralph and Thomas Gray, claimed to be descended from a Reconstruction
legislator. (Like many nineteenth-century predecessors, Ralph Gray paid
with his life for challenging the South's social order — he was killed in a
shootout with a posse while guarding a union meeting.)

Twenty more years elapsed before another generation of black Southerners launched the final challenge to the racial system of the New South.
A few participants in the civil rights movement thought of themselves as
following a path blazed after the Civil War. Discussing the reasons for his
involvement, one black Mississippian spoke of the time when "a few
Negroes was admitted into the government of the State of Mississippi and
to the United States." Reconstruction's legacy was also evident in the
actions of federal judge Frank Johnson, who fought a twelve-year battle
for racial justice with Alabama Gov. George Wallace. Johnson hailed from
Winston County, a center of Civil War Unionism, and his great-grandfather
had served as a Republican sheriff during Reconstruction. By this time,
however, the Reconstruction generation had passed from the scene and
even within the black community, memories of the period had all but
disappeared. Yet the institutions created or consolidated after the Civil
War — the black family, school, and church — provided the base from
which the modern civil rights revolution sprang. And for its legal strategy,
the movement returned to the laws and amendments of Reconstruction.

"The river has its bend, and the longest road must terminate." Rev.
Peter Randolph, a former slave, wrote these words as the dark night of
injustice settled over the South. Nearly a century elapsed before the
nation again attempted to come to terms with the implications of emancipation and the political and social agenda of Reconstruction. In many
ways, it has yet to do so.

## Elliott West

### from Reconstructing Race    [2003]

**ELLIOTT WEST** (1945– ) is the Distinguished Professor of History at the
University of Arkansas, Fayetteville. He is the author of five books including
*Growing Up with the Country: Childhood on the Far Western Frontier* (1989) and
*The Contested Plains: Indians, Gold Seekers, and the Rush to Colorado* (1998).

I would like to look again at race in America during the crucial middle
years of the nineteenth century and wonder aloud what that story might
look like if expanded to more of a continental perspective. Specifically, I

Elliott West, "Reconstructing Race," *Western Historical Quarterly* 34 (Spring 2003): 1–14.
Copyright © by Western Historical Quarterly. Reprinted by permission of Western Historical
Quarterly.

will bring the West more into the picture. If I have a general premise, it is that the acquisition of the Far West in the 1840s influenced, much more than we have credited, our racial history — how people have thought about race, how racial minorities have fared, and what policies our government adopted. In fact, since race is always a bellwether of larger forces, I think we need to consider that the great gulping of land in the 1840s had as much to do with shaping the course of our history as any event of that century, including the Civil War that dominates the story as we tell it today.

Taken together, the acquisitions of 1845–1848 comprised our greatest expansion. The annexations of Texas and Oregon and the Mexican Cession made the United States much larger and richer — and far more ethnically mixed. Languages are one crude measure. While the United States grew in area by about 66 percent, the number of languages spoken within it increased by more than 100 percent. That number would grow still more during the next few years as tens of thousands flooded into the California gold fields. In the 1850s, no nation on earth had a region with so rich an ethnic stew as the American West.

Expansion triggered an American racial crisis. We have always taught that to our students, of course, but we have missed at least half the point. The connection we make is between expansion and slavery. We say that new western lands, full of opportunity, made the question of black slavery dangerously concrete outside the South. That, in turn, set loose disputes that by 1861 would tip us over the edge of catastrophe. This sequence seems to give the West a prominent role in America's racial history, but the effect is ironic. Because race remains strictly a matter of black and white, and because its prime issue is African American slavery and its central event is the Civil War, western expansion is important only on eastern terms. Once the Mexican War does its mischief, the focus quickly swings back East and stays there. The West has its consequential moment, then remains at the edge of the action.

But that's nothing close to the whole story. Expansion was double trouble. It not only sped up the old conflict between North and South. By complicating so hugely America's ethnic character it raised new questions on the relation between race and nation. These questions centered on the West. . . .

The term for this era, Reconstruction, has always thrummed with racial implications, but when broadened to apply seriously from coast to coast, the term strengthens and its implications deepen. In the twenty years of tumult after 1846, attitudes and institutions of race were in fact being reconstructed, and more thoroughly than we have recognized. Listening to the clatter of opinions, not merely about black-white relations but also, in the color code of the day, about red, brown, and yellow, the range of possible outcomes seems to me a lot wider than we have allowed. When I shift my attention from the idealism of Reconstruction's radicals toward what was being said and done out West, and when I remember how rapidly that idealism would wither by the late 1870s, I wonder whether this nation flirted more seriously than we have admitted with a racial order far more rigid than what we finally got. I wonder what kind of America we might have seen if the headhunters and racial purists had carried the day. Frankly (to use a boyhood phrase) it gives me the shivers.

But of course something else happened. We turned away from the western tendency toward absolute racial divides, even as we compromised an eastern ideal of a fuller racial equality for former slaves. Among the theorists, the hard lines of scientific racism softened. Polygenesis, the teaching that races were born separate and could never merge, fell from favor. Racial distinctions were as strong as ever, and so was the trust in sorting them out by skull volume and the length of fingers, but now everyone once again was called part of one humanity. Races were unequal at the moment, but they were all moving along the same path of development. We seemed to be back around 1800, back to the Jeffersonian faith in turning Indians into whites. But there were two big differences. The new ideas about race were full of pretensions from the new science, especially evolutionary notions of social Darwinism. And now the government was expected to take charge of racial development as it never had before. The federal government, newly muscular after the Civil War, would act within its borders much as other imperial powers did in their distant colonies of Africa and Asia. Washington would claim the jurisdiction and the know-how to be a kind of racial master, part policeman, part doctor, part professor.

The key to understanding this . . . story is the powerful drive toward national consolidation. This theme — the integration of a divided America into a whole — is the one our textbooks tell us ruled the late nineteenth century. And so it did. Those texts, however, usually tell us that the sectional crisis and Civil War were the prime causes behind that drive, while, in fact, consolidation took its energy at least as much from the expansion of the 1840s. Acquiring the West stretched our distances, enriched our variety, and uncovered enormous wealth on our farthest edge. That, as much as secession, compelled us to think in terms of pulling it all together and keeping it that way. Making a firmer, tighter union meant resolving questions about differences within this nation, and close to the top of the list were questions about race. Here, too, westward expansion, as much as the conflict of North and South, had churned up matters and pushed us toward some resolution. It follows that if we want to understand what happened — in national consolidation, in American race, and in how the two wove together — we need to keep our eyes moving in both directions, toward both West and South.

Consolidation, racial or any other kind, means finding common ground. There must be standards to measure the parts of the nation and to decide what fits where. In bringing West and South and their peoples more tightly into the union, two standards were most important. The first was economic. From Virginia plantations to Nevada mines and Nebraska homesteads, the nation would be pulled together under the ideals of free labor and yeoman agriculture and through the realities of corporate capitalism. The second standard was a union of mores — custom, religion, language, and the rest of what we call, inadequately, "culture" — nurtured from Boston to Charleston to Tombstone. A national economy and a national culture — together they would provide the common ground of the new America. America's racial parts would have to find their place, if they had a place to find, on that ground and inside its boundaries. Watching the results, West and South, is a revelation, not just about our racial drama, but also about the entire process of expansion and the remaking of a nation.

The case of the Chinese was the most extreme. They were America's most anomalous people. In language, dress, foodways, religion, and customs they seemed beyond the pale, and with their vast predominance of men, they lacked what all other groups, however different, had in common: the family as their central social unit. Culturally, then, the Chinese were uniquely vulnerable. Economically, their potential was much more promising, but ironically that made them a special threat. From early in the 1850s, some had compared Chinese work gangs to black slavery and had suggested them as a solution to the Far West's chronic labor shortage. An editor predicted (and he meant it positively) that the Chinese will "be to California what the African has been to the South." After the Civil War, some raised the possibility of Chinese playing the African in the South itself. In 1869, businessmen met in Memphis to consider importing Asia's rural workers into their cotton fields and factories. They heard that the Chinese, "industrious, docile, and competent," could be shipped in five hundred at a time at $44.70 per head. Bitter opposition, however, came from opponents of slavery and, more effectively, from champions of free white labor. Close to the heart of the Chinese image as hopelessly alien was the notion that they were sheeplike, easily controlled, and utterly without the individual gumption to stand up to their bosses. This made them free labor's ultimate nightmare: a race of automatons used by monopolists and labor-bashers to undercut wages or cast out honest workers altogether. The most vicious assaults on Asians came from spokesmen for white workingmen like Henry George and in political movements like California's Workingmen's Party. In the end, the Chinese found themselves without either a cultural or economic base in the new nation and with virtually no natural constituency. They suffered the most excessive answer to America's racial question. As of 1882, they were excluded.

The case of Hispanics was the oddest. Their numbers were greatest in relation to whites in the Southwest, our least populous region with resources that were, for the moment, the least exploitable. This corner of the nation consequently was the last to be brought close and consolidated, which in turn lessened somewhat the pressure to resolve its racial issues. Mexican-Americans still carried the burden of the old rhetoric, the images of listless, unenlightened people, but they were not as alien as the Chinese. After all they were Christian, albeit Catholic, and were family-oriented farmers. And they fit the emerging economy. They did the grunt labor in mines, and they worked the land in a system of debt peonage strikingly similar to southern sharecropping. Hispanics, that is, posed little cultural threat and played useful economic roles. The upshot was partly to ignore the racial issues raised by expansion and partly to turn vices into virtues.

Mexican-Americans were either rendered invisible, segregated in cities and countryside, or they were reimagined as a bit of American exotica in a region we could afford to fantasize as an escape from fast-paced modern life. In the land of *poco tiempo*, these people of color became what was much tamer: people of local color.

That left African and Native Americans. Their case was most revealing of all. Since the 1840s, southern blacks and western Indians had been counterpoised in our racial thinking: insiders and outsiders, enslaved and free-roaming, the essences of South and West. Now they converged. They were brought together as events of the 1860s shattered older arrangements and assumptions. Emancipated blacks still were insiders — they were, in the fine phrase of Frederick Douglass, close under the arm of white America — but they were no longer controlled through slavery. While not as free-roaming as Indians, they were definitely on the loose. Indians, meanwhile, contrary to the claims of the 1840s and 1850s, were obviously not vanishing. In fact, their lands were being pulled into the national embrace far more quickly than anyone had guessed possible. Indians were not as enmeshed in white society as the freedmen, but they *were* being brought inside the house. Blacks and Indians found themselves suddenly moving from opposite directions into the national mainstream. Paradoxically, liberation and conquest were carrying them to the same place.

Where exactly they would end up, and how they would get there, would be the self-appointed job of the newly centralized government, and nothing in the history of Reconstruction is more illuminating as the programs that resulted. As usual, we have treated events in the West and South as if they rolled along utterly independent of each other, while in fact Washington's treatment of blacks and Indians ran as a stunning parallel. Official strategies were virtually the same. Economic integration for freedmen was to come through forty acres and a mule, or at least some measure of agrarian self-sufficiency; for Indians, the answer was to be allotment in severalty. For cultural integration, ex-slaves would be educated under the Freedmen's Bureau; for Indians, it would be agency and boarding schools. (And sometimes, most famously in the Hampton Institute, the two were schooled in the same places.) For both, Christian service and evangelism directed and suffused the entire enterprise, mixing religious verities with the virtues of free enterprise, patriotism, and Anglo American civilization.

The differences were not in the government's goals and methods but in the responses to them. Freedmen, as insiders, had worked within private agriculture for generations and had been sustained by their own Christian worship. They found the government's stated goals perfectly fine. The Sioux and Apaches and Nez Perces and others, as outsiders, had their own traditions and cosmologies and relations with the land. They replied differently. Some accepted the new order, but for others the government finally had to turn to its strong arm to impose what former slaves wanted all along.

It takes a little effort, I will admit, to see Freedmen's schools and the Little Big Horn as two sides of the same process, but blink a few times and it makes perfect sense, once you look at Reconstruction's racial policies, not on strictly southern terms, narrowly, as an outgrowth of Civil War, but rather as a culmination of a development that began in the 1840s. Its first stage began with the expansion of the nation, and with that physical growth we were unsettled profoundly in our sense of who we were and might be. This stage raised a series of new racial questions and aggravated older ones. The second stage, the Civil War, brought those questions to the sticking place. By ending slavery and bringing the West closer into the union, the war left the nation as mixed and uncertain in its racial identity as it ever had been or would be. By revolutionizing relations of power, the war also opened the way for a settlement of a sort. In the third stage, from 1865 to the early 1880s, the government used its confirmed authority to flesh out the particulars of a new racial arrangement. Some peoples it excluded, some it left on the edges, some it integrated on the terms and by the means of its choosing, including in some cases by conquest and coercion.

This Greater Reconstruction was even more morally ambiguous than the lesser one. It included not one war but three — the Mexican War, Civil War, and War against Indian America — and while it saw the emancipation of one non-white people, it was equally concerned with dominating others. It included the Civil Rights Acts and the 13th, 14th, and 15th Amendments, but it began with U.S. soldiers clashing with a Mexican patrol on disputed terrain along the Rio Grande in 1846. And it closed, practically, with the Chinese Exclusion Act of 1882 and symbolically, in 1877, with Oliver Howard — former head of the Freedman's Bureau who had risked his life and given his arm for emancipation — running to ground Chief Joseph and the Nez Perces along our northern border, forty miles shy of freedom. Always the Greater Reconstruction was as much about control as liberation, as much about unity and power as about equality. Indians were given roles they mostly didn't want, and freedmen were offered roles they mostly did, but both were being told that these were the roles they *would* play, like it or not. There has always been a darker side to *e pluribus unum*, and when we look at the parallel policies toward Indians and blacks, we can see it in its full breathtaking arrogance. When the Lake Mohonk Conference of Friends of the Indians turned from its usual concerns to devote two annual meetings to answering the so-called "Negro Question," one of its members, Lyman Abbott, was asked why no African Americans would be attending. He answered: "A patient is not invited to the consultation of the doctors in his case."

I hope no one takes from what I have written any intent to lessen the enormity of southern slavery in our history or to devalue in the slightest its human costs. My southern friends, especially, might argue that the way I am telling the story neglects the sheer weight of black-white relations in our national consciousness and the scale of the calamities spun off by slavery. They might tell me also that my version misses the genuine idealism generated from abolition and the Civil War. They might say all that and more, and if they do I will admit that they might be right.

But there are a few things I know. I know we should put our foot down and not allow the Civil War to continue behaving as it does now in our texts and histories, sitting there like a gravity field, drawing to itself everything around it and bending all meanings to fit its own shape. I am certain that, while we call the mid-nineteenth century the Civil War Era, acquiring the West had at least as much to do with remaking America as the conflict between North and South. I know that race is essential to understanding what happened during those years, and I know that the conquest and integration of the West is essential to understanding race. I am sure that we will never grasp the racial ideas of that time without recognizing that they took their twisting shapes partly from exchanges between West and South — a vigorous, strange dialogue that included not only slavery apologists and the familiar tropes about black inferiority but also rhetorical flights on opium smoking, color-coded *Zeitgeists*, and headhunters and bodysnatchers in caps and gowns. And I am confident that when we bring the West more into the story, when we end the isolation of episodes like the California gold rush and the Indian wars and make them part of a genuinely coast-to-coast history of race in America, we will have learned a lot.

The lessons will teach us again how western history has plenty to say about America today. In the 1960s, movements for the rights of black Americans encouraged us to look back with new care at slavery, emancipation, and reconstruction. The situation today — when Hispanic Americans are our largest minority and Asian Americans are arriving in unprecedented numbers, when Pat Buchanan is fanning fears about brown and yellow hordes, when the fastest growing minority in southern cities is American Indians, and when I read in my local newspaper about rallies by an Arkansas anti-Hispanic group with the unintentionally ironic acronym of AIM (Americans for Immigration Moratorium) — this situation should encourage us to look yet again at those middle years of the nineteenth century, this time in search of the roots of racial thinking that goes beyond the simpler divisions of black and white.

The larger point, of course, is a broader awareness of the most troubling theme of our past. For many of us that awareness will mean a more intimate implication, especially if we live outside the South, or like me along its edges. Race is not the burden of southern history. Race is the burden of American history. Its questions speak to all of us, whichever region we call home, and press us all to ask where and how far we have fallen short in keeping promises we have made to ourselves. In 1869, near the end of the Great Reconstruction, the reformer and spiritualist Cora Tappan took this continental perspective when she offered her audience an observation that, in its essence, is still worth making today:

> A government that has for nearly a century enslaved one race (African), that proscribes another (Chinese), proposes to exterminate another (Indians), and persistently refuses to recognize the rights of one-half of its citizens (women), cannot justly be called perfect.

# Index